THE ROUTLEDGE INTERNATIONAL HANDBOOK OF CHILDREN, ADOLESCENTS AND MEDIA

The roles that media play in the lives of children and adolescents, as well as their potential implications for their cognitive, emotional, social, and behavioral development, have attracted growing research attention in a variety of disciplines.

The Routledge International Handbook of Children, Adolescents and Media analyzes a broad range of complementary areas of study, including children as media consumers, children as active participants in media making, and representations of children in the media. The *Handbook* presents a collection that spans a variety of disciplines including developmental psychology, media studies, public health, education, feminist studies, and the sociology of childhood. Essays provide a unique intellectual mapping of current knowledge, exploring the relationship of children and media in local, national, and global contexts.

Divided into five parts, each with an introduction explaining the themes and topics covered, the *Handbook* features 57 new contributions from 72 leading academics from 38 countries. Chapters consider vital questions by analyzing texts, audience, and institutions, including:

- the role of policy and parenting in regulating media for children
- the relationships between children's online and offline social networks
- children's strategies of resistance to persuasive messages in advertising
- media and the construction of gender and ethnic identities

The *Handbook's* interdisciplinary approach and comprehensive, international scope make it an authoritative, state of the art guide to the nascent field of Children's Media Studies. It will be indispensable for media scholars and professionals, policy makers, educators, and parents.

Dafna Lemish is Professor of Communication, Dean of the College of Mass Communication and Media Arts at Southern Illinois University Carbondale, USA and founding editor of the *Journal of Children and Media*. She is author of numerous books and articles on children, media and gender representations.

THE ROUTLEDGE INTERNATIONAL HANDBOOK OF CHILDREN, ADOLESCENTS AND MEDIA

Edited by
Dafna Lemish

Routledge
Taylor & Francis Group

LONDON AND NEW YORK

First published in paperback 2015
First published 2013
by Routledge
2 Park Square, Milton Park, Abingdon, Oxon OX14 4RN

Simultaneously published in the USA and Canada
by Routledge
711 Third Avenue, New York, NY 10017

Routledge is an imprint of the Taylor & Francis Group, an informa business

British Library Cataloguing in Publication Data
A catalogue record for this book is available from the British Library

Library of Congress Cataloging in Publication Data
The Routledge international handbook of children, adolescents and media / edited by Dafna Lemish.
pages cm
Includes bibliographical references.
1. Mass media and children. 2. Mass media and youth. I. Lemish, Dafna, 1951- editor of compilation.
HQ784.M3R88 2013
302.23083–dc23
2012042153

ISBN: 978-0-415-78368-2 (hbk)
ISBN: 978-1-138-84913-6 (pbk)
ISBN: 978-0-203-36698-1 (ebk)

Typeset in Bembo
by Taylor & Francis Books

To my mother, Chaya Barkai (Mishkov), who once insisted on pulling me away from my desk on the eve of a major exam because "there is this great nature documentary on TV. You can learn so much from it too!" She read me books and played *Famous Authors* and *Wild Flowers* card games with me when I was sick. We also went to the movies, theater, and concerts throughout my childhood. In fact, she continues to recommend books for my leisure reading over the phone in our cross-Atlantic calls, advising me that I absolutely "have" to read them. Thus, it is fair to say that it is from her that I learned first-hand about the role of media in children's lives – as well as about her abiding faith in my abilities to study and write about it (or anything else) – if I only want to.

With my deepest gratitude and love, forever.

CONTENTS

Contents

Contents

ACKNOWLEDGEMENTS

This handbook is a huge undertaking, one which would have been impossible without the scholarship, enthusiasm, talent, expertise, and hard work of the 71 contributors. Collectively, they represent the current status of scholarship, policy making, activism, education, and advocacy work conducted for, about and with children, over the last half a century.

This volume would have been impossible without the support I received throughout my academic journey from many institutions and colleagues around the world, and in particular in both Israel and the United States over the last 30 years. Collectively, they form an orchestra of voices, and should be considered to be leading partners and contributors. I am also indebted to Natalie Foster, Senior Editor of Media and Cultural Studies at Routledge, for her enthusiasm and support for this project, and to the Routledge editorial and production team, especially to Ruth Berry, Production Editor, for her professionalism and dedication. I am also grateful to Jennifer Butcher, a Ph.D. student at Southern Illinois University for her invaluable help in preparing this manuscript for print.

Finally, I acknowledge the important role of my own three children, Leeshai, Noam, and Erga, who taught me, first-hand, about media in the lives of young people growing up, and their father and my partner Peter Lemish, who shared in our efforts at home to maximize the positive potential of the media and minimize the negative implications. The ideas we bounced at each other, the experiences we mediated, the constant learning we shared – have made this – as all of my other books – a reality.

Dafna Lemish

CONTRIBUTORS

Pål Aarsand, Ph.D., works as an associate professor at the Department of Education, Norwegian University of Science and Technology, Norway. His research interest is in young people's use of digital technology in everyday lives. He has focused on game/play, identities, the parent–child relationship, and digital competences. Aarsand is also interested in methodological issues at the intersection between ethnography and discourse analysis.

Meryl Alper (B.S., Northwestern University) is a Ph.D. student at the Annenberg School for Communication and Journalism at the University of Southern California. Her research focuses on young children's evolving relationships with old and new communication technologies, intergenerational joint media engagement, and the multimodal literacy practices of children with disabilities. Prior to her graduate studies, she conducted formative research for Sesame Workshop and Nick Jr.

Erica Weintraub Austin (Ph.D. Stanford University) is Professor and Director of the Murrow Center for Media & Health Promotion in the Edward R. Murrow College of Communication at Washington State University. She is nationally recognized for her research on children's and young adults' uses of the media in decision making about health and civic affairs and has been cited by the American Academy of Pediatrics in policy statements about the media and young people.

Troels Fibæk Bertel is a Ph.D. candidate at the IT University of Copenhagen. His research is focused on the social uses of convergent mobile media among youth.

Tyler Bickford is a Lecturer in the Core Curriculum at Columbia University, where he received his Ph.D. in ethnomusicology in 2011. His dissertation is an ethnographic study of digital media practices and expressive culture among US schoolchildren. He has written articles and reviews for *Ethnomusicology*, *Popular Music*, *Journal of Folklore Research*, *Journal of Consumer Culture*, *Current Musicology*, and several edited volumes. He is currently working on a book about the tween music industry. See also http://www.tylerbickford.com

Bradley J. Bond, Ph.D., is a post-doctoral research fellow at the Children's Digital Media Center at Georgetown University. He studies the influence of media on adolescent health and identity development. He can be reached at bjb87@georgetown.edu.

Dina L.G. Borzekowski, Ed.D., is a Research Professor, Department of Behavioral and Community Health, School of Public Health, University of Maryland. Dr. Borzekowski's research and teaching focus on the impact of media on the health and well-being of children and adolescents. Her work is global and uses a range of methodologies.

David Buckingham, Ph.D., is Professor of Communications and Media Studies at Loughborough University, UK. His research focuses on children and young people's engagements with electronic media, and on media education. He has published very widely on numerous aspects of the field, including children's television, children's responses to sexual and violent content, the political dimensions of television and the internet, and learning in formal and informal settings. His most recent book is *The Material Child: Growing Up in Consumer Culture* (Polity Press, 2011).

Moniek Buijzen, Ph.D., University of Amsterdam, is Professor of Communication at the Radboud University Nijmegen, and affiliated with the Center for Research on Children, Adolescents, and the Media (CCAM). Her research focuses on the processes and consequences of the commercial media environment. She has published in leading journals, including *Communication Research*, *Communication Theory*, and *Media Psychology*. Her work has been recognized with awards from the Netherlands Association for Scientific Research and the International Communication Association. See also www.ccam-ascor.nl.

Sandra L. Calvert, Ph.D., Professor of Psychology at Georgetown University, is the Director of the Children's Digital Media Center, a multi-site center funded primarily by the National Science Foundation. Her current research focuses on media, early development, and children's health. She is a fellow of the American Psychological Association and the International Communication Association. She can be reached at calverts@georgetown.edu.

Cynthia Carter, Ph.D., is senior lecturer in the Cardiff School of Journalism, Media and Cultural Studies, Cardiff University, UK. She has written widely on children, news and citizenship, citizen journalism and human rights issues, and news, gender and power. She is co-editor of *The Routledge Companion to Media and Gender* (2014) and founding co-editor of *Feminist Media Studies*. She is on the editorial board of numerous journals, including the *Journal of Children and Media*. Email: cartercl@cardiff.ac.uk

Kara Chan (Ph.D., City University of Hong Kong) is Professor at the School of Communication, Hong Kong Baptist University. Her research areas are about cross cultural advertising, advertising and children, and gender portrayal. She has published over 100 journal articles and book chapters. She is the co-author of *Advertising to Children in China* (Chinese University Press, 2004) and author of *Youth and Consumption* (City University of Hong Kong Press, 2010).

Stephanie Hemelryk Donald, DPhil, is Head of the School of Arts, University of Liverpool, and was 2012 Leverhulme Visiting Fellow at the Centre for World Cinemas at the University of Leeds. Recent articles have appeared in *New Formations*; *Theory, Culture and Society*; and *The Chinese Journal of Communications*. She is currently writing a book on "The Dorothy Complex".

Kirsten Drotner, DPhil, is a Professor of media studies at University of Southern Denmark where she also directs a national research centre DREAM (Danish Research Centre on Education and

Advanced Media Materials). She has published widely in the area of children and media, inc. *The International Handbook on Children, Media and Culture* (2008, co-editor Sonia Livingstone), *Informal Learning and Digital Media* (2008, co-editors Hans S. Jensen and Kim C. Schrøder) and *Digital Content Creation: Creativity, Competence, Critique* (2010, co-editor Kim C. Schrøder).

Meenakshi Gigi Durham, Ph.D., is a professor in the School of Journalism and Mass Communication at the University of Iowa, jointly appointed in the Department of Gender, Women's and Sexuality Studies. Her work has appeared in leading peer-reviewed journals. She is the co-editor of *Media and Cultural Studies: KeyWorks* (2011), author of *The Lolita Effect* (2008) and the forthcoming *TechnoSex: Technologies of the Body, Mediated Sexualities, and the Quest for the Sexual Self.*

Nelly Elias, Ph.D., is Senior Lecturer and chair of the Department of Communication Studies, Ben-Gurion University, Israel. She specializes in the FSU immigrants (adults and youth) in Israel and beyond, with particular interest in immigrants' cultural integration, Russian-language media outlets and media in immigrant families. She has various academic publications including a book entitled *Coming Home: Media and Returning Diaspora in Israel and Germany* (SUNY Press, 2008). More details can be seen on: http://www.arikonga.co.il/bgu/nelly_elias/main_en.htm

Shalom Fisch, Ph.D., is President and Founder of MediaKidz Research & Consulting, and former Vice President of Program Research at Sesame Workshop. For more than 25 years, he has applied educational practice and empirical research to help create effective educational television series, interactive games, print, and hands-on materials for children.

JoEllen Fisherkeller (MA/Ph.D., University of California at Berkeley; BA, University of California at San Diego) is Associate Professor in the Department of Media, Culture, and Communication at New York University. Her research and teaching interests are: young people's everyday experiences with popular media and communication technologies; identity negotiation and cultural learning in context; media education principles and practices including media analysis and production. She has two books and many articles in the disciplines of communication, culture, media studies, education, and anthropology.

Joelle Gilmore, Ph.D., was the Gloria T. and Melvin J. Chisum postdoctoral fellow of the Annenberg Public Policy Center of the University of Pennsylvania. Her current research focuses on food and beverage marketing aimed at children, childhood weight problems and obesity, and child consumers.

Maya Götz, Ph.D., is Head of the International Central Institute for Youth and Educational Television (IZI) at the Bavarian Broadcasting Corp., Munich, Germany, and of the PRIX JEUNESSE Foundation. Her main field of work is research in the area of "children/youth and television", gender-specific reception research, and counselling the public broadcasting service's children's television (ARD-network).

Kristen Harrison, Ph.D., is Professor of Communication Studies and Director of the Media Psychology Group at the Institute for Social Research at the University of Michigan. She studies child and adolescent media exposure in relation to body image, eating/weight disorders, and nutritional beliefs. She co-founded the University of Illinois STRONG Kids Program on childhood obesity and the Illinois Transdisciplinary Obesity Prevention Program. In 2011 she launched Michigan STRONG Kids to explore preschoolers' conceptions of healthy eating.

Uwe Hasebrink, Ph.D., is the Director of the Hans Bredow Institute for Media Research and full professor for empirical communication research at the University of Hamburg; research fields: patterns of media use and media repertoires, media convergence from the user's perspective, consequences of online media for established media, media use of children and young people, forms of user interest vis-à-vis the media as well as European media and European audiences.

Becky Herr Stephenson, Ph.D., is a media researcher focused on teaching and learning with popular culture and technology. Currently, Becky is a Research Associate at the Annenberg Innovation Lab at USC. Her position is jointly supported by the Cooney Center and the Innovation Lab; therefore, her current research aims to bridge the goals of both organizations and focuses on participatory learning for elementary school students.

Renee Hobbs, Ed.D., is Professor and Founding Director of the Harrington School of Communication and Media at the University of Rhode Island. She has authored four books and dozens of journal articles and professional publications and offers staff development programs to educators across the US and the world. Research interests include digital and media literacy education, teacher education, technology in education, and the relationship between critical thinking about media and academic achievement.

Mariëtte Huizinga, Ph.D., is Associate Professor of Youth and Media in the Amsterdam School of Communication Research (ASCoR) and the Center of Research on Children, Adolescents and the Media (CCaM) at the University of Amsterdam. Her research interests include the relationship between children's individual differences, media use, and behavior.

Amy Beth Jordan, Ph.D., is the Director of the Media and the Developing Child Sector of the Annenberg Public Policy Center of the University of Pennsylvania. Her current research focuses on children's media policy and the effects of beverage industry advertising and public health counter-marketing on the beverage choices made by children and parents.

Barbara Kolucki (MA, Teacher's College, Columbia University, 1975) is a trainer and educator in children's media, holistic child development, child protection, disability awareness, and prejudice reduction, primarily in the developing world. Barbara developed or facilitated several landmark communication projects for and about children, and has taught some of the first courses on Children and Media at Hong Kong University and Fordham University. She has written several UNICEF reports, articles, and media reviews. She is the co-author of UNICEF's Resource Package *Communicating with Children: Principles and Practices to Nurture, Inspire, Excite, Educate and Heal.*

Marina Krcmar (Ph.D., University of Wisconsin-Madison) is an associate professor at Wake Forest University. Her research focuses on children, adolescents and the media. Her current research examines the effect of videos targeting infants, (e.g., *Baby Einstein*) on preverbal children and the effect of violent video games on adolescents. Her research has appeared in *Journal of Communication, Human Communication Research, Media Psychology, Communication Research*, and other journals. Her book: *Living Without the Screen* was recently published by Routledge.

Alexis Lauricella (Ph.D. in Developmental Psychology and her Master's in Public Policy from Georgetown University), is a Research Associate working with Dr. Ellen Wartella in the Center on Media and Human Development at Northwestern University. Her research focuses on children's learning from media and parents' and teachers' attitudes toward and use of media with young children. Recent publications include articles in *Journal of Applied Developmental Psychology, Journal of Children and Media, Media Psychology, Merrill Palmer Quarterly* and reports for the Fred Rogers Center and the Center on Media and Human Development.

Dafna Lemish, Ph.D., is Interim Dean of the College of Mass Communication and Media Arts at Southern Illinois University Carbondale and founding editor of the *Journal of Children and Media*. She is author of numerous books and articles on children, media and gender representations including most recently: *Screening Gender on Children's Television: The Views of Producers Around the World* (Routledge, 2010); *Children and Television: A Global Perspective* (Blackwell, 2007); *Children and Media at Times of Conflict and War* (co-edited with Götz, Hampton Press, 2007); *Media and the Make-Believe Worlds of Children: When Harry Potter Meets Pokémon in Disneyland* (with Götz, Aidman, and Moon; Lawrence Erlbaum, 2005).

Sun Sun Lim (Ph.D., London School of Economics) is Associate Professor and Deputy Head of the Department of Communications and New Media at the National University of Singapore. She studies technology domestication by young people and families in Asia and has conducted fieldwork in China, Japan, Korea, and Singapore. She has a particular interest in studying the media use of marginalized and/or understudied communities such as juvenile delinquents and youths at-risk, as well as transnational families.

Siân Lincoln, Ph.D., is Senior Lecturer in Media Studies at Liverpool John Moores University, UK. Her research interests are in young people, youth cultures and private space, specifically teenage bedroom cultures. Her first book *Youth Culture and Private Space* (Palgrave Macmillan) will be published in 2012 and she is currently working on her second book *Rethinking Youth Cultures*. She has published in and edited journals including *YOUNG, Leisure Studies, Journal of Sociology, Information Technology*, and *People and Continuum*.

Deborah L. Linebarger, Ph.D. (1998, University of Texas, Austin) is Associate Professor of Education and Director of the Children's Media Lab at the University of Iowa. She studies children's use of media (especially educational media) by conducting experimental studies to detect media features that elicit attention and support comprehension, and descriptive and intervention studies that evaluate media effects in real-world contexts. She disseminates her research in education, psychology, communication, and medical forums, books, and journals.

Rich Ling is a Professor at the IT University of Copenhagen. He has focused on the analysis of mobile communication and its consequences for society. Ling has written several books on the subject including *The mobile connection* (Morgan Kaufmann, 2004), *New tech, new ties* (MIT Press, 2008) and *Taken for grantedness* (MIT Press, 2012). In addition Ling is a founding co-editor of the Sage Journal *Mobile Media and Communication*.

Sonia Livingstone, DPhil, (Department of Media and Communications, LSE) researches children, young people, and the internet; media and digital literacies and the mediated public sphere. She directs the 33 country network, EU Kids Online, and is author or editor of 16 books, including *The Handbook of New Media* (edited, with Leah Lievrouw, Sage, 2006), *Children and the Internet* (2009, Polity) and *Children, Risk and Safety Online* (edited, with Leslie Haddon and Anke Görzig, 2012, Policy).

Katalin Lustyik, Ph.D., is Assistant Professor of Media Studies at the Roy H. Park School of Communication, Ithaca College, USA. Her publications on international children's television, youth culture, television formats and Eastern European media have appeared in book collections and academic journals. She is the co-editor of *Popular Television in Eastern Europe During and Since Socialism* (Routledge, 2012) with Timothy Havens and Anikó Imre.

Nicole Martins, Ph.D., (2008, University of Illinois, Urbana-Champaign) is an Assistant Professor in the Department of Telecommunications at Indiana University. Her research interests include the social and psychological effects of the mass media on children and adolescents. She is currently working on several studies that examine the amount and nature of social aggression in programs popular with children, and the impact of socially aggressive portrayals on children's aggressive behaviors.

Sharon R. Mazzarella, Ph.D., is Professor in the School of Communication Studies at James Madison University, United States. She is editor or co-editor of five academic books including the recently published *Girl Wide Web 2.0: Revisiting Girls, the Internet, and the Negotiation of Identity* (2010). Her published articles in the area of youth and girls' studies appear in a range of academic journals.

Gustavo S. Mesch received his Ph.D. in Sociology at Ohio State University (1993). He is Professor of sociology at the University of Haifa. His areas of study include young people's adoption and use of the internet, and its effects on social network structure and sociability. He is a co-author of *Wired Youth: The Social World of Adolescence in the Information Age*, and served as the Chair of the Communication and Information Technology section of the American Sociological Association.

Máire Messenger Davies, Ph.D., FRSA, MBPsS, is Emerita Professor of Media Studies at the University of Ulster, Northern Ireland, Visiting Professor at the University of Glamorgan, Cardiff, Wales, a former Associate Professor at Boston University, USA and former Annenberg Fellow at the University of Pennsylvania. A psychologist and trained journalist, she is the author of several books on children and media including *Children, Media and Culture* (Open University Press/McGraw Hill, 2010) and *Dear BBC: Children, Television Storytelling and the Public Sphere* (Cambridge University Press, 2001).

Claudia Mitchell, Ph.D., is a James McGill Professor in the Faculty of Education, McGill University, Canada and an Honorary Professor at the University of KwaZulu-Natal, South Africa. Her research focus is on participatory visual methodologies; youth and sexuality in the age of AIDS, girlhood studies, and teacher identity. Along with authoring and co-editing 20 books in these areas, she is the co-founder and co-editor of *Girlhood Studies: An Interdisciplinary Journal*.

Amy I. Nathanson, Ph.D., is an Associate Professor of Communication in the School of Communication at Ohio State University. She studies media and children with a particular focus on how parent–child communication shapes the effects of television on children.

Sanne W. C. Nikkelen, M.Sc., is a Ph.D. candidate in the Amsterdam School of Communication Research (ASCoR) and research associate of the Center of Research on Children, Adolescents and the Media (CCaM) at the University of Amsterdam. Her Ph.D. project focuses on the relationship between media use and ADHD-related behavior in children and adolescents.

Brian O'Neill, Ph.D., is Senior Research Fellow at Dublin Institute of Technology and Head of the School of Media. He is a member of EU Kids Online, funded under the Safer Internet Programme and leads the work package on policy. He is also a member of Ireland's Internet Safety Advisory Council and is the author of reports on media literacy for the Broadcasting Authority of Ireland and UNICEF.

Debbie Olson is a Ph.D. candidate and a lecturer at University of Texas at Arlington. Her research interests include West African film, images of African/African American children in film and popular media, Race and Identity politics, Cultural Studies, and Hollywood film. She is the Editor-in-Chief of *Red Feather Journal: an International Journal of Children's Visual Culture* (www.redfeatherjournal.org), and co-editor of *Lost and Othered Children in Contemporary Cinema* (2012).

Tao Papaioannou, Ph.D., is Assistant Professor/Associate Head of the Department of Communications at the University of Nicosia, Cyprus. Prior to moving to Cyprus, she practiced public relations and taught communication in the US. Her current research interests include social networking sites and youth practices, media literacy and youth civic participation. She has written several papers on these subjects. Also, individually and in collaboration with others, she has obtained a number of large grants from the EU.

Radhika Parameswaran, Ph.D., is Professor in the School of Journalism and adjunct faculty in the Cultural Studies and India Studies programs at Indiana University, Bloomington, USA. She is editor of the encyclopedia *Audience and Interpretation in Media Studies* (2012, Wiley-Blackwell). She has authored eight book chapters and published her research in leading journals in communication and cultural studies. She is the recipient of three outstanding teaching awards from the School of Journalism.

Ingrid Paus-Hasebrink, Ph.D., is full professor for audio-visual communication and dean of the Faculty for Social and Cultural Sciences at the University of Salzburg; research fields: analyses of audio-visual content (television, radio, film, internet), of genres and formats; audience and reception analyses (e.g., daily talks, daily soaps, real life formats); she is head of a panel study on media socialization of socially disadvantaged children in Austria (from 2005 to 2012) and head of the Austrian team of the European research network EU Kids Online.

Norma Pecora, Ph.D. is Professor Emerita at the School of Media Arts and Studies, Ohio University. Her research interests include the children's media industry, questions of gender in children's media, and the history of children's media research. All of her work is informed by feminist theory. Among her recent works are *African media, African child* (edited with Enyonam Osei-Hwere) and *Children and Television: 50 years of research* (edited with John P. Murray and Ellen Wartella).

Kylie Peppler, Ph.D., is an Assistant Professor of Learning Sciences at Indiana University. An artist by training, Peppler engages in research that focuses on interest-driven arts learning at the intersection of the arts, computation, and new media. Peppler recently co-edited a book titled, *The Computer Clubhouse: Constructionism and Creativity in Youth Communities* (Teachers College Press), and has several forthcoming volumes, including *Textile Messages: Dispatches from the World of E-Textiles and Education* (Peter Lang).

Jochen Peter (Ph.D. 2003, University of Amsterdam, The Netherlands) is a Professor in the Amsterdam School of Communication Research (ASCoR) at the University of Amsterdam, The Netherlands. His research interests focus on adolescents' use of digital media and their psychosocial development as well as their sexual socialization.

Jeanne Prinsloo, Ph.D., is Professor in Journalism and Media Studies at Rhodes University in Grahamstown and an independent researcher/consultant working in the broad fields of media, identity, and critical literacy with issues of childhood and gender being particular interests.

Giselle Rampaul, Ph.D., is a literary scholar at The University of the West Indies, St Augustine Campus. Her research interests include representations of childhood in Caribbean Literature, intersections between British and Caribbean Literatures, and the work of Samuel Selvon. She is the producer and editor of the podcast series, "The Spaces between Words: Conversations with Writers" (www.spaceswords.com); and the co-editor of a collection of multidisciplinary essays, *The Child and the Caribbean Imagination* (forthcoming, UWI Press, 2012).

Rivka Ribak, Ph.D., is Chair of the Department of Communication at the University of Haifa. She has written on the ways in which media are implicated in parent–child relationships, particularly around issues of privacy, care, and control. She is now involved in a project that explores media avoidance and ambivalence, asking for example how families reduce screen time or use internet filters.

Michael Rich, MD, MPH, is Director of the Center on Media and Child Health (www.cmch.tv) at Boston Children's Hospital (BCH). He is an Associate Professor of Pediatrics at Harvard Medical School, an Associate Professor of Society, Human Development, and Health at the Harvard School of Public Health, and practices Adolescent Medicine at BCH. A father of four and former filmmaker, he also speaks and writes as The Mediatrician® at www.askthemediatrician.org.

Melissa N. Richards, MPP, is a doctoral student at Georgetown University. Her research interests include studying how children learn from media. She is currently investigating how children form bonds with media characters and if these relationships are associated with children's learning from these characters on screens. Prior to arriving at Georgetown, Melissa studied the effects of media on youth sleep patterns. She can be reached at (202) 687–7019 or at mnr25@hoyamail.georgetown.edu.

Michelle M. Rivera is a doctoral candidate in the Institute of Communications Research at the University of Illinois at Urbana-Champaign. Her research focuses on pan-ethnic constructions of Latina/o identity in popular culture, music fandom, and digital representations online. She is currently writing her dissertation on the global crossover of reggaetón music in the digital age. Michelle has published on the visual culture of the anti-reggaetón movement online.

Michael Robb, Ph.D. in psychology from the University of California, Riverside, is Director of Education and Research at the Fred Rogers Center for Early Learning and Children's Media. He oversees the Early Learning Environment™, a website that provides high-quality digital resources to families and educators of children from birth to age five. He has published research on the impact of electronic media on young children's language development, early literacy outcomes, and problem solving.

Esther Rozendaal, Ph.D., is Senior Assistant Professor of Communication at the Radboud University Nijmegen and affiliated with the Center for Research on Children, Adolescents, and the Media (CCAM). Her research focuses on children's advertising literacy and advertising processing. She has published in leading journals, such as *Human Communication Research*, *Media Psychology*, and *Journal of Children and Media*. Her work on advertising literacy has been recognized with awards from the *National Communication Association* and *International Communication Association*. See also www.ccam-ascor.nl.

Erica Scharrer (Ph.D., Syracuse University, 1998) is Professor in the Department of Communication at the University of Massachusetts Amherst. She studies media content, opinions of media, media effects, and media literacy, especially pertaining to gender and violence. She is co-author (first author, George Comstock) of *Media and the American Child* (Elsevier, 2007) and editor of the forthcoming *Media Effects/Media Psychology* (Wiley-Blackwell). Her work appears in *Journal of Children and Media*, *Communication Research*, and other journals.

Kirsten Seale, Ph.D., is a senior researcher in the School of Media and Communications, RMIT University, Melbourne. Her work considers the role of literature in the formation and communication of place in urban spatial and media economies.

Linda Simensky, MA, is Vice President of Children's Programming at PBS. She collaborates with producers, co-production partners, and distributors throughout development, production, and broadcast of PBS KIDS programming. Before joining PBS, Simensky was Senior Vice President of Original Animation for Cartoon Network, where she oversaw development and series production of *The Powerpuff Girls*, among other shows. She began her career working for nine years at Nickelodeon, where she helped build the animation department and launch the popular series *Rugrats*, *Doug*, and *The Ren & Stimpy Show*.

Jeannette Steemers, Ph.D., is Professor of Media and Communications and Co-Director of the Communication and Media Research Institute (CAMRI) at the University of Westminster. She has worked as an industry analyst (CIT Research) and Research Manager (HIT Entertainment). Her books include *Creating Preschool Television* (2010), *Regaining the Initiative for Public Service Media* (co-editor with G.F. Lowe, 2012), *Media in Europe Today* (co-editor 2011), *Selling Television* (2004), and *European Television Industries* (2005 with P. Iosifidis and M. Wheeler).

Jean Stuart, Ph.D., heads the Media discipline and co-directed the Centre for Visual Methodologies for Social Change, in the Faculty of Education, University of KwaZulu-Natal. Her research focus is participatory and arts-based approaches to address education and health issues. She leads Youth as Knowledge Producers: Arts-based approaches to HIV and AIDS prevention and education in rural KwaZulu-Natal and publishes on visual methodologies and innovative teaching approaches in the age of HIV and AIDS.

Carol Tilley, Ph.D., is an assistant professor in the Graduate School of Library and Information Science at the University of Illinois, where she teaches courses in youth services librarianship, media literacy, and comics. A former high school librarian, Tilley's scholarly interests include the intersection of young people, comics, and libraries, particularly in the US during the mid-twentieth century. She is co-editor of *School Library Research*, the peer-reviewed journal of the American Association of School Librarians.

Angharad N. Valdivia, Ph.D., is Research Professor and Head of Media and Cinema Studies and Interim Director of the Institute of Communications Research at the University of Illinois. She has published on issues of gender and popular culture with a current emphasis on Transnational Latina Media Studies. Her books include *A Latina in the Land of Hollywood, Feminism, Multiculturalism and the Media, A Companion to Media Studies*, and *Latina/o Communication Studies Today*, and *Latina/os and the Media*. She is the editor of *Communication Theory* and the *International Encyclopedia of Media Studies*, a 7-volume full-length article encyclopedia forthcoming with Wiley.

Patti M. Valkenburg, Ph.D., is a Distinguished Professor of Communication in the Amsterdam School of Communication Research (ASCoR) and director of the Center of Research on Children, Adolescents and the Media (CCaM) at the University of Amsterdam. Her research interest involves the cognitive, emotional, and social effects of media on children and adolescents.

Eva A. van Reijmersdal, Ph.D., is Senior Assistant Professor of Marketing Communication at the Amsterdam School of Communication Research (ASCoR), University of Amsterdam. Her research focuses on the effects of branded media content on audience acceptance and brand responses. She has published in leading journals, including *Psychology & Marketing, Journal of Advertising Research*, and *Computers in Human Behavior*. She received several awards for her research from the *International Communication Association* and the *European Advertising Academy*. See also www.ccam-ascor.nl.

Elizabeth A. Vandewater, Ph.D., is Associate Professor in Health Promotion and Behavioral Sciences at the University of Texas School of Public Health, Austin Regional Campus. Her research focuses on the impact of media and technology on children's health behaviors and health outcomes, with a special focus on trajectories of media use, obesity, and physical activity across childhood and adolescence at the population level.

Karen Orr Vered, Ph.D., is Associate Professor of Screen and Media. She has published on television aesthetics, Australian TV, feminism, Shirley Temple, and *Supernanny*. Her essays appear in *Camera Obscura, Continuum, Convergence, Television & New Media* and several anthologies. *Children and Media Outside the Home* (Palgrave, 2008) is an ethnographic study of children's media use in Australian after-school care settings.

Cecilia von Feilitzen, Ph.D., is Professor in Media and Communication Studies, School of Culture and Communication, Södertörn University, Sweden, and Scientific Co-ordinator of The International Clearinghouse on Children, Youth and Media, Nordicom, University of Gothenburg, Sweden. As a media researcher since 1964, she has published about 250 research reports, articles, and books. A great deal of her research has been devoted to children, young people, and media.

Ellen Wartella, Ph.D., is Al-Thani Professor of Communication, Professor of Psychology, and Professor of Human Development and Social Policy at Northwestern University. She is a leading scholar of the role of media in children's development and serves on a variety of national and international boards and committees on children's issues. She is co-principal investigator of the Children's Digital Media Center project funded by the National Science Foundation and was co-principal investigator on the National TV Violence Study.

FOREWORD

Máire Messenger Davies

Once upon a time, scholarly discussion about children and media focused primarily on one issue: did watching screen media cause them harm, and in particular, did it make them aggressive? The emphasis was on violence, and the medium most subject to accusations of harm was television.

This collection shows how far this debate (particularly prominent in the 1970s and 80s, but still with contemporary echoes) has moved on. Television is no longer the sole focus of concerned scholarly attention. Nor is the focus of academic inquiry about popular media primarily about negative effects. As this collection makes clear, we now recognize that children's relationship with their culture is conducted through a whole variety of media, from books to music to YouTube, to their own creative productions. This relationship, too, is no longer represented as a matter of simple, usually negative, social impact, but as an integral and complex part of their cognitive, social, cultural, civic and imaginative development over time.

The academic discipline most closely associated with earlier studies was social and developmental psychology – and the contribution of this always important field is well represented in this volume both in Part I, and Part III. But scholars from other disciplines involved in the study of childhood and society have now joined and broadened the debate about children and media. Studies from these other fields – sociology, history, literature, political economy – are not necessarily concerned with the direct impact of particular media products on different kinds of children. They also concern themselves with how children are represented in the media and they contribute the important insight that childhood is not a unitary concept; there are many childhoods, and different countries and cultures will have different ways of perceiving and constructing the idea of 'the child'. As Part I of this volume demonstrates, the centrality of all forms of media in children's socialization is recognized by ecologists, feminists, critical theorists and scholars of globalization. As their chapters show, the media's centrality in 'constructing' and circulating images of childhood, can, in turn, powerfully influence the ways in which actual children are perceived and treated within their cultures.

Certainly it is still recognized by scholars that media consumption in some circumstances can involve direct potential harm to children themselves, not just to the ways in which they are represented. These effects – to use a contentious term – are discussed in a series of important chapters in Part III, 'Concerns and Consequences'. Issues of both physical and mental health such as obesity, drug taking, eating disorders and ADHD, as well as the perennial topic of the representation of anti-social behaviour – some of it more graphic, interactive and intrusive than ever in the internet age – are discussed. In this context, it is good to see children represented not just as passive victims of adult media corruption, but as active potential citizens, with a role to play in determining their own destinies. This is acknowledged in chapters on politics and on news.

The study of children's relationship with media and culture also involves recognizing the ways in which media products are a source of enrichment and pleasure, contributing to cognitive and language development, and inspiring imagination and fantasy. Despite the rhetoric of increasing 'convergence' of all media on computer screens, this book's section on 'Channels and Convergence' distinguishes between 'Channels' as well as discussing the implications of 'Convergence'. These 'channels' include books, cinema, music, gaming and television (as a creative medium, rather than as a social influence). Each of these media are acknowledged as discrete objects of serious critical attention. It is important that media are seen in this inclusive way precisely because of the commercial imperatives of convergence: stories, characters and related merchandise appearing in one medium will be found in money-spinning forms in other media too. This is certainly a way of enhancing the profits of media organizations, but from the child's point of view, being able to meet well-loved characters and situations across and beyond different media can be a source of positive educational enrichment.

The other major change in the study of children's relationship to the media as illustrated in this volume is a recognition that there is a media world of childhood beyond the United States of America. Earlier widely-cited debates about the social impact of the media, especially television, were particularly focused on the situation in the USA. Given that the media are global, and given that the US remains the primary source of imported programming for countries everywhere, we must continue to recognize the impact of Hollywood in shaping our children's cultural worlds. Thus it is not surprising that many American scholars contribute to this book and discuss at length the different regulatory and commercial situations prevailing in the USA. However, this collection has a much broader international flavour than many books on children and media, with contributions from the UK, the Netherlands, Israel, Canada, Australia, Sweden, Germany, Denmark, Norway, Austria, Ireland, Cyprus, South Africa, Trinidad, Hong Kong and Singapore. This diversity recognizes that, despite the global nature of much of children's media, children grow up with specific local, national and regional cultures which can differ widely from each other and which will affect how global media are received and understood. Contributions from these other countries focus on the representation of children in media, as well as on their consumption of media products. In different chapters, race, ethnicity, nationality, religion, class and disability are each acknowledged as determinants of how children are perceived and of how they behave.

Cecilia von Feilitzen (Sweden) argues in her concluding chapter that international initiatives continue to be important. Although childhoods differ culturally and in many ways across the world, there are many areas of common concern for those who have the well-being of children at heart. All need to work towards: 'quality in children's media; better representation of children in other media; protection of children from harmful media content; and promotion of awareness, media literacy and children's right to communication through the media.'

The scholarly conversation in this volume will surely help to raise this awareness throughout the academic community worldwide.

INTRODUCTION

Children, adolescents, and media: creating a shared scholarly arena

Dafna Lemish

Introduction

The study of children, young people, and the media can be viewed as a microcosm of media studies. First, our field is occupied with the conventional three main realms of research of the field – audiences, texts, and institutions. Second, our research, policy debates, and initiatives, such as media literacy, demonstrate the importance of understanding the needs and capabilities of different types of audience. Third, in regard to audiences, media studies as a whole can learn from our field the importance of understanding that characterizations of populations, such as childhood, are socially constructed and culturally and historically situated. Thus, we understand that children are perceived to be a special, evolving, and dynamic group of people – characterized by unique developmental stages – who are gradually accumulating life experiences and developing knowledge as well as critical skills. All of these processes distinguish children and young people from older audiences. Indeed, they are often considered to be more vulnerable than adults to the influences of media. Hence the debate about whether some forms of protection and supervision should be required in order to insure the realization of young people's most basic of human rights – healthy social, physical, and mental development and well-being.

Living with a global media culture is one of the characteristics of childhood in the beginning of the third millennium, as screens – of television, cinema, computers, mobile devices, and hand-held electronic games – are all part of everyday life. Sixty years of research of the most central screen in children's lives, television, identified trends and key issues in regard to the roles of this medium, such as: long-term implications for behavior (e.g., violence, eating disorders, sexual experiences, consumer practices, pro-social behavior); cultivation of worldview and values (e.g., perception of gender, political attitudes, stereotypes of minorities); potential for learning (e.g., language, school-related curricula, cognitive skills); and, centrality in family and social life (e.g., structuring everyday routine, providing conversation topics, creating youth culture). Interestingly, while television continues to be dominant in families as well as for many individuals, this multifaceted medium is changing in front of our eyes. The device is now manufactured in every size and shape; audio-visual quality improves constantly and continues to perfect the illusion of mirroring a reality; and, perhaps, most important of all, the content offered is being integrated into the rapidly evolving media worlds of converging and mobile multiple screens.

What then, characterizes this new reality of screen culture as we focus on the study of children, adolescents, and media? The following six themes run as undercurrents through much of the current scholarship in this area: Multiple realities, technological convergence, consumer culture, globalization, literacy, and the positive/negative effects debate. We examine each of them briefly below.

Multiple realities

Screen culture is characterized by its omnipresence in every aspect of young people's lives – at home, in school, in the workplace, in places of leisure, on the roads. As such, scholars note that the distinction between our existence in concrete reality and the mediated one is often blurred, as the media seem to move smoothly and fluently between the two states. One set of key questions that can be raised in this regard asks: What effect does this seamless transition between two realities have on children? From another perspective, how do children navigate between these two realities? Or, can it be the case that the separation between the two kinds of reality is artificial and meaningless, as both "flow" one into the other and are reciprocal. As a result, the understanding of the "real" and "authentic" in such a culture may change its meaning. Indeed, according to post-modern approaches, one might argue that screen representations of reality are more attractive than the concrete ones in which we live.

According to Baudrillard, we live in a kind of "hyper-reality" in which concrete reality is replaced with its representations. For example, romantic love as portrayed in a soap opera may create longing and aspirations that are unrealistic in comparison with that experienced by an adolescent viewer. As a result, a teen may state "I can really be myself" when engaged in an internet chat since the partners to the chat are not influenced by his/her external appearance (e.g., race, gender, normative beauty, and sexiness), and strangers can play with their identities while they crystallize their very own internal core of what they perceive to be the "real me".

The borders between accepted and common social divisions are blurred in this hyper-reality, such as the division between the private and the public spheres. For example, while in her bedroom a pupil searches the net for information for a school project; during class she sends an intimate text message on her mobile phone. Or, a love declaration appears on a huge billboard beside the road in a major urban area, and scenes of war and natural disasters broadcast on CNN worldwide are captured by a personal phone-camera. Reality shows on television allow us the illusion of peeking into people's private lives. Uploading personal YouTube videos and writing blogs or even "sexting" – sending personal sexual messages and images via texting – move our private lives into the public sphere. Each one of the various screens can serve a variety of needs ranging from the private to the public, and each one can do so in spaces defined as private or public.

Technological convergence

The convergence of communication functions into one screen is one of the dominant aspects of screen culture facilitating the aforementioned processes. Thus, the mobile phone, tablet screen, or computer can serve multiple and concurrent functions: a "library" accessed through an internet connection, a video service, a television/DVD server, a radio and music player, a photo album, a phone, a personal calendar, a still or video camera, a games console, and an endless array of application functions. As a result, other forms of blurring are occurring with formerly presumed categories such as information, entertainment, and advertising; formal and informal learning; study and play. Similarly, distinctions between media that supposedly encourage passivity and those allowing for reciprocity and interactivity are becoming less convincing: One can choose to be passive or active on various levels with each screen, depending on interest, context, personality, and circumstances. For example, the computer and the internet allow interactivity, but it is also possible to consume them only for escape from reality and for momentary gratifications. Television may allow relaxation and relief, but can also allow the tailoring of a personal viewing schedule and encourage interactivity, such as the selection of a preferred idol, signing a petition, submitting home videos for competition, and even choosing a particular ending for a favorite series.

Children move between screens according to personal interest, accessibility, and the experiences each allows. They watch their favorite "celeb-singer" on television, save his/her photo on their desktop, surf the net to find "behind the scene" clips about their performance, write Facebook messages expressing views, download a favorite MP3 song or a ringtone to their mobile phone. The traditional assumption according to which a specific medium has a preference for a specific kind of content or role is redundant: For example, claims that books are more suitable for conveying complicated messages for the acquisition of formal knowledge, while television is more suitable for passive and non-demanding entertainment; or, that mobile phones are for making phone calls. In summary, each screen can serve a full range of needs and roles.

Consumer culture

Complex inter-relationships between popular culture and consumer culture exist, characterized by privatization, individualism, and commercialization. Young people are, themselves, important consumers, but they also influence purchases by adults in their lives. Public debates around children's place in the commercialized world fluctuate between anxiety over their possible role as victims of manipulative marketing to celebration of their consumer competency and sophistication. Children, so the argument goes, are treated by commercial forces not as future citizens developing values, capabilities, and skills vital for functioning in a democratic society, but as consumers immersed in a leisure culture with an insatiable appetite for consumerism. In doing so, media producers adapt the civic discourse of empowerment to serve commercial purposes. For example, children's independence is touted by advertisers as encouraging development of their own consumerist lifestyle in order to actualize the "right" to express their own individual "voice" in matters of culture and taste in music, fashion, food, and entertainment.

In addition, economic interests drive the construction of newly invented sub-periods of childhood. For example, the new "tween" period of pre-adolescence is deemed to be a distinct period of childhood with its own popular culture and tastes. Similarly, babies and toddlers are framed as representing a consumer market requiring its own technological developments (e.g., keyboards for babies, special DVDs, satellite channels devoted to them, internet sites for babies and toddlers seated on adults' laps; baby-games, mobile applications). There is also clear consumer segregation between girlhood and boyhood in the worlds of toys, fashion, music, TV programs, advertising, and so forth.

The consequences of the consumer culture extend well beyond questions regarding product purchases and the development of consumer literacy. Scholars raise questions regarding the promotion of a hedonistic culture among the young; encouragement of children's inability (or need) to postpone gratifications; cultivation of a self-image dependent upon appearance and ownership rather than qualities and achievements; internalization of a worldview according to which products are framed to offer cures for every human problem – psychological or social; the exhortation to youth to focus on the world of glamour and celebrities, and the construction of future aspirations as located within screen culture itself (e.g., the desire to be a famous "celeb", a fashion model, a sports-news anchor).

Globalization

Globally, children watch similar television programs and movies, play similar computer games, surf similar popular websites, and download similar popular music. Many of these texts originate in North America, and hence diffuse worldviews, values, and interests promoted in American culture. Interestingly, other texts traveling throughout the world originate elsewhere (e.g., Japanese anime, Korean computer games, African music, Latin American telenovelas) but undergo an adaptation process manifested by companies in the United States that function as a "megaphone" to legitimize and intensify their distribution. The result of this process is cultural mainstreaming and homogenization. Thus, children around the world sing similar pop songs, wear similar clothes, drink similar soft drinks, and adore the same mega-celebrities. If so, is it possible to argue that children worldwide live today in the global village portrayed by Marshall McLuhan? If so, as a result, do they perceive the world in similar or different ways? Is their local identity eroded? Do they dream the same scripts for their own futures?

While scholarly study and debate over the processes of cultural globalization is broad and is taking place in multiple disciplines, for many children and young people growing up today the tension between globalization and localization does not seem to be problematic. Globalization is integrated through "glocalization" processes; here, audiences grounded in specific local cultural contexts adopt and adapt global texts through processes of local meaning construction and interpretation. One such significant process involves the creation of hybrid cultures as children creatively integrate global contents and identities from other cultures with elements from their own specific culture, as characterized through its history, language, tradition, religion, ethnicity, and so forth. These processes of intercultural and transnational exchanges have been advanced significantly through technologies that include satellites, the internet, and mobile communication.

Literacy and education

The emergence of new forms of popular culture has led to redefining media literacy as a multi-modal literacy that requires a variety of skills in interpretation, comprehension, critical thinking, application, and creativity in multiple languages. Thus, the claim is made that the literate person needs to be a master of verbal language – oral, reading and writing (and preferably in more than one language), audio-visual languages, computation, information resourcing, along with the capacity to integrate all of these modalities simultaneously when functioning as an engaged citizen or "prosumer" (production-consumer). The realities of multi-modality challenge conventional formal schooling and normative ways of teaching, and dictate a new agenda for educational systems in the rapidly evolving media-saturated world. For example, unidirectional and hier-archical pedagogies, situating the teacher as the primary source of knowledge, requirement for unity of place and time for classroom teaching, and other verbal language-oriented educational systems are challenged by these new realities and require creative and bold adaptation strategies.

Positive and/or negative potential

Most parties to the ongoing debate over the positive and negative potential of media in children's lives assume technological determinism; that is, technology dictates social structures and processes. An alternative view admits that media culture is central to contemporary life, and has a potential for a wide range of complicated influences, most of which cannot be dichotomized as good or bad. Indeed, in support of this second view, we can claim that our accumulated knowledge about the role of media in children's lives suggests that they can have both positive and negative effects on children, depending on content, the context in which they are enjoyed, the use made of them, and the individual characteristics of children using them. Media have both positive and negative potential to make a difference in children's lives in all areas of their development: behaviorally (e.g., imitating sharing or aggression), socially (e.g., making new friends and strengthening existing relationships through social media or bullying their classmates on the internet); cognitively (e.g., learning school preparedness skills or developing short attention spans); creatively (e.g., creating computer graphics, writing blogs, and uploading their own videos or reproducing clichéd commercial formulas and stereotypical messages); or even physically (e.g., learning balanced nutrition or developing bad eating habits). Clearly, popular cultural influences are not simply either good or bad. They are complicated and interlinked with many gray areas open to multiple interpretations that depend upon different cultural value systems and worldviews. For example, is corresponding with strangers over the internet dangerous or does it widen horizons? Is sex education for adolescents in the media life-saving or morally inappropriate? Does watching an American TV series expand cultural experiences or damage other cultural identities? Does addressing topics like trauma or death help children cope with difficult experiences or traumatize them and make them even more fearful and distrustful of adults?

These overriding, complicated themes capture a moment in time in the dynamic process of change and reflect where we seem to be in this second decade of the third millennium. It poses exciting challenges to scholars of *children, adolescents, and media* if we are to break new ground in both theory and practice. In the next section, I propose admittedly subjective proposals of where I think we should proceed if we are to engage such challenges and, in doing so, strengthen our scholarly arena.

Creating a shared scholarly arena

The roles media play in children's and adolescents' lives, as well as potential implications of their use by children that contribute to their cognitive, emotional, social, behavioral, and health development continue to attract and advance research in a variety of disciplines. However, these endeavors are for the most part fragmented efforts grounded in different disciplines (e.g., developmental psychology, mass media, public health, education, cultural studies, feminist studies, sociology of childhood) with limited interdisciplinary cross-fertilization. This state of affairs is now changing dramatically with the founding in 2007 of the *Journal of Children and Media* (Routledge), the Children, Adolescents and the Media (CAM) Division of the International Communication Association (ICA), and the recent Children, Youth and Media Temporary Working Group, in the European Communication Research and Education Association (ECREA). There are also established as well as relatively new research centers across the world, such as: Center on Media and Child Health (CMCH), Children's Hospital Boston and Harvard Medical School (USA); Center for Research on Children, Adolescents and the Media (CcaM), University of Amsterdam (The Netherlands); Children's Digital Media Center (CDMC), Georgetown University (USA); Fred Rogers Center of Early Learning Environment, St. Vincent College (USA); the International Center Institute for Youth and Educational Television (IZI) in the Bavarian Broadcasting Corporation (Germany); Nordicom's International Clearinghouse on Children, Youth and Media, University of Gothenburg (Sweden); UNICEF's Communication for Development Unit; World Summit Movement on Media for Children; among others.

The booming interest in creating a shared international arena for scholarship presents an unusual challenge at this time, and an opportunity for revitalizing our field and redefining its goals, focus, and vision. This handbook was envisioned, initially, as a long-term goal and an outcome of the *Journal of Children and Media*. The Journal's mission statement reads as follows:

It is an interdisciplinary and multi-method collection that provides an integrative state-of-the-art discussion of the field by scholars from around the world and across theoretical and empirical traditions who are engaged in the study of media in the lives of children and adolescents. It is a unique intellectual mapping of current knowledge and future research directions about all forms and contents of media in regards to all aspects of children's lives, and especially in three complementary realms: Children as consumers of media, as active participants in media making, and representations of children in the media. It is committed to the facilitation of international exploration and dialogue among researchers, students, policy makers, health and education professionals, the media industry, parents and caregivers, and other invested stakeholders, through discussion of interaction between children and media in local, national, and global contexts; concern for diversity issues; a critical and empirical inquiry informed by a variety of theoretical and empirical approaches; and dedication to ensuring the social relevance of the academic knowledge it presents to the cultural, political, and personal welfare of children around the world.

This collection of chapters, created especially for this volume, is a mapping of the field in the most up-to-date, integrative, and creative ways possible. As you read, I propose keeping in mind the following five central challenges that I believe need to be engaged in order for us to be able to realize the capacity of this important field to thrive and to realize its potential contribution to improving the lives of children, parents, and educators, as well as the endeavors of media producers.

From multi–disciplinary – to – interdisciplinary study

At the heart of this handbook is the longstanding call for the interdisciplinary study of communication, a call with burning relevancy to its application in the current study of children and media.

Many colleagues in this field come from developmental psychology traditions, with "strong effects" theoretical grounding. They may study the effects of violence on children or kindergartners' ability to understand the persuasive intent of advertising. Others, who apply cultural studies methods, approach this field based on an identity-centered theoretical perspective (gender, race/ethnicity, class) and frame their work in terms of "meaning-making". They often explore the contribution of popular culture texts to identity construction or the way young audiences negotiate the meanings of such texts. Applying what may well be an overly-generalized distinction, these two approaches are often set off from one another as an American versus European divide; or via a conceptualization of children as "becoming" (i.e. a deficit model suggesting children should be viewed in the process of becoming adults) versus children as "being" (i.e., children as entities in their own right). To this we can add a third, rapidly growing body of work rooted in medical and health disciplines, with which quite frankly many of us in communication studies are unfamiliar (and vice versa; that is, researchers employing this approach seem to be unaware of these previously mentioned traditions). Here, researchers apply an epidemiological approach to media effects on children, leading many to endorse a protectionist ideology. Studies in this tradition have explored, for example, the effect early screen-viewing has on the brain development of babies and toddlers, or the effect of television viewing on obesity.

Each of these three approaches is dominated by a particular methodological preference: experimental, ethnographic, and correlational. Furthermore, scholars read and submit their work to journals in their separate disciplines, attend their own conferences, and network with one another.

The consequences of these divisions are grave: Not only does each ground understanding in one slice of the knowledge pie and prioritize a particular methodology of study, but scholars are mostly unaware of each other. Or, when they are aware, they are deeply suspicious and often even plainly disrespectful of these other approaches. In returning to the overview of the field, we observe that there are few bridging or integrative efforts in the literature. As such, each approach mostly stews in its own proverbial theoretical and empirical juices, while preaching to its own choirs and ignoring vast accumulations of knowledge in parallel tracks.

From national – to – international and transnational study

The study of media and children can no longer remain bound within national borders, as media, children, and young people's well-being is an international as well as a transnational phenomenon involving important issues such as the political economy of media corporations; the implications of the centrality of new, border-free technologies; massive migration movements; and the rapidly changing understandings and theorizing of multiculturalism, cultural-hybridity, and diasporic identities.

As many have argued in other fields, cross-cultural studies have the proven potential to make obvious the deep ethnocentrism and cultural biases we all assume, to some degree. Such studies help us understand the complicated intertwining of culture and media, and at the same time highlight those aspects of children's lives – such as their needs, aspirations, pleasures, anxieties – that seem to be shared universally.

Political economy analyses of these trends suggest that the monies invested in children and media advance a global business of enormous proportions and varying value. For huge entertainment corporations, children are not future citizens, rather they are first and foremost consumers. From such a point of view, childhood is not viewed as a distinct period in the life cycle, with attendant developmental needs that require development-oriented programing. On the contrary, this population is viewed as a distinct market opportunity requiring aggressive socialization to a consumer-centered lifestyle. Thus, as a number of authors in the handbook argue, any attempts to advance or lobby for change in the content of television programs and movies directed at children, to legislate internet safety policy, or to develop less violent and more creative computer games for children are no longer matters to be addressed in national isolation.

From description – to – social change

Furthermore, many scholars now point out that we cannot remain content to study only questions of privileged media use among children being raised in media-saturated environments. My own recent study of producers of children's TV around the globe (Lemish, 2010) and co-authorship of an international development-oriented media project for UNICEF (Kolucki and Lemish, 2011) reinforced my awareness of the multiple and important ways in which media for children are employed globally, such as: promoting schooling for girls; educating for sexual safety and rape-prevention in HIV/AIDS struck regions of the globe; providing alternative masculine role models in societies driven by domestic and general violence; reaffirming the value and self-image of diverse appearances in the face of the pressure of the Anglo-European "Beauty Myth"; involving young generations in participatory democracy. The list is as long as the issues facing children growing up in the world today.

In a global society in which children's basic survival is still a major issue, I submit that we privileged researchers of media need to roll up our sleeves and pitch in to link our research to social change efforts. Indeed, I believe that in the spirit of action research, the field of children and media studies needs a renewed commitment to create, integrate, and disseminate knowledge that will assist in efforts to empower children and young people through media, particularly those from underprivileged segments of global and national societies.

From research *about* children – to – research *for* and *with* children

As we came to understand that children occupy a very unique period in the human cycle, one deserving of special scholarly attention and resources, we realized that children, in each stage of their development and in all cultural contexts of diversity, need to be encountered and fully recognized as having a unique personal voice that deserves to be listened to, and understood with empathy. Children's voices need to be accounted for in our research questions, included in methods we choose and apply in our studies, in the ways we present our findings, and in recommendations we make for both further research and for applied implications. This involves disclosing and confronting the power relationships that exist between researchers and the children being researched. This requires developing more inclusive and egalitarian participatory methodologies – from the inception of the study to its assessment – while remaining ethically committed to promoting the well-being of those studied, attempting to avoid exploitive strategies, and guarding participants from possible research related harm.

For example, new technologies that blur traditional distinctions between the "sender and receiver" of text have immediate implications for our field. Many children and young people are regularly engaged with producing, as well as consuming, media texts – be it via emailing, instant-messaging, text-messaging, blogging, uploading, phone-photographing, videoing, designing personal web pages, and a host of other creative expressions. Since this is the case, it is no longer appropriate for us to study them as solely receivers of messages imposed from the outside or as negotiators of texts. Rather, we must understand them to be either potentially or actively involved in new and exciting uses of media. Naturally, the more alarming cases gain public attention (e.g., "sexting" – sexual texting, or the self-distribution of nude pictures and pedophilia), and thus become a pretext for legislating public policies that threaten a wide range of children's rights. In addition, much more remains for us to understand about children and the various ways media can better serve their healthy growth into productive and engaged citizens of the human globe.

From the margins – to – the center

The proposals addressed thus far have far-reaching implications within and beyond the academic world. As long as various branches of the study of children and media fail to attain and present an integrated, persuasive, and holistic picture of children, young people, and the media in their lives – the discipline will remain unsuccessful in producing a strong, empirically-grounded voice that influences media policy and media literacy on national as well as global levels. Our voice is desperately absent in the public sphere as witnessed by politicians and policymakers who wave the consensual "violence" and "sex" red flags, while continuing to ignore the intricate and complex matrix of media related issues so crucial for the well-being of children and young people.

The absence of a strong, multifaceted disciplinary voice may also contribute to the reasons why this sub-area of media studies is finding difficulty in engaging with other disciplines that focus on children and young people, such as education, health, and sociology. But even within our own disciplinary field of media studies, there seems to be limited flow between the study of children and other sub-areas. This seems quite surprising given that many of the questions asked in these fields are quite similar. A partial explanation for this situation may be the feminist explanation for the devaluation of questions pertaining to the private sphere of family and children (in comparison, for example, to the study of media, politics, the economy, and news). The fact that the vast majority of researchers in this sub-area are women continues to perpetuate the traditional gender division of interests and responsibilities. Yet, in a conceptual world in which adult identities are understood to be fluid, flexible, and ever-evolving – and where adulthood too is constructed as an unfinished developmental business – the study of children and media should really be at the heart of media studies as it pertains to the development of a better humanity.

The Handbook

Organizing such a vast area of multi-disciplinary research is a complicated task. Obviously, there are different ways of charting the field to the one I created. The following rationale was employed in developing this volume.

The Handbook structure

The Handbook is structured around five main sections, each divided into individual chapters: *Childhoods and Constructions, Channels and Convergence, Concerns and Consequences, Contexts and Communities, Collaborations and Companions.* You will note the use of capitalized C words as an organization tool. I did so because these terms assist me in pinpointing the anchor of each section.

Childhoods and Constructions: The opening section sets the stage for the study of this field by discussing the nature of childhood as a social construction and the various roles media play in such constructions. It offers a variety of approaches to studying children and media from a variety of disciplines.

Channels and Convergence: introduces the main media-cultures in children's lives individually; including their history, characteristics, content preferences, and unique contributions to the study of children and media. Despite valid arguments about media convergence, there is still much to be learned by looking at each group of media independently, as this clarifies their unique contributions to debates about media and children. We also learn about their roles in different regions of the world.

Concerns and Consequences: of media in the lives of children contains chapters that assess specific areas of consequences from various theoretical perspectives. However, as arguments presented in this section make clear, the discussion of children and media needs to be grounded in their many social and cultural contexts and communities.

Contexts and Communities: from dominant national and local cultures as well as the cultural communities of minorities and immigrants to family and peer groups, and to micro-contexts, such as the bedroom. This section also contains discussion of the role media play in children's ability to voice their own interests and concerns and their involvement in civic engagement.

Collaborations and Companions: presents a variety of initiatives whose shared mission is to maximize the benefits of media for children and to minimize potential harm. The exemplars selected function locally and/or worldwide in the realms of policy, quality and educational media, and media literacy.

Finally, many of the chapters in the book "correspond" to one another: They complement theory and empirical findings, offer alternative frames of reference, criticize and debate ideas and research presented just a few pages away. Such *connections* are noted at the end of each chapter in order to call your attention to those chapters particularly relevant for the issues discussed. Altogether, the handbook aims to provide as wide a horizon as possible on how media are integrated in children's and adolescents' lives around the world.

The authors

Two principles guided the selection of authors: First, researchers who were at a relatively early stage of what seemed to be a promising career path were invited along with established scholars who were prominent authorities in the field. Second, special efforts were made to select a broad and diverse collection of contributors representing relevant disciplines and methodological approaches, as well as different cultural backgrounds and geographical regions of the world. Thus, collectively, the contributors represent a diversity of disciplinary groundings, including communication and media studies, cinema and photography, literary studies, education, public health, medicine, sociology, child development, anthropology, policy, and the media industry.

While this handbook does contain a substantial representation of United States-based researchers, nearly half of the contributors, 34 out of 72 authors, reside outside the US; including Austria, Australia, Canada, Cyprus, Denmark, Germany, Hong Kong, Ireland, Israel, Netherlands, Norway, Singapore, South Africa, Sweden, Trinidad, and the United Kingdom.

This having been noted, several gross imbalances remain, despite my genuine efforts to assemble a global representation of contributors. First, vast regions of the world are not represented adequately; in particular, Latin America, Africa, the Middle East. As a result, high resource societies have a much stronger presence. The second imbalance is gender related: Only 12 of the contributors are male, again reflecting the dominance of women in this area, as noted above. Finally, despite the high priority I gave to including a wide range of persons from a variety of cultural and racial groups, there are only a few non-Caucasian contributors.

These observations call readers' attention to the nature of this field of inquiry and the large lacunae still in existence.

References

This introduction is based on my earlier writings, including:

Bloch, L.R. and Lemish, D. (2003). The Megaphone Effect: International culture via the US of A. *Communication Yearbook*, 27, 159–90. Mahwah, NJ: Lawrence Erlbaum.

Kolucki, B. and Lemish, D. (2011). *Communicating with Children: Principles and Practices to Nurture, Inspire, Excite, Educate and Heal*. NY: UNICEF.

Lemish, D. (2006). Rethinking childhood. *Panim*, 37, 14–21. (In Hebrew)

Lemish, D. (2007). *Children and television: A global perspective*. Oxford, UK: Blackwell.

Lemish, D. (2009). Media, children, and young people's wellbeing: Where should we go from here? *Connections: The future of media studies conference*, Media Studies Department, University of Virginia, Charlottesville, VA.

Lemish, D. (2010) *Screening gender in children's TV: The views of producers around the world*. New York and Abingdon: Routledge.

Lemish, D. (2012). Popular screen culture and childhood. In S. Nowak (Ed.), *MOCAK Forum 3*. Krakow, Poland: Museum of Contemporary Art in Krakow (MOCAK), pp. 28–31. (In Polish)

PART I

CHILDHOODS AND CONSTRUCTIONS

EDITOR'S INTRODUCTION

The field of children, adolescents, and media has been approached from diverse theoretical traditions and perspectives. Each perspective is grounded in a unique scholarly history, frames research questions in accordance with its assumptions, and focuses on different aspects of the relationships between children and media. We start this fascinating journey by introducing some of the most important of these perspectives, by focusing on the different ways in which childhood has been constructed, socially and culturally, and how these constructions contribute to the way we understand children's relationships with media today.

Kirsten Drotner's opening chapter focuses on media and constructions of childhood. Her overview explains how concepts of childhood and media are co-constructed in modernity through two major discursive domains. First, in everyday life, media serve as important, public means of articulating selective representations of childhood (e.g., through print news reporting, advertisements, television, and film). She demonstrates how these representations operate as catalysts in defining, handling, and regulating social problems as moral problems. Second, when new media enter the social scene, stark public reactions often follow. Her analysis focuses on situations in which these reactions turn into so-called media panics about children's media use, employing binary projections of the proper childhood and the future direction of society.

Debbie Olson and **Giselle Rampaul**'s chapter discusses representations of childhood in the media. They argue that childhood is, and has always been, an unstable concept, variously interpreted and represented according to historical, social, cultural, political, and economic contexts. Social and economic changes led to development of a theory of childhood innocence in which children came to be assigned a "special" status. Along with childhood innocence, *whiteness* was also implicitly idealized in early representations of childhood. Thus, images of a white childhood came to be considered universal and desirable. Such pictorial representations of children established a standard of what children were expected to look like, as well as contributing to idealized conceptions of childhood itself. However, technological advancement and ideological shifts inevitably changed the way childhood is imagined and understood. This, in turn, created new representations of childhood, particularly within a global context. Such images in the news media and elsewhere reinforce changing attitudes about childhood as it is culturally imagined.

Moving from constructions and representations of childhood to children as media audiences, **Uwe Hasebrink** and **Ingrid Paus-Hasebrink** map long-term trends in childhood consumption of media. They argue that changes in media environments and in children's media use led to changes in childhood and socialization, as well as children's development of their view of the world. Through their analysis of how each medium entered children's everyday lives and how it is used today, they demonstrate how the historical development of media technologies has played a key role in children's media. Placed in the current context of an increasingly converging media environment, the chapter sets out to develop a more holistic view of children's media use.

A different perspective to children's relationship with media is rooted in developmental psychology approaches, as **Marina Krcmar** discusses in her chapter. She examines four assumptions at work in research on children and media conducted through this perspective: Children and adolescents are qualitatively different from adults; age is a primary variable; all differences are related to development; developmental phenomena and developmental theory are applied selectively in research on children and media. Directives from each assumption are presented. The importance of environment and the roles of quantitative and qualitative research approaches, too, are discussed.

These chapters make for a smooth transition to **Elizabeth Vandewater**'s review of ecological approaches to the study of children and media. She discusses how and the extent to which ecological perspectives (as represented in ecological theory, systems-theory, and life-course developmental theory) have been incorporated in research on media and children. Brief outlines of the main ideas of these theories are presented, and the ways in which they have informed and generated developmental science systems perspectives is discussed. This review leads to her discussing the current state of scholarship on media and children, and proposing directions for future collective endeavors as media scholars.

A central thread in the current interest in children relates to their construction as consumers. **David Buckingham** explores the diverse ways in which children are constructed or defined as consumers in both popular and academic discourse. His chapter begins by contrasting the arguments of popular campaigners, who tend to construct children as victims of commercial marketing, with those of marketers, who tend to see children as active and "empowered" by consumer culture. This overview is followed by a discussion of two dominant perspectives within academic research: media effects research and consumer socialization research. Buckingham argues for the extension of these approaches via accounts that look at the social contexts of children's consumer practices. The final section presents several alternative theoretical approaches that might be developed, drawn from cultural studies, actor network theory, and the anthropology of consumer culture. Each of these approaches moves beyond the polarized approaches presented at the beginning of the chapter.

Seamlessly, **Karen Orr Vered** continues this argument by demonstrating how the multi-disciplinary and multi-methodological practice of critical studies scholarship intersects with studies of children, childhood, and media. The counter-hegemonic critique implicit in this scholarly practice is traced back to roots in Marxist critical theory seeded by the Frankfurt School scholars, and extended through the Birmingham Centre for Contemporary Cultural Studies (UK) and French critical traditions. Research conducted in the critical tradition is discussed with examples derived from different methodological approaches.

Another variant of a critical approach to scholarship is offered by the extension of feminist theories to the study of children and media. **Dafna Lemish** argues that feminist theory can offer the field of children and media significant and original perspectives, in the following four domains: A mapping of gender segregation of children's leisure culture and explanation of the mechanism driving this segregation; a theoretical understanding of gender as a form of social construction rather than limited biological assumptions; a particular view on the form and role of methodology in the study of children and media; and a model of engaged scholarship attempting to advance progressive social change.

A final perspective in this first section of the book is offered by **Radhika Parameswaran** who discusses approaches from globalization theory to the study of children and media. She argues that the spread of globalization and its precipitation of intensified cross-border flows in migrants, currencies, media culture, technologies, and ideologies is resulting in a much more deeply connected world for children. Political economy studies of global media companies and their products demonstrate the potential impact of cultural imperialism – the hegemony of Euro-American culture – on children, which continues to be a serious concern for scholars. Moderating powerful models of cultural imperialism, ethnographic studies reveal children's agency as active audiences and uncovers the ways in which glocalization and hybridity play important roles in shaping youthful audiences' responses to global media culture. The chapter concludes by highlighting neglected geographic and academic areas in existing knowledge, hence suggesting productive directions for future work on childhood and media globalization.

1

THE CO-CONSTRUCTION OF MEDIA AND CHILDHOOD

Kirsten Drotner

Charting ways in which mass media represent children and ways in which the media orchestrate claims about children's uses of new media offers analytical prisms through which we may address wider societal discourses of, and contestations over, what counts as proper media and proper childhood and youth. Such discourses are powerful frames within which children's actual media practices play out, and the discourses are therefore important to understand if we want a full insight into children's relations to media. My main claim, which I will substantiate in the following, is that modernity witnesses an ongoing co-construction of mass media, childhood and youth. Media are at once material and symbolic social resources (Carey, [1989]1992) whose main characteristic is their semiotic properties. So, media are not merely conduits for the transmission of information, they are institutionally embedded meaning-making tools that connect people across time and space (Thompson, 1995).

The nexus between media and childhood may be seen to operate along a continuum of positions. The chapter will focus on two poles in that continuum. First, on a day-to-day basis media serve as an important public means of articulating selective images of childhood, for example through print news reporting, advertisements, television and film. I will discuss how these popular mediated perceptions are articulated and may be understood. Second, notably with the uptake of a new medium, media may concentrate on certain aspects of children's media uses, and such interest may develop into what may be termed a media panic (Drotner, 1992). Positions within the two poles shift over time as the empirical contexts within which they operate change. But the two poles also share important similarities to do with the structural issues they tackle, issues that the chapter will spell out.

My focus will be on media discourses that are both public and popular by which I mean discourses promulgated through media that are publicly accessible and have a wide circulation and use. Conversely, I have nothing to say about children's responses to media nor their actual media practices. Since demarcations between childhood and youth change over time, I include examples of adolescence or youth when they are deemed relevant, although my main interest is with articulations of childhood; and while media serve as public arenas of debates on childhood in relation to, for example, education, work and leisure, I focus my analysis on those aspects of the nexus where the media operate directly as means or ends of childhood perceptions. Last, but not least, my account is a partial one, limited to the global North and its specific empirical constellations between media and childhood development that may have little relevance to other parts of the world.

Mediated childhood

Art historians, literary historians and cultural historians have a long tradition of using representations of children in books and paintings as sources documenting historical change (Coveny, 1967; McGraw, 1941). Indeed, the main proponent of the invention of childhood thesis, the French historian Philippe Ariès, uses painted portraits of children to claim that in premodern times children were socially marked as adults writ small, dressed out in robes and with adornments in the same manner as adults (Ariès, 1962). This claim has been contested. For example, the British art critic Peter Fuller argues that many child portraits produced in Europe's courts in the fifteenth and sixteenth centuries were tokens in negotiations of political marriages. So the images projected potentials of future beauty and wealth in order to literally optimise the purchasing power of the portrait (Fuller, 1979, p. 78). Apart from the validity of the empirical evidence, the analytical differences testify to two markedly different approaches to understanding the relation between childhood and representation. While Ariès largely uses paintings as documentation about *which* adult perceptions held sway at particular times, Fuller and others are at pains to illuminate *how* adult perceptions are constructed, circulated and socially embedded (Brown, 2002; Higgonet, 1998).

While Western art and literature have offered a rich source in charting shifting modes of child representation through the history of childhood, much less is made of the ways in which popular mass media as meaning-making technologies serve to advance shifting perceptions of childhood. To chart these perceptions, we need to look into the historical situatedness of the earliest forms of mass media, namely print. Books together with periodicals, prints, posters and postcards offer the earliest form of popular and publicly available media. Many forms of print include images as illustrations and embellishments, yet most rely on text. So, the uptake and use of print media is dependent on and serves to advance an ability to read if not to write. While many people have learned literacy and numeracy through family members or peers, the modern notion of childhood is closely related to training of literacy and numeracy during a sphere of life separated from adult affairs, and requiring institutional spaces of development such as home, school, playground and clubs, yet nevertheless preparing for the child's future functions with the family as an unquestioned base. The co-construction of early mass media and literate child audiences at a remove from the adult (male) world of work is key to the shaping of modern perceptions of childhood.

So, for example the American cultural critic Neil Postman has suggested that in Western Europe the spread of literacy through the invention of the printing press has been the principal force in shaping a widely accepted consensus around the meaning of childhood. Mastering book reading became a sign of maturity toward which the young must be trained (Postman, 1982). According to the historian John Gillis (1996), it was primarily the advent of hugely popular media in the nineteenth century – greeting cards, postcards, calendars and family magazines – that helped disseminate an idealised image of childhood as a domestic phase of innocent bliss, an image that became a constant source of identity for adults to the extent that it overshadowed the reality of children's lives.

This childhood image of domesticated innocence resonates with us today. It is perhaps most widely seen with babies and small children and most strikingly appropriated by advertising – from nappies and food to toys and cars. Many commercial TV serials and family films equally subscribe to the ideal in the sense that its aberrations act as dramaturgical drivers which the plot ultimately sets straight: wild or unruly children are tamed and socialised into "proper" behaviour, and childlike adults end up by shouldering the responsibilities of "proper" parenting.

The good, the bad and the ugly

British media scholar Patricia Holland is among the relatively few professionals who study how popular visual media articulate such normative images of childhood and how these articulations change over time. Importantly, she documents how the image of innocence is inscribed into wider divisions in terms of class, gender and ethnicity, divisions which popular media serve to naturalise through their selective discourses. Drawing on the childhood historian Hugh Cunningham (1995), she sees the child as an "other" against which not only adults' fantasies may be projected but equally their fears. Popular media draw on and serve to enhance representations of children that are idle, perverse, pitiful or abused, in short beyond the normative range of the middle-class family. Working-class children are represented as aberrant and in need of correction because of their public presence; girls – especially in public – appear aggressive or sexualised and in need of counselling; while children from non-Western cultures are seen as exotic victims in need of protection (Holland, 2004). She cogently demonstrates how the commercial pressures underlying much news reporting play into these contrasting representations of juvenile otherness by simultaneously stimulating audiences' sentiments of anxiety and attraction.

Young people top the list when it comes to problem-oriented portrayals in the media. Perhaps because they verge on the boundary to adulthood, their marking as carefree, natural and spontaneous others seems more difficult to sustain, and mediated gendering seems on the increase with age. Indeed, public news reports and documentaries routinely represent young people, and particularly young men from working-class and non-Western backgrounds, as sources of crime, unemployment and general disorder, nurturing sentiments of concern (Hendrick, 1990; Springhall, 1998). Conversely, these same groups have a long tradition of being represented as, for example, cunning aces in mass-circulation serials (Denning, 1987; Drotner, [1985]1988). Today, that tradition continues with streetwise male protagonists in reality shows on television, with glossy adverts featuring computer game geeks, and with young male and non-Western idols pushing normative boundaries in popular gossip forums on the internet and in the realm of popular music. Images of young women adhere to a similar genre distinction between fact and fiction, between problems and permissiveness, but with persistently different gender connotations. Sex, not crime, offers a standard frame of reference for the popular perception, understanding and interpretation of young women's actions as seen in titillating presentations of flower girls in popular nineteenth century magazines and on to contemporary make-over programmes on television. Although class and ethnic aspects play decisive roles in media articulations about young women, they are less transparent and acknowledged than in the case of young men (Walkerdine, 1997).

Co-creation: a two-way street

Modern media operate as powerful vehicles in the display, dissemination and discussions of childhood. Why is this so? A primary reason may be found in the simple fact that every adult can, and does, relate to articulations about children, whether visual, oral or in print. Childhood matters are simply good selling points and one of the key ingredients for commercial media to increase their sales; and the vast majority of media, in the past as today, are commercial. Moreover, the media employ a set of concepts about childhood that have some purchase on social reality. As public and easily accessible technologies, they operate as spaces for the voicing of competing perspectives on this reality, and hence media are catalysts of often mundane negotiations and reappropriations of what count as proper social and cultural boundaries for children. On a day-to-day basis popular media are prime catalysts in defining, handling and regulating social problems as moral problems (Hunt, 1999; Loseke, 2003).

The middle-class definition of childhood and its related "others" has equally influenced the shaping of modern media. As children in industrialised societies gradually, and conflictually, lose control as contributors to the family economy, they gain control over their leisure (Drotner, [1985]1988); and through the twentieth century juvenile leisure culture increasingly becomes a culture of domestic consumption with commercial media including advertising taking centre stage. Moreover, the middle-class norm of childhood comes to operate as a boundary space of genre, by which I mean that its normative demarcations of public and private, adult and child, girl and boy, play into a mapping of different genres. Perhaps the clearest example is the way in which, from the eighteenth century on, fairy tales develop from communal, oral narratives enjoyed by young and old into a hugely popular genre for the nursery, a genre that proves viable also for new media such as film, as testified, for example, in the early development of the Walt Disney corporation (Wasko, 2001).

In wider terms, fiction ties in with perceived notions that young children display imaginative faculties not enjoyed by older children, who mature into the use of more realistic fiction, news and documentaries. Media producers gradually establish genre hierarchies that are attuned to careful, parental and educational monitoring of proper media fare – books, magazines, film, television on to contemporary computer games and internet use – based on widespread notions of child development. Through the nineteenth and twentieth centuries, some media producers have traded in catering to such genre hierarchies while others have excelled in undermining the very same hierarchies to reach new audiences. For in the past, as today, children rarely keep only to children's media. When their media practices transgress what at any given time are deemed key boundaries of media, genres or uses, the moral regulation of mediated childhood may turn into more intense debate and, indeed, struggle.

Media panics: beyond dialogue

Particularly when a new medium emerges on the social scene, it provokes stark reactions in public debate, reactions that are persistently framed as normative discourses of optimism and pessimism, celebration and concern (Jensen, 1990). Chief among the optimists are proponents of the new medium, including publishers, producers, service providers and others with a vested interest in its wide uptake and success. Pessimists include a range of individuals and interest groups among which are often teachers, parent organisations, cultural critics and experts such as psychologists and doctors. What is specific about such discourses is that media are both objects of the discourse and the means of its articulation. Over time, pessimists have been the most persistent claims-makers, and such discourses of concern over the putative ill-effects of (new) media may aptly be termed media panics (Drotner, 1992, 1999). The term may be seen as a variation of the concept moral panic, which denotes the social processes shaping the public identification and handling of a perceived threat to the moral order of society. Coined by the British sociologist Stanley Cohen (1973) in his study of British youth movements in the mid-1960s, the concept specifies moral panics as being essentially normative discourses ("moral") that are marked by intense, emotional claims ("panics") and play out in public, often mediated, arenas with multiple claims-makers labelling the problem, and suggesting routes of political, legal or pedagogical action whose result is a fading of public interest – until a new problem is identified. Media panics serve to raise analytical key questions, including the role played by media in orchestrating the panics, the rhetorical strategies employed by different interest groups and the power relations involved in prompting some and not other issues to become panics at particular moments (Crichter, 2003; Thompson, 1998).

While media panics follow similar trajectories and share key analytical issues with the study of moral panics, media panics, as I noted above, are special in the sense that the media not only operate as discursive catalysts for rivaling claims-makers, (new) media and their perceived implications for particular social groups are the very focus of the panic. Social concern over popular media and their users is as old as popular media themselves. For example, in eighteenth-century Britain broadside ballads and chapbooks with emotionally charged and politically subversive tales enjoyed a wide readership. By the end of the century, Evangelical groups began to publish so-called cheap repository tracts – readable ballads, tales and Bible stories – as an antidote to the pernicious influence which the commercial fare was believed to have; and the tracts that were often given away as prizes to poor children in the newly established Sunday schools and other places of moral reform (Drotner, [1985]1988; Neuburg, 1977).

In many countries, the nineteenth century saw the first wave of a mass-reading public and mass-circulation print media, including new weeklies catering to young readers with their exciting tales and offering profitable export opportunities (Denning, 1987; Drotner, 1988). These combined developments paved the way for the so-called Nick Carter panic (Boëthius, 1994). Named after a popular American serial featuring a private detective, it unfolded in the Nordic countries of Europe in the early 1900s when mass schooling was under way and when the proper upbringing of girls and of working-class and poor children were objects of vigorous social attention. The Nick Carter panic is perhaps one of the earliest, but by no means the last (Lent, 1999), transnational media panics developing in several countries at nearly the same time. In Sweden and Denmark, for example, the panic resulted in anti-Nick Carter societies, publishers designed special series of counter-publications and library associations pushed for children's sections.

Similar media panics have accompanied the emergence of, for example, film (Smith, 2005), comics (Barker, 1984), videos (Crichter, 2003) and computer games (Sandywell, 2006). The detailed studies of these processes suggest important differences in terms of the socio-cultural contexts prompting the panics and the actions taken. The media landscape itself plays a key role in the sense that its degree of commodification, technological convergence and regulatory conventions play into the actual panic processes. Sweden's limited publishing industry and import options in the early 1900s is very different from the multi-platform game narratives and global marketing strategies employed by today's computer game industry – including a harnessing of panic discourses to attract potential fans. Moreover, the media offer prime venues for rapid interaction and coordination among interest groups with stakes in the panic discourses. Even so, the media panics also display striking similarities across time and space, similarities that are to do with the media, with the perceptions of childhood and with the panic discourse itself.

Through the panic discourses of a new medium, a hierarchy of media and genres is set up. At the pinnacle is the oldest medium – print – and especially the quality book. At the bottom of the hierarchy is most likely the new medium in question. So, when VCRs entered the home in the 1980s, family television was deemed better than the time-shifting of videos (Crichter, 2003). Moreover, factual genres hold pride of place, at least for older children, as is the case in the day-to-day debate over children and media. So, when children's cinema-going caused public outrage in the 1910s and 1920s, one of the recurrent concerns was the alleged emotional charge of the visual narratives. A normative dichotomy was set up between text as a means of insight and image as a source of entertainment. The panic hierarchies operated as ways of negotiating quality in the face of new modes of mediated communication, and the familiar media and genres offered obvious points of reference and assessment.

Since the late nineteenth century, media panics have been particularly concerned with young audiences. As we saw, the norms of middle-class childhood gain wide social currency in tandem with an institutionalisation of children's lives. Childhood becomes a phase for regulated protection and transformation, and the upbringing of the young (to adult status) becomes a key object of social interest: their individual development through ages and stages is seen as a harbinger of society's futures. The persistent panics targeted at the young are exercises in normative negotiations of what counts as a proper childhood and, on a wider canvas, what counts as the proper directions society should take. Theorists of moral panics have seen the panic focus on children as an exercise in symbolic politics, diverting attention to paedophilia not homosexuality, for example (Jenkins, 1992, p. 10). In terms of media panics, at least, childhood seems no area of normative diversion, but an area of normative projection, pushing at, and seeking to reaffirm, societal boundaries of moral futures.

The panic discourses themselves are marked by stark binary positionings based on emotion more than documentation; and what documentation is brought forward is often decontextualised. One of the best-known examples is provided by the American psychiatrist Frederic Wertham whose *Seduction of the Innocent* from 1954 is a powerful voice in the 1950s anti-comics campaigns. His analysis hinges on selected images with no sustained narrative or visual analysis (Barker, 1984); and on that basis he makes generalised claims about the psychological damage wrought on young and malleable minds. Still, the emotional nature and the claims-makers' selective evidence should not lead one to believe that panic discourses are pure fabrication or that they are not grounded on very real issues of concern. Rather, the discursive format obscures an illumination of more structural aspects of the issues at stake, including for example children's economic and social inequalities or the properties of media production.

Some new media have enjoyed a relatively rapid uptake with rather little public fuss. Radio, for example, entered people's living rooms from the 1920s on without large-scale debates on its implications for the young. A main reason may be that sound in popular perceptions is less powerful than images which are seen as defining elements of film, television, comics and computer games.

Voice and effect

The present chapter has studied some key historical discourses relating childhood and media. Children's own voices are not heard in such an approach, but they may be louder in the future. Young people's wide, if unequal, uptake and uses of social networking sites testifies to possible changes in the media images of the young. Shaping and sharing text, images and sound are ways in which the young make their mark on a media landscape modelled on adult perceptions for children, not by children. Still, empirical studies of what is actually uploaded and shared by whom and for what purposes quickly lessens the most celebratory conclusions. For example, the visual genre conventions shaping mass mediated images of hedonistic childhood tend to operate as aesthetic guides for their own snapshots and clips. But the youthful voices of mediated production nevertheless serve to further complicate the co-creation of media and childhood.

The ongoing moral regulation of social problems through discourses of media representation display very different rhetorical strategies and outcomes from the ones seen with the intermittent, short-lived media panics. Yet, in their different ways they address the same fundamental social issues to do with shifting power relations of age, gender, class and ethnicity. They address the same cultural issues to do with taste and quality. Last, but not least, they address the same issues to do with the implications of mediated interaction and its changes. In terms of children, notably effects studies in the United States have focused on this important issue with health, sex and violence as recurrent themes (Jamieson and Romer, 2008). The co-creation approach outlined in the present chapter offers a different inroad to studies of effect in three capacities. First, a historical perspective facilitates an attention to aspects of media change as well as stability. Second, the conceptual perspective – looking at childhood, not children – allows a constructivist approach open to discourses of contestation including silences. Third, the relational perspective – investigating the imbrications between childhood and adulthood, childhood and media discourses – invites us to remember that discourses and practices are interlaced. While the chapter has underlined continuities rather than changes in this account, the real intellectual insights lie in the context-sensitive and theoretically reflexive studies which are fortunately growing in number.

SEE ALSO in this volume chapter by Olson and Rampaul.

References

Ariès, P. (1962). *Centuries of childhood*. Harmondsworth: Penguin. (Original work published 1960).

Barker, M. (1984). *A haunt of fears: The strange history of the British horror comics campaign*. London: Pluto.

Boëthius, U. (1994). Youth, media and moral panics. In J. Fornäs and G. Bolin (Eds), *Youth culture in late modernity*. London: Sage, pp. 39–57.

Brown, M. R. (Ed.). (2002). *Picturing children: Constructions of childhood between Rousseau and Freud*. Aldershot: Ashgate.

Carey, J. ([1989]1992). A cultural approach to communication. In J. Carey, *Communication as culture: Essays on media and society*. New York: Routledge, pp. 13–36.

Cohen, S. (1973). *Folk devils and moral panics*. St Albans: Paladin.

Coveny, P. (1967). *The image of childhood: The individual and society. A study of the theme in English literature*. Harmondsworth: Penguin.

Crichter, C. (2003). *Moral panics and the media*. Buckingham: Open University Press.

Cunningham, H. (1995). *Children and childhood in Western society since 1500*, London: Longman.

Denning, M. (1987). *Mechanic accents: Dime novels and working-class culture in America*. New York: Verso.

Drotner, K. ([1985]1988). *English children and their magazines, 1751–1945*. New Haven, CT: Yale University Press.

——(1992). Modernity and media panics. In M. Skovmand and K.C. Schrøder (Eds), *Media cultures: Reappraising transnational media*. London: Routledge, pp. 42–62.

——(1999). Dangerous Media? Panic Discourses and Dilemmas of Modernity. *Paedagogica Historica*, *35*(3), 593–619.

Fuller, P. (1979). Uncovering childhood. In Martin Hoyles (Ed.), *Changing childhood*. London: Writers and Readers Publishing Cooperative, pp. 71–108.

Gillis, J.R. (1996). *A world of their own making: Myth, ritual, and the quest for family values*. New York: HarperCollins.

Hendrick, H. (1990). *Images of youth: Age, class, and the male youth problem 1880–1920*. Oxford: Clarendon Press.

Higgonet, A. (1998). *Pictures of innocence: The history and crisis of ideal childhood*. London: Thames & Hudson.

Holland, P. (2004). *Picturing Childhood: The myth of the child in popular imagery*. London: I.B. Tauris.

Hunt, A. (1999). *Governing morals: A social history of moral regulation*. Cambridge: Cambridge University Press.

Jamieson, P. E. and D. Romer (Eds). (2008). *The changing portrayals of adolescents in the media since 1950*. Oxford: Oxford University Press.

Jenkins, P. (1992). *Intimate enemies?: Moral panics in contemporary Great Britain?*. New York: Aldine de Gruyter.?

Jensen, J. (1990). *Redeeming modernity: Contradictions in media criticism*. Thousand Oaks: Sage.

Lent, J. A. (Ed.). (1999). *Pulp demons: International dimensions of the postwar anti-comics campaign*. Madison, NJ: Fairleigh Dickinson University Press.

Loseke, D. R. (2003). *Thinking about social problems: An introduction to constructionist perspectives*. New Brunswick, NJ: Aldine Transaction.

McGraw, M. (1941). *The child in painting*. New York: Greystone.

Neuburg, V. E. (1977). *Popular literature: A history and guide*. Harmondsworth: Penguin.

Postman, N. (1982). *The disappearance of childhood*. New York: Vintage.

Sandywell, B. (2006). Monsters in cyberspace: Cyberphobia and cultural panic in the information age. *Information, Communication and Society*, *9*(1), 39–61.

Smith, S. J. (2005). *Children, cinema and censorship.* London: I.B. Tauris.

Springhall, J. (1998). *Youth, popular culture and moral panics.* Basingstoke: Macmillan.

Thompson, J. B. (1995). *The media and modernity: A social history of the media.* Cambridge: Polity.

Thompson, K. (1998). *Moral Panics.* London: Routledge.

Walkerdine, V. (1997). *Daddy's girl: Young girls and popular culture.* London: Palgrave Macmillan.

Wasko, J. (2001). *Understanding Disney: The manufacture of fantasy.* Cambridge: Polity.

2

REPRESENTATIONS OF CHILDHOOD IN THE MEDIA

Debbie Olson and Giselle Rampaul

Introduction—visualizing childhood

Childhood is, and has always been, an unstable concept, variously interpreted and represented according to historical, social, cultural, political and economic contexts as Philippe Ariès shows in his ground-breaking work, *Centuries of Childhood* (1962). Ariès' work is regarded as a fundamental text informing study on representations of childhood, as it opens up discussions about the concept of childhood in history as well as in the contemporary period. By examining representations of childhood in visual media, Ariès showed that childhood is a relatively new idea, and that the concept of childhood changed and developed over time. Social and economic changes led to the development of a theory of childhood innocence; depictions of children as miniature adults in the sixteenth century were eventually replaced with depictions of children as distinct from adults. Children, then, came to be assigned a "special" status. Although such pictorial representations of children established a standard for what children were expected to look like and contributed to certain idealized conceptions of childhood, the idea of childhood innocence is now being questioned by some and contested by others. Images of children appearing more recently demonstrate an ideological shift as they interrogate the earlier taken-for-granted ideas about childhood innocence by presenting children as knowing, adultified, and sometimes menacing. This chapter explains how representations of children and childhood are historically and culturally situated, both reflecting values and contributing to their continual change and renewal.

In her historical overview of the emergence of the concept of the modern child in America, Viviana Zelizer (1985) explores how this "special status" led to "sacralized" images of children (objects invested with sentimental or religious value) in the media that consequently affected their economic market value. Profound changes in the modern family and the rise of industrial capitalism contributed to the cultural process of "sacralization" of the child as seen, for example, in the way that child deaths in the nineteenth century took on more emotional value, evident in consolation literature and funerary art during that period—although portraits and triptychs of dead children appeared as early as the sixteenth century (Avery and Reynolds 2000). Childhood, constructed as a vulnerable state in need of adult protection, was consequently domesticated. The endurance of this domesticated middle class childhood is evident in its visual representation in reading primers of the early twentieth century, although these images were few and were limited to line drawings. The Scott Foresman *Dick and Jane* series used by public schools for decades until the 1970s perpetuated this idealized childhood in its rich colorful depictions of a white middle class American family. Carole Kismaric and Marvin Heiferman (1996) argue that "Dick and Jane were meant to represent Everyboy and Everygirl" (p. 21). Millions of American children became literate and acculturated with these images that mapped onto the modern cultural imaginary about what constitutes the American Dream and the associated place of childhood and children.

Anne Higgonet (1998), who focuses on an analysis of childhood through an examination of paintings and photographs, argues that an ideal of innocence is presented in the (Western) Romantic conceptions of childhood as feminine, passive, and associated closely with nature and the belief that these images somehow captured the essence or "truth" of childhood. She, however, points to a significant social change under way in which images of the traditional innocent child are morphing into "knowing images" that "endow children with psychological and physical individuality at the same time as they recognize them as being distinctively child-like" (p. 12). Whereas paintings like Joshua Reynolds' *The Age of Innocence* (1788) and John Everett Millais' *Cherry Ripe* (1879) and Kate Greenaway's illustrations portray the Romantic innocent child, Anne Geddes' photographs exploit the irrational fetishization of this image by drawing attention to the disconnection between childhood and its associations in dragging babies "into the realms of the bizarre and grotesque" (Holland, 2004, p. 25). Higgonet also points to the issues of consent, commercialization, and child pornography that are bound up in the photography of real children as in the work of Sally Mann who portrays her own children as knowing or adultified. Child pornography has as much to do with the ways in which children are presented in the media as the ways in which these representations are perceived and produced, as Patricia Holland (2004) argues. By focusing on contemporary popular visual images of childhood and arguing that "there has been a growth in imagery that deliberately sets out to shock," she attempts to make sense of the resultant pleasure and the contemporary "crisis of looking" (p. xiii). These ephemeral but persistent images of children—such as Christmas cards portraying the Virgin Mary and Child, children's clothing advertisements, and Save the Children posters—are publicly available and "feed comfortably into the consciousness of the age" (p. 1). This imagery reveals "an abstract, shifting and heavily ideological *concept*" (p. xiv) which tells stories, mythologizes, and recreates the dream of childhood for adults.

Racialized childhoods

Along with childhood "innocence", whiteness was also implicitly idealized in early representations of childhood and images of a white childhood came to be considered universal and desirable. Non-white children have, therefore, traditionally been subject to stereotypical and caricatured representations or have simply been excluded from cultural productions of media images, being replaced instead by images of white childhood. More recently, in predominantly white societies such as in America and Australia, there have been deliberate corrective attempts to distribute multicultural images of nationhood that include representations of non-white children. However, in countries where whiteness is in the minority, depictions of the racial majority are still rare as images of white children dominate the media. Both the inclusion and exclusion of non-white children in different parts of the world are in response to the early establishment of a whiteness paradigm in visual representations of childhood. The depiction of race and color in images of childhood is, therefore, important to wider social, cultural, and political issues.

Michelle H. Martin (1998) argues that the Black-a-Moor of *Struwwelpeter* and Little Black Sambo of *The Story of Little Black Sambo* were perhaps the first illustrations of black children in European picture books. Although these writers were venturing into "uncharted territory"

(p. 147) by writing about children of color, their presentations of blackness are very similar to each other because they relied on and perpetuated established stereotypes. These works influenced the ways in which African American children came to be represented at the turn of the century. Many of these caricatured images of black children participated in the more generalized racist discourses of the early twentieth century, as Carolyn Dean (2000) shows in her examination of literary, pictorial and musical representations. Children of color were, in fact, absent from all but "folk" representation for some time. Because they drew attention to "physiognomic alterity" (p. 18) and prejudice was characterized as "natural" and "innate," these images "helped naturalize the extant American social order and obfuscate institutionalized racist practices" (p. 29). In the popular media of the time, such images sanitized themes of race relations, racial prejudice, victimization, and miscegenation, offering reassuring interpretations of contemporary social conditions. The eventual inclusion of children of color in mainstream representation—such as in school reading primers—was politically motivated and had political implications and consequences in America.

Studies of media representations of childhood elsewhere in non-Western countries show that the influence of the Western Romantic concept of white childhood is widespread. In countries where whiteness is the minority, white babies are still presented as the dominant and paradigmatic image of childhood. For example, Maila Stivens (2010) explores the racial content of media images, which are predominantly of white babies, in Malaysia and Singapore. She argues that within the global circulation of images and meanings, the white baby, especially within advertising, is the dominant image in parenting magazines, baby fairs and expos. Although Singaporean children make up 19 percent of the general population, Marjory Ebbeck and Sheela Warrier (2008) find that images of these children comprise only 2.5 percent of visual media (p. 250). If present, local children are regularly portrayed as helpless, vulnerable, and problematic, and are insensitively used as a draw for adult themes. Images of the white baby, interpreted within these local contexts, however, also complicate discussions about the exclusionary power of post-colonial whiteness. Stivens suggests that such images may constitute a move toward a post-nationalist, non-ethnicized space for childhood (para 35).

Although there have been attempts at increasing multicultural and multiracial presence in the media in white majority populations, problems of representation, stereotyping, and allegorizing still emerge. For example, while the popular and long running Australian children's show, *Play School*, might include a more racially inclusive agenda that is consistent with the multiculturalism of Australia, Elizabeth Mackinlay and Katelyn Barney (2008) deconstruct the show's representations of Aboriginal Australians to reveal a simultaneous "respect for the 'other'" and "an objectification" of that "other" (p. 280). In the case of the three 2006 films by border-crossing Mexican directors (Alfonso Cuarón's *Children of Men*, Alejandro González Iñárritu's *Babel*, and Guillermo del Toro's *Pan's Labyrinth*) explored by Allison Mackey (2010), "the figure of the child is utilized to signal an intense preoccupation with the future of democratic public life." The films' depictions of the oscillating discourses of childhood innocence and fear of children emanating from North America signal the increasing "disposability" of Other childhoods (p. 172).

Representations of childhood in news media

Historically, newspapers have had a major role to play in the sacralization of childhood through their sensationalism of certain stories about childhood. Apart from publicizing childhood deaths, they opened debates about child labor, including the issue of child actors who paradoxically were working children who "represented the new, sentimentalized view of children," as Zelizer shows (p. 95). Sentimental adoption was also sympathetically presented in newspaper headlines and in the rags-to-riches, fairy-tale presentations of adoption in magazines. The blonde, blue-eyed girl child was advertised as the most desirable and, therefore, most valuable, as she was the ultimate representation of domesticated and sentimental childhood. This section examines how news media construct childhood, how conceptions of childhood influence media production and sales, and how the media can contribute to a better understanding of the lives of real children.

Surveying newspaper articles and other news media coverage of child murders in the UK, Chris Greer (2007) argues that children are often presented as "ideal victims" as they are portrayed as "vulnerable, defenceless, innocent and worthy of sympathy and compassion" (p. 22), perpetuating the sacralization of childhood. Similarly, Cristina Ponte (2007), in her transnational study of children in the news, argues that the media present the child victim as "the *perfect innocent*" (p. 738). Valerie Youssef (2011) and Nada Korac (2009) also observe that children are often represented as "passive" in the news media of Trinidad and Tobago and Serbia respectively. Victim photographs, that often accompany these reports, further present "an idealized personification of innocence and loss" (Greer, p. 31). At the same time, by analyzing case studies, Greer points out that not all childhoods are created equally in the news. Factors such as age, gender, class, notions of "respectability," and race all contribute to the legitimacy of victim status and thus the extent of media coverage and interest.

While sexual abuse of children has become a "news staple," Greer notes that only certain kinds of stories, such as abuse by individuals outside the home or through grooming on the internet, are given significant media attention as external threats seem less emotionally problematic (p. 41). Dwelling on the gruesome details of the mutilation and sexual assault upon the child's body can function as a disturbing and powerful marketing tool in raising local news ratings and viewership, as Youssef (2011) argues. Such studies of representations of children in the news media draw attention to the issues involving the rights of the child as defined by the UN although, most times, these rights are not taken into consideration. In her analysis of representations of children in conflict and disaster situations, Karen Wells (2009) argues that images of suffering children simultaneously elicit anxiety and feelings of voyeurism and sadism and, therefore, "offend[s] the Western gaze." She takes issue, however, with attempts "to avoid depictions of suffering, repeating stereotypical discourse" as she regards this censorship and "protection" of Western sensibilities as counterproductive and unethical (p. 6).

Other representations of the child as victim appear in news stories about illness, health and medical carelessness, poverty, missing and abandoned children. In stories that feature the "Olympic child" (children of famous people) and the "Disputed child" (custody battles), children are defined according to their relationships with their adult parents (Ponte, 2007. pp. 746, 748). Ponte, however, draws attention to a paradox in the way contemporary societies imagine children and conditions of childhood. While children are portrayed as victims, they can also be portrayed as "the *black sheep* child" (p. 738) or menace, as in stories about delinquents, child soldiers, and child murderers who kill other children such as the Columbine, Colorado, teens, and the two ten-year-old boys, Robert Thompson and Jon Venables, who were convicted for the murder of two-year-old James Bulger in the UK. The "Child of Science" stories (about artificial insemination and fetal capacities, for example), however, can be associated with empowerment or potential although they, too, are often presented "under contradictory frames" (Ponte, 2007, p. 746) in science versus religion debates.

Global images of childhood

Some scholars have argued that media images of children on the global stage promote cultural homogenization or cultural imperialism, particularly because Disney and Western media dominate the children's media landscape worldwide, as Katalin Lustyik (2010) suggests. Janet Wasko et al. (2001) found that across cultures, audiences articulate a "commonly shared understanding of what Disney means" and that, despite cultural differences, audiences tend to interpret Disney's images of childhood along similar value lines: romantic love, good triumphs over evil, and happily-ever-afters (p. 334). Disney's dominance around the world has affected "indigenous media and cultural production" by setting a (Western) standard by which local children's image media are measured (p. 336). Such domination of childhood images by the Western-based Disney corporation can influence the way childhood is portrayed within local contexts. In a study focused on gender in children's television around the world, Maya Götz and Dafna Lemish (2012) found that images of children on television tended to follow universal stereotypes: more overweight males are portrayed than overweight females, females are usually portrayed in groups and are disproportionately blonde, male antagonists are more often portrayed as dark, and the majority of characters are Caucasian. As these studies suggest, however, cultural homogenization can occur in both reception and local production of images of children and childhood.

A contrasting trend in scholarship about global children's media complicates the homogeneity argument and suggests that the viewer actively engages and interprets media images within a local context. The viewer's role in unlocking local meanings within visual media contributes to new images of children as active social participants, producers and consumers of culture who participate in constructing visual images and narratives through their global participation on the internet (Youtube, Facebook, etc). David Buckingham (2007) studies the changing nature of childhood against the backdrop of ever-advancing global media, which in turn leads to new discourses about images of children and the ways those images represent childhood. Buckingham suggests that the "production, circulation, and consumption" of the child image is a complex process, challenging previous notions of cultural homogenization (p. 43). For instance, Fran Hassencahl (2012) argues that children are frequently used in Iranian cinema to express social criticism as the free expression of children is more accepted in Iran. Ammu Joseph (2007) criticizes the absence of children's voices in India's media and argues that if the dominant media allowed children a voice instead of only co-opting their images, children could experience a discourse that reflects a real desire to include them in cultural production as active and autonomous participants (p. 289). This sentiment is echoed by Anne Kjorholt (2007) who believes children have the potential to shape ideas about national identity beyond what their traditional images represent (pp. 36–37). The popularity of such films as *Slumdog Millionare* (2008) makes visible Joseph's call for the inclusion of children's voices as a mediating influence in the reception and construction of popular images of childhood. For Xuelin Zhou (2007), images of disaffected youth in Chinese cinema reflect cultural changes and a growing cosmopolitanism among young people. Zhou shows that images of youth in rebellion films critique the social order and its "orthodox morality" in favor of a purposelessness that is reflected by images of "hedonistic youth" heroes who suffer from a "cultural inferiority complex" (p. 61) as young people negotiate changing social conditions. The figure of the child outside Western media contributes to a growing landscape of visualized childhood, the discursive nature of which necessitates its critical location within local socio-political, cultural, and geographic arenas.

New media and the future of childhood's image

Technological advancement has inevitably changed the way childhood is imagined and understood, which in turn, creates new representations of childhood. In *No Future*, Lee Edelman (2004) takes a unique look at the way the child image is used within historical, political, and cultural discourses as a symbol of heteronormative futurity (p. 2). Edelman explores the ways in which images of children and childhood comprise what he calls a "secular theology" that ultimately shapes collective narratives and narrative meanings (p. 12). Edelman argues that it is the universalized image of the child—the "Cult of the Child"—that shapes a society's historical and political cultural discourse (p. 19). Modern children, according to Jyotsna Kapur (2005), have been "cyborgized"—they are more technologically competent than their predecessors, and have access to a wide world of information and experiences that blur the boundaries between child and adult (pp. 122–23). Such children are represented in films like the popular *Home Alone* series as independent of adult protection and guidance (p. 120). Images of children permeate the advertising landscape contributing to the "routinization" of the child image within multimedia formats. The vast amount of images of children in media circulation have blurred the distinction between conceptions of the child as consumer and producer, as Sarah Banet-Weiser (2009) argues, "forcing us to rethink the subject position of the [child] audience" (p. 76) and of the images of childhood within global media.

Though numerous images continue to reinforce the notion of childhood innocence, a new trend in today's global media sensationalizes the child image in multiple ways. Jane O'Connor (2009) argues that the rise of the child star, or celebrity child, is one instance that seems to contradict the cultural need to elevate the child to a "symbol of natural goodness and a connection to the divine" (p. 223). For O'Connor, today's child celebrity is an "object of pity, ridicule, and disdain" that symbolizes "lost childhood and disastrous adult lives" (p. 214). Adultified images of children are prevalent in today's media, including sexualized images of young girls, exemplified by the French *Cosmo* magazine's photos of ten-year-old child model, Thylane Loubry Blondeau. Popular reality shows that spectacalize the adultification and sexualization of young girls, notably TLC network's "Toddlers and Tiaras," frequently replace more traditional childhood images with images that question the very meaning of "child".

Another change in the traditional child image is the urbanization of children through politicized images of child soldiers or child criminals. In their study of global youth cinema, Timothy Shary and Alexandra Seibel (2007) found that delinquency was the most common representation of children in national media. Such images in the news media and elsewhere reinforce changing attitudes about childhood as it is culturally imagined. Giroux (2009) believes there is a new "global social order" in which children, rather than representing a possible future, are instead "demonized and criminalized" (p. 29) in popular imagery. Olson (2007) argues that the urbanization of the child image is also visually expressed by the changing color palette used to frame and contextualize modern images of childhood. Traditional pastel pinks, blues, yellows, and other soft colors are replaced by deeply saturated dark reds, greens, blues, magentas, and other non-traditional color schemes. One significant change in the global landscape of the child image is the child actively creating images of him/herself for public consumption. From Youtube videos to internet blogs to social networking, children who have access are able to present their own images and voice their own stories outside the control of adults. Such images testify to the complex site of childhood in ways the mythologized traditional child images do not.

Finally, the digital environment gives rise to new conceptions of the child image. One prevailing digital image is that of the starving child of color used in humanitarian fundraising. Kate Manzo (2008) shows that such images demean the dignity of childhood itself, as well as reinforcing negative stereotypes about peoples in the global South. James R. Kincaid (1992, 1998) has argued that the vast amount and availability of the child image via the internet has generated a "set of remarkable cultural narratives [and] ... ways of seeing children" (p. 5) that gives rise to a culture of child eroticism. Some digital images of children reflect the contradictory relationship adults have with childhood, which finds expression in some popular video games where the child player is required to "kill" the child image on screen (for example, Dead Space, 2008, Electronic Arts); a symbolic identity destruction of sorts. Visualizations of demonic or criminal childhood perhaps reflect new tensions and moral panics by adults about the perceived insidious nature of today's youth. As Jan Jagodzinski (2004) and Henry Giroux (2009) conclude, today's youth are positioned as the source of adult anxieties to such an extent that images of childhood innocence and futurity are more often, and unfairly, replaced with images of the delinquent or disconnected adultified child who inhabits a childhood space dominated by hyper-consumerism and rampant technology. The sheer magnitude of child images on the internet, often sexualized and adultified, encourage discussions about the ways in which children and adults negotiate, consume, and produce those images.

SEE ALSO in this volume chapter by Drotner.

References

Ariès, P. (1962). *Centuries of Childhood*. New York: Alfred A. Knoff, Random House.

Avery, G. and Reynolds K. (2000). *Representations of Childhood Death*. London: Macmillan.

Banet-Weiser, S. (2009). Home is where the brand is. In A.D. Lotz (Ed.), *Beyond Prime Time: Television in the Post-Network Era*. New York: Routledge, pp. 75–93.

Buckingham, D. (2007). Childhood in the age of global media. *Children's Geographies*, 5(1–2), 43–54.

Dean, C. (2000). Boys and girls and "boys": popular depictions of African–American children and childlike adults in the United States 1850–1930. *Journal of American & Comparative Cultures*, 23(3), 17–35.

Ebbeck, M. and Warrier, S. (2008). Image of the Singapore child. *Early Childhood Education Journal*, 36(3), 247–51.

Edelman, L. (2004). *No Future*. Durham: Duke UP.

Giroux, H. (2009). *Youth in a Suspect Society*. New York: Palgrave Macmillan.

Götz, M. and Lemish, D. (Eds) (2012). *Sexy Girls, Heroes and Funny Losers: Gender representations in children's TV around the world*. New York: Peter Lang.

Greer, C. (2007). News media, victims and crime. In P. Davies, P. Francis and C. Greer (Eds), *Victims, Crime and Society*. London: Sage, pp. 20–49.

Hassencahl, F. (2012). Experiencing *Hüzün* through the loss of life, limb, and love in Bahman Ghoboadi's *Turtles Can Fly* (2004). In D. Olson and A. Scahill (Eds), *Images of Lost and Othered Children in Contemporary Cinema*. New York: Lexington, p. 319.

Higgonet, A. (1998). *Pictures of Innocence: The History and Crisis of Ideal Childhood*. New York: Thames & Hudson.

Holland, P. (2004). *Picturing Childhood*. London: I.B. Tauris.

Jagodzinski, J. (2004). *Youth Fantasies: the Perverse Landscape of the Media*. New York: Palgrave Macmillan.

Joseph, A. (2007). Why Children Should be Seen and Heard: an Indian Perspective. *Journal of Children and Media*, 1(3), 289–93.

Kapur, J. (2005). *Coining for Capital: Movies, Marketing, and the Transformation of Childhood*. New Brunswick, NJ: Rutgers UP.

Kincaid, J. R. (1992). *Child-loving: The erotic child and Victorian culture*. New York: Routledge.

——(1998). *Erotic Innocence: The culture of child molesting*. Durham, NJ: Duke.

Kismaric, C. and Heiferman, M. (1996). *Growing up with Dick and Jane*. San Francisco: Harper Collins.

Kjorholt, A. T. (2007). Childhood as symbolic space: searching for authentic voices in the era of globalisation. *Children's Geographies*, 5(1–2), 29–42.

Korac, N. (2009). The invisible child. In conference report on media: Representations of children in news media: revisiting the Oslo challenge. Retrieved from http://www.crin.org/resources/infodetail.asp?id=20123

Lustyik, K. (2010). Transnational children's television: the case of Nickelodeon in the South Pacific. *International Communication Gazette*, 72(2), 171–90.

Mackey, A. (2010). Make it public! Border pedagogy and the transcultural politics of hope in contemporary cinematic representations of children. *College Literature*, 37(2), 173–85.

Mackinlay, E. and Barney, K. (2008) "Move over and make room for Meeka": The representation of race, otherness, and indigeneity on the Australian children's television program "Play School". *Discourse: Studies in the Cultural Politics of Education*, 29(2), 273–88.

Manzo, K. (2008). Imaging humanitarianism: NGO identity and the iconography of childhood, *Antipode*, *40*(4), 632–57.

Martin, M. H. (1998). "Hey, who's the kid with the green umbrella?" Re-evaluating the Black-a-Moor and Little Black Sambo. *The Lion and the Unicorn*, *22*(2), 147–62.

O'Connor, J. (2009). Beyond social constructionism: A structural analysis of the cultural significance of the child star. *Children in Society*, *23*(3), 214–25.

Olson, D. (2007). Little Burton Blue: Tim Burton and the product(ion) of color in the fairy tale films The Nightmare Before Christmas and The Corpse Bride. *MP: an International Feminist Journal*, *1*(6), 32–40.

Ponte, C. (2007). Mapping news on children in the mainstream press. *European Societies*, *9*(5), 735–54.

Shary, T. and Seibel, A. (Eds) (2007). *Youth Culture in Global Cinema*. Austin: University of Texas press.

Stivens, M. (2010). White babies and global embodiments. *Intersections: Gender and Sexuality in Asia and the Pacific 23*. Retrieved from http://intersections.anu.edu.au/issue23/stivens.htm

Wasko, J., Phillips, M. and Meehan, E. R. (2001). *Dazzled by Disney? The Global Disney Audience Project*. London: Leicester UP.

Wells, K. (2009). Images of children in conflict and disaster: The ethics and politics of representation. In conference report on MEDIA: Representations of children in news media: Revisiting the Oslo challenge. Retrieved from http://www.crin.org/resources/infodetail.asp?id=20123

Youssef, V. (2011). Child murder in the press of Trinidad and Tobago. *Tout Moun: Caribbean Journal Cultural Studies*, *1*(1). Retrieved from http://www.mainlib.uwi.tt/epubs/toutmoun/index1.htm

Zelizer, V. A. (1985). *Pricing the Priceless Child: The Changing Social Value of Children*. New York: Basic Books.

Zhou, X. (2007). Chinese "youth problem" films of the 1980s: The apolitics of rebellion. In T. Shary and A. Seibel (Eds), *Youth Culture in Global Cinema*. Austin, TX: University of Texas Press, pp. 59–70.

3

TRENDS IN CHILDREN'S CONSUMPTION OF MEDIA

Uwe Hasebrink and Ingrid Paus-Hasebrink

Introduction

Within the framework of this volume this chapter deals with children's media consumption and how it changes over time. A reconstruction of long-term trends in children's media use meets two challenges. First, it cannot rely on long-term data, which cover several decades or even centuries and provide comparable data over a longer period of time. Second, as a rule the existing data, which cover at least several years, reflect the situation only in a specific country and do not enable general conclusions on a global level. Thus, our approach has to build on a synopsis of a large body of research from different historical and cultural backgrounds. In order to identify relevant trends which can serve as meaningful interpretations of the history of children's media use, this synopsis has to be highly selective.

Our approach combines two steps: first we take the historical development of media technologies as a key condition for children's media use, starting with the earliest media; we will follow the historical development. For each relevant media technology we will sketch how it entered children's everyday lives and how it is used today. This way of telling the story of children's media use as distinct stories of individual media technologies is linked with the risk of a deterministic view of technology. Therefore, against today's backdrop of an increasingly converging media environment, our second step sets out to develop a more holistic view of children's media use. We will focus on function rather than on technology. This means that we try to identify comprehensive media repertoires of children, for example the composition of different media that children select for themselves. This perspective helps to better understand the particular role of the different media and the interrelations between "old" and "new" media, as well as the changing functions that media fulfill in children's everyday lives.

Single media technologies in children's media use

From a historical perspective, children's media consumption is most obviously shaped by the particular media available in a certain time period. In the following we will briefly sketch the most important media innovations, when they first appeared, what has been particular about them for children's media consumption, and how they are used in today's multimedia environments.

Due to space limitations we have had to make a decision here: around the world, technical development is not at all synchronous; while, for instance, radio and television have been normal presences for children in the Western world in their families' households for several decades, this is not the case for many children in some developing countries even today. For this chapter we decided to take the Western or American/European perspective as the reference point, but at some points we will emphasize the substantial differences among different parts of the world.

Print media

Although there were different forms of mediated communication for and with children before Gutenberg invented the printing press (for example, theater or orally presented fairy tales), in this chapter we take print media as the earliest form of media. The development of children's media started with periodical magazines for children. In Germany, for instance, the first weekly magazine for children was published in Leipzig between 1772 and 1774. During the nineteenth century more and more magazines and books for children were illustrated with colored drawings. This development builds the early starting point for the new genre of comic strips. Walt Disney's cartoon movies, including *Mickey Mouse*, first presented in 1928, became so popular that the company started to distribute them by using a wide range of media and merchandising products, including printed magazines or short strips in newspapers. Since the 1980s Japanese *Manga* comics have also become quite popular in the Western world.

Compared to books and comics, other print media like newspapers and magazines are less popular among young children; however, teenagers tend to read books and comics less often, and increasingly turn to newspapers and magazines. In some countries, youth-oriented magazines have become particularly important platforms for all aspects of youth culture. Reading books is clearly more frequent among girls than among boys; regarding age there is a decreasing trend after the age of 8 to 10 years (Rideout et al., 2010, p. 30). In a comparative European study, Beentjes et al. found that among 9- to 10-year-olds in Europe, 85 percent read books. However, this figure decreases to 73 percent among 15- to 16-year-olds (2001, p. 94).

Cinema

The advent of cinema was a starting point for a still increasing interest in empirical research on how children deal with any new medium and what effects this might have (Paik, 2001, p. 7). In the first decades of the twentieth century, cinema proved to be quite attractive, also for children. Paik (2001, p. 9) reports that in 1929 the average American child was attending 1.6 movies per week. Cinema attendance in general was highest between the late 1920s and late 1940s. After the advent of television the number of people going to the movies substantially decreased.

While younger children go to the movies together with their parents, the core function of going to the movies is related to teenagers' increasing need to develop their own social network and to experience social events outside their families' homes. Recent figures reflect a stable role of cinema within children's lives, at least in the United States. A recent Kaiser Family Foundation study on American children's media use in 2009 (Rideout et al., 2010) reports that 12 percent of children aged 8 to18 report watching a film in a cinema on a normal day. This figure is the same as five years ago.

Radio

Starting in the early 1920s radio entered households in the US quite quickly: In 1930 46 percent of American households had a radio; in 1940 the figure was 80 percent, and in 1970 it reached

98 percent (Paik, 2001, p. 11). In the first decades of its development radio proved to be a highly attractive medium, for children as well as adults; many dedicated children's programs were developed. An American study in the 1950s showed that listening to the radio was the most frequent evening activity of young people aged between 8 and 16 (Lyness, 1952, quoted from Paik, 2001, pp. 11f.).

As a consequence of the advent of television the relative importance of radio for children and young people decreased. Although in most countries there are still some dedicated children's programs, the main function of young people's use of the radio is listening to music. This is particularly true for older teenagers: according to most studies the amount of time devoted to listening to the radio increases with age. Girls tend to spend a bit more time with radio than boys (e.g., Medienpädagogischer Forschungsverbund Südwest [MPFS] 2011a, p. 22; Rideout et al., 2010, p. 28).

Television

Television's rapid diffusion in the United States started in the late 1940s; the strongest growth occurred in the 1950s. Globally the proportion of households owning a television set reached 79 percent in 2009. Whereas there is almost full availability in Europe, the Commonwealth of Independent States (former Soviet Union), and The Americas, only three quarters of the households in the Asia and Pacific region and less than one third in Africa can view a TV set at home (International Telecommunication Union [ITU], 2010a).

From early childhood, children have spent quite a long time with the screen medium, more than with any other media activity. Even today with the availability of a wide variety of media, television viewing time is still high. In this respect, it is important to define what we mean by viewing television. In many statistics the amount of viewing only includes the time that children spend watching TV programs on a TV set when they are broadcast. By contrast, the recent Kaiser Family Foundation studies use the category *TV content*, which includes watching TV programs on a TV set at the time of their broadcast, or by means of time-shifted TV (on demand or self-recorded), DVDs/videos watched on TV or on a computer, and TV on other platforms like the internet, iPods/MP3 players, and cell phones (Rideout et al., 2010, p. 15). In 2009, 8- to 18-year-olds in the US spent 4.5 hours per day with TV content; this figure was more than half an hour higher than five years earlier. The overall viewing time reaches a peak for 11- to 14-year-olds. Boys tend to watch slightly more than girls.

Audiovisual and audio recording devices

Children's options to make use of electronic media were substantially enhanced by audio recorders in the early 1970s and by video recorders in the late 1970s. Over a relatively short time both devices entered the majority of children's bedrooms in most Western countries. There were two functionalities which made these new devices so attractive for young audiences. Firstly, particularly for younger children, they offered "repeatable pleasures" (Wood, 1993, p. 184): children love to listen to or watch the same story again and again, although (or because) they know the content by heart. This constellation allows them to experience exactly the degree of suspense that they like. Secondly, particularly for teens, these recording devices allowed them to collect or sample or re-mix their own content from different sources, and by doing so to express themselves and their identities.

Since then the specific technical devices and features for recording audio(visual) content have changed substantially: VCR technology has been widely replaced by DVD, Blu-Ray, DVR and other standards; the path from cassette recorders and LPs to CD players to MP3 was similar. Nevertheless, the respective older technical devices stayed quite popular for children: The typical development was that families bought the latest technology, e.g., a CD or DVD player for the living room, and moved the old technology, e.g., a cassette recorder or VCR, into the children's room.

Almost every American household has at least one DVD player or video recorder and 57 percent of 8- to 18-year-olds have one in their own bedroom; this figure has been increasing over the last ten years (Rideout et al., 2010, p. 9). The amount of use of these devices (0:41 hours per day) is lower than the use of TV programs on a TV set at the time of their broadcast (2:39 hours); nevertheless, it fills a substantial part of children's everyday lives. This is even more true for different audio media, which are mainly used for music.

Electronic games

When in the middle of the 1970s electronic games left public amusement halls and entered private households, they immediately became an important new element in children's media repertoires. Although – from today's perspective – rather simple, early games like *Mario* or *Pac-Man* in the 1980s fascinated millions of children worldwide. The first years were dominated by games consoles to be linked with a TV set, and small handheld games. In the second half of the 1980s, computers increasingly made their way into private households, with games of all kinds being the main function for children. The games market and particularly the most successful Japanese companies like Nintendo (e.g., *Game Boy* and later *Wii*) and Sony (*PlayStation*) grew exponentially, until annual turnover with electronic games exceeded that of the complete movie industry. On the one hand the consequence of this development was a strong fragmentation of the market with fast innovations in technology, design, and game genres; on the other hand, very few products became overwhelmingly successful on a global scale. One example is *Pokémon*, which started as a game on the Nintendo *Game Boy*, was then adapted for bigger consoles, TV series, play cards, and a wide range of merchandising products, and in the process became a globally distributed cultural brand (see Tobin, 2004).

Today, electronic games are available on all new digital platforms, particularly cell phones. An important step in technical development has been the increasing use of online games. Particularly the so-called Massively-Multiplayer-Online-Role-Playing-Games (MMORPG) like *World of Warcraft* have attracted many young people. Gaming is highest between 10 and 13 years; boys play considerably longer than girls. Because of their persistence and the highly time-consuming tasks that have to be fulfilled in these online worlds, they have generated intense public and academic debate on whether they might lead to excessive gaming behavior (e.g., Gentile, 2009).

Internet

In 2009, 15 years after the start of the public diffusion of the internet, 84 percent of 8- to 18-year-olds in America had internet access in their family; one third even had their own access in their bedroom (Rideout et al., 2010, p. 9).

Before dealing with some findings on how children use the internet, it has to be emphasized that until now internet diffusion is extremely imbalanced across the world. According to the ITU statistics from 2010 (ITU, 2010b), Europe is the continent with the highest proportion of internet users (65 percent of the total population). The Americas follow with 55 percent, the Commonwealth of Independent States with 46 percent, and the Arab States with 25 percent.

The Asia and Pacific region has 19 percent internet users, Africa 10 percent. Given the fact that some of these continents include pioneer countries in terms of internet use, e.g., the United States, or Japan and South Korea, these figures indicate that there are many countries in Asia or in the Americas where internet distribution is still very low.

A recent European study which investigated the online behavior of 9- to 16-year-olds and their parents in 25 European countries (EU Kids Online, see Livingstone et al., 2011) provides a rich empirical basis: use of the internet for school work is the top online activity (85 percent). Playing games against the computer (83 percent), watching video clips (76 percent), and social networking (62 percent) are the next most popular online activities. This contrasts with the various ways of creating user-generated content: posting images (39 percent) or messages (31 percent) for others to share, using a webcam (31 percent), file-sharing sites (18 percent), spending time in a virtual world (16 percent) or writing a blog (11 percent) are all less common (ibid.).

Gender differences are generally small; boys overall have a slightly wider repertoire of online activities, and they play more games. Age differences are greater, with the exception of using the internet for school work: 9- to 12-year-olds are much less likely than 13- to 16-year-olds to use the internet for watching or posting video clips or messages, reading or watching the news, instant messaging, social networking, and email or downloading music or films. In terms of the amount of use, children's internet use is dedicated mainly to communication (MPFS 2011b, p. 33).

Comprehensive trends of children's media use

While children's media consumption has obviously been shaped by the media technologies available at a given point in history, the technology-oriented perspective applied in the previous section has its limitations. Given the broad availability of different services, one relevant phenomenon regarding children's media use is that children actively combine different services and build their personal *media repertoire* (Hasebrink and Popp, 2006). This perspective helps to better understand the relationship between different media, particularly between so-called "old" and "new" media. As the history of media-related discourses shows, this relationship is usually expected to be competitive, with new media replacing the earlier media. Many findings regarding trends in children's media consumption contradict this assumption. Even if today's children devote quite a lot of time to social networking sites or online gaming, they continue to read books, listen to music, and watch television. If we take this perspective and observe general patterns of children's media use, several relevant trends can be identified.

Availability of media services

Children's everyday lives are particularly affected by the meta-process of mediatization (Krotz, 2009; Livingstone, 2009). An increasing number of media devices, in their own bedroom and elsewhere in the family's household, the expanding range of functionalities offered by new services, the continuous and omnipresent availability of services which overcome temporal and spatial limits – these aspects mark a significant trend in the conditions for children's media use. Today's children have far more options to communicate than any generation before them.

Amount of media use

One consequence of the omnipresence of media services seems to be that the time children spend with media continues to increase. In 2009 8- to 18-year-olds in the United States spent more than 7.5 hours per day with media (Rideout et al., 2010, p. 11); this is more than one hour longer than five years earlier. In the same time period the proportion of multitasking increased, indicating that young people increasingly use two or even more media at the same time, so that the total time of media exposure adds up to 10.75 hours, which is 2.25 hours more than five years ago. According to the methodology of the Kaiser Family Foundation (KFF) study, these figures do not include the time spent using the computer for school work, or time spent texting or talking on a cell phone. While 8- to 10-year-olds use the media for fewer than eight hours per day, 11- to 14-year-olds spend almost 12 hours and those 15 to 18 years of age about 11.5 hours with the media (ibid.). These figures are one of the strongest indicators for the wider process of mediatization of children's lives.

Cross-media patterns of use

The media industry increasingly develops cross-media strategies, the ideal being to distribute content on as many platforms as possible. Famous media brands for children, which may originate from games, movies, television, comics, or even books (e.g., *Harry Potter*), are available almost everywhere; the same content is now marketed across different media platforms. Such media brands build the integrating and characterizing elements of children's media repertoires.

Relationship between parents' and children's media use

Children's media repertoires are increasingly independent from their parents' influence. The availability of media in children's bedrooms, individualized media services such as digital games or social networking platforms as well as parents' lack of knowledge about modern digital media allow children to decide rather independently what media they use. This phenomenon has been described as "bedroom culture" (Bovill and Livingstone, 2001, p. 179), and stresses the importance of children's bedrooms as their own social spaces. Bedrooms can be constructed (e.g., decorated) according to a child's own conception, and they provide an unsupervised and private place to spend their leisure time. This leads to fewer opportunities for shared media experiences of parents and children (Bovill and Livingstone, 2001, p. 195; Livingstone et al., 2011, p. 19).

Entertainment and education as functions of children's media use

As a consequence of the developments mentioned above, pedagogical approaches to children's media are becoming less influential; educational services are giving way to entertainment and fun-oriented content (Buckingham and Scanlon, 2005, p. 46).

Consequences of recent trends in children's media use

Changes in media environments and in children's practices of use lead to changes in childhood and socialization and in the development of their view of the world as well. Today the idea of childhood as a preparatory stage for adult life is increasingly modified by the notion of the child as a competent, self-socialized being in its own right who steers and fosters his or her own development largely independently. Thus, more significance is attached to the independence or "agency" of children. This change in the understanding of childhood is closely related to the trends in media use mentioned above.

Not least due to discovering young people as a target group, childhood increasingly turns into a self-determined as well as market-oriented form of life, in the context of which media again play a decisive role. On the one hand, children are addressed as active and supposedly competent media users, and on the other, they are regarded as future consumers in a globalised media system. Therefore, the phase of growing up manifests itself not only as a mediated but also as a consumer childhood.

Nowadays, communication largely equals media communication; and as studies concerned with early childhood media use show (Rideout et al., 2003), even toddlers use a wider range of media. Media offer children and adolescents an area of projection for their dreams, emotions and fantasies, which they use according to their age, gender, and development status (e.g., Beentjes et al., 2001, p. 86; Paus-Hasebrink, 2007). Moreover, media provide a broad repertoire for identification and action that adds to children's identity construction. As media are agencies of symbols and meanings, they provide children with orientation and the potential for identification (Lemish, 2007). Children choose their personal favorites among these heroes and champions and use them in their own identity formation (Paus-Hasebrink, 2007). The trends in children's media use as highlighted in this chapter suggest that media play an ever increasing role in children's socialization and in developing their view of the world.

SEE ALSO in this volume chapter by Drotner, chapter by Nathanson, and chapter by Livingstone.

References

Beentjes, J. W. J., Koolstra, C. M., Marseille, N. and van der Voort, T. H. A. (2001). Children's Use of Different Media: For How Long and Why? In S. Livingstone and M. Bovill (Eds), *Children and Their Changing Media Environment. A European Comparative Study*. Mahwah, NJ: Lawrence Erlbaum, pp. 85–111.

Bovill, M. and Livingstone, S. (2001). Bedroom Culture and the Privatization of Media Use. In S. Livingstone and M. Bovill (Eds), *Children and Their Changing Media Environment. A European Comparative Study*. Mahwah, NJ: Lawrence Erlbaum, pp. 179–200.

Buckingham, D. and Scanlon, M. (2005). Selling Learning: towards a political economy of edutainment media. *Media, Culture and Society, 27*(1), 41–58.

Gentile, D. A. (2009). Pathological Video-Game Use among Youth Ages 8 to 18. A National Study. *Psychological Science, 20*(5), 594–602. Retrieved June 9, 2012, from http://www.drdouglas.org/drdpdfs/Gentile_Pathological_VG_Use_2009.pdf

Hasebrink, U. and Popp, J. (2006). Media Repertoires as a Result of Selective Media Use. A conceptual approach to the analysis of patterns of exposure. *Communications, 31*(3), 369–87.

International Telecommunication Union [ITU] (2010a). *World Telecommunication/ICT Development Report 2010 – Monitoring the WSIS targets*. Retrieved June 9, 2012, from http://www.itu.int/ITU-D/ict/publications/wtdr_10/index.html

International Telecommunication Union [ITU] (2010b). *The World in 2010: ICT Facts and Figures*. Retrieved June 9, 2012, from http://www.itu.int/ITU-D/ict/material/FactsFigures2010.pdf

Krotz, F. (2009). Mediatization: A Concept to Grasp Media and Societal Change. In K. Lundby (Ed.), *Mediatization: Concept, Changes, Conflicts*. New York City, NY: Lang, pp. 21–40.

Lemish, D. (2007). *Children and Television: A global perspective*. Malden, MA: Blackwell.

Livingstone, S. (2009). On the Mediation of Everything. *Journal of Communication, 59*(1), 1–18.

Livingstone, S., Haddon, L., Görzig, A. and Ólafsson, K. (2011). *Risks and safety on the internet: The perspective of European children. Full findings*. London: EU Kids Online. Retrieved June 9, 2012, from http://www2.lse.ac.uk/media@lse/research/EUKidsOnline/EU%20Kids%20II%20(2009–11)/EUKidsOnlineIIReports/D4FullFindings.pdf

Lyness, P. (1952). The Place of the Media in the Lives of Boys and Girls. *Journalism Quarterly, 29*(1), 43–54.

Medienpädagogischer Forschungsverbund Südwest [MPFS] (2011a). *KIM-Studie 2010. Kinder + Medien, Computer + Internet. Basisuntersuchung zum Medienumgang 6-bis 13-Jähriger in Deutschland*. [KIM-Study 2010. Children + media, computer + internet. Media usage of 6- to 13-year-olds in Germany.]. Stuttgart: MPFS. Retrieved June 9, 2012, from http://www.mpfs.de/fileadmin/KIM-pdf10/KIM2010.pdf

Medienpädagogischer Forschungsverbund Südwest [MPFS] (2011b). *JIM-Studie 2011. Jugend, Information, (Multi-)Media. Basisuntersuchung zum Medienumgang 12-bis 19-Jähriger*. [JIM-Study 2011. Youth, information, (multi-)media. Media usage of 12- to 19-year-olds.]. Stuttgart: MPFS. Retrieved June 9, 2012, from http://www.mpfs.de/fileadmin/JIM-pdf11/JIM2011.pdf

Paik, H. (2001). The History of Children's Use of Electronic Media. In D. G. Singer, and J. L. Singer (Eds), *Handbook of Children and the Media*. Thousand Oaks, CA: Sage, pp. 7–27.

Paus-Hasebrink, I. (2007). Heroes, Identity and para-social Interaction. In J. Arnett (Ed.), *Encyclopedia of Children, Adolescents, and the Media*. Thousand Oaks, London, New Delhi: Sage, pp. 375–77.

Rideout, V. J., Vandewater, E. A. and Wartella, E. A. (2003). *Zero to Six. Electronic Media in the Lives of Infants, Toddlers and Preschoolers*. Menlo Park, CA: Kaiser Family Foundation.

Rideout, V. J., Foehr, U. G. and Roberts, D. F. (2010). *Generation M². Media in the Lives of 8- to 18-Year Olds. A Kaiser Family Foundation Study*. Menlo Park, CA: Kaiser Family Foundation.

Tobin, J. (Ed.) (2004). *Pikachu's Global Adventure: The Rise and Fall of Pokémon*. Durham: Duke University Press.

Wood, J. (1993). Repeated Pleasures: notes on young people's use of video. In D. Buckingham (Ed.), *Reading Audiences. Young People and the Media*. Manchester: Manchester University Press, pp. 184–201.

4

EXAMINING THE ASSUMPTIONS IN RESEARCH ON CHILDREN AND MEDIA

Marina Krcmar

In a landmark article, Peters (1986) argued that because communication applies concepts and theories from other fields, it cannot be thought of as a distinct, coherent discipline. Gonzales (1988) countered that communication has its roots in interdisciplinarity and, rather than being a source of intellectual poverty, the interdisciplinary nature of communication is one of its main strengths. Nowhere is this more evident than in the area of children and media. Typically, a sound piece of scholarship that examines children and media looks not only at the child, but at the child as a developmentally influenced and constrained individual. Many scholars (e.g., Byrne et al., 2009; Cantor, 2002; Krcmar, 2010) take developmental theory as a starting point. Research on children and media has worked consistently and intentionally to apply work from developmental psychology. However, surprisingly little has been written that examines this interplay between developmental psychology and media research or the theoretical and methodological assumptions that hold sway in this area of study. In fact, it is perhaps evidence of the strength of these assumptions that they have not been considered or examined at length. In this chapter I will examine these assumptions and discuss how environment influences child development and how methodological issues influence our understanding of both child development and of the interplay between media and child development.

Implicit assumptions in research on children and media

In any area of research, indeed, epistemologically speaking, in any area of life, the assumptions that we hold most strongly are the most difficult to see. In research on children and media, many of the assumptions derive from those rooted in developmental psychology itself. Although these assumptions are not necessarily incorrect, they bear periodic examination to help us move forward more creatively in our research enterprise.

Children and adolescents are qualitatively different from adults. One of the most straightforward assumptions that guides work in developmental psychology and has thus been adopted by research on children and media is the assumption that *children are qualitatively different from adults.* Before this idea made it into scientific consciousness, children were not focused on as a separate class of persons. More recently, however, there have been political and economic reasons to assume that children lack knowledge and ability that requires them to have a (female) caretaker for a lengthy period (Burman, 2008). This results in a freeing of jobs for an adult, male work force. These social and political forces define childhood (Burman, 2008), generating assumptions about it: namely that childhood exists, and these assumptions remain embedded in our cultural beliefs about children.

This assumption is inherent in the work of developmental psychologist Jean Piaget (Harris, 1997). Piaget popularized the idea that young children think, conceptualize, and understand differently from adults and therefore their perceptions of the world and their interactions in it all deserve distinct attention (Piaget, 1926). Much of the research that focuses on young children and mass media takes as a premise that children *do* think differently from adults; however, this assumption has been questioned, if not directly then at least in its effect. Specifically, we assume that if young children think differently, and are constrained by cognitive limitations (e.g., Inhelder and Piaget, 1964) then they are in need of adult protection. Educational media and prosocial television targeting young children assume that children are in need of guidance and shaping. A contrasting view is that children are increasingly sophisticated as they encounter newer technologies and a greater variety of media content (Livingstone, 2002). While some scholars have taken this approach, arguing that children should be empowered as sophisticated media consumers (e.g., Livingstone, 2002) the dominant approach in media effects research, which itself takes developmental psychology and its experimental methods as a basis, has been a more protectionist approach (Buckingham, 2000).

If, as Piaget has argued, young children's thinking has certain characteristics that are some-what resistant to environmental training, simply empowering them with information is not enough. For example, Cantor and colleagues (e.g., Cantor, 2002) have argued that to calm a preschooler frightened by an image on television, simply explaining that the image is not real does little to calm their fears due to these very cognitive limitations. Instead, until children have made a certain amount of cognitive developmental progress that allows them to distinguish between reality and fantasy, it may be more productive to calm their fears with behavioral strategies such as hugs (Cantor, 2002).

Assumptions regarding young children's difference from adults are also implicit in the literature on adolescence. However, the fact that adolescents exist as a distinct age group is also an assumption worth examining. Although puberty as a physical change has obviously always been with us, adolescence as a concomitant social and emotional period is somewhat new. At the beginning of the twentieth century, children often began paid employment at age 10. A minimum age for leaving school (15 years) was not introduced in Europe until 1944 (Harris and Butterworth, 2002). However, as technological advancements required more skilled workers and more specialized education, the years of schooling needed to maintain a technologically advanced society increased. Requirements for advanced schooling necessitated postponement of reproduction. Thus, biological changes came face to face with economic, political, and social necessity and the years of adolescence were ultimately extended. Amidst these forces, an academic interest in a period of life known as adolescence became greater (Saltman, 2005).

The middle of the twentieth century, then, saw a meeting of several occurrences. First, adolescence as a social construction, influenced by the dominant political, economic, and moral mores of the day emerged (Saltman, 2005), with a continued emphasis on adolescence as a difficult time in child development (Arnett, 2007). Next, television quickly became the mass medium of the decade, with approximately 65 percent of homes owning a set by 1955 (Paik, 2001, p. 15). Third, the field of mass communication was in its infancy and interest in media and children was among the early topics of interest (e.g., Schramm, et al., 1961). Thus, it was inevitable that an interest in the effects of television on adolescents would emerge, with a majority of focus on the negative effects and how to mitigate them.

Certainly this is not to argue that adolescence is not a time of physical, emotional, and psychological change. Rather, it is important to examine our assumption that adolescence as a period of development exists somehow outside of the social and cultural contexts that helped define it. In sum, one major assumption is that children and adolescents think in ways that differ from adults. It is crucial to understand that this is an assumption in order to recognize when developmental theory provides us with shoulders to stand on, or when the weight of the extant theory clouds our vision.

Age is taken as a primary variable. A second major assumption, one intrinsically related to the first, is that age is often utilized as a key variable in studying children. To perhaps state the obvious, this practice is less common in media research that examines adults' responses to media. Thus, we assume that not only do children think differently from adults but that the way they process media differs as they age. Furthermore, with only some exceptions, we assume that audience processing strategies and outcomes change with age during childhood and adolescence, but do not do so during adulthood. Whereas it is true that processing changes with the age of the child, it is crucial, still, to view this as an assumption. A sizeable body of literature does support this contention from the very youngest viewers (e.g., 6-month-olds, Krcmar et al., 2007) to adolescents (Borzekowski and Strasburger, 2008). However, despite compelling evidence that age is an important variable in research, often-times age is used as a proxy for development without the recognition that age is confounded by experience, and perhaps other relevant variables. As children age, not only do they grow and develop biologically, but their experience with media typically increases; their interactions with the world outside of their immediate families expand; they may be exposed to a greater number of stimuli that are more varied in nature. Thus, age is an indicator of and corollary of development, but so too is it a corollary of many environmental and experiential variables. Thus, it is important to question and empirically examine the assumption that age differences are inevitably linked to individual development and recognize when it is a confound, hiding other relevant factors.

All differences are related to development. A third assumption, one also rooted in developmental psychology, is that we tend to look for changes in children over time and then take any differences as evidence for development or progress towards adulthood. Unlike the assumption above, where age may mask more important or interesting variables, research on child development must be vigilant about not assuming that any change is evidence of development. Consider, for example, research on adults and media. Differences between older and younger adults, when they are examined, are taken as evidence for social differences, economic differences or differences in the subculture of a cohort. None of this is to imply that development does not occur; however, it is important to consider when changes over time or differences between age groups are related to something other than cognitive, emotional or social development.

For example, more than three and a half decades ago, researchers suggested that due to cognitive limitations, very young children, those aged 3 to 5, did not understand the persuasive and selling intent of advertising (Ward et al., 1977). By today's standards, when toddlers and preschoolers are exposed to arguably more advertising on more media platforms than ever before, it is possible to construe this classic research as dated. It is possible that with access to more media and more sophisticated advertising campaigns, young children have become more aware and critical of advertising. If such is the case, then scholars such as Livingstone (2002) are correct: we underestimate children and are unduly protective of them. Research from 1977 (i.e., Ward et al., 1977) should be replicated because the content of the media under investigation—advertising—has changed dramatically in the ensuing years. In fact, McAlister and Cornwell (2009) set out precisely to test this claim. They found that 3 to 5-year-olds still do not understand the persuasive intent of advertising, despite the more sophisticated media climate in which they have been raised. However, 35 years of research provided support for this finding; one study did not. Thus, as researchers we must consider that simply because differences between older and younger children exist, these differences are not necessarily related to development.

Selective application of developmental phenomena and developmental theory in understanding children and media. The fourth issue, which I might categorize as a problem, and not an assumption, per se, carries with it two problems. First, researchers tend to focus on children's cognitive processing of media, assuming that other developmental factors such as emotional and moral development are outcome variables. Perhaps this is related to scholars' focus on a narrow group of developmental scholars and theorists (e.g., Piaget). For example, Vygotsky (1896–1934) is often overshadowed by his more well-known contemporary, Piaget. However, Vygotsky's work is valuable to media researchers due to several of his insights. Vygotsky stressed that certain cognitive processes in children, such as voluntary memory, problem-solving, and self regulation, have their origins in social interaction and social activity. To researchers interested in studying how children learn from an increasingly diverse array of media, both traditional and social, theorists who emphasize the dynamic nature of development may help in our understanding of the process. Thus, Vygotsky offers a possible starting place for thinking about children's learning from new media, especially, perhaps, from social media. As a result of this somewhat narrow focus, work by Piaget on cognitive development has often been used exclusively to inform our understanding of children's sense-making of media. However, there appears to be a subtle assumption at work: theory on children's cognitive development tends to be used in order to understand how children *process and understand* media; children's emotional, moral, and social development is often measured as a dependent variable.

Despite this assumption, recent theorists paint a more holistic, more integrated picture of children that media researchers would be wise to attend to. For example, past developmental literature has assumed that children are passive recipients of development, with development emerging either innately or from their social world that either provided or did not provide them with what they needed (Shonkoff and Phillips, 2000). More recent approaches see children as active participants in their own development, due to a drive to explore and understand their world. Furthermore, it is not necessarily accurate to atomize the developmental process, assuming that cognitive, emotional, social, and moral development are distinct processes. Instead, cognitive development may inform moral development which in turn may influence children's interactions with peers.

In terms of media research, we must recognize, for example, that cognitive development influences children's attention to media, but emotional development may influence their attraction to a media character which in turn may affect their attention. Similarly, social development may influence their willingness and ability to "talk" to an on-screen character which may then influence their learning from that character. Thus, if we as researchers continue to assume that 1) media are processed primarily cognitively and 2) media influence primarily emotional, social, and learning outcomes, we may become stagnant in our research. Therefore, that we are somewhat selective and limited in our application of developmental theory should act as a call to expand the boundaries of use and application of theories in order to understand how children make sense of media and how they are influenced by them, socially, emotionally, cognitively, and morally.

The importance of environment

Another area to be considered in our exploration of children and media is the importance of integrating children's environment into all research and theory building. A sizable amount of research regarding children and media does not consider the family as a featured variable. This decision is sometimes made for the sake of expediency and sometimes for reasons of internal validity. In either case, family and environment is left out. Although the elimination of certain variables is an inherent property of experimental design this may not always be appropriate.

There are reasons both practical and theoretical to claim that it is invalid to remove children from a social environment in the name of experimental validity. First, children rarely consume media in isolation; very young children are rarely completely alone. Furthermore, many children's programs attempt to engage children socially by asking questions, eliciting verbal and physical interaction, and building social relationships between the main character and the child (Lauricella et al., 2011). Thus, for young children, social interaction is part of the experience of consuming and learning from media.

Second, according to some theorists (e.g., Vygotsky, 1978, 1986) children's development cannot be considered isolated from social interaction. Specifically, "human learning presupposes a specific social nature and a process by which children grow into the intellectual life of those around them" (1978, p. 88). In the end, then, the social world and learning are so intertwined that to attempt to take them apart would be difficult and meaningless. Drawing on family systems theory (Bertalanffy, 1972) I argue that to atomize something that occurs in the family (i.e., television viewing), especially when studying children who cannot survive outside of the context of a support system, is to destroy it beyond recognition.

In addition, another problem with the way family environment has been studied is that social interaction is likely a broader concept than we conceptualize it in, say, the mediation literature (e.g., Nathanson, 2002). Strasburger et al. (2009) define mediation simply as "the ways in which parents try to buffer children's exposure to media content" (p. 506). However, perhaps even this broad definition misses some of what we need to look at in understanding how families interact with media. Yes, parents mediate in explicit ways (e.g., by helping children interpret content) but they also engage in ways that remain mostly unexplored. Is there a difference in a child's processing of media between sitting in a high chair or being rocked and kissed by a parent while viewing? Is one condition more supportive of learning or more distracting to it? Certainly an experiment could attempt to answer that question, but perhaps we consider it too irrelevant or strange to ask. In any case, family environment, social interaction, and mediation may be conceptualized in ways that must be broadened.

The criticisms noted above withstanding, the study of children and media and the application of development to media research on children has offered some very practical insights. For example, *Sesame Street* was the first children's program to be designed based on research that indicated what worked in terms of children's learning from television (Fisch and Bernstein, 2001; Lesser and Schneider, 2001). Thus, research on children and media has offered insights, design recommendations, and assistance to those who design it. As researchers ourselves, can our research be improved?

The perfect study?

The subheading above is intended to be ironic. Most researchers who have worked in the field understand that each study requires a solid design in which decisions, practical limitations, and sacrifices typically lead to a strong, but not perfect study. For example, questionnaires and experiments allow for data collection that can examine relationships between variables. Questionnaires allow for systematic data collection regarding reliably measured variables from large numbers of participants. Experiments are often viewed as an excellent method: by randomly assigning participants to the treatment or control condition, isolating and manipulating a causal variable, and then measuring some outcome potentially associated with the cause, one can attempt to make claims regarding causality. The strength of these designs is that in their approach, they are able to increase precision. However, this level of precision for particular variables necessitates ignoring other potentially meaningful factors. We are left with a carefully wrought but somewhat narrow examination of the phenomenon. Consider, instead, how ethnographers may approach the study of children's use of the internet.

Livingstone (2009) conducted " … an in-depth study of thirty families as they went on-line at the turn of the century, marking their struggles and pleasures as they appropriated the internet into their homes and their daily lives. … [the researchers] observed the child using the internet in an informal and unstructured manner for up to two hours" (p. 239). This research revealed how parents and children perceived and used the internet, revealing a great deal of variation in the technological skills that parents and children had in setting up and maintaining the system that influenced how much and how effectively they used it. Similarly, Lemish (1987) conducted an in-depth ethnographic study of toddlers and television, that informed our understanding of children's earliest media use, a prescient study for its time given the early age at which children are introduced to media in the current environment. Thus, through careful in-home observation we are able to see not only how media function in an ideal situation such as a laboratory but in real situations where parents and children bring many different perceptions and skill levels to bear on their use.

For those who argue that one method is inherently more effective because, for example, a laboratory tells us only about laboratory behavior, I would argue that to address any research question the first issue is the selection of the correct research tool. Detailed information about use, family dynamics surrounding internet use, validity assessment of self-reported data in actual situations (when possible) are much more effectively answered through careful ethnographic studies that allow a detailed look at lived experiences. Tests of the effectiveness of a particular variable, such as advergames effects on recall for a product, are better tested with an experiment. Limiting our research to a single method is appropriate only if we are interested in a single kind of question. Ultimately, answering research questions fully requires the application of several methods, both micro and macroanalytic. And to best continue to build our body of knowledge concerning children and media, we must repeatedly see and question our assumptions.

SEE ALSO in this volume chapter by Vandewater.

References

Arnett, J. J. (Ed.) (2007). *International encyclopedia of adolescence*. New York: Routledge.

Bertalanffy, L. Von. (1972). The history and status of general systems theory. In G. J. Klit (Ed.), *Trends in general systems theory*. New York, NY: Wiley-Interscience.

Borzekowski, D. G. and Strasburger, V. C. (2008). Adolescents and media messages about tobacco, alcohol, and drugs. In S. L. Calvert and B. J. Wilson (Eds), *The handbook of children, media, and development*. Malden, MA: Blackwell, pp. 432–52.

Buckingham, D. (2000). *After the death of childhood*. Cambridge, UK: Polity Press.

Burman, E. (2008). *Deconstructing developmental psychology (2nd ed.)*. New York, NY: Routledge/Taylor & Francis.

Byrne, S., Linz, D. and Potter, W. J. (2009). A test of competing cognitive explanations for the boomerang effect in response to the deliberate disruption of media-induced aggression. *Media Psychology, 12*(3), 227–48.

Cantor, J. (2002). Fright reactions to mass media. In J. Bryant and D. Zillmann (Eds), *Media effects: Advances in theory and research (2nd ed.)*. Mahwah, New Jersey: Lawrence Erlbaum, pp. 287–306.

Fisch, S. M. and Bernstein, L. (2001). Formative research revealed: Methodological and process issues in formative research. In S. M. Fisch and R. T. Truglio (Eds), *"G" is for growing: Thirty years of research on children and Sesame Street*. Mahwah, NJ: Lawrence Erlbaum, pp. 39–61.

Gonzales, H. (1988). The evolution of communication as a field. *Communication Research*, *15*(3), 302–8.

Harris, M. and Butterworth, G. (2002). *Developmental psychology: A student's handbook*. Hove, UK: The Psychology Press.

Harris, P. (1997). Piaget in Paris: From 'autism' to logic. *Human Development*, *40*(2), 109–23.

Inhelder, B. and Piaget, J. (1964). The early growth of logic in the child, classification and seriation. E. A. Lunzer and D. Papert, Trans. New York, NY: Harper & Row.

Krcmar, M. (2010). Assessing the research on media, cognitive development and infants: Can infants really learn from television and videos? *Journal of Children and Media*, *4*(2), 119–34.

Krcmar, M., Grela, B. and Lin, K. (2007). Can toddlers learn vocabulary from television? An experimental approach. *Media Psychology*, *10*(1), 41–63.

Lauricella, A. R., Gola, A. H. and Calvert, S. L. (2011). Toddlers' learning from socially meaningful video characters. *Media Psychology*, *14*(2), 216–32.

Lemish, D. (1987). Viewers in diapers: The early development of television viewing. In Lindlof, T. (Ed.), *Natural audiences: Qualitative research of media uses and effects*. Norwood, NJ: Ablex, pp. 33–57.

Lesser, G. S. and Schneider, J. (2001). Creation and evolution of the Sesame Street curriculum. In S. M. Fisch and R. T. Truglio (Eds), *"G"is for growing: Thirty years of research on children and Sesame Street*. Mahwah, NJ: Lawrence Erlbaum, pp. 25–38.

Livingstone, S. (2002). *Young people and new media: Childhood and the changing media environment*. London, UK: Sage.

Livingstone, S. (2009). A rationale for positive online content for children. *Communication Research Trends*, *28*(3), 12–17.

McAlister, A. R. and Cornwell, T. (2009). Preschool children's persuasion knowledge: The contribution of theory of mind. *Journal Of Public Policy & Marketing*, *28*(2), 175–85.

Nathanson, A. I. (2002). The unintended effects of parental mediation of television on adolescents. *Media Psychology*, *4*(3), 207–30.

Paik, H. (2001). The history of children's electronic media. In D. G. Singer and J. L. Singer (Eds), *Handbook of Children and Media,* Thousand Oaks, CA.: Sage, pp. 7–28.

Peters, J. D. (1986). Institutional sources of intellectual poverty in communications research. *Communications Research*, *13*(4), 527–59.

Piaget, J. (1926). *Language and the thought of the child*. London, UK: Paul Kegan.

Saltman, K. J. (2005). The social construction of adolescence. In E. R. Brown and K. J. Saltsman (Eds), *The critical middle school reader*. New York, NY: Routledge, pp. 15–20.

Schramm, W., Lyle, J. and Parker, E. B. (1961). *Television in the lives of our children*. Stanford, CA: Stanford University Press.

Shonkoff, J. and Phillips, D. (Eds). (2000). *From neurons to neighborhoods: The science of early childhood development*. Washington, DC: National Academy Press.

Strasburger, V. C., Wilson, B. and Jordan, A. (2009). *Children, adolescents, and the media (2nd Ed.)*. Thousands Oaks, CA: Stage.

Vygotsky, L. S. (1978). *Mind in society*. Cambridge, MA: Harvard.

Vygotsky, L. S. (1986). The genetic roots of thought and speech. In A. Kozulin (Trans. & Ed.), *Thought and language*. Cambridge, MA: MIT Press.

Ward, S., Wackman, D. B. and Wartella, E. (1977). *How children learn to buy: The development of consumer information processing skills*. Beverly Hills, CA: Sage.

5

ECOLOGICAL APPROACHES TO THE STUDY OF MEDIA AND CHILDREN

Elizabeth A. Vandewater

This research was supported by funding from The Michael and Susan Dell Center for Healthy Living, the William T. Grant Foundation (WTG 7236), the National Science Foundation (BCS-1139527), and the National Institute of Child Health and Human Development (1R01HD053652). The author is especially grateful to Emily Hebert for her help and editing assistance.

Introduction

The United States became a nation of television viewers between 1950 and 1960, and the popularity of television has continued unabated to this day. Indeed, the American public has maintained its love affair with media and technology of all kinds since the introduction of television, as evidenced by the dizzying array of technology and the wide range of devices currently available for the delivery of media content (Vandewater and Denis, 2011). Around the same time America was falling in love with television, Urie Bronfenbrenner (Bronfenbrenner, 1944) was beginning to formulate some of the main tenets of what is now widely referred to as "Ecological theory" (Bronfenbrenner, 1979, 1986). Presaging the basic tenet of his ecological approach in 1944, Bronfenbrenner lamented " … piecemeal analysis, fixed in time and space, of isolated aspects, is insufficient and even misleading … " (1944, p. 75).

From the mid-1970s to the early 1990s, Bronfenbrenner and his colleagues developed and refined a more articulated ecological perspective, which acknowledged and attempted to account for the influences of the multiple contexts in which lives are lived. Ecological approaches explicitly model the developmental influences of environmental contexts and the ways in which such contexts intersect to importantly shape development and developmental outcomes (Bronfenbrenner, 1979, 1986; Bronfenbrenner and Crouter, 1983). Other influential and intimately related theories include systems theory (Cox et al., 2010; Cox and Paley, 2003; Sameroff, 1995, 2010) and life-course developmental theory (Elder et al., 2003).

Over the years, many pages have been dedicated to delineating and describing the basic tenets of these theories. Thus, a full and detailed review of each of these perspectives is neither necessary nor within the scope of this chapter. Rather, my purpose here is to outline the main ideas of these three closely related ecological perspectives (ecological theory, systems theory, and life-course developmental theory) and the ways in which they have informed and generated developmental systems perspectives as a prelude to discussion of the ways in which they have (or have not) been applied to research on media and children, and suggest some directions for future research in this area.

Ecological theory

Ecological theory, as outlined by Bronfenbrenner and his colleagues (Bronfenbrenner, 1979, 1986, 1989; Bronfenbrenner and Ceci, 1994; Bronfenbrenner and Crouter, 1983; Bronfenbrenner and Evans, 2000), is not, from a conceptual perspective, particularly complicated. The basic notions include: 1) individuals develop in many, often nested, contexts (e.g., individuals within families, families within neighborhoods, neighborhoods within larger communities, and so on); 2) the multiple contexts in which lives are lived, and the intersections among these many contexts, importantly shape development; 3) individuals actively choose the contexts in which they live their lives, and these choices have developmental implications, and 4) experiences of important others in contexts not touched by the developing individual (such as parental experiences at work) can have developmental consequences for the individual (such as when parents' work stresses impinge upon their ability to parent or the quality of family life). In later writings, Bronfenbrenner and his colleagues explicitly incorporated underlying biological processes in the model, giving rise to what is sometimes called the "Biopsychosocial ecological model" (Bronfenbrenner and Ceci, 1994). Ecological models are often presented in figures as concentric rings of influence, at the center of which is the developing child. For illustrative purposes, an example of such a model is presented in Figure 5.1.

Systems theory

Systems theory (sometimes called family systems theory) is an outgrowth of the clinical insight that problems in the parent–child relationship were often the result of problems in the marital

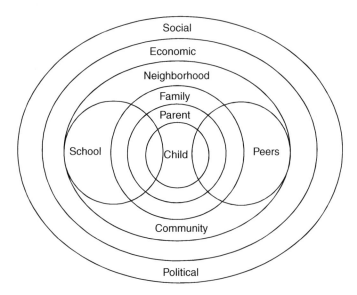

Figure 5.1 A commonly portrayed ecological model

relationship (Cox and Paley, 2003). The basic tenet of systems theory is that in order to understand the developing child, one must gain a broader perspective on the whole family, and seek to understand the wider processes and exchanges at the familial level and among various family members, rather than focusing almost exclusively on the mother–child dyad (Sameroff, 1995).

Life-course developmental theory

Like ecological and systems theory, life-course developmental theory emphasizes the interplay among multiple contexts of development (Benson and Elder, 2011; Crosnoe and Riegle-Crumb, 2007; Elder et al., 2003; Umberson et al., 2010). However, as the name implies, life-course developmental theory is concerned with development over the entire life course of the individual—from birth to death. Moreover, life-course theory explicitly focuses on the influence of historical period and historical context, and attempts to place the developing individual in a social and cultural milieu which is shaped by historical and social forces of both the past and the present, at both the societal and individual level (Elder et al., 2009). Life-course developmental theory has five main principles: 1) life span development—the notion that development and aging are life long processes, 2) agency—the notion that individuals construct their own life course through choices and behaviors made within the constraints and opportunities of social and historical circumstance, 3) time and place—the notion that the life course is embedded and shaped by the historical times and places in which individual lives are lived, 4) timing—the notion that the developmental antecedents and consequences of events, behaviors, and life transitions vary according to their timing in a person's life, and 5) linked lives—the notion that as intensely social animals, human lives are lived interdependently, and socio-historical influences are expressed within social networks (Elder et al., 2003).

Developmental science and developmental systems

Although they each have their own supporters, the fundamental truths inherent in ecological, systems, and life-course perspectives, and the substantial overlap among their truths have given rise to what is referred to by some as developmental science, and by others as developmental systems perspectives (Huang and Glass, 2008). Noting the inadequacies of much of the research to date (on almost any topic one cares to choose) many have called for a developmental systems perspective, which would attend to (or at least not simply ignore) all of the important elements influencing development in attempts to examine developmental outcomes (Glass and McAtee, 2006; Huang et al., 2009; Huang and Glass, 2008); though there are many figurative models of such approaches. However, in addition to representing the environmental contexts in which lives are lived, the most useful of these models also incorporate: 1) representations of both genomic and biological influences on development, 2) an axis representing life-course development, and 3) an explicit representation of the ways in which these influences combine to present opportunities and constraints and ultimately affect human behavior (see, e.g., Glass and McAtee, 2006). A representation of such a systems model is shown in Figure 5.2.

The devil is in the details: the challenges of empirical examination using ecological theory and systems perspectives

The essential point of ecological and developmental systems perspectives should come as no surprise to anyone even remotely self-aware or self-reflective: the many sources and contexts (both proximal and distal, current and past) of human experience matter. They affect who we

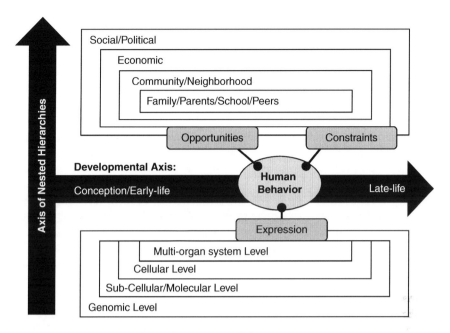

Figure 5.2 A developmental ecological systems model

are and who we will become—we choose and shape them through our own behaviors and actions, and are simultaneously shaped by them. Though the fundamental truth of this observation is not at question—the fact that development is obviously the result of the ebb, flow, intersection, and separation of many simultaneously operating contextual forces has proven to be somewhat problematic for science and scientific inquiry.

First, giving full and deep attention to the biological, social, and psychological forces we know are acting in concert to affect development would require doctoral training in a minimum of at least three to five disparate fields. Second, even the increasingly sophisticated analytic techniques available for understanding growth, change and flow—such as growth-curve modeling (Blozis and Cho, 2008; McArdle et al., 2002), social networks analysis (Balasubramaniam et al., 2010; Wasserman and Faust, 1994), and agent-based modeling (Bonabeau, 2002)—offer poor and crude imitations of the complex developmental processes under scrutiny. Even using the most sophisticated modeling algorithms available today amounts to an analytic sledge hammer on the delicate and reciprocal developmental processes we seek to understand. I suspect that even with continued exponential leaps in our computing and processing abilities, this will continue to be the case for some time to come. Third, by the rules of scientific inquiry and hypothesis testing, a theory where everything matters is not much of a theory. Ecological perspectives and/or models are sometimes disparaged as "the kitchen sink model" (because everything matters)—and the criticism rings true.

The state of research on media and children

Though many fields suffer from a general failure to conceptually include or empirically account for the effects of context, the study of media and children seems to suffer more than most. This may be at least partly due to the status of research on media and children's development as a "poor step-child" to other research areas in developmental science—particularly developmental psychology. Media research has long been categorized as "applied" (versus basic) research, and thus viewed as less important or central to the study of child development than other influences, such as parent–child interactions.

A direct consequence of this view is that media researchers have been so intent on proving that media in fact *do* matter for child development, that they have focused almost exclusively on the impact of media on developmental outcomes, with little to no attention paid to the family contexts in which much of children's media use occurs (Huston and Wright, 1997). To the extent that family contexts are included in analyses, they are most often treated as covariates or confounding factors. Though this approach has its utility, it obviates one's ability to examine how relationships may differ for children with different experiences or from different groups. In other words, it relegates contextual influences to the realm of error—the very antithesis of an ecological approach. For their part, scholars concerned with child development have (almost uniformly) simply ignored children's media use. By and large, children's media use appears neither in their conceptual models nor in their empirical examinations, even as a covariate. This is true despite both the veritable mountain of devices available for the delivery of media content available in most homes today, and the enormous amount of media use that takes place in the home. Thus, the child development literature and the literature on media and children, both deeply concerned with understanding adjustment and developmental outcomes in children, have largely proceeded independently of one another, with little sharing of ideas and information (Vandewater et al., 2005).

Taken together, this amounts to a striking lack of accounting for important ecological contexts in both literatures. The consequences of this mutual lack of ecological perspective in the extant literature are very real—and not trivial. The true cost lies in the enormous loss of scientific knowledge and understanding of the role media play in development and developmental processes. Because child development and family scholars have generally failed to account for children's media use, media's potential to change the very nature of parenting, family interactions, and peer socialization—and thus the influences of such factors on child development—remains largely unknown. Likewise, and despite over fifty (or more) years of research focusing on media and children, we know little about how family contexts and family interactions change the nature of media's impact on development. Other important questions remain similarly unexamined, such as the ways in which the media use of parents and others shapes children's media use, or the ways in which family processes contribute to children's media use, media choices, or media content preferences. The loss to science and empirical knowledge resulting from such unanswered questions is very great—and both scholarly and popular understanding of the role of media in children's lives and child development have suffered greatly for it.

Of course, as with any broad statement, exceptions to these claims do exist. Perhaps the largest exception lies in the area of parental mediation of children's media use. For example, Nathanson and colleagues have documented the ways in which parental mediation of aggressive content can change children's reactions to such content (Nathanson, 1999; Nathanson and Yang, 2003), as well as documenting the role of parental mediation on adolescent body-image and reactions to sexual media content (Nathanson, 2002; Nathanson and Botta, 2003). Valkenburg and her colleagues have examined the ways in which parental mediation can alter the impact of media on children (Valkenburg et al., 1999). There is also evidence that parental mediation of children's media can improve children's media literacy and thus, for example, help children to understand the intent of advertising (Buijzen and Valkenberg, 2005; Singer and Singer, 1998). There is also literature examining the impact of parental co-viewing on young children's learning from television (Kirkorian et al., 2008). There are also certainly scattered individual studies examining some of the relationships I mention above. But overwhelmingly, and as a group, we have largely dropped the ball on this one. Thus, due to inadequacies of much of the research to date, we have gained little understanding of the developmental connections between media use and various developmental outcomes across childhood, the extent to which these developmental connections may be different for different groups of children, and the processes or mechanisms linking media use and developmental outcomes across childhood.

A call for change: it's time to "walk the walk"

It seems rather obvious to state that children's use of media and exposure to media content does not happen in a vacuum; rather, it occurs in the wider contexts in which they live their lives. From early to middle childhood, the family is perhaps the most important context of media use. In fact, children's primary contact with media occurs informally as part of the home and family environment, rather than in structured settings and activities (Huston and Wright, 1994). During middle childhood and late adolescence—as school, peers, and friends begin to loom larger in developmental processes—children's media use is both shaped by, and importantly shapes, their social networks and social relations at school, among peers, and with friends. Yet, a deeper understanding of the developmental connections between media use and children has been severely hindered by a distinct dearth of studies which include such developmental (particularly longitudinal) and contextual information in explanatory models.

These ideas are not new. Many cogent and eloquent calls for the use of ecological and developmental frameworks to examine a broader range of possible interpersonal and familial context influences on the connections between media use and developmental outcomes already exist (Jordan, 2004; Linebarger and Vaala, 2010; McHale et al., 2009).

Yet, somehow, Bronfenbrenner's (1944) lament, made an astonishing 68 years ago, remains disturbingly valid: " … piecemeal analysis, fixed in time and space, of isolated aspects, is insufficient and even misleading … " (1944, p. 75). The fundamental truth of Bronfenbrenner's (1944) observation that scientific inquiry is often lacking in consideration of developmental context, historical context, biological context, and social context remains both disturbingly common and disturbingly accurate. In the intervening years since ecological theory was first elucidated (Bronfenbrenner, 1979), many studies have been published with the word "ecological" in their title, and/or generally claimed to rely on an ecological approach. Sadly, few of these studies stand up to close examination (see however, Conger et al., 2002; Vandewater and Lansford, 2005).

A final appeal

Collectively, as scholars who care deeply about both producing good science, and true understanding of the role of media in children's lives and in child development, we must widen our lens. We must eschew the endless procession of correlational or cross-sectional analyses that add little to nothing to deeper and more nuanced understandings of media and children. We must think deeply and comprehensively about how best to incorporate and test the ebb and flow of developmental processes in our research on children and media. This is not a trivial undertaking. It is especially difficult to examine the myriad of influences and the dynamic nature of their influences empirically. Yet, if it were easy to document developmental processes, we would have done so already—and there would be no need for yet another plea for more nuanced approaches to the study of media and children based on ecological theory.

Yet, media scholars must meet this challenge, or simply fade into irrelevance. The ubiquitous nature of a seemingly exponentially growing array of new media technologies has changed the nature of children's daily lives, including their connectivity with others, how they spend their time, and their access to an ever-growing amount of content for information and entertainment (Vandewater and Denis, 2011)—radically and forever. Though the very popularity of media among youth has fostered a great deal of debate and controversy (Strasburger et al., 2010)—one thing is abundantly clear—they are here to stay. Media are no longer an experience for children that is separable from other areas of their lives. They are everywhere, and at all hours of the day. As a field this means that we can no longer treat media use as if it were an isolated experience. Thus, though always important, understanding and examining the context of media use is now even more critical to understanding the developmental effects of media. Current and future generations of children will never know life without the internet, Wi-Fi, computers, touchscreens, tablets or smartphones. We ignore the power of these new technologies to shape, and be shaped by, ecological contexts at our (and their) peril.

SEE ALSO in this volume chapter by Krcmar, chapter by Vered and chapter by Nathanson.

References

Balasubramaniam, P., Vembarasan, V. and Rakkiyappan, R. (2010). Delay-dependent robust exponential state estimation of Markovian jumping fuzzy Hopfield neural networks with mixed random time-varying delays. *Communications in Nonlinear Science and Numerical Simulation, 16*(4), 2109–29.

Benson, J. E. and Elder, G. H. (2011). Young adult identities and their pathways: A developmental and life course model. *Developmental Psychology, 47*(6), 1646–57.

Blozis, S. A. and Cho, Y. (2008). Coding and centering of time in latent curve models in the presence of interindividual time heterogeneity. *Structural Equation Modeling, 15*(3), 413–33.

Bonabeau, E. (2002). Colloquium paper: Agent-based modeling: Methods and techniques for simulating human systems. *Proceedings of the National Academy of Sciences, 99*, 7280–87.

Bronfenbrenner, U. (1944). A constant frame of reference for sociometric research: Part II experiment and inference. *Sociometry, 7*(1), 40–75.

——(1979). *The ecology of human development: Experiments by nature and design.* Cambridge: Harvard University Press.

——(1986). Ecology of the family as a context for human development: Research perspectives. *Developmental Psychology, 22*(6), 723–42.

——(1989). Ecological systems theory. In R. Vasta (Ed.), *Theories of child development: Revised formulations and current issues.* Greenwich, Connecticut: JAI Press.

Bronfenbrenner, U. and Ceci, S. J. (1994). Nature-nurture reconceptualized in developmental perspective: a bioecological model. *Psychological Review, 101*(4), 568–86.

Bronfenbrenner, U. and Crouter, A. C. (1983). The evolution of environmental models in developmental research. In P. Musen (Ed.), *The Handbook of Child Psychology* (Vol. 1). New York: Wiley, pp. 358–414.

Bronfenbrenner, U. and Evans, G. W. (2000). Developmental science in the 21st century: emerging questions, theoretical models, research designs and empirical questions. *Social Development, 9*(1), 115–25.

Buijzen, M., and Valkenberg, P. M. (2005). Parental mediation of undesired advertising effects. *Media Psychology, 49*(2), 153–65.

Conger, R. D., Wallace, L. E., Sun, Y., Simons, R. L., McLoyd, V. C. and Brody, G. H. (2002). Economic pressure in African American families: A replication and extension of the family stress model. *Developmental Psychology, 38*(2), 179–93.

Cox, M. J., Mills-Koonce, R., Propper, C. and Gariépy, J. L. (2010). Systems theory and cascades in developmental psychopathology. *Development and Psychopathology, 22*(3), 497–506.

Cox, M. J. and Paley, B. (2003). Understanding families as systems. *Current Directions in Psychological Science, 12*(5), 193–96.

Crosnoe, R. and Riegle-Crumb, C. (2007). A life course model of education and alcohol use. *Journal of Health and Social Behavior, 48*(3), 267–82.

Elder, G., Johnson, M. J. and Crosnoe, R. (2003). The emergence and development of the life course theory. In J. Mortimer and M. Shanahan (Eds), *Handbook of the life course.* New York: Kluwer Academic, pp. 3–19.

Elder, G. H., Clipp, E. C., Brown, J. S., Martin, L. R. and Friedman, H. W. (2009). The life-long mortality risks of World War II experiences. *Research on Aging*, *31*(4), 391–412.

Glass, T. A. and McAtee, M. J. (2006). Behavioral science at the crossroads in public health: Extending horizons, envisioning the future. *Social Science and Medicine*, *62*(7), 1650–71.

Huang, T. T., Drewnoskski, A., Kumanyika, S. and Glass, T. A. (2009). A systems-oriented multilevel framework for addressing obesity in the 21st century. *Preventing Chronic Disease*, *6*(3), A82.

Huang, T. T. and Glass, T. A. (2008). Transforming research strategies for understanding and preventing obesity. *JAMA*, *300*(15), 1811–13.

Huston, A. C. and Wright, J. C. (1994). Educating children with television: The forms of the medium. In D. Zillman, J. Bryant and A. C. Huston (Eds), *Media, Children, and the Family: Social Scientific, Psychodynamic, and Clinical Perspectives*. Hillsdale, NJ: Lawrence Erlbaum, 73–84.

——(1997). Mass media and children's development. In I. E. Sigel and K. A. Renninger (Eds), *Handbook of Child Psychology* (Vol. 5): John Wiley, pp. 999–1058.

Jordan, A. B. (2004). The role of media in children's development: An ecological perspective. *Journal of Developmental and Behavioral Pediatrics*, *25*(3), 196–212.

Kirkorian, H. L., Wartella, E. A. and Anderson, D. R. (2008). Media and young children's learning. *Future of Children*, *18*(1), 39–61.

Linebarger, D. L. and Vaala, S. E. (2010). Screen media and language development in infants and toddlers: An ecological perspective. *Developmental Review*, *30*(2), 176–202.

McArdle, J. J., Ferrer-Caja, E., Hamagami, F. and Woodcock, R. W. (2002). Comparative longitudinal structural analyses of the growth and decline of multiple intellectual abilities over the life span. *Developmental Psychology*, *38*(1), 115–42.

McHale, S. M., Dotterer, A. and Kim, J.-Y. (2009). An ecological perspective on the media and youth development. *American Behavioral Scientist*, *52*(8), 1186–1203.

Nathanson, A. I. (1999). Identifying and explaining the relationship between parental mediation and children's aggression. *Communication Research*, *26*(2), 124–43.

——(2002). The unintended effects of parental mediation of television on adolescents. *Media Psychology*, *4*(3), 207–30.

Nathanson, A. I. and Botta, R. A. (2003). Shaping the effects of television on adolescents' body image disturbance. *Communication Research*, *30*(3), 304–31.

Nathanson, A. I., and Yang, M. S. (2003). The effects of mediation content and form on children's responses to violent television. *Human Communication Research*, *29*(1), 111–34.

Sameroff, A. J. (1995). General systems theory and developmental psychopathology. In D. Cichetti and D. J. Cohen (Eds), *Developmental psychopathology* (Vol. 1). New York: Wiley, pp. 659–95.

——(2010). A unified theory of development: A dialectic integration of nature and nurture. *Child Development*, *81*(1), 6–22.

Singer, D. G. and Singer, J. L. (1998). Developing critical viewing skills and media literacy in children. *The Annals of the American Academy of Political and Social Science*, *557*(1), 164–79.

Strasburger, V. C., Jordan, A. B. and Donnerstein, E. (2010). Health effects of media on children and adolescents. *Pediatrics*, *125*(4), 756–67.

Umberson, D., Crosnoe, R. and Reczek, C. (2010). Social relationships and health behavior across life course. *Annual Review of Sociology*, *36*, 139–57.

Valkenburg, P. M., Krcmar, M., Peeters, A. L. and Marseille, N. M. (1999). Developing a scale to assess three styles of television mediation: "Instructive mediation," "restrictive mediation," and "social coviewing". *Journal of Broadcasting and Electronic Media*, *43*(1), 52.

Vandewater, E. A. and Denis, L. M. (2011). Media, social networking, and pediatric obesity. *Pediatric Clinics of North America*, *58*(6), 1509–19, xii.

Vandewater, E. A. and Lansford, J. E. (2005). A family process model of problem behaviors in adolescents. *Journal of Marriage and Family*, *67*(1), 100–109.

Vandewater, E. A., Lee, J. H. and Shim, M. (2005). Family conflict and violent electronic media use in school-aged children. *Media Psychology*, *7*(7), 73–86.

Wasserman, S. and Faust, K. (1994). *Social network analysis: Methods and applications*. New York, NY: Cambridge University Press.

6

CONSTRUCTING CHILDREN AS CONSUMERS

David Buckingham

Over the past few decades, children have become increasingly important both as a market in their own right and as a means to reach adult markets. Commercial companies are targeting children more directly and at an ever-younger age; and they are using a much wider range of techniques that go well beyond conventional advertising. Marketers often claim that children are becoming 'empowered' in this new commercial environment: the market is seen to be responding to needs and desires on the part of children that have hitherto been largely ignored or marginalized, not least because of the social dominance of adults. However, critics have expressed growing concern about the apparent 'commercialization' of childhood. Popular publications, press reports and campaigns have addressed what are seen to be the damaging effects of commercial influences on children's physical and mental health. Far from being 'empowered', children are typically seen here as victims of a powerful, highly manipulative form of consumer culture that is almost impossible for them to escape or resist.

This debate inevitably reflects broader assumptions about childhood – about what children are, or what they should be. Children, it is assumed, are different from adults in key respects: they possess particular characteristics, needs or vulnerabilities, which mean they should be treated in different ways. These claims can in principle be subjected to empirical examination. Yet this debate is also to some extent a normative one: in making claims about what we want children to be or to become, we are also asserting fundamental values to do with the kind of society we want. The theories and methods that researchers use in exploring such phenomena – and indeed the issues and questions they choose to explore in the first place – are also bound to reflect these broader values and assumptions. This chapter aims to explore some of the ways in which the figure of the child consumer is defined or constructed, by campaigners, by marketers and by academic researchers. In doing so, it argues that we need to move beyond the polarized terms in which this debate is typically framed, and to address the social and cultural contexts of children's consumption practices.

Campaigners and marketers

In recent years, there has been a flurry of popular critical publications about children and consumer culture: prominent examples include Schor's *Born to Buy* (2004), Linn's *Consuming Kids* (2004) and Mayo and Nairn's *Consumer Kids* (2009). Other popular books in this vein include discussions of children's consumption alongside broader arguments about the apparent demise of traditional notions of childhood – as in the case of Palmer's *Toxic Childhood* (2006). The arguments in these publications are, by and large, far from new. One can look back to similar arguments being made in the 1970s, for example by groups like Action for Children's Television in the United States (Hendershot, 1998); or to announcements of the 'death of childhood' that have regularly recurred throughout the past two centuries (e.g., Postman, 1983). Even so, there now seems to be a renewed sense of urgency in these claims.

Such books typically presume that children used to live in an essentially non-commercial world, or a kind of idyllic 'golden age'. Many of them link the issue of consumerism with other well-known concerns about media and childhood: as well as turning children into premature consumers, the media are accused of promoting sex and violence, obesity, drugs and alcohol, gender stereotypes and false values, and taking children away from other activities that are deemed to be more worthwhile. Of course, this is a familiar litany, which tends to conflate very different kinds of effects and influences. It constructs the child as innocent, helpless, and unable to resist the power of the media. Thus, these texts describe children as being bombarded, assaulted, barraged, even subjected to 'saturation bombing' by media: they are being seduced, manipulated, exploited, brainwashed, programmed and branded. And the predictable solution here is for parents to engage in counter-propaganda, to censor their children's use of media, or simply keep them locked away from corrupting commercial influences. These books rarely include the voices of children, or try to take account of their perspectives: this is essentially a discourse generated by adults *on behalf of* children.

Meanwhile, there has been a parallel growth in marketing discourse specifically focused on children. Again, there is a long history of this kind of material. As Cook (2004) and Jacobson (2004) have shown, the early decades of the twentieth century saw marketers increasingly addressing children directly, rather than their parents. In the process, they made efforts to understand the child's perspective, and began to construct the child as a kind of authority, not least by means of market research. In recent years, however, this kind of marketing discourse has proliferated, most notably in relation to the newly-identified category of the 'tween'. More recent examples would include del Vecchio's *Creating Ever-Cool* (1997) and Sutherland and Thompson's *Kidfluence* (2003); although perhaps the most influential account is Lindstrom's *BRANDchild* (2003), which is the basis of a major consultancy business that has effectively become a brand in its own right.

The most striking contrast between these accounts and those of the critics of consumer culture is their very different construction of the child consumer. The child is seen here as sophisticated, demanding and hard-to-please. Tweens, we are told, are not easily manipulated: they are an elusive, even fickle market, sceptical about the claims of advertisers, and discerning when it comes to getting value for money – and they need considerable effort to understand and to capture. Of course, given the political pressure that currently surrounds the issue of marketing to children (most notably around so-called 'junk food'), marketers are bound to argue that advertising has very little effect, and that children are 'wise consumers'. Yet this idea of the child as sovereign consumer often elides with the idea of the child as a citizen, or an autonomous social actor, and with the notion of children's rights; and it is often accompanied by a kind of 'anti-adultism' – an approach that is very apparent, for example, in the marketing of the global children's television channel Nickelodeon (Banet-Weiser, 2007). To use one of Nickelodeon's key marketing slogans, in the new world of children's consumer culture, *kids rule*.

Theories of consumer culture: beyond the binaries

There is a polarization here between two diametrically opposed views of children: the child as innocent victim *versus* the child as competent social actor. Yet there are also some similarities. It seems to be assumed that there is a natural state of childhood that has been destroyed or corrupted by marketers – or alternatively that children's 'real' innate needs are somehow being acknowledged and addressed, even for the first time. It is also believed that there is something particular to the condition of childhood that makes children necessarily more vulnerable – or indeed spontaneously more wise and sophisticated, for example in their dealings with technology; and that adults are somehow exempted from these arguments.

These contrasting views of consumption are also played out in academic theories and debates. On the one hand are accounts that see consumption as a kind of betrayal of fundamental human values. From this point of view, the pleasure of consumption is something to be suspected, a matter of inauthentic, short-term gratification – unlike the apparently authentic pleasures of human interaction, true culture, or spontaneous feeling. This argument stands in a long tradition of critical theory, from Adorno and Marcuse (and indeed more conservative critics like Leavis and Ortega y Gasset) through to contemporary authors such as Bauman (2007) and Barber (2007). For such critics it is generally *other people's* consumption that is regarded as problematic: the argument is informed by a kind of elitism, whereby largely white, male, middle-class critics have stigmatized the consumption practices of others – women, the working classes and now children (Seiter, 1993).

On the other hand, there are accounts that emphasize the agency of consumers – their ability to define their own meanings and pleasures, and to exercise power and control. Such accounts were particularly prominent in 'postmodernist' Cultural Studies at the beginning of the 1990s (e.g. Fiske, 1990), although they have arguably resurfaced with some more celebratory accounts of fandom and so-called 'participatory culture' (Jenkins, 2006). Far from being passive dupes of the market, consumers are regarded here as active and autonomous; and commodities are seen to have multiple possible meanings, which consumers can select, use and rework for their own purposes. In appropriating the 'symbolic resources' they find in the marketplace, consumers are engaging in a productive and self-conscious process of creating an individual 'lifestyle' and constructing or 'fashioning' their identities. In the process, they are seen to be evading or resisting the control of what Fiske (1990) calls 'the power bloc'.

In many respects, these contrasting views replay a much wider polarization within the social sciences, between structure and agency (Buckingham and Sefton-Green, 2003). Yet this fails to acknowledge some of the paradoxes here. For example, it is entirely possible that children (or indeed adults) might be active and sophisticated readers of media, but might nevertheless still be influenced – or indeed that an *illusion* of autonomy and choice might be one of the prerequisites of contemporary consumer culture. *Activity* is not necessarily the same thing as *agency*. At the same time, we need to acknowledge the genuine difficulties and uncertainties that are entailed for marketers in actually targeting children – and the possibility that the power of marketers may be more limited than is often assumed.

On the side of structure, the market clearly does attempt to construct and define the child consumer: it offers children powerful definitions of their own wants and needs, while purporting to satisfy them. Yet on the side of agency, children also construct and define their own needs and identities – not least by how they appropriate and use consumer goods. The paradox of contemporary marketing is that it is bound to construct children as active, desiring and autonomous, and in some respects as resisting the imperatives of adults, while simultaneously seeking to make them behave in particular ways. As such, it is positively misleading to see this in terms of a simple *opposition* between structure and agency, or as a kind of 'zero-sum game', in which more of one automatically means less of the other. Structure requires agency, but agency only works through structure: each, in this sense, actively produces the other.

Consumption out of context

In seeking to move beyond such binary thinking, we also need to develop a broader and more contextualized analysis of children's consumer practices. Much of the research in this area focuses on children's responses to advertising – especially television advertising – rather than on other aspects of marketing or of consumption. A great deal of it is also concerned with purchasing (or aspects of 'pre-purchasing' such as information-seeking, preference and choice); and relatively little with how children appropriate and use products in their everyday lives. As such, this work focuses on a relatively narrow aspect of the broader nexus of production, distribution, circulation and consumption.

Much of this work has been conducted by psychologists, within two main traditions: media effects and consumer socialization. Both approaches have been widely challenged on methodological grounds, which do not need to be rehearsed here. More significant in this context are the theoretical questions that can be raised about these approaches. Effects research is self-evidently premised on a view of children's relationship with media as a matter of cause and effect. A classic behaviourist perspective (which is sometimes termed 'social learning theory') conceives of this process in terms of stimulus and response – of which the most obvious example would be imitation. From this perspective, television advertising would be seen to produce direct effects on viewers – not only in terms of purchasing behaviour, but also in terms of attitudes and values. More sophisticated exponents of this approach posit the existence of 'intervening variables' (both individual differences and social factors, such as personality, gender or family background) that come between the stimulus and the response, and thereby mediate any potential effects; although the basic 'cause-and-effect' model continues to apply (see Gunter and Furnham, 1998).

By contrast, consumer socialization research tends to draw on developmental psychology in proposing a sequence of 'ages and stages' in maturation (John, 1999). From this perspective, children's development as consumers is related to the development of more general cognitive skills and capacities, such as the ability to process information, to understand others' perspectives, to think and reflect in more abstract ways, and to take account of multiple factors that might be in play in decision-making. Influenced by parents and peers, as well as media and marketing, children's consumer behaviour is seen to become gradually more autonomous, consistent and rational. This approach inevitably leads to a 'deficit model' of the ways in which children understand, interpret and act upon their world: they are seen primarily in terms of what they lack, as compared with adults. The view of socialization here is fundamentally teleological: it regards development as a linear progression towards the final achievement of adult rationality. In common with developmental psychology more broadly, this approach also neglects the emotional and symbolic aspects of consumer behaviour, in favour of cognitive or intellectual ones.

Critics of this approach argue that a more sociocultural account of consumer socialization is required. Ekstrom (2006), for example, proposes that consumer socialization is an ongoing, lifelong process, rather than something that is effectively concluded at the point of entry to adulthood; that it varies among different social and cultural groups, and over time; and that it involves different life experiences and contexts of consumption. As such, there can be no single definition of what counts as a 'competent' consumer. Ekstrom also argues that children should be seen as active participants in the process of socialization, not as passive recipients of external influences. Likewise, Cook (2010) proposes that the notion of socialization should be replaced by the notion of 'enculturation', which he suggests would help to move beyond the normative, monolithic approach of consumer socialization research. He argues that children are already implicated in consumer culture from before the point of birth; and that rather than seeking to assess children's knowledge in the abstract, we need to consider how that knowledge is used (or not used) in everyday social practice.

As objects of psychological inquiry, then, children tend to be perceived and defined in particular ways. The primary interest is in *internal* mental processes of cognition or emotion: the 'social context' is predominantly understood as an external variable or influence. Children are also conceptualized principally in terms of *development* – that is, in terms of their progression towards the goal of adult maturity. And methodologically, much of the focus is on what children *think* – or say they think, often in response to psychometric tests – rather than in what they *do*, or even on how their knowledge is used in everyday life. By and large, children are not seen here as independent social actors: as sociologists of childhood would have it, they are seen not as *beings*, but only as *becomings* (Lee, 2001).

Consumption in context

The key point here is that it makes little sense to abstract children's relationship with advertising, or their consumer behaviour, from the broader social and historical context. Indeed, the distinction between consumption and the 'context' in which it occurs may itself be misleading: it might be more appropriate to regard consumption as a form of *social practice*, and a dimension of other social practices, which collectively *construct* 'contexts'. In a capitalist society, almost all our social activities and relationships are embedded within economic relations. The children's market works through and with the family, the peer group and – increasingly – the school. We need to address how consumption practices are carried out in these different settings, how they help to define the settings themselves, and how they are implicated in the management of power, time and space. In the process, we need to move beyond the notion of the consumer as a self-contained individual, and beyond individualistic notions of desire, identity and lifestyle, to focus instead on relationships and reciprocity.

Johansson (2010) points to Actor Network Theory as an alternative to this individualistic view, by virtue of its emphasis on connections, networks and flows. Agency is seen here, not as a possession of the individual, but rather as something that is exercised in specific situations and events, and via 'assemblages' of human and non-human actors (including objects, artefacts and texts, as well as people). This approach has much in common with the 'circuit of culture' that is characteristic of Cultural Studies (see Buckingham, 2008), not least in that it moves beyond the dichotomy of structure and agency: power is not seen to lie either with consumers or with producers, but precisely in the interrelationships between them.

Anthropological and sociological studies of childhood have begun to address these dynamics in other areas of children's lives (see Qvortrup et al., 2009); and in some recent studies, this approach has begun to be applied to children and parents' everyday consumption practices as well (see Martens et al., 2004). This work addresses central questions to do with the construction of childhood identities and the wider 'generational order', drawing on the Sociology of Childhood as well as on Cultural Studies and on anthropological studies of 'material culture' (see Buckingham, 2011; Buckingham and Tingstad, 2010).

One particular focus of interest here is how consumption produces and sustains hierarchies of status and authority in children's peer groups. Thus, some research shows how children's clothing purchases can be a site of play and creativity but also of anxiety about status and belonging (Boden et al., 2004). To what extent does knowledge of consumer culture function as a kind of cultural (or subcultural) capital for children? How do the hierarchies of taste and 'cool' within the peer group relate to the hierarchies within adult culture (for example, of class, ethnicity or gender)? How might such hierarchies work with or against the imperatives of consumer culture (for example, by rendering the 'cool' uncool overnight)? How do we interpret the anti-consumerist rhetoric of some forms of youth culture – and the ways in which it has been appropriated for so-called 'ethical' consumption, for example in the case of Fairtrade produce (see Banaji and Buckingham, 2009)?

Another focus here is the changing role of parenting, and the social expectations that surround it. Cross (2004) has identified the symbolic tension here between parents' desire to shelter the child, to use childhood as a place for pedagogic nurturing, and their desire to allow the child a space for expression, to indulge the freedom they themselves have lost. As parents spend less and less time with their children, they may be more inclined to compensate by providing them with consumer goods. As such, contemporary parenting is now increasingly implicated with the operations of the market – and yet parents often regard this with considerable ambivalence (Pugh, 2009).

Other studies have addressed the experience of young people who are excluded from peer group culture because of their lack of access to consumer goods (e.g. Croghan et al., 2006). Not all consumers are equally able to participate, since participation depends not just on one's creativity but also on one's access to material resources: the market is not a neutral mechanism, and the marketized provision of goods and services (not least in the media and in education) may exacerbate existing inequalities. In this context, it is particularly important to understand the consumption practices of children and parents in disadvantaged communities and low resource societies, for whom 'consumer choice' may be a fraught and complex matter. While many children may be able to access some aspects of the goods that become the *lingua franca* of children's culture – for instance, by being part of the audience for the advertising that surrounds them – their experience of the actual products is likely to vary widely with material purchasing power. Chin's work (2001) on poor African-American children usefully challenges the idea that less wealthy children are somehow more at risk from the seductions of consumer culture, exploring how their strikingly altruistic consumption practices – during a shopping trip she arranged as part of the research – are embedded within their social and familial relationships.

Conclusion

Contemporary childhoods are always-already commercial childhoods. Childhood is not, and cannot be, a pure space that is somehow held apart from the market relations that surround and help to define it. Children are being constructed as consumers, not just through advertising and marketing but also through the commercialization, privatization and marketization of other aspects of their lives, including education, leisure and welfare services, and public broadcasting. These developments may well accentuate inequalities between children, even if they do not create them. The market clearly does have a considerable power to determine the meanings and pleasures that are available to children; but children themselves also play a key role in creating those meanings and pleasures, and they may define and appropriate them in very diverse ways. Despite the often melodramatic claims of campaigners and the generalized optimism of the marketers, the outcomes of children's increasing immersion in consumer culture are by no means the same for all.

SEE ALSO in this volume chapter by Chan and chapter by Buijzen, Rozendaal and van Reijmersdal.

References

Banaji, S. and Buckingham, D. (2009). The civic sell: young people, the internet and ethical consumption. *Information, Communication and Society*, *12*(8), 1197–1223.

Banet-Weiser, S. (2007). *Kids rule! Nickelodeon and consumer-citizenship*. Durham, NC: Duke University Press.

Barber, B. (2007). *Consumed*. New York: Norton.

Bauman, Z. (2007). *Consuming life*. Cambridge: Polity.

Boden, S., Pole, C., Pilcher, J. and Edwards, T. (2004). New consumers? The social and cultural significance of children's fashion consumption. *Working Papers: Cultures of Consumption Series*, 16. London: Birkbeck College.

Buckingham, D. (2008). Children and media: a Cultural Studies approach. In K. Drotner and S. Livingstone (Eds), *Handbook of children, media and culture*. London: Sage, pp. 219–36.

——(2011). *The material child: Growing up in consumer culture*. Cambridge: Polity.

Buckingham, D. and Sefton-Green, J. (2003). Gotta catch 'em all: structure, agency and pedagogy in children's media culture. *Media Culture & Society*, *25*(3), 379–99.

Buckingham, D. and Tingstad, V. (Eds) (2010). *Childhood and consumer culture*. London: Palgrave Macmillan.

Chin, E. (2001). *Purchasing power: Black kids and American consumer culture*. Minnesota: University of Minnesota Press.

Cook, D. T. (2004). *The commodification of childhood*. Durham, NC: Duke University Press.

——(2010). Commercial enculturation: moving beyond consumer socialization. In D. Buckingham and V. Tingstad (Eds), *Childhood and consumer culture*. London: Palgrave Macmillan, pp. 63–79.

Croghan, R, Griffin, C., Hunter, J. and Phoenix, A. (2006). Style failure: consumption, identity and social exclusion. *Journal of Youth Studies*, *9*(4), 463–78.

Cross, G. (2004). *The cute and the cool*. New York: Oxford University Press.

Del Vecchio, G. (1997). *Creating ever-cool*. Louisiana: Pelican.

Ekstrom, K. (2006). Consumer socialization revisited. In R.W. Belk (Ed.), *Research in consumer behavior, Volume 10*. Oxford: Elsevier, pp. 71–98.

Fiske, J. (1990). *Understanding popular culture*. London: Unwin Hyman.

Gunter, B. and Furnham, A. (1998). *Children as consumers*. London: Routledge.

Hendershot, H. (1998). *Saturday morning censors*. Durham, NC: Duke University Press.

Jacobson, L. (2004). *Raising consumers*. New York: Columbia University Press.

Jenkins. H. (2006). *Convergence culture*. New York: New York University Press.

Johansson, B. (2010). Subjectivities of the child consumer: beings and becomings. In D. Buckingham and V. Tingstad (Eds), *Childhood and consumer culture*. London: Palgrave Macmillan, pp. 80–93.

John, D. R. (1999). Consumer socialization of children. *Journal of Consumer Research*, *26*(3), 183–213.

Lee, N. (2001). *Childhood and society*. Buckingham: Open University Press.

Lindstrom, M. (2003). *BRANDchild*. London: Kogan Page.

Linn, S. (2004). *Consuming kids*. New York: Anchor Books.

Martens, L., Southerton, D. and Scott, S. (2004). Bringing children (and parents) into the sociology of consumption. *Journal of Consumer Culture*, *4*(2), 155–82.

Mayo, E. and Nairn, A. (2009). *Consumer kids*. London: Constable.

Palmer, S. (2006). *Toxic childhood*. London: Orion.

Postman, N. (1983). *The disappearance of childhood*. London: W.H. Allen.

Pugh, G. (2009). *Longing and belonging: Parents, children and consumer culture*. Berkeley: University of California.

Qvortrup, J., Corsaro, W. and Sebastian-Honig, M. (Eds) (2009). *The Palgrave handbook of childhood studies*. London: Palgrave Macmillan.

Schor, J. (2004). *Born to buy*. New York: Scribner.

Seiter, E. (1993). *Sold separately: Children and parents in consumer culture*. New Brunswick, NJ: Rutgers University Press.

Sutherland, A. and Thompson, B. (2003). *Kidfluence*. New York: McGraw Hill.

7

CRITICAL STUDIES: PRACTICE NOT DISCIPLINE

Karen Orr Vered

Practising across multiple disciplines and employing a variety of methods, media researchers in a Critical Studies tradition may have formal training in literary criticism, history, film-making, art history, philosophy, aesthetics, anthropology, narratology, pedagogy, linguistics or other fields. Given this diversity, Critical Studies is best understood as an approach to the object of study and a way to practice scholarship rather than a discipline in its own right. The chapter offers a broad background to the tradition of Critical Studies and is informed by my own multi-disciplinary training and its application in practice to the exploration of children's media use. This chapter focuses on an intellectual heritage with roots in Marxist Critical Theory and a view that the economic, social, political, and cultural are inseparable and mutually constitutive. Media are understood here as cultural forms that express broader social patterns (Williams, 1974) and Critical Studies examine the cultural forms and cultural practices that take shape in the nexus of technology, text, and context.

The critique inherent to Critical Studies is an activist one with aims to identify and address social problems, particularly those to do with inequality and power. Like Feminist Studies and early Cultural Studies, Critical Studies is a counter-hegemonic practice that often questions the received wisdom and challenges the dominant paradigm or discourse (Kincheloe and McLaren, 2002; Fay, 1987). Critical Studies acknowledges that children's relatively subordinate and dependent status in society limits their opportunity to speak on their own behalf and to participate fully in society. Their access to media is often circumscribed and restricted, their opinions and preferences are not often sought after, and yet children are spoken for and about, particularly through media regulation and policy. As part of its counter-hegemonic practice, Critical Studies scholarship often highlights children's media practices, and tries to do so in the words of children and with their participation, to understand how children make media meaningful. In this way, Critical Studies emphasizes children's agency in media interactions and economies.

Broadly, Critical Studies scholarship has explored images of children in media (representations) and what they indicate about our understanding of children and childhood at particular historical moments; how children understand media (meaning construction); what children do with media (as consumers and producers); how industrial systems of media treat children (as consumers) – and it has looked reflectively at scholarship itself by examining the construction of children and media as a specialized area of inquiry. Often the subject of inquiry is focused at the intersections and interfaces of such concerns.

One might pose the following research question: "Given the commercial imperative for repetition that results in stereotype, under what circumstances and in what ways do children resist or respond to the uniformity and conformity promoted by commercial media?" This complex question implies that production and consumption practices are co-constitutive and dialogic. To address the interwoven issues here, a researcher might look at the fictional characters that children create in their drawings and other media production and ask whether children make characters with features and behaviors similar to those that already exist or if they create characters to fill gaps or blend the characteristics from different franchises and properties in their own creations? Examining what children do is important because what they make is a form of expression and marks their participation in the cultural economies of media in material ways. To elicit a richer understanding of children's views, researchers sometimes ask children to draw pictures of concepts, stories, or experiences. Children's illustrations can elaborate on their oral comments or serve as a prompt to guide research (Götz et al., 2005). This is to suggest but one example of how scholars might go about gaining knowledge of the meaning that children construct with and through their media use and play.

Intellectual heritage

The Marxist critical theory set out by the Frankfurt School scholars in the early part of the twentieth century explains that media communications and their industries are part of the broader culture industries and critical to the maintenance of society through the cultural work that media perform. The works of Max Horkheimer, Theodor Adorno, Herbert Marcuse, Jürgen Habermas, and Walter Benjamin on mass culture, media, and communication are among the earliest influential writings that have contoured this approach to media research. While the scholarly traditions of art history and literary criticism were well-established before the industrial revolution, twentieth century scholarship was confronted with the consequences of industrialization and commercial intensification for media markets, producers, consumers, readers, audiences, and citizens. The forms of media, the associated structures and systems of production and distribution, as well as consumption practices changed with industrialization. Mass production and industrial systems of distribution allowed for mass media – media accessible to many. The question then arose, was this necessarily a unidirectional system in which the public could only receive and never produce?

The critical project that the Frankfurt School scholars established has evolved over time and has subsequently been criticized for overstating the hegemonic power of media and too narrowly limiting individual agency, particularly our ability to participate in resistance (Fay, 1987). While many researchers in the Critical Studies tradition today might not explicitly link their work to the Frankfurt scholars, the attention they brought to media production and consumption in a capitalist context is an ongoing concern; how children are positioned, addressed, and participate in media cultures often reflects other features of their socio-economic context and position.

Our understanding of childhood and what it means to be a child were also affected by the industrial revolution. As children were removed from the work force "for their protection," their ability to earn was curtailed. Gradually, but eventually, they became valued for their sentimental qualities rather than their usefulness (Zelizer, 1985). The non-productive but sentimentally "priceless" child replaced the useful wage earning child. While they could no longer earn, children were soon recognized as powerful consumers and subsequently addressed as a market in their own right (Seiter, 1993). Critical Studies acknowledges children's participation in consumer-media culture and seeks to understand the positions that children occupy within it, how they are addressed, and how they respond (Banet-Wiser, 2007; Kinder, 1991; Sammond, 2005).

Across the twentieth century, art history and literary criticism models were applied in the examination of commercial mass media and allowed scholars to take seriously what might otherwise have been deemed "low culture" objects or "cheap amusements." Although I would distinguish between Cultural Studies as a discipline and Critical Studies as a practice, the British tradition of Cultural Studies scholarship associated with the Birmingham Centre for Contemporary Cultural Studies (CCCS) and the works of Raymond Williams (1974), Stuart Hall (1980), Dick Hebdige (1979), Paul Willis (1977), and Angela McRobbie (1990) helped shape current practices in Critical Studies scholarship of media (on Cultural Studies, see Buckingham, 2008). The role of popular culture in shaping and experiencing subjectivity, first articulated for working class identity and later youth, has been extended to children as a unique group and consumer population. On the one hand the working classes were marginalized from the central operations and ownership of mass media but, on the other hand, they were ideal consumers. Cultural Studies research demonstrated that consumer-media practices and the meanings derived from mass media were not scripted by producers, but rather that individuals made media meaningful within the context provided by their own lived experiences – gender, class, ethnicity, and so forth (Hall, 1980). Rather than being dominated by a singular meaning regime enforced from elsewhere, Cultural Studies scholarship has demonstrated how individuals participate in the construction of meaning through their everyday practices. Angela McRobbie (1990) was critical of the masculine bias in the research on youth cultures and focused her work on female youth culture to demonstrate the significance of gender in this arena. Studies of children and youth media cultures have benefited from her contributions.

Children's relative dependence and the associated special status they occupy results in their individual rights being compromised rather than complete in many circumstances. The difference attributed to children, as distinct from adults, is institutionalized as deficiency and children's likes, preferences, tastes, and opinions are often seen to be flawed or ill-informed; children's tastes are disrespected and associated with low culture. Challenging the hegemonic view of children as dependent, Critical Studies grants agency and autonomy to children and understands that although children may be marginal to the industrial practices of production they are active as consumers, and sometimes producers. Through their consumer practices and their production activities, including media play and modification of media objects, children inscribe commercial media with meaning that makes sense in the context of their experiences both immediate and mediated. Michael Dezzuani (2011), however, cautions that gaining access to the means of media production and "having a voice" do not necessarily result in greater power and he highlights the need for ethical reflection in media education programs that incorporate production activities and agendas.

French scholarship has also influenced studies of children and media by drawing attention to the fine tensions between the ubiquitous nature of media within our everyday routines and environs, and the industrial features of contemporary mass media and individual agency. The works of Henri Lefebvre and Michel de Certeau on everyday life and those of Michel Foucault and Roland Barthes on power and agency in discourse have been most influential. This strand of intellectual heritage suggests that it is important to recognize children's autonomy and agency and the limitations that are placed on both with respect to media consumption and production.

An important distinction in critical media scholarship since the late 1980s is a focus on what people do with media and where they do it. The contexts in which media engagements occur contour those media experiences and consequently contribute to shaping the meaning that is made from specific content. Examining media practices as situated social activity makes us aware that while observations in family homes reveal something about media use at home, such insights cannot be applied without qualification to other contexts. In after-school care services, for example, children "watch" television, and other recorded material, as a karaoke-like activity. They sing along and dance to the TV shows and movie theme songs, often replaying the same scene repeatedly on DVD (Vered, 2008, 2011). Unlike family homes, after-school care services expect children to be rambunctious and active, even when they are indoors. Television is not understood as a quiet activity or necessarily something for "down time." TV viewing is not a sedentary activity in the public and child-centered spaces of childcare services for school aged children.

Following from the fundamental assumption that media exist as complex combinations of technology, text, and context, making the text and making sense of the text are equally dependent upon human agency. Thus, meaning is actively produced rather than received and media content cannot have fixed meaning. Qualitative and descriptive methods in addition to, or instead of, quantitative methods have been important in revealing how meaning is ascribed in particular contexts.

Counter-hegemonic research

Whatever their motivation, arguments about the media in relation to children tend to conceive of media as a powerful force in children's socialization, in some ways more powerful than parents and schools. Whether that power is used for good or evil – whether it does them good or turns them bad – it is essentially pedagogical: it is about instructing children in the ways of the adult world and their eventual place within it (Bazelgette and Buckingham, 1995, p. 3).

This emphasis on children as little learning sponges, absorbing all the time, is often coupled with a fear that rather than learning mainly positive lessons, children's development and behavior will be influenced by what are perceived to be media's "harmful effects." The dominant paradigm in the discourse on children and media relies on the combination of three views: 1) the pedagogical imperative, as above; 2) a rather lopsided belief in harmful media effects; and, 3) the view that children, more than adults, are vulnerable to media influences. This persists despite the impossibility of isolating media influences from other influences (Fowles, 1999). Critical Studies scholarship challenges oversimplified constructions of children, childhood experience, and functionalist media studies. The most recent concern to marshal the power of the dominant discourse is the question of what contribution media might have to the rise in childhood obesity. The worst of this approach seeks to link media use and media content to children's increased size by proffering a substitution thesis: time spent with media is sedentary and replaces physical activity; children literally consume the foods represented on TV. Such formulations end up laying blame on "the Media" by oversimplifying a complex condition that has many dimensions, including those of social class and its associations with both food culture and media culture.

An earlier concern about media influence on children circulated around the possibility that children would imitate violent behavior that they had experienced through narrative fiction. This has been applied to television since the 1950s, to digital games since the late 1980s, and to movies, comics, and pulp fiction before that. Importantly, Critical Studies can help us to understand the affective and expressive dimensions of children's relationships with media and draw attention to what children do with media, not what media do to children.

Central to the practice of Critical Studies is an understanding that media objects or properties are, like paintings or works of literature, cultural objects. The production and consumption of media are cultural practices that occur in multiple and complex contexts. The contextual focus may be local and intimate, like children's friendship networks that develop and maintain themselves around a shared interest and activities associated with a media property like Pokémon, Harry

Potter, Club Penguin or the next phenomenon over the horizon. Looking at government regulation or industrial practices of publishing, film distribution, media marketing and exhibition the focus is on a macro-level context. Dafna Lemish's (2010) investigation of how gender is understood by children's television producers around the world demonstrates how national, regional, and cultural agendas inform an understanding of gender, which in turn influences many aspects of children's programming.

What does it mean "to do" critical studies of children and media?

Following Foucault's method, Carmen Luke (1990) makes an important contribution by explaining how the child viewer has been constructed, constrained, defined, and delimited by dominant trends in research and its dissemination in both the academic and popular press. In *Constructing the Child Viewer: A History of the American Discourse on Television and Children, 1950–1980*, Luke argues that the disciplines of sociology, psychology, and education primarily viewed media as a social information source for children in the early years of media research between 1917–53. That is, movies, radio, comic books, and later television were understood as information sources through which children learned social lessons. Luke explains that the Payne Fund studies of 1933 set the research agenda for many years to come and by the late 1940s,

> [C]hildren and adolescents had been transformed into consumers of mass culture and mass media. For social critics, academics, and the public, the problem with children's access to and relationship with popular culture and mass media was their susceptibility to the messages of a cultural text directed at mass society, not necessarily or solely directed at children …
>
> *(p. 57)*

Current debates about children and media continue to bear this legacy as popular discourse creates an image of children as fundamentally vulnerable in their relations with media, as consumers of meaning not producers, and with limited agency characterized as reactive rather than proactive. Media policy and regulation often reflect these views and are consequently framed as protectionist – keeping children safe from possible influences and the effects of media. But perhaps an even more important incentive to scholars in the Critical Studies tradition, children have been silenced by this set of beliefs and were only marginal to Media Studies for some time (Buckingham, 2008).

An important strand of Critical Studies research on children and media has assumed a counter-hegemonic posture to explore and document the agency that children exercise in their media engagements. One aspect of this emphasis can be summarized as a focus on "affect not effect." Learning how children feel and what they think about the media that they engage with is distinct from seeking to identify the fixed consequences (effects) of those engagements. While "affect" is sometimes affiliated with certain psychological schools of thought, the word is used here in its vernacular sense to suggest not only immediate emotional response but the longer-term and more reflective dimensions of feeling *and* thinking. Children actively construct meaning from the media they engage with, irrespective of the medium: digital games, trading cards, broadcast television and radio, print forms, film, and a wide range of on-line media that are both replicating and transforming earlier formats.

My research has focused on children's recreational use of media at school and in after-school care settings and Pokémon provides a rich example. In many Australian school classrooms, at the height of its popularity at the start of this century, Pokémon was seen to be a disruptive force, distracting children from their work and, as a consequence, teachers prohibited all things Pokémon during class time. Children secreted their precious Pokémon cards in hip pockets, backpacks, and desks until the bell rang. At after-school care, Pokémon cards and knowledge of the narrative world and its characters became a Rosetta stone yielding entry to friendship networks and exchanges of immeasurable value. The narrative world of the Pokémon cross-media franchise provided a base from which children developed a play-yard run and chase game of intense physical activity that combined skills in throwing, catching, and recitation (Vered, 2008). Contrary to the view that media play is sedentary and replaces physical activity, Pokémon was so well liked that, when the children had reached the limit of their turn at the video game, they extended their Pokémon play outside on the playground.

Had I not carefully observed the children and then asked them to explain, in their own words, what they were doing, I never would have discovered the game of playground Pokémon. I noticed that the Pokémon video game playing group often played a chase/tag game, running about and tossing yellow tennis balls at each other, freezing and performing lengthy recitations. I asked them about the playground game and learned about this elaborate performance of embodying Pokémon characters in narratives derived from the TV series and customized to meet the geographic and physical affordances of the climbing equipment. This activity was a game specific to this friendship group and this playground. It could only be discovered in its natural setting.

Engaging with human subjects to generate data comes to Media Studies from two main sources. One is the tradition borrowed from market research whereby consumer input is solicited to inform the design of products. These techniques have been used extensively within media industries to develop stories, characters, and extended product lines for media properties and have been important in the exploration of questions about digital games and gender: what do girls want? (Cassell and Jenkins, 1998). Secondly, and arguably more important, is what has been called the "ethnographic turn" in the Humanities and Social Sciences since the early 1980s. With the rise of new disciplines and an increase in interdisciplinary research, the anthropological methods of ethnography were adopted and transformed to suit emerging research agendas and practices.

Ethnography literally means "writing culture" but the term is more often used in media studies to imply the specific method of participant observation, in which the researcher has close involvement with a community over an extended period of time and observes while participating in the activities of that community. The goal of participant observation is to develop an insider's perspective on cultural practices and to relay that understanding to an audience outside the cultural community of study. Ethnography is both descriptive and interpretive.

Other qualitative methods adopted by Critical Studies of Media are semi-structured interviews, focus group discussions, and oral history collection. Here again, industry and market research on product development has often deployed focus group techniques to discover what appeals to their market. A point of distinction for Critical Studies scholarship is that it seeks to understand the preferences of those who might not form the majority, who are often overlooked by an industry seeking the largest or the most prestigious audience. Returning to the hypothetical question posed at the beginning of this chapter: how do children respond to or resist the stereotypes that are generated by industry practices that seek the widest possible audience? Not surprisingly, work about women and girls has been essential in this regard (Baker, 2004a, 2004b; Kearney, 2006) and owes much to earlier feminist scholars.

Critical Studies is a counter-hegemonic scholarly practice with a complex intellectual heritage and a rich diversity of influences and traditions. Its application to studies of children and media has been groundbreaking, provocative, and challenging. With the emergence of each new media platform we encounter new interests and develop new questions. Among the more interesting questions for the near term are those that engage with aspects of the miniature and mobile in media formats and children's everyday lives.

SEE ALSO in this volume chapter by Drotner and chapter by Lemish.

References

Baker, S. (2004a). It's not about candy: Music, sexiness and girls' serious play in after school care. *International Journal of Cultural Studies*, 7(2), 197–212.

——(2004b). Pop in(to) the bedroom: Popular music in pre-teen girls' bedroom culture. *European Journal of Cultural Studies*, 7(1), 75–93.

Banet-Wiser, S. (2007). *Kids Rule!: Nickelodeon and Consumer Citizenship*. Durham: Duke University Press.

Bazelgette, C. and Buckingham D. (1995). *In Front of the Children: Screen Entertainment and Young Audiences*. London: British Film Institute.

Buckingham, D. (2008). Children and Media: A Cultural Studies Approach. In K. Drotner and S. Livingstone (Eds), *The International Handbook of Children, Media & Culture*. London: Sage, pp. 219–36.

Cassell, J. and Jenkins, H. (1998). *From Barbie to Mortal Kombat: Gender and Computer Games*. Cambridge, MA: MIT Press.

Dezzuani, M. (2011). Youth Media Production and Technology Skills Acquisition: Opportunities for Agency. In J. Fisherkeller (Ed.), *International Perspectives on Youth Media: Cultures of Production & Education*. New York: Peter Lang, pp. 121–37.

Fay, B. (1987). *Critical Social Science*. Ithaca, NY: Cornell UP.

Fowles, J. (1999). *The Case for Television Violence*. Thousand Oaks, CA: Sage.

Götz, M., Lemish, D. Aidman, A. and Moon, H. (2005). *Media and the Make-Believe Worlds of Children: When Harry Potter meets Pokémon in Disneyland*. New Jersey: Lawrence Erlbaum.

Hall, S. ([1973] 1980). Encoding/decoding. In Centre for Contemporary Cultural Studies (Ed.), *Culture, Media, Language: Working Papers in Cultural Studies, 1972–79*. London: Hutchinson, pp. 128–38.

Hebdige, D. (1979). *Subculture: The Meaning of Style*. London: Methuen.

Kearney, M. C. (2006). *Girls Make Media*. New York: Routledge.

Kincheloe, J. L. and McLaren, P. (2002). Rethinking Critical Theory and Qualitative Research. In Y. Zou and E. T. Trueba (Eds), *Ethnography and Schools: Qualitative Approaches to the Study of Education*. Boston: Rowman & Littlefield, pp. 87–138.

Kinder, M. (1991). *Playing with Power in Movies, Television and Video Games*. Berkeley: University of California Press.

Lemish, D. (2010). *Screening Gender in Children's TV: The Views of Producers Around the World*. New York and Abingdon: Routledge.

Luke, C. (1990). *Constructing the Child Viewer: A History of the American Discourse on Television and Children, 1950–1980*. New York: Praeger.

McRobbie, A. (1990). *Feminism and Youth Culture*. Basingstoke: Macmillan.

Sammond, N. (2005). *Babes in Tomorrowland: Walt Disney and the Making of the American Child, 1930–1960*. Durham: Duke University Press.

Seiter, E. (1993). *Sold Separately: Parents & Children in Consumer Culture*. New Brunswick, NJ: Rutgers UP.

Vered, K. O. (2008). *Children and Media Outside the Home: Playing & Learning in After-school Care*. London: Palgrave Macmillan.

——(2011). Center or Margin? The Place of Media Play in Children's Leisure: Case Studies in Sweden and Australia. In J. Fisherkeller (Ed.), *International Perspectives on Youth Media: Cultures of Production and Education*. NY: Peter Lang, pp. 228–45.

Williams, R. (1974). *Television: Technology and Cultural Form*. London: Fontana.

Willis, P. (1977). *Learning to Labor: How Working Class Kids Get Working Class Jobs*. New York: Columbia University Press.

Zelizer, V. A. (1985). *Pricing the Priceless Child: The Changing Social Value of Children*. New York: Basic Books.

8

FEMINIST THEORY APPROACHES TO THE STUDY OF CHILDREN AND MEDIA

Dafna Lemish

The heavily gendered nature of childhood is obvious to any naïve passer-by who views the clothes children wear as well as the toys and games with which they play; who listens to their language and mannerisms, assesses their interests and make-believe worlds, and reflects on their media habits and preferences. Indeed, many scholars have observed that the gendered nature of the lives of young audiences is so distinct that it could be claimed that they live in two very different cultural worlds.

The latter claim draws heavily on developmental theories and extensive media research findings. Both bodies of research suggest that the tendency of children to segregate themselves by gender and play more compatibly with members of the same sex is already evident in early childhood, around the third year, and that it solidifies progressively by mid-childhood. While boys and girls are intensely conscious of each other as future partners and spend a large proportion of their time as they grow up attempting to satisfy their curiosity about the other group, they experience tremendous social pressure to remain separate during childhood (Maccoby, 1998).

The causes and consequences of this segregation are a major topic of investigation in child psychology and education, and lie beyond the scope of our discussion here. Suffice it to say that gender-segregated childhoods provide different contexts for the social development of children, which do not necessarily prepare them for mutual understanding and collaboration.

So what can gender theory and research contribute to our understanding of children and media? What explanatory power does it bring to the interdisciplinary table as an original perspective? The claim advanced here is that gender studies, and more specifically feminist theory, can offer the field of children and media significant and original perspectives, at least in the following four domains: First, a mapping of gender segregation of children's leisure culture and an explanation of the mechanism driving this segregation; second, a theoretical understanding of gender as a form of social construction rather than a biological fact; third, a particular view on the form and role of methodology in the study of children and media; and fourth, a model of engaged scholarship that is attempting to advance progressive social change.

Gendered mediated childhoods

An overview of the research from a gender perspective (see Lemish et al., 2001) reveals two seemingly opposed conclusions. First, boys and girls differ in their access to media, patterns of use, and content preferences as well as in the social practices and meanings they attach to them. At the risk of over-generalizing, we can argue that boys are more technologically oriented; girls are more likely to listen to music and read; boys prefer action/adventure and sports genres; girls prefer human relationships and romance; boys hang out more with groups of friends outdoors or at their computers, while girls spend more time with their best friends in the intimacy of their own rooms; boys' culture is "game-dominated" (including video, computer games, and internet surfing), while girls' culture is more about relationships, communication, and talk (including their preferred use of new technologies like the internet and the mobile phone). Parents reinforce these trends by their own gendered behavior: Boys and fathers share similar interests in sports, action-adventure, and computers; girls and mothers share similar interests in human relationships and more romantic genres. In short, there is mounting evidence that confirms the claim that traditional gender differences are being maintained with new media as well as with conventional technologies.

At the same time, we can argue quite easily for a very different conclusion. While many of the differences found in quantitative studies are rather small (even if they are statistically significant), in-depth qualitative explorations provide us with what I submit is a richer understanding of gender differences and similarities. Many girls as well as boys play outdoors and many boys as well as girls read books. Many girls show a strong interest in computer technology and gaming, and are proficient in their use of the internet. Some like sports and electronic games that feature action and adventure. True, fewer girls than boys have such tastes, but nevertheless, girls too are exploring and engaging in the new media environment. Furthermore, more and more boys are retreating into their bedrooms, once a female territory, to play electronic games alone or with friends and siblings.

The equalizing role television may be playing in this process provides us with insights into these changes. Boys and girls watch television programs, both intensively and extensively, in similar amounts and on multiple platforms. This is a change from previous research that suggested that boys are heavier television viewers. One possible explanation for this finding draws on the expansion of viewing alternatives through cable and satellite channels, as well as DVDs and the internet, to a saturation point in some parts of the world. One implication of this situation is that, currently, the media provide girls with a wider selection of attractive contents to suit their interests. In addition, the social world presented on the television screen has been changing. Although far from being a world with equal opportunities and justice, television nevertheless offers girls today a greater variety of role models that show independent women in positions of power, engaged in adventures, and enjoying successful careers.

Moreover, while boys and girls continue to have very different content interests, there is increasing evidence that genre preferences can cross generational gaps. Thus, girls do watch the same programs as their sisters and mothers, creating a feminine commonality of interests; and, boys watch the same programs as their brothers and fathers, so guarding their own masculine space at home. Yet, it is probably not so much the case that media technologies create gender segregation: Instead it is the contents and meanings these technologies offer, as well as the viewing contexts of their consumption, that are important. When girls are offered attractive options that serve them, they too use the computer, visit internet chat rooms, and play outdoors. Indeed, the interpretation that attributes differences to content rather than to media may be specifically observed in the case of the computer. There are many possible factors that contribute to the image of computers as a sphere dominated by males. The computer market, similar to the broadcast one, has neglected to cater to girls' specific interests and needs. In addition, parents seem to be less inclined to encourage their daughters to experiment with computers. Other studies found that household practices (such as giving boys priority over computer use; negative role models provided by mothers; boys' superior networking with other computer users, etc.) strengthen gender segregation in relation to computer use. The relatively unchallenged assumption that operating a computer requires technological skills for which boys are more inclined, is deeply rooted in the historical perception of technology as essentially masculine. However, a social analysis of technological usage from a feminist perspective suggests that technology is much more than hardware; it is also a process of production and consumption, a form of knowledge, a site of gender and racial domination as well as of power struggle. Gender relations in the household and its characteristic division of labor shape the way technologies, including leisure technologies such as computers, are adapted and used domestically.

What complicates this situation of domestic consumption is the fact that media, toy, and merchandising industries capitalize very successfully on these popular notions; indeed, stated more succinctly, they are intricately involved in enculturation, primarily through their extensive advertising and merchandising efforts in pursuit of ever-expanding markets and profits. Indeed, their understanding of "implied audiences" is based on interpretations of market findings seeking to identify children's tastes, desires, and pleasures as mechanisms that serve these industries' goals (Lemish, 2010).

Commercial industries build upon the well established research finding of the gendered nature of media consumption by children and young people: Overall, girls develop an interest in traditional masculine genres whereas, on the whole, boys continue to show no interest in female ones. While this descriptive evidence does provide empirical support for the popular axiom applied by children's entertainment industry and media professionals – "girls will watch boys' programs but boys will not watch girls'" – we lack a critical analysis that is the product of identifying, deconstructing, and analyzing the mechanisms creating this phenomenon. For example, according to the feminist analysis of social change, this process can be partly explained through the observation that girls as well as women, more generally, have learned to gradually incorporate typical male perspectives and values into their lives, without necessarily abandoning traditional female responsibilities and interests. This echoes other situations where efforts at improving status and position are advanced through the process of subordinated social groups adjusting "up" socially. Perhaps the trend of girls' interest in boys' genres represents their growing sensitivity to the advantageous position that boys hold in our society and the higher value associated with their tastes and interests (Lemish, 2010).

In conclusion, I argue that feminist studies could provide us with a valuable perspective and interpretation and a deeper understanding with which to examine the gendered cultures of boys and girls growing up in a mediated world.

Construction of childhood

The second major domain of interrelationships between feminist studies and our field is in the more theoretical understanding, now common place in the sociology of childhood, that this period in our lives is highly socially constructed, and often has very little to do with the biological variable of age (James et al., 1998). While clearly children of different ages differ greatly from each other, and from adults, in all aspects of life (cognitive, social, emotional, physical, behavioral), age in itself does not provide us with an explanation for these differences. Thus, today we understand that the definition of childhood is fluid, is ever changing, and is greatly dependent on cultural and temporal circumstances. For example, while a nine-year-old child in certain countries in Africa can be a soldier, using machine guns to kill civilians and enslave girls for the sexual pleasures of his commanders, a college student in his twenties in the US could be still living at home, enjoying free rent and parental laundry and cooking services. And an under-21-year-old adult in the US may not be allowed to drink alcohol or vote in certain states, but he can serve as a combat soldier in Iraq. In many societies, consensual sex under the age of 16 is criminal, while in others a 16-year-old may have already fathered four children or might be considered to be "over-the hill" in the sex industry. Multiple examples abide of differing definitions of "childhood" worldwide, with attendant legal and human rights as well as responsibilities and social expectations. Furthermore, the definition of childhood is constantly reinvented by political, religious, and market forces. Take, for example, the relatively new category of "tweens" – the pre-adolescent age: This period was invented as a marketing strategy to target this age group by creating a profit-driven identity to be realized through the consumption of goods, accessories, clothing, specific media tastes, and the like. Similarly, a redefinition of babies' and toddlers' developmental needs has emerged in recent years, largely through the efforts by a now booming industry that targets parents urging them to consume baby videos, cable channels, computer games, and related merchandising in order to advance, so they claim, their newborn child's development, and, subtextually, capacity to compete for social and economic rewards from birth.

Recognition of the social construction of "childhood" draws part of its theoretical grounding from the introduction of the construct of "gender" as a social category. Together, both childhood and gender have replaced the centrality of biology – as in children's age and reproductive organs – in understanding this young period of life. The French philosopher Simone de Beauvoir's formative statement – "One is not born a woman, but becomes one" (de Beauvoir, 1989) – captures the essence of this process. Accordingly, gender is not viewed as something originally extant in human beings, but rather it is a set of understandings that organize how we relate to our bodies; one that is produced through behaviors and social relations in the production and practice of everyday life. As such, gender is distinct from biological, sexual differences that characterize humans from birth. Accordingly, gender is considered to be a socially-determined production, and consequently differs from culture to culture. Hence, paraphrasing de Beauvoir's statement regarding this understanding of childhood, we can claim that one is not born a child, but one becomes one through socializing processes within a particular cultural context.

Only through such an understanding does "childhood" have meaning and significance, and only within these differing contexts can childhood be studied and interpreted. Clearly, gender studies are not the only theoretical school that introduced the notion of "social construction," but they had a central role in pushing it to the forefront of the discussion of biological categories. These have been also picked up by theories of race and post-colonialism. It reminds us that gender is deeply intertwined with all other human identities – be they race, ethnicity, religion, class, disability, all being perceived as social constructions that are open to multiple interpretations. The good news is that this approach offers an optimistic view of the human condition – if the meaning of biology – be it age, race, sex, disability – is socially constructed – it can also be changed. Compare it to a deterministic view that offers very little hope for progress – once you are born with a womb, or black skin, or Down syndrome – you are stuck with it and with all it entails (except for the rare case of sexual reassignment or skin implantation, for example). Thus, in the fundamental nature/nurture debate, the feminist approach weighs heavily on the side of nurture, and its liberating potential.

In conclusion, I argue that feminist studies contribute to an understanding of childhood as a social construction which is non-deterministic and opens the door to the possibility of change.

Methodological approaches to the study of children and media

Being change-oriented by definition, feminist media research is in natural alliance with social-action theoretical approaches to research. Therefore, it rejects many of the central assumptions of normative science regarding the search for universal laws, absolute truths, and objective knowledge. Instead, it recognizes that all knowledge is partial, relative, and socially situated, and all forms of scholarship are ideological by nature and political by implication. It values the researcher's own subjectivity and reflexive abilities and renounces the presumed (positivist) scientific goal to achieve objectivity and value-free research. It is greatly concerned with power relationships between researchers and those being researched, and searches for more egalitarian participatory methodologies – from the inception of the study to its assessment. Finally, it is committed, ethically, to promoting the well-being of those studied, attempts to avoid exploitive strategies, and seeks all in its power to guard them from possible research-related harm (Lemish, 2002).

All such feminist methodological concerns are immediately translatable to the study of children and media: Rather than thinking of children as little people in the process of becoming fully grown adults, we think of them as young people in their own right: we need to allow children, in each stage of their development, to be fully recognized as having unique needs and skills, as well as a personal voice that deserves to be listened to as well as understood – with respect and empathy. Therefore, when considering media research that has the child's well-being as its goal, feminist research is committed to research not only ABOUT children and their special developmental needs, but also to research WITH children and FOR children. The accumulated knowledge from years of studying children and media demonstrates that children are active users of media: They react to, think, feel, and create their own meanings out of them. They bring to media encounters a host of predispositions, abilities, desires, and experiences. They watch television, surf the internet, or play a computer game in diverse personal, social, and cultural circumstances that also influence what they get out of the experience. We can never assume that what we, as adults, need and take from a television program, a magazine article, a news report, or an internet site is what children will get out of it. Too often children themselves are absent from research on children and media, and – amazingly – it remains too rare that we hear expressions in their own voices of their concerns, interests, views, and so forth as well as exemplars of children's agency in these media. Symbolically, in feminist research, rather than referring to children as "subjects" of study, they are seen and related to, in fact, as participants in the study. This is more than a linguistic sensitivity, it is a commitment deeply rooted in non-hierarchal values of feminist approaches to social science (Lemish, 2007).

As discussed above, feminist research is particularly concerned with the social construction of gender and the conditions of individual children, diversified by race, class, sexual orientation, religion, disability and the like. While there is no unified definition of what makes up feminist thinking or feminist methodologies, there are several principles that are central to those defining themselves as feminist researchers. Their work attempts to uncover and challenge male dominance and patriarchal structures, and advocates gender equality. It rejects Western binary oppositions such as public/private, rational/emotional, spirit/body, subject/object, culture/nature, west/east and re-shifts interests to the devaluated and ignored domains of the private sphere, the emotional realm, and the taboos surrounding sexuality. As a result, new areas of investigation in children and media are blooming, beyond the traditional red flag phenomena of violence and sex, concern for cognitive and language development, and recently with obesity.

Take for example recent studies on girls' use of the internet (Mazzarella, 2010). These studies exemplify the interdisciplinary nature of the flourishing field of girlhood studies, as it requires integrating work undertaken in multicultural contexts through a variety of scholarly research traditions. Doing so requires engagement with questions about the gendered nature of technology, the democratic potential of the internet, the implications of the digital divide, empowerment and agency, identity construction, the roles of leisure and popular culture, networking, and sociality. Studies of these phenomena advance the agenda that considers girls to be active producers of texts and meanings, rather than solely passive victims of hegemonic culture. At the same time, we are advised to recognize the limitations of celebratory discourses of "active meaning making" by girls and to also pay close research attention to the implications of the limited cultural narratives offered to them on their well-being – be it for the proliferation of hypersexuality and the promotion of unhealthy approaches to human sexuality, the push for attaining an unrealistic and highly Caucasian "Beauty Myth," and the erasing of indigenous cultures (Lemish, 2010). Similarly, there is an emergence of boys' studies, concerned with the unique meaning making processes of their own engagement with favorite media texts (Winter and Neubauer, 2008). Both promising lines of research provide us with insights into children's private and hidden lives, from their – rather than our – perspectives, including their relationships with their bodies, developing sexualities, and pleasures.

In conclusion, I argue that feminist studies of children and media foreground gender related issues, as part of a general concern for the role media play in the early socialization of children and youth into social inequalities and intolerance for diversity. They recognize that these are deeply rooted in social structures and thus they examine media content, production, and audiences in context. They thus encourage cross-cultural and comparative methodologies that can highlight universal as well as cultural differences, and a methodology that is democratic, empowering, and mostly grounded and inductive.

Commitment to social change

One of the salient characteristics of feminist theory is its commitment not only to contribute to research and social theory, but also to be a catalyst for deep social change, thus emphasizing the emancipatory potential of combining knowledge and action. Feminist research is highly politicized and ideologically committed to obtaining, disseminating, and integrating knowledge in the eventual form of specific change recommendations, oriented to liberating and empowering women and other underprivileged segments of society. It embraces the concept of critical consciousness as a prerequisite for resistance and for the possibility of change through confrontation with social forces producing the naturalization of social repression. Accordingly, it seeks to problematize existing social orders that produce unequal opportunities offered in the media world for boys and girls and the differentiated uses they make of the media; the gendered risks around media effects and implications and the like. It attempts to contribute to social change via introducing change in the social structures producing gender inequality in the area of children and media: be they the professional industry producing and distributing the media, the related toy and merchandising industry, the caregivers and educators socializing children, the legislative system, and policy-makers.

As a result, feminist studies have encouraged collaborative non-hierarchical work that is both interdisciplinary in nature as well as multi-dimensional. Such efforts seek the integration of all forms of knowledge, academic and professional, that can contribute to the well-being of children and improve their media interactions. Thus, responsible production, together with engaged parenting and education, may provide the fertile ground necessary for a media world that provides a "safe haven" and an enriching symbolic environment for children and young people. Many contributions in this handbook offer illustrations of such efforts, including the applications of research to policy making, media literacy, production of content, youth made media, social change, and educational interventions.

In conclusion, I argue that feminist studies have highlighted the need for and directed scholarly efforts toward seeking to make a difference in the real world.

Concluding note

This discussion has sought to highlight four of the major contributions that, I believe, feminist studies have made and continue to make to the field of children and media. It has also attempted to dispel several misconceptions regarding feminist theory, and in particular, that it is only concerned with girls and women. Indeed, the examples in this chapter demonstrate that this is far from the truth. Furthermore, feminist approaches have also been accused of being too ideological and thus not "good" science. True, feminist theorists could be considered ideological, but only in the sense that they stress human equality and the right of each and every child (regardless of gender, race, geographical location, disability or any other determinants of human conditions) to realize his or her full potential. And, according to this logic, it would be fair to claim that the science of medicine is ideological because researchers and doctors are committed to sustain life and well-being, as is the science of law for its commitment to social justice. Accordingly, feminist scholars are as ideological as any discipline dedicated to the improvement of the human condition.

SEE ALSO in this volume chapter by Mazzarella.

References

This chapter is based on my earlier work and includes excerpts from Lemish, 2002, p. 64; Lemish, 2010; Lemish et al, 2001, pp. 277–279.

De Beauvoir, S. (1989[1949]). *The second sex.* New York: Vintage.

James, A., Jenks, C. and Prout, A. (1998). *Theorizing childhood.* Cambridge: Polity.

Lemish, D. (2002). Gender at the forefront: Feminist perspectives on action theoretical approaches in communication research. *Communications: The European Journal of Communication Research*, 27(1), 63–78.

——(2007). *Children and television: A Global perspective.* Oxford, UK: Blackwell.

——(2010). *Screening gender in children's TV: The views of producers around the world.* New York and Abingdon: Routledge.

Lemish, D., Liebes, T. and Seidmann, V. (2001). Gendered media meaning and use. In Livingstone, S. and Bovill, M. (Eds), *Children and their changing media environment.* Hillsdale, NJ: Lawrence Erlbaum, pp. 263–82.

Maccoby, E. E. (1998). *The two sexes: Growing up apart – coming together.* Cambridge, MA: The Belknap Press of Harvard University Press.

Mazzarella, S. (Ed.) (2010). *Girl Wide Web 2.0: Revisiting girls, the internet, and the negotiation of identity.* New York: Peter Lang.

Winter, R. and Neubauer, G. (2008). Cool heroes or funny freaks: Why certain programmes and TV characters appeal to boys. *TelevIZIon*, 21(E), 30–35.

9

MEDIA CULTURE AND CHILDHOOD IN THE AGE OF GLOBALIZATION

Radhika Parameswaran

Children are living today in the age of "globalization," a ubiquitous term that has as many definitions as there are proliferating programs and disciplines in the academy. Anthropologist Appadurai's vision of globalization as an interactive matrix of economic, political, historical, and cultural relations or "scapes" that illuminate "disjuncture and difference" rather than linear, unitary, or singular domination has had a significant impact on many scholars of media globalization. According to Appadurai (1996), in an era when the global geopolitical order is characterized by criss-crossing and morphing hierarchies of power that travel within and across territorial borders, the new global cultural economy has to be envisioned as a complex, overlapping, disjunctive order, which does not conform easily to existing center-periphery models. Appadurai's normative framework for investigating globalization proposes five dimensions of global flows: 1) ethnoscapes, the continuous and shifting traffic in people who migrate and move for a multitude of reasons 2) technoscapes, the technologies that facilitate the rapid transfer of information across previously impermeable borders 3) financescapes, the global grid of economic institutions, commodities, currency speculation, and capital transfer 4) mediascapes, the infrastructure and repertoire of popular culture and news narratives that both connect *and* fragment audiences and 5) ideoscapes, ideologies of corporations, states, religions, and social movements that feed into, sustain, and challenge various political cultures. Appadurai stresses that globalizing and localizing processes, or various forms of global homogenization and local heterogenization, feed into and reinforce each other rather than act in a mutually exclusive fashion, and hence he calls for more research on the complex cultural production of different localities (1996). Among media scholars, Tomlinson (1999) defines globalization as the complex connectivity and integration of work and consumer modalities in modern social life in the midst of rapidly developing and ever more intricate social and economic networks of interconnections and interdependencies.

A brief overview of research on globalization and children's mediascapes

Media scholars Dafna Lemish et al. (1998), pioneers in investigating the influences of globalization on children's media culture, note as far back as in 1998 that the complexities and contradictions of globalization offer rich opportunities for empirical work on children and media. More recently, social historian Paula Fass (2007) argues that children represent a forgotten population in academic research on globalization: "It is odd that children and childhood should be nowhere on the agenda of those who currently discuss globalization ... Children are everywhere present in this debate, but never heard from or addressed" (p. 202). Going a step further, she also asserts, "It is simply foolhardy to discuss globalization, the cultural politics of globalization, and the social consequences of globalization without firmly situating children in that discussion" (p. 217). Responding to the challenge of inserting children into concerns over globalization's spreading orbit, a modest corpus of research, which includes a handful of books (de Block and Buckingham, 2007; von Feilitzen, 2002; Fisherkeller, 2011; Lukose, 2009; McMillin, 2009), has inaugurated the project of studying children's engagement with global consumer and media culture, or in other words, children's imaginative "mediascapes," in order to investigate how historical processes— homogenization, heterogenization, glocalization, commodification, hybridity, and creolization— associated with media globalization intersect with the other "scapes" or global flows—ethno-, finance-, ideo-, and techno-scapes—that Appadurai has identified in his model of globalization. Advancing an understanding of children's media culture not only fills a yawning gap in empirical work on globalization (von Feilitzen, 2002), but more importantly, global media research on childhood promises to yield a richer and deeper portrait of globalization itself because children are often conceived simultaneously as the most vulnerable global population (subject to the authority of adults and strong media effects) and as future global citizens- and leaders-in training, who embody the best aspirations of their families and communities.

A brief survey of the geographic terrain of scholarship published in English on childhood, globalization, and media culture reveals that scholars have addressed primarily urban locations in the following nations: Australia, Austria, Belgium, Britain, Canada, Chile, Czech Republic, Denmark, France, Estonia, Germany, Greece, Haiti, India, Indonesia, Ireland, Israel, Italy, Japan, Malta, Myanmar, Netherlands, New Zealand, Nigeria, Pakistan, Poland, Portugal, Sierra Leone, Slovenia, South Africa, Spain, Sweden, Thailand, and the United States. Echoing a larger trend in interdisciplinary research on globalization's fluid and shifting ethnoscapes, researchers have focused on immigrant (largely non-Western and non-white) children's immersion and interest in media and popular culture and on the role that media play in facilitating diasporic children's multicultural identity formation (de Block and Buckingham, 2007; Durham, 2004; Elias and Lemish, 2008; Kabir, 2008; Katz, 2010; Luttrell et al., 2011; Moran, 2007; Vargas, 2006). On a refreshing note, despite the greater burdens and challenges (obtaining human subjects' approvals and permissions from adult authority figures) that researchers have to frequently negotiate in order to gain access to children in different institutional settings, many studies of globalization and media are based in interactions and interviews with children and in observations of their everyday lives, thus registering to a certain extent children's individual and collective agency in the knowledge that gets produced about them (Bosch, 2007; Buckingham, 2007; Drotner, 2004; Durham, 2004; Elias and Lemish, 2008; Grixti, 2006; Kabir, 2008; Katz, 2010; Lukose, 2009; McMillin, 2009; Miller, 2010; Salo, 2003; Strelitz, 2004). At the same time, some social science research on globalization that includes parents' and other authority figures' efforts to monitor and control children's media practices also reminds us that constructions of "childhood" continue to emerge from and are shaped by the minds and behaviors of adults, who raise and educate children (Bosch, 2007; Elias and Lemish, 2008; Kirwil, 2009). On parsing out the artifacts and objects of study—media genres, technologies, and spectacular commodities—in the global mediascape of childhood that have attracted the attention of scholars and critics, it becomes readily apparent that the global multimedia and integrated enterprises of Barbie, Bratz, Bollywood, Disney, Dora the Explorer, Harry Potter, Pokémon, Sesame Street, and Teletubbies have steadily expanded their footprints in Europe, Asia, North America, and Africa (de Block and Buckingham, 2007; Cross and Smits, 2005; Drotner, 2004; Durham, 2004; Grewal, 1999; McAllister, 2007,

Tobin, 2004; Valdivia, 2009) and that television viewing (Elias and Lemish, 2008; Hendriyani et al., 2011; Kapur, 1998; McMillin and Fisherkeller, 2009; Moran, 2007; Melnick and Jackson, 2002; Salo, 2003; Strelitz, 2004; Valdivia, 2008; Wai, 2002) and internet and digital media (Donoso and Ribbens, 2010; Kirwil, 2009; Menten, 2009; Newman, 2010; Stornaiuolo et al., 2011) use have become almost inescapable aspects of a majority of children's everyday lives.

Political economy, production, and children's global media culture

Research on and critiques of the political economy (business models, marketing, and distribution of media commodities, and state/government regulation and policies) and production aspects of children's mediated culture demonstrates that neoliberal economic globalization—the gradual weakening and removal of regulations and laws constraining foreign media ownership in Europe, Asia, and Africa—has facilitated the global proliferation of capitalist media and commodities based in advertising models that target children as homogenous consumer subjects, who are driven by a relentless and universalized quest for upward mobility. To some degree, the political economy critiques (Hamelink, 2002; Hendriyani et al., 2011; McAllister, 2007; McChesney, 2002; Sigismondi, 2009; Wai, 2002; Westcott, 2002) of the limited media options and choices available for children testifies to the continued relevance of earlier concerns over cultural imperialism as fueling the "Americanization" of the world although, illustrating the rise of new nodes of global power or counter-flows in the sphere of children's global media, scholars (Buckingham, 2007; Cross and Smits, 2005; Durham, 2004; Levine, 2009; Tobin, 2004; Ugor, 2009; Wai, 2002) also document the rising global influence of media culture originating from such countries as Japan (Pokémon, Mighty Morphin Power Rangers, anime visual productions), India (Bollywood), Canada (television series *Caillou* and *Degrassi*), and Nigeria (Nollywood). In general, children around the world lack wholesome and entertaining indigenous media that are produced specifically for them, and due to this problem some adolescents and younger children in India and Sierra Leone often seek out inappropriate adult media and popular culture (Joseph, 2007; Wai, 2002). Turning the critical lens on the nation-state's neglect of children's educational and developmental needs, Hamelink (2002) and McChesney (2002) advocate for state-sponsored solutions to curb the growth of global commercial media, create advertising free zones, and increase the availability of unrestricted "free" high quality content for children in the global public domain.

An interesting subset of research on children, globalization, and media production investigates the positive impact of children's active participation in production processes—creating their own media and exchanging media artifacts with children of other nations and cultures—on their identities, psychological growth and development, and global consciousness (Bosch, 2007; Donoso and Ribbens, 2010; Luttrell et al., 2011; Menten, 2009; Miller, 2010; Stornaiuolo et al., 2011). For example, interrupting the flow of popular culture from the United States, South African children's productions of radio and audio stories in educational settings allows them to create media that speak to urgent local issues including ethnic and national pride, African role models for children, racial and generational conflict and tensions, sexuality and dating, bullying and violence, and HIV/AIDS in families (Bosch, 2007). Producing and posting photography and exploring their peers' animated reactions in the online spaces of Fotologs—the technoscapes of globalization—assisted Chilean youth in affirming their personhood, receiving social validation, gaining social control, and achieving self clarification and self expression (Donoso and Ribbens, 2010). In a poignant and moving article that explores a Kenyan-American girl's discourses on her own photographs of life at school and home, researchers document the gratitude this immigrant child expresses for women who care for her (mother and female cook and teachers), her determination to work hard and succeed, and her desire to stay connected to extended family in Kenya (Luttrell et al., 2011). Media literacy projects, which chronicle cross-cultural exchanges of biographical audio, video, and digital media among Indian, Indonesian, African, European, South African, and British children, document the productive ways in which children's authorship of media narratives for different national or cultural audiences encourages young people to embrace a more cosmopolitan, empathetic, sympathetic, and critically self-aware and self-reflective outlook (including consciousness of poverty and class and race privilege) on the world (Menten, 2009; Miller, 2010; Stornaiuolo et al., 2011).

Glocalization, hybridity, and the agency of young audiences

Perhaps the most interesting and original contributions of research on children and media globalization lies in scholars' nuanced and complicated accounts of "glocalization" and "hybridization" in children's media audience practices, that is, in the multi-layered ways in which children express their agency and critical capacities when they speak about their use and interpretations of media texts (Buckingham, 2007; Lemish et al., 1998; Vargas, 2006). Extending the arguments of globalization theorists, who have contested simplistic and linear approaches to modern cultural (read Western) and media imperialisms as troubling reincarnations of Euro-American histories of colonialism, research on young people's and children's responses (verbal, non-verbal, interactive, and behavioral) to media illustrates an ongoing dialectic among audiences' pro or anti-Western, national, regional, class, religious, and ethnic affiliations and loyalties. Immigrant Muslim youth in Australia criticize mainstream Australian culture and media for stereotyping and criminalizing their community, yet they also call upon their identities as Australian citizens to argue that diasporic Muslim communities and their leaders should respect their Western host country's norms, err on the side of moderation, and facilitate bi-cultural dialogues (Kabir, 2008). Diasporic South Asian girls in the United States experience their gender and sexuality as complex sites of hybridization, cultural spaces in which they stitch together media preferences for Bollywood and for select forms of American popular culture in order to carve out empowering collective immigrant identities and to negotiate parents' control of and surveillance over girls' sexuality (Durham, 2004).

For Russian immigrant children in Israel, integration into their new homeland is neither a monolithic nor a homogenous experience of domination by the host Israeli culture or media. Instead, as the researchers argue, "the mass media fulfill very central and varied roles in the life of the immigrant family," but children in these families engage with Russian-language media, Israeli media, and global media in multiple ways (dependent on time spent in the host culture, language skills, family structure, gender relations, and parenting styles) that produce different outcomes for the two parallel processes of inward integration (use of media to strengthen family and community identity) and outward integration (use of media to enable integration into host society and local peer/youth culture) (Elias and Lemish, 2008, p. 35). While most work on children's media practices points to the affirmative role of "hybridity" as a resource for young immigrants to negotiate multiple identities, one rare study of lower income bilingual Hispanic children in the United States uncovers the burden of "media brokering" that these children have to shoulder in order to help their families adjust and integrate to life in their new homelands (Katz, 2010). For some of these children, their stressful hybrid adult work of cultural and linguistic translation (between families and employers and health/immigration/school bureaucracies) sometimes ends up hindering their educational and developmental progress.

A variety of global media products including Disney and Pokémon (Buckingham, 2007; Drotner, 2004; Lemish, 2002; Tobin, 2004) are often read through the lenses of regional and local experiences and cultures while very young European children find the production context or cultural locatedness of imported American media texts irrelevant to their enjoyment and understanding of popular culture. On a related note, the content of global media and popular culture texts themselves resist easy conflation with dominant or hegemonic constructions of nation or race although such progressive or multicultural iterations of global media do not imply escape from capitalist commodification; for example, Disney's *Lion King* is about South Africa, *Aladdin* is about the Middle East, *Mulan* is about China (Buckingham, 2007) and the Bratz dolls Sasha, Jade, and Yasmin with their varying skin tones signify ambiguous and globally accessible ethnicities (McAllister, 2007). Youth in South Africa, India, and Malta use, enjoy, and consume imported and indigenous media to sustain both global and local identity formations, and class, race, and gender shape and differentiate adolescents' tastes for popular culture with older, middle- and upper-class youth expressing greater preferences for English-language, American, and other imported programs (Grixti, 2006; McMillin, 2008; McMillin and Fisherkeller, 2009; Salo, 2003; Strelitz, 2004). Children's eclectic, hybrid tastes for global and national popular music in Denmark, France, and Israel are giving rise to a "joint culture which is created through music, and the easy acceptance of a large diversity of musical styles, ethnic flavors, innovative appearances, and marketing strategies" (Lemish et al., 1998, p. 549). For some black South African girls, glocalized television programs (imitative global formats with indigenous content and actors)—a reality dating show and a soap opera—even encouraged opposition to local sexist and patriarchal norms of courtship and also supported their desire for greater freedom in crafting flexible racial identities and in transgressing normative racial boundaries in romantic relationships (Salo, 2003).

Minding the gaps: future directions for research

What are some productive future directions for scholarship on children, media, and globalization? The review of knowledge in this area shows that political economy critiques and audience research have privileged particular nations in different regions of the world; for example, South Africa remains the hegemonic representative nation in scholarship on Africa (Nyamnjoh, 2002), India outnumbers work on any other nation in South Asia, and Japan leads studies of children in East Asia. Addressing neglected nations in these regions, including the dearth of knowledge on children and media globalization in the Middle East and in China, a nation that is poised to become a leading global superpower, would fill large gaps in the scope of existing empirical research. Apart from a few studies that have explored representations of children in conjunction with globalization in the news media (Montgomery, 2011), very few textual or content analyses target global journalism's cross-cultural production of childhood in relation to human rights discourses, violence, consumer culture, educational attainment, or public health. Similarly, we need more knowledge that takes into account children's voices and practices, including their interpretations of global cinema and their uses of such newer forms of global technology as cell phones and videogames. Middle-class children in urban and metropolitan locations are the primary subjects of most work on media and globalization with the result that poor and rural children's media experiences throughout the world remain relatively invisible. By pursuing new questions and revisiting established theories, research on media culture and childhood in the age of globalization can make vital contributions to interdisciplinary work on globalization at a time when conceptions of childhood and youth have become powerful semiotic signifiers of such aspirational and utopian ideas as the global village, global activism, global consumerism and citizenship, global prosperity, and global harmony (Levine, 2009).

SEE ALSO in this volume chapter by Drotner and chapter by Fisherkeller.

References

Appadurai, A. (1996). *Modernity at large: Cultural dimensions of globalization*. Minneapolis: University of Minnesota Press.

Bosch, T. E. (2007). Children, culture and identity on South African community radio. *Journal of Children & Media*, *1*(3), 277–88.

Buckingham, D. (2007). Childhood in the age of global media. *Children's Geographies*, *5*(1/2), 43–54.

Cross, G. and Smits, G. (2005). Japan, the U.S. and the globalization of children's consumer culture, *Journal of Social History*, *38*(4), 873–90.

de Block, L. and Buckingham, D. (2007). *Global children, global media: Migration, media and childhood*. New York: Palgrave Macmillan.

Donoso, V. and Ribbens, W. (2010). Identity under construction: Chilean adolescents' self-disclosure through the use of Fotolog. *Journal of Children & Media*, *4*(4), 435–50.

Drotner, K. (2004). Disney dilemmas: Audience negotiations of media globalization. *Nordicom Review*, *25*(1/2), 137–48.

Durham, M. G. (2004). Constructing the new ethnicities: Media, sexuality, and diaspora identity in the lives of South Asian immigrant girls. *Critical Studies in Media Communication*, *21*(2), 140–61.

Elias, N. and Lemish, D. (2008). Media uses in immigrant families: Torn between "Inward" and "Outward" Paths of Integration. *International Communication Gazette*, *70*(1), 21–40.

Fass, P. S. (2007). *Children of a new world: Society, culture and globalization*. New York: New York University Press.

Fisherkeller, J. (Ed.) (2011). *International perspectives on youth media: Cultures of production and education*. New York: Peter Lang.

Grewal, I. (1999). Traveling Barbie: Indian transnationality and new consumer subjects. *Positions*, *7*(3), 799–827.

Grixti, J. (2006). Symbiotic transformations: Youth, global media and indigenous culture in Malta. *Media, Culture & Society*, *28*(1), 105–22.

Hamelink, C. J. (2002). Media globalisation: Consequences for the rights of children. In C. von Felitzen and U. Carlsson (Eds), *Children, young people and media globalization*. Göteborg, Sweden: UNESCO International Clearing House on Media, pp. 33–42.

Hendriyani, H. E., d'Haenens, L. and Beentjes, J. (2011). Children's television in Indonesia: Broadcasting policy and the growth of an industry. *Journal of Children & Media*, *5*(1), 86–101.

Joseph, A. (2007). Why children should be seen and heard. *Journal of Children & Media*, *1*(3), 289–93.

Kabir, N. A. (2008). The media is one-sided in Australia. *Journal of Children & Media*, *2*(3), 267–81.

Kapur, J. (1998). A small world after all: Globalization and the transformation of childhood in India. *Visual Anthropology*, *11*(4), 387–97.

Katz, V. S. (2010). How children of immigrants use media to connect their families to the community: The case of Latinos in South Los Angeles. *Journal of Children & Media*, *4*(3), 298–315.

Kirwil, L. (2009). Parental mediation of children's Internet use in different European countries. *Journal of Children & Media*, *3*(4), 394–409.

Lemish, D., Drotner, K., Liebes, T., Maigret, E. and Stald, G. (1998). Global culture in practice: A look at children and adolescents in Denmark, France and Israel. *European Journal of Communication*, *13*(4), 539–56.

Lemish, D. (2002). Between here and there: Israeli children living cultural globalization. In C. von Felitzen and U. Carlsson (Eds), *Children, young people and media globalization*. Göteborg, Sweden: UNESCO International Clearing House on Media, pp. 125–34.

Levine, E. (2009). National television, global market: Canada's Degrassi: The next generation. *Media, Culture & Society*, *31*(4), 515–31.

Lukose, R. A. (2009). *Liberalization's children: Gender, youth, and consumer citizenship in globalizing India*. Durham, NC: Duke University Press.

Luttrell, W., Dorsey, J., Shalaby, C. and Hayden, J. (2011). Transnational childhoods and youth media: Seeing with and learning from one immigrant child's visual narrative. In J. Fisherkeller (Ed.), *Youth on media: International perspectives*. New York: Peter Lang, pp. 192–210.

McAllister, M. P. (2007). "Girls with a passion for fashion": The Bratz brand as integrated spectacular consumption. *Journal of Children & Media*, *1*(3), 244–58.

McChesney, R. W. (2002). Children, globalisation, and media policy. In C. von Felitzen and U. Carlsson (Eds), *Children, young people and media globalization*. Göteborg, Sweden: UNESCO International Clearing House on Media, pp. 23–32.

McMillin, D. C. (2008). Girls as the new global currency. *Journal of Children & Media*, 2(1), 83–85.

——(2009). *Mediated identities: Youth, agency, and globalization.* New York: Peter Lang.

McMillin, D. and Fisherkeller, J. (2009). Local identities in globalized regions: Teens, everyday life, and television. *Popular Communication*, 7(4), 237–51.

Melnick, M. J. and Jackson, S. P. (2002). Globalization American-style and reference idol selection. *International Review for the Sociology of Sport*, 37(3/4), 429–48.

Menten, A. (2009). Youth voice in an age of globalization: How youth media programs can prepare young people for an interconnected world. *Youth Media Reporter*, 3(3), 382–85.

Miller, S. (2010). "I am what you make me. I am who I am": Self-reflection and self-expression in a cross-cultural youth media project in the United Kingdom and South Africa. *Journal of Children & Media*, 4(4), 418–34.

Montgomery, H. (2011). Rumors of child trafficking after natural disasters. *Journal of Children & Media*, 5(4), 395–410.

Moran, K. C. (2007). The growth of Spanish-language and Latino-themed television programs for children in the United States. *Journal of Children & Media*, 1(3), 294–300.

Newman, M. Z. (2010). New media, young audiences and discourses of attention: From Sesame Street to "snack culture." *Media, Culture & Society*, 32(4), 581–96.

Nyamnjoh, F. B. (2002). Children, media and globalization: A research agenda for Africa. In C. von Felitzen and U. Carlsson (Eds), *Children, young people and media globalization*. Göteborg, Sweden: UNESCO International Clearing House on Media, pp. 43–52.

Salo, E. (2003). Negotiating gender and personhood in the new South Africa. *European Journal of Cultural Studies*, 6(3), 345–65.

Sigismondi, P. (2009). Global strategies in the children's media market. *Journal of Children & Media*, 3(2), 152–65.

Stornaiuolo, A., Hull, G. A. and Sahni, U. (2011). Cosmopolitan imaginings of self and other: Youth and social networking in a global world. In J. Fisherkeller (Ed.), *Youth on media: International perspectives*. New York: Peter Lang, pp. 263–82.

Strelitz, L. (2004). Against cultural essentialism: Media reception among South African youth. *Media, Culture & Society*, 26(5), 625–41.

Tobin, J. (2004). (Ed.). *Pikachu's adventure: The rise and fall of Pokémon.* Durham, NC: Duke University Press.

Tomlinson, J. (1999). *Globalization and culture.* Cambridge, UK: Polity Press.

Ugor, P. (2009). Small media, popular culture, and new youth spaces in Nigeria. *Review of Education, Pedagogy & Cultural Studies*, 31(4), 387–408.

Valdivia, A. (2008). Girls and global television: Notes on a collaborative effort. *Journal of Children & Media*, 2(2), 175–79.

——(2009). Living in a hybrid material world: Girls, ethnicity and doll products. *Girlhood Studies: An Interdisciplinary Journal*, 1(3), 173–93.

Vargas, L. (2006). Transnational media literacy: Analytic reflections on a program with Latina teens. *Hispanic Journal of Behavioral Sciences*, 28(2), 267–85.

von Feilitzen, C. (2002). Children, young people and media globalisation: Introduction. In C. von Feilitzen and U. Carlsson (Eds), *Children, young people and media globalization*. Sweden: UNESCO International Clearing House on Media, pp. 13–22.

Wai, M. Z. (2002). Globalisation and children's media use in Sierra Leone. In C. von Felitzen and U. Carlsson (Eds), *Children, young people and media globalization*. Göteborg, Sweden: UNESCO International Clearing House on Media, pp. 171–88.

Westcott, R. (2002). Globalisation of children's TV and strategies of the "big three." In C. von Felitzen and U. Carlsson (Eds), *Children, young people and media globalization*. Göteborg, Sweden: UNESCO International Clearing House on Media, pp. 69–76.

PART II

CHANNELS AND CONVERGENCE

EDITOR'S INTRODUCTION

In this section we turn from a discussion of theories of childhoods and children to those focusing on media technologies themselves. While we acknowledge the convergent nature of media in children's lives, we also try to pull them apart and highlight the unique aspects of each medium and the contributions it has made to children's culture and leisure.

We start chronologically with children's print culture, an often forgotten medium in collections of articles on media and children. **Carol L. Tilley** surveys the history and current state of children's print culture, focusing on the United States and Great Britain. She touches on the divide between literary and mass-market publishing, the rise of contemporary realism, and the development of digital book applications. Although print culture as a subject encompasses a broad range of social, cultural, historical, and material considerations surrounding the production and consumption of texts, this survey addresses a more narrow question: how have books and related texts for youth developed to their current status?

Stephanie Hemelryk Donald and **Kirsten Seale** discuss the importance of film in children's imaginative lives, and the role of film in the memories of childhood entertained and promulgated by adults. In doing so, they differentiate between film for children and films that feature childhood, but acknowledge that the difference between these modes of address is not always clear. While they do not support the argument that film is a reflection or accurate representation of children's experience, they do suggest that certain ways of being are created, made legible, or legitimated through narrative fiction film. They also discuss the notions of "showing" and "seeing" the world through film, according to which adults show and children see, and film making heightens that divide of perception and power.

The subject of **Jeanette Steemers'** chapter is television. Thus, her analysis deals with the most central medium in children's lives for several decades. Furthermore, in terms of media studies, television has received the most research and public attention to date, and in doing so has established the legitimacy of our discipline. Steemers argues that children's television culture today is shaped by those who work in an increasingly globalized TV industry, dominated by US-based transnationals. Her chapter explores the connections between industry, content, and audiences that define children's television culture in the US and Western Europe. One key difference between US and European children's television culture has been the supremacy of commercial broadcasting in the US and the tradition of European public service broadcasting (PSB). While PSBs are an important source of domestic content in Europe, differences between commercial and PSB approaches are blurring. For example, while television remains an important pastime, children today watch less broadcast TV. Instead, they access it through other platforms (mobiles, computers) and via multi-tasking on computers and mobile phones. Thus, children's TV is also impacted by changes in consumption.

Sonia Livingstone argues that children's homes, timetables, relationships, education, and entertainment are being reshaped now that everyday activities are conducted on and through the internet. The rapid pace of change occasions considerable hopes and fear in public discourses of childhood. This chapter critiques popular discourses of "digital natives" and of wholesale transformations introduced by the internet. It then analyzes three key terms – "children," "internet" and "culture" – by contrasting them with their opposite terms – "adult," "offline" and "political economy." Livingstone argues that children's internet culture is further cross-cut by three key tensions: power (a central theme in analyzing culture), change (central to the internet), and vulnerability (much discussed in relation to children). Embedded in global and commercial processes, children's internet culture is, on the one hand, subject to a market-logic, distinct from the organic needs of children and childhood. Yet, on the other hand, it is shaped by children's agency and creativity in enacting their own culture.

In a closely related chapter, **Pål Aarsand** discusses children's digital gaming culture. Central to this discussion are the notions of the "child perspective" and how the concept of "gaming cultures" can be understood. Arguing from the perspective of children, Aarsand claims that children's digital gaming cultures consist of both games produced for children (by adults) and children's own production of games or game activities. The chapter situates studies of children's gaming cultures around three central questions: Who are the players? Where do children play digital games? How do children play? In prior studies, gaming practices have often been seen as children's subcultures. However, this chapter argues that one can also see gaming practices as integrated parts of children's everyday life.

The mobile phone, argue **Rich Ling** and **Troels Bertel**, has become an important and taken-for-granted part of children's and adolescents' lives. The vast majority of children and teens in many countries have a mobile phone, and use it to coordinate their activities, as a safety link to significant others, as well as to weave their social networks and interact with their parents. The authors discuss how the mobile phone has also been associated with less positive behaviors such as sexting, bullying, and distracted driving. They argue that perhaps more than any other medium, the mobile phone is an illustration of the proliferation of convergent technology in children's lives.

Music, argues **Tyler Bickford**, is an important part of the social, emotional, and political lives of children and adolescents. Teenagers have long been the primary audience for popular music, and musical media for children of all ages have expanded greatly in the last generation. Children's role as music audiences is a key aspect of their expanding public status as consumers, and music listening is a key practice for working through social relationships with peers and articulating identities around gender, race, class, and sexuality. Children integrate musical media into their longstanding cultural traditions, such as handclapping games and play with toys, and products from music and consumer industries are designed to cultivate these sensibilities. This chapter provides an overview of how these phenomena have been addressed in the US and Europe, while focusing on recent technological and commercial developments that point to important changes for children's status in public culture.

All the media discussed above are part of children's consumer culture and the reality that children are growing up in a commercialized world. **Kara Chan**'s chapter reminds us that there is continuing debate about whether children are victims of marketing or competent participants in consumer culture. Her chapter outlines the historical development of a child consumer culture and toy market in the US and its influences worldwide. She also discusses the segmentation of children's and youth markets as well as symbolic meanings of consumption of products and brands associated with them. The chapter concludes by examining how children in different cultures relate to Disney products, as a case study to illustrate how a global brand adjusts its product benefits to cater to the local consumer culture.

Meryl Alper's chapter focuses on youth, new media, and learning within convergence culture, or the current era of accelerated, complex, and interconnected flows of information across old and new media systems. Within the last decade, there has been a growing body of research on the technological and social contexts supporting or constraining children's learning, participation, and connections within their everyday media ecologies. However, thus far, the nascent digital media and learning field has been limited in its approach to studying children's learning in developmentally, socially, culturally, and globally nuanced manners. She argues specifically for greater inclusion of the diverse ways in which young children and youth with disabilities experience technology in various contexts. In order for the field of digital media and learning to advance, scholarship must take into account how the experiences of children both complement and conflict with dominant discourses.

Finally, **Meenakshi Gigi Durham** develops the concept of children's technologized bodies. She argues that children's engagement with technology is embodied: mobile technologies are effectively parts of the child's anatomy, and technologies play a crucial role in children's social lives. Because children's lives are defined by this "mixed reality" and marked by an ongoing reciprocity between the material and the cybernetic, red flags have been raised regarding the potential perils associated with children's bodies in a technologized landscape. One such discursive flashpoint has been the practice of "sexting." The chapter analyzes this practice vis-à-vis children's relationships with virtual selves, or avatars, as well as their invention of sexual practices that seem safe in an "abstinence only" environment. She concludes, however, by noting that although technologies promise libertarian freedoms, it is crucial to recognize that they are part of a system of multinational technological production and capitalist hegemonies. Thus, she argues, a theory and praxis of children's technologized bodies must address their political, economic, and ideological contexts.

10

CHILDREN'S PRINT CULTURE

Tradition and innovation

Carol L. Tilley

The social, cultural, and material transformations that followed in the wake of the development of movable type came later for children and adolescents than they did for adults. Prior to the eighteenth century, authors and publishers took little interest in the particular needs of youth, in part because these needs were seldom distinguished from those of adults until Enlightenment philosophers such as Jean-Jacques Rousseau posited that childhood was separate and distinctive from adulthood. This intellectual shift accompanied—in Western Europe and North America at least—both a rise in literacy and a growing entrepreneurial spirit among publishers that led to child-centered publications such as the English book merchant and publisher John Newbery's *A Little Pretty Pocket Book* (1744). Newbery's book combined alphabetic structure with rhyming descriptions of children's games, profuse illustrations, and moral lessons. Although the book was not wholly original, building as it did on various moral and educational texts from preceding centuries (cf. Darton, 1932), it fulfilled Newbery's purpose of *Delectando monemus* (Latin, "instruction with delight") and marked a starting point for a distinctive print culture for young people.

Broadly conceived, print culture includes complex and interwoven social, cultural, historical, and material considerations surrounding the production and consumption of texts including literary novels, popular magazines, and educational manuals. Print culture historian Wayne Wiegand (1998) proposes that this discipline incorporates diverse aspects that include changing conceptions of literacy, book as commodity, the impact of technological developments on authorship and reading practices, and the circulation of printed texts. The concept of print culture itself is not antithetical to technological innovation—moving type was just such an innovation—but the term can obscure the role of technology. Thus, one must be clear that print culture includes not only "traditional" printed texts but also developments such as digital books. Similarly, the concept of print culture can sometimes seem to privilege "print" over "orality," although scholars such as Betsy Hearne (1991) have demonstrated the artificiality of this distinction, especially regarding folktales, where a story may cross between orality and print multiple times.

Given its broad scope, print culture as it pertains to children and adolescents requires significant delimitation for a chapter such as this one. This overview of print culture for children and adolescents will emphasize contemporary issues in the material culture of print while indicating their historical precedents. Taking Newbery as a starting point, the chapter focuses on books, periodicals, and related products published and distributed by trade publishers, as opposed to educational and textbook publishers. Its emphasis will be on the United States (US) and Great Britain, which dominate many aspects of children's print culture on a global level, although examples from other countries and regions will be integrated where possible. There will be no attempt to address child-produced materials, self-published works, materials produced chiefly for the educational market, reference works for or about young people, or games and toys that are often part of the broader youth print culture.

Children's print culture in history: an establishing shot

Prior to John Newbery's ventures into children's publishing, books for children tended to privilege spiritual and religious didacticism. Protestantism argued for individual accountability for salvation and moral rectitude, thus impelling persons of all ages to read the Bible and encouraging the publication of works such as minister Issac Watts' *Divine Songs, Attempted in Easie Language for the Use of Children* (1715), which was quickly reprinted in hundreds of editions. Comparatively few texts were published expressly for younger readers, so children also read from adult-focused works such as John Bunyan's widely translated allegory *The Pilgrim's Progress (from This World to That Which Is to Come)* (1678). Popular books with a moral, but not proselytizing, intent including *Aesop's Fables*—published in more than one hundred editions by the early sixteenth century—and Charles Perrault's fairy tale collection *Histoires ou contes du temps passé* (*Stories or tales from past times*) (1687). Many of these texts were intended for both child and adult readers, but gradually they were published in chapbook form—inexpensive and often abridged pamphlet editions—that targeted child readers more exclusively.

Newbery's marketing acumen—*The History of Little Goody Two-Shoes* (1765) was an even greater commercial success than *A Little Pretty Pocket Book*—encouraged a blooming print culture for young people. Beginning in the late eighteenth century, authors, editors, and publishers introduced more diverse texts to young audiences. Collections of folk and fairy tales found wide audiences, especially in Germany where multiple editions of Grimms' *Kinder-und Hausmärchen* (*Children's and Household Tales*) (1812) were joined by other compilations including E.T.A. Hoffman's *Nachtstücke* (*Nocturnes*) (1816–17). Juvenile periodicals, which typically combined literature, history, and science, thrived especially in England and the US, where titles including *The Children's Friend* (1824–c. 1930) and *St. Nicholas* (1873–1940) enjoyed publication runs that spanned decades. Toy books and similar ephemera like harlequinades—single sheets of illustrated paper that required special folds to reveal the stories—were also common. McLoughlin Brothers (1828–1920), an American children's publisher, issued a variety of brightly colored movable books, toys, and games. Moral and cultural didacticism lingered—and remains a formidable presence in children's print culture—but the most successful Western works tempered it with growing playfulness and imagination, a consequence of the continuing reconceptualization of childhood.

Advances in printing, improved standards of living, and increased literacy rates helped hasten an international "golden age" of children's literature beginning in the late nineteenth century. In the US, Louisa May Alcott's *Little Women* (1868/1869) and Thomas Bailey Aldrich's *The Story of a Bad Boy* (1870) introduced young readers to morally imperfect characters who did not always suffer dire consequences. Along with Mark Twain's *The Adventures of Tom Sawyer* (1876), these books characterized the twin themes of domestic life and adventure that dominated much of juvenile fiction in the US for decades. In Great Britain, fantasies incorporating domestic and folkloric elements including Lewis Carroll's *Alice's Adventures in Wonderland* (1865) and George MacDonald's *The Princess and the Goblin* (1872) flourished. Juvenile literature published elsewhere during the late nineteenth and early twentieth centuries evokes similar themes and styles. For instance, Iwaya Sazanami's *Kogane-maru* (*Tale of the Brave Dog, Kogane-Maru*) (1891) wove together Western and Japanese folklore to tell the story of a dog bound to avenge the deaths of its parents. Similarly the Italian author Carlo Collodi blended folklore, puppet theater, and domestic morality in *Le avventure di Pinocchio* (*The Adventures of Pinocchio*) (1883).

Children's print culture deepened in the twentieth century, particularly as children's literature grew in its recognition as a distinctive category of publishing. The number of juvenile books published each year in the US climbed from fewer than 400 in 1900 to about 1,300 in 1955 and above 4,000 by the early 1990s. The regularization of book reviewing serves as one marker of this expanding formalization. Although the English writer Sarah Trimmer reviewed books for children in her magazine *The Guardian of Education* beginning in 1802 and periodicals on both sides of the Atlantic such as England's *Macmillan's Magazine* and *Scribner's Monthly* in the US occasionally recommended children's books, *The Horn Book*, first published in 1916 and still published in 2012, was the first journal to focus solely on the review and discussion of youth literature. Respect for the growing corpus of children's literature is also reflected in the establishment of literary awards. The John Newbery Medal given for excellence in children's literature was first awarded in the US in 1922, its British counterpart the Carnegie Medal in 1937, New Zealand's Esther Glen Award in 1944. In 1956, the International Board of Books for Young People (IBBY) awarded its first Hans Christian Andersen Award, the primary transnational award for youth literature.

School and public libraries consistently comprised the largest market for mainstream children's literature, but consumers were hungry for children's books. Throughout the twentieth century, publishers responded with inexpensive reprints of children's classics, juvenile series fiction, Little Golden Books, and other low-priced books shunned by the library market. Nevertheless, sales for these books regularly accounted for the majority of juvenile publishing's annual revenue. The development of more distinctively market-oriented publications together with the increase of children's literature further divided the publishing industry and children's print culture by highlighting a perceived dissonance between "literary" and mass-market publications for young people.

Starting in the late nineteenth century, a variety of low-cost publications—some specifically targeting youthful audiences and others that found their way to young readers—inundated the market. Named for the cheap quality of their paper, pulp publications included sensational British penny dreadfuls, juvenile series fiction, science fiction stories, and comic books. Guardians of youth reading disparaged publications like these, which were more widely available than their "literary" counterparts and often had content—slang, titillating adventure, and more mature themes—that departed from the status quo of children's literature (cf. West, 1988). Some pulp materials such as comic books were not only rejected by libraries but became the sources for moral panic. Prejudices persist—in the US, for instance, it was common into the 1970s for libraries to exclude series such as *Nancy Drew*—against materials perceived to be more overtly commercial than literary in nature, even though the Newbery Medal's namesake sold small toys together with children's books as a marketing tool.

Contemporary children's print culture: perspectives and phenomena

During the late 1950s increases in state funding to schools and libraries in both the US and Britain spurred further growth in the market for young people's books. From 1956 to 2011, sales of children's and young adult trade books in the US increased from approximately $45 million (~ $360 million adjusted for current prices) to more than $2.75 billion (US). Virtually all categories of publishing for young people grew during this past half-century, but several notable trends arose, especially in the US. First, authors and publishers introduced increasingly robust and authoritative works of nonfiction, especially in the sciences, social studies, and biography. In contrast to the fictionalized and text-dense works they succeeded, contemporary nonfiction books like Russell Freedman's *Kids at Work: Lewis Hine and the Crusade Against Child Labor* (1994) marshaled documentary evidence and included profuse illustrations; often these titles emphasized marginalized persons or specialized subjects. Second, juvenile publishing has developed significant segmentation, particularly in terms of age and reading ability. Thus, consumers can now choose among publishing formats such as board books for toddlers, leveled series fiction for new readers, picture books for both younger and older children, short and long-form comics, and chapter books for early fluent readers. The generally improved quality of children's books and the increased segmentation in formats has also encouraged a proliferation of awards. Many countries now have national awards—Brazil's Fundação Nacional do Livro Infantil e Juvenil (National Book Foundation Children and Youth) award and China's Feng Zikai Children's Picture Book Award are examples—often decided by librarians, teachers, or members of the publishing industry.

One of the most profound changes, however, came in the literary fiction aimed at young readers. Some of the pulp stories that young people favored focused on the grit and tragedy of everyday lives, but it was not until the 1960s that realism became a consistent feature. In the US, Maurice Sendak's picture book *Where the Wild Things Are* (1963), Louise Fitzhugh's middle grades novel *Harriet the Spy* (1964), and S. E. Hinton's young adult novel *The Outsiders* (1967) established the trend toward a more modern realism in books for youth. In England this trend occurred later in the 1980s, although some earlier novels such as John Rowe Townsend's *Gumble's Yard* (1961) signaled the changes to come. Earlier calls for realism by some factions in both the US and the Soviet Union during the 1930s were focused on making settings and action of these books more recognizable to children. This subsequent movement toward realism, however, further pushed the boundaries in more varied ways such as by openly acknowledging differences in social and economic class, incorporating issues related to emotional and physical violence, and allowing that adults sometimes harm young people. These changes have not been without controversy. For teachers, librarians, and parents, who are often the gatekeepers of youth reading, the introduction of subject matter such as a portrayal of an openly homosexual romance— Nancy Garden's *Annie on My Mind* (1982)—or heroin-addicted and homeless teens—Melvin Burgess' *Junk* (US, *Smack*) (1996)—led to protests and calls for censorship. However, honest subject matter does not always equate with sensationalism, and books such as *Junk*, which was awarded Britain's Carnegie Medal, can have recognized literary value.

The growing children's book market is notable for its English-language imperialism. Youth literature has fewer national and regional variations today than it did a century ago with popular titles translated and sold internationally. For example, almost all of the juvenile bestsellers in India are imports. A popular title such as Cornelia Funke's children's fantasy *Herr der Diebe (The Thief Lord)* (2000) is available in languages including English, Indonesian, Arabic, and Faroese, along with its native German. Part of the growth has been coordinated through the annual Bologna Children's Book Fair, established in 1963, and a key site for the purchase and sale of publishing / licensing rights for juvenile books and related media. Although the Fair regularly holds sessions on issues such as translation and reading practices in various countries, titles originally published in English—especially ones from the US—dominate the market. Changes are slowly taking place, though; for instance, Korean author Hwang Sun-mi's children's book *Leafie: A Hen into the Wild* (2000) was published in Poland in 2011 and plans exist for its publication in other countries, including the US and Vietnam. Other exceptions include the Japanese market where Western juvenile literature in translation is unpopular partly because of strong reader preferences for indigenous manga. Even in Britain, US selections frequently occupy bestseller lists. For instance, in the first decade of this century, bestselling children's authors in Britain included Americans Stephanie Meyer, R.L. Stine, and Lemony Snicket alongside domestic favorites such as Jacqueline Wilson and J.K. Rowling.

As the market for young people's books has grown in recent decades, the publishers have consolidated so that a handful dominate the market including Random House (Bertelsmann A.G.), Disney, and Scholastic. Although Scholastic remains a family-owned company, its recent revenues exceed $2 billion (US) annually, driven by successes such as the *Harry Potter* and *Hunger Games* series. Like many other major publishers, Scholastic also has a number of imprints, smaller divisions that now function as specialty publishers; PUSH is one such imprint, publishing teen fiction by first time authors such as Tanuja Desai Hidier's *Born Confused* (2002) about an Indian-American teenager negotiating cultural and familial boundaries. Small and independent publishers certainly do still exist—Candlewick in the US, Groundwood Books in Canada, and l'école des loisirs in France are examples—but they lack the corporate resources to compete financially. Still smaller and regional publishers play important roles in developing children's print culture. Consider, for instance, Dar al-Hadaeq, an independent publisher of children's books founded in 1989 in Lebanon and focused on nurturing the publication of Arabic-language books that give younger readers a better sense of shared cultural identity.

The successes of children's print culture—and in particular, children's literature—belie broad concerns that young people are not reading for pleasure. Research into children's pleasure reading offers no easy response. For instance, a review commissioned by Britain's National Literacy Trust found that girls read for pleasure more than boys and that the frequency of pleasure reading decreases with age (Clark and Rumbold, 2006). Data from the 2009 PISA (Programme for International Student Assessment) survey of 15-year-olds from the more than 70 OECD (Organization for Economic Cooperation and Development) member countries suggest that two-thirds read for pleasure daily and confirms a gender gap. The same report shows that young people in the US, the United Kingdom, and other highly industrialized nations typically report lower rates of pleasure reading than their counterparts in countries such as Kazakhstan, Albania, Tunisia, and Peru. A study on youth media use in the US (Kaiser Family Foundation, 2010) suggests that although daily pleasure reading has slowly decreased over the past decade, there are commensurate increases in screen-based reading. Producers of popular children's television shows and related media still view print as a valuable means of reaching young people. For instance, the Nickelodeon cable television network launched a magazine for British children in 2011 and the same network has a variety of book series based on popular shows like *Dora the Explorer*.

Current phenomena

Children's print culture is not static. Just as technological and social changes in the nineteenth century encouraged the development of a robust field of youth literature, advances in technologies coupled with a vast and changing media landscape are altering contemporary children's print culture.

E-books, digital apps, and social media

Complications impede the direct movement of young people's books from print to digital. Many e-readers cannot adequately display illustrations and double-page spreads from children's picture books or other visually intensive texts such as comics. Further, few young people own e-readers, as fewer than 20 percent of US teen readers use e-books (Intrator, 2012). Consequently many of the bestselling e-books are young adult titles that need little visual augmentation and have significant numbers of adult readers (e.g. Suzanne Collins' *Hunger Games* trilogy). Some publishers like Disney, which have established branding and assertive marketing, are experiencing significant growth in e-book sales.

   Digital book-related applications, or apps, are a more popular platform, as they allow young readers to explore texts that are augmented by narration, animation, music, and other interactive features. Often these apps are based on standard texts such as nursery rhymes and folktales or content from established children's brands like Sesame Street and Disney. Dr. Seuss-related apps from Oceanhouse Media, for instance, have sold more than a million units (Intrator, 2012). According to Kate Wilson, the director of Britain's Nosy Crow, a publisher of both traditional books and digital apps for children, creating apps requires a different skill set for creators and publishers, one that includes coding, interaction design, animation (Abrams, 2012). This suggests that successful creators and publishers will need to retool in order to compete successfully in this marketplace. Beyond engaging young people with existing stories, digital apps such as Launchpad Toys' *ToonTastic* and *StoryKit*, a product of the International Children's Digital Library project based at the University of Maryland, encourage and support young people in creating their own stories, comics, and books.

   Authors and publishers are also building on social media tools' pervasiveness to connect with young people and offer enhanced content. Again, *Harry Potter* is notable for its *Pottermore* website, which launched publicly in 2012. Here users can work their way through the series' universe, access background content, and compete against others in skill-based tournaments. Some authors use existing platforms like Twitter and YouTube to reach readers. Author John Green and his brother Hank, for instance, have more than 750,000 subscribers to their frequently updated YouTube channel, Vlog Brothers, and are active on Twitter, Facebook, and their self-produced website. Tools such as Skype also allow authors to stage virtual visits with readers in schools and libraries.

New forms of storytelling

Undergirding the technology that enables digital apps and e-readers is a longterm trend in hybrid storytelling. Scholar Eliza Dresang (1999) coined the term "radical change" to describe the ambiguity, nonlinearity, and multiple perspectives that have increasingly characterized youth literature in the past three decades. David Macauley's (1990) picture book *Black and White*, for instance, simultaneously tells four complementary stories from differing points of view, requiring the reader to choose how to proceed through the book. The features of radical change, along with the use of interactivity and multiple genres in a single work, are creating new forms of storytelling in youth literature. Exemplifying these changes are works such as the picture books *123 Piano!* (2005) and *Briek* (2008) by Belgian author Pieter Gaudesaboos, which mix fact and fiction together with stills from family films, invented advertising images, unique book design, and sometimes accompanying music CDs. Comics, a classic medium for hybrid storytelling, have moved from the margins into the fold of respectable children's print culture in the US. Although comics are an accepted staple of children's reading in countries such as Japan, India, and France, they were long derided in the US for their perceived violent and insipid content. Since 2000, publishers including First Second and Toon Books have been issuing long-form (e.g. Dave Roman's *Astronaut Academy* (2011)) comics and novels that incorporate comics (e.g. Jeff Kinney's *The Diary of a Wimpy Kid* (2007)).

Blockbusters and media franchises

In 1930, Edward Stratemeyer published the inaugural volume of the *Nancy Drew* girl sleuth series. Still in print in the US and internationally, having undergone several revisions in content to update the cultural references, total sales number at least eighty million volumes. In addition, Nancy Drew has been translated across media into film, television shows, and computer games. Although not the first popular juvenile series, it serves as a forerunner of contemporary blockbusters and media franchises in the youth literature world, perhaps best exemplified by J.K. Rowling's *Harry Potter* books. This seven book series—originally published in Britain between 1997 and 2007—is available in dozens of translations, selling half a billion books worldwide. Like *Nancy Drew*, *Harry Potter* has been adapted into other media including video games and film, but it has also spawned theme park attractions, museum exhibits, and branded merchandise ranging from jellybeans to replica wizarding wands. All told, the *Harry Potter* series cum brand has an economic value in excess of $15 billion (US), making it a touchstone for the world of children's print culture. Yet, while *Harry Potter*'s eye-popping monetary value makes it unique, the blockbuster status it achieved and the media franchise it originated are no longer unusual.

Series books and those with recurring characters allow publishers to capitalize on readers' familiarity to enhance marketing and promotion. Series books were long outside the purview of "literary" children's publishing, though books like Susan Cooper's *The Dark is Rising* series and Beverly Cleary's *Ramona* books are exceptions. Publishers now seek out stories like Stephanie Meyers' *Twilight Saga* and Eoin Colfer's *Artemis Fowl* that can sustain serialization and show promise of franchise and branding success. Series books are such a significant force in juvenile publishing that since 2008 the bestseller lists in *The New York Times* distinguish among series and non-series fiction for young people in ranking sales. Notably the newspaper lacked any juvenile bestseller list until 2000 when it instituted one because *Harry Potter* books were lingering on the adult list. Stand-alone fiction still plays a role: books like Newbery winner Kate DiCamillo's *The Tale of Despereaux* (2003) and Caldecott winner Brian Selznick's *The Invention of Hugo Cabret* (2007) have received literary accolades, met with popular success, and been made into feature films.

Research in children's print culture

At least three disciplines have significant investments in the study of children's print culture: education, children's literature, and library and information science (LIS). As detailed in Wolf et al. (2011), scholars working in these disciplines necessarily take differing perspectives, but all are engaged in understanding how young people engage with texts; the familial, peer, institutional, social, and cultural contexts in which that engagement occurs; and how those texts are created, produced, and received. Professional societies supporting scholarship in children's print culture include the International Research Society for Children's Literature (IRSCL), the International Board on Books for Young People (IBBY), the International Reading Association (IRA), and the Children's Literature Association (ChLA). Among the journals with significant content in this field are *Children's Literature in Education*, *International Research in Children's Literature*, and *The Lion and Unicorn*. Rich scholarship exists for understanding the material forms and intellectual substance of children's print culture, especially as it has developed in North America and Western Europe, as well as on reading preferences and frequency. This latter scholarship is often of limited value because it frequently relies on adult-constructed survey instruments that may not reflect children's perspectives. Many important questions remain, especially surrounding young people's everyday activities and experiences with print culture. As the field moves forward, it is imperative that scholars find ways to conduct research that reflects children's agency and understanding.

References

Abrams, D. (2012, August 22). How is writing a children's book different than writing an app? *Publishing Perspectives*. Retrieved from http://publishingperspectives.com/2012/08/how-is-writing-a-childrens-book-different-than-writing-an-app/

Clark, C. and Rumbold, K. (2006). *Reading for Pleasure: A Research Overview*. London: National Literacy Trust.

Darton, F. J. H. (1932). *Children's Books in England: Five Centuries of Social Life*. Cambridge: Cambridge University Press.

Dresang, E. (1999). *Radical Change: Books for Youth in a Digital Age*. New York: H.W. Wilson.

Hearne, B. G. (1991). *Beauty and the Beast: Visions and Revisions of an Old Tale*. Chicago: University of Chicago Press.

Hunt, P. G. (Ed.). (1996). *International Companion Encyclopedia of Children's Literature*. London: Routledge.

Intrator, P. (2012, February 15). Children's books go multimedia, multinational, multi … everything. *Publishing Perspectives*. Retrieved from http://publishingperspectives.com/2012/02/childrens-books-go-multimedia-multinational-multi-everything/

Kaiser Family Foundation. (2010, January). *Generation M2: Media in the Lives of 8- to 18-Year-Olds*. Menlo Park: Author.

Macauley, D. (1990). *Black and White*. New York: Houghton Mifflin Harcourt.

Organization for Economic Cooperation and Development (2011). Do students today read for pleasure? *PISA In Focus* 2011/8 (September). Paris: Author. Retrieved from http://www.oecd.org/pisa/pisaproducts/48624701.pdf

West, M. I. (1988). *Children, Culture, and Controversy*. New Haven: Archon.

Wiegand, W. A. (1998). Theoretical foundations for analyzing print culture as agency and practice in a diverse modern America. In J. Danky and W. A. Wiegand (Eds). *Print Culture in a Diverse America*. Champaign: University of Illinois Press, pp. 1–16.

Wolf, S. A., Coats, K., Enciso, P. and Jenkins, C. A. (Eds). (2011). *Handbook of Research on Children's and Young Adult Literature*. London: Routledge.

11

CHILDREN'S FILM CULTURE

Stephanie Hemelryk Donald and Kirsten Seale

Childhood is often seen as another world. Although it is a world we have all visited, it has become inaccessible to us except through the distortions of memory.

(Bazalgette and Buckingham, 1995, p. 1)

Defining childhood through film memory

It is a rainy November evening in Sydney and Donald's seventeen-year-old daughter is preparing for exams. She is ten months away from her eighteenth birthday, legally adult. But this particular evening she has one thing on her mind. She has seen "George" (or it could have been "Fred" – they are after all identical twins) in Sydney's Town Hall railway station on her way home. She and her friend pursued him, to no avail, through the station. "Mum," she exclaims, "What was I supposed to do? It was George, that's my childhood!" By now the reader may have worked out that George is George Weasley, a significant character in the Harry Potter saga. A seventeen-year-old, born in 1994, has indeed grown up with him. She has read and reread, seen and re-seen seven books and eight films, carefully spaced by the author and then the film producer to maximize expectation and identification since publication of the first volume in the United Kingdom in 1998. What may be surprising to the reader is the degree to which fictional entertainment premised on a nostalgic, even colonial, view of boarding school and Little England should so powerfully define contemporary childhood and adolescence across the world. In 2002, one year after the first film was released, children at a Beijing primary school informed us that their favourite fictional characters in film were Hermione Grainger and Harry Potter. If there was any remaining doubt that this franchise was not only spectacularly successful but that it also relied on the capacity of spectators to identify with characters at the various stages of their young lives, the decision by the distributors to restrict access to the films after 29 December 2011 and withdraw DVDs from sale except in specially packaged staged releases dismisses that doubt. Their decision re-engineers the status of the films as events within the temporal passage of new childhoods and new teens, and supports the observation that growing up with Harry Potter is both a transcultural experience and a commercially astute premise.

The importance of familiarity

Deborah Cartmell (2007) suggests that a defining characteristic of children's books is that they are "more loved" than adult fiction. Multiple readings, and the associated mimetic practices of identification and playing out of stories and character, contribute to this definition of "loved". Similarly, since the innovations of video and DVD, favourite films can be watched more than once. The careful re-release of Disney animations supports this "to-be-loved-ness" – to rephrase Laura Mulvey's (1975) famous dictum. The connoisseurship of recognition and familiarity with the plot and the characters adds pleasure and even a sense of internalized ownership to the original excitement of the first viewing. We can contrast this aspect of contemporary children's film culture with the much stronger sense of the cinematic event, which dominated previous generations. Thus, a Dutch woman (Interview, Melbourne, 2011) in her early seventies recalls that her favourite film as a child was the social drama *Ciske de Rat* (Staudte, 1955). She remembers the viewing as a major treat, and recalls only the bare bones of the plot, and indeed as discussion ensues it emerges that she has conflated that title with another earlier film about a street child, *Boefje* (Sirk, 1939). What she also recalled, we would surmise, was the pleasure of identification with the child's persona and the attention paid to him in the formal aesthetic structure of the film. In another interview, an elderly Chinese man recalls:

> Compared with my contemporaries, I saw films earlier. I saw a movie for the first time before 1949 when I was a kid. Our nursery school principal took me to a movie theater in the 1940s. … I remember vividly that the movie I saw was produced by China and called *Snow White*. The movie had no sounds, just pictures. There was a Russian movie named *700 Years Ago*. The film told of Russians resisting the Mongol invasion. I did not entirely understand the movie at that time. I just remember that our principal held me in her arms.
>
> *(Interview, Shanghai, 2011)*

For many older people in Britain and the United States, the first animated children's film they recall seeing was Walt Disney's *Snow White and the Seven Dwarves* (Cottrell et al., 1937). The film set the pace for merchandising as well as for an ideological undercurrent of automated domesticity (Kuhn, 2010). Henry Giroux (1999, pp. 4–5) writes that the "recognition of the pleasure that Disney provides should not blind us to the realization that Disney is about more than entertainment", whilst Jack Zipes cautions against Disney's focus on narratives that resolve, "according to rigid sexist and racist notions that emanate from the nineteenth century and are recalled in the film with nostalgia" (1995, p. 112), and Ian Wojcik-Andrews laments the "infantile, narcissistic and violent underside of Disney culture" (2000, p. 81). Giroux, Zipes and Wojcik-Andrews remind us that Disney films enunciate and reiterate a conservative version of power relations that reference a limited view of society, whilst maintaining firm control of a young consumer base. Thus, *The Lion King* (Allers and Minkoff, 1994) deploys bizarrely jumbled symbolic imagery and tropes – goose-stepping hyenas, a fluttering mane/flag under a rising crescent moon, a plummy English accent – in a single sequence chronicling the rise to power of the usurper, Scar. Presumably derived from post-Gulf War US Islamophobia, *and* a generalized positioning of the English as prone to evil, *and* the Nuremberg rallies, the confused and angry ideological assault on the audience is benignly forgiven and forgotten in a chorus of "Hakuna Matata".

Laying aside Disney's hold over mid-twentieth century American dreaming, it appears curious that the many children's films predicated upon a nostalgic remembrance or depiction of the world order, and of childhood itself, are supposedly directed at an audience for whom nostalgia is presumably irrelevant. Yet the success of the Harry Potter films suggests a type of what we might call "flattened" or "immediate nostalgia", where children, as they grow up with new iterations on new media platforms, refer back to earlier films and texts, as proof of "their childhood". Children's film culture surely belongs to children, but it is also a space of intense nostalgia and delight for many adults. One of the surprising joys of parenthood in the age of digital reproduction is the sharing of screen memories – and thereby one's own childhood memories – with younger family members. Indeed, as the family film becomes an increasingly important part of the global film market, generations are strongly encouraged to encounter films for the first time together.

The (im)possibility of children's film?

As we observe below there is, however, conceptual difficulty, or even impossibility, in determining what meaning is created for which audience segment and with what intention and nuance. When a children's film is made and marketed as a family film, is it still a children's film at all? Or, does it necessarily compromise its efforts to aestheticize, narrativize, and identify with children's experience? And, if all these aspects of film-making are carefully addressed to child spectators, or even entrusted to children (which is enabled by the epistemic shift to ubiquitous and accessible digital visual technologies), surely one must always acknowledge the powerful structural conditions underlining young people's access to any screen material, given the extremely unequal relations of production and consumption for this particular demographic.

Despite these caveats, it is clear that many children do enjoy film culture, and that in spite of the attractions of television and internet content the possibility of cinema is still an important aspect of the media sphere for the young. In the following discussion of what we call the *possibility* of children's film, we first reference global phenomena, such as Harry Potter and the Disney stable. In so doing we recognize that the tyranny of distribution, language and narrative norms creates further inequalities of attention from producers, critics and audiences. We also mention films that are not in the global market, to remind ourselves that children are occasionally offered alternatives to the international mainstream. Whether or not these opportunities for a different notion of cinematic pleasure change the structural relationship between adult nostalgia and children's film culture remains open to question.

Simply put, a children's film is a film produced for a primary audience of children. In thinking about children's films, we consider spectators up to the age of seventeen. Bazalgette and Staples (1995) use the age of twelve as a marker. Our emphasis will often fall on this younger demographic of children, whilst recognizing that phenomena like the *Harry Potter* series and the popular *McDull* films (Toe Yuen, 2001; 2004) complicate this as children are exposed to the books and films (in the case of Harry Potter), and the animations in television shows (in the case of McDull) at a young age, and then approach adolescence with the characters and narratives as they are re-mediated through additional cinematic adaptations and cross-media platforms. Although children's films are consumed in public and private spaces – in television broadcasts, on DVD, and through the internet – we consider a children's film to be one that is directed towards exhibition in cinemas. We note that the cinematic event is a crucial aspect of film affect, and that, while children may see films many more times on DVD and other home technologies, spectatorship in the cinema remains an experience of special significance.

The literary scholar Ian Wojcik-Andrews (2000), who has contributed a history of children's film to the field, outlines six perspectives from which to analyse the children's film: personal, pedagogical, critical, textual, institutional, and cultural. To this we would add political, aesthetic, and historical, while also noting that the cultures of children's film spectatorship and pleasure range widely between local and global experience, and across class groups, in developing and developed media ecologies. With those categories of attention in mind, we attempt to provide a platform from which to delineate the actuality of children's film in world cinema.

Jacqueline Rose (1998) has posited the impossibility of children's fiction through a devastating analysis of classic English language texts. In doing so she has laid the ground for the argument that the impossibly ruptured relationship between adults and children perseveres in cultural production created by adults for children. She sees this as an ontological betrayal, "Children's fiction sets up the child as an outsider to its own process, and then aims, unashamedly to take the child *in*" (pp. 58–59), and as an act of appropriation, " ... the idea [...] of a primitive or lost state to which the child has special access. The child is, if you like, something of a pioneer who restores these worlds to us, and gives them back to us with a facility or directness which ensures that our own relationship to them is, finally, safe" (p. 64). Rose's scepticism prepares us for A. S. Byatt's *The Children's Book* (2009), which fictionalizes the neuroses of the children's author in a saga of twentieth century bohemian disorder, but notably without acceding to the view that the process of writing for children is necessarily infantile or perverse, nor that the love that children bestow on their favourite texts, literary or filmic, is misdirected.

The indeterminacy of childhood and children's texts seems affirmed by the lack of explicit acknowledgement of the child audience by the entertainment industry, despite the importance of the youth market to box office receipts. This is reflected in the absence of a "children's film" category in compilations of international film box office figures (the categories used are "Rated G" and "Family Film"), and by national ratings approaches that emphasize censorship over a proactive address to the pleasures and fascinations of the child spectator. The (im)possibility of the children's film/text is challenged by the "blockbuster" status of many animated films such as the *Toy Story* trilogy (Lasseter, 1995; 1999; Unkrich, 2010), and the international and critical success of the delicate characterizations and robust adventures of Studio Ghibli's feature animations such as *Spirited Away* (Miyazaki, 2001) and *Howl's Moving Castle* (Miyazaki, 2004). Firmly centred on child protagonists and animal spirits, Miyazaki's narratives essay Shinto animism, temporal disjuncture, familial discord, and social decay. Yet there persists a general absence of critical attention to films for children, or for families with children. Bazalgette and Buckingham (1995) have noted this conundrum, pointing out that "Amid the extensive public debates about the effects of the media on children, very little attention is paid to the material that is produced explicitly for them." (p. 5) Media panics routinely bewail the availability of X or R rated violent or pornographic material to children. Yet, the insinuations of "General Audience" films, which entertain but also proselytize the worldviews of anxious adults, are not widely understood to be dangerous to young minds (Giroux, 1999).

Socialization and the "seeing child"

To extrapolate from Rose without losing sight of her original insights, we could say that children's films are never for children alone. There are other prerequisites. They are conceived and constructed by adults with the intention to socialize, instruct, educate and inform children on, for example, their position in the social and political order, how to be consumers, how to negotiate interpersonal relationships, how to play within the culture in which they are located, and how to "show" difference. In choosing the word "show", we echo Karen Lury's (2005) insights on the adult capacity to show what is constructed as true or acceptable within certain social contexts, against a child's capacity to "see" the constituent elements of the world on view. As Lury understands, the interaction between showing and seeing is a core aspect of learning and growing across generations, an interaction which is not a one way street. The little boy who recognizes the king's nudity in Hans Christian Andersen's cautionary tale of the *Emperor's New Clothes* epitomizes the social value of the seeing child.

The predominant practice of annexing and adapting fairy tales for children's film is an outstanding example of the socialization of the child's eye view. Rose's stance is substantiated by Zipes' extensive work in this area where he argues that the "domestication" of fairy tales for an audience of children starts with the material itself – "The fairy tale was never a genre intended for children" (2011, p. 17) – and is subordinate to a number of other concerns. According to Zipes, fairy tales lend themselves to children's film because they contain narratives on social hierarchies and the proper conduct within those structures. They present encounters between narrative, symbolism, and the dark side of human failure, trouble, and desire, yet the resolutions veer towards retribution or social stability at all costs. That such stories should be the staple for children is both appropriate (this is the world they live in after all) and strangely counter-intuitive. In film for children, fairy stories and archetypes are revisited, partly with new social prerogatives, but also to reproduce the sense of belonging to a wider, older adult world. The Chinese epic *Journey to the West* (*Xi You Ji*) has been filmed 12 times to date, with two more versions due in 2012 and 2013. It tells the story of a magic Monkey, born from a stone egg, who travels westwards across the world in search of Buddhist scriptures, with the monk Tripitaka, Horse, and two companions, Sandy and Piggy. The story concerns the expansion of Buddhism from India and the west of China into the Han heartlands, but it is framed as an adventure-fairy-fantasy-epic. The characters are an imperfect and troublesome group. Monkey himself is violent, disobedient and untrustworthy, but nonetheless ends up as the popular hero of the story. Piggy is a sexual predator, Horse is a dragon in disguise, and Sandy is a rough but well-meaning warrior. The constant re-enactment and re-embodiment of these types for generation after generation of young Chinese (and indeed international audiences) demonstrates that, even as the adult world seeks to manage children's investment in culture and sociability, it indulges in a carnivalesque celebration of misbehaviour and improper conduct.

The film *Where the Wild Things Are* (Jonze, 2009) is another study of the carnivalesque. Based on Maurice Sendak's much-loved 1968 picture book of the same name, it, too, has intergenerational resonance. The boy and the monsters dance all night, the world turns upside down. Childhood fantasies of escape, rebellion and return are imagined through a boy's night-time adventure. His frenzied dance enunciates the fraught tension between adult desires for a perfect, and so impossible childhood, and children's imaginative and actual journeys within childhood – both wonderful and catastrophic. The film adaptation concentrated on the moral lessons for the protagonist Max – no-one can be king without first dealing with his own bad temper, and that goes for children and monsters both – but perhaps its major contribution is to reiterate to a child audience the subjective despair of the adult world, which is where the wild things really are.

Special insights of protagonists notwithstanding, national bombast, hubris and bias, as well as some gentler characteristics or nobler aims, are frequently coded into films for child spectators. Early children's film in the UK supported First World War propaganda, the Beijing Children's Film Studio (founded 1981) made films specifically to re-articulate patriotism and social stability for the post-Cultural Revolution child in Reform China, and the aforementioned *Ciske de Rat* was very much concerned with enunciating social progress in the post-war state in the Netherlands. In Australia, the Children's Television Foundation (ACTF) is a publicly funded organization that was founded to lobby for, and ultimately create, high quality programming for local children. The foundation branched into cinema with *Yolngu Boy* (Johnson, 2001), a feature film motivated by the desperate need to increase screen representation of minorities, indigenous children and stories of indigenous lives that exceed the *Pocahontas* (Gabriel and Goldberg, 1995) moment in Disney. Found actors, local slang, and rap music are used to build a bridge between the Indigenous

Australian subjects of the film, and the wider population of teenage viewers. The film's "after life" is supported by its web presence, and its continuing impact in pedagogical regimes of cross-cultural understanding. The ACTF's rationale is that the local, circumscribed by national boundaries and points of view, renders the child's world legible and legitimate:

> The Australian Children's Television Foundation believes that children should have access to their own culture and their own stories through film and television. [...] They should encourage an understanding of the child's world interpreting the joys and the hardships and the range of human emotion and experience.

Quality programs can contribute positively to a child's development and creativity and to a child's sense of personal and national identity by presenting a diversity of places, ideas and values reflecting the rich multicultural heritage of Australia (Australian Children's Television Foundation, 2000).

Hierarchies of development

The rub here is that institutions such as the ACTF, regardless of their politics of inclusion and representation, are nevertheless predicated on a hierarchy of development that places childhood in a conceptual prison of perpetual incompleteness, which may only be escaped through the doors of adult perception and guidance. In order to entertain the idea of a children's cultural field – indeed of many such fields of socialization, judgement and affect – one must first remove the temporal and teleological bias of the adult as a destination point. Taken logically, if we retain this bias, then we cannot truly discuss any cultural field without deferring to the oldest segment of any population (unless also deferring to the seven ages of man and the presumption of a second childhood).

The seven ages of man, values placed on different age groups, and the notion of ideal co-chronicity, are explored cinematically in *The Curious Case of Benjamin Button* (Fincher, 2008), a free adaptation of a short story by F. Scott Fitzgerald (1922). The narrative draws on certain preoccupations of children's literature and film to explore its central premise: that time might travel backwards. A boy is born an old man and grows younger. In the film, his wife loves him when he seems "older" than her, but they have to part as she grows too old and he too young. The film's premise is fantastic – that a clockmaker can make clocks run anticlockwise and so force time backwards, the material object dictating the processes of nature. The original short story is, however, closer to the theme of impossibility. It interrogates the determinism of the body and the fixedness of generational relationships. In Fitzgerald's telling, there is no magical reason for the boy's fate, and people's love (a father, a wife, a son) is circumscribed by the boundaries of what seems reasonable to them and their age-group.

Fitzgerald's story reveals the shift between *seeing* and *showing*. In children's literary culture we might talk about the stages of being read to, reading aloud, and reading to oneself; of the different types of address, privacy, intimacy, and knowingness that each allows (Donald, 2001). In a segue from Rose's determination of impossibility, Linda Hutcheon advances the notion of "double address". While allowing for demarcations between adult and child, Hutcheon admits a much more fluid negotiation between adult, text, and child than Rose. She detects

> a double audience of both child and adult, the adult experiencing with the child or the adult the child becomes. [...] And then there is the child in the process *becoming* the adult, whose expanding consciousness is being shaped by his or her experience.
>
> *(2008, pp. 174–75)*

Hutcheon's observations are most obviously pertinent to family films, where the film-maker is deliberately placing attractions for the adult viewer within the scope of a film addressed to children. To that extent, she does not countermand Rose's remarks on the subordination of a child's taste to an adult's preconception and internal longings. However, Hutcheon does clear conceptual space in which to challenge the overdetermined break between adult and child status. In children's film culture there is a less familiar articulation between seeing, watching for oneself, watching in the company of children, and watching in the presence of adults – who may be seeing a "different" film. In the words of one online commentator on *Stuart Little* (Minkoff, 1999), a film about an anthropomorphized mouse:

> Not one of my favourites, but the kids seem to like watching it over and over.

References

Allers, R. and Minkoff, R. (Directors) (1994). *The Lion King* [Motion Picture]. USA: Walt Disney Pictures.

Australian Children's Television Foundation. (2000). *The ACTF: Introduction.* Retrieved from http://www.yolnguboy.com/directory/htm/frameset3.htm

Bazalgette, C. and Buckingham, D. (1995). The Invisible Audience: Introduction. In C. Bazalgette and D. Buckingham (Eds), *In front of the children: screen entertainment and young audiences.* London: BFI (British Film Institute) Publishing, pp. 1–14.

Bazalgette, C. and Staples, T. (1995). Unshrinking the Kids: Children's Cinema and the Family Film. In C. Bazalgette and D. Buckingham (Eds), *In front of the children: screen entertainment and young audiences.* London: British Film Institute, pp. 92–108.

Byatt, A. S. (2009). *The children's book.* London: Chatto & Windus.

Cartmell, D. (2007). Adapting children's literature. In D. Cartmell and I. Whelehan (Eds), *The Cambridge companion to literature on screen.* Cambridge: Cambridge University Press, pp. 16–180.

Cottrell, William, Jackson, Wilfred, Morey, Larry, Pearce, Perce and Sharpsteen, Ben (Directors) (1937). *Snow White and the Seven Dwarfs.* New York: RKO Radio Pictures, 1937.

Donald, S. H. (2001). The necessary privations of growing up. *New Formations, 41*(2), 131–41.

Fincher, D. (Director) (2008). *The Curious Case of Benjamin Button* [Motion Picture]. USA: Warner Bros.

Fitzgerald, F. S. (27 May 1922). *The curious case of Benjamin Button.* Collier's.

Gabriel, M. and Goldberg, E. (Directors) (1995). *Pochahontas* [Animated Feature]. USA: Walt Disney Pictures.

Giroux, H. A. (1999). *The mouse that roared: Disney and the end of innocence.* Lanham, MD: Rowman & Littlefield.

Hutcheon, L. (2008). Harry Potter and the Novice's Confession. *The Lion and the Unicorn, 32*(2), 169–79.

Interview, Melbourne (2011). Interviewee wished to remain anonymous. Authors, September 15, 2011.

Interview, Shanghai (2011). Interviewee wished to remain anonymous. Authors, March 26, 2011.

Johnson, S. (Director) (2001). *Yolngu Boy* [Motion Picture]. Australia: Australian Children's Foundation.

Jonze, S. (Director) (2009). *Where the Wild Things Are* [Motion Picture]. USA, Australia and Germany: Warner Bros.

Kuhn, A. (2010). Snow White in 1930s Britain. *Journal of British Cinema and Television, 7*(2), 183–99.

Lasseter, J. (Director) (1995). *Toy Story* [Animated Feature]. USA: Pixar Animation Studios, Walt Disney Pictures.

Lasseter, J. (Director) (1999). *Toy Story 2* [Animated Feature]. USA: Pixar Animation Studios, Walt Disney Pictures.

Lury, K. (2005). The child in film and television: introduction. *Screen, 46*(3), 307–14.

Minkoff, R. (Director) (1999). *Stuart Little* [Motion Picture]. USA: Columbia Pictures.

Miyazaki, H. (Director) (2001). *Spirited Away* [Animated Feature]. Japan: Studio Ghibli.

Miyazaki, H. (Director) (2004). *Howl's Moving Castle* [Animated Feature]. Japan: Buena Vista International.

Mulvey, L. (1975). Visual Pleasure and Narrative Cinema. *Screen, 16*(3), 6–18.

Rose, J. S. (1998). The Case of Peter Pan: The impossibility of children's fiction. In H. Jenkins (Ed.), *The children's culture reader.* New York; London: New York University Press, pp. 58–66.

Sirk, Douglas (Director) (1939). *Boefje.* Netherlands: Leo Meyer.

Staudte, Wolfgang (Director) (1955). *Ciske de rat.* Netherlands: Filmproductie Maatschappij, Amsterdam; Hans Boekman en Co ter Linden.

Unkrich, L. (Director) (2010). *Toy Story 3* [Animated Feature]. USA: Pixar Animation Studios, Walt Disney Pictures.

Wojcik-Andrews, I. (2000). *Children's films: history, ideology, pedagogy, theory.* New York: Garland.

Yuen, T. (Director) (2001). *My Life as McDull* [Animated Feature]. Hong Kong: Bliss Picture.

Yuen, T. (Director) (2004). *McDull, Prince de la Bun* [Animated Feature]. Hong Kong: Bliss Picture.

Zipes, J. (1995). Once Upon a Time Beyond Disney: Contemporary Fairy-tale Films for Children. In C. Bazalgette and D. Buckingham (Eds), *In front of the children: screen entertainment and young audiences.* London: British Film Institute, pp. 109–126.

Zipes, J. (2011). *The enchanted screen: the unknown history of fairy-tale films.* London: Routledge.

12

CHILDREN'S TELEVISION CULTURE

Jeanette Steemers

Children's television culture is quite different from the shared values of adult television culture. As Buckingham points out, children's television is "not produced *by* children, but *for* them" and as such children's television is often more a "reflection" of adult "interests or fantasies or desires" (1995, p. 47) and their view of childhood, rather than what children would choose themselves. This is a television culture where one group (adults) create content for another group (children), who have little or no say about what is produced for their benefit. Indeed children's television culture invariably mirrors the commercial motivations and/or concerns and beliefs held by adults, and the key players in defining this culture are those who work in the children's television industry.

A second important observation is that children's television culture, which is not that old, is one of the most globalized forms of television, seemingly dominated by US-based transnational corporations and animation, conceived for North American audiences. For reasons of space this short article concentrates on the development of children's television culture in the US and Western Europe, because the US is a key source of children's programming around the world, and because Europe has been a key recipient of this content. Television content dedicated to children as a "special" audience, "with distinctive characteristics and needs" (Buckingham, 2005, p. 468) did not emerge in these countries until after 1945. Initially provision was patchy and limited to short blocks on generalist television channels at times when more valuable adult audiences were not available. Yet the advent of multichannel, multiplatform services from the 1980s onwards has created a large contemporary children's television culture, based around dedicated children's channels and programming that is at once transnational and local in its content, audiences and industry structures. In this chapter I will explore the connections between industry, content and audiences that define children's television culture.

Defining children's television culture from an industry perspective

Yet what do we mean by children's television culture? Buckingham (2005) writes about three related aspects of that culture. In the first instance there is the institutional and industry context of production. Second there is the content, based on an "age and stage-related organization of television" (Messenger Davies, 2001, p. 79) rather than a classification focused on genres such as drama, information and entertainment. Third, there is the child audience, which has been subject to evolving definitions and constructions in much the same way as childhood itself over the years. This outline of three different yet connected levels provides a useful starting point for exploring a children's television culture shaped by policy, regulation, production practices, technology, funding, changing content and consumption practices. Children's television culture is a broad interpretation involving industry, content and audiences. The production ecology of children's television refers to the different industry players involved in shaping children's television.

From an industry or institutional perspective we can identify a children's television culture that is shaped by a complex ecology or ecosystem (Steemers, 2010; also Cottle, 2003), comprising a "community" of industry, regulatory and civil society players (Bryant, 2007), who "coexist, cooperate and compete" within an increasingly disintegrated and globalized production environment (Steemers, 2010, p. 16). These relationships shape the organization, production practices and content of children's television. Yet this is also an ecology, which is constantly evolving, reflecting changing industry relationships and the search for new sources of funding in the wake of a children's media market which has fragmented into hundreds of channels available on different digital platforms.

Who then are the main players in this ecology which functions across broadcasting, content creation, ancillary rights exploitation (including merchandise licensing), regulation and lobbying for children's media (see Table 12.1)?

As shown in Table 12.1 large US transnationals like Disney, Nickelodeon (owned by Viacom) and Cartoon Network (owned by Time Warner) are active across different platforms (TV, online, mobile) as broadcasters, content creators and brand managers. They commission and broadcast content for their own domestic children's channels; they produce content in-house; they sell their content to overseas broadcasters; they run their own branded channels in overseas markets; and they or their subsidiaries are involved in consumer product licensing and home

Table 12.1 Industry players in the children's television production ecology

Broadcasting/TV channel operation	• Globally active US transnationals (Disney, Nickelodeon, Cartoon Network). • Regional transnationals (Al Jazeera, JimJam, KidsCo) • Nationally available public service broadcasters (PSBs e.g. BBC, ARD/ZDF, PBS) • Nationally available commercial channels with children's blocks • Toy companies with broadcasting interests (Hasbro)
Content creation/ production	• US transnationals • National PSBs • Independent producers • Content/brand managers/facilitators • Toy companies (Hasbro, Mattel)
Licensees	• Toy companies • Publishers • Electronic games industry • Other licensees (apparel, stationery)
Regulators	• E.g. FCC, Ofcom
Lobbyists	• E.g. Children Now; Campaign for a Commercial-Free Childhood; American Center for Children and Media (US); Children's Media Foundation (formerly Save Kids' TV) (UK); Youth Media Alliance (formerly Alliance for Children and Television) (Canada)

entertainment, generating more revenues from this activity than from broadcast revenues. Even the non-profit US Public Broadcasting Service (PBS) recycles content originally shown on its PBS Kids block on PBS Kids Sprout, a commercial US joint venture digital channel and video-on-demand service.

In Europe the dedicated channels and blocks of public service institutions are involved in both broadcasting and content creation (see Table 12.1). The UK's BBC through its commercial subsidiary, BBC Worldwide, is also involved like US transnationals in branded channels overseas and consumer product licensing. Dedicated children's channels are run by the BBC (CBeebies for the under 6s, and CBBC for those aged 7 to 12); ARD/ZDF in Germany (KiKa); France TV (Gulli); RAI in Italy (RAI Yoyo for the under 8s, and Rai Gulp for older children); Ketnet in Belgium; NRK Super in Norway and the Z@pp and Z@ppelin blocks run by NPS in the Netherlands. These broadcast mostly European content with national content often exceeding 50 percent of transmissions (D'Arma and Steemers, 2012, p. 155). However, alongside these domestic public broadcasters, there are the US transnationals (Disney, Nickelodeon, Cartoon Network), who provide local versions of US-originated channels, with their own US-produced content usually exceeding 70 percent of transmissions (Ibid, p. 151). This is used to leverage other business opportunities in consumer products. Commercial domestic broadcasters in Europe have largely retreated from the broadcasting and production of children's television because of strong competition from PSB and the US transnationals, as well as bans or restrictions on advertising around children's content which have made it an unprofitable enterprise.

Alongside content creation (See Table 12.1) by large transnationals and public service broad-casters, there is a diverse community of independent producers, ranging from large production companies involved in international co-production, distribution and merchandise licensing to many smaller production entities, focused primarily on creative production and the associated skills of animation, writing, directing and producing. In this wider ecology smaller producers depend on broadcasters and larger producer-distributors to part-fund their projects through presales, com-missions, co-funding and licensing deals, because they do not have the infrastructure, skills and resources to do this themselves. In turn larger broadcasters and content managers are often dependent on smaller creative entities to take on the risk of creative development.

Beyond broadcasting and the creation of content there are other players who impact children's television. Licensees like toy companies create consumer products based on children's programmes and in turn are dependent on retailers who provide the limited shelf space to sell these products. Licensing has become an important funding stream for globally marketed shows, with some producers earning up to 90 percent of their turnover from consumer products and home entertainment (Steemers, 2010, p. 79). Advertisers are an important player in the US, but in Europe restrictions or bans on TV advertising around children's TV content limit their influence. Legislative and regulatory bodies, who are part of this ecosystem, shape the nature of children's television culture through policy and law-making. Finally lobby groups play a role in keeping debates about children's television and media in the public domain. Examples include campaigns for educational content in the US, and campaigns against fast food advertising and in support of home-grown content in Britain.

Yet this ecosystem is changing and so are the relationships within it as children's entertain-ment, retail and IP licensing start to converge around consumer brands. Nickelodeon, Disney and Cartoon Network own and create up to 70 percent of their channel output in the US in order to maintain control of their global brands (Grant, 2009). Major US toy companies Hasbro and Mattel have moved into broadcasting and content creation, where they had previously confined their activities largely to acquiring the licenses needed to produce toys based on television properties owned by others. In October 2010 Hasbro, the company behind *GI Joe, Transformers* and *My Little Pony* launched a joint venture US children's network, The Hub, with Discovery Communications. For smaller producers there is concern that toy companies will simply develop their own toy brands for TV rather than commissioning new ideas. This fear deepened with the purchase by Mattel in October 2011 of HIT Entertainment, the UK-based production and brand management company behind global preschool franchises *Thomas the Tank Engine, Bob the Builder* and *Barney*.

These developments come at a time of declining financial contributions from traditional broadcasters for commissions, dwindling advertising revenues and a general economic downturn in North America and Europe, which has affected the consumer products market across developed economies. With more players fighting over smaller budgets, producers now have to locate funding from multiple sources including international co-production, pre-sales and where appropriate licensing advances. This in turn dilutes creative control, rights and future revenues. In search of revenues many production companies risked large swathes of investment in the hope of generating a global licensing hit in the US, which is estimated to account for 50–70 percent of global licensing revenues (Grant, 2009). In Europe and North America there have been business failures (4Kids Entertainment, Entertainment Rights, TV Loonland) and redundancies (Chapman Entertainment, Chorion) as production companies struggle to raise funding for future productions or to service their debts from previous acquisitions and investments. To minimize risk and maximize their own gains the US transnationals are keeping production in-house or favouring larger producers. The appearance of toy companies as producer-broadcasters suggests that the business will become more concentrated among larger organizations, who have easier access to funding and can withstand the long lead times needed to develop content, particularly if licensing revenues do not materialize until three to five years after launch. Toy companies recognize that children are shifting their attention from action figures and plush toys to screen-based games on tablet devices, and this underpins their move into screen entertainment as toy revenues decline. However, consolidation and closer alignment to the toy industry raises concerns about the genre diversity and future quality of children's media, if commercial priorities take greater precedence. These developments also reveal the frailties of smaller nationally-based production companies, who do not own multiple platforms and lack the resources or experience to develop brands which work beyond television.

What remains key from all of this is that the way that children's television culture is understood and evaluated cannot really be understood without some sense of what constitutes the broader industry ecology of children's media, the forces/actors that operate within it, the assumptions about what children's television should deliver as a business, and how these factors are negotiated by different players.

Key stages in the development of children's television content – perspectives from the US and Western Europe

The previous breakdown of the industry ecosystem that shapes children's television culture is useful when looking at the US and Western Europe because it raises questions about the degree of difference and similarity between these two systems. These differences are clearly apparent in the different developmental trajectories of children's television in both regions. Initially the focus in both was almost entirely driven by domestic considerations, which shaped children's television in distinctive ways, because the institutional basis of television was quite different – grounded on the supremacy of commercial broadcasting in the US, and the initial dominance of publicly-funded public service monopolies in Western Europe. In Western Europe children's television was viewed as one small component of a public service remit, which was not meant to be driven by commercial imperatives. US children's television culture by contrast, was embedded in a different commercial broadcasting history with different traditions – not least the lack of a strong public service ethos in children's television.

In Britain for example, the BBC was focused from the start on providing a public service schedule in miniature for its young audiences, based on their perceived needs with a varied diet of drama, information programmes and some animation that protected them from commercial exploitation and "from the consequences of their own vulnerability and ignorance" (Davies et al., 2004, p. 479). However, with the arrival of its commercial rival, ITV, in 1955, the BBC was forced to become more responsive to its audience and less paternalistic. The commitment to a diverse schedule continued, but there was also investment in more child-centred programmes such as the preschool magazine, *Play School* in the 1960s, and Saturday morning entertainment shows in the 1970s that reflected children's love of popular music and culture. In the rest of Western Europe public service broadcasters retained monopolies until the 1980s (Germany, France, Benelux) and 1990s (Scandinavia, Spain), so there was arguably less incentive to radically alter the scale or type of service they were providing for children. This changed once the forces of commercial competition were unleashed, and PSBs took a keen interest in dedicated children's channels once US players moved into their markets.

In the US advertising-funded commercial network television reigned supreme. As the 1950s progressed, children's television was marginalized to Saturday morning slots comprising mainly of animation, because children were not sufficiently attractive to advertisers. Broadcasters and producers were not expected to fulfil public service or educational goals, as this was a business that satisfied the commercial goals of advertisers and the networks rather than the needs of the audience. By 1961 Newton Minow, Chair of the FCC was describing children's TV as a "vast wasteland", which served children poorly with "massive doses of cartoons, violence, and more violence". The wasteland was enriched in 1969 with the launch of the educational preschool format *Sesame Street* on newly established non-profit network, PBS. PBS and the producers it commissioned, embraced an educational remit for children's programming and consulted educational and child development experts. However, mainstream children's television on the US networks became more commercialized in the 1980s with animation series that were produced in collaboration with toy companies (e.g., *Transformers, Care Bears, He-Man*).

Yet in both the US and later in Western Europe the introduction of multi-channel, commercially-led television heralded a shift from scarcity to digital abundance. A combination of commerce, technology, deregulation and globalizing markets brought new players into the children's television market in the late 1980s and early 1990s including Nickelodeon, Cartoon Network and Disney in the US and later worldwide. Over time there has been a shift away from children's slots on generalist channels to dedicated children's channels, which are now increasingly targeted at different age groups – infants (under 2s), preschoolers (3 to 6), tweens and teens. Dedicated channels increased supply, but fragmented the children's market, forcing content producers to target international sales and consumer products much more intensively to raise revenues and sustain economic viability. The US transnationals have been the most successful at internationalizing their operations and leveraging their television franchises worldwide. However, domestic commercial broadcasters in both America and Europe have either reduced or withdrawn their commitment to children's television because of declining advertising revenues.

A fundamental change in Western Europe has been a shift of emphasis from content aimed at the domestic market and produced from within a public service television culture to a market which is more commercially oriented and aligned to international audiences and multiple platforms.

The clear distinction between "public" and "commercial" is becoming less clear. PSBs in Europe compete with domestic commercial channels as well as the US transnationals and buy programming from these companies as well. PSBs work closely with independent producers because they are required by EU and national legislation to commission certain levels of programming from independent producers, but these are the same producers who are trying to sell to commercial broadcasters. Restricted funding is also compelling PSBs in Europe to seek co-production funding. So their investments in originations are often shaped by the commercial considerations of others, including international sales and consumer products.

These developments are relevant in as far as they impact the nature of children's content. Children's television culture does not exist in a vacuum. It is promoted or constrained by policy, regulation and economics with far-reaching effect. This is evident in the different historical development of children's television in the US and Europe where as we have seen commercial and public service priorities respectively have defined the different nature and scope of children's output. But over the years this distinction has blurred as European television has become more commercially oriented. What we are seeing now are two different historical and institutional cultures of children's programming converging as funding pressures result in a more globalized production environment, transforming children's television production in Europe, in particular, from an essentially non-commercial domestic activity into a more international enterprise, focused much more on funding issues, brand management and IP ownership. In both the US and Europe this has laid bare tensions between the desire to make quality programming that satisfies the educational, informational and socio-emotional needs of children and young people, and the operation of television as a business. In Europe concerns are focused on domestic origi-nations for children, particularly drama and factual programming, whose future looks uncertain other than from public service broadcasters.

Where is children's television culture going now?

However, the great unknown in all of this is where children's television culture is going next as broadcasters fight over fragmenting audiences and funding sources. Properties that are successful in licensing, particularly globally, are few in number, and the recession in developed markets has dented licensing revenues. We have already established that the children's television industry is moving away from the traditional broadcaster-producer model to encompass a broader array of toy companies, content brokers and brand managers. However a business model for sus-tainable content on the web and mobile platforms remains elusive. Catch-up services like Tivo, online on-demand services like Netflix and the streaming of children's content, often at no cost, have decimated DVD revenues and reduced the ability to generate income from multiple windows without generating substantial alternative revenues. Online revenues remain uncertain and secondary with television delivering the greatest impact initially and feeding other important revenue streams in merchandise licensing.

What we do know is that the target audience for children's television has become younger. Generally children's television culture finishes at twelve, because the industry sees no financial incentive in servicing older children, who are thought to be watching non-children's content. At the same time younger children are being targeted in infancy in spite of concerns about the possible negative impact on infant development before the age of two (see American Academy of Pediatrics, 1999; 2011).

We also know that children's media consumption is changing and complex, and that they are now using a variety of platforms (mobile phones, computers, tablets) and applications (VoD, time-shifting DVRs) to view television. In theory this poses a threat to the industry, particularly as older children migrate to online and mobile media. According to one report, European children aged 9 to 16 spend 88 minutes a day online (Livingstone et al., 2011, p. 12), and 86 percent watch video clips online (p. 15). However research suggests that television is still an important part of children's lives. The key shift is that they are no longer viewing television primarily as broadcast television, and they are undertaking other activities alongside their TV viewing.

Research in the US by the non-profit Kaiser Family Foundation in 2010 established that children aged 8 to 18 spend 7 hours and 38 minutes a day consuming media (Rideout et al., 2010). However, through multitasking on computers and mobile phones they managed to fit 10 hours and 45 minutes of media activity into this time, which included 4 hours and 29 minutes spent viewing television (p. 2), an increase on 3 hours and 51 minutes in 2004. However, only 2 hours and 39 minutes of TV viewing was made up of scheduled broadcasts with the remainder viewed on the internet (24 minutes), mobile phones (15 minutes) and IPods (16 minutes). Television continued to take up the majority of children and young people's media consumption, but 41 percent of viewing was either time-shifted or viewed on devices or platforms other than the television set (p. 3).

In summary children's television continues to be an important part of children's lives. Yet there are clear shifts in this culture, driven by the changing production ecology and business of children's television, but also by changing consumption patterns. New technologies have increased opportunities to watch television. Children's television culture has moved from scarcity to abundance; from blocks on general channels to dedicated niche services; from local to more globalized content; and from linear television shows to more multimedia experiences accessed on various platforms and devices. Children's television content is still characterized by programming designed to meet the needs of children. However, it is also connected to commercial demand and corporate strategies, where the child audience is segmented in ways that appeal primarily to commercial interests; with new digital and online spaces increasingly colonized by the largest international companies. Children's television is becoming more commercialized and internationalized because of the complexity of its funding which relies increasingly on ancillary and overseas revenues. In Europe this leaves less room for smaller creative producers who have become dependent on public service broadcasters for commissions. Broadcast distribution remains key to marketing, but other digital platforms are becoming noticeable (online), but not profitable. With consolidation among existing players and expansion by large US toy companies, plurality of supply is likely to diminish as the largest players constantly repurpose their own content for a variety of platforms.

References

American Academy of Pediatrics (1999). Media education. *Pediatrics*, *104*(2), 341–43.
——(2011). Media use by children younger than 2 years. *Pediatrics*, *128*(5), 1040–45.
Bryant, J. A. (2007). Understanding the children's television community from an organizational network perspective. In J. A. Bryant (Ed.), *The children's television community*. Mahwah: Lawrence Erlbaum, pp. 35–55.
Buckingham, D. (1995). On the impossibility of children's television. In C. Bazalgette and D. Buckingham (Eds), *In front of the children*. London: British Film Institute, pp. 47–61.
——(2005). A special audience? Children and television. In J. Wasko (Ed.), *A companion to television*. London: Blackwell, pp. 468–86.
Cottle, S. (2003). Producing nature(s): The changing production ecology of natural history TV. In S. Cottle (Ed.), *Media organization and production*. London: Sage, pp. 170–87.
D'Arma, A. and Steemers, J. (2012). Localisation strategies of US-owned children's television networks in five European markets. *Journal of Children and the Media*, *6*(2), 146–63.

Davies, H., Buckingham, D. and Kelley, P. (2004). In the worst possible taste. Children, television and cultural value. In R. Allen and A. Hill (Eds), *The television studies reader*. London: Routledge, pp. 479–93.

Grant, J. (2009) California Dreaming, 24 February. *C21 Media*. Retrieved November 5 2011, from http://www.c21media.net/features/detail.asp?area=2&article=47815

Livingstone, S., Haddon, L. Görzig, A. and Olafsson, K. (2011). *EU Kids Online*. Retrieved 29 September 2011, from www.eukidsonline.net.

Messenger Davies, M. (2001). *Dear BBC: Children, television storytelling and the public sphere*. Cambridge: Cambridge University Press.

Rideout, V, Foehr., U. and Roberts, D. (2010). *Generation M2: Media in the lives of 8- to 18-Year-Olds*. A Kaiser Family Foundation Study. Retrieved 15 June 2012, from http://www.kff.org/entmedia/upload/8010.pdf

Steemers, J. (2010). *Creating preschool television. A story of commerce, creativity and curriculum*. Basingstoke: Palgrave Macmillan.

13

CHILDREN'S INTERNET CULTURE

Power, change and vulnerability in twenty-first century childhood

Sonia Livingstone

The internet as harbinger of change in children's lives

The early twenty-first century witnessed the emergence of a new form of children's culture. Children's internet culture is, in one sense, a form of children's media culture like any other, yet it now intersects all dimensions of childhood, at least in developed countries. In recent years, children's homes, timetables, relationships, education and entertainment have been rearranged such that everyday activities are conducted on and through the internet. While, traditionally, children were expected to accommodate to adult cultural norms, in relation to the internet they are celebrated for their pioneering exploration – sanctioned or otherwise – of the unfolding digital opportunities for identity, sociality, learning and participation. However, the highly combustible mix of rapid change, youthful experimentation and technological complexity has reignited the moral panics that typically accompany media change, amplifying public uncertainty, parental anxiety and policy attention to the risks accompanying children's internet use.

In the UK, for example, internet adoption has risen with astonishing rapidity from just 13 percent of 7 to 16-year-olds accessing the internet at home in 1998 to 41 percent in 2000 and plateauing at 87 percent in 2011 (ChildWise, 2012). Although the pace and nature of change vary across cultures, in many countries children, parents, teachers, youth work professionals, marketing companies and media providers have all responded energetically by incorporating the internet into their activities with children. In developing countries too, children are gaining internet access, often via a mobile phone rather than a computer, swept along in the apparently relentless global trend towards personalized, portable, networked media ownership (Gasser et al., 2010; Ito et al., 2005). But as technology becomes differentiated, with ever more devices becoming internet-enabled, content appears increasingly mainstreamed. Notwithstanding public hyperbole regarding the internet's extraordinary breadth, children devote their energies to a few highly corporate sites developed for adults: among UK 7 to 16-year-olds, for example, the top websites are Facebook, YouTube, and Google (ChildWise, 2011).

How shall we analyse children's internet culture? A few years ago, Corner (1995, p. 5) observed 'the powerful capacity of television to draw towards itself and incorporate (in the process, transforming) broader aspects of the culture' and also 'to project its images, character types, catchphrases and latest creations to the widest edges of the culture, permeating if not dominating the conduct of other cultural affairs'. Today we might say the same of the internet, for these centrifugal and centripetal forces seem to be rewriting the values, practices and ambitions of a generation. Faced with clamorous voices on all sides – from the sceptics (children are still children, there's nothing new under the sun), to the anxious (our children are under threat, the good old days are gone) and the optimists (children are leading the way into a bright new dawn, existing institutions must reshape themselves for the digital future) – it is a timely moment to examine children's internet culture critically in relation to the emerging evidence base (Livingstone, 2009).

Theorizing children's internet culture

Consider the terms that comprise children's internet culture (see Figure 13.1). Each term requires unpacking to recognize its heterogeneity across contexts. The first and third bring a sizeable legacy of academic analysis, while the middle term refers to a phenomenon that changes faster than research is published. The intersections among these terms also invite attention: many scholarly books on 'culture' say little about the internet, many on the 'internet' have no index entry for 'children' and only recently have the sociology of childhood and the psychology of socialization acknowledged that internet use is already embedded in contemporary childhoods. Any term marks an analytic distinction from its obverse and this helps us to pinpoint some fascinating debates in relation to children's internet culture, as also shown in the figure.

Specifically, *children* are most simply defined as *not adults*, though the nature of the difference varies by age, psychosocial development and socioeconomic context. The costs and benefits of distinguishing child and adult domains online are much contested because, in some respects but not others, children are vulnerable – or, put positively, they merit special consideration to ensure their well-being.

As for the *internet*, early research made a strong distinction between the so-called cyber or virtual world and the real or *offline world*, a distinction that is no longer tenable. Today's researchers ask whether the online extends, amplifies or transforms phenomena previously occurring offline, opening up a host of questions about the emerging opportunities and risks online, along with policy proposals about how to manage them.

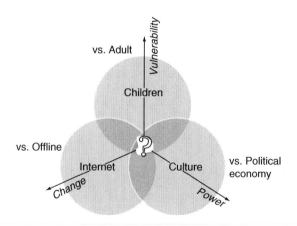

Figure 13.1 Intersecting concerns regarding children's internet culture

Thirdly, note that the question of *culture*'s dependence on *political economy* has long proved fraught, as has the distinction between elite and quotidian conceptions of culture. There are, therefore, tensions surrounding the cultural versus political economic factors shaping children's internet cultures and, within the cultural factors, there are also tensions over whether to provide content and services for children according to normative ideals or children's expressed preferences.

Spurred in part by public fascination with 'digital natives' (Prensky, 2001; see also Buckingham, 2006; Palfrey and Gasser, 2008; Selwyn, 2009) along with public anxieties over paedophiles, pornography and other online risks, society has found itself asking – and researchers have found themselves investigating – basic questions of change, power and vulnerability, as also shown in Figure 13.1. Specifically, are online opportunities and risks genuinely unique to the digital age? Who or what is responsible for these changes? What type of special interventions, if any, do children require?

Cultural vs. political economic dimensions of children's internet *culture*

Children's internet culture is strongly marked by the commercial imperatives now mediating information and communication processes that were, until recently, both more private (i.e. personal) and yet more public (i.e. non-profit). Where once children phoned their friends, visited relatives, kept a photo album, shared music tapes or wrote a diary, today they do this in a commercially-owned online environment, and this also has implications for control over personal information and rights to free expression (Livingstone, 2005). The commercial is linked to the global: for example, national, culturally-appropriate, linguistically-specific social networking sites are being displaced by one global company, *Facebook*, resulting in huge critical attention to *Facebook*'s proprietary protocols for data protection, networking and privacy management (boyd and Hargittai, 2010). Relatedly, searching for information – once an admittedly elite process of visiting a library or consulting an authoritative reference book – is displaced by 'Googling' within an advertising-heavy space according to opaque algorithms that may not serve the public interest. Consider too how the traditional staples of childhood – picture books, board games, sports, painting and craft activities as well as more recent mass media – are gaining online versions that may supplement but may also displace the offline original. On the one hand, the online world greatly extends children's opportunities (including for intimacy, expression and participation), but on the other, since content is ever more detached from medium, it also amplifies the success of today's hugely profitable children's content brands (e.g. Disney, Barbie, Nickelodeon, The Simpsons, McDonalds, Harry Potter; Wasko, 2008).

Twentieth-century analyses of culture commonly start from Raymond Williams' (1983) dissection of 'culture' as 'one of the two or three most complicated words in the English language'. Two complexities are especially relevant to children's internet culture. First, culture encompasses both the material (goods, products, media, technologies) and the symbolic (images, narratives, discourses, imaginaries), necessitating the integration of disciplines which compete in their accounts of power. The former tend to emphasize structural determinisms (especially informed by political economic analysis) while the latter tend to emphasize agentic processes of meaning creation (as developed by cultural studies), although both shape children's internet culture (Curran et al., 1996). Second, culture connotes both that which is superior or refined (as in civilized or high culture) and that which is ordinary (as in popular or folk culture). For children, the question of values is particularly fraught since it has long been the responsibility of adult society to provide children with the optimal resources to support their development and yet today's liberal multiculturalism suspects such effort to be paternalistic or elitist, instead seeking to validate children's own activities and interests.

The possibilities opened up by conjoining these theoretical positions are now being explored in the analysis of children's internet culture, whether taking a more political economic (e.g. Grimes and Shade, 2005; Wasko, 2008) or cultural studies position (e.g. Stern, 2008). For example, David Buckingham applies the 'circuit of culture' to reveal how newly profitable but technocratic opportunities for online edutainment are either successfully imposed or to some degree renegotiated by parents and children in building their meaningful domestic learning environments (Buckingham et al., 2001). Ito et al.'s (2010) ethnographic approach to youthful 'hanging out' online helps to identify whether and when interest-driven or 'geeky' activities harbour the potential for new modes of learning among those alienated by established, hierarchical pedagogy. Henry Jenkins (2003) reveals the lively clashes between transgressive but highly literate young fans and litigious content owners desperate for new ideas that enable some unexpected innovations in cultural forms and experiences.

The online vs. offline shaping of children's *internet* culture

Almost uniquely in relation to the internet, children's knowledge is widely recognized as being both valuable and exceeding that of adults. Is the internet effecting a reversal of traditional power relations among the generations in a world where adults are digital immigrants, the grandchild teaches the grandparent to Skype, the pupil challenges the teacher's knowledge, and even commerce tries to 'get down with the kids'? The largely unanticipated growth of peer-to-peer culture, user-generated content, social networking and remix culture is stamping a youthful imprint on cultural domains hitherto dominated by adults. Is this to the benefit of children or, as also argued of television (Postman, 1992), is something lost as children increasingly participate in the adult world? Children still love to play outside with their friends, learn to swim or kick a ball, snuggle in front of the television with their family and daydream in places hidden from adult eyes. Teenagers still flirt, worry about their appearance, skimp their homework and get drunk. So how shall we understand the changes wrought by widespread use of the internet?

Early research conceived of virtual or cyber worlds as entirely 'other', disconnected from 'reality' (and so open to radical postmodern speculation about the end of identity, representation, inequality, morality and more). But empirically grounded research soon recognized significant continuities between life online and offline, especially the ways in which the offline shapes the online socially, economically and politically through processes of design, usage or appropriation and regulation (Wellman, 2004; Woolgar, 2002). Does this mean the internet itself is not a player in social change? As already noted, incorporating the internet into the very fabric of society exacerbates processes of globalization, commercialization and individualization in children's lives. Yet it is salutary to reflect that after half a century of mass television, Katz and Scannell (2009) struggled to identify just what difference even half a century of television made, and so it is unsurprising that social science is not ready to pronounce on the consequences of internet use for children, despite the pundits' many claims. Sober assessments of 'what difference the internet has made' to children's social relations (Valkenburg and Peter, 2009), parenting (Clark, 2011), civic participation and educational outcomes (Livingstone, 2012) or personal risks and safety (Wolak et al., 2008) tend to claim contingent and modest effects only.

But, just as media studies has long argued that television is far from a neutral window on the world, the same should be argued for the internet. Its characteristics, its anticipation of its users, its design features (for example, shaping privacy, authenticity, safety or networking) are, on the one hand, shaped by the institutions that developed them, but also they mediate the relations among people in particular ways. To recognize, critique and intervene in the power of media representations, scholars have long sought to promote media literacy to the wider public (especially through media education for children). Now, too, internet scholars are promoting digital literacy alongside their critical scholarship (Frau-Meigs and Torrent, 2009). For not-withstanding the excitement about children's digital expertise, the online environment is far more complex – sophisticated, yet treacherous – than most people can competently navigate, evaluate or contribute to, and a critical engagement with the online environment is therefore crucial for today's citizens, young and old.

Adapting boyd's (2008) analysis, we can recognize the internet's distinctive communicative affordances as including *persistence* (content is recorded, always visible, difficult to erase), *scalability* (simple interactions can be rapidly made available to vast audiences), *asynchronicity* (enabling interaction management), *replicability* (permitting seamless editing and manipulation of content), *searchability* (both extending and permitting specialization within networks of information and relationships), *audience uncertainty* (regarding who is listening and who is speaking) and *collapsed contexts* (absence of conventional boundaries for social situations, a key consequence being public/private blurring). These features pinpoint how the internet's affordances mediate children's experiences. Telling cases include: the extraordinary focus among youth on self-presentation and relationship management newly enabled by social networking sites' exploitation of persis-tence, scalability, asynchronicity and replicability; the deepened pain of bullying once extended into cyberbullying and so now, too, persistent, scalable and visible to uncertain audiences across home and school contexts; the unprecedented potential for children with niche interests (whether chess or photography, a diasporic identity or a desire for self-harm) to harness the 'long tail' of the internet (Anderson, 2006) via the features of searchability and self/audience anonymity. In short, the possibility is not merely that children's lives are increasingly filled by online activities, but that the main aspects of their lives (identity, pleasure, pain, relationships) are altered by the fact of their digital, networked, online mediation.

The specificity of childhood (vs. wider adult society) in *children*'s internet culture

Children's online opportunities and risks depend substantially on their familial, socio-economic and national contexts, making for considerable heterogeneity in children's internet cultures, even though the power of the global brands provides a counter-veiling homogenizing effect. The EU Kids Online project proposes the metaphor of the ladder to capture the commonalities within this diversity (Livingstone et al., 2011). Its survey of 9 to 16-year-olds' online activities found that when they first use the internet, children tend to look up information for school and play games alone or against the computer; most also check out YouTube or similar sites for watching video clips. These activities involve engaging with mass mediated content, and young children do little more than this. Older children take the further step of peer to peer communication (social networking, instant messaging, email), and teenagers more than younger children do more complex interactive activities such as playing games with others online, downloading content and sharing it via webcam or message boards, for instance. The most advanced and creative step – file-sharing, blogging, visiting virtual worlds – is reached by only a minority of teenagers. Thus despite the hype, it seems that few children undertake new kinds of creative, fan-based or remixed 'produsage' (Bruns, 2008) or contribute to civic activism (Dahlgren and Olsson, 2007). What does progression up the ladder depend upon? The importance of age reveals how children's motivations and interests matter, as do their digital skills and literacies. Some variation by country can be attributed to contextual factors such as the degree of internet adoption, the level of national investment in digital resources for education, or the size of the language community (that provides online content for children). Most within-country variation in amount of use is attributable to socioeconomic status, though once children gain access, age differences matter more, with gender adding some nuances through the relative preference for games (boys) or communication (girls) (McQuillan and D'Haenens, 2009).

In relation to online opportunities, there is a policy debate over whether children should share in the online resources available to adults or whether they require – and have a right to – specific, age-appropriate provision (for whom, funded by whom, to what end?). But in the online world as in the offline world, opportunities go hand in hand with the risk of harm – because the internet has been designed in this way (for example, searching for 'teen sex' produces useful health information and violent pornography), because the internet is populated not only by children but also by those who would harm them, and because children use their maturing skills and inventiveness to take risks, as they must if they are to develop resilience. In relation to risks as for opportunities, age is crucial, far more than either gender or socioeconomic status.

Figure 13.2 shows findings from EU Kids Online for the proportion of children by age who have encountered online opportunities, risks or – a crucial mediator between the two – risky opportunities (such as looking for new friends online, adding contacts that one hasn't met face to face, pretending to be a different kind of person online, disclosing personal information to 'strangers'). From this we learn that children's internet cultures are (i) heavily differentiated by age, (ii) that risks and opportunities are positively correlated, so that seeking to reduce the former may jeopardize the latter too, (iii) and that risky opportunities – 'playing with fire', perhaps – are part of the overall experience. However, accounting for experiences of risk and, even more so, of harm to children requires consideration of a further set of factors that differentiate among children, namely the psychological and social sources of vulnerability in children's lives. For as research confirms, children who suffer particular problems or difficulties in their lives are also more vulnerable to online risk of harm (Livingstone et al., 2012), and identifying ways of

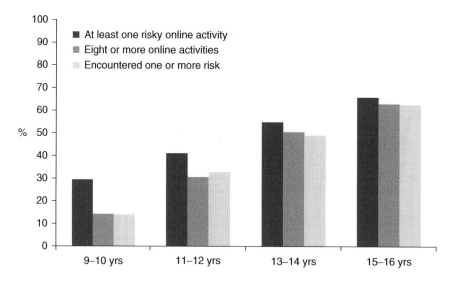

Figure 13.2 Children's online activities and risks, by age
Source: EU Kids Online, see www.eukidsonline.net
Base: 25,142 9–16 year olds in 25 European countries, surveyed in 2010.

redesigning the internet to enhance safety without costing more resilient children their rightful opportunities is proving an interesting policy-relevant challenge (Wolak et al., 2008).

Conclusion

It may be argued that children's internet culture differs little from any other area of consumer culture. As is the case for late modernity writ large, it is shaped by the fundamental processes of social change – globalization, commercialization, individualization and mediatization (Krotz, 2007). Thus children's internet culture is embedded within the global flows of people, technology and finance. It is increasingly subject to a market logic distinct from the organic needs of children and childhood. It is ever more focused on the child as individual divorced from community structures and affiliations (Beck and Beck-Gernsheim, 2002). And it is thoroughly mediatized – for beyond extending children's culture to the internet, the affordances of the online environment are also reshaping children's culture both online and offline.

But as we have seen, this analysis underplays the contribution of the everyday activities of children themselves, for which we must mobilize a conception of culture that emphasizes ordinary activities 'under the radar' of both culturally normative and political economic perspectives. Indeed, a closer examination of children's internet culture reveals counter processes that qualify grand claims about childhood engulfed by increasing commercialisation and globalization – the embedded nature of local meanings, the agency and creativity of children's activities and meaning-making online and offline, the emergence of new publics and non-commercial spaces, the elaboration of ever widening social and civic networks, and even a renewed appreciation for face to face interaction (Turkle, 2011). In short, a more satisfactory analysis of children's internet culture recognizes (but does not overstate) children's agency in contributing to their culture as well as the power of social structures beyond media and market (family, school, religion, tradition, politics).

Scholarly analysis of children's internet culture has tended to illustrate, complicate and contextualize but not entirely transcend the oppositional thinking (optimistic versus pessimistic, virtual versus real, opportunities versus risks) that characterized the early years of internet studies (Wellman, 2004). In introducing our *International Handbook of Children, Media and Culture* (2008), Kirsten Drotner and I argued for three principles to guide the analysis of children's media cultures:

- Research must transcend technologically-determinist discourses of celebration and anxiety and develop multi-disciplinary, empirically-grounded accounts of the complex relations among children, media and culture;
- Media-specific research should be contextualized within a comparative account of children and young people's life worlds, recognizing the multiple influences upon children and their diverse positioning in relation to these influences;
- Research should include child-centred methods, seeking to recognize children's own agency, experiences, perspectives and priorities rather than imposing an adult agenda or adult values.

These surely provide a good guide for children's internet cultures also. Already, no aspect of children's lives is entirely untouched by the internet, yet society's exploitation of the internet is still unfolding. The public and policy spotlight will remain on children's internet cultures for some time and, given the many difficulties children face in their lives, it seems incumbent on researchers not only to track their internet use but also to use this knowledge in the wider effort to optimize the benefits.

SEE ALSO in this volume chapter by Alper and chapter by O'Neill.

References

Anderson, C. (2006) *The long tail: Why the future of business is selling less of more*. New York: Hyperion.

Beck, U. and Beck-Gernsheim, E. (2002). *Individualization*. London: Sage.

boyd, d. (2008). Why youth ♡ social network sites: The role of networked publics in teenage social life. In D. Buckingham (Ed.), *Youth, identity, and digital media* (Vol. 6). Cambridge: MIT Press, pp. 119–42.

boyd, d. and Hargittai, E. (2010). Facebook privacy settings: Who cares? *First Monday, 15*(8). Last accessed 12 July 2012 at http://www.firstmonday.org/htbin/cgiwrap/bin/ojs/index.php/fm/article/view/3086

Bruns, A. (2008). *Blogs, Wikipedia, Second Life, and beyond: From production to produsage (Digital Formations)* New York: Peter Lang.

Buckingham, D. (2006). Is there a digital generation? In D. Buckingham and R. Willett (Eds), *Digital generations*. Mahwah, New Jersey: Lawrence Erlbaum, pp. 1–13.

Buckingham, D., Scanlon, M. and Sefton-Green, J. (2001). Selling the digital dream: Marketing educational technology to teachers and parents. In A. Loveless and V. Ellis (Eds), *Subject to change: Literacy and digital technology*. London: Routledge, pp. 20–40.

ChildWise (2011). ChildWise Monitor. *The Trends Report 2011*: ChildWise www.childwise.co.uk.

ChildWise (2013). ChildWise Monitor Report 2012-13. ChildWise www.childwise.co.uk.

Clark, L. S. (2011). Parental mediation theory for the digital age. *Communication Theory, 21*(4), 323–43.

Corner, J. (1995). *Television form and public address*. London: Edward Arnold.

Curran, J., Morley, D. and Walkerdine, V. (Eds) (1996). *Cultural studies and communications*. London: Edward Arnold.

Dahlgren, P. and Olsson, T. (2007). From public sphere to civic culture: Young citizens' internet use. In R. Butsch (Ed.), *Media and public spheres*. New York: Palgrave Macmillan, pp. 198–209.

Drotner, K. and Livingstone, S. (Eds) (2008). *The international handbook of children, media and culture*. London: Sage.

Frau-Meigs, D. and Torrent, J. (Eds) (2009). *Mapping media education policies in the world: visions, programmes and challenges*. New York: The United Nations Alliance of Civilizations and Grupo Comunicar.

Gasser, U., Maclay, C. M. and Palfrey, J. G. (2010) *Working towards a deeper understanding of digital safety for children and young people in developing nations*. Harvard, MA: Berkman Center Research Publication No. 2010–17.

Grimes, S. M. and Shade, L. R. (2005). Neopian economics of play: children's cyberpets and online communities as immersive advertising in NeoPets.com. *International Journal of Media and Cultural Politics, 1*(2), 181–98.

Ito, M., Okabe, D. and Matsuda, M. (Eds) (2005). *Personal, portable pedestrian: Mobile phones in Japanese life*. Cambridge, Mass.: MIT Press.

Ito, M., and others (2010). *Hanging out, messing around, and geeking out: Kids living and learning with new media*. Cambridge: The MIT Press.

Jenkins, H. (2003). *Quentin Tarantino's Star Wars*? Digital cinema, media convergence, and participatory culture. In D. Thorburn and H. Jenkins (Eds), *Rethinking media change: The aesthetics of transition*. Cambridge, MA: MIT Press, pp. 281–312.

Katz, E. and Scannell, P. (2009). The end of television? Its impact so far. *The Annals of the American Academy of Political and Social Science, 625* (whole issue).

Krotz, F. (2007). The meta-process of 'mediatization' as a conceptual frame. *Global Media and Communication, 3*(3), 256–60.

Livingstone, S. (2005). In defence of privacy: Mediating the public/private boundary home. In S. Livingstone (Ed.), *Audiences and publics: When cultural engagement matters for the public sphere*. Bristol: Intellect Press, pp. 163–85. At http://eprints.lse.ac.uk/505/

——(2009). *Children and the internet: Great expectations, challenging realities*. Cambridge: Polity.

——(2012) Critical reflections on the prospects for ICT in education. *Oxford Review of Education, 38*(1), 9–24.

Livingstone, S., Haddon, L., Görzig, A. and Ólafsson, K. (2011) *EU Kids Online II: Final report*. LSE, London: EU Kids Online. Available at www.eukidsonline.net

Livingstone, S., Haddon, L. and Görzig, A. (Eds.) (2012) *Children, risk and safety online: Research and policy challenges in comparative perspective.* Bristol: The Policy Press.

McQuillan, H. and D'Haenens, L. (2009). Young people online: gender and age influences. In S. Livingstone and L. Haddon (Eds), *Kids online: Opportunities and risks for children.* Bristol: The Policy Press, pp. 95–106.

Palfrey, J. and Gasser, U. (2008). *Born digital: Understanding the first generation of digital natives.* New York: Basic Books.

Postman, N. (1992). *The disappearance of childhood: How TV is changing children's lives* (2 ed.). New York: Viking.

Prensky, M. (2001). Digital natives, digital immigrants. *On the Horizon, 9*(5), 1–2.

Selwyn, N. (2009). The digital native – myth and reality. *Aslib Proceedings, 61*(4), 364–79.

Stern, S. (2008). Producing sites, exploring identities: Youth online authorship. In D. Buckingham (Ed.), *Youth, identity, and digital media.* Cambridge: MIT Press, pp. 95–117.

Turkle, S. (2011). *Alone together: Why we expect more from technology and less from each other.* Philadelphia: Perseus Running Press.

Valkenburg, P. M. and Peter, J. (2009). Social consequences of the internet for adolescents: a decade of research. *Current directions in psychological science, 18*(1), 1–5.

Wasko, J. (2008). The commodification of youth culture. In K. Drotner and S. Livingstone (Eds), *International handbook of children, media and culture.* London: Sage, pp. 460–74.

Wellman, B. (2004). The three ages of internet studies: Ten, five and zero years ago. *New Media and Society, 6*(1), 123–29.

Williams, R. (1983). *Keywords: A vocabulary of culture and society.* London: Fontana.

Wolak, J., Finkelhor, D. and Mitchell, K. (2008). Online "predators" and their victims: myths, realities, and implications for prevention and treatment. *American Psychologist, 63*(2), 111–28.

Woolgar, S. (2002). Five rules of virtuality. In S. Woolgar (Ed.), *Virtual society? Technology, cyberbole, reality.* Oxford: OUP, pp. 1–22.

14

CHILDREN'S DIGITAL GAMING CULTURES

Pål Aarsand

An essential feature of work within the sociology of childhood paradigm is to view children as competent actors in their own right (James et al., 1998), and thereby producers of culture (e.g. Corsaro 1997). From this point of view, the present text discusses how children's digital gaming cultures are produced and sustained. In order to do this, focus is placed on: who is playing, where this takes place and how the game playing is accomplished.

Gaming cultures

When discussing children and gaming culture, one can differentiate between culture produced for children by adults and children's own production of culture (Mouritsen, 2002). Even though there are problems with such clear-cut distinctions, it is useful to differentiate between the digital games produced by adults and directed at children – serious games (educational) as well as entertainment games – and children's use of digital games in the context of their own practices.

Children's gaming cultures can be understood as subcultures in the sense of "groups of people who have some practices, values and interest in common and who form through their interaction a distinct group within a larger culture" (Mäyrä, 2008, p. 25). Studies of Massively Multiplayer Online Role-Playing Games (MMORPG) have focused on the production and reproduction of social communities where a certain type of terminology is often used among the players, and where formal and informal rules guide and regulate the social interaction in these groups (Karlsen, 2010; Linderoth and Bennerstedt, 2007). Gaming culture as a subcultural phenomenon can also be described as communities of play practices (Pearce, 2009), where members share experiences and develop ways to handle tasks and artefacts in games (Sjöblom, 2011) as well as participate in game-related activities (cf. Steinkuehler, 2006). When gaming is seen as a cultural activity, researchers are interested in topics such as identity, learning and competence (e.g. Pearce, 2009; Taylor, 2008).

Around the latest turn of the century, there was a tendency to regard children's use of digital media, particularly games, as an age-related phenomenon (Prensky, 2001; Tapscott, 1998). It was claimed that not only did children understand and treat digital media differently than other age groups did, but also that it was easier for them to learn how to handle the technology. As a result of this ease of learning, they were more knowledgeable and competent than adults in handling media like digital games. In terms of learning and competence it has been argued that there is a generational gap, a digital divide, between children and adults. In this way, children have become "the Other", those who are unlike the rest of the population. This approach treats children as though they were part of a homogenous group, indicating that it is age that determines how one handles games. Such a stance also treats digital games as though they were all identical. Moreover, when children's gaming cultures are discussed in general terms like "generational gap", gaming practices are turned into "black boxes", which does not explain what the cultures look like or how they function.

Children's game cultures are not to be seen as subcultures in the sense of being located "outside" society or in isolated spaces. They are not a sort of tribal childhood that renders some parts of children's lives separate from the adult world (James et al., 1998). Rather, children's gaming cultures can be seen as related to other practices that restrict and encourage game activities – practices such as parenting, formal learning, racism, bonding, bullying and sporting. In this way, gaming culture is seen as cultural practices in which children use digital games for their own purposes and relate to other cultural phenomena in their everyday lives (Shaw, 2010). But, who are these game playing children?

Who is the player?

The player is often investigated with regard to age, gender, ethnicity, socioeconomic background and parents' education. In studies of children's media use in the Western world, it can be seen that between 80 percent and 100 percent of children in the age range 9–17 years play digital games (Medietilsynet, 2010; Medierådet, 2010a; Rideout et al., 2010). Thereby, more or less all children play digital games, or are part of game playing cultures. Nordic studies report significant differences when it comes to gender and gaming (Medietilsynet, 2010; Medierådet, 2010a). More boys than girls tend to play digital games. Boys play more sports and car games, shooting and action, and MMORPG, while girls tend to play party and humour/animated games. The Swedish Media Council (Medierådet 2010b) reports that popular games among girls in the age group 5–9 years were "Sing a Star", Barbie and horse games. It is interesting to note that none of the boys played the two last types of games. A US study shows that boys tend to play more often and for longer periods than girls do (Rideout et al., 2010). The studies above also reported that age matters and that the youngest half of their population was more likely to play games and spend more time on games. Despite the fact that age is marked as one of the key factors in describing children's gaming, only a few surveys actually consider young children. One exception to this is the Swedish Media Council (Medierådet 2010b), which has studied the media use of children aged 2–9 years. When this group is divided into two groups, 2–5 and 5–9 years, significant age and gender differences are found concerning what games children play. The age and gender differences are explained as being a consequence of the fact that games target certain age groups and genders. Put differently, the youngest children are less likely to play games that target older children.

The questions of gender and age have been, and still are, important topics in studies of gaming practices. Feminist researchers have studied the types of games boys and girls play, game design and identities, as well as the large proportion of girls who do not play games. One reason why attention has been focused on digital games and gender is that games have been seen as an important path to working with technology (in the context of education and future jobs, particularly in STEM disciplines). Cassell and Jenkins (1998) discuss how gender stereotypes matter in games as well as in the game industry's views on the female gamer. Ten years later, Kafai et al. (2008) argue that gender is still an important aspect of game practices that has to be considered and discussed. At the same time, they stress that merely noting gender differences runs the risk of essentializing the (fe)male gamer. In addition, it draws on assumptions about what boyish games are like, whereby certain kinds of logic are related to what is considered feminine and masculine.

Ethnicity is a dimension found in North American studies (e.g. Rideout et al., 2010). In these studies, it can be seen that Hispanic and African-American children spend significantly more time on digital games than Caucasian children do. Thus, both ethnicity and social class are topics that may matter when it comes to who is playing with whom – how, when and where. Age, gender and ethnicity are also relevant in relation to game characters, or avatars. One of the recurring statements in feminist game research is that girls dislike games in which women are sexualized, victims, and not heroes (Denner and Campe, 2008). A large-scale study of 95 percent of all games sold in the US during 2005 shows that Caucasian adult males are over-represented as primary and secondary characters in games compared to their actual proportion of the US population (Williams et al., 2009). Earlier studies have shown that when African-Americans (men) are the primary characters in games, these are usually sports games. Otherwise, African-American and Latino characters usually have marginal roles, either as criminals or victims (Leonard, 2006).

Children are not one homogenous group of players but rather vary with regard to age, gender and ethnicity. These are even identity categories that matter in virtual landscapes. The question of game players' identities in online and offline communities brings us to the next questions: where, and how, do children produce gaming cultures?

Where and how do children play?

Children play different game genres, and they play online as well as offline (Apperley, 2006; Juul, 2010; Lenhart et al., 2008; Medietilsynet, 2010; Rideout et al., 2010). Studies show that popular genres among children are "sport and car games", "shooting and action games", "puzzles", "role playing games", "adventure", "strategy games", "simulation games", "party games" and "humour/cartoon games", and "MMORPGs". To make sense of how games work within children's gaming culture, researchers have investigated where and how they are used.

Where do children play?

Game activities are situated within particular games, but also at places such as homes, preschools, schools, after school centres, internet cafés and friends' houses. Playing digital games at home is common to most children, because this is where they have access to game equipment. The social environment consists of parents and perhaps siblings, all of whom claim access to the console or the place where it is located (Aarsand and Aronsson, 2009), and all of whom influence how gaming is accomplished. It has also been shown that children use parents as a resource for solving problems, or for getting started when they are playing at home (e.g. Fatigante et al., 2010). When children play games in families, they often have to deal with local rules that guide/govern what they play and how long they are allowed to play (Aarsand, 2011), and conflicts and negotiations in relation to these rules seem to be a recurring topic in families (Vandewater et al., 2005). Studies of games in school have mainly focused on children and educational games – primarily because these are the kinds of games officially permitted in this context – and on how children are restricted from entering possible game sites. Research on internet cafés shows that this social and material environment serves as a place where children can meet and play together. Internet cafés and after school gaming clubs have been described as places where children learn to play, where they create and display their game competences as well as social hierarchies (Kafai et al., 2008;

Sjöblom, 2011). At these places they are introduced to games and reviews of games, and learn how to evaluate games and game play. Studies of children's use of games in preschool are still rare, but there are exceptions. For instance, both Agneta Ljung-Djärf (2008) and Polly Björk-Willén (2011) focus on how children participate in game play through positioning and mutual problem-solving.

Where does the action take place? The question of "where" has to deal with how the distinction between online and offline is handled in game activities (Aarsand, 2010). Online games, particularly children's use of MMORPGs, have been discussed in the public press. Lately, games studies have paid attention to where and how children are playing MMORPGs. Games like "Whyville" (e.g. Kafai, 2010), "Habbo Hotel" (e.g. Mäntymäki and Salo, 2011) and "Neopets" (e.g. Dumitrica, 2011) have been studied with a focus on different social practices such as learning, cheating, identity performances and purchasing. Although considerable attention has been paid to online games, it is still most common among children to play offline, at home, or at their friends' places (Lenhart et al., 2008; Medierådet, 2010a; Medietilsynet, 2010). Moreover, children seem to play digital games in well-known social environments. Instead of making a clear distinction between online and offline games, one can discuss the use of games in terms of participation (Ito et al., 2008; Jenkins, 2006). This points to how game cultures can be studied by paying attention to embodied game playing practices situated in time and space to capture participants' perspectives on their own playing (Aarsand and Aronsson, 2009; Bennersted and Ivarsson, 2010; Piirainen-Marsh, 2010; Sjöblom, 2011). In short, it can be argued that we need to look at where and how average gamers use digital games in their everyday life within and across practices (cf. Corliss, 2010).

How do children play?

There is a tradition within games studies to regard gaming as an activity that is cut off from the surroundings, and that takes place within the "magic circle" (Caillois, 2001; Huizinga, 1998; Juul, 2005; Salen and Zimmerman, 2004). According to this perspective, the game is guided by specific rules meant to keep the "world" outside the game. The rules are what constitute and sustain the borders of the game. The players need to respect and play by the rules to keep the game going. This means that aspects like gender, age, ethnicity, social class and religion are of no relevance to succeeding in the game. Consalvo (2007) has studied the phenomenon of cheating, and argues that games cannot be understood in terms of magic circles because the rules of the game always have to compete with "other rules and in relation to multiple contexts, across varying cultures, and into different groups, legal situations, and homes" (p. 416). Thus, Consalvo argues that we have to look beyond the activity of gaming to understand why it looks like it does and what gaming means to those who are involved. Consalvo's study also illustrates that the rules of the game are situated, and that there is a tension between game designers' intentions regarding how to play the game by the rules and how players actually play it.

Jenkins (2006) discusses the use of media in terms of participatory culture, that is "culture in which fans and other consumers are invited to actively participate in the creation and circulation of new content" (p. 331). He demonstrates how digital games and game play are followed by other practices, such as writing fan fiction or creating YouTube movies. In this way, Jenkins also tells us that game culture involves much more than playing games within their respective virtual landscapes. Moreover, games can be used in many different ways and for many different purposes. This has been described by Ito et al. (2008), who show three different forms of media engagement among children: "hanging out", "messing around" and "geeking out". "Hanging out" is described as children's using digital games to get together, thus with the main motive of socializing. "Messing around" is described as an interest-driven orientation to games that is supported both socially and materially. The main interest is to get to know and master the game, but players tend to stay within the context of peer sociability. "Geeking out" is explained as "an intense commitment to or engagement with media or technology" (Ito et al., 2008, p. 28). "Geeking out" requires time, space and resources so that the child has the opportunity to pursue his/her interest. When the focus is on patterns of participation, it is not directed at the game technology as such but rather at how the technology is used in the context of children's everyday lives.

Participation has also been central in interactional studies of digital games in children's everyday lives. Here, the focus has been on how gaming is accomplished in interaction. For instance, it is shown how switching between languages works as a resource in orienting to aspects of the game and coordinating action (Piirainen-Marsh, 2010), how the use of response cries works to create an intersubjective understanding of the game situation (Aarsand and Aronsson, 2009), and how children display competences in collaborate game action in front of the screen (Sjöblom, 2011). Moreover, seeing children's gaming cultures as participatory cultures indicates that these cultures involve much more than just playing the game.

Children's gaming cultures

Playing digital games involves learning, but what do the children learn? Research on games and learning has been pursued by two camps (Connolly et al., 2012): those who focus on negative outcomes, such as aggression and sexualization (Anderson, 2004; Gentile and Gentile, 2008), and those who focus on positive outcomes such as problem-solving and social skills (Steinkuehler and Duncan, 2008).

The discussion on what is learnt by playing games in terms of outcome is a rather narrow one, particularly if one is interested in children's gaming culture. Instead, learning can be seen as the production and reproduction of gaming cultures. For instance, it has been claimed that by playing games one simply becomes good at playing games (Juul, 2005). Such statements have caused researchers to focus on the pedagogical principles that games build upon, which help players make progress and thereby learn to become better players (Gee, 2003; Gentile and Gentile, 2008). But being a good game player has also been discussed in terms of game literacies (Gee, 2003; Squire, 2007). Game literacies can be broadly explained as players' ability to read, understand and act in a relevant manner within games, indicating that literacy concerns technical as well as social and cultural competences that are needed to be able to participate in game practices (e.g. Jenkins, 2006). Consalvo (2007) underlines this when she uses the concept "gaming capital" to describe the system of preferences and dispositions that gamers develop when playing games, which can be seen as similar to game literacies. According to her, the notion captures the "dynamism of game play as well as the evolving game and paratextual industry" (p. 4). The notion of gaming capital is used in an attempt to broaden the scope of what matters to the participants in game practices, and how these values are produced and sustained in interaction with other players and the game industry. Moreover, it could be argued that game literacy implies that players learn to produce and reproduce gaming cultures, which is done in relation to their understanding of gaming practices, access to technology and social settings (Pearce, 2009). Along this line, what is learnt is something that has to be answered by investigating what qualifies someone as a competent player (e.g. Consalvo, 2007; Ito et al., 2008; Sjöblom, 2011).

To understand children's gaming cultures, researchers have studied important questions including who is playing games, what they are playing and with whom they are playing, and there is even some research on how they are playing. Together, this gives us insights into aspects of how children's gaming cultures are produced, sustained and changed, but we are still only at the beginning of this research.

SEE ALSO in this volume chapter by Alper.

References

Aarsand, P. (2011). Parenting and digital games: On children's game play in US families. *Journal of Children and Media*, 5(3), 318–33.

——(2010). Young boys playing digital games: From console to the playground. *Nordic Journal of Digital Literacy*, 4(1), 38–55.

Aarsand, P. and Aronsson, K. (2009). Response cries and other gaming moves: Toward an intersubjectivity of gaming. *Journal of Pragmatics*, 41(8), 1557–75.

Anderson, C. A. (2004). An update on the effects of playing violent video games. *Journal of Adolescence*, 27(1), 113–22.

Apperley, T. H. (2006). Genre and game studies: Toward a critical approach to video game genres. *Simulation & Gaming*, 37(1), 6–23.

Bennerstedt, U. and Ivarsson, J. (2010). Knowing the way. Managing epistemic topologies in virtual game worlds. *Computer Supported Cooperative Work*, 19(2), 201–30.

Björk-Willén, P. (2011). Händelser vid datorn. Förskolebarns positioneringsarbete och datorspelets agens ("Happenings around the computer. Preschool children's positioning and computer games agency"). *Barn*, 21(3–4), 75–92.

Caillois, R. (2001). *Man, play and games*. Urbana and Chicago, IL: University of Illinois Press.

Cassell, J. and Jenkins, H. (1998). *From Barbie to Mortal Kombat: Gender and computer games*. Cambridge, MA: MIT Press.

Connolly, T. M., Boyle, E. A., MacArthur, E., Hainey, T. and Boyle, J. M. (2012). A systematic literature review of empirical evidence on computer games and serious games. *Computers & Education*, 59(2), 661–86.

Consalvo, M. (2007). *Cheating: Gaining advantage in videogames*. Cambridge, MA: MIT Press.

Corliss, J. (2010). Introduction: The social science study of video games. *Games and Culture*, 6(1), 3–16.

Corsaro, W. A. (1997). *The sociology of childhood*. Thousand Oaks, CA: Pine Forge Press.

Denner, J. and Campe, S. (2008). What games made by girls can tell us. In Y. Kafai, C. Heeter, J. Denner and J. Y. Sun (Eds), *Beyond Barbie and Mortal Kombat: New perspectives on gender and gaming*. Cambridge, Mass.: MIT Press, pp. 129–40.

Dumitrica, D. D. (2011). An exploration of cheating in a virtual gaming world. *Journal of Gaming & Virtual Worlds*, 3(1), 21–36.

Fatigante, M., Linerati, V. and Pontecorvo, C. (2010). Transitions in and out of games: How parents and children bracket game episodes at home. *Research on Language & Social Interaction*, 43(4), 346–71.

Gee, J. P. (2003). *What video games have to teach us about learning and literacy*. New York: Palgrave Macmillan.

Gentile, D. A. and Gentile, R. (2008). Violent video games as exemplary teachers: A conceptual analysis. *Journal of Youth and Adolescence*, 37(2), 127–41.

Huizinga, J. (1998). *Homo ludens: A study of the play-element in culture*. London: Routledge.

Ito, M., Horst, H., Bittanti, M., Boyd, D., Herr-Stephenson, B. and Lange, P. G. (2008). *Living and Learning with New Media: Summary of Findings from the Digital Youth Project*. Retrieved June 10, 2012, from: http://digitalyouth.ischool.berkeley.edu/files/report/digitalyouth-WhitePaper.pdf

James, A., Jenks, C. and Prout, A. (1998). *Theorizing childhood*. Cambridge; New York: Polity Press: Teachers College Press.

Jenkins. (2006). *Convergence culture*. New York and London: New York University Press.

Juul, J. (2005). *Half-real: Video games between real rules and fictional worlds*. Cambridge, MA: MIT Press.

——(2010). *A casual revolution: Reinventing video games and their players*. Cambridge, MA: MIT Press.

Kafai, Y. B. (2010). World of Whyville: An introduction to tween virtual life. *Games and Culture*, 5(3), 3–22.

Kafai, Y. B., Heeter, C., Denner, J. and Sun, J. Y. (2008). *Beyond Barbie and Mortal Kombat: New perspectives on gender and gaming*. Cambridge, MA: MIT Press.

Karlsen, F. (2010). Addiction and randomness: A comparative analysis of psycho-structural elements in gambling games and massively multiplayer online role-playing games. In U. Carlsson (Ed.), *Children and youth in the digital media culture: From a Nordic horizon*. Göteborg: The International Clearinghouse on Children, Youth and Media.

Lenhart, A., Kahne, J., Middaugh, E., Macgill, A. R., Evans, C. and Vitak, J. (2008). *Teens, video games, and civics: Teens' gaming experiences are diverse and include significant social interaction and civic engagement.* Retrieved November 10, 2009, from: www.macfound.org/atf/cf/%7BB0386CE3–8B29-4162-8098-E466FB856794%7D/PEW_DML_REPORT_080916.PDF

Leonard, D. J. (2006). Not a hater, just keeping it real: The importance of race- and gender-based game studies. *Games and Culture, 1*(1), 83–88.

Linderoth, J. and Bennerstedt, U. (2007). *Living in World of Warcraft: The thoughts and experiences of ten young people.* Stockholm: The Swedish media council.

Ljung-Djärf, A. (2008). The owner, the participant and the spectator: Positions and positioning in peer activity around the computer in preschool. *Early Years, 28*(1), 61–72.

Mäntymäki, M. and Salo, J. (2011). Teenagers in social virtual worlds: Continuous use and purchasing behavior in Habbo Hotel. *Computers in Human Behavior, 27*(6), 2088–97.

Mäyrä, F. (2008). *An introduction to game studies: Games in culture.* Los Angeles; London: Sage.

Medierådet (2010a). *Ungar & Medier 2010* (The Swedish Media Council, 'Children & Media 2010'). Stockholm: Medierådet.

Medierådet. (2010b). *Småungar & Medier.* (The Swedish Media Council, 'Young children & Media 2010'). Stockholm: Medierådet.

Medietilsynet (2010). *Barn og digitale medier 2010* (The Norwegian Media Council, 'Children and digital media 2010'). Oslo: Medietilsynet.

Mouritsen, F. (2002). Child culture – play culture. In F. Mouritsen and J. Qvortrup (Eds), *Childhood and children's culture.* Odense: University Press of Southern Denmark, pp. 14–42.

Pearce, C. (2009). *Communities of play: Emergent cultures in multiplayer games and virtual worlds.* Cambridge, Mass.: MIT Press.

Piirainen-Marsh, A. (2010). Bilingual practices and the social organisation of video gaming activities. *Journal of Pragmatics, 42*(8), 3012–30.

Prensky, M. (2001). *Digital game-based learning.* New York: McGraw-Hill.

Rideout, V. J., Foehr, U. G. and Roberts, D. F. (2010). *Generation M2: Media in the lives of 8-to 18-year-olds.* The Kaiser Family Foundation Study.

Salen, K. and Zimmerman, E. (2004). *Rules of play: Game design fundamentals.* Cambridge, MA: MIT.

Shaw, A. (2010). What is video game culture? Cultural studies and game studies. *Games and Culture, 5*(4), 403–24.

Sjöblom, B. (2011). *Gaming interaction: Conversations and competencies in internet cafés.* Linköping: Linköping University.

Squire, K. (2007). Video games literacy: A literacy of expertise. In J. Coiro, M. Knobel, C. Lankshear and D. Leu (Eds), *Handbook of research on new media literacies.* New York: Macmillan, pp. 635–70.

Steinkuehler, C. A. (2006). Why game (culture) studies now? *Games and Culture, 1*(1), 97–102.

Steinkuehler, C. and Duncan, S. (2008). Scientific habits of mind in virtual worlds. *Journal of Science Education and Technology, 17*(6), 530–43.

Tapscott, D. (1998). *Growing up digital: The rise of the net generation.* New York: McGraw-Hill.

Taylor, T. L. (2008). Becoming a player: Networks, structure, and imagined futures. In Y. B. Kafai, C. Heeter, J. Denner and J. Y. Sun (Eds), *Beyond Barbie and Mortal Kombat.* Cambridge, MA: The MIT Press, pp. 51–66.

Vandewater, E. A., Park, S.-E., Huang, X. and Wartella, E. A. (2005). No – you can't watch that: Parental rules and young children's media use. *American Behavioral Scientist, 48*(5), 608–23.

Williams, D., Martins, N., Consalvo, M. and Ivory, J. D. (2009). The virtual census: Representations of gender, race and age in video games. *New Media Society, 11*(5), 815–34.

15

MOBILE COMMUNICATION CULTURE AMONG CHILDREN AND ADOLESCENTS

Rich Ling and Troels Bertel

Introduction

In the developed world, and increasingly in the developing world, children and teens have grown up with ready access to mobile phones. The mobile phone has become *de rigueur* in teens' and increasingly children's lives. It has changed the way that they experience youth compared to previous generations. This essay summarizes research on mobile phone use among children and teens in their daily lives. Though mobile phones are increasingly multidimensional devices that allow for not only communication but also portable gaming, music, and a variety of other functions, we will largely focus on mobile telephones in their role as communication devices.

Children and teens are both similar and different, a fact that is reflected in their mobile communication practices. Castells et al. (2007, p. 128) thus argue that children and teens share "a common culture of communication with various emphases in its manifestation depending on age."

While there are undoubtedly similarities between the groups it is clear that they are also different in important areas as regards mobile communication. At the most basic level, texting, a distinctive feature of the mobile phone, requires the user to master writing. This limits the use of this aspect of the mobile phone for the youngest children.

There are also differences in adoption between the groups. While ownership among teens has been very widespread in many developed countries, ownership among younger children has been less common. The tendency, however, seems to be that the mobile phone is steadily being adopted at earlier ages. In 2004 in the UK, Davie et al. (2004) found that 45 percent of 10 to 11-year-olds had a mobile phone. In the same year in the US only 18 percent of 12-year-olds had a mobile phone. In 2005 in Norway over 80 percent of 10-year-olds owned one (Vaage, 2010). By 2009 US mobile phone ownership among 12-year-olds was up to 58 percent.

When compared with children, teens in general enjoy greater autonomy. They have more independence from parents and develop more elaborate peer cultures (Fine, 2004; Ito et al., 2010, p. 8). Their mobile communication is directed towards peers to a higher degree than children's which is primarily oriented toward the family (Green and Haddon, 2009, p. 98). Indeed teens text and use voice calls more than any other age group (Ling et al., 2011). In addition, they use the internet on the mobile phone more than younger children. The teen period is also characterized by negotiations of identity that is less common among children (Fine, 2004; Ito et al., 2010, p. 8). Teens, because of their different life situation, use mobile media to manage social life to a higher degree than do children. For these reasons most research about mobile culture to date has focused on teens while explicit research on young children's use remains less common. This fact will be reflected in the material reviewed in this essay.

Review of research on mobile telephony use among youth

The study of social uses of mobile communication is relatively new and before the year 2000 there was little research. Since then there has been considerable and growing interest in the field (Green and Haddon, 2009, p. 1). Geographically, European research has been predominant although significant early contributions were also made in Asia and in the US (Green and Haddon, 2009, p. 10). Today, the study of the social uses of the mobile phone has become a much more widespread endeavor.

Teen use was among the first issues to be investigated (Ling, 2001) in works from Norway (Johnsen, 2003; Ling and Yttri, 2002), Hong Kong (Leung and Wei, 1999), Finland (Kasesniemi and Rautiainen, 2002; Oksman and Rautianen, 2003), the UK (Green and Smith, 2004; Grinter and Eldridge, 2001) and Japan (Ito, 2001). More recently the Pew Internet and American Life project has been active in examining teen use of mobile communication.

Teens are central in these works because they were early, and unexpected, adopters of mobile telephony. They helped drive the mass adoption of the technology and helped shape its use (Ling, 2004). They remain the most active users today, a point consistently found by research (see for instance Ling et al., 2011). The mobile phone with voice calls and particularly texting has become a central medium for teen interaction. It is a device used extensively for interaction with the same gendered friends (Lenhart et al., 2010). In addition, it has been shown to be a tool for developing and maintaining romantic relationships. In some cases this is seen with forbearance by parents, but in societies where interaction between the genders is more controlled, the mobile phone has posed a threat to this system of authority (Ellwood-Clayton, 2003; Hijazi-Omari and Ribak, 2008).

The majority of research on mobile phone use among children and youth focuses on texting (SMS) and voice calls. It is clear that with the rise of smart phones, the mobile internet and other advanced mobile media, mobile communication is increasingly melding into broader forms of mediated interaction. Activities that were formerly restricted to personal computers (such as the use of social network sites, e.g. Facebook) are now increasingly available on mobile phones, tablets, etc. In addition, new mobile technologies such as location based services are becoming available. The research about these phenomena, however, is still sparse.

Social functions of the mobile phone

The use of the mobile phone in many countries today is near ubiquitous among teens and growing among younger children. This raises the question of why it is important for children and teens to have a mobile phone. In considering this, several distinctive functions of the mobile phone emerge including coordination, expressive uses, safety, texting, and multimedia uses.

Coordination. Perhaps more than anything else, the mobile phone facilitates coordination (Ling and Yttri, 2002) providing users with the ability to make and remake agreements on the fly. This has changed the way that youth sort out the logistics of daily life and has led to a type of iterative planning that is particularly common among teens where agreements can be made and adjusted as needed. This provides mobile phone users with temporal and spatial flexibility (Haddon, 2000).

Expressive uses. Among teens a main motivation for having a mobile phone is often simply to have social access to peers (Ling, 2009; Miyata et al., 2008). Indeed, analysis done by Lenhart et al. indicates that this is perhaps the dominant motivation (Lenhart et al., 2010). These "expressive" exchanges include important emotional discussions as well as simple idle chat. While sometimes appearing superficial or even meaningless, the exchange of texts and calls is an important way for youth to build cohesion with their peers (Matsuda, 2005). Further, it is used to explore romantic interactions (Ito et al., 2010) with the relative absence of interpersonal cues (texts do not blush) and the asynchronous nature of texting (texts give pause to think) giving teens a sense of greater control with their interaction in emotional situations (Madell and Muncer, 2007).

These expressive messages constitute a large part of the total volume of teen texting (Ling, 2005).

Safety. The mobile telephone is seen as a safety link (Ling, 2007; Palfrey, 2008). Youth often describe an imagined or actual quasi-serious episode (i.e. missing a bus, running out of gas, etc.), as the triggering event for getting a phone. The latent ability to use it in the case of an actual emergency is an important justification for having a mobile phone for both parents and children (Cohen et al., 2007; Ling, 2012).

Texting. Any discussion of mobile phones needs to take special note of texting, the exchange of short text messages between mobile phones. A main attraction of texting is that it functions "under the radar" providing a channel where friends can gossip, make agreements, flirt, and generally communicate while simultaneously engaged in other activities. It is also a venue where youth can develop creative linguistic flourishes and styles through which they can show their membership in particular social groups (Baron, 2008; Ling, 2008). Despite the fears of some, texting does not seem to result in poor language skills (Plester et al., 2008). Rather the majority of studies show that it encourages written communication.

Multimedia and internet uses. Recently, mobile phones have evolved into highly capable multimedia devices. So-called smart phones (e.g. the iPhone, Android phones) now come equipped with a camera for snapping photos or recording videos, applications for music and video playback, mobile games and an internet browser similar in capability to those found on the personal computer. Different networked apps (built-in or user added) provide youth with tools for social interaction and sharing multimedia content, e.g. Facebook, Skype, and Twitter. While the multimedia and internet uses are undoubtedly a main motivation for the rapid rise of smart phones, little research has yet been published on the topic.

The social effects of mobile telephony

The social uses of the mobile phone among children and particularly teens are also associated with broader social issues, the most important of which we list here.

Social cohesion. The mobile phone facilitates adolescents' contact with one another, through both instrumental and expressive uses. The sum of these many small communications is to form and strengthen the links in their social networks. The circle of friends with whom teens text and call, however, is rather small. Half of all calls and texts go to a select group of only 5–8 persons (Ling et al., 2011).

Social exclusion. The flipside of the connectivity and social cohesion afforded by the mobile phone is that its use may be a source of social exclusion for those who do not master the technology or cannot afford it. As the mobile phone has become ubiquitous to the point of being a taken-for-granted social fact in the lives of the large majority of the population in many societies, lack of access to the technology may become a serious social impediment (Castells et al., 2007, p. 256).

Emancipation. The mobile phone has changed the way that teens become emancipated from their parents (Clark 2013). The mobile phone allows teens freedom from their parents' surveillance and privacy in making and receiving calls and texts. It is a conditional freedom however (Haddon, 2000), since parents can call their child via the mobile phone whenever there is a need to, for example to remind them of an unfinished chore (Ling, 2007). Thus, the mobile phone is an arena for the negotiation of dependence and independence between young people and their parents.

Problematic issues

It is possible to adopt a generally positive gloss associated with the use of mobile communication. This, however, is not the whole story. Mobile telephony has also contributed to different nefarious activities.

Mobile phones in the public sphere. At the broadest, and perhaps the most innocent level mobile phone use is often linked with disruption of the public sphere (Ling, 1997). It can ring at inopportune moments and the person receiving the call can be guilty of discussing inappropriate, private or perhaps trivial themes for all to hear (Haddon, 2000; Monk et al., 2004).

Money use. Another issue that can be difficult and a potential cause for conflict in the family is teens' use of money for mobile telephony. Many children and teens have either a set number of minutes or texts they can use or they have a prepaid subscription that prevents them from overusing their phones (Lenhart et al., 2010). The cost of sending and receiving data (and the cost of buying a smart phone) also limits the use of the mobile internet.

Sexual uses and sexting. The diffusion of camera phones has led to the practice of sexting (a portmanteau of sex and texting). Sexting is the practice of using the mobile phone to send sexually suggestive materials such as nude or partially nude photos or video. Sexting has, in some cases, become a part of teen dating/courting (Lenhart et al., 2010). Lenhart in a study of sexting among 12–17-year-old teens in the US found that 15 percent had received such "sexts" while 4 percent admitted to sending them (2009). Livingstone et al. in a pan-European study using a broader definition of sexting (where sexting can occur on other platforms than the mobile phone, can be text rather than images and video, and is not necessarily self-produced) found that 15 percent of 11–16-year-olds have received material from their peers that was seen as sexual using this definition (Livingstone et al., 2011, p. 7). The same study found that 3 percent of the 9–16-year-olds had seen sexual images on their mobile phone in the past 12 months (Livingstone et al., 2011, p. 50).

The taking and exchange of sexually suggestive pictures can be the source of trouble. If there is improper pressure or if the trust between partners is broken and the sexting material is shared with outsiders to the relationship, sexting becomes a problem. The individual can lose control over the circulation of the material and, in some cases, can be publicly shamed. A related issue is that teens who record sexual behavior on their mobile phones, showing themselves or others under the age of majority, may be considered producers of child pornography with severe legal problems as a consequence (Xiaolu, 2010).

Much of the media attention towards sexting has focused on the negative aspects of the practice in a "burgeoning moral panic" (Chalfen, 2010, p. 350). However, recent research has pointed to mobile phones and their content also being just another venue for youth to use in developing a gendered (and sexual) identity (Bond, 2010; Schulz, 2012).

Mobile bullying. For children and teens who become the object of bullying, the direct access provided by the mobile phone can become an intractable problem. The child or teen who is bullied via the mobile phone is never outside the reach of his or her tormenters who can call and send messages at any time (Smith and Slonje, 2010, p. 259). Further, the lack of direct feedback in texting (due to the reduced interpersonal cues mentioned previously) may make the consequences less clear for the bully, and make cyberbullying easier (Smith and Slonje, 2010, p. 259). Livingstone et al. in a pan-European study found that 1 percent of the 9–10-year-olds, 2 percent of the 11–12-year-olds, 3 percent of the 13–14-year-olds and 6 percent of the 15–16-year-olds had been bullied by "mobile phone calls, texts or image/video texts" in the past 12 months (2011, p. 62).

Distracted driving. Many teens pride themselves on the ability to multitask (Foehr, 2006). Research has shown, however, that multitasking can negatively affect the efficiency of carrying out individual tasks (Blakemore and Choudhury, 2006). While some teenage drivers may feel that they can command a motor vehicle adequately while texting at the same time, this is a grave misconception. Indeed, distracted driving as a result of texting is perhaps one of the most dangerous dimensions of mobile communication (Strayer et al., 2006).

Radiation. Though we do not discuss it here, there is a major, and largely inconclusive discussion regarding the effects of electromagnetic radiation from mobile phones. This is a medical discussion that is beyond the limits of this article.

The future of mobile communication

Since the mid 1990s the mobile phone has developed a well established place in children's and teens' lives in many countries. The technology, however, has not stood still. Mobile devices have gained functionality including cameras, music and video players, internet browsers, terminals for social network sites such as Facebook and a host of other functions. Increasingly, the mobile internet and special purpose apps are opening up other functionality. Cloud computing, access to social network sites and the like mean that the role of the personal computer is being challenged by the highly portable mobile phone. In this guise, the individual can upload a photo of their new boy/girl friend to their Facebook account only seconds after their first kiss. Likewise they can tell their circle of friends about the break-up just as quickly. Beyond this, newer mobile computing devices such as tablets are changing the way that young people consume news, watch television, interact with friends, and consume a wide variety of goods and services.

SEE ALSO in this volume chapter by Mesch and chapter by Ribak.

References

Baron, N. (2008). *Always On: Language in an online and mobile world*. Oxford: Oxford University Press.

Blakemore, S.-J. and Choudhury, S. (2006). Development of the adolescent brain: implications for executive function and social cognition. *Journal of Child Psychology and Psychiatry*, 47(3/4), 296–312.

Bond, E. (2010). The mobile phone = bike shed? Children, sex and mobile phones. *New Media & Society*, 13(4), 587–604.

Castells, M., Fernández-Ardèvol, M., Linchuan, J. Q. and Sey, A. (2007). *Mobile Communication and Society*. Cambridge, MA: MIT Press

Chalfen, R. (2010). Commentary sexting as adolescent social communication. *Journal of Children & Media*, 4(3), 350–54. doi:10.1080/17482798.2010.486144

Clark, Lynn Schofield. (2013). *The Parent App: Understanding Families in the Digital Age*. Oxford: Oxford University Press.

Cohen, A., Lemish, D. and Schejter, A. M. (Eds). (2007). *The Wonder Phone in the Land of Miracles: Mobile telephony in Israel*. Cresskill, NJ: Hampton Press.

Davie, R., Panting, C. and Charlton, T. (2004). Mobile phone ownership and usage among pre-adolescents. *Telematics and Informatics, 21*(4), 359–73.

Ellwood-Clayton, B. (2003). Virtual strangers: Young love and texting in the Filipino archipelago of cyberspace. In K. Nyiri (Ed.), *Mobile Democracy: Essays on Society, Self and Politics*. Vienna: Passagen Verlag, pp. 35–45.

Fine, G. A. (2004). Adolescence as cultural toolkit: High school debate and the repertoires of childhood and adulthood. *The Sociological Quarterly, 45*(1), 1–20.

Foehr, U. G. (2006). *Media Multitasking among American Youth: Prevalence, predictors and pairings*. Henry J. Kaiser Family Foundation.

Green, N. and Haddon, L. (2009). *Mobile Communications*. Oxford: Berg.

Green, N. and Smith, S. (2004). "A spy in your pocket"? Monitoring and regulation in mobile technologies. *Surveillance & Society, 1*(4), 573–87.

Grinter, R. and Eldridge, M. (2001). y do tngrs luv 2 txt msg? In W. Prinz, Y. Jarke, K. Rogers, K. Schmidt and V. Wulf (Eds), *Proceedings of the Seventh European Conference on Computer-Supported Cooperative Work ECSCW '01*, Bonn, Germany. Dordech, Netherlands: Kluwer, pp. 219–38.

Haddon, L. (2000). The social consequences of mobile telephony: Framing questions. In R. Ling and K. Thrane (Eds), *Sosiale konsekvenser av mobiletelefoni: proceedings fra et seminar om samfunn, barn og mobile telefoni*. Kjeller: Telenor FoU, pp. 2–7.

Hijazi-Omari, H. and Ribak, R. (2008). Playing with fire: On the domestication of the mobile phone among Palestinian teenage girls in Israel. *Information, Communication & Society, 11*(2), 149–66. doi:10.1080/13691180801934099

Ito, M. (2001). Mobile phones, Japanese youth and the re-placement of social contact. Boston. Retrieved from http://www.itofisher.com/PEOPLE/mito/Ito.4S2001.mobile.pdf

Ito, M., Baumer, S., Bittani, M., Boyd, D. M., Cody, R., Herr-Stephenson, B., Horst, H. A., et al. (2010). *Hanging Out, Messing Around, and Geeking out – Kids Living and Learning with New Media*. Cambridge MA: MIT Press.

Johnsen, T. (2003). The social context of the mobile phone use of Norwegian teens. In L. Fortunati, J. E. Katz and R. Riccini (Eds), *Mediating the Human Body: Technology, Communication and Fashion*. London: Lawrence Earlbaum, pp. 161–70.

Kasesniemi, E.-L. and Rautiainen, P. (2002). Mobile culture of children and teenagers in Finland. In J. E. Katz and M. Aakhus (Eds), *Perpetual Contact: Mobile communication, private talk, public performance*. Cambridge: Cambridge University Press, pp. 170–92.

Lenhart, A. (2009). Teens and sexting. *A Pew Internet & American Life Project Report, Retrieved July 4*, 2010.

Lenhart, A., Ling, R., Campbell, S. and Purcell, K. (2010). *Teens and Mobile Phones*. Washington, D.C.: Pew Research Center.

Leung, L. and Wei, R. (1999). Who are the mobile phone have-nots? Influences and consequences. *New Media & Society, 1*(2), 209–26.

Ling, R. (2012). *Taken for Grantedness*. Cambridge, MA: MIT Press.

Ling, R. (1997). "One can talk about common manners!": The use of mobile telephones in inappropriate situations. In L. Haddon (Ed.), *Themes in Mobile Telephony Final Report of the COST 248 Home and Work group*. Stockholm: Telia.

Ling, R. (2001). *Adolescent Girls and Young Adult Men: Two sub-cultures of the mobile telephone* (No. R 34/2001). Kjeller: Telenor R&D.

Ling, R. (2004). *The Mobile Connection*. San Francisco: Morgan Kaufman.

Ling, R. (2005). The socio-linguistics of SMS: An analysis of SMS use by a random sample of Norwegians. In R. Ling and P. Pedersen (Eds), *Mobile Communications: Renegotiation of the social sphere*. London: Springer, pp. 335–49.

Ling, R. (2007). Children, youth and mobile communication. *Journal of Children and Media, 1*(1), 60–67.

Ling, R. (2008). *New Tech, New Ties: How mobile communication is reshaping social cohesion*. Cambridge: MIT Press.

Ling, R. (2009). Mobile communication and teen emancipation. In G. Goggin and L. Hjorth (Eds), *Mobile Technologies: From telecommunications to media*. New York: Routledge, pp. 50–61.

Ling, R. and Yttri, B. (2002). Hyper-coordination via mobile phones in Norway. In J. E. Katz and M. Aakhus (Eds), *Perpetual Contact: Mobile communication, private talk, public performance*. Cambridge: Cambridge University Press, pp. 139–69.

Ling, R., Bertel, T. F. and Sundsøy, P. R. (2011). The socio-demographics of texting: An analysis of traffic data. *New Media & Society*. doi:10.1177/1461444811412711

Livingstone, S., Haddon, L., Görzig, A. and Ólafsson, K. (2011). *Risks and Safety on the Internet – the perspective of European children*. The London School of Economics and Political Science.

Madell, D. E. and Muncer, S. J. (2007). Control over social interactions: An important reason for young people's use of the internet and mobile phones for communication? *CyberPsychology and Behavior, 10*(1), 137–40.

Matsuda, M. (2005). Mobile communication and selective sociality. In M. Ito, D. Okabe and M. Matsuda (Eds), *Personal, Portable, Pedestrian. Mobile Phones in Japanese Life*. Cambridge: MIT Press, pp. 123–42.

Miyata, K., Boase, J. and Wellman, B. (2008). Handbook of mobile communication studies. In J. Katz (Ed.), *The Social Effects of Keitai and Personal Computer E-Mail in Japan*. Cambridge, MA: MIT Press, pp. 209–22.

Monk, A., Carroll, J., Parker, S. and Blythe, M. (2004). Why are mobile phones annoying? *Behavior and Information Technology, 23*(1), 33–41.

Oksman, V. and Rautianen, P. (2003). "Perhaps it is a body part": How the mobile telephone became an organic part of the everyday lives of Finnish children and teenagers. In J. E. Katz (Ed.), *Machines that Become Us*. New Brunswik, NJ: Transaction, pp. 293–308.

Palfrey, J. (2008). *Child Safety & Online Technologies: Final report of the internet safety technical task force to the Multi-State Working Group on Social Networking of State Attorneys General of the United States*. Cambridge, MA: Berkman Center for Internet & Society at Harvard University. Retrieved from http://cyber.law. harvard.edu/pubrelease/isttf/

Plester, B., Wood, C. and Bell, V. (2008). Txt msg n school literacy: does texting and knowledge of text abbreviations adversely affect children's literacy attainment? *Literacy, 42*(3), 137–44.

Schulz, I. (2012). Visual mobile phone content and developmental challenges. In C. Martin and T. Pape (Eds), *Images in Mobile Communication*. Wiesbaden: VS Verlag für Sozialwissenschaften, pp. 41–55. Retrieved from http://www.springerlink.com/ content/h3x3451504282g60/export-citation/

Smith, P. K. and Slonje, R. (2010). Cyberbullying – the nature and extent of a new kind of bullying, in and out of school. In S. R. Jimerson, S. M. Swearer and D. L. Espelange (Eds), *Handbook of Bullying in Schools: an International Perspective*. New York: Routledge.

Strayer, D. L., Drews, F. A. and Crouch, D. J. (2006). A comparison of the cell phone driver and the drunk driver. *Human Factors, 48*(2), 381–92.

Vaage, O. (2010). *Mediabruks undersøkelse, 2009*. Oslo: Statistics Norway.

Xiaolu, Z. (2010). Charging children with child pornography – Using the legal system to handle the problem of "sexting." *Computer Law & Security Review, 26*(3), 251–59. doi:10.1016/j.clsr.2010.03.005

16

CHILDREN'S MUSIC CULTURE: COMMERCE, TECHNOLOGY, AND TRADITION

Tyler Bickford

Music is an important part of the social, emotional, and political lives of children and adolescents. Teenagers have long been the primary audience for popular music, and musical media for children of all ages have expanded greatly in the last generation. Children's role as a music audience is a key aspect of their expanding public status as consumers, and music listening is a key practice for working through social relationships with peers and articulating identities around gender, race, class, and sexuality. Children integrate musical media into their long-standing cultural traditions, such as handclapping games and play with toys, and products from music and consumer industries are designed to cultivate these sensibilities. This chapter provides an overview of how these issues have been addressed in the US and Europe by scholars from ethnomusicology, music education, popular music, media and cultural studies, and communication, while focusing on recent technological and commercial developments that point to important changes for children's status in public culture. This chapter does not address children's musical culture in non-Western contexts.

Children's commercial music industry in the US

The US commercial children's music industry has grown dramatically in the last few years, but these recent trends build on a long history. Predating the recording industry, music publishers in Europe and the United States commissioned original music and printed and distributed collections of music for children. As today, commercial music for children was part of a larger consumer ecology that, for instance, associated children and music with holidays like Christmas (see Kok, 2008, for a discussion of just one such example). Recordings for children were among the very earliest music recordings sold, and they were often cross-marketed with toy phonographs and illustrated books (Tillson, 1994, 1995). In addition to such consumer-oriented products, record labels marketed educational recordings (largely classical music curated for "music appreciation" curricula) to schools and music educators (Dunham, 1961). In the post-war era, more explicitly commercial music, tied to animated Disney movies and television shows, became popular. In parallel, independent labels with ties to the folk-revival movement began producing frequently anti-commercial music for children, and the folk-singing style of artists such as Tom Glazer and Raffi came to characterize the genre of children's music (Bonner, 2008). In the 1990s Disney's animated musicals had a resurgence, and the 1996 launch of Radio Disney, an FM station programmed with music from young mainstream recording artists as well as child-friendly "oldies" and novelty songs, pointed to that company's renewed commitment to cultivating child music audiences. By the next decade Disney was developing its own artists and releasing pop music—not just musical theater numbers—on its own labels, and its cable TV station The Disney Channel became a key site for launching new musical offerings. While children's media companies like Nickelodeon and Nintendo successfully cultivated the niche kids' market in the 1980s and 1990s, in the last decade pop music made for kids has taken a step further, and broken through into broader commercial dominance. One week early in 2006, for example, the three top-selling records on the Billboard sales charts were children's albums (Levine, 2006), and the top-selling album in the US for the entire year was the soundtrack to the massively popular Disney Channel original movie *High School Musical.*

Traditional children's music—in the folk-revival style, using simple acoustic arrangements and emphasizing singable songs—has grown along with popular music genres for children. A new generation of children's music artists, such as Laurie Berkner and Dan Zanes, have achieved widespread success producing recordings in this tradition, which maintain the basic characteristics of the tradition popularized by singers such as Raffi, but are frequently described as being more sophisticated and adult-friendly. To some extent these artists achieve adult tolerance by doubling down on the folk music and roots-rock elements that have characterized children's music for half a century, as folk music provides a bridge between musical characteristics that are seen as appealing to children and those that upper-middle-class white adults are disposed to see as markers of authentic and legitimate cultural traditions. The schlocky and saccharine style of acts such as Barney and the Australian group The Wiggles, popular in the 1990s, is increasingly uncommon in the US even in music for very young children.

A key dynamic in the changing music industry for children is the emergence of the demographic marker "tween," describing children especially from 9–12 years old, but which reaches out to include children as young as 4 and as old as 15 (Cook and Kaiser, 2004). (The term highlights the status of children this age as be*tween* childhood and adolescence.) "Tween" music is freed from some of the "childish" elements of music for young children, and stylistically resembles mainstream pop music, though with somewhat less emphasis on overtly sexual themes (but still emphatically retaining pop's heteronormative focus on romantic love). The age ambiguity of tween music makes room for child-oriented artists to appeal to a wider listenership. Artists such as Justin Bieber and Taylor Swift, who became celebrities as young teenagers and continue to be associated with young audiences, now command much broader audiences and have become uniquely successful figures in the popular music industry. At times this leads to visible conflict between artists associated with children and "mainstream" artists, such as a moment onstage at MTV's 2009 Video Music Awards in which prominent rapper Kanye West interrupted Taylor Swift's speech accepting an award for best music video, and was loudly criticized by many in language that emphasized Swift's relative youth and corresponding vulnerability, while other children's media figures explicitly expressed support and solidarity with Swift and against West.

In addition to tween musicians appealing to older audiences, the tween music industry makes mainstream popular music available to children. In part this is through original products from artists such as Swift, Bieber, and the various Disney acts, which direct music with professional songwriting and high production values toward children, whose media have long been characterized by low budgets and indifferent production. In parallel, brands such as Kidz Bop and Radio Disney (mentioned above) market mainstream popular music directly to children, curating it moderately to address adult concerns about inappropriate content. Kidz Bop re-records Top 40 pop songs with choruses of children singing along to the choruses and hooks, and occasionally with slightly altered lyrics. Songs on their CD compilations frequently appear within months of the original song's popularity, and present such music, which parents might normally be disinclined to purchase for their children, as legitimate and appropriate for children. From 2002–5, in the years leading up to the release of *High School Musical* and other original tween acts, Kidz Bop was the top-selling children's music act, and in 2005 and 2006 had records among the ten highest-selling albums in any category (for an overview and theoretical account of the contemporary tween music industry see Bickford, 2012). While international data is limited, the US culture industries are a major exporter of media, and popular music for children is no exception. Many of the US acts described in this section are popular especially in Europe, and tour around the world.

Children as music audiences

Teenagers and adolescents have long been the primary audiences for "mainstream" popular music, which remains true today. There is significant overlap between children and teenagers in the audiences for acts like Taylor Swift, and in many cases high school and even college students in 2011 (as this chapter was being written) would have been enthusiastic fans of tween music acts in 2006 and 2007, and continued to follow stars like Miley Cyrus or *High School Musical*'s Zac Efron as they take on more mature personas and roles. But while some boundary-crossing clearly happens, distinctions based on age identities are particularly salient for school-aged people, and in my research and teaching I often find that explicit denunciations of child- or tween-oriented artists are a common discursive technique for expressing maturity and rejecting markers of immaturity. Similarly, the hyper-sexualization and other explicit themes of mainstream popular music may appeal to older teenagers in part because they express a break from the largely adult-imposed limits of "appropriateness" that children and pre-adolescents bear.

A generation ago children in the US and Europe could be seen to move through age-graded musical preferences, with the youngest expressing interest in children's music (Raffi etc.) and classical music, pre-adolescents preferring popular music in general, and adolescents eventually settling into preferences for specific genres of popular music (von Feilitzen and Roe, 1990). A move from children's and classical genres to pop is correlated with movement away from parental influence, as children report less interest in genres their parents prefer (Christenson, 1994). My own ethnographic research on children's popular music consumption in a small community in the northeastern United States bears this point out in its broad outlines, but suggests that musical taste remains a space for expressions of parental affiliations among middle-school age children (Bickford, 2011). Such children's expressed *favorite* genre is frequently from mainstream popular music, but like anyone kids' tastes are not monolithic; many have strong secondary interests in genres like classic rock (bands such as AC/DC or Led Zeppelin), and enthusiastically point out that their enjoyment of such music is learned from and connects them to their parents.

More recent data on large-scale trends is limited, but as discussed in the previous section, the range of pop music offerings oriented to children has expanded significantly in the last decade, so kids likely become aware of and interested in such genres of pop music at an earlier age. (Even 6- and 7-year-old kids sometimes reject music by groups such as The Wiggles as "baby music," in an expression of maturity not unlike older youth's rejection of tween pop.) If tween pop is increasingly popular in middle childhood, it is possible that the standard progression from children's music, to generic pop, to specific genres has changed so that tween pop either replaces the generic pop phase, or pushes it back, with potential implications for the timing when teenagers settle into specific genre preferences. A 15-year-old who is primarily interested in the Jonas Brothers or Justin Bieber may be following a somewhat different track than the one seen by previous researchers.

Music's influence on children and young people's attitudes, behavior, and development is the subject of frequent adult and scholarly concern, especially for genres of music associated with racial minorities or counter/subcultures. In addition to age, musical preferences are significantly correlated with gender and race (Roberts and Christenson, 2000), and to the extent that music listening habits are correlated with violent or misogynistic behavior, it is difficult to sort out correlation from causation. Experimental studies (in which researchers ask subjects to listen to certain types of music and measure their aggression or other characteristics within a relatively short time frame, and against a control group who listen to other genres of music) suggest that there are some measurable short-term effects of heavy metal listening on young men's expression of aggressive and misogynistic traits (Roberts et al., 2003). Studying the larger-scale effects of sustained listening across time in an experimentally rigorous way is not feasible (research subjects are unlikely to be willing or able to change their listening habits in randomized and controllable ways, for instance), and with issues such as personality and social behavior music is necessarily one smallish influence, and confounding effects proliferate.

In addition to experimental studies of "media effects," ethnographic studies of the social and cultural contexts of children's music listening demonstrate that young people's music listening is embedded in meaningful social relationships. For children from immigrant families in the US, for instance, the "mainstream" music heard on Top 40 radio stations and emphasized among peers in school settings can become a powerful marker of unmarked white middle-class "American" identities (Minks, 1999). For pre-teen and teenage girls, "serious play" with popular music in bedrooms and other spaces provides opportunities to develop understandings of their gender and sexual identities in wider contexts (Baker, 2004a, 2004b; Willet, 2011). For very young children, music listening provides soundtracks for play, scripts for understanding emotions, and opportunities for working through relationships with peers (Vestad, 2010).

Musical media and children's own cultural traditions

Children's traditional culture, including playground songs and toys, increasingly incorporates musical media, and elements of these traditions are increasingly taken up in mainstream popular music. Children's handclapping and singing games, for instance, are a classic topic of folkloristic inquiry. These traditions are still practiced in playgrounds around the world, and children incorporate textual and musical elements from advertisements, television shows, popular songs, and the internet into their playground songs (Grugeon, 2001; Harwood, 1994; Marsh, 1999). Children's handclapping games also become educational media, as educators and folklorists collect and distribute collections for use in the classroom, and these games are themselves a form of media that creates opportunities for transnational and cross-cultural interaction and understanding among children around the world (Marsh, 2008).

Like handclapping games, play with physical toys is a key element of children's traditional culture, and musical media for children are increasingly embedded in toys to appeal to children, facilitating children's integration of musical media into their own play practices. Electronic toys for young children commonly include musical elements, often in the form of snippets that play in response to an infant or young child's action. The music in such toys is often in the classical style, reflecting the association of such genres with young children, mentioned above, and pieces like Rossini's *William Tell Overture* seem to have become canonical in these settings (Young, 2008). Older children's uses of portable music devices like MP3 players often resemble toy-play too, as kids decorate their devices, trade and share them, and tinker with their physical form (Bickford, 2013). Musical media are also a very common part of children's physical and kinesthetic play, accompanying dancing or games like musical chairs (Young and Gillen, 2007).

Elements from children's cultural traditions also filter into mainstream popular media in various ways. Textual elements from children's musical games, such as "Down Down Baby," are found in mass media products like the 1988 movie "Big" and the 2000 song "Country Grammar" by rapper Nelly (Marsh, 2006). Characters and themes from children's literature and nursery rhymes can be found in mainstream popular music throughout its history (Cooper, 1989). And it is increasingly common for mainstream artists, such as Nicki Minaj and Cee Lo Green, to dress in childlike colorful and playful costumes (that are doll-like; and one performance by Green included accompaniment by The Muppets) that increase their appeal to children, even if kids are not the primary audience for such music.

Music and digital media

Digital technologies have created new contexts for children and young people to engage with musical media. In fact music and young people frequently figure centrally in discourses of technological change. Napster, a 1990s file-sharing service on which young people would exchange music, was a prominent early example of panicked discourses about challenges the internet might pose for traditional media industries. File-sharing discourses participate in common anxious and celebratory tropes of children as both problems and sources of promise (Stephens, 1995), framing children and youth in terms of theft, piracy, and the break-down of legal order, but also in terms of sociality, sharing, cooperation, and collaboration. In the era since courts ordered Napster to shut down, social network sites like Facebook that appeal to youth encourage sharing information about listening habits among friends as a form of social advertising.

Portable music devices like MP3 players are also prominent in discussions of technological change and are commonly associated with young people. Apple's iPod is an icon of new media, and commentators often link the iPod to young people as a marker of their identities as "digital natives." In fact, the iPod is such a prominent image in these discourses that nearly every study of young people and digital media mentions the device in the introduction (e.g., Palfrey and Gasser 2008; Ito et al., 2009; Montgomery 2007). Palfrey and Gasser, for instance, define digital natives as "those who wear the earbuds of an iPod on the subway to their first job, not those of us who still remember how to operate a Sony Walkman" (2008, p. 4). Interestingly, none of these studies builds on this initial reference to the iPod and youth in the body of the study, ignoring iPod practices in favor of discussions of the internet and mobile phones.

So music is associated prominently in images of youth and digital technology, but young people's musical practices are largely understudied. What studies of youth and digital music have been done suggest that music-editing software affords young people increasing abilities to produce music, while technological complexity encourages collaboration, and online social networks create opportunities for distribution and public performances (Mahendran in Ito et al., 2009, pp. 270–72). My own research on children's uses of MP3 players demonstrates that physical interaction and face-to-face sociability are key values that structure children's portable music listening, and common practices like sharing earbuds so that two friends can listen together create new contexts for intimacy in the joint consumption of music (Bickford, in press). In such ways, children and teenagers' uses of portable musical media are dramatically different than the isolated, cocooning practices that scholars have found among adult users of similar technologies (Bull, 2008; Ito et al., 2008). But at the same time, such an emphasis on face-to-face sharing is perhaps of a kind with the importance of real-world social relation-ships to young people's uses of social network sites and other information communication technologies.

Conclusion

Children's music culture is thoroughly intertwined with all aspects of children's media culture. Children's commercial music is among the most visible elements of children's expanding consumer role and the dramatic changes this role has had for the entertainment and consumer industries. Music is an important element connecting children's long-held cultural traditions with an ever-changing mass media and technological environment. As audiences for music, children locate themselves in increasingly powerful positions in mass culture, and in everyday listening practices they express personal investments and organize relations among friends and peers. Music is a key element linking youth and technological change, while children's uses of new technologies emphasize their existing social relationships and cultural traditions. Music often goes unnoticed in studies of media, but music is among the most important and meaningful forms of media in children and adolescents' lives, and links children's small-scale face-to-face sociality to national and transnational configurations of commerce and mass media.

SEE also in this volume chapter by Mesch and chapter by Lim.

References

Baker, S. (2004a). "It's *not* about Candy": Music, sexiness, and girls' serious play in after school care. *International Journal of Cultural Studies*, 7(2), 197–212.

——(2004b). Pop in(to) the bedroom: Popular music in pre-teen girls' bedroom culture. *European Journal of Cultural Studies*, 7(1), 75–93.

Bickford, T. (2011). *Children's music, MP3 players, and expressive practices at a Vermont elementary school: Media consumption as social organization among schoolchildren.* Doctoral dissertation, Columbia University.

——(2012). The new "tween" music industry: The Disney Channel, Kidz Bop, and an emerging childhood counterpublic. *Popular Music*, *31*(3), 417–36.

——(2013). Tinkering and tethering in the material culture of children's MP3 players. In P. S. Campbell and T. Wiggins (Eds), *The Oxford handbook of children's musical cultures.* New York: Oxford University Press, pp. 527–42.

——(In press). Earbuds are good for sharing: Children's headphones as social media at a Vermont school. In J. Stanyek and S. Gopinath (Eds), *The Oxford handbook of mobile music studies.* New York: Oxford University Press.

Bonner, D. (2008). *Revolutionizing children's records: The Young People's Records and Children's Record Guild Series, 1946–1977.* Lanham, MD: Scarecrow Press.

Bull, M. (2008). *Sound moves: iPod culture and urban experience.* New York: Routledge.

Christenson, P. G. (1994). Childhood patterns of music uses and preferences. *Communication Reports*, 7(2), 136–44.

Cook, D. T. and Kaiser, S. B. (2004). Betwixt and be Tween: Age ambiguity and the sexualization of the female consuming subject. *Journal of Consumer Culture*, 4(2), 203–27.

Cooper, B. L. (1989). Rhythm 'n' rhymes: Character and theme images from children's literature in contemporary recordings, 1950–85. *Popular Music and Society*, 13(1), 53–71.

Dunham, R. L. (1961). *Music appreciation in the public schools of the United States, 1897–1930.* PhD dissertation, University of Michigan.

von Feilitzen, C. and Roe, K. (1990). Children and music: An exploratory study. In K. Roe and U. Carlsson (Eds), *Popular music research: An anthology from NORDICOM-Sweden.* Göteborg: Department of Political Science, University of Göteborg, pp. 53–70.

Grugeon, E. (2001). "We like singing the Spice Girl songs … and we like Tig and Stuck in the Mud": Girls' traditional games on two playgrounds. In J. Bishop and M. Curtis (Eds), *Play today in the primary school playground.* Buckingham: Open University Press, pp. 98–114.

Harwood, E. (1994). Miss Lucy meets Dr. Pepper: Mass media and children's traditional playground song and chant. In H. Lees (Ed.), *Musical connections: Tradition and change.* Auckland: International Society for Music Education, pp. 187–93.

Ito, M., Baumer, S., Bittani, M., boyd, d., Cody, R., Herr-Stephenson, B., et al. (2009). *Hanging out, messing around, geeking out: Living and learning with new media.* Cambridge, MA: MIT Press.

Ito, M., Okabe, D. and Anderson, K. (2008). Portable objects in three global cities: The personalization of urban places. In R. Ling and S. W. Campbell (Eds), *The reconstruction of space and time: Mobile communication practices.* Piscataway, NJ: Transaction, pp. 67–87.

Kok, R.-M. (2008). Negotiating children's music: New evidence for Schumann's "charming" late style. *Acta Musicologica, 80*(1), 99–128.

Levine, R. (2006, March 6). The top-selling tunes on Billboard, sung by children for children, *New York Times.* Retrieved November 8, 2011, from http://www.nytimes.com/ 2006/03/06/business/06music.html

Marsh, K. (1999). Mediated orality: The role of popular music in the changing tradition of children's musical play. *Research Studies in Music Education, 13*(1), 2–12.

——(2006). Cycles of appropriation in children's musical play: Orality in the age of reproduction. *World of Music, 48*(1), 9–32.

——(2008). *The musical playground: Global tradition and change in children's songs and games.* New York: Oxford University Press.

Minks, A. (1999). Growing and grooving to a steady beat: Pop music in fifth-graders' social lives. *Yearbook for Traditional Music, 31*, 77–101.

Montgomery, K. C. (2007). *Generation digital: Politics, commerce, and childhood in the age of the internet.* Cambridge, MA: MIT Press.

Palfrey, J. and Gasser, U. (2008). *Born digital: Understanding the first generation of digital natives.* New York: Basic Books.

Roberts, D. F. and Christenson, P. G. (2000). Popular music in childhood and adolescence. In D. G. Singer and J. L. Singer (Eds), *Handbook of children and the media.* Thousand Oaks, CA: Sage, pp. 395–413.

Roberts, D. F., Christenson, P. G. and Gentile, D. A. (2003). The effects of violent music on children and adolescents. In D. A. Gentile (Ed.), *Media violence and children: A complete guide for parents and professionals.* Westport, CT: Praeger, pp. 153–70.

Stephens, S. (1995). Children and the politics of culture in "late capitalism." In S. Stephens (Ed.), *Children and the politics of culture.* Princeton: Princeton University Press, pp. 3–48.

Tillson, D. R. (1994). Children's musical play: The role of the phonograph. *The Ephemera Journal, 6*, 86–98.

——(1995). The golden age of children's records. *Antique Phonograph News* (March–April), 3–6, 12.

Vestad, I. L. (2010). To play a soundtrack: How children use recorded music in their everyday lives. *Music Education Research, 12*(3), 243–55.

Willet, R. (2011). An ethnographic study of preteen girls' play with popular music on a school playground. *Journal of Children and Media, 5*(4), 341–57.

Young, S. (2008). Lullaby light shows: Everyday musical experience among under-two-year-olds. *International Journal of Music Education, 26*(1), 33–46.

Young, S. and Gillen, J. (2007). Toward a revised understanding of young children's musical activities: Reflections from the "Day in the Life" project. *Current Musicology, 84*, 79–99.

17

CHILDREN AND CONSUMER CULTURE

Kara Chan

Children represent three markets: a primary market with their own income to spend, an influencer market that gives direction to parental purchases, and a future market for all goods and services (McNeal, 1992). The parent–child relationship in Western societies changes from authoritative to mutual understanding. Children's voices are taken seriously in family purchases (Valkenburg and Cantor, 2001).

The development of a children's consumer culture in the U.S.

The development of children as a consumer market in the United States can be traced to the period 1890 to 1940 (Leach, 1993a). As mass production of consumer goods outpaced consumer demand, marketers looked to children as a neglected demographic group at which they could target their products (Strasser, 1989). Social transformations including the democratization of middle-class family life, the increasing salience of children's peer relations and group activities, and growing regard for the legitimacy of children's self-expression convinced marketers that children were an important consumer market (Jacobson, 2008).

That market witnessed explosive growth in the variety and supply of children's toys and clothing (Leach, 1993a), the establishment of children and teens' toys and clothing sections in department stores (Cook, 2004), as well as mail-order catalogues (Jacobson, 2008), the allocation of retail space for children's playgrounds to attract shoppers (Leach, 1993a; 1993b), the development of personalized customer relationship programs for young consumers (Formanek-Brunell, 1993), the publication of consumer magazines for children and teens (Jacobson, 2004), and the promotion of products at schools through commercialized teaching materials (Manning, 1999). To gain access to the parents, marketers in the early 1930s used visual images that idealized the companionate family and associated their products with children's developmental needs (Jacobson, 2008). Advertisers positioned themselves as friendly advisers that helped youth succeed in the trials of peer culture. Advertisers offered young people tips on impression management and immediate solutions to their concerns about personal appearance and popularity (Jacobson, 2004).

In the new media age, marketers gain access to the juvenile market using digital tools including buzz marketing, developing web sites for children and sponsoring trendsetters to influence discussions in chat rooms (Jones and Reid, 2010). The prevalence of media in children's bedrooms and the omnipresent images of consumer goods for children are influencing their perceptions of a good life and personal well-being (Jacobson, 2008).

The global toy market

Besides food and beverages, the first group of commercial products that a child comes into contact with is toys. Infants are introduced to stuffed animals and mobiles at the crib. Toddlers learn to touch, feel, and play with play items (McNeal, 1987). Toys are part of children's consumer culture as they are bought and consumed to display a certain lifestyle and identity (Bondebjerg and Golding, 2004). Playing is an integral part of childhood. Due to the marketing efforts of a small number of mega-corporations for toys, a child's form of play changes from a spontaneous and unsupervised form to a commercialized and branded form. This results in bigness and sameness in children's consumer culture (Schor, 2004).

The following paragraphs identify the trends of the global toy market and discuss its impacts on children's consumer culture. The toy market worldwide is estimated to have been worth about US$83 billion in 2010, an increase of 5 percent over the previous year (NPD Group, 2011). The United States remained the largest toy market with US$22 billion in sales, followed by Japan, China, the U.K., and France. Economic growth and the large child populations in those countries accounted for their market size. Toy sales in emerging markets including Brazil, Russia, India, and China grew 13 percent, more than double of the growth of the global toy market. Analysis of 1,477 items requested by U.S. children as holiday gifts reveals that the most frequently mentioned were Barbie dolls and Lego blocks. This indicates that the children's consumer culture is brand-oriented (Getzier, 2011).

Marketers often position themselves and their products as children's allies (Cook, 2007). They have adopted child empowerment discourse that values children not as a vulnerable audience susceptible to exploitation, but as a group of knowing, active consumers who exercise choice (Kunkle and Roberts, 1991). The child empowerment approach leads to positive identification with children and adopting their point of view (Cook, 2007). In ads for children's products, child empowerment is typically communicated through the use of language that addresses children directly as "you" or "you and your family." Children are typically in the foreground of the visuals, which encourage children to experience the products or services before their peers. Children are the presenters in the advertising stories (Gram, 2011).

Marketers involve children in the design and production of their products so as to recognize children's choices. For example, a candy producer allowed children to combine flavors in their own manner (Dahm, 2002). Internet technology has facilitated children's expressing their interests and choices in promotions through online platforms. Post-campaign studies have found that children participate with enthusiasm in such marketing efforts (Angrisani, 2002; Cuthbert, 2002).

The toy market witnessed a convergence of toy manufacturers, the media industry, and the high-tech industrial economy. Older children are now playing with mobile phones, the internet, and online games. So, the media becomes the toy. The children's consumer culture is becoming global as the media and the contents creation process is being globalized (Bondebjerg and Golding, 2004).

Children and youth market segments

The children and youth market is usually segmented by age, sex, and perhaps race or ethnicity (McGinnis et al., 2006). For example, the online Toys "R" Us shop uses eight age segments:

birth–12 months, 12–24 months, 2-year-olds, 3–4, 5–7, 8–11, 12–14, and "big kids" (Toys "R" Us, 2011). Marketing scholars and market research agencies have proposed alternative segmentations based on lifestyles, or the activities-interest-opinion framework (Wells and Tigert, 1971). Lauffer (2003) constructed four primary play dimensions of inner-directedness (playing alone), other-directedness (playing with others), playing in a reality context, and playing in a fantasy context. The four dimensions were used to define four discrete child mindsets: Achievers who were motivated by individual ability and success; Dreamers who were motivated by unstructured play and imagination; Leaders who were driven by goals and winning over peers; and Collaborators who enjoyed interaction with peers and cooperation in a group (Lauffer, 2003). Lauffer further proposed that a child's mindset is influenced by the dominant culture of their country (Lauffer, 2003).

Narang (2010) collected psychographic data from 264 respondents aged 16 to 26 in India using Kahle's (1983) consumption-related List of Values instrument. The data resulted in four clusters: Get-going Adopters who were extremely fond of company, enjoyed excitement, and wanted to enjoy life to the full; Inner Value-oriented Conservatives who possessed a well-defined internal set of religious values; Politics and Sports Enthusiasts who shared a keen interest in political activities and enjoyed various kinds of sports; and Independent Life Lovers who exhibited a strong liking for a lot of variety in their lives and were serious about arts and culture (Narang, 2010). Narang compared these results with findings from psychographic studies of Chinese adults (Ma, 2004), and of adults from Thailand, Malaysia, and The Philippines (Ewing et al., 1998). Much similarity was found, while the Politics and Sports Enthusiasts cluster was unique to Indian youth.

While such segmentations attempt to classify children and youth into meaningful groups, we should not forget the underlying commonality among all children and youth. The children and youth consumer culture demonstrates increasing similarity in terms of technology focus, a deep interest in the process of becoming who or what they will be in the future, being experience-driven, and a desire to get connected with peers in physical as well as virtual communities (Ekstrom and Tufte, 2007; Gram, 2011; Stock and Tupot, 2006).

Children today are active internet users as well as consumers, and marketers are developing internet strategies to engage children and youth. Children willingly play online games on brand websites, download commercials and jingles, seek solutions to games or puzzles on product packages, create their own versions of brand-related content, and enroll as members or friends of their favorite brands (Jones and Reid, 2010). Integrating interactive content with product promotions supported by cartoon spokesmen encourages young consumers to develop a strong and playful connection with a brand. In this way, brands have been successfully woven into the everyday life of the children and the youth that marketers are targeting (Chester and Montgomery, 2008).

Parents are aware of the symbolic meaning of consumption for children. They are eager to spend money on their children because they want them to have a sense of social belonging in terms of owning the right kinds of goods and living the right experiences. They worry that if their children do not have the right possessions they will look and feel abnormal (Pugh, 2009).

Consumption and identity

Children perceive toys as possessions. What they own tells who they are. When children in mainland China were asked to draw pictures about a child with a lot of toys and a child with few, the drawings and the subsequent interviews demonstrated that the children most often associated toys with fun and excitement. They also perceived that having the right toys would help them attract friends, be successful, and enjoy self-confidence. Older children had a more complex association between toys and social significance. They perceived that more toys could bring more fun and more friends, but at the same time could also trigger selfishness, envy, and arrogance. Older Chinese children believed strongly that having a lot of toys would have a negative impact on their schoolwork (Chan, 2005).

Brands are playing a role in defining, expressing, and communicating self-concepts among children and adolescents (Chaplin and John, 2005). A series of experiments with U.S. children and adolescents aged 8–18 found that self-brand connections developed with age. Children in middle childhood made a limited number of self-brand connections, and those connections were based mainly on concrete associations with the brands, such as owning the branded item. Adolescents demonstrated stronger self-brand connections, and those connections were based on abstract qualities of personality, user characteristics, or reference group affiliation (Chaplin and John, 2005). Children's immersive involvement with brands can affect them socially and emotionally, as well as leading to endorsement of materialistic values (Marshall, 2010).

The Disney brand

Children all over the world are consuming branded goods produced by the major toy and media companies. Is their similar relationship with the product resulting in homogeneity of consumer values? This section uses Disney as a case study to answer this question.

The renowned Disney brand is one of only two of the top ten global brands aimed primarily at children. McDonald's ranks no. 6 and Disney no. 9 (Interbrand, 2011). The Walt Disney Company is one of the world's largest media conglomerates (Siklos, 2009). Its promise of "magic and imagination" brought in net income of US$4.8 billion in 2011 (Oregon Public Broadcasting, 2011). Disney is a leader in film production, television, travel, publishing, and online media (Nigel Wright Consultancy Limited, 2011). It owns the ABC television network and cable networks such as the Disney Channel and ABC Family. It owns or licenses 14 theme parks, including its own parks in Los Angeles, Orlando, Tokyo, Paris, and Hong Kong (Nigel Wright Consultancy Limited, 2011). A sixth Disneyland is expected to open in Shanghai in 2016 (TravelChinaGuide, 2011). The five Disneyland parks in operation are estimated to attract 84 million visitors each year (TravelChinaGuide, 2011). Disney products are available in more than 220 Disney owned or licensed retail shops in North America, more than 100 shops in Europe, and 40 in Japan (Disney Consumer Products, 2011). The Disney online store sells toys, dolls, home decorations, "art works," and collectables, as well as theme park products to every corner of the world (Disney Store, 2011).

Some scholars have criticized Disney for its worldview and values, including distorted female images, and its potential negative impact on young children. For example, scholars comment that the female characters in Disney films are often weak, passive and highly dependent on the approval of (or even rescue by) the male characters (e.g., Bell et al., 1995; Kasturi 2002). Baker-Sperry (2007) analyzed the text of Disney's official *Cinderella* story book and found the following themes: romantic love at first sight, the expectation that the females and not the males would take up domestic work, magical transformation, rescuer and rescued roles, the importance of physical beauty, as well as the lack of a pivotal male role. Martin and Kazyak (2009) analyzed Disney's G-rated films and found that heterosexuality was favored through portraying heterosexual romantic love as powerful and transformative, as well as through different ways of depicting men's and women's bodies. The sexiness of feminine Disney characters was always defined by the gaze of masculine characters (Martin and Kazyak, 2009). Characters in Disney's stores are instrumental in children's learning of sex roles. Gender reception studies found that Disney fairy tales provided the child audience with the social meaning of romance and marriage (Baker-Sperry, 2007; Lee, 2008).

Wasko (2001) argued that Disney's extensive use of synergies such as licensing agreements for merchandise, vigilant protection of its copyright, and the straight control of its workforce helped to promote a deliberate and standardized vision of fantasy. However, its insistence on the commitment and sacrifice of workers in Disney theme parks and the extensive surveillance of park visitors were being criticized (Wasko, 2001).

Consumption of Disney products varies in different cultural contexts. Disney emphasizes fun and imagination, but it also pays attention to the needs and the cultural norms of the target market. In China, an emerging economy that places tremendous emphasis on education, Disney launched a chain of English language schools called Disney English. It was the first Western media company to operate a school in China (D'Altorio, 2010). There were 23 Disney English centers in China as of August 2011, and more were planned (Disney English, 2011). Chinese parents view English as a ticket to the world, and aspire to equip their children with fluent English as early in childhood as possible (The Economist, 2010). The strategy of positioning Disney products as educational tools helps Disney react to the stringent publishing rules and rampant infringement of intellectual piracy in China (D'Altorio, 2010). Because of China's restriction of foreign media, Disney was not able to start a television channel or distribute the full series of Disney movies (Areddy and Sanders, 2009). Thus, Disney English became an alternative for reaching child consumers and their parents. Chinese children attended Disney English classes as an after school activity. Disney characters, books, songs, TV shows, and movies are incorporated as teaching materials. Classrooms are even named after Disney movie characters. Students who perform well are rewarded with stationery, flash cards, and other items especially designed as incentives for the Chinese market (Areddy and Sanders, 2009). Parents trust the Disney brand because of its strong international image, and Disney English has developed an online "parent portal" to inform parents about the progress of their child and engage them in the learning process (Disney English, 2011). Parents are encouraged to log on to the portal to find ways to encourage their children to pick up the language (Areddy and Sanders, 2009). Chinese parents appreciate Disney English's ability to engage children in learning English in a fun way, perhaps triggering a passion for English (Xiudadad, 2009).

Previously, the success of Disney cartoons in China brought criticism of cultural imperialism (Mufson, 1996). For example, Chinese people were not happy with the portrayal of the national heroine Mulan in Disney's film (Liu, 2009). Today, some parents worry that the overemphasis on fun may erode Chinese children's commitment to the traditional virtues of hard work, discipline, and moral integrity (Mufson, 1996).

To conclude, children are recognized as important targets for commercial products and services. The development of the children's consumer market is sometimes criticized as the commercialization of childhood. Using the toy market as an example, we identify that the children's consumer culture is moving toward brand and technology focus, homogeneity, and multimedia formats. There is emphasis on market segmentation, meaning children of similar age, the same sex, and similar psychographics are assumed to be attracted by a uniform product and benefit appeal. A review of children and consumer culture led us to a question about how children of different cultures interact with brands with different consumer values. Further analysis can focus on the ways children in different cultures respond to marketing communications of leading global brands of interest to them.

SEE ALSO in this volume chapter by Buckingham and chapter by Buijzen, Rozendaal, and van Reijmersdal.

References

Angrisani, C. (2002). The tween scene: Highlighting demographic appeal. *Supermarket News*, September 12. Retrieved from http://supermarketnews.com/archive/tween-scene

Areddy, J. T. and Sanders, P. (2009). Chinese learn English the Disney way. *The Wall Street Journal*, April 20, B1.

Baker-Sperry, L. (2007). The production of meaning through peer interaction: Children and Walt Disney's Cinderella. *Sex Role*, 56(11/12), 717–27.

Bell, E., Hass, L. and Sells, L. (Eds) (1995). *From mouse to mermaid: The politics of film, gender, and culture*. Bloomington: Indiana University Press.

Bondebjerg, I. and Golding, P. (Eds) (2004). *European Culture and the Media*. Portland, Oregon: Intellect Books.

Chan, K. (2005). Material world: Attitudes towards toys in China. *Young Consumers*, 6(1), 54–65.

Chaplin, L. N. and John, D. R. (2005). The development of self-brand connections in children and adolescents. *Journal of Consumer Research*, 32(1), 119–29.

Chester, J. and Montgomery, K. (2008). No escape: Marketing to kids in the digital age. *Multinational Monitor*, 29(1), 11–16.

Cook, D. T. (2004). *The commodification of childhood: The children's wear industry and the rise of the child-consumer, 1917–1962*. Durham, NC: Duke University Press.

——(2007). The disempowering empowerment of children's consumer "choice": Cultural discourses of the child consumer in North America. *Society and Business Review*, 2(1), 37–52.

Cuthbert, W. (2002). Cartoon and Kellogg milk kid empowerment with Big Pick. Retrieved from http://kidscreen.com/2002/10/01/bigpick-20021001/

Dahm, L. (2002). Upping the ante on candy: The newest candy from impact confections offers kids a multi-sensory experience. *Stagnito's New Products Magazine*, 2(6), 16.

D'Altorio, T. (2010). Disney works its magic on China: No wishing on a star required. *Investment U*. Retrieved from http://www.investmentu.com/2010/July/disney-works-its-magic-on-china.html

Disney Consumer Products. (2011). *Disney store*. Retrieved from https://www.disneyconsumerproducts.com/Home/display.jsp?contentId=dcp_home_ourbusinesses_disney_store_us&forPrint=false&language=en&preview=false&imageShow=0&pressRoom=US&translationOf=null&region=0

Disney English. (2011). *Fact sheet*. Retrieved from http://disneyenglish.disney.com.cn/EN/press/20110830442.html

Disney Store. (2011). *Home page*. Retrieved from http://www.disneystore.com/

The Economist (2010). Disney's schools in China: Middle kingdom meets magic kingdom. *The Economist*. August 26. Retrieved from http://www.economist.com/node/16889262

Ekstrom, K. M. and Tufte, B. (Eds) (2007). *Children, media, and consumption: On the front edge*. Göteborg: International Clearinghouse on Children, Youth and Media, Nordicom, Göteborg University.

Ewing, M. T., de Bussy, N. M. and Leyland, P. F. (1998). *White collar Asia: A cross-national psychographic exploration*. Retrieved from http://smib.vuw.ac.nz:8081/www/ANZMAC1998/Cd_rom/Ewing168.pdf

Formanek-Brunell, M. (1993). *Made to play house: Dolls and the commercialization of American girlhood, 1830–1930*. New Haven: Yale University Press.

Getzier, W. G. (2011). *Toys: More kids want 'em this holiday*. Retrieved from http://kidscreen.com/2011/11/23/toys-more-kids-want-em-this-holiday/

Gram, M. (2011). Approaching children in experience advertising: Danish amusement parks 1969–2008. *Young Consumers*, 12(1), 53–65.

Interbrand. (2011). *2011 ranking of the top 100 brands*. Retrieved from http://www.interbrand.com/en/best-global-brands/best-global-brands-2008/best-global-brands-2011.aspx

Jacobson, L. (2004). *Raising consumers: Children and the American mass market in the early twentieth century*. New York: Columbia University Press.

——(2008). *Children and consumer culture in American society: A historical handbook and guide*. Westport, Conn: Praeger.

Jones, S. C. and Reid, A. (2010). Marketing to children and teens on Australian food company web sites. *Young Consumers*, 11(1), 57–66.

Kahle, L. R. (1983). *Attitudes and social adaptation: A person-situation interaction approach*. London: Pergamon.

Kasturi, S. (2002). Constructing childhood in a corporate world: Cultural studies, childhood, and Disney. In G. Canella and J. Kinchella (Eds), *Kid world: Childhood studies, global perspectives, and education*. New York: Peter Lang, pp. 39–58.

Kunkle, D. and Roberts, D. (1991). Young minds and marketplace values in children's television advertising. *Journal of Social Issues*, *47*(1), 57–72.

Lauffer, R. (2003). A new approach to segmenting the global child. *Advertising and Marketing to Children*, *4*(2), 3–8.

Leach, W. (1993a). Child-world in the Promised Land. In J. Gilbert, A. Gilman, D. M. Scott and J. W. Scott (Eds), *The mythmaking frame of mind: Social imagination and American culture*. Belmont, CA: Wadsworth, pp. 209–38.

Leach, W. (1993b). *Land of desire: Merchants, power, and the rise of a new American culture*. New York: Pantheon.

Lee, L. (2008). Understanding gender through Disney's marriages: A study of young Korean immigrant girls. *Early Childhood Education Journal*, *36*(1), 11–18.

Liu, L. W. (2009, December 3). China vs. Disney: The battle for Mulan. *Time World*. Retrieved from http://www.time.com/time/world/article/0,8599,1944598,00.html

Ma, F. (2004). *Lifestyle segmentation of Chinese consumers*. ESOMAR Asia Pacific Conference, Shanghai. Retrieved from http://www.tgisurveys.com/knowledgehub/papers.aspx?id=3

McGinnis, J. M., Gootman, J. and Kraak, V. I. (Eds) (2006). *Food marketing to children and youth: Threat or opportunity?* Washington, DC: The National Academies Press.

McNeal, J. U. (1987). *Children as consumers: Insights and implications*. Lexington, MA: Lexington Books.

McNeal, J. U. (1992). *Kids as customers: A handbook of marketing to children*. Lexington, MA: Lexington Books.

Manning, S. (1999). Students for sale: How corporations are buying their way into America's classrooms. *The Nation*, *269* (September 27), 11–18.

Marshall, D. (Ed.) (2010). *Understanding children as consumers*. London: Sage.

Martin, K. A. and Kazyak, E. (2009). Hetero-romantic love and heterosexiness in children's G-rated films. *Gender & Society*, *23*(3), 315–36.

Mufson, S. (1996). China's "soccer boy" takes on foreign evils: Cartoon hero gets home-field advantage. *The Washington Post*, October 9, A31.

Narang, R. (2010). Psychographic segmentation of youth in the evolving Indian retail market. *The International Review of Retail, Distribution and Consumer Research*, *20*(5), 535–57.

Nigel Wright Consultancy Limited (2011). *About the Walt Disney Company*. Retrieved from http://www.nigelwright.com/TheWaltDisneyCompany/

NPD Group. (2011). *World toy sales in 2010 were $83.3 billion, an increase of nearly 5 percent over 2009*. Retrieved from https://www.npd.com/wps/portal/npd/us/news/pressreleases/pr_110702

Oregon Public Broadcasting. (2011). "Investors all ears as Disney reports positive earnings." Retrieved from http://opb.giftlegacy.com/?pageID=32& docID = 634

Pugh, A. J. (2009). *Longing and belonging: Parents, children, and consumer culture*. Los Angeles: University of California Press.

Schor, J. B. (2004). *Born to buy: The commercialized child and the new consumer culture*. New York: Scribner.

Siklos, R. (2009). Why Disney wants DreamWorks. *CNNMoney*, February 9. Retrieved from http://money.cnn.com/2009/02/09/news/companies/disney_dreamworks.fortune/index.htm

Stock, T. and Tupot, M. L. (2006). Common denominators: What unites global youth? *Young Consumers: Insight and Ideas for Responsible Marketers*, *7*(2), 36–43.

Strasser, S. (1989). *Satisfaction guaranteed: The making of the American mass market*. New York: Pantheon.

Toys "R" Us. (2011). *Shop by age*. Retrieved from http://www.toysrus.com/category/index.jsp?categoryId=2269725

TravelChinaGuide. (2011). *Shanghai Disneyland*. Retrieved from http://www.travelchinaguide.com/attraction/shanghai/disneyland-park.htm

Valkenburg, P. U. and Cantor, J. (2001). The development of a child into a consumer. *Journal of Applied Developmental Psychology*, *22*(1), 61–72.

Wasko, J. (2001). *Understanding Disney: The manufacture of fantasy*. Cambridge, UK: Polity Press.

Wells, W. D. and Tigert, D. J. (1971). Activities, interests and opinions. *Journal of Advertising Research*, *11*(4), 27–35.

Xiudadad. (2009). Review baby's first graduation ceremony: The days at Disney English. *Onlylady*. Retrieved from http://bbs.onlylady.com/thread-758081-1-1.html [in Chinese]

18

CHILDREN AND CONVERGENCE CULTURE

New perspectives on youth participation with media

Meryl Alper

"Convergence culture," as employed by US media scholar Henry Jenkins, encompasses "technological, industrial, cultural, and social changes in the ways media circulate" (Jenkins, 2006, p. 322). In contrast to the digital revolution paradigm of the 1990s, which predicted that the internet would supplant broadcast media (Negroponte, 1995), a key tenet of convergence culture is that old media are not being *displaced* by the introduction of new content delivery systems, but rather *shifted* in terms of their function and status (Gitelman, 2006). New media has not caused cultural convergence, but it has certainly accelerated and widened the circulation or "spreadability" of media content at all levels of culture (Jenkins et al., 2013).

Personal and collective acts of circulation, consumption, creation, and appraisal of media in everyday life shape the logics of information flows across old and new mass media platforms, from families separated by distance reading bedtime stories over Skype (Ballagas et al., 2010) to interactive cross-cultural classroom pen pal programs such as The Flat Stanley Project (Hubert, 2005). The hypothesis guiding the nascent research on children's opportunities and risks growing up within contemporary convergence culture is that the increasingly ubiquitous, embedded, and social nature of digital media and networks has led to diverse forms and practices of children's literacy, learning, and play. Much of the research in this area has been funded by the US-based MacArthur Foundation's initiative on digital media and learning (DML), and is defined by a constellation of theoretical, interdisciplinary, and methodological approaches. Research questions in this field primarily explore how young people learn in formal and informal ways to navigate technology, develop cultural competencies, and hone social skills in online and offline spaces (Jenkins et al., 2006). Inquiry also focuses on how best a growing spectrum of learning institutions and stakeholders can support and guide children's development.

This chapter will focus on key discourses and debates around "participatory culture" within an era of media convergence. A participatory culture is "a culture with relatively low barriers to artistic expression and civic engagement, strong support for creating and sharing one's creations, and some type of informal mentorship whereby what is known by the most experienced is passed along to novices" (Jenkins et al., 2006, p. 3). Convergence culture refers to a specific interplay across media platforms and the reconfiguration of the relationship between mass media and participatory culture.

The first half of this chapter outlines the leading theoretical, interdisciplinary, and methodological frameworks for researching young people's engagement with participatory culture, as well as the major accumulated knowledge to date in this burgeoning area. The remainder of this chapter focuses on two significant omissions within these discourses regarding the obstacles to and the opportunities for access and participation for various populations of children. I argue specifically for greater inclusion of young children and children with disabilities in the digital media and learning research agenda. Their inclusion productively complicates existing research in the DML field and broadens the potential to re-imagine children's learning with old and new media in a convergence culture.

Theoretical and applied frameworks

Theoretical base

The theories grounding youth participatory culture relate to the ways in which children develop a sense of self-identity and self-expression, exercise judgment, and think systematically. This work draws heavily on sociocultural and ecological perspectives on child development (Bronfenbrenner, 1979), sociocultural learning theory (Lave and Wenger, 1991; Rogoff, 2003), and situated learning (Gee, 2004). A specific learning ecology framework recognizes that children learn both through explicit instruction in formal settings and also through informal, social, and recreational activities in out-of-school domains (Barron, 2004, 2006). Other relevant paradigms focusing on cultural participation and social relationships include distributed cognition (Clark, 2003; Hutchins, 1995), collective intelligence (Lévy, 1997), new literacy studies (New London Group, 1996), and more broadly, youth participation in local and global public culture (Appadurai and Breckenridge, 1988; Maira and Soep, 2004).

The scholarship on digital media and learning has been collaborative and interdisciplinary from the outset. A great deal of DML research, design, and practice incorporates the work of scholars and practitioners in education, communication, anthropology, sociology, critical race studies, queer studies, game studies and game design, transmedia production, learning sciences, and computer science (e.g., Bennett, 2008; Everett, 2008; Salen, 2008).

Methodologies

Research on children's engagement with participatory culture is conducted using a variety of qualitative and quantitative data collection methodologies and analyses, with particular sensitivity to language differences and power differentials between researchers and often-younger research subjects. Ethnographic methods such as participant observation and "photovoice" (Wang and Burris, 1994) provide rich detail and documentation to situate children's media use within embedded social structures, cultural patterns, and grassroots issues. Historiography helps researchers gain perspective on today's cultural fears and hopes alongside their historical antecedents (e.g., moral panics in the early twentieth century about young girls using the "new" landline telephone) (Cassell and Cramer, 2008). Digital time-diary studies using text messages, mobile phones, and one-on-one attention allow for adolescents to provide more accurate self-reports of media use (Hargittai and Karr, in press). The examples above reflect just a few of the mixed methods and strategies used, and approaches taken, by researchers when studying young people's cultural participation with media.

Participatory culture

Jenkins originally proposed the idea of "participatory media cultures" in the 1970s and 1980s to describe popular culture fan communities (Jenkins, 1992), and has more recently traced participatory fan practices to reconfigured relationships between media production and consumption (Jenkins, 2006). Jenkins has also applied this participatory culture framework to issues of play, learning, and literacy, describing the benefits of young people's engagement with participatory culture and the skills and competencies needed for children and their teachers to fully participate in creative, civic, and professional life (Jenkins et al., 2006; Reilly et al., 2012).

Discussions around participatory culture play out across various debates within digital media and learning research, and more broadly to children and media research in general. Participatory culture challenges the notion that children's media consumption is passive (Dyson, 1997; Kinder, 1991; Seiter, 1999), and conversely, the proposition that media production should be the foundation of children's active participation in media. Media consumption is embedded in networked communication and social media ecologies – making it difficult to thread apart and judge young people's media creation, consumption, circulation, and critiquing independently from one another. The voluntary or involuntary terms of children's participation are also greatly debated, as scholars note both the pleasures and perils of participatory culture. Risks include the commoditization and surveillance of youth participation for corporate interests and targeted advertising; centralization and consolidation of commercial power; and labor exploitation and copyright issues of children's "user-generated content" (e.g., Sandvig, 2003).

The Digital Youth Project proposed a complementary construct to participatory culture of "genres of participation" with new media (Ito, 2008). Ito and her colleagues make distinctions between "friendship-driven" and "interest-driven" genres of participation (Ito and colleagues, 2009). The former refers to the shared practices that grow out of young people's friendships in their local social worlds such as school, sports, clubs, camps, and religious groups. The latter construct consists of niches and affiliations that are driven by youth interests, hobbies, and career aspirations, which then lead to new friendships and the formation of peer networks. Ito et al. (2009) detail the way adolescents and teens "hang out" with media (more friendship-driven) "mess around," (blended friendship- and interest-driven) and "geek out" (interest-driven). Young people are not categorized into just one typology, as each child makes multiple types of investments with different media and technological genres as they grow up.

Gaps in the digital media and learning research agenda

Some scholars question how many children are hanging out most of the time, and postulate that perhaps only a small number are actually messing around and geeking out (Warschauer and Matuchniak, 2010). The hard reality is that most young technological innovation and geeking out in post-industrial countries comes from very privileged white, male worlds. Scholars can only begin to chart a forward path for supporting all children and adolescents' engagement in participatory culture practices if these underlying theories incorporate what "participation" and "culture" might mean to more diverse groups of young people and their communities.

Jenkins et al. (2006, p. 3) identity the "participation gap," or "the unequal access to the opportunities, experiences, skills, and knowledge that will prepare youth for full participation in the world of tomorrow." While the "digital divide" construct has primarily focused on technological access, research on the participation gap seeks to incorporate children's unequal opportunities to cultivate new media literacies. Such social skills and cultural competencies build upon the foundation of traditional literacies, critical analytic literacies, research skills, and technical skills.

A growing body of research addresses the participation gap, focusing on factors of social class, ethnicity, race, gender, and sexuality in shaping children and adolescents' opportunities to engage, experiment, and collaborate with new media (e.g., boyd, 2007; Gray, 2009; Seiter, 2005; Watkins, 2009). In the remainder of this chapter, I argue that *age* and *disability* are other important but vastly understudied factors intertwined with the availability and accessibility of opportunities for children to participate through today's networked and digital media.

Young children

Within the US, "K-12" (kindergarten through high school) and "K-16" (kindergarten through college) are terms that often signify learning at all grade levels. Most DML research focuses on middle and high school age children, but to date, how young children grow up with digital media, for better or worse, at home, school, and within their communities is a significantly under-researched area in the DML space (Alper, in press; Blanchard and Moore, 2010).

It is imperative to incorporate young children into the DML research agenda for a number of reasons. Research on primary and secondary school age children may not directly apply to children younger than six due to developmental differences in social, emotional, cognitive, and physical development. Families with younger children can also mutually support one another's learning through viewing, reading, playing, creating, searching, and contributing with diverse forms of digital media, or "joint media engagement" (Takeuchi, 2011; Takeuchi and Stevens, 2011). Intergenerational experiences with old and new media forms provide social, emotional, and cognitive resources for fostering children's curiosity, interests, and passions.

Opportunities and gaps to engage in participatory culture also start before children begin kindergarten. This is evidenced by recent research on the "app gap," a new widening of unequal access to mobile devices and use of applications for lower-income children ages 0 to 8 (Rideout, 2011). This is in addition to a "scaffolding gap," in which low-income children receive far less age-appropriate mentoring or direction from adults in their media use than higher-income youth (Neuman and Celano, 2006), underscored by government defunding of many social services in the US intended to support families. There is an ongoing need for longitudinal studies, both in the US and internationally, to determine if inequalities in access and use of new media also relate to inequalities in learning outcomes in young children's later primary and secondary school educations.

The diverse stakeholders in early childhood education are under-represented in the DML space and should have more opportunities to contribute and speak on their own behalf. Organizations such as the Fred Rogers Center for Early Learning and Children's Media, the Joan Ganz Cooney Center at Sesame Workshop, and the International Clearinghouse on Children, Youth, and Media are leading rich and interesting conversations across the globe on developmentally appropriate ways that digital media can best support young children's learning, as opposed to issuing monolithic recommendations for "no screen time" (e.g., National Association for the Education of Young Children and Fred Rogers Center for Early Learning and Children's Media, 2012). Collaborations with these groups, as well as parents, teachers, and early childhood-focused scholars can help foster a greater plurality of voices into DML research.

Youth with disabilities

Younger and older students with various cognitive, physical, social, and emotional needs, as well as their teachers, parents, and other caregivers, are often unintentionally marginalized from digital media and learning studies (Alper et al., 2012). The media ecologies of children with disabilities have become increasingly complex in recent years. Major gaps in access and institutional support exist between children with disabilities in the Global North and South (e.g., Pal et al., 2011). Private sector ventures in educational and assistive technologies targeting children with disabilities have recently grown tremendously, particularly mobile apps designed for the iPad and iPhone (e. g., Lee, 2012). These tools potentially provide a customizable and flexible platform for enhancing independence and quality of life, social participation, and educational experiences (Alper et al., 2012; Druin, 2002; Guha et al., 2008). A more critical dialogue is needed in the DML space about how all children with disabilities, in developed and developing nations, can more fully participate in media-based learning opportunities such as gaming and online communities, as young people and later on as independent adults (e.g., Pitaru, 2008).

One specific example of this nuanced critical dialogue is exploring the ways in which young people with disabilities also "geek out" with media. One case study is that of Christopher Hills, an adolescent boy and unabashed Apple "fan boy" with cerebral palsy in Australia. Christopher produced a video entitled "One Head, One Switch, The World" in 2012 about the dynamics between technology and his disability. This video had nearly 100,000 views on YouTube as of January 2013 (Hills, 2012a). Christopher has severe motor impairments, but full cognitive and intellectual abilities. He uses his head to control a system of switches mounted to the headrest of his wheelchair, which then controls his MacBook video-editing suite. Christopher's father helps him shoot the video footage and type subtitles, and together they co-create a web series on Christopher's creative media practices.

Christopher expands and diversifies the DML notion of kids who "geek out," as well as those who potentially benefit from interest-driven, intergenerational learning. He is a budding vlogger, creating webisodes driven by his interest in Apple technology. Christopher also demonstrates a willingness to challenge social and technological rules. For example, in one vlog entitled "Why Touchscreens Scare Me," Christopher reports,

> Touch screens have helped many people with disabilities as we've seen with the iPad, but for me they don't help at all. I keep reading things about touch screens taking over the mouse and keyboard. This really scared me because most assistive ware is designed for the classic desktop.
>
> *(Hills, 2012b)*

Those who feel frustrated by the top-down boundaries imposed on their abilities regularly challenge and resist standing media policy and drive the demand for technological innovation (Verlager, 2008). Christopher is an exemplar case of youth participation in civic life and cultural production.

Christopher's new media practices as a means to shift the norms of digital spaces are an example of emerging "hacker literacies" (Santo, in press). The hacker literacies paradigm fuses critical media and participatory media literacies to support young people's cultivation of an empowered stance in relation to the way technology is formulated, coded, and designed, as well as a critical perspective on how that technology impacts society. The DML research agenda needs to be more inclusive of narratives like Christopher's and the lenses provided by other children and adolescents with various disabilities if the field is going to innovate beyond its promising beginnings.

Conclusion

Participatory culture focuses not solely on the platforms through which young people engage with media, but the social, emotional, and cultural motivations and investments driving their everyday play, learning, and experimentation among networks of friends, peers, family members, and mentors. A growing body of research is addressing the participation gap but there are still areas that need to be addressed. Many types of variations exist between and within diverse groups of children (e.g., children of color with multiple disabilities, young children in rural and urban settings). Young children and youth with disabilities all may have unique media ecologies, relationships to mainstream and assistive technologies, and contributions to make to civic life. In order for the DML field to advance, scholarship (university-based and independent) must take into account how the experiences of these children both complement and conflict the discourses dominant in digital media and learning research. Future directions proposed in this chapter are by no means extensive, but are a starting point for imagining new paradigms for learning within convergence culture and the processes for achieving that vision of change.

SEE ALSO in this volume chapter by Livingstone, chapter by Fisherkeller, and chapter by Stuart and Mitchell.

References

Alper, M. (in press). Developmentally appropriate new media literacies: Supporting cultural competencies and social skills in early childhood education. *Journal of Early Childhood Literacy*.

Alper, M., Hourcade, J. P. and Gilutz, S. (2012). Interactive technologies for children with special needs. Workshop presented at the *11th International Conference on Interaction Design and Children*, IDC '12. Bremen, Germany: ACM.

Alper, M., Hourcade, J. P., Israel, M., Basham, J. D., Lee, S. and Dunn, A. (2012, March 2). Universal designs for DML: Innovations for students with disabilities. Panel presented at the *3rd Annual Digital Media and Learning Conference,* San Francisco, CA. Retrieved from http://dml2012.dmlcentral.net/content/dml-universal-designs-dml-innovations-students-disabilities

Appadurai, A. and Breckenridge, C. (1988). Why public culture? *Public Culture*, *1*(1), 5–9.

Ballagas, R., Raffle, H., Go, J., Revelle, G. L., Kaye, J., Ames, M., Horii, H., et al. (2010). Story time for the 21st century. *IEEE Pervasive Computing*, *9*(3), 28–36.

Barron, B. (2004). Learning ecologies for technological fluency: Gender and experience differences. *Journal of Educational Computing Research*, *31*(1), 1–36.

——(2006). Interest and self-sustained learning as catalysts of development: A learning ecologies perspective. *Human Development*, *49*(4), 193–224.

Bennett, W. L. (Ed.) (2008). *Civic life online: Learning how digital media can engage youth.* The John D. and Catherine T. MacArthur Foundation Series on Digital Media and Learning. Cambridge, MA: MIT Press.

Blanchard, J. and Moore, T. (2010). *The digital world of young children: Impact on emergent literacy*. Mill Valley, CA: Pearson Foundation. Retrieved from http://www. pearsonfoundation.org/downloads/Emergent Literacy-WhitePaper.pdf

boyd, d. (2007). Why youth (heart) social network sites: The role of networked publics in teenage social life. In D. Buckingham (Ed.), *MacArthur Foundation Series on Digital Media and Learning – Youth, identity, and digital media*. Cambridge, MA: MIT Press, pp. 119–42.

Bronfenbrenner, U. (1979). *The ecology of human development: Experiments by nature and design*. Cambridge, MA: Harvard University Press.

Cassell, J. and Cramer, M. (2008). High tech or high risk: Moral panics about girls online. In T. McPherson (Ed.), *Digital youth, innovation, and the unexpected*, The John D. and Catherine T. MacArthur Foundation Series on Digital Media and Learning. Cambridge, MA: MIT Press, pp. 53–76.

Clark, A. (2003). *Natural-born cyborgs: Minds, technologies, and the future of human intelligence*. New York: Oxford University Press.

Druin, A. (2002). The role of children in the design of new technology. *Behaviour and Information Technology*, *21*(1), 1–25.

Dyson, A. H. (1997). *Writing superheroes: Contemporary childhood, popular culture, and classroom literacy*. New York: Teachers College Press.

Everett, A. (Ed.) (2008). *Learning race and ethnicity: Youth and digital media*. The John D. and Catherine T. MacArthur Foundation Series on Digital Media and Learning. Cambridge, MA: MIT Press.

Gee, J. P. (2004). *Situated language and learning: A critique of traditional schooling*. New York: Routledge.

Gitelman, L. (2006). *Always already new: Media, history and the data of culture*. Cambridge, MA: MIT Press.

Gray, M. L. (2009). *Out in the country: Youth, media, and queer visibility in rural America*. New York: New York University Press.

Guha, M. L., Druin, A. and Fails, J. A. (2008). Designing *with* and *for* children with special needs: an inclusionary model. *Proceedings of the 7th International Conference on Interaction Design and Children*, IDC '08. New York, NY, USA: ACM, pp. 61–64.

Hargittai, E. and Karr, C. (in press). WAT R U DOIN? Studying the thumb generation using text messaging. In E. Hargittai (Ed.), *Research methods from the trenches*. Ann Arbor, MI: University of Michigan Press.

Hills, C. (2012a, March 20). "One switch. One head. The world." Retrieved May 25, 2012, from http://www.youtube.com/watch?v=cSSgndQ5mVs

———(2012b, April 3). "Intersection: Why Touch Screens Scare Me." Retrieved May 25, 2012, from http://www.youtube.com/watch?v=j5H4TV-2-Tw412.

Hubert, D. (2005). The Flat Stanley Project and other authentic applications of technology in the classroom. In R. Karchmer, M. H. Mallette, J. Kara-Soteriou, & D. J. Leu (Eds.), *Innovative approaches to literacy education: Using the internet to support new literacies*. Newark, DE: International Reading Association.

Hutchins, E. (1995). *Cognition in the wild*. Cambridge, MA: MIT Press.

Ito, M. (2008). Mobilizing the imagination in everyday play: The case of Japanese media mixes. In K. Drotner & S. Livingstone (Eds.), *International Handbook of Children, Media and Culture* (pp. 397–412). Los Angeles: Sage.

Ito, M., Baumer, S., Bittanti, M., boyd, d., Cody, R., Herr-Stephenson, B., Horst, H. A., et al. (2009). *Hanging out, messing around, and geeking out: Kids living and learning with new media*. Cambridge, MA: MIT Press.

Jenkins, H. (1992). *Textual poachers: Television fans and participatory culture*. New York: Routledge.

———(2006). *Convergence culture: Where old and new media collide*. New York: New York University Press.

Jenkins, H., Ford, S. and Green, J. (2013). *Spreadable media: Creating value and meaning in a networked culture*. New York: New York University Press.

Jenkins, H., Purushotma, R., Clinton, K., Weigel, M. and Robison, A. J. (2006). *Confronting the challenges of participatory culture: Media education for the 21st century*. Chicago, IL: The John D. and Catherine T. MacArthur Foundation.

Kinder, M. (1991). *Playing with power in movies, television, and video games: From Muppet Babies to Teenage Mutant Ninja Turtles*. Berkeley, CA: University of California Press.

Lave, J. and Wenger, E. (1991). *Situated learning: Legitimate peripheral participation*. Cambridge, UK: Cambridge University Press.

Lee, S. (2012). Project Injini: Developing cognitive training games for children with special needs. *Games for Health Journal*, *1*(1), 69–73.

Lévy, P. (1997). *Collective intelligence*. Cambridge, MA: Perseus.

Maira, S. and Soep, E. (Eds.) (2004). *Youthscapes: The popular, the national, the global*. Philadelphia, PA: University of Pennsylvania Press.

National Association for the Education of Young Children and Fred Rogers Center for Early Learning and Children's Media (2012). Technology and interactive media as tools in early childhood programs serving children from birth through age 8. Position statement adopted January 2012.

Negroponte, N. (1995). *Being digital*. New York: Knopf.

Neuman, S. B. and Celano, D. (2006). The knowledge gap: Implications of leveling the playing field for low-income and middle-income children. *Reading Research Quarterly*, *41*(2), 176–201.

New London Group. (1996). A pedagogy of multiliteracies: Designing social futures. *Harvard Educational Review*, *66*(1), 60–93.

Pal, J., Pradhan, M., Shah, M. and Babu, R. (2011). Assistive technology for vision-impairments: An agenda for the ICTD community. *Proceedings of the 20th international conference companion on world wide web*. New York, NY, USA: ACM, pp. 513–22.

Pitaru, A. (2008). E Is for everyone: The case for inclusive game design. In K. Salen (Ed.), *The ecology of games: Connecting youth, games, and learning*, The John D. and Catherine T. MacArthur Foundation Series on Digital Media and Learning. Cambridge, MA: MIT Press, pp. 67–88.

Reilly, E., Vartabedian, V., Felt, L. and Jenkins, H. (2012). PLAY *(Participatory learning and* YOU*!)*. Los Angeles, CA: University of Southern California Annenberg Innovation Lab.

Rideout, V. J. (2011). *Zero to eight: Children's media use in America*. San Francisco, CA: Common Sense Media.

Rogoff, B. (2003). *The cultural nature of human development*. Oxford: Oxford University Press.

Salen, K. (Ed.) (2008). *The ecology of games: Connecting youth, games, and learning*. The John D. and Catherine T. MacArthur Foundation Series on Digital Media and Learning. Cambridge, MA: MIT Press.

Sandvig, C. (2003). Public Internet access for young children in the inner city: Evidence to inform access subsidies and content regulation. *The Information Society, 19*(2), 171–83.

Santo, R. (in press). Hacker literacies: User-generated resistance and reconfiguration of networked publics. In J. Avila and J. Zacher-Pandya (Eds), *Critical digital literacies as social praxis: Intersections and challenges.* New York: Peter Lang.

Seiter, E. (1999). Power Rangers at preschool: Negotiating media in child care settings. In M. Kinder (Ed.), *Kids' Media Culture*. Durham, NC: Duke University Press, pp. 239–62.

——(2005). *The Internet playground: Children's access, entertainment, and mis-education.* New York: Peter Lang.

Takeuchi, L. (2011). *Families matter: Designing media for a digital age.* New York: The Joan Ganz Cooney Center at Sesame Workshop.

Takeuchi, L. and Stevens, R. (2011). *The new coviewing: Designing for learning through joint media engagement.* New York: The Joan Ganz Cooney Center at Sesame Workshop.

Verlager, A. K. (2008). Literacy as process: The multiple literacies of blind readers. *Journal of Media Literacy Education, 55*(1 & 2). Retrieved http://www.journalofmedialiteracy.org/index.php/past-issues/2-cultural-diversity-v55-n1a2/23-literacy-as-process-the-multiple-literacies-of-blind-readers

Wang, C. and Burris, M. A. (1994). Empowerment through photo novella: Portraits of participation. *Health Education & Behavior, 21*(2), 171–86.

Warschauer, M. and Matuchniak, T. (2010). New technology and digital worlds: Analyzing evidence of equity in access, use, and outcomes. *Review of Research in Education, 34*(1), 179–225.

Watkins, S. C. (2009). *The young and the digital: What the migration to social-network sites, games, and anytime, anywhere media means for our future.* Boston: Beacon Press.

19

CHILDREN'S TECHNOLOGIZED BODIES: MAPPING MIXED REALITY

Meenakshi Gigi Durham

In some sense, children have always been active participants in technoculture. Archaeological evidence indicates that children were involved with technology as far back as prehistoric times: excavations reveal that children used flints, axes, and other stone tools in the Paleolithic era (Grimm, 2000; Högberg, 2008; Montagu, 1976; Shea, 2006), wielded daggers and needles in the Bronze Age (Rega, 2000), threw pots in the first century C.E. (Kamp, 2001). During the Industrial Revolution, children "toiled in early mills, mines and manufactories" (Humphries, 2010, p. 1), handling lathes, looms, and lethal equipment. Child labor laws put an end to all that, but children turned to technological tools for recreation in the twentieth century: Boy Scouts rigged amateur radios (Arceneaux, 2009), children snapped pictures with Brownie cameras (Olivier, 2007), and budding DeMilles pointed home movie cameras at their parents and siblings to create amateur films (Luckett, 1995).

It should not surprise us, then, that in the contemporary moment children have taken to technologies like the proverbial ducks to water, programming smartphones, downloading applications, and reconfiguring laptops before they're even out of preschool. Children's worlds are now pervaded by digital technologies to an extent that certain traditional boundaries—between the "real" and the "virtual," body and machine, subject and object—are beginning to blur and break down, for better or worse.

In fact, the media scholar Mark Hansen argues that in today's media environment, "all reality is mixed reality" (2006, p. 1)—composed of "fluid and functional crossings between virtual and physical realms" (p. 2). No longer can we draw clear lines between the "real world" and "cyberspace," for it is largely through our engagements with technologies that we experience the world. As Hansen points out, "technologies work to expand the body's motile, tactile, and visual interface with the environment," mediating "our embodied coupling with the world" (2006, p. 26).

The ease with which children of all ages handle technology is a taken-for-granted aspect of contemporary life. Although it is important to recognize that children's access to, and uses of, technology differ depending on contextual features such as location, socioeconomic status, and developmental stage (Selwyn, 2009), it is still arguable that in technologically advanced cultures, these toys and tools are seamlessly integrated into the surfaces of everyday life, unremarkable features of children's lifeworlds.

Mobile technologies, especially, are becoming essential elements of daily life. These technologies and the communicative conduits they offer wield significant symbolic value in the social worlds of youth: they constitute the basis of roles, relationships, support systems, and status among peers (Blair and Fletcher, 2011; Livingstone and Bovill, 2001; Stern, 2007; Thulin and Vilhel, 2007). Technologies—especially cell phones—are "imperative in the formation, maintenance and manipulation of close, intimate relationships" among children and adolescents, and—perhaps more importantly—provide an "alternate space," akin to a backyard bike shed, for explorations of sex and desire (Bond, 2010). Children and adolescents also use the internet, via social networking and other sites, as a resource for exploring identities (Elias and Lemish, 2009; Rademacher, 2005), developing and maintaining friendships (Tsoulis-Reay, 2009; Valkenburg and Jochen, 2009), and sexual education, interactions, and communication (Cohn, 2009; Livingstone, 2008; Peter and Valkenburg, 2006, 2008, 2010).

In the lives of children and adolescents, then, technologies don't figure as mere objects—they are not perceived to be machines or ancillary pieces of equipment. Rather, they are organisms appended to bodies, functioning with the body as naturally as the cerebral cortex or the limbs. There is no clear boundary between the child and the cell phone or computer; the technology is in every way an extension of the child's body and consciousness. Children have remarkable physical dexterity with the keypads and screens of these devices, handling them with casual skill, and they are keenly attuned to their faintest sounds, lights, and vibrations. For many children and teens, the cell phone is an "organic thing" that operates as part of their lived materiality: "the mobile phone constitutes an important part of themselves" (Oksman and Rautiainen, 2003, p. 307; see also Ribak, 2009, who describes the phone as an "umbilical cord" and Green and Singleton, 2007, whose studies of British youth identify the phone as a "mobile self"). The spaces children and teens enter, create, and engage with via computer screens and gaming consoles similarly constitute interfaces that conjoin embodiment and virtuality.

These interfaces serve as portals for journeys between "real world" and virtual environments. Technologically, they require physical activity and attention; mentally, they immerse the user in alternative spaces and experiences. Waggoner (2009) describes technological interfaces as "a fluid ground between real-world and virtual conceptions" (p. 33).

Because children's lives are defined by this "mixed reality" and marked by an ongoing reciprocity between the material and the cybernetic, red flags have been raised regarding the potential perils and problems associated with children's bodies in a technologized landscape. These concerns begin with the health risks associated with the use of technology—seizures, attention deficit problems, behavioral and emotional disorders—and extend to the social, legal, and cultural implications of children's technological activities.

Sexting and sexual subjectivities

One such discursive flashpoint has been the practice of "sexting." Periodically, news stories narrate cases of young teens sending provocative cellphone pictures of themselves to peers; these pictures sometimes "go viral," circulating widely among consociates and eventually on the internet. While adults agonize over the legal and personal consequences of minor children sexting, kids engage in it for reasons that are often misconstrued as either defiant or guileless. "No, [it's not a big deal], we are not having sex, we are sexting," explained one ninth-grade boy; and a high school girl surmised, "I think it's fairly common in my school for people to do this. They see it as a way of flirting that may possibly lead to more for them" (Lenhart, 2009). Sexting scenarios are varied: sometimes young couples in romantic relationships exchange explicit photographs; sometimes messages are sent in the hope of sparking such a relationship; sometimes text and photos are shared for a sensual thrill or a lark; sometimes they are circulated vindictively to punish or humiliate an individual, usually a girl. In recent high-profile cases, three Pennsylvania high school girls took topless photographs of themselves for their boyfriends (Zirkel, 2009); in Milton, Vermont, teenage girls sent nude or semi-nude videos and pictures of themselves to male classmates who asked for them (Rathke, 2011). In both cases, the photos were then circulated widely to schoolmates and others; in other recent incidents, boys who forwarded sexts were charged under child pornography statutes, and teenage girls committed suicide after the photographs went viral (Forbes, 2011; Hoffman, 2011; Quaid, 2009; Christian Science Monitor, 2009).

In most peer-to-peer sexting cases, the creation and initial transmission of the images are not coerced—kids themselves take and send the pictures to their peers. Wireless connections are imagined to prefigure sensual bonds, impulsive intimacies, loving liaisons. The cell phone photo or video is intended to perform the seduction.

The image of oneself on a cell phone screen is not unlike a first-person avatar in an online game; avatars become para-authentic selves whose existences blur with "real" or embodied selves (Jin, 2010; Mallan, 2009). New media scholars use the term "presence" to indicate the illusory state where users no longer perceive the medium as a separate entity. This effect is greater given the perception of the cell phone as an integral part of one's anatomy. Sending a risqué picture of oneself to a paramour, then, is the virtual equivalent of the intimate act of undressing before a lover. The difference between the two erotic acts is, in one sense, indiscernible to the young digital operant; yet the distinction is also of crucial importance in the contemporary sexual climate.

Sexting thus can be construed as an act of ardor, a flirtatious exchange between intimates. And the texts and images personify and symbolize the sender. For the sexter, the act is a one-on-one interaction, a private communication from one individual to another. To the young adolescent, the sexted message is a love letter of sorts.

It matters, too, that sexting involves no physical contact: no touching, no kisses or caresses, no exchange of body fluids. "We are not having sex, we are sexting," emphasized the boy in the Pew Center study quoted earlier; and in the same study, many teens dismissed the practice as "not a big deal." A survey conducted by the National Campaign to Prevent Teen Pregnancy (2008) found that a quarter of their teen respondents viewed sexting as harmless, while the vast majority saw it as "fun" and "flirtatious," even when they were aware of the risks. For teens and preteens, who use technology in ways that are often obscure and incomprehensible to adults, sexting represents a version of sexuality that dodges the embodied dangers of sex in "real life"— the perilous prospects of teen pregnancy, rape, and sexually transmitted infections that have been hammered home to them in an "abstinence only" era. Sexting, thus, is "safe sex:" virtual, disembodied, digitized and sanitized, it offers the possibility of erotic play without the perils of real-world sexual activity.

This is a logical move for teenagers and children raised in a conservative climate where they have been taught to fear sex as the site of disease, coercion, and unplanned parenthood. Research indicates that "sex positive" sex education—that is, a program of education that acknowledges the pleasures and prerogatives of sex, as well as the risks—would empower children to make better decisions about sexual activity (Gresle-Favier, 2010). But the United States is, on the whole, still light years away from such progressive approaches to dealing with the sexuality of children and adolescents, and so young people invent ways of exploring sexuality without the physical entanglements they have been warned against. Sexting is one such invention.

Children and teenagers sext even when they are aware that their messages are likely to be circulated to unintended recipients. The appeal of translating their sexual bodies into virtual realms is seemingly irresistible; they are reacting, too, to peer pressure and cultural norms. Girls report sexting as a response to requests from boyfriends or other males; boys report forwarding sexts as a response to male peer pressure. But boys sext girls, as well, seeing it as a way to initiate a relationship. LGBT (lesbian, gay, bisexual, and transgender) teens sext, often to pursue relationships hidden from parents and heterosexual peers. And in a media environment rife with erotic imagery—in advertisements, music videos, movies, video games, TV shows and toys—the sexy image is the coin of the realm.

Erotic images play a complex role in contemporary youth cultures. Most people come into contact with sexually explicit media in adolescence, and they are a tacitly acknowledged element of sexual education as well as peer group socialization. Young adults in the twenty-first century are not particularly offended or disturbed by pornography, seeing its use as normal and acceptable (Carroll et al., 2008)—indeed, erotic imagery is so much part of mainstream media culture that it would be difficult to reject it out of hand, and children are exposed to it almost from birth, it is such an entrenched part of a media-saturated environment. The pervasiveness of erotica may explain the open attitudes toward pornography among youth, as the distinctions between mainstream imagery and softcore pornography are growing increasingly blurred and ambiguous. And though the images are not "real"—in the sense that they are representations, commercially driven signs, technologically created, manipulated and disseminated via artifices that even young audience members recognize—they are also "real" in that they comprise the lived environment of the twenty-first century. The photographed, airbrushed, digitally altered bodies of the women and men in magazines and music videos epitomize desirability and gendered ideals: they offer cues to viewers about how best to perform femininity and masculinity. Following Guy Debord's (1983) observation that we live in a society of the spectacle, where social relationships among people are "mediated by images," lived sexualities must be understood as deeply imbricated by visual imagery.

Research indicates that mediated sexualities are influential in young people's understandings of real-world sexual interactions (Ward, 2003), and this convergence appears to include visual self-presentation, at least within the phenomenon of sexting, and to some extent in other online forums. As Mendelson and Papacharissi (2010) pointed out in a study of Facebook, young women "often posed in exaggerated sexy poses with each other, showing leg or exaggerating their cleavage. … Their sexy poses were often recognized and complimented through comments from both male and female friends" (p. 263). This observation dovetails with the overall gendered patterns of sexting, where girls sext more frequently than boys, and also offers some insight into the cultural capital associated with sexy self-presentation.

User-generated content is a key aspect of digital media today, and for youth creating avatars in online spaces is a way to explore the identity questions that beleaguer adolescence (Beals, 2010). It is not a leap to construe the sexted image as an avatar of sorts—a fabrication that offers the same possibilities of pleasure and fantasy, but one even more closely bound to the human creator than a figure in a game, in that it is a conscious self-representation of reality, a literal self-image. Virtual worlds like Habbo, WeeWorld, and Second Life offer tools for users to customize and activate their online personae; so the act of translating oneself into an uploadable and transmissible image is at once familiar and affirming to young digital operants.

The interactive play between gamer and avatar offers a chance to experiment with selfhood, to "toy with subjectivity, play with being," as the media scholar Bob Rehak (2003, p. 123) puts it; on his analysis, the avatar is conjoined with the user's embodiment, enabling players "to think through questions of agency and existence, exploring in fantasy form aspects of their own materiality" (p. 122). The sexted image serves the same purpose for young adolescents exploring issues of gender and sexuality in a climate that restricts and represses such explorations in reality.

To understand sexting as adolescent exploration does not mean that sexting is harmless. Precisely because we live in an era where the sexuality of minor children is regulated by law and stigmatized by cultural convention, these images have serious social implications. The circulation of sexted images is often intended to shame and disgrace the "sextee," and sexters can face legal sanctions. The cultural historian Leo Marx (2010) reminds us that technology is hazardous: "By consigning technologies to the realm of things, this well-established iconography distracts attention from the human—socioeconomic and political—relations which largely determine who uses them and for what purposes" (p. 577). When children translate their bodies into technological forms, they concede them to the caprices of those who use the technologies for their own, often nefarious, purposes, from bullying to cyberporn. My analysis of the phenomenon of sexting offers insights into these contradictory dimensions of children's engagements with technologies—their liberatory potential as well as their regressive and repressive significations.

Mapping children's sexualities in the contemporary mediascape

The sexting issue is just one aspect of the technological landscape that today's youth constantly navigate. Though handheld technologies offer the illusion of individual control over this land-scape, these technologies are elements of a larger system of technological production whose political, economic, and ideological premises demarcate and permeate tech usage even to the micro-level of the individual user. Bound up in the workings of global capital hegemonies, information communication technologies (ICTs) cannot be viewed naïvely as apolitical machines or through a utopian vision of progress. Handheld devices—iPads, e-readers, cell phones, laptops—are conduits for information, some of which can be generated by users, but much of which is still produced by multinational media corporations with avaricious economic and ideological investments; as Jameson (1984) has pointed out,

> The technology of contemporary society is therefore mesmerizing and fascinating, not so much in its own right, but because it seems to offer some privileged representational shorthand for grasping a network of power and control even more difficult for our minds and imaginations to grasp—namely the whole new decentred global network of the third stage of capital itself.
>
> *(p. 79)*

The signs and images that flicker on miniature screens are elements of the broader global mediascape, defined by Appadurai (1996) as "the distribution of the electronic capabilities to produce and disseminate information ... and the images of the world created by these media" (p. 35). The videos, games, apps, and icons downloaded to small screens replicate and reiterate the larger-scale images and ideographs of movie screens, jumbotrons, and billboard advertisements; content-sharing and multiplatform products blur the lines among these media. Increasingly, the mediascape forms the contemporary terrain: the contours of our geospatial locations are cell phone towers, LED displays, satellite dishes, and corporate logos; GPS systems drive our movements among these simulated landmarks; pixilated images dominate our everyday interactions.

For Jameson, spatial issues are "the fundamental organizing concern" of a postmodern era (p. 89); evolving societies are characterized by spatial mutations that challenge our very subject positions. In the contemporary moment, in an environment permeated by the apparatus of media and flooded by mediated images, children translate and retranslate their embodied loca-tions via cyberspaces and cyberselves that move across dimensions to act and interact. Children engage actively with technologies, creating avatars and self-representations, scoring points in games, communicating across time and space with friends and strangers. At the same time, the ideological undercurrents of media representations pervade these processes. Video games, for example, are notorious for the hyper-masculinity and hyper-femininity of the characters (e.g. Cassell and Jenkins, 1998; Ivory, 2006; Kang and Yang, 2006), offering patterns of gendered appearance that reinscribe regressive stereotypes. Images of women and men in advertising idealize hypersexualized bodies: slender and voluptuous for females, muscular and powerful for men. And while media technologies valorize these physical forms, biotechnologies are easily available as a means of attaining them, for they are not readily found in nature. Plastic surgeries among minors have risen significantly in the past decade: in 2010, over 200,000 plastic surgeries were performed on 13- to 19-year-olds in the U.S., the most common of which were optional cosmetic procedures such as rhinoplasty and breast augmentation (American Society of Plastic Surgeons, 2011). Biotechnologies and media technologies thus function seamlessly in concert to reshape children's embodied selves to conform to the mediated images; in these ways, children's embodiment, too, is a form of "mixed reality," an amalgamation of image and tissue, flesh and fabrication. These engagements of the physical and the technological are dynamic, fluid, iterative and ongoing, destabilizing environments, corporealities, and subjectivities.

Jameson posited that we need new "cognitive maps" in order to learn to function in mutating and shifting social spaces—maps that would disabuse us of the illusion that we exist in a libertarian utopia, free of power-based hierarchies and capital hegemonies. The recognition that children's lives are imbricated by technologies underscores the urgency of developing models of theory and praxis that locate children's technologized bodies in their political, economic, and social contexts.

SEE ALSO in this volume chapter by Ling and Bertel and chapter by Jochen Peter.

References

American Society of Plastic Surgeons (2011). Plastic surgery for teenagers briefing paper. Retrieved at http://www.plasticsurgery.org/news-and-resources/briefing-papers/plastic-surgery-for-teenagers.html

Appadurai, A. (1996). *Modernity at large: Cultural dimensions of globalization*. Minneapolis: University of Minnesota Press.

Arceneaux, N. (2009). Paul Reveres of early radio: The Boy Scouts and the origins of broadcasting. *Studies in Popular Culture*, *31*(2), 81–100.

Beals, L. M. (2010). Content creation in virtual worlds to support adolescent identity development. *New Directions for Youth Development*, *2010*(128), 45–53.

Blair, B. L. and Fletcher, A. C. (2011). "The only 13-year-old on Planet Earth without a cell phone:" Meanings of cell phones in early adolescents' everyday lives. *Journal of Adolescent Research*, *26*(2), 155–77.

Bond, E. (2010). The mobile phone = bike shed? Children, sex, and mobile phones. *New Media and Society*, *13*(4), 587–604.

Carroll, J. S., Padilla-Walker, L. M., Nelson, L. J., Olson, C. D., Barry, C. M. and Madsen, S. D. (2008). Generation XXX: Pornography acceptance and use among emerging adults. *Journal of Adolescent Research*, *23*(1), 6–30.

Cassell, J. and Jenkins, H. (1998). *From Barbie to Mortal Kombat: Gender and computer games*. Cambridge, Mass.: MIT Press.

Christian Science Monitor (2009). Sexting overreach, April 28, p. 8.

Cohn, D. (2009). *Teens, sex and the Internet: A pilot study on the Internet and its impact on adolescent health and sexuality*. (Unpublished Master of Public Health thesis). Drexel University: Philadelphia.

Debord, G. (1983). *Society of the spectacle*. Detroit: Black and Red.

Elias, N. and Lemish, D. (2009). Spinning the web of identity: the roles of the internet in the lives of immigrant adolescents. *New Media & Society*, *11*(4), 533–51.

Forbes, S. G. (2011). Sex, cells, and SORNA: Applying sex offender registration laws to sexting cases. *William and Mary Law Review*, *52*(5), 1717–46.

Green, E. and Singleton, C. (2007). Mobile selves: Gender, ethnicity and mobile phones in the everyday lives of young Pakistani-British women and men. *Information, Communication and Society*, *10*(4), 505–26.

Gresle-Favier, C. (2010). The legacy of abstinence-only discourses and the place of pleasure in US discourses on adolescent sexuality. *Sex Education, 10*(4), 413–22.

Grimm, L. (2000). Flintknapping: Relating material culture and social practice in the Upper Paleolithic. In J. S. Derevenski (Ed.), *Children and material culture*. New York: Routledge, pp. 53–71.

Hansen, M. (2006). *Bodies in code: Interfaces with digital media*. New York: Routledge.

Hoffman, J. (2011, March 27). A girls' nude photo, and altered lives. *The New York Times*, p. A1.

Högberg, A. (2008). Playing with flint: Tracing a child's imitation of adult work in a lithic assemblage. *Journal of Archaeological Method and Theory, 15*(1), 112–31.

Humphries, J. (2010). *Children and child labour in the British Industrial Revolution*. New York: Cambridge University Press.

Ivory, J. D. (2006). Still a man's game: Gender representation in online reviews of video games. *Mass Communication and Society, 9*(1), 103–14.

Jameson, F. (1984). Postmodernism, or the cultural logic of late capitalism. *New Left Review, 146*, 54–92.

Jin, S. A. (2010). Parasocial interaction with an avatar in second life: A typology of the self and an empirical test of the mediating role of social presence. *Presence, 19*(4), 331–40.

Kamp, K. A. (2001). Prehistoric children working and playing: A Southwestern case study in learning ceramics. *Journal of Anthropological Research, 57*(4), 427–50.

Kang, H. and Yang, H. (2006). The visual characteristics of avatars in computer-mediated communication. *International Journal of Human-Computer Studies, 64*(12), 1173–83.

Lenhart, A. (2009, December 15). Teens and sexting: Attitudes toward sexting. Philadelphia, PA: Pew Internet and American Life Project. Retrieved at http://www.pewinternet.org/Reports/2009/Teens-and-Sexting/Main-Report/3-Attitudes-towards-sexting.aspx

Livingstone, S. and Bovill, M. (2001). *Families and the Internet: An Observational Study of Children and Young People's Internet Use – A Report for BTexact Technologies*. London: London School of Economics.

Livingstone, S. (2008). Taking risky opportunities in youthful content creation: Teenagers' use of social networking sites for intimacy, privacy and self-expression. *New Media and Society, 10*(3), 393–411.

Luckett, M. (1995). Filming the family: Home movie systems and the domestication of spectatorship. *Velvet Light Trap, 36*(Fall), 21–32.

Mallan, K. (2009). Look at me! Look at me! Self-representation and self-exposure through online networks. *Digital Culture and Education, 1*(1), 51–56.

Marx, L. (2010). Technology: The emergence of a hazardous concept. *Technology and Culture, 51*(3), 561–77.

Mendelson, A. and Papacharissi, Z. (2010). Look at us: Collective narcissism in college student facebook photo galleries. In Z. Papacharissi (Ed.), *A networked self: Identity, community, and culture on social network sites*. New York: Routledge.

Montagu, A. (1976). Toolmaking, hunting, and the origin of language. *Annals of the New York Academy of Sciences, 280*(1), 266–74.

National Campaign to Prevent Teen Pregnancy (2008). *Sex and Tech: Results from a Survey of Teens and Young Adults*. Washington DC: National Campaign to Prevent Teen Pregnancy.

Oksman, V. and Rautiainen, P. (2003). "Perhaps it is a body part:" How the mobile phone became an organic part of the everyday lives of Finnish children and teenagers. In J. E. Katz (Ed.), *Machines that become us: The social context of personal communication technology*. New Brunswick, NJ: Transaction, pp. 293–308.

Olivier, M. (2007). George Eastman's modern Stone Age family: Snapshot photography and the Brownie. *Technology and Culture, 48*(1), 1–19.

Peter, J. and Valkenburg, P. M. (2006). Adolescents' exposure to sexually explicit online material and recreational attitudes toward sex. *Journal of Communication, 56*, 639–60.

——(2008). Adolescents' exposure to sexually explicit Internet material, sexual uncertainty, and attitudes toward uncommitted sexual exploration: Is there a link? *Communication Research, 35*, 579–601.

——(2010). Processes underlying the effects of adolescents' use of sexually explicit Internet material: The role of perceived realism. *Communication Research, 37*(3), 375–99.

Quaid, L. (2009, December 4). Many young people 'sexting,' poll finds. *San Jose Mercury News*, p. 1A.

Rademacher, M. (2005). Am I a punk? Communication of punk identity in online message boards. Paper presented at the annual meeting of the International Communication Association, May 26–30, New York.

Rathke, L. (2011, August 18). 22 teens involved in Vt. sexting ring. Associated Press.

Rega, E. (2000). The gendering of children in the early Bronze Age cemetery at Mokrin. In M. Donald and L. Hurcombe (Eds), *Gender and material culture in archaeological perspective*. New York: Palgrave Macmillan, pp. 238–49.

Rehak, B. (2003). Playing at being: Psychoanalysis and the avatar. In M. J. P. Wolf and B. Perron (Eds), *The video game theory reader*. New York: Routledge, pp. 103–28.

Ribak, R. (2009). Remote control, umbilical cord, and beyond: The mobile phone as a transitional object. *British Journal of Developmental Psychology*, *27*(1), 183–96.

Selwyn, N. (2009). The digital native: myth and reality. *Aslib Proceedings: New Information Perspectives*, *61*(4), 364–79.

Shea, J. (2006). Children's play: Reflections on the invisibility of children in the Paleolithic record. *Evolutionary Anthropology*, *15*(6), 212–16.

Stern, S. T. (2007). *IM me: Adolescent girls and the world of instant messaging*. New York: Peter Lang.

Thulin, E. and Vilhel, B. (2007) Mobiles everywhere: youth, the mobile phone, and changes in everyday practice. *Young: Nordic Journal of Youth Research*, *15*(3), 235–53.

Tsoulis-Reay, A. (2009). OMG I'M ONLINE … AGAIN! MySpace, MSN and the everyday mediation of girls. *Screen Education 53*(Autumn), 48–55.

Valkenburg, P. M. and Jochen, P. (2009). The effects of instant messaging on the quality of adolescents' existing friendships: A longitudinal study. *Journal of Communication*, *59*(1), 79–97.

Waggoner, Z. (2009). *My avatar, my self: Identity in video role-playing games*. Jefferson, NC: McFarland.

Ward, L. M. (2003). Understanding the role of entertainment media in the sexual socialization of American youth: A review of empirical research. *Developmental Review*, *23*(3), 347–88.

Zirkel, P. A. (2009). All atwitter about sexting. *Phi Delta Kappan*, *91*(2), 76.

PART III

CONCERNS AND CONSEQUENCES

EDITOR'S INTRODUCTION

The vast majority of research in the field of children and media has been dominated by concerns for the effects media might have on them, the implications of media use, and the consequences for individuals and society at large. This part of the book introduces the main areas of effects research most heavily investigated.

Deborah L. Linebarger opens this section with the claim that babies' exposure to screen media has intensified considerably in the last 15 years. This serves to reinforce the need to focus research on the youngest of audiences and, in particular, the implications of media use for early cognitive and language development. Linebarger argues that because infants have a limited developmental repertoire, their ability to learn from screen content is challenged. Prior to 18 months old, infants learn significantly more from a physically-present adult than a screen presentation. This phenomenon is referred to as the video deficit. But, screen media are not unique in this regard, as infants have similar difficulty learning from other symbolic media (e.g., books, pictures). Still, processing and learning from screen content is possible at this early age. Therefore, in order to advance learning, it is recommended that screen content incorporate realistic objects and events, social contingency coupled with language-promoting strategies, and production techniques that highlight key contents. Infants also learn more when they view the same content repeatedly, when their parents co-view with them, and when TVs are turned off while they are in the room.

A widely held concern is whether there is a relationship between children's media use and the development of ADHD (attention deficit hyperactivity disorder). The chapter by **Mariëtte Huizinga**, **Sanne W.C. Nikkelen**, and **Patti M. Valkenburg** reviews the literature on this issue. They focus on what they consider to be the most promising hypotheses regarding this possible effect and review the main results of the empirical studies by combining a qualitative literature review with the results of a formal meta-analysis. The authors conclude that studies have found the presence of a negative relationship between media use and the presence of ADHD-symptoms (i.e., inattention, hyperactivity, and impulsivity). More specifically, use of violent saturated media was significantly associated with ADHD. An effect of fast-paced media use on ADHD could not be established, as the number of available studies that examined this relationship was too limited. This meta-analysis underlines the crucial need for future research to systematically investigate individual differences that may moderate the relation between children's media use and ADHD.

While the media are, undoubtedly, part of the fantasy world of children, the nature of their influence on children's fantasizing continues to be discussed at length in public and in academia. The chapter by **Maya Götz** presents the state of research regarding this domain and, in addition, focuses on methodological approaches used to study children's inner worlds. She argues that recent research proposes considering children's media use and their fantasy worlds as an integration process. For example, children adopt the perspective of characters in the story during media reception and imagine how they would act in the situation. The degree of intensity with which children enter into stories can differ greatly between individuals. Following reception, they integrate parts of the media into their daily life, especially if the story and characters are highly attractive. Thus, researchers have found that children incorporate elements of the media in their fantasy worlds and in identity development processes.

Discussions of fantasy-worlds have often been intertwined with that of the development of creativity. The proliferation of digital media has given new impetus to this field of research. **Kylie Peppler** explores how social media spaces can be leveraged for creativity, focusing on the ways in which social media support youths' creative production. The chapter examines these ideas by, first, presenting relevant research in both the fields of creativity and social media, followed by examples of notable online youth communities dedicated to innovative endeavors, and, finally, with a concluding argument for the importance of vernacular forms of creativity for learning and development as well as discussion of the implications of these new media developments for research on creativity.

Nicole Martins' chapter addresses the role of entertainment media, particularly television and film, in emotional development. First, she briefly reviews content analyses of emotional portrayals on television. Her review of studies of children's recognition and learning of emotional portrayals on television concludes that there are developmental differences in children's ability to comprehend characters' emotional experiences. She continues to review the positive and negative impacts of exposure to emotionally charged portrayals, with particular attention to the research on fear and desensitization. The chapter concludes with suggestions for future research, such as the role of emotions as an impetus for media selection.

Issues relating to media violence and youth are perennially important, and have inspired decades of social science research. Acknowledging recent controversies and concerns, **Erica Scharrer** explores the ways in which young people at various locations across the globe receive (and even participate in) aggressive and violent content via media. Three categories of potential influence of violent media that emphasize cognitive, affective, and behavioral implications for young people are discussed: aggression, desensitization, and fear (also known as the *mean world* syndrome). The author demonstrates how meta-analyses provide an efficient means of covering rather vast and extensive literatures on the topic, though these presentations are supplemented in the chapter by prominent individual studies. Finally, two major means of disrupting media effects of violence are discussed – parental mediation and media literacy.

The second oft-mentioned "red flag" in discussions of media and children is the effect they might have on sexual development. **Jochen Peter** argues that despite scholarly discussions about the relationship between media and adolescents' sexual development, little research on the issue exists. His chapter synthesizes what is currently known about the association between adolescents' use of sexual media content (SMC) and their sexual development (i.e., changes in adolescents' sexual cognitions, affect, and behavior). In terms of cognitions, more frequent use of SMC has been found to be related to more permissive sexual attitudes, stronger gender stereotypes, and improved sexual knowledge. In terms of sexual affect, the literature shows gender differences regarding arousal to sexually explicit material and a complex association between SMC and sexual satisfaction. In terms of sexual behavior, studies have found that the use of SMC is linked to earlier sexual activities. In contrast, the relation between the use of SMC and sexual risk behavior is still unclear. The chapter concludes by outlining the shortcomings of existing research and the possibilities for future research.

In relation to the issue of media effects on child and adolescent development of body image, **Kristen Harrison**'s chapter summarizes research concerning the *lean body* ideal prevalent in Western media and disordered eating in connection with media exposure. The chapter begins by making the case for the continued study of thinness-oriented disordered eating, followed by discussion of thin-ideal media as a key sociocultural influence. This discussion is followed by a review of ongoing debates about whether effects are strong enough to merit concern, and whether pro-eating-disorder websites function as support systems or recruitment tools? The chapter concludes with a discussion of future research directions including the need for increased attention to family, peer, and community agents as moderators and mediators of exposure outcomes; developmental processes from early childhood though young adulthood; global trends in thin-ideal media content and effects; and modes of resistance.

A closely related concern for the contribution of media to obesity is discussed in the chapter by **Bradley J. Bond, Melissa N. Richards**, and **Sandra L. Calvert**. Obesity has become an epidemic, affecting the health and well-being of children throughout the world. Media exposure is one of the main environmental factors often imputed as a contributor to childhood obesity. This chapter summarizes the research on media and obesity by detailing five major mechanisms by which media may contribute to childhood obesity: food advertising's influence on increased caloric intake, overeating during media exposure, lower metabolic rates during exposure, increased sedentary behavior during exposure, and sleep patterns disrupted by media. The chapter also presents theories employed to explain the influence of food marketing on the dietary habits of children. The chapter concludes by suggesting future areas of research in the realm of media and obesity.

Another health-related issue concerns media and substance abuse; such as, alcohol, smoking, and drugs. In her review of the research, **Dina L.G. Borzekowski** argues that media messages about substance use are ubiquitous. First, the majority of these environmental cues communicate powerful and positive reasons to initiate and continue the use of tobacco, alcohol, and recreational drugs. Second, children and adolescents are very familiar with these media messages. Thus, given clear influence on their attitudes and behaviors, there are growing efforts and interventions to change the media environment in order to lessen the impact of these messages on substance abuse among children and youth.

From topics focusing on physical well-being, discussion moves into the realm of the implications of media use to children's understanding of the social and political world. **Jeanne Prinsloo**'s chapter offers an overview of research into media and children's learning about the social world. The chapter presents an account of two traditions of research. First, the *effects* tradition assumes the child is vulnerable and therefore there is concern with the negative impact of media on children. For example, both *cultivation* and *social learning* theories attend to how children are socialized along lines of race, though these studies focus on blackness as though whiteness is not at issue. Thus, these studies investigate the extent of exposure, the nature of racialized representations, and the media preferences of black children. In contrast, the *cultural* research tradition assumes that the child is an active agent, acting within complex historical and cultural contexts. Studies investigate how young people negotiate and produce meaning from the contesting discourses they encounter. Finally, this overview points to the limitations of our knowledge in relation to children's learning about their social worlds and cites the need for broad and localized research.

Cynthia Carter focuses specifically on news consumption and meaning. She argues that it has become something of a truism that children regard the news as "boring." Thus, no matter where they live in the world, researchers find that they refuse to read newspapers, tune into television or radio news, or search out news on the internet. The term "boring" is ideologically loaded with assumptions about children's civic apathy, and runs the risk of becoming a self-fulfilling prophecy. If adult news is "boring," argues Carter, it is because it represents a world of adults doing incomprehensible things, where children's interests and opinions are rarely regarded as noteworthy or valuable, and thus are absent. When news is produced with children's civic development in mind, it has the potential to enable them as citizens and empower them to develop an ongoing interest in the world. This chapter assesses the contributions of research investigating issues associated with the role of news for adults and children in facilitating or hindering children's development and participation as citizens.

In reviewing an effect that has been drawing increasing attention from policymakers, **Erica Weintraub Austin** discusses the processes and impacts of media on children's political socialization. She, too, argues that despite commonly expressed concerns that young people are apathetic and cynical about public affairs, evidence shows instead that they find the world around them to be of interest, even if they do not find traditional-style news coverage compelling. Indeed, as civic participation among young people has been increasing steadily, we learn that they tend to engage especially when participation is convenient and they believe their efforts will be fruitful. Furthermore, youth seek information independently and in doing so learn from an ever widening variety of media platforms and genres. For example, entertainment news and satire can motivate additional information-seeking and discussion. In turn, this helps youth contextualize what they learn and helps them develop media literacy skills. Finally, while parental influence often takes place through role modeling and communication style, rather than through the explicit discussion of public affairs, politically-oriented discussion has been found to be especially valuable when solicited by youth themselves.

Political socialization is often juxtaposed to consumer socialization. **Moniek Buijzen, Esther Rozendaal**, and **Eva A. van Reijmersdal** move us to that realm of scholarship by reviewing the research literature on young people and persuasion. They focus specifically on the contemporary commercial media environment, which has changed dramatically over the past decade. Advertisers targeting the youth market have rapidly adopted new advertising techniques including branded websites, brand placement in video games, and viral marketing in social media. These newer advertising practices typically rely on affect-based mechanisms and are often embedded within the medium context, which may have important consequences for young people's processing of advertising. The chapter focuses on three important domains: child and adolescent persuasion processing; persuasion and resistance; and advertising literacy. The authors conclude the chapter with a reconceptualization of advertising literacy that contends with the current commercial media environment, and also serves as the foundation for setting the agenda for future research.

In discussing media and gender identities, **Sharon R. Mazzarella** begins with a brief discussion of the difference between biological sex and the cultural construct of gender and maps the body of scholarship on media and children's gender identities. Specifically, Mazzarella addresses the gender roles presented to children in the media they consume; the differences between girls' and boys' media preferences; and how children and adolescents incorporate digital media in their gender identity work. The chapter concludes with a call for scholarship on children and identity work to fill in the gaps with more of a focus on boys, a range of technologies, and cross-cultural studies.

This section of the book concludes with **Gustavo Mesch**'s discussion of media and peer sociability. This chapter reviews the theoretical perspectives about and empirical research on the role of online communication in youth culture and its effects on young people's social life. The discussion focuses on sociability, a concept that refers to the psychological inclination and behaviors that are used when one is involved in social relationships. Mesch argues that online and face-to-face ties overlap to a great extent and that online communication generally has a positive effect on participation in peer networks. Young people who do not participate in online communication risk social exclusion. Finally, rather than isolating individuals, online ties facilitate access to important information and resources that do not exist in the offline peer network.

20

SCREEN MEDIA, EARLY COGNITIVE DEVELOPMENT, AND LANGUAGE

Babies' learning from screens

Deborah L. Linebarger

Introduction

Screen media exposure (i.e., any audio-visual content that can be viewed on TVs, DVDs, iPads, mobile devices, computers) for children under three years is prevalent. Recent surveys of infants and toddlers in the US indicate that more than 99 percent of families have TVs in their homes and 74 percent of infants are exposed to TV before the age of two (Rideout and Hamel, 2006). Babies under two spend about 1½ hours per day watching screen media turned on specifically for them (Rideout and Hamel, 2006) and spend about 5.5 hours per day in a room where the television is on in the background (Lapierre et al., 2012). A majority of parents believe that particular types of screen media content (e.g., infant-directed DVDs like *Brainy Baby* or *Baby Einstein*) can be educational and beneficial to their infant's development (Rideout et al., 2003; Zimmerman et al., 2007). Standing in contrast to these parents' beliefs about the benefits of infant screen use is the American Academy of Pediatrics' (AAP, 2011) position statement that viewing by infants and toddlers is not recommended and is likely harmful. Some researchers have argued that any exposure to screens leads to over-stimulation and later developmental problems (e.g., Christakis et al., 2004; Zimmerman et al., 2007) although more recent evidence indicates that the relations among viewing, infant capacities, and developmental outcomes are more complex and nuanced (e.g., Barr, 2010; Linebarger and Vaala, 2010).

Babies and learning

Babies are a special audience. During the first two years of life, an extraordinary amount of development across multiple domains occurs. Of these domains, the ability to use language to communicate feelings, thoughts, ideas, and experiences is considered a privileged domain (i.e., infants are uniquely primed to rapidly acquire language; Bransford et al., 2000). Coupled with and inextricably linked to language development is cognition. Cognition is defined as a set of mental processes used to acquire knowledge and learn. These processes include perception, attention, memory, problem-solving, reasoning, and decision-making. Babies typically speak their first words around 12 months. Getting to this developmental point requires considerable growth and integration between cognition and language. Both sets of skills work independently and in concert to facilitate infants' exploration and understanding of their everyday worlds.

Infants' burgeoning cognitive abilities guide their initial conceptual understanding of objects and events. They will categorize these early experiences along a number of salient perceptual dimensions including shape, color, texture, motion, and function (Clark, 2004). While these early encounters with objects and events are primarily perceptual in nature, language use by adults during these encounters assists category formation (e.g., Ferry et al., 2010; Fulkerson and Waxman, 2007; Waxman and Markow, 1995). As early as three months old, researchers determined that babies were more likely to categorize objects after hearing words about these objects versus perceptually-matched tones (Ferry et al., 2010). Infants' frequent exposure to everyday language likely confers a special status to words by highlighting commonalities and differences among groups of objects (Clark, 2004). As infants' interactions with their worlds continue and their linguistic knowledge grows, language will shape and further refine their conceptual understanding (Clark, 2004) and their conceptual understanding will help them make inferences about the probable meanings of unfamiliar words. Eventually, language becomes a representational resource; that is, it can serve as a framework for encoding or mentally depicting new information. Representational thought is an important precursor to learning from screen media (DeLoache et al., 2010).

Learning from screen media

Prior to 18 months of age, learning from screen content is challenging (Barr and Hayne, 1999; Hayne et al., 2003; Meltzoff, 1988; Robb et al., 2009). Research documents that infants learn more from live interactions (i.e., someone is physically present with the infant during the learning trials) versus interactions modeled by an onscreen actor ("video deficit"; Anderson and Pempek, 2005; Barr, 2010). This deficit has been observed across a number of learning paradigms including imitation (e.g., Barr and Hayne, 1999; Hayne et al., 2003; Meltzoff, 1988), problem-solving (e.g., Schmitt and Anderson, 2002), and language-learning (DeLoache et al., 2010; Kuhl et al., 2003; Krcmar et al., 2007; Robb et al., 2009).

One difficulty in the interpretation of this evidence lies in the conditions under which learning was contrasted. Studies that found a video deficit typically compared learning from video to learning from a "live" actor. This comparison invariably set up learning from screen media to fail. Infants lack experience with, prior knowledge of, and have limited cognitive capacity for understanding screen content. Conversely, they have extensive experience with, have developed prior knowledge about, and can subsequently devote greater cognitive capacity toward understanding objects or events introduced during interactions with a physically-present adult. The video deficit is not unique to screen-based media. Rather, screen media are one of a variety of symbols used to represent particular persons, objects, or events not physically present. Babies have difficulty learning from any symbols because they cannot simultaneously process content as both a concrete entity and a symbol of that particular entity, a phenomenon labeled dual representation (e.g., DeLoache and Burns, 1994). More comparable exemplars for evaluation would be other symbolic media like books or pictures. When comparisons are made across symbolic media, the "video deficit" effect is similarly reproduced (Barr, 2010; Barr and Hayne, 1999; DeLoache and Burns, 1994; Kuhl et al., 2003; McCall et al., 1977; Simcock and DeLoache, 2006). For instance, infants' difficulty in learning from picture books developmentally parallels their difficulty in learning from screen media (e.g., Simcock and DeLoache, 2006). More recently,

Barr has referred to the deficit as a "transfer" deficit (Barr, 2010); that is, infants experience difficulty transferring their understanding of two-dimensional content to a three-dimensional learning situation.

The difficulty in processing and learning from screen content can be overcome. Evidence suggests that the degree of correspondence between an infant's everyday life and screen media's unfamiliar forms and content determine whether, how, and how much an infant will learn. By engaging in numerous daily interactions with persons, objects, and events, infants develop a framework or routine for what to expect and how to process and learn from these interactions. Once formed, a routine provides structure for interpreting events, anticipating temporal sequencing, and drawing inferences from new experiences. Developing a routine around interactions with screen media, book reading, or other symbol systems provides a framework through which infants can learn, build, and organize concepts, patterns, and relationships. As knowledge of and experiences with screen media accumulate, infants' representational understanding of screen media grows. Initially, the formation of a routine leads to content-specific learning because early learning is concretely tied to a stimulus presentation. In fact, research indicates that learning is more likely to be demonstrated if the same sets of cues present during initial encoding are also present during the testing phase (Barr, 2010; Barr and Hayne, 1999). Over time and with experience, content-specific learning will generalize to situations outside the immediate screen media context. Boosting the degree of correspondence between what an infant knows or has previously experienced and onscreen content occurs through content-specific manipulations and by participation in supportive contexts surrounding screen media use.

Screen media content manipulations

The major difficulty associated with learning screen content involves babies' ability to adequately represent depicted content in memory for later retrieval. There are a number of studies that demonstrate learning can be improved by manipulating the presentation of content at both macro- and micro-levels.

Macro-level characteristics

Screen media are typically presented in one of three macro-level formats: narratives (e.g., *Arthur and Friends*), expositories (e.g., *Zoboomafoo*) or narrative/expository hybrids (e.g., *Barney & Friends*). Narratives feature characters engaging in numerous language exchanges. These exchanges provide viewers with multiple opportunities to "overhear" conversations. Experimental research indicates that babies learn new words equally well from overhearing two adults talking and directly engaging in talk with an adult (Akhtar, 2005; Akhtar et al., 2001; Floor and Akhtar, 2006). This research has been recently extended to screen media with similar success; that is, infants acquire language by "overhearing" onscreen adults speaking (O'Doherty et al., 2011). Commercially-produced narratives create similar "overhearing" opportunities. Correlational research indicates that babies' narrative viewing predicts more sophisticated language use during play and larger vocabularies at 30 months (Linebarger and Walker, 2005).

Conversely, viewing expository programs predicted poorer language outcomes (Linebarger and Walker, 2005). The purpose of an expository program is to convey information. There are a number of expository types including compare/contrast, sequencing, cause/effect, and descriptive. Young children's lack of familiarity with an expository's organizing features combined with the sheer volume of information is likely to overwhelm their cognitive resources leading to the formation of incomplete representations and subsequent difficulties in retrieving learned content.

Associations between viewing narrative/expository hybrids and language outcomes are mixed. Watching one hybrid (i.e., *Barney & Friends*) predicted more sophisticated use of language while playing, but smaller vocabularies, whereas viewing a different hybrid (i.e., *Teletubbies*) predicted less sophisticated language use during play and smaller vocabularies (Linebarger and Walker, 2005). Hybrids generally link a number of small but narratively-oriented vignettes. While hybrids contain typical narrative elements (e.g., characters, setting, plot) and dialogue, their modest level of coherence and their differing organizational structures (characteristic of expositories) likely contributed to the inconsistent findings.

Micro-level characteristics

Micro-level characteristics are features that have been embedded within screen content to deliver that content. Three different sets of characteristics have been linked to learning from screen content: the use of realistic depictions, the use of social contingency and higher-order language strategies, and the strategic and judicious use of production techniques.

Infants learn more from interactions with live persons; therefore, creating screen content that incorporates more realistic portrayals or situations should result in more learning. Evidence indicates that learning from screen media, pictures, and picture books was more likely to occur with content that was more realistic when compared with animation or cartoons (Barr and Hayne, 1999; DeLoache et al., 1997; Ganea et al., 2008; Schmitt and Anderson, 2002; Simcock et al., 2011).

Social contingency involves efforts to simulate a direct interaction with the viewer or to provide some type of contingent response after potential viewer interaction. Research investigating the effectiveness of higher-order language strategies tested requests for language or action from the viewer and voiceovers that narrated onscreen activity. Both experimental and correlational studies indicate that social contingency and language strategies improved infant learning from screen media (Cleveland and Striano, 2008; Hayne and Herbert, 2004; Houston-Price et al., 2006; Krcmar, 2010; Krcmar et al., 2007; Lauricella et al., 2011; Linebarger and Walker, 2005; Seehagen and Herbert, 2010; Troseth et al., 2006).

Production techniques include both auditory and visual cues that, due to their perceptually salient nature, attract and sustain babies' attention (e.g., sound effects, music; Gola and Calvert, 2011). Unfortunately, these techniques are not always matched to important content. Consequently, children are likely to learn whatever content is paired with these techniques including unimportant or incidental content (Piotrowski, 2010). Experimentally, learning was more likely to occur when clips were created by researchers because these clips were simpler and contained fewer production techniques when compared to commercially-produced screen content. In a recent content analysis, researchers documented that infant-directed screen media were filled with high concentrations of perceptually salient production features (Goodrich et al., 2009). Studies examining commercially-available screen content indicate that little learning occurs (DeLoache et al., 2010; Krcmar et al., 2007; Robb et al., 2009) with the exception of one study that found language-learning benefits only after extended viewing (Vandewater et al., 2010). Recent research has begun to disentangle the variety of production cues found in media to determine which cues help and which hinder learning. For instance, Barr and colleagues determined that background music hindered learning, sound effects matched to key content helped learning, and a combination of background music and sound effects helped learning as long as the sound effects were matched to key content (Barr et al., 2010; Barr et al., 2009). Collectively, this research suggests that production techniques can support learning when used judiciously to mark key content or to enhance the match between onscreen content and real life.

The contexts surrounding screen media use

A number of direct and indirect experiences shape the contexts in which infants' exposure to screen media occurs. Some of these experiences are supportive of learning from screen media while others are more likely to diminish learning. Direct learning effects have been linked to repetition, co-viewing, and constant interruptions from a TV on in the background whereas indirect learning effects have been linked to TV's interference with parental attention to and involvement with their infants.

Repetitive exposure to screen media has been causally linked to babies' increased learning from screen media across several experimental contexts including imitation (Barr et al., 2007; Barr et al., 2009); problem-solving (Robb et al., 2009); and word learning (Krcmar et al., 2007; Vandewater et al., 2010). Because babies have very little background knowledge and experience with screen media, repeated exposure is crucial if any learning is to occur.

Parents interact in a variety of ways with their infants while co-viewing screen media especially child-directed educational content (Mendelsohn et al., 2008, 2010). Interactions consisted of labeling and clarifying content, responding to infant-initiated verbalizations, and extending content beyond the screen to make connections with infants' everyday lives (Barr et al., 2008; Fidler et al., 2010; Lemish and Rice, 1986). Three experimental studies found that infants of parents who used these strategies while co-viewing evidenced better language outcomes (Fender et al., 2010; Mendelsohn et al., 2010; Seehagen and Herbert, 2010).

Exposure to background TV has been linked to shorter play episodes and less focused attention during this play as well as fewer and lower-quality parent–child interactions (Christakis et al., 2009; Kirkorian et al., 2009; Schmidt et al., 2008; Setliff and Courage, 2011). It is likely that these results stem from the nature of the auditory content originating from the TV. Because auditory cues are generated intermittently, they are able to repeatedly recruit attention with little habituation, causing constant attention-shifting and difficulty concentrating or playing.

Background TV exposure also indirectly affects learning by disrupting parental attention and decreasing the quantity and quality of parent–child interactions. Other research indicates that infants and toddlers living in households where there is infrequent and lower-quality parental talk evidence substantially smaller vocabularies by age three (Hart and Risley, 1995) and diminished academic achievement in elementary school (Walker et al., 1994). Correlational evidence documents similar associations among exposure to high levels of adult-directed content, infrequent parent–child talk, and poor language outcomes (Mendelsohn et al., 2010).

Final thoughts

Babies' exposure to screen media has intensified considerably since 1997 due in large part to the introduction of Baby Einstein's infant-directed videos that year. Infants have limited developmental competencies that make learning screen content challenging. Cognitive overload rapidly occurs when the volume and complexity of information typical of screen media exceeds processing capacity (Goodrich et al., 2009). To learn from screen media, infants must navigate a myriad of visual and verbal stimuli as well as understand the dual nature of screen media; that is, they must understand that the screen and its content are both concrete entities and abstract symbols or representations of these entities (DeLoache et al., 2010). Processing and learning from screen media can be enhanced through content-specific manipulations and through changes to the contexts surrounding babies' media use. Onscreen content that incorporates more realistic depictions of persons and objects, social contingency and higher-order language strategies, and the strategic and judicious use of production techniques facilitate learning. Supportive learning contexts arise when infants view the same content repeatedly, when parents co-view with them, and when TVs are turned off while infants are in the room.

Screen media use is pervasive in babies' lives. Moving forward, it is critical to continue to investigate infants' use of it, the specific structural features and content types that impede or improve learning from it, and the contexts surrounding its use that can support or inhibit learning. Much remains to be learned in this regard.

SEE ALSO in this volume chapter by Fisch.

References

Akhtar, N. (2005). The robustness of learning through overhearing. *Developmental Science, 8*(2), 199–209.

Akhtar, N., Jipson, J. and Callanan, M. (2001). Learning words through overhearing. *Child Development,* 72(2), 416–30.

American Academy of Pediatrics (2011). Media use by children younger than 2 years. *Pediatrics, 128*(5), 1–6.

Anderson, D. R. and Pempek, T. A. (2005). Television and very young children. *American Behavioral Scientist, 48*(5), 505–22.

Barr, R. (2010). Transfer of learning between 2D and 3D sources during infancy: Informing theory and practice. *Developmental Review, 30*(2), 128–54.

Barr, R. and Hayne, H. (1999). Developmental changes in imitation from television during infancy. *Child Development, 70*(5), 1067–81.

Barr, R., Muentener, P., Garcia, A., Fujimoto, M. and Chavez, V. (2007). The effect of repetition on imitation from television during infancy. *Developmental Psychobiology, 49*(3), 196–207.

Barr, R., Zack, E., Muentener, P. and Garcia, A. (2008). Infants' attention and responsiveness to television increases with prior exposure and parental interaction. *Infancy, 13*(1), 3–56.

Barr, R., Wyss, N. and Somanader, M. (2009). The influence of electronic sound effects on learning from televised and live models. *Journal of Experimental Child Psychology, 103*(10), 1–16.

Barr, R. E., Shuck, L., Salerno, K., Atkinson, E. and Linebarger, D. L. (2010). Music interferes with learning from television during infancy. *Infant and Child Development, 19*(3), 313–31.

Bransford, J., Brown, A. and Cocking, R. (2000). *How people learn: Brain, mind, experience, and school.* Washington, DC: National Academy Press.

Christakis, D. A., Zimmerman, F. J., DiGuiseppe, D. L. and McCarty, C. A. (2004) Early television exposure and subsequent attentional problems in children. *Pediatrics, 113*(4), 708–13.

Christakis, D. A., Gilkerson, J., Richards, J. A., Zimmerman, F. J., Garrison, M. M., Xu, D., Gray, S. and Yapanel, U. (2009). Audible television and decreased adult words, infant vocalizations and conversational turns: A population-based study. *Archives of Pediatric & Adolescent Medicine, 163*(6), 554–58.

Clark, E. V. (2004) How language acquisition builds on cognitive development. *Trends in Cognitive Sciences, 8*(10), 472–78.

Cleveland, A. and Striano, T. (2008). Televised social interaction and object learning in 14- and 18-month-old infants. *Infant Behavior and Development, 31*(2), 326–31.

DeLoache, J. S. and Burns, N.M. (1994). Symbolic functioning in young children. *Journal of Applied Developmental Psychology, 15*(4), 513–27.

DeLoache, J. S., Miller, K. F. and Rosengren, K. S. (1997). The credible shrinking room: Very young children's performance with symbolic and non-symbolic relations. *Psychological Science, 8*(4), 308–13.

DeLoache, J. S., Chiong, C., Sherman, K., Islam, N., Vanderborght, M., Troseth, G.L., Strouse, G.A. and O'Doherty, K. (2010). Do babies learn from baby media? *Psychological Science, 21*(11), 1570–74.

Fender, J. G., Richert, R. A., Robb, M. B. and Wartella, E. (2010). Parent teaching focus and toddlers' learning from an infant DVD. *Infant and Child Development, 19*(6), 613–27.

Ferry, A., Hespos, S. J. and Waxman, S. (2010). Language facilitates category formation in 3-month-old infants. *Child Development, 81*(2), 472–79.

Fidler, A., Zack, E. and Barr, R. (2010). Television viewing patterns in 6- to 18-month-olds: The role of caregiver-infant interactional quality. *Infancy 15*(2) (2010), 176–96.

Floor, P. and Akhtar, N. (2006). Can 18-month-old infants learn words by listening in on conversations? *Infancy, 9*(3), 327–39.

Fulkerson, A. L. and Waxman, S. R. (2007). Words (but not tones) facilitate object categorization: evidence from 6- and 12-month-olds. *Cognition, 105*(1), 218–28.

Ganea, P. A., Bloom-Pickard, M. and DeLoache, J. S. (2008). Transfer between picture books and the real world by very young children. *Journal of Cognition and Development, 9*(1), 46–66.

Gola, A. A. H. and Calvert, S. L. (2011). Infants' visual attention to baby DVDs as a function of program pacing. *Infancy, 16*(3), 295–305.

Goodrich, S. A., Pempek, T. A. and Calvert, S. (2009). Formal production features of infant and toddler DVDs. *Archives of Pediatric & Adolescent Medicine, 163*(12),1151–56.

Hart, B. and Risley, T. (1995). *Meaningful differences in the everyday experiences of young American children.* Baltimore: Paul H. Brookes.

Hayne, H. and Herbert, J. (2004). The effect of adults' language on long-term retention by 18-month-old infants. *Journal of Experimental Child Psychology, 89*(2), 127–39.

Hayne, H., Herbert, J. and Simcock, G. (2003). Imitation from television by 24- and 30-month-olds. *Developmental Science, 6*(3), 254–61.

Houston-Price, C., Plunkett, K. and Duffy, H. (2006). The use of social and salience cues in early word learning. *Journal of Experimental Child Psychology, 95*(1), 27–55.

Kirkorian, H. L., Pempek, T. A., Murphy, L. A., Schmidt, M. E. and Anderson, D. R. (2009). The impact of background television on parent-child interaction. *Child Development, 80*(5), 1350–59.

Krcmar, M. (2010). Can social meaningfulness and repeat exposure help infants and toddlers overcome the video deficit? *Media Psychology, 13*(1), 31–53.

Krcmar, M., Grela, B. and Lin, K. (2007). Can toddlers learn vocabulary from television? An experimental approach. *Media Psychology, 10*(1), 41–63.

Kuhl, P. K., Tsao, F. M. and Liu, H. M. (2003). Foreign-language experience in infancy: Effects of short-term exposure and social interaction of phonetic learning. *Proceedings of the National Academy of Sciences, 100*(15), 9096–101.

Lapierre, M., Piotrowski, J. T. and Linebarger, D. L. (2012). Background television in the homes of US children. *Pediatrics, 130*(5), 1–8.

Lauricella, A. R., Gola, A. A. H. and Calvert, S. L. (2011). Toddlers' learning from socially meaningful video characters. *Media Psychology, 14*(2), 216–32.

Lemish, D. and Rice, M. L. (1986). Television as a talking picture book: A prop for language acquisition. *Journal of Child Language, 13*(2), 251–74.

Linebarger, D. L. and Walker, D. (2005). Infants' and toddlers' television viewing and relations to language outcomes. *American Behavioral Scientist, 48*(5), 624–45.

Linebarger, D. L. and Vaala, S. (2010). Infants and toddlers, screen media, and language development: An ecological perspective. *Developmental Review, 30*(2), 176–202.

McCall, R. B., Parke, R. D. and Kavanaugh, R. D. (1977). Imitation of live and televised models by children one to three years of age. *Monographs of the Society for Research in Child Development, 42* (5, Serial No. 173).

Meltzoff, A. N. (1988). Imitation of televised models by infants. *Child Development, 59*(5), 1221–29.

Mendelsohn, A. L, Berkule, S. B, Tomopoulos, S., Tamis-Lemonda, C. S., Huberman, H. S., Alvir, J. and Dreyer, B. P. (2008). Infant television and video exposure associated with limited parent–child verbal interactions in low socioeconomic status households. *Archives of Pediatrics & Adolescent Medicine, 162*(5), 411–17.

Mendelsohn, A. L., Brockmeyer, C. A., Dreyer, B. P., Fierman, A. H., Berkule-Silberman, S. B. and Tomopoulos, S. (2010). Do verbal interactions with infants during electronic media exposure mitigate adverse impacts on their language development as toddlers? *Infant and Child Development, 19*(6), 577–93.

O'Doherty, K., Troseth, G., Shimpi, P., Goldenberg, E., Akhtar, N. and Saylor, M. (2011). Third-party social interaction and word learning from video. *Child Development, 82*(3), 902–15.

Piotrowski, J. T. (2010). Evaluating preschoolers' comprehension of educational television: The role of viewer characteristics, stimuli features, and contextual expectations. Publicly accessible Penn Dissertations, Paper 106.

Rideout, V. and Hamel, E. (2006). *The media family: Electronic media in the lives of infants, toddlers, preschoolers and their parents.* Menlo Park, CA: Kaiser Family Foundation.

Rideout, V., Vandewater, E. and Wartella, E. (2003). *Zero to six: Electronic media in the lives of infants, toddlers, and preschoolers.* Menlo Park, CA: Kaiser Family Foundation.

Robb, M. B., Richert, R. A. and Wartella, E. A. (2009). Just a talking book? Word learning from watching baby videos. *British Journal of Developmental Psychology, 27*(1), 27–45.

Schmidt, M. E., Pempek, T. A., Kirkorian, H. L., Lund, A. F. and Anderson, D. R. (2008). The effect of background television on the toy play behavior of very young children. *Child Development, 79*(4), 1137–51.

Schmitt, K. L. and Anderson, D. R. (2002). Television and reality: Toddlers' use of visual information from video to guide behavior. *Media Psychology*, *4*(1), 51–76.

Seehagen, S., and Herbert, J. S. (2010). The role of demonstrator familiarity and language cues on infant imitation from television. *Infant Behavior and Development*, *33*(2), 168–75.

Setliff, A. E. and Courage, M. L. (2011). Background television and infants' allocation of their attention during toy play. *Infancy*, *16*(6), 611–39.

Simcock, G. and DeLoache, J. S. (2006). The effects of iconicity on re-enactment from picture books by 18- to 30-month-old children. *Developmental Psychology*, *42*(6), 1352–57.

Simcock, G., Garrity, K. and Barr, R. (2011). The effect of narrative cues on infants' imitation from television and picture books. *Child Development*, *82*(5), 1607–19.

Troseth, G. L., Saylor, M. M. and Archer, A. H. (2006). Young children's use of video as a source of socially relevant information. *Child Development*, *77*(3), 786–99.

Vandewater, E. A., Barr, R. F., Park, S. E. and Lee, S. J. (2010). A US study of transfer of learning from video to books in toddlers. *Journal of Children and Media*, *4*(4), 451–67.

Walker, D., Greenwood, C., Hart, B. and Carta, J. (1994). Prediction of school outcomes based on early language production and socioeconomic factors. *Child Development*, *65*(2), 606–21.

Waxman, S. R. and Markow, D. B. (1995). Words as invitations to form categories: Evidence from 12- to 13-month old infants. *Cognitive Psychology*, *29*(3), 257–302.

Zimmerman, F. J., Christakis, D. A. and Meltzoff, A. N. (2007). Television and DVD/video viewing in children younger than 2 years. *Archives of Pediatric and Adolescent Medicine,* *161*(5), 473–79.

21

CHILDREN'S MEDIA USE AND ITS RELATION TO ATTENTION, HYPERACTIVITY, AND IMPULSIVITY

Mariëtte Huizinga, Sanne W. C. Nikkelen, and Patti M. Valkenburg

Children's media environment has changed considerably in the past decades. It has become more fast-paced, violent, and arousing, and has been targeting children at an ever younger age (e.g., Allen et al., 1998; Koolstra et al., 2004). During these same decades, the frequency of the diagnosis of Attention Deficit Hyperactivity Disorder (ADHD) among children has also significantly increased, from about 1.5 percent in the 1970s to 1980s to about 8.5 percent in the 1990s and early 2000s (Akinbami et al., 2011; Kelleher et al., 2000). ADHD is a behavioral disorder characterized by elevated levels of inattentiveness, hyperactivity, and impulsivity that (a) are age-inappropriate, (b) pervasive, and (c) impair a child's cognitive and social-emotional functioning (American Psychiatric Association, 2000).

A widely held concern related to these parallel occurring changes is whether there is a relationship between children's media use and the development of ADHD. Knowledge of this relationship is essential not only for academics, but also for parents, educators, and society at large. Only if we know whether, and (if so) how and why, media influence children, can we develop tailored prevention and intervention strategies. A recent literature search into the relationship between children's media use and ADHD or ADHD-related behavior indicated a rapid increase of studies published between the 1970s and 2011 (see Nikkelen et al., 2013). The results of these studies are however very inconsistent. Some have reported a positive relationship between media use and ADHD, whereas others have found no relationship at all (for similar observations, see Kirkorian et al., 2008; Schmidt and Vandewater, 2008).

The aim of this chapter is to review the literature on the relationship between media use and ADHD or ADHD-related behavior. In the next sections, we will first identify the most important hypotheses on the relationship between media use, ADHD, and ADHD-related behavior. Then, we will review the main results of the empirical studies that address the relationship between media use and ADHD and the three symptoms of ADHD: inattentiveness, hyperactivity, and impulsivity. Finally, we will discuss some limitations in previous literature and present some suggestions for future research.

Conceptualizations and measures of ADHD and ADHD-related behavior

Studies on the relationship between media use and ADHD differ greatly in their conceptual and operational definitions of ADHD. Moreover, many of these studies have treated media-effects studies on inattentiveness, impulsivity, and hyperactivity as identical and interchangeable. It is however quite possible that media-exposure is differentially related to inattentiveness, hyper-activity, and impulsivity. In this chapter, we therefore not only review the studies that investigated the effects of media on ADHD as a composite, but also those studies that specifically focused on one of the three ADHD-symptoms. We define inattentiveness as the inability to focus deliberate, conscious attention to organizing and completing a task (i.e., children do not pay attention to what they are doing). Impulsivity is defined as children's inability to control immediate actions (i.e., children do not think before they act and/or are impatient). Hyperactivity is conceptualized as excessive physical activity (i.e., children are continuously in motion) (Barkley, 1997; Nigg, 2006).

The majority of empirical studies used a self-report measure to assess ADHD and/or ADHD-related behavior, such as parent ratings (e.g., the distractibility/hyperactivity scale of the Parenting Stress Index) (Abidin and Brunner, 1995; Levine and Waite, 2000), or the Conner's Parent Rating Scale (CPRS) (Chan and Rabinowitz, 2006). Other studies used teacher ratings (Levine and Waite, 2000; Ullmann et al., 1991), classroom observations (Levine and Waite, 2000), or other scales based on the Diagnostic and Statistical Manual of Mental Disorders (American Psychiatric Association, 2000) (Miller et al., 2007).

Hypotheses on the media–ADHD relationship

Many studies on the effect of media use on ADHD have failed to argue precisely why media and ADHD could be related (e.g., Chan and Rabinowitz, 2006; Miller et al., 2007; Özmert et al., 2002). The effects of media use on ADHD have typically been attributed to two important characteristics of media: its fast pace (i.e., frequently occurring cuts, edits or scene changes, and highly active characters), and its violent content.

Fast pace

Two hypotheses may explain the relationship between watching fast-paced media and ADHD or ADHD-related behaviors. The *Arousal-Habituation Hypothesis* states that the fast pace of entertainment media may increase arousal during and after exposure. Arousal is caused by eliciting frequent shifts in attention and renewed orienting responses during watching (Lang et al., 2000). It is assumed that in the long term children get habituated to this media-induced arousal stimulation. After repeated exposure, their arousal system adjusts itself to this continuous stimulation. In the long run, their baseline arousal level decreases, which in turn leads to boredom, inattention or hyperactivity during other, less arousing activities.

The second hypothesis, which we refer to as the *Scan-and-Shift Hypothesis*, proposes that fast-paced entertainment media teach the child to develop an attentional style that can be characterized by scanning and shifting rather than selecting and focusing. As a result, children are less prepared to cope with other attentional tasks that require effortful attention, such as playing, reading, or homework (Jensen et al., 1997).

Violent content

Two hypotheses may account for a relationship between violent media content and ADHD. The *Violence-Induced Script Hypothesis* argues that violent content in entertainment media hinders the development of self-control (Zimmerman and Christakis, 2007). Several studies have found that exposure to violent media is related to self-control and the activation of brain regions underlying self-control (Hummer et al., 2010; Mathews et al., 2005; Wang et al., 2009). An explanation for this finding may be that violent media activate an aggressive script in the individual (Hummer et al., 2010; Kronenberger et al., 2005). Since aggressive behavior is associated with proactive, impulsive behavior with no inhibition of inappropriate responses, the frequent activation of such a script may lead to a learned behavioral style of poor self-control.

A second hypothesis on the relationship between the violent content of media and ADHD is the *Violence-Induced Arousal-Habituation Hypothesis*. This hypothesis argues that media violence can induce high arousal levels in the viewer (Anderson and Bushman, 2001; Fleming and Rickwood, 2001). Furthermore, the more violent the content is, the higher the increase in arousal (Barlett et al., 2008). However, after some time a *desensitization effect* may occur. For example, playing an arousing video game causes a high increase in arousal at first, but this increase may become less when playing the game several times (Ballard et al., 2006). As with fast-paced programs, high exposure to violent content may cause such high levels of arousal that after frequent exposure the baseline arousal level becomes significantly lower, possibly leading to attention problems and hyperactivity.

Empirical evidence

The literature search of Nikkelen et al. (2013) included 33 studies (20 cross-sectional, 11 longitudinal, and 2 experimental studies). Three of these studies focused on a separate, specific measure of inattentiveness. One study included a specific measure of hyperactivity, and three studies included a specific measure of impulsivity. The numbers of the studies into the separate ADHD-symptoms proved to be too small to justify a formal meta-analysis. Therefore, we used a qualitative meta-analysis to integrate these studies, and a formal quantitative meta-analysis (Comprehensive Meta-Analysis 2.2; Borenstein et al., 2005) to review the media-effect studies focusing on ADHD as a composite.

Media effects on inattentiveness

Three cross-sectional studies investigated the relationship between media use and inattentiveness. One study examined the effect of adolescents' violent television viewing and violent video game playing habits on executive function and attention (Kronenberger et al., 2005), one study focused on the link between time spent watching television and playing videogames and inattentiveness in adolescents (Chan and Rabinowitz, 2006), and the third study examined the correlation between TV viewing and attention among 9-year-old children (Schittenhelm et al., 2010). The results of Kronenberger et al. (2005) indicated a significant negative association between violent media use and attentional skills ($r = -.47$). Schittenhelm et al. (2010) found a negative relationship between TV viewing and attentional skills ($r = -.41$), whereas Chan and Rabinowitz (2006) found a negative relationship for videogames only ($r = -.37$). Finally, Kronenberger et al. (2005) found a significant moderating effect of aggression on the media-violence by attention relation ($p < .05$), indicating that the media-violence effect was stronger in aggressive adolescents.

One longitudinal study investigated the relationship between media use and inattentiveness (Maaβ et al., 2010). This study indicated that TV viewing by preschool children was negatively related to attention skills four years later ($r = -.26$). Thus, these four studies suggest a negative association between media use and attention skills, which may be stronger for aggressive children (see Kronenberger et al., 2005).

Media effects on hyperactivity

Only one study examined the relationship between media use and hyperactivity (Miller et al., 2007), by investigating the association between high levels of television viewing and activity level in preschool children. The results indicated a positive relation between children's daily television viewing and their activity level ($r = .20$).

Media effects on impulsivity

Three studies examined the relationship between media use and impulsivity. One study found no significant effect (Anderson et al., 1977), the other two studies yielded a negative effect (Anderson and Maguire, 1978; Lin and Lepper, 1987). Anderson et al. (1977) experimentally tested whether the pacing of a television program influenced 4-year-old children's behavior post-viewing. One cross-sectional study by Anderson and Maguire (1978) examined whether the amount of time spent watching different types of television programs was related to teacher's ratings of third and fourth graders' impulsivity, compared to fifth and sixth graders. The other cross-sectional study examined the relationship between home video game usage and teacher ratings of impulsivity of children from fourth to sixth grade (Lin and Lepper, 1987). Anderson et al. (1977) predicted that children who had seen a fast-paced episode of *Sesame Street* were more likely to be impulsive, compared to children who had seen a slow-paced episode of Sesame Street. This prediction was however rejected, as the amount of impulsive children in the fast-paced condition (5 out of 24) was not significantly larger than in the slow-paced condition (7 out of 24). In contrast, the results of Anderson and Maguire (1978) indicated that the number of violent television programs that children regularly watched was positively related to children's impulsivity, although this effect accounted only for the younger age group ($r = .29$). In the older age group however, violence did not play a significant role, but only the total number of regularly watched television programs was positively related to impulsivity ($r = .35$). Finally, the results of Lin and Lepper (1987) indicated no significant correlations between home video game use and impulsivity in either boys ($r = .00$) or girls ($r = .09$). Summarized, the pacing of media (i.e., *Sesame Street*) is not related to children's impulsivity (Anderson et al., 1977). In contrast, one cross-sectional study found a negative link between media violence and impulsivity. This study also suggested that media effects on impulsivity are stronger for younger children and for boys.

Media effects on ADHD as a composite

As discussed, only the media-effects literature on ADHD as a composite variable allowed for a formal meta-analysis. A detailed description of the meta-analytic approach falls beyond the scope of this chapter (but see for an in-depth discussion, Nikkelen et al., 2013). The meta-analysis revealed a positive relationship between general media use and violent media use and ADHD, although the strength of this relationship was small ($r = .12$ and $r = .12$, respectively). The effect of fast-paced programs could not be assessed because only two studies measured fast media use (Anderson et al., 1977; Tower et al., 1979). A comparison of the effects of television viewing and videogame playing revealed no significant differences. Further, the strength of the relationship between media use and ADHD did not differ as a function of age. However, the meta-analysis indicated a marginal effect, suggesting that the media-ADHD effect is stronger for boys than for girls. The effects of the current meta-analysis are considerably smaller compared to the review of the empirical studies that separately address the ADHD-symptoms. Our meta-analysis however provides a more reliable conclusion, as the outcome reflects the pattern among the study results (i.e., the true effect size), as opposed to a less precise effect size derived from single studies, under a given single set of assumptions and conditions (e.g., Borenstein et al., 2005).

Conclusions and suggestions for future research

The general picture that arises from our review of the few empirical studies that specifically examined one of the three ADHD-symptoms (inattention, hyperactivity, and impulsivity) suggests a negative relationship between media use and the presence of these ADHD-symptoms. Violent media use seems to hinder attentional skills (e.g., Kronenberger et al., 2005), and to stimulate hyperactivity (Singer et al., 1984), and impulsivity (e.g., Anderson and Maguire, 1978; Lin and Lepper, 1987). In addition, the results of a meta-analysis that focused on the effects of fast pace and violent content of media on a composite score of ADHD indicated that violent media use was significantly, albeit weakly, associated with ADHD. The effect of fast-paced media use on ADHD could not be established, because the number of available studies that examined this relationship was too small. Age did not moderate the effects of violent and fast-paced media use on ADHD. Finally, gender and aggressive tendency might moderate the effect of media on ADHD, but the evidence is too weak to draw decisive conclusions.

The finding that hardly any study has focused on fast-paced media as a cause of the media-ADHD relationship is remarkable. After all, most explanatory hypotheses that are available in the literature attribute the effects of media to its fast pace (e.g., Jensen et al., 1997; Lang et al., 2000). Moreover, the great majority of the studies on media and ADHD are based on simple input–output designs, which only investigate the relationship between general media use (input) and ADHD (output) without exploring what underlies this relationship. None of the available studies have actually addressed the mediating role of the underlying mechanisms that they propose, such as arousal and executive functioning (e.g., Anderson and Bushman, 2001; Barkley, 1997; Barlett et al., 2008; Kronenberger et al., 2005). Therefore, there is an urgent need for future research that examines the differential effects of violent content and fast pace on ADHD and ADHD-related behavior, while testing the specific mechanisms that may explain these relationships.

The media effects of the meta-analysis of Nikkelen et al. (2013) are smaller than those found in meta-analyses on the relationship between media violence and aggression (e.g., Anderson et al., 2004). However, unlike in the field of media violence and aggression, the far majority of the studies on media use and ADHD employed cross-sectional designs. Therefore, unlike the media-violence-aggression literature, the media-ADHD literature does not allow us to decisively single out the causal direction of the relationships. Thus, despite the results of the meta-analysis, it remains unclear whether media use is the cause or the consequence of ADHD or ADHD-like behavior. To solve this gap in the literature, there is a vital need for future research that applies experimental or longitudinal designs.

The results of the current literature review yielded no evidence for moderating effects of age on ADHD. This may be due to the fact that hardly any studies investigated differences between different age groups. In addition, there are some indications that gender and trait aggression may enhance the relationship between media use and ADHD-related behavior. However, the evidence for these latter moderating relationships is too weak to allow decisive conclusions, as the moderating effect of trait aggression has been investigated in only one study (Kronenberger et al., 2005). The moderating effect of gender on ADHD was however found in the meta-analysis of Nikkelen et al. (2013), and this effect is based on the percentages of boys and girls in the empirical studies included in the meta-analysis. In general, such an approach to detect gender differences is however not the most reliable method (e.g., Bushman et al., 2009).

To date, hardly any of the empirical studies have investigated whether the media–ADHD relationship differs for boys and girls and for other possible individual-difference variables. This is remarkable, because it is highly conceivable that children differ in their susceptibility to media effects on ADHD. For example, it is likely that violent and rapidly paced media have a small and negligible influence on the great majority of children but a large influence on a small subgroup of children. Therefore, there is crucial need for future research to systematically investigate whether and how age, gender, and other individual-difference variables may enhance (or reduce) media effects on ADHD and ADHD-like behavior. After all, only if we know which children are particularly susceptible to specific media are we able to adequately target prevention and intervention strategies at these children.

References

Abidin, R. R. and Brunner, J. F. (1995). Development of a parenting alliance inventory. *Journal of Clinical Child Psychology, 24*(1), 31–40, doi:10.1207/ s15374424jccp2401_4

Akinbami, L. J., Liu, X., Pastor, P. N. and Reuben, C. A. (2011). Data from the national health interview survey, 1998–2009. *NCHS Data Brief* No. 70, 1–8.

Allen, J., Livingstone, S. and Reiner, R. (1998). True lies – changing images of crime in British postwar cinema. *European Journal of Communication, 13*(1), 53–75.

American Psychiatric Association (2000). *Diagnostic and statistical manual of mental disorders (4th ed., text revision).* Washington, DC: Author.

Anderson, C. C. and Maguire, T. O. (1978). Effect of TV viewing on the educational performance of elementary school children. *Alberta Journal of Educational Research, 24*(3), 156–63.

Anderson, C. A. and Bushman, B. J. (2001). Effects of violent video games on aggressive behavior, aggressive cognition, aggressive affect, physiological arousal, and pro-social behavior: A meta-analytic review of the scientific literature. *Psychological Science, 12*(5), 353–59.

Anderson, D. R., Levin, S. R. and Lorch, E. P. (1977). The effects of TV program pacing on the behavior of preschool children. *AV Communication Review, 25*(2), 159–66.

Anderson, C., Carnagey, N., Flanagan, M., Benjamin, A., Eubanks, J. and Valentine, J. (2004). Violent video games: Specific effects of violent content on aggressive thoughts and behavior RID D-8583-2011. *Advances in Experimental Social Psychology, 36*(36), 199–249, doi:10.1016/S0065–2601(04)36004–1

Ballard, M. E., Hamby, R. H., Panee, C. D. and Nivens, E. E. (2006). Repeated exposure to video game play results in decreased blood pressure responding. *Media Psychology, 8*(4), 323–41.

Barkley, R. A. (1997). Behavioral inhibition, sustained attention, and executive functions: Constructing a unifying theory of ADHD. *Psychological Bulletin, 121*(1), 65–94.

Barlett, C. P., Harris, R. J. and Bruey, C. (2008). The effect of the amount of blood in a violent video game on aggression, hostility, and arousal. *Journal of Experimental Social Psychology, 44*(3), 539–46.

Borenstein, M., Hedges, L., Higgins, J. and Rothstein, H. (2005). *Comprehensive meta-analysis version 2.* Englewood, NJ: Biostat.

Bushman, B. J., Huesmann, L. R. and Whitaker, J. L. (2009). Violent media effects. In R. L. Nabi and M. B. Oliver (Eds), *The Sage handbook of media processes and effects.* Thousand Oaks, CA: Sage, pp. 361–76.

Chan, P. A. and Rabinowitz, T. (2006). A cross-sectional analysis of video games and attention deficit hyperactivity disorder symptoms in adolescents. *Annals of General Psychiatry, 5* (16), doi:10.1186/1744–1859X-5-16

Fleming, M. J. and Rickwood, D. J. (2001). Effects of violent versus nonviolent video games on children's arousal, aggressive mood, and positive mood. *Journal of Applied Social Psychology, 31*(10), 2047–71.

Hummer, T. A., Wang, Y., Kronenberger, W. G., Mosier, K. M., Kalnin, A. J., Dunn, D. W. and Mathews, V. P. (2010). Short-term violent video game play by adolescents alters prefrontal activity during cognitive inhibition. *Media Psychology, 13*(2), 136–54.

Jensen, P. S., Mrazek, D., Knapp, P. K., Steinberg, L., Pfeffer, C., Schowalter, J. and Shapiro, T. (1997). Evolution and revolution in child psychiatry: ADHD as a disorder of adaptation. *Journal of the American Academy of Child and Adolescent Psychiatry, 36*(12), 1672–79, doi:10.1097/00004583-199712000-00015

Kelleher, K., McInerny, T., Gardner, W., Childs, G. and Wasserman, R. (2000). Increasing identification of psychosocial problems: 1979–96. *Pediatrics, 105*(6), 1313–21, doi:10.1542/peds.105.6.1313

Kirkorian, H. L., Wartella, E. A. and Anderson, D. R. (2008). Media and young children's learning. *Future of Children, 18*(1), 39–61.

Koolstra, C. M., van Zanten, J., Lucassen, N. and Ishaak, N. (2004). The formal pace of Sesame Street over 26 years. *Perceptual and Motor Skills, 99*(1), 354–60.

Kronenberger, W. G., Mathews, V. P., Dunn, D. W., Wang, Y., Wood, E. A., Giauque, A. L. and Li, T. Q. (2005). Media violence exposure and executive functioning in aggressive and control adolescents. *Journal of Clinical Psychology, 61*(6), 725–37, doi:10.1002/jclp.20022

Lang, A., Zhou, S. H., Schwartz, N., Bolls, P. D. and Potter, R. F. (2000). The effects of edits on arousal, attention, and memory for television messages: When an edit is an edit can an edit be too much? *Journal of Broadcasting and Electronic Media, 44*(1), 94–109.

Levine, L. E. and Waite, B. M. (2000). Television viewing and attentional abilities in fourth and fifth grade children. *Journal of Applied Developmental Psychology, 21*(6), 667–79.

Lin, S. and Lepper, M. R. (1987). Correlates of children's usage of videogames and computers. *Journal of Applied Social Psychology, 17*(1), 72–93, doi:10.1111/j.1559–1816.1987.tb00293.x

Maaβ, E. E., Hahlweg, K., Naumann, S., Bertram, H., Heinrichs, N. and Kuschel, A. (2010) Sind moderne Bildschirmmedien ein Risikofaktor für ADHS? Ein Längsschnittuntersuchung an Deutschen Kindergartenkindern. *Vierteljahresschrift für Heilpädagogik und ihre Nachbargebiete, 79*(1), 50–65.

Mathews, V. P., Kronenberger, W. G., Wang, Y., Lurito, J. T., Lowe, M. J. and Dunn, D. W. (2005). Media violence exposure and frontal lobe activation measured by functional magnetic resonance imaging in aggressive and nonaggressive adolescents. *Journal of Computer Assisted Tomography, 29*(3), 287–92.

Miller, C. J., Marks, D. J., Miller, S. R., Berwid, O. G., Kera, E. A., Santra, A. and Halperin, J. M. (2007). Brief report: Television viewing and risk for attention problems in preschool children. *Journal of Pediatric Psychology, 32*(4), 448–52, doi:10.1093/jpepsy/jsl035

Nigg, J. T. (2006). *What causes ADHD? Understanding what goes wrong and why.* New York, NY: The Guilford Press.

Nikkelen, S. W. C., Valkenburg, P. M., and Huizinga, M. (2013). Media use and ADHD-related behaviors in children and adolescents: A meta-analysis. Paper presented at the Etmaal, the Annual Conference of NeFCA, the Dutch-Flemish Organization of Communication Science, Rotterdam, the Netherlands.

Özmert, E., Toyran, M. and Yurdakok, K. (2002). Behavioral correlates of television viewing in primary school children evaluated by the child behavior checklist. *Archives of Pediatrics and Adolescent Medicine, 156*(9), 910–14.

Schittenhelm, R., Ennemoser, M. and Schneider, W. (2010). Aufmerksamkeit als mediator der beziehung zwischen fersehverhalten und schulleistung. *Zeitschrift Für Entwicklungspsychologie Und Pädagogische Psychologie, 42*(3), 154–66, doi:10.1026/0049–8637/a000016

Schmidt, M. E. and Vandewater, E. A. (2008). Media and attention, cognition, and school achievement. *Future of Children, 18*(1), 63–85. doi:10.1353/foc.0.0004

Singer, J. L., Singer, D. G. and Rapaczynski, W. S. (1984). Family patterns and television viewing as predictors of children's beliefs and aggression. *Journal of Communication, 42*(3), 107–89.

Tower, R. B., Singer, D. G., Singer, J. L. and Biggs, A. (1979). Differential effects of television programming on preschoolers' cognition, imagination, and social play. *American Journal of Orthopsychiatry, 49*(2), 265–81.

Ullmann, R., Sleater, E. and Sprague, R. (1991). *ADD-H comprehensive teacher's rating scale (ACTeRS).* Champaign, IL: Metri Tech.

Wang, Y., Mathews, V. P., Kalnin, A. J., Mosier, K. M., Dunn, D. W., Saykin, A. J. and Kronenberger, W. G. (2009). Short term exposure to a violent video game induces changes in frontolimbic circuitry in adolescents. *Brain Imaging and Behavior, 3*(1), 38–50.

Zimmerman, F. J. and Christakis, D. A. (2007). Associations between content types of early media exposure and subsequent attentional problems. *Pediatrics, 120*(5), 986–92.

22

MEDIA, IMAGINATION AND FANTASY

Maya Götz

Children grow up in a media saturated world. What does this mean for their fantasy life? The premise underlying much of the research studying this question is that humans have capabilities to form a private inner reality: "(...) We can play and replay memories, link memories, shape and reshape organized mental structures such as schemas and scripts, anticipate future encounters or adventures, and, in general, privately inhabit a self-constructed world of life narratives."

(Singer and Singer, 2008, p. 290)

Influence of television on imaginative activities

In the first decades of television research, a series of studies attempted to answer the question of how far media constrain fantasies, creativity or, for instance, forms of role play. These studies were concerned with evaluating the probably negative impact of the new electronic media, which were becoming increasingly significant.

Several early correlational as well as experimental studies found negative relationships between television viewing and children's scores on tasks considered to be indicators of creativity and imagination. In one influential study, Williams (1986) began a comparative natural experiment prior to the arrival of television in a Canadian town she named Notel. Comparisons between children in the pre- and post-television period in Notel, as well as with children in two other communities, revealed that the Notel children rated higher on tests of creativity in comparison with children in the two other towns. The Notel scores declined in tests performed two years after the introduction of television (Williams, 1986).

Valkenburg's (2001) review of the literature discussed the Reduction Hypothesis that suggested several possible connections between television and children's imagination: Television viewing reduces the time children spend "practicing" other more creative things; the fast-pace and action-oriented stories on television sometimes frighten and stress young viewers, and so disrupt more imaginative involvement in contemplative activities; and, the nature of the medium with its "readymade pictures" provides input that is less stimulating.

Researchers investigated how various media differ as stimuli of creativity and imagination. One research area focused on whether a televised version of a story stimulates more or fewer creative ideas, storylines and problem-solving solutions than the same story told verbally (as in audio or print forms). A series of studies that compared the influence of television with radio (Greenfield and Beagles-Roos, 1988; Greenfield et al., 1986) confirmed the hypothesis that processes of imagination (operationalized as any form of representational activity that creates new entities such as characters or events) were better stimulated by radio than television. Rolandelli (1989) explained in the review of these and other studies that the visual superiority effect of television is confounded by the advantages of the auditory-verbal track for comprehension.

Studying television as a stimulant for imaginative play, Singer and Singer claimed that television's visually concrete presentational forms inhibit children's daydreaming in comparison to the abstract nature of words in print or spoken language (e.g. Singer, 1980; Singer and Singer, 1981; Singer et al., 1984). They assumed that the ready-made fantasy world of television does not require a lot of mental effort and the fast pace of the programmes does not leave room for daydreaming while watching. The researchers claimed that the findings suggest that children who are heavy electronic media users are less likely to engage in pretend play or other forms of creativity (Singer and Singer, 2005). A study by Kumari and Ahuja (2010) added that they score lower in tests on creative imagination.

Complementary to this conclusion is the hypothesis that television may stimulate programme-bound daydreaming. Therefore, daydreaming by heavy viewers of violence, for example, will be preoccupied with aggressive themes and superheroes closely related to their favourite television narratives (Huesmann and Eron, 1986). Thus, children who watched more educational programs specifically designed to foster fantasy were more imaginative than the children in the control group (Singer and Singer, 1998).

Electronic media and the content of fantasy-activities

These studies set the ground for later investigations as the focus of research has been shifting toward study of the relation of content and children's fantasy life. Valkenburg and her colleagues surveyed 354 children three times, in one-year intervals, and found that exposure to non-violent programmes was related to an increase in children's positive-intense fantasy style, while the preference for violent shows correlates with an aggressive-heroic style (Valkenburg et al., 1992). This conclusion supports the hypothesis that, ultimately, the types of content children watch are more important in determining outcomes of fantasy and imaginative play than the quantity of time spent viewing. A later study found that more imaginative children preferred programmes of an educational nature typically featured on public broadcasting stations in the United States while less imaginative children preferred action and adventure cartoons with a high level of violence (Singer and Singer, 2005, p. 67). This finding corresponds with studies that investigated the relationship between imagination, children and the computer. For example, violent thoughts seem to be related to playing violent video games (Carnagey and Anderson, 2005).

Many researchers of this area of investigation posit that media contents "enter" the imagination of children. This is particularly evident in studies of the everyday lives of children (see, e.g. Charlton and Bachmair, 1990). A number of case studies contain rich descriptions that illustrate the potential connections between media texts and children's imagination and play; for example, embracing Ernie from *Sesame Street* as an imaginary companion in the USA (Taylor, 1999); or playing Batman (Neuss, 1999); aspiring to be like a member of the *Spice Girls* pop group (Lemish, 1998); or a *Pokémon Master* in Israel (Lemish and Bloch, 2004). Yet, the analysis of interviews with parents and specialists (e.g. Jones, 2002), ascertained by collecting exemplars of anecdotal accounts of children's talk and play, indicates that there is more to the "story". Clearly these everyday experiences suggest the existence of an intense relationship between media culture and children's fantasy world.

Appropriation of media as an imaginative process

The term "fantasy" originates from the Greek "*phantazesthai*," meaning "to appear", "bring to light", or to "appear before the soul". "Phantasia–imagination" is the capacity to create inner appearances, for internal sense presentation, that resemble external perceptions (Brann, 1991, p. 21). Thus, the appropriation of media as an imaginative process refers to the ability of individuals to reproduce images or concepts derived originally from this basic sense, but now reflected in one's consciousness as memories, fantasies and future plans (Singer and Singer, 2005, p. 16).

Media use is a form of experience and involves a range of active imaginary processes, some of which are initiated with reception. As early as the mid-1950s, Horton and Wohl described the various imaginative activities of the recipient during the reception of television. They argued that, similar to role play, the spectator is freed from direct compulsion to act and therefore can act out behavioural options and roles in a notional sense (cf., e.g. Horton and Wohl, 1956; Maccoby and Wilson, 1957).

"Identification" is one of the "umbrella terms" used to describe a typical imaginative process going on during reception; as wanting to be and seeking to be like (similarity) (Liebes and Katz, 1990). Self-awareness is gradually set aside in this process and replaced, temporarily, by a strong emotional and cognitive connection to the media character (Cohen, 2001, p. 251). There are forms of identification that extend beyond actual reception of the text that are regarded as particularly important for identity development. For example, Rosengren and his colleagues focused on "long-term identification" with one or more characters (Rosengren et al., 1976, p. 349), while von Feilitzen and Linne (1975) investigated "wishful identification".

Qualitative studies with children and young people demonstrate that identification is just one of the possible forms of an imaginary relationship with media (see, e.g. Buckingham, 1993a). In this sense, media are used as a source of symbolic material that children utilize by extracting elements they consider to be useful for making meaning of their experiences, as well as in communicating about them and expressing agency (see, e.g. Buckingham, 1993b; Buckingham and Bragg, 2004; McMillin, 2009). In sensory terms, while this experience may be limited to particular senses, according to the particular medium, emotionally the experience is often intensely absorbed into inner images and concepts, and has deep involvement in identity work and self-empowerment (e. g., Fisherkeller, 2002; McMillin and Fisherkeller, 2009).

Individual case studies demonstrate via the media traces contained therein that children process current, social and biographical topics in their make-believe worlds (Götz et al., 2005, p. 99). It may be that these media fantasies are self-imposed ways that enable them to maintain their self-image and – at least for some time – to survive critical life situations (see, e.g. Götz, 1999).

These fantasies can be clichéd or characterized by aggression, as documented in a qualitative study of 70 Dragon Ball Z fans. However, the individual meaning of the fight-dominated anime series for a child's fantasy can assume many different directions, some unexpected by adults. For example, a rather shy boy who is small in stature (Torben, 10 years old) stated: "Dragon Ball is like a cushion – when I fall it doesn't hurt, because I imagine I'm a fighter." Here we see how inner imagination enables him to handle physical pain. While others like 10-year-old Bülent (with immigration background) related what he gets out of the Dragon Ball Z and daydreams related to it: "I feel stronger somehow. When someone hits me, for example at school, then I really scream and hit back hard, like in Dragon Ball. Before that I never defended myself." Bülent took from his favourite series an understandable but nonetheless aggressive script, about how to behave in a situation of conflict (Götz, 2003). Thus, for the child, the relationships between media content and the meaning are very complex and oftentimes unexpected (Buckingham, 1996; Tobin, 2000).

How to research the relationship of media and children's fantasies

One overarching question that can be asked in regard to this research domain is whether something as complex as fantasy can be understood adequately without letting children themselves articulate the natural social context in which it occurs in everyday life? This would include various forms of interpersonal interactions that occur naturally during play and daydreaming and so on. Some researchers have argued that in order to better understand the relationship between media and fantasies, spaces must be created that enable children to articulate and interpret their fantasies (Charlton and Bachmair, 1990).

There are a number of ways that children can share with us glimpses into their inner world of fantasies (e.g. via their symbolic transmission into play, conversation and artwork such as drawing). Götz et al. (2005) guided 197 children between the ages of eight and ten years of age from South Korea, Israel, the USA and Germany through a fantasy journey to their "big daydream". After this process, they were invited to paint a picture of what they imagined, write a few words about it and then explain during intensive individual interviews what their fantasies were about and if there was any connection to the media. Each of the children's daydream narrations were then assembled into "stories" in the analysis. The sensitizing concept used to investigate the relationship between fantasy and media in this study was the search for "media traces", defined as individually acquired pieces of the media. Traces were identified and compared with the original medium and with the way the child used them in his/her fantasy in reconstructing their subjective significance as well as in *working out* the meaning of media within them (Bachmair, 1990). Either explicit or clear implicit media traces were evident in approximately two thirds of the cases. These ranged from dream worlds that seemed to stem entirely from a media experience to those that revealed no direct traces whatsoever. In addition to occasional use of the typical aesthetics of a medium, children sometimes took a setting (e.g. a location or an environment) to host their own fantasy. They incorporated media characters in their worlds or imagined themselves to be one, and sometimes they imagined parts of media stories. Television was the primary medium referenced, but other media such as computer games or books served as the starting point and/or part of the dream world. Visual media (i.e. television, video cassettes and films) played the most significant role in the children's stories – led by television (Götz et al., 2005).

Collectively, these studies do affirm the major importance of visual media for children's fantasizing (e.g. Singer and Singer, 2005). Given this understanding, and the methodological approaches employed, researchers also investigated if there are generational differences. Götz (2006a) studied a research population of German adults, born across a spectrum of decades, including participants who did not grow up viewing television. In addition to conducting a biographical interview, participants recalled and then drew their Big Daydream when they were eight or nine years, just like the children in the study mentioned above did. One major finding was that the daydreams were structurally very similar to the fantasy worlds and activities imagined by children today: Whereas the latter fantasize themselves as "being special" and imagine that they are pop stars, soap actors or soccer players, adults in the study recalled imagining they were stars of the theatre or fighter pilots in World War II; whereas children today fantasize about travelling to alien planets in space ships, in post-war times they imagined they were sent in huge ships to explore foreign countries. Although the media traces in the imagined texts were structurally similar, in the past their origins were from fewer and other media than available today. Thus, while television and computer games are the sources for media traces in the fantasies of children living in the beginning of the new millennium, books, radio or even pictures from cigarette packets were the sources of material and the springboard for the imagination in post-war times. On the one hand, media traces point to the child's individual appropriation, and they are signs of identity construction and self-presentation. On the other hand, they point to the everyday culture in which the child is growing up and use of the various media available to him/her.

The significance of the latter point was demonstrated in an international study conducted during the first ten days of the Iraq War (2003). Children in the USA, Israel and Germany were asked to draw a picture of what they imagined was happening in Iraq and what they wanted to see about this war on television. Dominant national discourses were clearly reflected in the children's inner images: Children in the USA were hoping for a quick victory, and they had fantasies such as George Bush killing Saddam Hussein; children in Israel focused on their own safety and bomb attacks on their country or the role of their prime minister as peacemaker; children in Germany had sympathy for children and families in Iraq, and their fantasies of US soldiers included executing Iraqi children with a smile (cf. Lemish and Götz, 2007).

Permeation of national discourses was also evident in a corresponding international study of the relationship between imagination and natural/industrial disasters in Japan/Fukushima in 2011. Children throughout the world viewed the same media images, but nonetheless there were clear national differences. Children in Germany, for instance, concentrated much more frequently on the abolition of nuclear power. This topic was more central in public discourse in Germany than it was for children in the USA or Brazil. Similarly, particularly significant values or discourses central in their cultures were reflected, for instance, by children in the USA, who focused more on the loss of property; and children in Cuba and Ecuador, who focused on the death of farm animals and the loss of farmland, especially in the countryside. Beside reflecting national discourse, regional experiences shaped children's imagination of what happened. Children in the US Midwest, for example, linked the destruction to earthquakes, children in Brazil to heavy rainstorms and children in the Dominican Republic to waves and flooding (Götz et al., 2012).

Conclusion

Imagination and fantasy are complex processes that involve various cultural aspects and the child's individuality in the topics with which he or she is dealing. These topics and the materials employed are influenced by the child's specific social context, family, peers, school, community and all the child's previous experiences. Media consumption is part of these experiences and can take up much of a child's leisure time activities, depending on the quantity of time spent with the media and the content chosen. Children learn how to process these topics through their cultural experiences and, here too, the media are of central importance; for example, in offering pictures and stories that reflect norms and values. Children acquire these actively and then select, reinterpret and incorporate the acquired materials into their fantasies. This is not a simple stimulus-response-mechanism, but nevertheless children do seem to absorb and use parts of the discourses, values and forms of textual constructions presented through the media.

Given public concern and scholars' participation in discussions about children's well-being, as well as academic curiosity, it behooves us to continue our studies and to engage in discussion about media, their content and the question of how they are involved in children's fantasies and perspectives.

SEE ALSO in this volume chapter by Krcmar and chapter by Martins.

References

Bachmair, B. (1990). The function of interpretation and expression in television experience and television symbolism. In M. Charlton and B. Bachmair (Eds), *Media communication in everyday life. Interpretative studies on children's and young people's media actions.* Munich, New York: Saur, pp. 81–115.

Brann, E. T. H. (1991). *The world of the imagination: Sum and substance.* Savage, MD: Rowman & Littlefield.

Buckingham, D. (1993a). *Children talking television: The making of television literacy*. London, England: Falmer.

Buckingham, D. (Ed.) (1993b). *Reading audiences: Young people and the media*. Manchester, England: Manchester University Press.

Buckingham, D. (1996). *Moving images: Understanding children's emotional responses to television*. Manchester, England: Manchester University Press.

Buckingham, D. and Bragg, S. (2004). *Young people, sex and the media: The facts of life?* New York, NY: Palgrave Macmillan.

Carnagey, N. and Anderson, C. (2005). The effects of reward and punishment in violent video games on aggressive affect, cognition, and behavior. *Psychological science*, *16*(11), 882–89.

Charlton, M. and Bachmair, B. (Eds) (1990). *Media communication in everyday life. Interpretative studies on children's and young people's media actions*. Munich, New York: Saur.

Cohen, J. (2001). Defining identification: A theoretical look at the identification of audiences with media characters. *Mass Communication and Society*, *4*(3), 245–64.

Fisherkeller, J. (2002). *Growing up with television. Everyday learning among young adolescents*. Philadelphia: Temple Univ. Pr.

Götz, M. (1999). *Mädchen und Fernsehen: Facetten der Medienaneignung in der weiblichen Adoleszenz* [Girls and television: Facets of media appropriation in female adolescence]. Munich: KoPäd.

——(2003). Fantasies of fighting and fighters. The fascination of Dragon Ball Z in between strong inner pictures and a heightened readiness to resort to aggression. *TelevIZIon*, *16*(1), 18–21.

Götz, M. (2006a). "Radio, das war absolute Magie" – Kinderträume zu Zeiten ohne Fernsehen ["Radio, that was absolute magic" – children's dreams in times without television]. In M. Götz (Ed.), *Mit Pokémon in Harry Potters Welt. Medien in den Fantasien von Kindern* [With Pokémon in Harry Potter's world. Media in children's fantasies]. Munich: KoPäd, pp. 342–64.

Götz, M., Lemish, D. Aidman, A. and Moon, H. (2005). *Media and the make-believe worlds of children: When Harry Potter meets Pokémon in Disneyland*. Mahwah, NJ: Erlbaum.

Götz, M., Holler, A., Nastasia, D. and Nastasia, S. (2012). I want to know how high the wave really was: Children worldwide and their perceptions of the catastrophes in Japan in March 2011. *TelevIZIon*, *25*(1), 49–53.

Greenfield, P. and Beagles-Roos, J. (1988). Radio vs. television: Their cognitive impact on children of different socio-economic and ethnic groups. *Journal of Communication*, *38*(2), 71–72.

Greenfield, P., Farrer, D. and Beagles-Roos, J. (1986). Is the medium the message? An experimental comparison of the effects of radio and television on imagination. *Journal of Applied Developmental Psychology*, *7*(4), 237–55.

Horton, D. and Wohl, R. R. (1956). Mass communication and para-social interaction: Observations on intimacy at a distance. *Psychiatry*, *19*(3), 215–29.

Huesmann, L. R. and Eron, L. D. (Eds) (1986). *Television and the aggressive child: A cross-national comparison*. Hillsdale, NJ: Erlbaum.

Jones, G. (2002). *Killing monsters: Why children need fantasy, super heroes, and make-believe violence*. New York, NY: Basic Books.

Kumari, S. and Ahuja, S. (2010). Video viewing and cognitive development in preadolescents. *Social Science Computer Review*, *28*(2), 170–76.

Lemish, D. (1998). Spice Girls' talk: A case study in the development of gendered identity. In S. A. Inness (Ed.), *Millennium girls: Today's girls around the world*. New York, NY: Rowman & Littlefield, pp. 145–67.

Lemish, D. and Bloch, L. R. (2004). Pokémon in Israel. In J. Tobin (Ed.), *Pikachu's global adventure: Making sense of the rise and fall of Pokémon*. Durham, NC: Duke University Press, pp. 165–86.

Lemish, D. and Götz, M. (Eds) (2007). *Children and media in times of war and conflict*. Cresskill, NJ: Hampton.

Liebes, T. and Katz, E. (1990). *The export of meaning*. New York, NY: Oxford University Press.

Maccoby, E. E. and Wilson, W. C. (1957). Identification and observational learning from films. *Journal of Abnormal Social Psychology*, *55*(1), 76–87.

McMillin, D. C. (2009). *Mediated identities. Youth, agency, and globalization*. New York, NY: Lang

McMillin, D. C. and Fisherkeller, J. (2009). Local identities in globalized regions: Teens, everyday life, and television. *Popular Communication*, *7*(4), 237–51.

Neuss, N. (1999). Batman, Michael Jordan und "the different Mexico". Wesen und Bedeutung von Phantasiegefährten und Phantasieländern [Batman, Michael Jordan and "the different Mexico". Nature and meaning of fantasy mates and fantasy countries]. In N. Neuss (Ed.), *Ästhetik der Kinder – Interdisziplinäre Beiträge zur ästhetischen Erfahrung von Kindern* [Esthetics of children – interdisciplinary contributions on esthetic experience of children]. Frankfurt am Main, Hessen: GEP, pp. 47–62.

Rolandelli, D. R. (1989). Children and television: The visual superiority effect reconsidered. *Journal of Broadcasting and Electronic Media*, *33*(1), 69–81.

Rosengren, K. E., Windahl, S., Hakansson, P.-A. and Johnsson-Smaragdi, U. (1976). Adolescents' TV relations. Three scales. *Communication Research*, *3*(4), 347–66.

Singer, D. G. and Singer, J. L. (2005). *Imagination and play in the electronic age*. Cambridge, MA: Harvard University Press.

——(2008). Make-believe play, imagination, and creativity: Links to children's media exposure. In S. L. Calvert (Ed.), *The handbook of children, media, and development*. Oxford, UK: Blackwell, pp. 290–308.

Singer, J. L. (1980). The power and limitation of television: A cognitive-affective analysis. In P. H. Tannenbaum (Ed.), *The entertainment functions of television*. Hillsdale, NJ: Erlbaum, pp. 31–65.

Singer, J. L. and Singer, D. G. (1981). *Television, imagination, and aggression: A study of preschoolers*. Hillsdale, NJ: Erlbaum.

——(1998). Barney and Friends as entertainment and education. Evaluating the quality and effectiveness of a television series for preschool children. In J. K. Asamen (Ed.), *Research paradigms, television, and social behavior*. Thousand Oaks, CA: Sage, pp. 305–67.

Singer, J. L., Singer, D. G. and Rapaczynski, W. S. (1984). Children's imagination as predicted by family patterns and television viewing: A longitudinal study. *Genetic Psychology Monographs*, *110*(1), 43–69.

Taylor, M. (1999). *Imaginary companions and the children who create them*. Oxford, UK: Oxford University Press.

Tobin, J. (2000). *"Good guys don't wear hats": Children's talk about the media*. New York, NY: Teachers College Press.

Valkenburg, P. M. (2001). Television and the child's developing imagination. In D. G. Singer and J. L. Singer (Eds), *Handbook of children and the media*. Thousand Oaks, CA: Sage, pp. 121–34.

Valkenburg, P. M., Vooijs, M. W., van der Voort, T. H. A. and Wiegman, O. (1992). The influence of television on children's fantasy styles. A secondary analysis. *Imagination, Cognation and Personality*, *12*(1), 55–67.

von Feilitzen, C. and Linne, O. (1975). The effects of television on children and adolescents: A symposium: Identifying with television characters. *Journal of Communication*, *25*(4), 51–55.

Williams, T. M. (Ed.) (1986). *The impact of television: A natural experiment in three communities*. New York, NY: Academic Press.

23

SOCIAL MEDIA AND CREATIVITY

Kylie Peppler

Introduction

Today's youth, aged 8–18, are avid media consumers, as evidenced by usage trends on sites like YouTube and Facebook, and from ever-increasing participation in online videogame communities (Rideout et al., 2010). New social tools for creating and viewing user-generated content present a substantial shift in the ways that participants in youth culture leverage electronic media to interact and learn from each other. The Kaiser Family Foundation suggests that social media participation is relatively universal among high-school-aged youth across the United States, irrespective of race or class (Rideout et al., 2010). Furthermore, the lines between consumers and producers are being blurred in such spaces, what Jenkins and others refer to as the new "participatory culture" (Jenkins et al., 2009). The extent to which youth move fluidly between consuming and producing media is a by-product of widely available creative tools and Web 2.0 platforms that enable youth to experiment with technology that was previously the exclusive domain of professionals. Notable pockets of youth are creating and sharing media, with some studies even suggesting that 77 percent of social network teens are creating some type of content (Lenhart and Madden, 2007). Though some studies argue that teens use social media platforms primarily for consumption (Chau, 2010; Pempek et al., 2009), longitudinal trends indicate that production practices are steadily on the rise; for example, 39 percent of online teens electronically share original artistic creations (such as artwork, photos, stories or videos) up from 33 percent in 2004, and one in four teens also report remixing content they found online into their own creations, up from 19 percent in 2004 (Lenhart and Madden, 2007).

This type of media production denotes a "creative turn" (Sefton-Green et al., 2011) in our uses of new technologies and brings often overlooked aspects of creativity to the fore. The purpose of this chapter is to take a look at the ways in which social media spaces can be leveraged for creativity, paying particular attention to the ways in which social media support youths' creative production. Creative production within online learning communities highlights the ways in which youth are appropriating, critiquing, and making novel contributions today. We examine these ideas by first highlighting relevant research in both the fields of creativity and social media. We then present examples from notable online communities, including Do-It-Yourself (DIY), Multi-User Virtual Environments (MUVEs), and other online communities where youth are actively involved in creative activity and discuss the implications for research on creativity.

Finally, we discuss the implications for today's youth, the potential social media holds, and why such vernacular forms of creativity are important for learning and development.

Social media and Web 2.0

The term "social media" denotes a wealth of types of online spaces and participation. Barnes, for example, defines social media as the "organizational and software procedures that control the exchange of interpersonal information" in social networking sites like Facebook or MySpace, online Role-Playing Games (RPGs), instant messaging programs, and bulletin boards, among others (2006, para. 2). The term social media is quite broad and is used as an umbrella to describe a range of social software and social networking applications that allow individuals to communicate with one another and track discussions across the Web.

Social media were made possible by, and are considered by some to be synonymous with, the general shift from Web 1.0 to Web 2.0 technology (Greenhow et al., 2009). "Web 2.0," a term coined in 2004 by O'Reilly Media (O'Reilly, 2005), characterizes a transition from the predominantly read-only Web 1.0 into a more social and collaborative Web 2.0 space, where individuals can now read content that others have posted as well as post their own text and multimedia content (Greenhow et al., 2009). As increasing numbers of youth come to see the potential of social media to showcase and garner feedback about their band's new recording, their photography project, or their latest poem, these online communities are becoming important sites of creativity that need to be better understood in the research.

Social media and creativity

Common to definitions of creativity is an emphasis on original or novel contributions that involve divergent processing (Valkenberg and van der Voort, 1994). Traditionally, research on creativity has been dominated by cognitive perspectives, which are tied to the study of exceptional cases and have situated the source of creativity in the individual (Guilford, 1950). More recently, scholarship on creativity has moved to recognize the genesis and development of creative ideas as being part of a broader, socially determined process (Sawyer, 2006). Consistent with Csikszentmihalyi's (1996) systems model, creativity is becoming increasingly understood as a system, composed of (a) individuals, (b) knowledge domains, and (c) a field of informed experts. In Csikszentmihalyi's model of creativity, individuals build on culturally valued practices and designs to produce new variations of the domain, which, if deemed valuable by the community (i.e., the field), become part of what constitutes the evolving domain. Each of the three components of the system continue to impact one another over time. The presence of a field of experts implies that colleagues and domain norms are essential to the realization of individual creativity. Such a view removes the aura of mystery around creativity and, instead, emphasizes the importance of sustained discussion with peers and an appreciation of the constraints that one works within while producing creative work.

Up until now, most research that has utilized a systems model of creativity refers to a *panel of experts* to act as proxy for the "field," providing evaluations of creative contributions within the community. In social media, however, several problems emerge, the first of which is that the "field" becomes more difficult to define. Expertise, for example, is *distributed amongst members* and crowd-sourcing is becoming an increasingly common way to determine what constitute the most creative contributions (e.g., ratings on Amazon.com, Rotten Tomatoes and others). Furthermore, what crowds gravitate toward may not be what we consider to be the most creative contributions. This raises key questions about whether a YouTube video that receives the most views is indeed the most "creative" contribution to the community. If not, then how does widespread viewing and sharing of artifacts online relate to the creativity of the contribution?

Secondly, social media call notions of originality, intellectual property, and ethics into question when remixing (the combination of semiotic resources into new digital or multimodal texts [Erstad et al., 2007] proliferates online). Reflective of a Web 2.0 culture where people are expected to add, change, and interact with the contributions of others, much of the work posted by youth in social media spaces leverages content created by someone else – to what extent is their creation original when it is not entirely their own? What happens when several hundred people collaborate, as is often the case in Web 2.0 communities, and collectively produce a novel contribution? This brings some tensions that have always been true of creative work to the fore; namely, that history has shown us that creative ideas build on ideas that came before them. Every invention represents a novel synthesis of ideas floating around at the time. Remix, when you think about it as a novel synthesis of ideas and not pure imitation, is a reflection of most, if not all, creative contributions, in that no innovation exists outside of the cultural and historical context in which it was created.

Attempting to resolve some of these tensions, Gauntlett and others argue for contextualized views of creativity, where creativity is defined in direct relationship to one's personal history and perspective, a process "which brings together at least one active human mind, and the material or digital world, in the activity of making something which is novel in that context, and is a process which evokes a feeling of joy" (2011, p. 76). This notion defines creativity as a novel act as judged by the individual in respect to their *own personal history*, not the field's. Such a perspective is salient especially with regard to youth communities, where the personal act of creativity is a driving force in production. Whether a youth's work is on par with the contributions of famous artists or Nobel Prize winners is somehow beside the point. What matters more to youth, and arguably to anyone who dabbles in the act of creative production, is the feeling of creating something that is novel *to them*, a personal view of creativity that is perhaps more conducive to healthy development and learning than seeking the appraisal of a field of (likely inaccessible) experts.

The focus of this chapter is on creative acts that align with this emerging view of creativity (Gauntlett, 2011), works that sit at the intersection of collaborative practice, digital media production, and online peer-to-peer evaluations. In the following, we present three examples of creativity in social media that span a range of social media environments, including youth work in a Multi-User Virtual Environment (MUVE) called "Quest Atlantis," a digital art/computer programming community called "Scratch," and a DIY online community called "LilyPond."

Multi-User Virtual Environment (MUVE): Quest Atlantis

Quest Atlantis (www.questatlantis.org) (QA) is a Multi-User Virtual Environment (MUVE) where young people aged 9–16 immerse themselves in educational and socially negotiated activities. Units within QA are sets of missions that target a larger narrative. One unit, Architecture, was developed to explore youths' relationships with the themes of social alignment and creative expression, and provides players with the tools to create their own 3D virtual buildings (Peppler and Solomou, 2011). The Architecture unit was situated within an area of QA that hosted a number of media production and consumption trajectories, and is unique among other QA environments in that it was designed to be player-run, emphasizing creative production (in the form of building 3D architecture within the game environment) as a means of evolving one's identity in the play space.

A recent study of creativity within this environment took a closer look at how ideas emerge and spread throughout this community, calling our attention to the ways that creativity is a cultural endeavor, shaped and persisted through the actions and values of many people (Peppler and Solomou, 2011). Analysis of the building trends within the unit points to the ways that youth took up creative ideas in the form of remixing – the more creative (i.e., "spreadable") the original contribution, the more widely the idea was emulated by others. For example, the rate that youth adopted trends that emerged elsewhere in the community provided a measure of an original designs' creative value in the absence of public rating systems (like those found on YouTube). The analysis of building activity within the Architecture unit also revealed that spreadable ideas have a limited lifespan, as determined by the evolving tastes and values of a community – a phenomenon amplified by the rapid dissemination of new ideas afforded in online environments. This study additionally provided insight into how a domain can evolve over time with the addition of new members of a community, who build on the ideas of prior work and try things in new combinations. Generational development of creativity within a domain is further explored in recent research that suggests that, under certain conditions, online creative content generation actually improves with each successive generation of work (Nickerson et al., 2011) and that generally, creative output increases with increased exposure to the domain (Amabile, 1996). Findings from Architecture point to the successful development of a dynamic social media platform designed to promote engagement on behalf of distinct creative cultures and sustain engagement among individuals new to the domain of virtual architecture.

An online digital art community: Scratch

Since its introduction in 2008, the online Scratch community (scratch.mit.edu) has quickly grown to over a million registered users and over two million uploaded projects. Scratch, the multimedia-rich programming environment, was designed for youth in urban areas to create their own interactive stories, animations, games, and art by combining and manipulating stacks of building-block-like commands (Resnick et al., 2009). Programmed objects can be any imported two-dimensional graphic image, hand-drawn or downloaded from the Web, making Scratch particularly appealing to novice programmers wanting to create culturally meaningful and per-sonally expressive work (Peppler, 2010). Furthermore, what makes the Scratch virtual com-munity particularly vibrant is the open-source nature of project creation, which affords easy remixing of older projects into newer ones. In fact, over 40 percent of all projects posted on the website are remixes of existing Scratch projects (Senivirate and Monroy-Hernández, 2010). All projects on Scratch are given a Creative Commons Attribution Share-Alike License by default, which stipulates that anyone can reuse assets and/or code from a project as long as they credit the originator of the design being remixed. Furthermore, Scratch remembers this: modifying another user's project and resaving it automatically generates a note that credits and links back to the original project. This provides an entree into the benefits of open-source licensing, particularly in a global context where heated discussions around intellectual property and copyright pervade multiple industries. While educators often bemoan remix practices as cheating, others have argued that this type of production is a form of everyday creative activity, requiring interpretive flexibility or re-purposing the functionality of everyday objects (Kafai et al., 2011).

The online social media space has become much more than just a space to display creativity through unique projects in Scratch. For example, there are large numbers of youth that work together in the online environment to create a series of projects called Role-Playing Games or RPGs. These groups consist of several hundred to several thousand members and typically participate through text-based role play in the gallery comments. In 2011, over 1,600 galleries had the word "RPG" in their titles, the largest RPG of which, called Anthros Unite, had over 500,000 comments and nearly 2,000 associated Scratch projects (Roque, 2011). The group comprised over 400 project creators and over 1,200 comment writers, who collaboratively made over 1,900 projects and over a half million comment posts. Such expansive online collaboration practices were not intended by Scratch's creators, which speaks to the power of online communities of determining how designs are enacted, as well as inspiring large numbers of people to participate across multiple modes; in this case, not just youths' work in Scratch, but the exploration of the medium (i.e., the Scratch social platform) can elicit creative modes of thinking and interaction. Certainly, the collective contribution of Anthros Unite is novel within the Scratch community, and yet we can't attribute the creative act to any particular individual, or quantify it using any traditional measures of creativity; in such cases, the notion of the "individual" in the system's view of creativity is lost. However, as the 10-minute credits sequence at the end of a film indicates, a creative act does not *have to* be fueled by the individual acting in isolation, but rather in the coordinated efforts of a collective.

Youth online DIY community: LilyPond

Do-It-Yourself (DIY) tools and communities are playing a crucial role in the social media landscape, bridging the traditional divide between digital and physical media. Particularly relevant to this discussion are tools and communities that extend beyond the screen and into the physical world (c.f., Gershenfeld, 2005). Vibrant online communities are organized around the design and creation of a wide range of real-world artifacts, including robots, technology-enhanced clothing, scrapbooks, and scientific instruments. Participants build projects and then document, discuss, and display them on DIY sites like Instructables and Ravelry, along with more traditional media sites like Flickr, Vimeo, and YouTube. These communities attract and support adult hobbyists as well as budding youth scientists, designers, and engineers.

One such website is called LilyPond (http://lilypond.media.mit.edu), which enables young people to document and share their unique electronic textile (e-textile) constructions. This particular community primarily uses the LilyPad Arduino toolkit in their creations – a sewable, programmable microcomputer and its corresponding sensors and actuators – that novice engineers/ designers can embed into textiles for aesthetic and/or functional effect (Buechley and Eisenberg, 2008). Users sew LilyPad modules together with conductive thread instead of using traditional tools like insulated wire and soldering materials. To define the behaviors of the project, users employ the popular Arduino (www.arduino.cc) or Modkit (www.modk.it) development environment, enabling them to program the LilyPad microcontroller to manage sensor and output modules (like LEDs) employed in their designs. Reflective of the growing popularity of the e-textile movement in fashion, engineering and design industries, the LilyPond provides a platform for sharing basic e-textile project documentation, including a project title, a descriptive text, images, and LilyPad Arduino programming code. While the site is still in its infancy, youth across the country have started posting their projects as part of their school, after-school, or free time.

Recent studies have empirically explored creativity within this new domain, specifically observing the work posted by the LilyPond virtual community. Experts in the domain and youth with limited experience evaluated the creativity of a random selection of electronic textile artifacts from the LilyPond online gallery (Peppler, Kafai, Fields, Shively, and Searle, under review). We were not only interested in how consistent (or divergent) youth and experts were in their ratings of creativity but also in what rationales they employed in judging the designs. Results of the study indicated that there were high levels of inter-judge reliability among youth and experts in the domain, suggesting that youth can be a valuable resource for assessing the creative dimensions of innovative products in new domains like e-textiles. The reliability amongst the two groups was much higher than one might expect, which suggests that the crowd-sourcing found in these domains might prove to produce reliable critiques of creative work.

Conclusions and implications

Today's youth use whatever is at hand in their production practices, including the tools and networked social media spaces to share work with a distributed online network. In doing so, youth are becoming avid consumers and producers of media, garnering increasing levels of expertise with new media and broad exposure to cultural forms of production (Peppler, 2010, 2011). Though this type of media engagement falls out of scope of traditional schooling curricula, this represents a missed opportunity for educators to connect to youths' out-of-school learning. For example, there is good reason to believe that youth are learning about various art forms through online participation and social media (Peppler, 2011).

There is a need for further research to investigate how exposure and production is distributed among youth across a variety of demographics. Current research suggests that while all youth have heavy media exposure (including social media), youth from high-income, well-educated families are more likely to be producers of this media (Lenhart and Madden, 2007). This gap is a potential place where schools and after-school communities could contribute by allowing youth more time for open, meaningful exploration of tools and communities.

As Bers argues (2012), this type of everyday creativity is important for youths' learning and development as it's closely related to the building of self-confidence. Moreover, creativity can be cultivated through engaging in conscious, purposeful activity aimed at fostering creativity. Despite early concerns that computers might stifle creativity (Cordes and Miller, 2000), computers have been shown to help foster creativity, particularly when used in a creative way. As Resnick and others argue, when computers are used "more like paintbrushes and less like televisions," they open "new opportunities for children to playfully explore, experiment, design, and invent" (2006, p. 192). As Bers argues, computers like all learning environments, need to be constructed in such a way as to promote positive youth development (2012).

While much of our discussion has focused on the positive implications of social media for creativity, there are some caveats as well that call for further research. For example, prior research has demonstrated that there are clear dangers of assessing acts of creativity: once ideators are recognized they are also less likely to produce additional creative ideas, at least in the immediate future (Audia and Goncalo, 2007). As youth, for example, create work that is deemed creative in the online community, they may be less likely to produce additional creative ideas. Closer examination is needed of the impact that external reward systems (like stars or "liking") in social media have on creative output. Current research suggests that these rating systems might create a drop in creative production for the individual. However, clear tensions exist as these types of rating systems are closely related to the quality of the community as a whole and can deter off-topic or offensive commentary of works shared online (Shirky, 2011).

SEE ALSO in this volume chapter by Livingstone and chapter by Alper.

References

Amabile, T. (1996). *Creativity in Context: Update To The Social Psychology Of Creativity.* Boulder, CO: Westview.
Audia, P. and Goncalo, J. (2007). Past Success and Creativity Over Time: A Study of Inventors in the Hard Disk Drive Industry. *Management Science, 53*(1), 1–15.

Barnes, S. (2006). A Privacy Paradox: Social Networking in the United States. *First Monday*, *11*(9). Retrieved from: http://firstmonday.org/htbin/cgiwrap/bin/ojs/index.phpfm/article/view/1394/1312

Bers, M. U. (2012). *Designing Digital Experiences for Positive Youth Development: From Playpen to Playground*. London, UK: Oxford University Press.

Buechley, L. and Eisenberg, M. (2008). The LilyPad Arduino: Toward Wearable Engineering for Everyone. Wearable Computing Column in *IEEE Pervasive*, *7*(2), 12–15.

Chau, C. (2010). YouTube as a participatory culture. *New Directions for Youth Development*, *2010*(128), 65–74.

Cordes, C. and Miller, E. (2000). *Fool's Gold: A Critical Look at Computers in Childhood*. Early Childhood Alliance.

Csikszentmihalyi, M. (1996). *Creativity: Flow and the psychology of discovery and invention*. HarperCollins: New York, NY.

Erstad, O., Gilye, Ø. and de Lange, T. (2007). Re-mixing Multimodal Resources: Multiliteracies and digital production in Norwegian media education. *Learning, Media and Technology*, *32*(2), 183–98.

Gauntlett, D. (2011). *Making is Connecting: The social meaning of creativity, from DIY and knitting to YouTube and Web 2.0*. Cambridge, UK: Polity Press.

Gershenfeld, N. (2005). *FAB: the coming revolution on your desktop—from personal computers to personal fabrication*. New York, NY: Basic Books.

Greenhow. C., Robelia, B. and Hughes, J. (2009). Web 2.0 and Classroom Research: What path should we take now? *Educational Researcher*, *38*(4), 246–59.

Guilford, J. P. (1950). Creativity. *American Psychologist*, *5*(9), 444–54.

Jenkins, H. with Purushotma, R., Clinton, K., Weigel, M. and Robison, A. (2009). *Confronting the Challenge of Participatory Culture: Media Education for the 21st Century*. Occasional Paper. Boston: MIT/MacArthur Foundation.

Kafai, Y., Fields, D. and Searle, K. (2011). *Everyday Creativity in Novice E-Textile Designs: Remixing as Interpretive Flexibility*. Published in the ACM Proceedings for the Creativity and Cognition Conference, Atlanta, GA.

Lenhart, A. and Madden, M. (2007). *Social Networking Websites and Teens: An overview*. Washington, DC: Pew Internet and American Life Project.

Lenhart, A., Purcell, K. and Smith, A. (2010). *Social Media & Mobile Internet Use among Teens and Young Adults*. Washington DC: Pew Internet and American Life Project.

Nickerson, J., Sakamoto, Y. and Yu, L. (2011). *Structures for Creativity: The crowdsourcing of design*. CHI 2011 Workshop on Crowdsourcing and Human Computation: Systems, Studies, and Platforms, May 8, 2011, Vancouver, BC, Canada.

O'Reilly, T. (2005). *What is Web 2.0: Design Patterns and Business Models for the Next Generation of Software*. O'Reilly Media. Available at: http://oreilly.com/web2/archive/what-is-web-20.html (Last accessed December 1, 2011).

Pempek, T., Yermolayeva, Y. and Calvert, S. L. (2009). College Students' Social Networking Experiences on Facebook. *Journal of Applied Developmental Psychology*, *30*(3), 227–38.

Peppler, K. (2010). Media Arts: Arts Education for a Digital Age. *Teachers College Record*, *112*(8), 2118–53.

——(2011). *New Opportunities for Interest-Driven Arts Learning in a Digital Age*. (Deliverable to the Wallace Foundation). Bloomington, Indiana: Indiana University.

Peppler, K. and Solomou, M. (2011). Building Creativity: Collaborative Learning and Creativity in Social Media Environments. *On the Horizon*, *19*(1), 13–23.

Peppler, K., Kafai, Y., Fields, D., Shively, K. and Searle, K. (under review). Understanding Creativity in Digital Media and Learning: Youth and Expert Assessments of e-Textiles Designs.

Resnick, M. (2006). Computer as Paintbrush: Technology, Play, and the Creative Society. In D. Singer, R. Golikoff and K. Hirsh-Pasek (Eds), *Play = Learning: How play motivates and enhances children's cognitive and social-emotional growth*. London, UK: Oxford University Press, pp. 192–208.

Resnick, M., Maloney, J., Monroy-Hernandez, A., Rusk, N., Eastmond, E., Brennan, K., Millner, A., Rosenbaum, E., Silver, J., Silverman, B. and Kafai, Y. (2009). Scratch: Programming for All. *Communications of the ACM*, *52*(11), 60–67.

Rideout, V., Foehr, U. and Roberts, D. (2010). *Generation M2: Media in the Lives of 8- to 18-Year-Olds*. Menlo Park, CA: Kaiser Family Foundation.

Roque, R. (2011). Creating Worlds Together from Scratch: A Study of Role Playing Games in an Online Creative Community. Unpublished manuscript.

Sawyer, R. K. (2006). *Explaining Creativity: The Science of Human Innovation*. New York: Oxford University Press.

Sefton-Green, J., Thomson, P., Jones, K. and Bresler, L. (2011). *The International Handbook of Creative Learning*. London: Routledge.

Senivirate, O. and Monroy-Hernández, A. (2010). Remix Culture on the Web: A Survey of Content Reuse on Different User-Generated Content Websites. *Web Science*. Retrieved http://journal.webscience.org/392/

Shirky, C. (2011). Course Syllabus for the Design of Conversational Spaces. Retrieved June 7, 2011 from http://journalism.nyu.edu/assets/Syllabi/2011/Fall/Conversation-Syllabus.doc

Valkenburg, P. M. and van der Voort, T. H. A. (1994). Influence of TV on Daydreaming and Creative Imagination: A review of research. *Psychological Bulletin, 116*(2), 316–39.

24

MEDIA AND EMOTIONAL DEVELOPMENT

Nicole Martins

Without a doubt, the mass media provide countless ways for children to observe, experience, and learn emotions. Young children may experience some of their first fears as a result of exposure to a scary movie or television program, whereas older children may turn to the internet as a way to cope with teen angst and anxiety. Children are likely to watch their favorite television character encounter a range of emotions like happiness and anger, and eventually learn to empathize with those characters. Given the sheer amount of time children spend with the media, perhaps it comes as no surprise that much of the social interaction they see appears on screen. In this chapter, I will address the role of entertainment media, particularly television and film, in children's emotional development and elucidate areas that are ripe for future research.

What is emotional development?

In the first few years of life, children rapidly acquire the social and emotional competencies that help guide them into adulthood (Cohen et al., 2005). These emotional competencies refer to a child's ability to experience, manage, and express both positive and negative emotions as well as recognize emotions experienced by others. These building blocks are integral to children's emotional development because they allow children to relate well to others. As a result, children who are emotionally healthy are able to form close and satisfying relationships with peers and adults (Cohen et al., 2005).

There are several factors that influence children's emotional development. One such factor is biology. Evidence indicates, for example, that infants who are born prematurely are at risk for developing social–emotional problems (Lester et al., 1985). Second, a child's environment plays a crucial part in emotional development. Children who are deprived of parents' exclusive focus and involvement are unable to form secure attachments to their parents. Consequently, these children are less likely to fashion meaningful relationships with other children or adults (Feldman and Eidelman, 2004).

Another environmental factor that may contribute to children's emotional development is exposure to the mass media. Indeed, several researchers have argued that television plays a pivotal role in children's understanding of emotions, their own emotional experiences, and their general emotional competence (Dorr et al., 1983; Huston et al., 1992). Despite this claim, little empirical research has examined the kind of emotional portrayals featured in programs popular with children and whether children actually learn about emotions from such displays.

Emotional portrayals in the mass media

A casual examination of the television landscape suggests that there are plenty of emotional presentations on television from which children can learn. *Sesame Street* teaches children about emotions by routinely encouraging the child viewer to identify, label, and express feelings. A recent episode, for example, featured a "Mad Men" parody where the Muppets struggled with anger, sadness, and finally happiness as they worked to get an advertisement just right. Emotional displays like these are not just limited to children's programming; they can also be found in prime-time. Prime-time sitcoms, dramas, and reality shows consistently feature actors trying to master their emotions in extreme social situations. The popular FOX program *Glee*, regularly depicts one of the program's male leads, Kurt, experience the emotional ramifications of being an openly gay teenager. Thus, these examples suggest that there are emotional depictions on television from which children can learn. However, only two published studies have systematically examined the amount and nature of these displays in programs that children watch.

In the first study, Houle and Feldman (1991) selected five episodes from five sitcoms that were popular among 6- to-11-year-old-children. The researchers coded the facial expression of emotion exhibited by each character, and the situational context (e.g., conflict, threats) in which the emotional displays occurred. The researchers found that happiness was the most frequently displayed emotion (35 percent) whereas fear was the emotion displayed the least (> 1 percent). However, negative emotions were just as common. Sadness and anger accounted for just as many emotional portrayals as did happiness. Conflict was the most frequent emotional situational context to elicit emotion (33 percent). In the second study, Weiss and Wilson (1996) conducted a content analysis to examine the emotions and emotional situations in five prime-time family-formatted situation comedies popular among 2- to-11-year-olds. Contrary to the popular conception that sitcoms feature predominately positive feelings, the authors found that negative emotions like anger and fear were nearly as common as positive emotions.

Can children learn about emotions from the media?

The two studies mentioned above suggest that both positive and negative emotional displays are common in programs that children watch. But do emotional portrayals actually teach children about emotions? The research, though scant, indicates that televised portrayals can teach children about emotions. However, there are several factors that influence what children will understand from an emotional display. One such factor is the child's level of cognitive functioning. A large body of evidence supports the notion that younger children interpret the same television program differently than older children do (see Dorr, 1986). A cognitive skill that is especially relevant to children's interpretations of emotional portrayals is perspective taking. Viewers often need to role take or imagine themselves in a character's situation to fully comprehend the emotion or behavior portrayed in a scene. The ability to role take has been shown to increase with age (Kurdek, 1977). In one early experiment, Wilson and Cantor (1985) examined whether younger (3–5) and older (9–11) children differed in their tendency to empathize with a television character in a scary movie clip. In one clip, a threatening stimulus was shown (e.g. a bee) and in the other clip, the character's fear in response to the stimulus was shown. The younger children were less physiologically aroused and less frightened by the character's fear than by the threatening stimulus. In contrast, older children responded emotionally to both versions of the movie clip. The results of this study suggest that preschoolers did not lack empathy because they failed to recognize the nature of the character's emotion – the vast majority did recognize that the character was afraid. Rather, the younger children did not have the role-taking skills that are considered necessary for true empathy to occur.

Another factor that may influence what children will actually learn from an emotional display concerns formal features of media presentations. Research demonstrates that the presence of a subplot further complicates young children's understanding of character emotions. Weiss and Wilson (1998) examined children's comprehension of and emotional responses to negative emotions portrayed in an experiment with children in grades K-5. Boys and girls viewed a family sitcom that featured one of two negative emotions (anger, fear) and varied the inclusion of a positive and humorous subplot. Results revealed that inclusion of the subplot reduced young children's (K-2), but not older children's (3–5), ability to understand the emotional event in the main plot. Among all children, the inclusion of the positive subplot distorted perceptions of how negative and persistent the main character's emotions actually were. Overall, these age differences in comprehension suggest that a subplot can interfere with understanding the major story line for children who are cognitively less sophisticated.

Given that young children in particular have a difficult time remembering and understanding televised emotional displays, some researchers have examined whether repeated exposure to the same story would help children understand emotions better. Thus, a final factor that may influence what children will actually learn from an emotional display is repeated exposure. Mares (2006) examined the effects of repeated viewing on children's comprehension of videos. Younger children (4- and 5-year-olds) and older children (6- to 8-year-olds) watched a short story about a lonely old woman who finds a stray cat inside her house. The old lady is pleased to see the cat and says she wishes that more people would come to visit. Results revealed that repeated viewing of the video helped children with simple tasks such as emotion recognition. Younger children (4- and 5-year-olds), were able to explicitly describe the emotions of the old lady (happiness upon seeing the cat, lonely overall), and these descriptions improved with repeated viewing (there was a ceiling effect for older children). However, children's understanding of more complex information, such as inferring the emotions of each character, remained low for all children, despite prior exposure. This study indicates that at least for younger children, repeated viewing of a program may help in recognizing basic character emotions. The ability to make inferences about emotions, however, requires children to engage in role taking with a character, a skill that emerges in middle childhood (Kurdek, 1977).

Negative responses to emotionally charged portrayals

In this review I have argued that little empirical research has examined the amount and kind of emotional portrayals featured in programs that children watch, and whether children can actually learn about emotions from such portrayals. Little attention has been paid to these issues because most of the research attention has focused on the media's ability to evoke fear and anxiety among young viewers.

Fear and anxiety. Children often experience fear while being exposed to emotionally charged or scary media portrayals. Indeed, a nationally representative survey found that 62 percent of parents of children aged 2 to17 reported that their child had become scared that something they saw on television or in a movie might happen to them (Gentile and Walsh, 2002). Research also demonstrates that fear and anxiety produced by media content impacts children's behaviors. For example, Cantor and Omdahl (1991) conducted an experiment to examine whether exposure to scary media events (e.g., house fire, drowning) influenced subsequent behavioral choices among children in grades K-5. In this study, exposure to a deadly house fire or drowning increased children's fear of a similar event occurring in their own lives. Also of note, children in the house fire or drowning exposure conditions expressed less willingness to go canoeing or build a fire in a fireplace than did children in the control group. Thus, the results of this study suggest that brief exposure to stories that are routinely featured on television (i.e., news) may result in fear and risk perception that parents may want to prevent.

There also is growing evidence that the fright-producing impact of media depictions is long-lasting. Harrison and Cantor (1999) asked 153 undergraduates whether they had seen a television program or movie that frightened them so much that the emotional effects persisted after the program was over. Ninety percent of the participants reported having such an experience. Notably, one-third of these respondents said that their fear lasted more than one year, and of these respondents 26 percent reported that they were still experiencing residual fear at the time of measurement. In another study, Valkenburg (2004) asked 75 undergraduates to write down a specific instance of media-induced fright. Although the results revealed moderately lower percentages than those reported by Harrison and Cantor (e.g., 70 percent reported a fright reaction), there were many similarities in the results. In particular, the type of program or movie that caused the fear was closely related to the viewer's age at the time of exposure (as was the case in the Harrison and Cantor study). The scariest programs for children younger than seven were programs that featured grotesque-looking characters (e.g., *The Incredible Hulk*), whereas programs and movies that featured realistic threats (e.g., *Jaws*) caused fear in older children and adolescents.

These findings mirror a more recent study that asked children themselves to report their experience with scary media content. Cantor et al. (2010) asked elementary school children to report a frightening media experience they had while watching a television program or movie. The researchers found that 76 percent of the children reported having been frightened by something they had seen in a movie or on TV. Of these children, 23 percent said that the fear was still ongoing at the time the study was conducted. Consistent with developmental differences in children's responses to frightening content, the most frequently mentioned element in programs or movies that induced children's fear was supernatural forces (e.g. zombies). The authors argued that supernatural elements are often scary to young children because they routinely feature monstrous-looking characters whereas supernatural forces elicit fear among older children because the possibility of their existence is often unclear.

Desensitization. Desensitization is the process by which repeated exposure to a stimulus results in a numbing or habituation of certain natural emotional reactions. Desensitization is a commonly cited concern among media violence researchers because empirical evidence indicates that prolonged exposure to media violence can reduce psychological reactivity in both the short- and long-term.

Why should we be concerned about reduced reactivity to fictional portrayals of violence? The concern here is that reduction in arousal to entertainment violence may impact viewers' reactions to violence in the real world. In their classic study, Thomas and Drabman (1975) showed first and third graders either a violent or non-violent TV program and then put them in charge of monitoring two preschool children at play. Older children who viewed the aggressive program took significantly longer to seek adult assistance to stop what they thought was an altercation between the two preschoolers, compared to children who viewed the non-violent program. This finding was replicated 20 years later by Moliter and Hirsch (1994) who concluded that children tolerate the aggressive behavior of others if exposed to media violence. More recently, Funk et al. (2004) examined whether there was a relationship between real-life and media violence exposure and desensitization in a sample of 150 4th and 5th grade students.

In this study, desensitization was operationalized as children's attitudes toward violence (e.g., People with guns or knives are cool) and children's empathic responses (e.g., When I see a kid who is upset, it really bothers me). The study found that exposure to video game and movie violence – but not real-life violence – was associated with lower empathy and stronger pro-violence attitudes. Thus, empathy was affected because exposure to media violence desensitized viewers to the true consequences of violent actions.

Positive responses to emotionally charged portrayals

Given that research demonstrates that the media can produce negative emotions among young viewers, it is also conceivable that the media have the ability to elicit positive responses to emotionally charged portrayals. The research on children's parasocial relationships supports this idea. A parasocial relationship is an emotional one-way attachment that develops between an audience member and a media personality (Horton and Wohl, 1956). Evidence indicates that young people often feel as though they know and have a special connection with their favorite media figures (e.g., Murray, 1999). The depth of this connection is revealed in the emotional reactions of audience members to the loss of their favorite characters. For example, a study of online fans of the series *My So-Called Life,* found that many teenaged girls experienced extreme sadness and loneliness when the show was cancelled, due to their parasocial attachment to the lead character, Angela (Murray, 1999). These bonds, then, have implications for children's learning about emotions. Lauricella et al. (2011) examined toddlers' learning of a seriation sequencing task from socially meaningful video characters. In their experiment, the researchers randomly assigned 48 toddlers to a socially meaningful character video demonstration (e.g., Elmo), a less socially meaningful character video demonstration, or a no exposure control group. The results revealed that toddlers learned the task better from the socially meaningful character video than from the less socially meaningful video. The authors argued that children in the less meaningful video condition performed worse on the sequencing task because the majority of the attentional resources went to trying to understand who the character was rather than focusing on what the character was doing. This line of research suggests, then, that teaching children about emotions on the screen may be facilitated by characters that elicit strong parasocial bonds with their audience.

Although often cited as a negative impact of emotionally charged media, desensitization can positively impact both younger and older children's ability to cope with frightening portrayals. In one study for example, gradual exposure to filmed footage of snakes reduced fear reactions to the snake pit scene from the film *Raiders of the Lost Ark* (Wilson and Cantor, 1987). In another experiment, exposure to a live lizard reduced children's expression of fear while watching a scene involving lethal lizards in *Frogs* (Wilson, 1989). Lastly, Weiss et al. (1993) found that exposure to graphic photographs of worms taken from the horror film *Squirm* reduced children's self-reported fear during a scene from that movie. Notably, the desensitization technique was effective for both younger and older children in all three studies.

Emotion as an impetus for media selection

Up until this point, I have discussed the positive and negative effects of the media on children's emotions. What has received far less attention, however, are the ways in which children's emotions may influence the selection of media fare. Mood management theory (Zillmann, 2000) assumes that people choose media content in order to regulate their affective states. Simply put, people choose media to maintain a good or positive mood, or to improve a bad or negative mood. Indeed, a large body of evidence suggests that viewers selectively expose themselves to media portrayals in order to better or maintain current moods and/or states (Knobloch-Westerwick, 2006).

It is not clear, however, how well mood management theory explains media selection in child and adolescent populations. To date, only one study has tested this theory with an adolescent sample. Dillman-Carpentier et al. (2008) examined media use and mood states in a sample of 7- to 17-year-old children. In the study, adolescents with major depressive disorder and control adolescents without psychiatric disorders were called on customized cell phones up to four times a day and asked about their current mood state and media use across an 8-week period. The study found that among adolescents who used media, the emotional quality of their media choice matched their prior mood. This finding was true of adolescents with and without depression, as well as for boys and for girls. The authors concluded that the adolescents in this study were choosing media that matched, rather than enhanced, their current mood level.

Concluding issues and directions for future research

The research presented here suggests that the media can influence children's emotional development. However, the bulk of this research has focused on the media's ability to produce fear and anxiety among children. We know very little about the media's power to generate more positive reactions like compassion and empathy. Future research should examine this issue, especially given some networks' focus on developing empathy and compassion in young children. For example, Sprout, the 24-hour preschool television channel, recently launched the "Kindness Counts" campaign. The campaign uses social media components and programming tie-ins to help encourage children and their parents to be kind to one another. The ultimate goal of the campaign is to log one million acts of kindness reported to Sprout from families across the country. In addition, PBS announced that an animated spin-off of *Mister Rogers' Neighborhood* entitled *Daniel Tiger's Neighborhood* will air on PBS Kids in 2012. Much like the original *Mister Rogers*, the program is designed to teach preschool children school readiness and prosocial skills. Given that empathy appears to be a developmental skill (Wilson and Cantor, 1985), future research should examine whether such skills can be taught to young audience members.

Another issue ripe for further investigation concerns desensitization. Little empirical research exists in this area, particularly with children. However, there has been a recent call for more work on this subject (see Brown and Tierney, 2011) given media violence's role in the dynamics of bullying. It is believed, for example, that repeated exposure to media violence may desensitize children to the point where they are slow or unwilling to stop real-life violence, like school bullying, when they encounter it. Future research should examine the role that media violence exposure might play in the trajectory of peer victimization in school.

Another issue concerns the role of electronic media on children's emotional development beyond television and film. For example, there are many horror-themed video games on the market, and the graphics of these games are comparable to horror movies. Does playing games like these, then, result in fright reactions similar to those observed after television exposure? In a similar vein, how do children's online experiences shape their emotional development? In an era where much of the content online is user generated, future research should examine the emotions experienced by the content generated by other users and peers.

A final issue concerns the role of emotions as the impetus for media selection. At least one study with children suggests that moods impact exposure to media messages. However, one study is clearly not enough. It is important to more fully explore the role of emotion in selection processes among children, particularly given the amount of time children spend with the mass media. And as Nabi (2009) notes, future research would do well to conceptually distinguish moods from emotions, so that we can consider how discrete emotions (e.g., anger, fear, happiness) result in the selection of different forms of content.

Emotional development is crucial in helping children form healthy mature relationships. Future research should continue to examine the role electronic media may play in children's emotion learning, their own emotional experiences, and their overall emotional competence.

SEE ALSO in this volume chapter by Scharrer.

References

Brown, P. and Tierney, C. (2011). Media's role in violence and the dynamics of bullying. *Pediatrics in Review, 32*(10), 453–54.

Cantor, J., Byrne, S., Moyer-Guse, E. and Riddle, K. (2010). Descriptions of media-induced fright reactions in a sample of US elementary school children. *Journal of Children and Media,4*(1), 1–17.

Cantor, J. and Omdahl, B. (1991). Effects of fictional media depictions of realistic threats on children's emotional responses, expectations, worries, and liking for related activities. *Communication Monographs, 58*(4), 384–401.

Cohen, J., Onunaku, N., Clothier, S. and Poppe, J. (2005). *Helping young children succeed: Strategies to promote early childhood social and emotional development.* Washington, DC: National Conference of State Legislatures and ZERO TO THREE.

Dillman-Carpentier, F., Brown, J., Bertocci, M., Silk, J., Forbes, E. and Dahl, R. (2008). Sad kids, sad media? Applying mood management theory to depressed adolescents' use of media. *Media Psychology, 11*(1), 143–66.

Dorr, A. (1986). *Television and children: A special medium for a special audience.* Beverly Hills, CA: Sage.

Dorr, A., Doubleday, C. and Kovaric, P. (1983). Emotions depicted on and stimulated by television programs. In M. Meyer (Ed.), *Children and the formal features of television.* New York: Saur, pp. 97–143.

Feldman, R. and Eidelman, A. I. (2004). Parent–infant synchrony and the social–emotional development of triplets. *Developmental Psychology, 40*(6), 1133–47.

Funk, J. B., Bechtoldt-Baldacci, H., Pasold, T. and Baumgartner, J. (2004). Violence exposure in real life, video games, television, movies, and the internet: Is there desensitization? *Journal of Adolescence, 27*(27), 23–39.

Gentile, D. and Walsh, D. (2002). A normative study of family media habits. *Applied Developmental Psychology, 23*(2), 157–78.

Harrison, K. and Cantor, J. (1999). Tales from the screen: Enduring fright reactions to scary media. *Media Psychology, 1*(2), 97–116.

Horton, D. and Wohl, R. R. (1956). Mass communication and parasocial interaction. *Psychiatry, 19*(3), 215–29.

Houle, R. and Feldman, R. S. (1991). Emotional displays in children's television programming. *Journal of Nonverbal Behavior, 15*(4), 261–71.

Huston, A. C., Donnerstein, E., Fairchild, H., Feshbach, N. D., Katz, P. A., Murray, J. P., Rubinstein, E. A, Wilcox, B.L. and Zuckerman, D. (1992). *Big world, small screen: The role of television in American society.* Lincoln: University of Nebraska Press.

Knobloch-Westerwick, S. (2006). Mood Management: Theory, evidence, and advancements. In J. Bryant and P. Vorderer (Eds), *The psychology of entertainment.* Mahwah, NJ: Erlbaum, pp. 239–54.

Kurdek, L. (1977). Structural components and intellectual correlates of cognitive perspective taking in first-through-fourth-grade children. *Child Development, 48*(3), 1503–11.

Lauricella, A. R., Gola, A. A. H. and Calvert, S. L. (2011). Toddlers' learning from socially meaningful video characters. *Media Psychology, 14*(2), 216–32.

Lester, B. M., Hoffman, J. and Brazelton, T. B. (1985). The rhythmic structure of mother–infant interaction in term and preterm infants. *Child Development, 56*(1), 15–2.

Mares, M. L. (2006). Repetition increases children's comprehension of television content—Up to a point. *Communication Monographs, 73*(2), 216–41.

Molitor, F. and Hirsch, K. W. (1994). Children's toleration of real-life aggression after exposure to media violence: A replication of the Drabman and Thomas studies. *Child Study Journal, 24*(3), 191–207.

Murray, S. (1999). Saving our so-called lives: Girl fandom, adolescent subjectivity, and *My so-called life.* In M. Kinder (Ed.), *Kids' media culture.* Durham, NC: Duke University Press, pp. 221–35.

Nabi, R. L. (2009). Emotion and media effects. In R. L. Nabi and M. B. Oliver (Eds), *The Sage handbook of media processes and effects.* Newbury Park, CA: Sage, pp. 205–22.

Thomas, M. H. and Drabman, R.S. (1975). Toleration of real-life aggression as a function of exposure to televised violence and age of subject. *Merrill-Palmer Quarterly*, *21*(3), 227–32.

Valkenburg, P. M. (2004). *Children's responses to the screen: A media psychological approach*. Mahwah, NJ: Erlbaum.

Weiss, A. J. and Wilson, B. J. (1996). Emotional portrayals in family television series that are popular among children. *Journal of Broadcasting & Electronic Media*, *40*(1), 1–29.

——(1998). Children's cognitive and emotional responses to the portrayal of negative emotions in family-formatted situation comedies. *Human Communication Research*, *24*(4), 584–609.

Weiss, A. J., Imrich, D. and Wilson, B. J. (1993). Prior exposure to creatures from a horror film: Live versus photographic representations. *Human Communication Research*, *20*(1), 41–66.

Wilson, B. J. (1989). Desensitizing children's emotional reactions to the mass media. *Communication Research*, *16*(6), 723–45.

Wilson, B. J. and Cantor, J. (1985). Developmental differences in empathy with a television protagonist's fear. *Journal of Experimental Child Psychology*, *39*(2), 284–99.

——(1987). Reducing children's fear reactions to mass media: Effects of visual exposure and verbal explanation. *Communication Yearbook 10*. Beverly Hills, CA: Sage, pp. 553–73.

Zillmann, D. (2000). Mood management in the context of selective exposure theory. In M. F. Roloff (Ed.), *Communication yearbook 23*. Thousand Oaks, CA: Sage, pp. 103–23.

25

THE BEHAVIORAL, AFFECTIVE, AND COGNITIVE IMPLICATIONS OF MEDIA VIOLENCE

Complex relationships between young people and texts

Erica Scharrer

Violence encountered through the media appears to be a fairly common experience for young people throughout the world. Television emerges as a frequent source. In the United States, content analyses (Signorielli, 2003, Smith et al., 1998) find an average of 13 to 22 acts of physical aggression per hour in Saturday morning television (a timeslot dominated by cartoons) and 4.5 to 6 per hour in prime-time (a time when many children and teens are present in the audience). In the United Kingdom, children's programs comprised the largest frequency of programs with violence in a large sample spanning ten channels, accounting for 35 percent of all the violence-containing programs (Gunter et al., 2003). An analysis of six Canadian networks between 1993 and 2001 found a 378 percent increase in violence over time (Paquette, 2004). Similar numbers of acts of violence are posted by Japan—and Asia, more generally—but programs tend to emphasize suffering caused by violence more so than programs from the United States (Goonasekera and Lock, 1990; Kodaira, 1998). Finally, the Global Media Violence Study, with data from 23 countries, found that in many global locations children and teens see an average of 5 to 10 aggressive acts per hour on television (Groebel, 1998).

Video games and films are also sources of exposure to violence and aggression for children and teens. In 90 percent of randomly selected T-(for Teen) rated games from 2001 played for one hour, the user must commit a violent act against another character to continue, and in 69 percent that violent act must be killing (Haninger and Thompson, 2004). Although the violence gets more graphic and realistic in nature in more restrictive games (such as those rated T or M for Mature; Smith et al., 2003), two-thirds of games rated E for Everyone have been found to contain violent acts in which one character intentionally harms another (Thompson and Haninger, 2001).

Coyne et al. (2010) studied 90 movies targeted toward adolescents (rated G for General Audiences, PG for Parental Guidance suggested, or PG-13 for Parents Strongly Cautioned, recommended for viewers age 13 or older) in the 1980s, 1990s, and 2000s and found an average of 28 acts of violence per film. Physical violence without weapons constituted 46 percent of all violent acts, followed by violence perpetrated with weapons at 39 percent. Coyne and Whitehead (2008) found all of the 47 animated Disney films in their sample contained social aggression, with the most frequent forms including social exclusion (occurring at a rate of 2.13 acts per hour) and malicious humor (1.22 acts per hour). Yokota and Thompson (2000) found physical violence in 100 percent of the 74 G-rated, animated films from 1937 to 1999 that comprised their sample.

Aggression takes on more proactive, participatory forms when one considers the internet, and the primary means appears to be cyberbullying. For the EU Kids Online Project (Livingstone et al., 2010), data were gathered from a random selection of 1,000 9- to 16-year-olds and their parents in each of 25 countries. Findings show 55 percent of those interviewed said the internet contains content that may bother kids their age, whereas just 12 percent report being disturbed by something they have seen on the internet. In 59 percent of the instances, parents were not aware of that outcome. Six percent report they have been bullied online and 3 percent admit to having bullied someone else online. Although bullying was relatively uncommon compared to other internet-related risks such as exposure to sexual content or meeting strangers online, it was much more upsetting to the young people interviewed.

Parallel studies were conducted in Russia and Australia, using the same methods (Livingstone et al., 2010). The Russian children reported more online bullying than the European children, both as victims and as perpetrators. In Australia, twice as many children compared to those in Europe reported experiencing something online that bothered them, and 13 percent indicated they had been bullied online. In the United States, estimates from a national sample of 13- to 17-year-olds find 43 percent report having experienced cyberbullying in the last year, and such reports were highest among 15- and 16-year-old girls (Harris Interactive, 2007). Worldwide, therefore, although less than half of children and teens report being bullied online (and sometimes far less than half), such an experience of aggression is upsetting and may occur without parental knowledge.

Major media effects

The bulk of the research on the effects of media violence on youth is conducted in the United States, the United Kingdom, Germany, the Nordic countries, and the Netherlands (Gentile et al., 2007). Among researchers in those countries who have studied media violence, just 4 percent are convinced there is no causal link between media violence and violence in society (Linné, 1998). There is wide consensus in the United States, for instance, that three main categories of potential effects can stem from exposure to media violence (Comstock and Scharrer, 2007; Potter, 1999; Smith et al., 1998). Media violence has been shown to (1) teach young people about aggression— by stimulating aggressive thoughts, attitudes that are favorable or facilitative toward aggression, and aggressive behavior; (2) desensitize audiences so that they become accustomed to violent exposures and such exposures no longer register as alarming; and (3) produce fear responses— which include nightmares and other sleep disturbances—and encourage the "mean world syndrome" in which television viewers increasingly view the world around them as dangerous and unsafe. For each of these main areas, this review will discuss an example of one or more single research studies (often chosen among a multitude of other options; the goal was to include studies conducted in multiple geographic locations) and will rely on meta analyses to summarize the research record as a whole.

Learning aggression

Huesmann and colleagues (e.g., Huesmann et al., 1984) have examined the effects of television violence longitudinally in samples of young people from six countries (Australia, Finland, Israel, the Netherlands, Poland, and the United States). Aggression was assessed by peer reports of physical and verbal acts and children were studied from the ages of 6 to 8 to the ages of 8 to 11. Some differences emerged based on country of origin, yet the overall trend was for positive and small- to moderate-sized cross-lagged correlations between television violence use and later aggression in all locations.

Slater et al. (2003) studied middle school students in 20 schools in 10 different regions of the United States, measuring longitudinally their aggression and their use of such media types as action films, violent computer and video games, and internet sites with violent content. Slater and colleagues found a mutually reinforcing "spiral" model: young people high in aggression appear to be drawn to violent media *and* violent media use predicts later aggression.

The conclusions from meta analyses in these areas are clear and compelling, and show that aggression has been measured behaviorally as well as through attitude formation and cognition. Paik and Comstock (1994) amassed 217 studies of television violence and aggression or crime and found an overall effect size of .31. Largest effects sizes were found for preschoolers (.49), followed by those 18 to 21 (.39), 6 to 11 (.32), 12 to 17 (.23) and, finally, adults (.18). Boys and men in the meta analysis produced a modestly larger effects size than girls and women (.36 vs. .26), and generally, the more severe the outcome (e.g., criminal activity compared to aggression in play or simulated aggression in the lab), the smaller the statistical relationship with television. In fact, in a more recent meta analysis in which outcome measures were restricted to only those behaviors that were both criminal and violent in nature ($n = 26$ independent samples), Savage and Yancey (2008) found only a modest effect size of media violence among males only in the data and no significant effects for females.

Anderson (2004) included 32 independent tests in a meta analysis of studies that encompassed over 5,000 subjects and found significant effects of violent game playing on aggression, arousal, and helping behaviors. Anderson et al. (2010) meta analyzed studies conducted in the United States, Australia, Germany, Italy, the Netherlands, Portugal, the United Kingdom, and Japan and found significant effects of violent video game playing on aggressive behavior and no differences based on country of origin (Western compared to Eastern) among the experiments or cross-sectional survey studies in the sample. The effects size from the longitudinal surveys was marginally larger for Western compared to Eastern regions of the world ($p = .07$).

Desensitization

A desensitization effect of media violence exposure has been considered variously as a cognitive (what do young people think about violence?), affective (how do they feel?), and physiological (how do their bodies register concern?) response (Potter, 1999). A related thread of literature has considered whether exposure to media violence interferes with helping behaviors when young people encounter an ostensibly aggressive encounter. Drabman and Thomas (1974) began this line of inquiry, and in their study third and fourth grade children who had been exposed to a violent stimulus took longer to respond when a staged fight broke out (as seen on a monitor) compared to those exposed to a non-violent stimulus. Molitor and Hirsch (1994) replicated the study among same-aged children. Bushman and Anderson (2009) substituted video games for television and college students for children, and found those who had played violent video games took longer to help, rated the staged fight as less serious, and were less likely to notice the staged fight than those who played non-violent games.

No meta analysis exists on the topic of media violence and desensitization (perhaps because it's not as commonly studied as aggressive effects and perhaps because the concept of desensitization has been defined and measured so differently). Yet, reviews on the topic find convincing evidence for the phenomenon, including the gradual reduction of elevated blood pressure and skin conductance over multiple violence exposures and views of violence as increasingly normative and common (Comstock and Scharrer, 2007; Potter, 1999).

Fear and the mean world syndrome

Researchers have shown that many children and adolescents can readily remember a media text that scared them, such affective effects have both temporary and lasting consequences, and news media, in particular, are likely to provoke a fear response (Buijzen et al., 2007; Cantor, 2009). Using interviews with more than 200 Finnish children, Korhonen and Lahikainen (2008) discovered that media-induced fears are quite common, cause nightmares and other disturbances, and stem from exposure to media depictions of monsters and imaginary creatures, guns, accidents, and war. Van der Molen and Bushman (2008) found, among a large sample of 8- to 12-year-olds from the Netherlands, that exposure to threats such as wars or house fires led to fear and worry, and such responses were heightened when the threat was presented as a news segment compared to a fictional portrayal.

Developmental differences emerge quite clearly in the media and fear literature, with different media texts viewed as more or less scary as children age, and different coping strategies as more or less effective (Cantor, 2009). Younger children tend to adopt behavioral ways of dealing with the fear they experience through media consumption (grabbing a comfort object, hiding their eyes) whereas older children can use cognitive means of convincing themselves what they are seeing is not real (Cantor and Wilson, 1988). Meta analysis shows that some children find frightening media appealing. Hoffner and Levine (2005) meta analyzed 38 studies of media, fright, and violence, and found young people who were high sensation seekers and had higher trait aggression, as well as boys more than girls, were more attracted to frightening media.

The concept of the "mean world syndrome" stems from cultivation theory, which predicts a largely cognitive process in which the amount of television individuals are exposed to gradually and cumulatively shapes their views of the "real world" (Morgan et al., 2009). For heavy viewers, boundaries are blurred between televised and social reality, and because television tends to show a great deal of violence, heavy viewers are more likely than lighter to view the world as dangerous, violent, and scary (Gerbner and Gross, 1976; Morgan et al., 2009). A meta analysis (Shanahan and Morgan, 1999) on the topic has found an overall effects size between television viewing and a cultivated outlook of .10, and found little variation for crime, violence and mean world syndrome outlooks compared to others (the theory has been applied to a wide range of television themes and therefore cultivated outlooks). Effects sizes also do not vary much by age of the research participants, with children and early adolescents having very similar effects sizes as older adolescents and adults.

Interventions

Having established a statistical link between media violence exposure and outcomes including aggression, desensitization, fear, and the mean world syndrome, research attention has increasingly turned toward methods and means of disrupting those relationships. Both parental mediation—efforts of parents, caregivers, and other adults to intervene in media experiences within the home—and media literacy—efforts of teachers to encourage critical thinking and active challenging of media in schools—have the potential to make negative effects of media violence less likely. Yet, both areas of research show that different approaches are differentially effective at different ages and, generally, the best means of reaching kids is to actively involve them directly in these efforts.

Parental mediation

Children's responses of fear, worry, and anger associated with exposure to violent events in the news can be lessened by parents' active mediation (defined as their attempts to help children understand and critique what they see), although such success was confined in one such study to the younger children within a sample of 8- to 12-year-olds (Buijzen et al., 2007). The insertion of critical comments or questions while young people are being exposed to media violence by parents in the home—or, by proxy, by adult researchers in the lab—can decrease the likelihood of an aggressive response (Corder-Bolz, 1980; Nathanson and Cantor, 2000). Yet, research with college students who were asked to think back upon their adolescence shows some attempts at mediation can backfire. Restrictive mediation—limiting or blocking access to media—increased positive attitudes toward the content and encouraged alternative means of accessing the content (Nathanson, 2002).

Media literacy

Long established in schools in the United Kingdom, Australia, and Canada, media literacy (or media education) is increasingly taking hold in Japan, the United States, and elsewhere (Komaya, 2012; Kubey, 1998). There is a small but growing body of evidence about the effectiveness of media literacy curricula in helping young people negotiate media violence. Huesmann et al. (1983) found that adding an essay writing activity about what had been learned about media violence to a three-hour curriculum for first- and third-grade children increased its effectiveness, in that participating children were less likely than control group members to perceive television violence as realistic. An equally effective strategy in reaching this young age group (first through third graders) was employed by Rosenkoetter et al. (2004) who used role playing, the analysis of media clips, and a video production exercise in their curriculum. They found differential effects by gender, although all outcomes were encouraging: girls consumed less violent media and became less inclined to identify with aggressive characters whereas boys displayed reduced peer-derived indicators of aggression. Critically viewing clips from popular television programs appeared to be an effective teaching tool for 10- to 12-year-olds in the Netherlands (Voojis and van der Voort, 1993) and mostly 12-year-olds in the Northeastern United States (Scharrer, 2006). Byrne (2009) also found that a "hands on" activity (with students writing and reciting a paragraph about what they had learned) increased the effectiveness of a media literacy curriculum on violence among fourth and fifth graders. Thus, it appears that media literacy instruction does have the potential to intervene in the formation of positive attitudes toward aggression, to increase critical thinking about media violence, and, in some cases, to inspire less violence exposure and reduce aggression levels.

Conclusions, current climate, and contemporary controversies

It is clear from this chapter that children and adolescents in multiple locations across the globe encounter substantial amounts of aggression and violence in the media they consume. It is also quite clear that such consumption has a number of troubling implications that span the usual categories of cognitive, affective, and behavioral effects, including the potential for learning aggression (from thoughts to facilitative attitudes to behavior), diminishing concern for aggression and violence (also known as desensitization), and either personal responses of fear or societal-level views of a threatening world.

School shootings—which seem tragically increasingly common on the world stage—are often discussed as possible repercussions of the effects of violent media, and anxieties related to the safety of our children are common in the current climate. Yet, it is important to recall that extreme forms of violence are less strongly linked to media use than to other psychosocial factors, and an enormous gap exists between actual violent crime rates (which, in many areas, are in decline) and the perceived likelihood of such events. Thus, while we should take seriously the effects of media violence, we should also resist an unquestioned "culture of fear." Some cultural studies scholars (e.g., Barker and Petley, 2001) and some psychologists (e.g., Ferguson, 2007; Ferguson and Kilburn, 2009) would caution media violence researchers against both overstating aggression-related media effects by inferring they are causal contributors to school shootings and, in general, operating from a position of "moral panic" regarding the role of the media in the lives of young people. Perhaps future research in this area will find a way to acknowledge the pleasures that media afford—even content containing violence—with the less desirable consequences that they may present, and do more to illuminate developmental stages at which the balances struck between gratification and critique can be calibrated.

In the future, research and practice are likely to continue to grow in the areas of media literacy and parental mediation and continue to refine our understandings of effective means of promoting resistant interactions with media violence. Additional content analyses and effects studies will likely be inspired by newer media forms, such as increasingly realistic video games and ever-larger roles in young people's lives for social media and internet use that—at the same time they provide enormous opportunities—pose risks related to bullying, aggression, and other threats to safety. And the connection between scholarly work on the topic of children and media violence is likely to continue to be in conversation with policy. A recent Supreme Court ruling that struck down a California law imposing fines on those who rented or sold rated M for Mature-rated video games to minors seems to strongly reinforce the industry-derived *self*-regulation of media violence in the United States thus far. The flows of policy formations in locations outside the United States, often with traditions of stronger governmental roles in media regulation, will be important to track, as well. Indeed, advocacy and attempts to sway policy are likely to continue to present an additional, more macro-level oriented means of intervention in the issue of media violence in the future, alongside the more micro-level practices of media literacy education and parental mediation reviewed in this chapter.

SEE ALSO in this volume chapter by Martins, chapter by Pecora and chapter by Lustyik.

References

Anderson, C. A. (2004). An update on the effects of playing violent video games. *Journal of Adolescence*, *27*(1), 113–22.

Anderson, C. A, Shibuya, A., Ihori, N., Swing, E. L., Bushman, B. J., Sakamoto, A., Rothstein, H. R. and Saleem, M. (2010). Violent video game effects on aggression, empathy, and prosocial behavior in Eastern and Western countries: A meta-analytic review. *Psychological Bulletin*, *136*(2), 151–73.

Barker, M. and Petley, J. (2001). *Ill effects: The media/violence debate* (2nd ed.). London: Routledge.

Buijzen, M., van der Molen, J. H. and Sondij, P. (2007). Parental mediation of children's emotional responses to a violent news event. *Communication Research*, *34*(2), 212–23.

Bushman, B. J. and Anderson, C. A. (2009). Comfortably numb? Desensitizing effects of violent media on helping others. *Psychological Science*, *20*(3), 273–77.

Byrne, S. (2009). Media literacy interventions: What makes them boom or boomerang? *Communication Education*, *58*(1), 1–14.

Cantor, J. (2009). Fright reactions to mass media. In J. Bryant and M. B. Oliver (Eds), *Media effects: Advances in theory and research, 3rd ed.* New York, NY: Routledge, pp. 287–303.

Cantor, J. and Wilson, B. J. (1988). Helping children cope with frightening media presentations. *Current Psychology: Research and Reviews*, *7*(1), 58–75.

Comstock, G. and Scharrer, E. (2007). *Media and the American Child*. San Diego, CA: Elsevier/Academic Press.

Corder-Bolz, C. R. (1980). Mediation: The role of significant others. *Journal of Communication*, *30*(3), 106–18.

Coyne, S. M. and Whitehead, E. R. (2008). Indirect aggression in animated Disney films. *Journal of Communication*, *58*(2), 382–95.

Coyne, S. M., Callister, M. and Robinson, T. (2010). Yes, another teen movie: Three decades of physical violence in films aimed at adolescents. *Journal of Children and Media*, *4*(4), 387–401.

Drabman, R. S. and Thomas, M. H. (1974). Does media violence increase children's toleration of real-life aggression? *Developmental Psychology*, *10*(3), 418–21.

Ferguson, C. J. (2007). Evidence for publication bias in video game violence effects literature: A meta-analytic review. *Aggression and Violent Behavior*, *12*(4), 470–82.

Ferguson, C. J. and Kilburn, J. (2009). The public health risks of media violence: A meta-analytic review. *Journal of Pediatrics*, *154*(5), 759–63.

Gentile, D. A., Saleem, M. and Anderson, C. A. (2007). Public policy and the effects of media violence on children. *Social Issues and Policy Review*, *1*(1), 15–61.

Gerbner, G. and Gross, L. (1976). Living with television: The Violence Profile. *Journal of Communication*, *26*(2), 173–99.

Goonasekera, A. and Lock, Y. K. (1990).Violence on television in Asia. *Asian Journal of Communication*, *1*(1), 136–46.

Groebel, J. (1998). *The UNESCO global study on media violence*. A joint project of UNESCO, the World Organization of the Scout Movement and Utrecht University, The Netherlands. Report presented to the Director General of UNESCO, UNESCO, Paris.

Gunter, B., Harrison, J. and Wykes, M. (2003). *Violence on television: Distribution, form, context, and themes*. Mahwah, New Jersey: Erlbaum.

Haninger, K. and Thompson, K. M. (2004).Content and ratings of teen-rated video games. *Journal of the American Medical Association*, *291*(7), 856–65.

Harris Interactive (2007). *Teens and cyberbullying: Executive summary of a report on research conducted for National Crime Prevention Council*. Accessed 11/29/11 at http://www.ncpc.org/resources/files/pdf/bullying/ Teens%20and%20Cyberbullying%20Research%20Study.pdf

Hoffner, C. A. and Levine, K. J. (2005). Enjoyment of mediated fright and violence: A meta-analysis. *Media Psychology*, *7*(2), 207–37.

Huesmann, L. R., Eron, L. D., Klein, R., Brice, P. and Fischer, P. (1983). Mitigating the imitation of aggressive behavior by changing children's attitudes about media violence. *Journal of Personality and Social Psychology*, *44*(5), 899–910.

Huesmann, L. R., Lagerspetz, K. and Eron, L. D. (1984). Intervening variables in the TV violence/ aggression relation: Evidence from two countries. *Developmental Psychology*, *20*(5), 746–75.

Kodaira, S. I. (1998). A review of research on media violence in Japan. In U. Carlsson and C. von Feilitzen (Eds) *Children and media violence*. The UNESCO International Clearinghouse on Children and Violence on the Screen. Nordicom: Göteborg, Sweden, pp. 81–105.

Komaya, M. (2012). Media literacy and media education. In D. G. Singer and J. L. Singer (Eds), *Handbook of children and the media, 2nd ed.* Thousand Oaks, CA: Sage, pp. 681–96.

Korhonen, P. and Lahikainen, A. R. (2008). Recent trends in young children's television-induced fears in Finland. *Journal of Children and Media*, *2*(2), 147–62.

Kubey, R. (1998). Obstacles to the development of media education in the United States. *Journal of Communication*, *48*(1), 58–69.

Linné, O. (1998). What do we know about European research on violence in the media? In U. Carlsson and C. von Feilitzen (Eds), *Children and media violence*. The UNESCO International Clearinghouse on Children and Violence on the Screen. Nordicom: Göteborg, Sweden, pp. 139–54.

Livingstone, S., Haddon, L., Görzig, A. and Ólafsson, K. (September, 2010). *EU Kids Online*. Accessed 11/19/11 at http://www2.lse.ac.uk/media@lse/research/EUKidsOnline/Home.aspx

Molitor, F. and Hirsch, K. W. (1994). Children's toleration of real-life aggression after exposure to media violence: A replication of the Drabman and Thomas studies. *Child Study Journal*, *24*(3), 191–207.

Morgan, M., Shanahan, J. and Signorielli, N. (2009). Growing up with television: Cultivation processes. In J. Bryant and M. B. Oliver (Eds), *Media effects: Advances in theory and research, 3rd ed.* New York, NY: Routledge, pp. 34–49.

Nathanson, A. I. (2002). The unintended effects of parental mediation of television on adolescents. *Media Psychology*, *4*(3), 207–30.

Nathanson, A. I. and Cantor, J. (2000). Reducing the aggression-promoting effect of violent cartoons by increasing children's fictional involvement with the victim: A study of active mediation. *Journal of Broadcasting & Electronic Media*, *44*(1), 125–42.

Paik, H. and Comstock, G. (1994). The effects of television violence on antisocial behavior: A meta-analysis. *Communication Research, 24*(2), 516–46.

Paquette, G. (2004). Violence on Canadian television networks. *Journal of the Canadian Academy of Child and Adolescent Psychiatry, 13*(1), 13–15.

Potter, W. J. (1999). *On media violence*. Thousand Oaks, CA: Sage.

Rosenkoetter, L. I., Rosenkoetter, S. E., Ozretich, R. A. and Acock, A. C. (2004). Mitigating the harmful effects of violent television. *Journal of Applied Developmental Psychology, 25*(1), 25–47.

Savage, J. and Yancey, C. (2008). The effects of media violence exposure on criminal aggression: A meta analysis. *Criminal Justice and Behavior, 35*(6), 772–91.

Scharrer, E. (2006). "I noticed more violence:" The effects of a media literacy program on knowledge and attitudes about media violence. *Journal of Mass Media Ethics*, 21(2), 70–87.

Shanahan, J. and Morgan, M. (1999). *Television and its viewers: Cultivation theory and research*. Cambridge: Cambridge University Press.

Signorielli, N. (2003). Prime-time violence 1993–2001: Has the picture really changed? *Journal of Broadcasting & Electronic Media, 47*(1), 36–58.

Slater, M. D., Henry, K. L., Swaim, R. C. and Anderson, L. L. (2003). Violent media content and aggressiveness in adolescents: A downward spiral model. *Communication Research*, 30(6), 713–36.

Smith, S. L., Lachlan, K. A. and Tamborini, R. (2003). Popular video games: Quantifying the presentation of violence and its context. *Journal of Broadcasting and Electronic Media, 47*(1), 58–76.

Smith, S. L., Wilson, B. J., Kunkel, D., Linz, D., Potter, W. J., Colvin, C. M. and Donnerstein, E. (1998). *National television violence study 3*. Thousand Oaks, CA: Sage.

Thompson, K. M. and Haninger, K. (2001). Violence in E-rated video games. *Journal of the American Medical Association, 286*(5), 591–98.

van der Molen, J. H. and Bushman, B. J. (2008). Children's direct fright and worry reactions to violence in fiction and news television programs. *The Journal of Pediatrics, 153*(3), 420–24.

Voojis, M. W. and van der Voort, T. H. A. (1993). Learning about television violence: The impact of a critical viewing curriculum on children's attitudinal judgments of crime series. *Journal of Research and Development in Education, 26*(3), 133–42.

Yokota, F. and Thompson, K. M. (2000). Violence in G-rated films. *Journal of the American Medical Association, 283*(20), 2716–20.

26

MEDIA AND SEXUAL DEVELOPMENT

Jochen Peter

Adolescents in high resource countries currently grow up in a media-saturated, technology-oriented environment (Rideout et al., 2010). One important consequence of this environment is that adolescents have gained easy access to sexual media content (SMC) of varying degrees of explicitness. Traditional media that adolescents use, such as television and magazines, increasingly feature sexual content (for summaries, see Brown, 2009; Ward, 2003). Similarly, sex and sexual themes often occur in movies and notably in music popular among adolescents (Pardun et al., 2005). Finally, pornographic content is easily available on the internet and is used by a substantial number of adolescents (e.g., Wolak et al., 2007).

The growing availability of SMC for adolescents has led to opposite reactions in the scholarly community. Some scholars have suggested that the easy accessibility of SMC, particularly of internet pornography, may have negative consequences for adolescents' sexual development (e.g., Zillmann, 2000). These concerns are typically based on three assumptions. First, content analyses have shown that the representation of sex and sexuality in SMC is unrealistic (for reviews, see Brown, 2009; Ward, 2003). Second, adolescents lack the emotional and social maturity, as well as the sexual experience, to put SMC, notably pornographic content, into perspective (e.g., Thornburgh and Lin, 2002). Third, along with peers, SMC has outperformed parents and schools as a source for sexual information (Kaiser Family Foundation, 2003).

Other scholars, in contrast, have emphasized that the worries about the negative effects of SMC on young people are, historically speaking, a recurring phenomenon (Duits and van Zoonen, 2011). Given also the far-reaching changes in sexual matters, these scholars have therefore argued that sex should not be seen as inherently dangerous and adolescents should not be regarded as necessarily vulnerable to SMC (Attwood and Smith, 2011). Rather, adolescents' use of SMC should be studied within an emphasis on their critical skills and active appropriation of the content (Lerum and Dworkin, 2009).

Despite ongoing scholarly discussions about media and adolescents' sexual development, as well as several policy reports on the issue (for a summary, see Duits and van Zoonen, 2011), relatively little research on the issue is available and, if so, it is scattered and not cumulative. This chapter, therefore, tries to synthesize what is currently known about the relationship between adolescents' use of SMC and their sexual development, but also outlines the shortcomings of existing research. The term SMC refers to any (audio)visual and/or verbal representation and depiction of sex and sexual themes in the media, regardless of its degree of explicitness. Sexual development can be defined as changes in adolescents' sexual cognitions, affect, and behavior. This definition guides the organization of the chapter.

Media and sexual cognitions

Sexual cognition is used, in this chapter, as a summarizing term that refers to beliefs and knowledge about sex-related issues. The majority of studies that dealt with the relation between SMC and sexual cognitions have focused on beliefs about the relational context of sex and stereotypical gender beliefs. Overall, the studies have shown that when young people use SMC more often, they more strongly believe that sex without relational commitment is acceptable. This association has been found for sexual content in various media; for sexual content of differing degrees of explicitness; and with different research designs. For example, in a survey study US adolescents were more likely to see sex as a game when they watched sex-oriented prime-time programming more frequently (Ward and Friedman, 2006). Likewise, a two-wave panel study showed that 12–14- year-old male adolescents who often used sexually explicit material in various media were likely to hold more permissive beliefs about sex (Brown and L'Engle, 2009). Similar findings also occurred for the use of pornography in cross-sectional studies conducted among Taiwanese adolescents (Lo and Wei, 2005) and Japanese college students (Omori et al., 2011). Finally, both in a cross-sectional (Ter Bogt et al., 2010) and a longitudinal survey study among Dutch adolescents (Peter and Valkenburg, 2010b), a more frequent use of internet pornography was associated with a notion of sex as a primarily physical, casual game in which one's own sexual pleasure is considered more important than the affectionate or relational aspects of engaging in sex.

In terms of the link between SMC and gender beliefs, consistent evidence has emerged that adolescents' use of SMC is associated with more stereotypical beliefs about men and women. For instance, both in experiments and surveys among adolescents and young adults in the US, the use of sex-oriented prime-time programming has been found to be linked to beliefs that men are sex-driven and women are sex objects (Ward, 2002; Ward and Friedman, 2006). Young people's use of specific music genres, such as hip hop and hardhouse (Ter Bogt et al., 2010) as well as hard rock (Hansen and Hansen, 1988), seems also to be related to more stereotypical gender beliefs, including the sexual double standard (Zhang et al., 2008). Finally, cross-sectional and longitudinal survey studies conducted in various countries have demonstrated that adolescents' use of sexually explicit material is associated with a stronger notion of women as sex objects (Brown and L'Engle, 2009; Omori et al., 2011; Ter Bogt et al., 2010). However, a recent three-wave panel study has suggested that the relationship is reciprocal. Adolescents who believed that women were sex objects tended to use more pornographic content, which in turn reinforced and strengthened these beliefs (Peter and Valkenburg, 2009a)

Although content analyses have shown that media representations of sexual issues are often biased and unrealistic (for reviews, see Brown, 2009; Ward, 2003), the few available studies suggest that media can affect young people's sexual knowledge positively. For example, watching an episode of *Friends* in which condom failure was portrayed increased teenagers' knowledge about condoms (Collins et al., 2003). Similarly, more frequent reading of mainstream magazines, such as *Marie Claire* and *GQ*, was positively linked to young adults' knowledge about sexual health (Walsh and Ward, 2010). Finally, information found on the internet, notably when it stems from peers, seems to positively influence adolescents' sexual knowledge (Suzuki and Calzo, 2004). That said, scholars have emphasized repeatedly that sexual information in the media still has to become more diverse and realistic before it can generally serve as a trustworthy source for adolescents (Brown and Keller, 2000). At the same time, adolescents need to acquire more media literacy skills in order to be able to evaluate the credibility and trustworthiness of sexual information in the media more competently (Subrahmanyam and Smahel, 2011, chapter 8).

Media and sexual affect

The term sexual affect is used in this chapter to summarize physiological reactions to SMC, such as sexual arousal, as well as feelings and emotions that adolescents experience while and after using SMC. Although arousal plays a crucial role in many models of how people react to SMC (e.g., the sexual behavior sequence: Byrne, 1977), it has infrequently been investigated in research on adolescents and SMC. The few studies that have studied arousal have typically dealt with pornography and found that the majority of adolescents, notably males, experience pornography as sexually arousing (Mansson and Lofgren-Martenson, 2007; Peter and Valkenburg, 2008). There is also some evidence that young people find both pornography and less explicit SMC generally pleasurable and involving (Carroll et al., 2008; Peter and Valkenburg, 2009a, 2010a; Ward and Rivadeneyra, 1999). However, female adolescents seem to be more ambivalent than male adolescents about their affective reactions to SMC, particularly to pornography. While female adolescents experience pornography as physically arousing, they also consider such reactions as embarrassing. Similarly, they feel repelled by the lack of intimacy and the male-centered portrayal of sex in pornography (Berg, 2007). The ambivalent reactions of girls to sexual content merge with research that has shown that pornography makes female adolescents, in particular, more uncertain about their sexuality (Peter and Valkenburg, 2010a). Moreover, the finding fits in the larger context of discussions about the ambivalence of girls' sexual socialization (Tolman, 2002) and deserves further attention.

Within research on emotional reactions to SMC, young people's sexual satisfaction has received the most attention. Overall, young people's interpretation of the content, personal characteristics, and the type of content seem to play a central role in whether and how SMC affects young people's sexual satisfaction. For example, in terms of young people's interpretation of SMC, college students have been found to be less satisfied with their sexual experiences when they perceived sex on television as enjoyable. Conversely, those who perceived sex on television as realistic were satisfied with their sexual experiences (Baran, 1976). In terms of personal characteristics, adolescents with no or little sexual experience have been found to be less satisfied with their sexual lives as a result of watching internet pornography than those with greater sexual experience (Peter and Valkenburg, 2009b). Finally, in terms of the type of content, Stulhofer et al. (2010) have shown that paraphilic pornography reduced young men's sexual satisfaction, while mainstream pornography had no influence.

Media and sexual behavior

Research on the link between SMC and adolescents' sexual behavior has typically focused on the initiation of sexual behavior, sexual harassment, and sexual risk behavior. Regarding the initiation of sexual behavior, several US studies have found that adolescents who are frequently confronted with sex on television (Collins et al., 2004), in X-rated sexual content (Brown and L'Engle, 2009), and in music (Martino et al., 2006) started having sex earlier. However, SMC tends to affect white adolescents more strongly than black adolescents (Brown et al., 2006). The relationship between the use of SMC and the progression of adolescents' sexual behavior seems reciprocal: Adolescents who were more sexually experienced used SMC more often, which, in turn, stimulated them to explore new sexual experiences (Bleakley et al., 2008).

In terms of sexual harassment, there is some evidence from the US that 12- to 14-year-old male adolescents who used more X-rated sexual content were more likely to sexually harass girls (Brown and L'Engle, 2009). Another US study obtained comparable results for both boys and girls, but additionally showed that the intentionality of the use of X-rated sexual content and its violent character are crucial for the emergence of such influences (Ybarra et al., 2011). When adolescents used violent X-rated sexual content intentionally, they were likely to harass others sexually. However, the use of non-violent X-rated sexual content was unrelated to adolescents' sexual harassment perpetration.

Regarding the link between SMC and adolescents' sexual risk behavior, research has produced inconsistent results. A longitudinal US study found that adolescents who watched a lot of sexual content on television were more likely to become pregnant in the subsequent three years than those who did not watch much sexual content on television (Chandra et al., 2008). Similarly, another longitudinal US study found that African American female adolescents who frequently watched rap music videos had a higher chance to contract a sexually transmitted disease than those who did not watch such videos (Wingood et al., 2003). European studies have elicited somewhat different findings. For example, in a survey among a representative sample of Swiss adolescents, adolescents' use of internet pornography was not associated with teenage pregnancy or a high number of sexual partners. However, male adolescents who used pornography frequently tended to not have used a condom during their last intercourse (Luder et al., 2011). Finally, a longitudinal comparison of a representative sample of Dutch adolescents and adults reported an influence of online pornography on having unprotected sex with an unknown partner only among adults, but not among adolescents (Peter and Valkenburg, 2011).

Shortcomings and future research

Existing research suggests that adolescents' use of sexual media content is linked with their sexual cognitions, affect, and behavior. This research, notably the studies done in the past decade, has increasingly been based on more sophisticated research designs and representative samples of adolescents rather than on college students. However, it needs to be strongly emphasized that the field as a whole still suffers from several methodological and conceptual issues that need urgent research attention. At least three methodological issues need to be tackled. First, the influences of SMC on sexual development typically have small effect sizes and the practical significance of the effects needs scrutiny. This issue is inherently linked to questions about the measurement of key concepts, appropriate research designs, and rigorous data analyses techniques (see, e.g., the recent debate about the appropriateness of traditional regression-type analyses, with Steinberg and Monahan's (2011) position on the one hand and Brown's (2011) as well as Collins et al.'s (2011) position on the other). Second, questions about the causal link between SMC and adolescents' sexual development are too easily reduced to notions of a unidirectional impact of SMC on sexual development. We need to pay more attention to reciprocal, long-term relations between SMC and sexual development. Third, the study of adolescent sexuality is not only inherently multi-disciplinary, drawing on disciplines such as sexology, sociology, psychology, and anthropology, but also confined to what may be studied among a protected group, such as minors, from an ethical point of view (e.g., it is ethically impossible to conduct experiments on pornography with adolescents). The complexity of the issue, along with ethical limits to what can be studied, require a stronger focus on triangulation. Existing research seems to be based either on quantitative or qualitative approaches, but the two are rarely combined.

At least five conceptual issues limit current research. First, although adolescence is a crucial developmental period, a genuine developmental perspective on the issue of SMC and sexual development is conspicuously absent from existing research. We know little about how developmental characteristics interact with adolescents' reactions to SMC. Second, the majority of research focuses on the negative implications of adolescents' use of SMC, notably on the risks and potential harm of such activities. Although these questions are important, they should not preclude questions about potentially positive effects of SMC, such as increased sexual self-efficacy, improved sexual knowledge, and more positive attitudes toward sexual diversity. As other research has suggested (Buckingham and Bragg, 2004), an exclusive focus on the negative consequences of SMC use may deny adolescents' agency and critical skills, and often implies that adolescents should be protected from such content rather than be educated about it. Third, if we pay stronger attention to adolescents' critical skills when using SMC, we also need to deal more strongly with adolescents' resistance to SMC. This, in turn, inherently implies that we better understand the conditions under which different types of adolescents process and interpret SMC in different ways. Essentially, this will also help us comprehend which adolescents are susceptible to SMC and which are not. Fourth, the conflicting results concerning the link between SMC and sexual risk behavior suggest that many existing findings may only hold in specific cultural contexts. We need cross-cultural research to deepen our insights into the extent to which cultural factors, such as the level of sexual restriction, sexual traditionalism, and the openness of public discourses about sexuality in a given culture, affect the link between media and adolescents' sexual development. Finally, the majority of studies tend to ignore the larger social and cultural changes that the transformation of adolescent sexuality is a part of. The shift in adolescent sexuality can only be understood by taking into account that adolescent sexuality is no longer controlled by traditional authorities, but has become a matter of personal taste and pleasure (Attwood and Smith, 2011).

In conclusion, our knowledge about how media and adolescents' sexual development are related has increased considerably in the past years. To date, we have much better insights into how adolescents use SMC and how this is associated with their sexual cognitions, affect, and behavior than some time ago. Still, we are only starting to fully grasp the complexities of these associations. To succeed in this endeavor, it is vital that we ask ideologically unbiased and conceptually open-minded questions and study them in methodologically rigorous and theoretically advanced ways.

References

Attwood, F. and Smith, C. (2011). Investigating young people's sexual cultures: An introduction. *Sex Education*, *11*(3), 235–42.

Baran, S. J. (1976). How TV and film portrayals affect sexual satisfaction in college students. *Journalism Quarterly*, *53*(3), 468–73.

Berg, L. (2007). Turned on by pornography – still a respectable girl? How fifteen-year-old girls deal with pornography. In S. V. Knudsen, L. Lofgren-Martenson and S.-A. Mansson (Eds), *Generation P? Youth, gender, and pornography*. Copenhagen, Denmark: Danish School of Education Press, pp. 293–308.

Bleakley, A., Hennessy, M., Fishbein, M. and Jordan, A. (2008). It works both ways: The relationship between exposure to sexual content in the media and adolescent sexual behavior. *Media Psychology*, *11*(4), 443–61.

Brown, J. D. (2009). Media and sexuality. In R. L. Nabi and M. B. Oliver (Eds), *The Sage Handbook of media processes and effects*. Los Angeles: Sage, pp. 409–22.

——(2011). The media do matter: Comment on Steinberg and Monahan (2011). *Developmental Psychology*, *47*(2), 580–81.

Brown, J. D. and Keller, S. N. (2000). Can the mass media be healthy sex educators? *Family Planning Perspectives*, *32*(5), 255–56.

Brown, J. D. and L'Engle, K. L. (2009). X-Rated: Sexual attitudes and behaviors associated with U.S. early adolescents' exposure to sexually explicit media. *Communication Research*, *36*(1), 129–51.

Brown, J. D., L'Engle, K. L., Pardun, C. J., Guo, G., Kenneavy, K. and Jackson, C. (2006). Sexy media matter: Exposure to sexual content in music, movies, television, and magazines predicts black and white adolescents' sexual behavior. *Pediatrics*, *117*(4), 1018–27.

Buckingham, D. and Bragg, S. (2004). *Young people, sex, and the media: The facts of life?* Basingstoke: Palgrave Macmillan.

Byrne, D. (1977). Social psychology and the study of sexual behavior. *Personality and Social Psychology Bulletin*, *3*(1), 3–30.

Carroll, J. S., Padilla-Walker, L. M., Nelson, L. J., Olson, C. D., Barry, C. M. and Madsen, S. D. (2008). Generation XXX: Pornography acceptance and use among emerging adults. *Journal of Adolescent Research*, *23*(1), 6–30.

Chandra, A., Martino, S. C., Collins, R. L., Elliott, M. N., Berry, S. H., Kanouse, D. E. et al. (2008). Does watching sex on television predict teen pregnancy? Findings from a national longitudinal survey of youth. *Pediatrics*, *122*(5), 1047–54.

Collins, R. L., Elliott, M. N., Berry, S. H., Kanouse, D. E. and Hunter, S. B. (2003). Entertainment television as a healthy sex educator: The impact of condom-efficacy information in an episode of Friends. *Pediatrics*, *112*(5), 1115–21.

Collins, R. L., Elliott, M. N., Berry, S. H., Kanouse, D. E., Kunkel, D., Hunter, S. B. et al. (2004). Watching sex on television predicts adolescent initiation of sexual behavior. *Pediatrics*, *114*(3), E280-E289.

Collins, R. L., Martino, S. C., Elliott, M. N. and Miu, A. (2011). Relationships between adolescent sexual outcomes and exposure to sex in media: Robustness to propensity-based analysis. *Developmental Psychology*, *47*(2), 585–91.

Duits, L. and van Zoonen, L. (2011). Coming to terms with sexualization. *European Journal of Cultural Studies*, *14*(5), 491–506.

Hansen, C. H. and Hansen, R. D. (1988). How rock music videos can change what is seen when boy meets girl: Priming stereotypic appraisal of social interactions. *Sex Roles*, *19*(56), 287–316.

Kaiser Family Foundation (2003). *National survey of teens and young adults on sexual health public education campaigns: Toplines*. Menlo Park, CA: Kaiser Family Foundation.

Lerum, K. and Dworkin, S. L. (2009). "Bad girls rule": An interdisciplinary feminist commentary on the report of the APA task force on the sexualization of girls. *Journal of Sex Research*, *46*(4), 250–63.

Lo, V.-h. and Wei, R. (2005). Exposure to internet pornography and Taiwanese adolescents' sexual attitudes and behavior. *Journal of Broadcasting & Electronic Media*, *49*(2), 221–37.

Luder, M.-T., Pittet, I., Berchtold, A., Akre, C., Michaud, P.-A. and Suris, J.-C. (2011). Associations between online pornography and sexual behavior among adolescents: Myth or reality? *Archives of Sexual Behavior*, *40*(5), 1027–35.

Mansson, S.-A. and Lofgren-Martenson, L. (2007). Let's talk about porn! On youth, gender, and pornography in Sweden. In S. V. Knudsen, L. Lofgren-Martenson and S.-A. Mansson (Eds), *Generation P? Youth, gender, and pornography*. Copenhagen, Denmark: Danish School of Education Press, pp. 241–58.

Martino, S. C., Collins, R. L., Elliott, M. N., Strachman, A., Kanouse, D. E. and Berry, S. H. (2006). Exposure to degrading versus nondegrading music lyrics and sexual behavior among youth. *Pediatrics*, *118*(2), E430-E441.

Omori, K., Zhang, Y. B., Allen, M., Ota, H. and Makiko, I. (2011). Japanese college students' media exposure to sexually explicit materials, perceptions of women, and sexually permissive attitudes. *Journal of Intercultural Communication Research*, *40*(2), 93–110.

Pardun, C. J., L'Engle, K. L. and Brown, J. D. (2005). Linking exposure to outcomes: Early adolescents' consumption of sexual content in six media. *Mass Communication & Society*, *8*(2), 75–91.

Peter, J. and Valkenburg, P. M. (2008). Adolescents' exposure to sexually explicit Internet material and sexual preoccupancy: A three-wave panel study. *Media Psychology*, *11*(2), 207–34.

——(2009a). Adolescents' exposure to sexually explicit internet material and notions of women as sex objects: Assessing causality and underlying mechanisms. *Journal of Communication*, *59*(3), 407–33.

——(2009b). Adolescents' exposure to sexually explicit internet material and sexual satisfaction: A longitudinal study. *Human Communication Research*, *35*(2), 171–94.

——(2010a). Adolescents' use of sexually explicit internet material and sexual uncertainty: The role of involvement and gender. *Communication Monographs*, *77*(3), 357–75.

——(2010b). Processes underlying the effects of adolescents' use of sexually explicit internet material: The role of perceived realism. *Communication Research*, *37*(3), 375–99.

——(2011). The influence of sexually explicit internet material on sexual risk behavior: A comparison of adolescents and adults. *Journal of Health Communication*, *16*(7), 750–65.

Rideout, V. J., Foehr, U. G. and Roberts, D. F. (2010). *Generation M2: Media in the lives of 8- to 18-year-olds.* Menlo Park, CA: Kaiser Family Foundation.

Steinberg, L. and Monahan, K. C. (2011). Adolescents' exposure to sexy media does not hasten the initiation of sexual intercourse. *Developmental Psychology, 47*(2), 562–76.

Stulhofer, A., Busko, V. and Landpriet, I. (2010). Pornography, sexual socialization, and satisfaction among men. *Archives of Sexual Behavior, 39*(1), 168–78.

Subrahmanyam, K. and Smahel, D. (2011). *Digital youth. The role of media in development.* New York: Springer.

Suzuki, L. K. and Calzo, J. P. (2004). The search for peer advice in cyberspace: An examination of online teen bulletin boards about health and sexuality. *Journal of Applied Developmental Psychology, 25*(6), 685–98.

Ter Bogt, T. F. M., Engels, R. C. M. E., Bogers, S. and Kloosterman, M. (2010). "Shake It baby, shake it": Media preferences, sexual attitudes and gender stereotypes among adolescents. *Sex Roles, 63*(11), 844–59.

Thornburgh, D. and Lin, H. S. (2002). *Youth, pornography, and the Internet.* Washington, DC: National Academy Press.

Tolman, D. L. (2002). *Dilemmas of desire: Teenage girls talk about sexuality.* Cambridge, MA: Harvard University Press.

Walsh, J. L. and Ward, L. M. (2010). Magazine reading and involvement and young adults' sexual health knowledge, efficacy, and behaviors. *Journal of Sex Research, 47*(4), 285–300.

Ward, L. M. (2002). Does television exposure affect emerging adults' attitudes and assumptions about sexual relationships? Correlational and experimental confirmation. *Journal of Youth and Adolescence, 31*(1), 1–15.

——(2003). Understanding the role of entertainment media in the sexual socialization of American youth: A review of empirical research. *Developmental Review, 23*(3), 347–88.

Ward, L. M. and Rivadeneyra, R. (1999). Contributions of entertainment television to adolescents' sexual attitudes and expectations: The role of viewing amount versus viewer involvement. *Journal of Sex Research, 36*(3), 237–49.

Ward, L. M. and Friedman, K. (2006). Using TV as a guide: Associations between television viewing and adolescents' sexual attitudes and behavior. *Journal of Research on Adolescence, 16*(1), 133–56.

Wingood, G. M., DiClemente, R. J., Bernhardt, J. M., Harrington, K., Davies, S. L., Robillard, A. et al. (2003). A prospective study of exposure to rap music videos and African American female adolescents' health. *American Journal of Public Health, 93*(3), 437–39.

Wolak, J., Mitchell, K. and Finkelhor, D. (2007). Unwanted and wanted exposure to online pornography in a national sample of youth Internet users. *Pediatrics, 119*(2), 247–57.

Ybarra, M. L., Mitchell, K. J., Hamburger, M., Diener-West, M. and Leaf, P. J. (2011). X-rated material and perpetration of sexually aggressive behavior among children and adolescents: Is there a link? *Aggressive Behavior, 37*(1), 1–18.

Zhang, Y. Y., Miller, L. E. and Harrison, K. (2008). The relationship between exposure to sexual music videos and young adults' sexual attitudes. *Journal of Broadcasting & Electronic Media, 52*(3), 368–86.

Zillmann, D. (2000). Influence of unrestrained access to erotica on adolescents' and young adults' disposition toward sexuality. *Journal of Adolescent Health, 27*(2S), 41–44.

27

MEDIA, BODY IMAGE, AND EATING DISORDERS

Kristen Harrison

Body image and eating disorders: definition and prevalence

Anorexia nervosa and bulimia nervosa are eating disorders characterized by thin-ideal internalization (embracing the thin body ideal as one's own), a strong drive for thinness, and an intense fear of fatness (American Psychiatric Association, 2000). Lifetime prevalence estimates in the United States for anorexia nervosa and bulimia nervosa are 0.9 percent and 1.5 percent among women, and 0.3 percent and 0.5 percent among men (Hudson et al., 2007), with an additional 4.4 percent overall for "eating disorders not otherwise specified" (EDNOS) (Lewinsohn, 2001). Far more young people—17 percent, according to the U.S. Centers for Disease Control and Prevention (2007)—are obese, so why should we be concerned about cultural influences on child body image and disordered eating? The reason is that the costs of poor body image and disordered eating are exceptionally high, and disordered eating may have permanent developmental consequences. In one study, the death rate of anorexia was 15.6 percent over 21 years (Zipfel et al., 2000). Other complications include depression, anxiety disorders, attempted suicide, chronic pain, infectious diseases, insomnia, cardiovascular and neurological problems (Johnson et al., 2002), strained interpersonal relationships (Holt and Espelage, 2002), and depleted bone density and delayed menarche (Nicholls, 2004). Disordered eating can also lead to obesity; in longitudinal research, normal-weight children who used unhealthful weight-loss tactics increased their risk of both disordered eating and obesity in adolescence (Neumark-Sztainer et al., 2006).

Media as sociocultural influence

Research on the media as a sociocultural influence on body image and disordered eating has been ongoing for more than 20 years. A full review of the corpus of relevant research is beyond the scope of this chapter, so articles described here comprise relatively recent studies that succinctly represent new or well-replicated research findings. The most comprehensive recent meta-analysis of media-body research (Grabe et al., 2008) summarized 141 studies involving 15,047 female participants. Media exposure was related to moderate decreases in satisfaction with the body and increased eating pathology. Effects for thin-ideal internalization were stronger for adolescents than for adults, whereas effects for eating behaviors and beliefs about eating were stronger for adults but still significant for adolescents. There is no comparable meta-analysis for males, but studies with boys have reported small-to-moderate effects (Harrison, 2000a; Harrison and Bond, 2007) indicating increased body image disturbance and eating pathology with greater media exposure.

Most research on media, body image, and disordered eating has employed adult and adolescent samples (Levine and Harrison, 2003). Only recently have researchers begun systematically studying pre-adolescent girls (Gilbert, 1998; Harrison, 2000a; Harrison and Hefner, 2006; Sands and Wardle, 2003) and boys (Harrison and Bond, 2007). Eating disturbances can begin in preschool (Stice et al., 1999), and anorexia and bulimia can appear prior to adolescence, especially among girls (American Psychiatric Association, 2000). Given the ubiquity of commercial media in children's lives, it is important to understand how media portrayals influence body image and disordered eating in childhood. This understanding begins with an assessment of body ideals in the media children use.

The media-portrayed thin ideal

Print media

Most research on body trends in print media has focused on the shrinking size of adults such as *Playboy* magazine centerfold subjects (Sypeck et al., 2006). Research on child-audience media reveals more complicated trends. Ballentine and Ogle (2005) conducted a rhetorical analysis of the way "body problems" were represented in *Seventeen* from 1992 to 2003. Problems like excess weight and flabbiness were framed as fixable with consumer products and services. However, over time articles focused more on making the most of one's natural beauty (e.g., "superskinny girls aren't typical … what your body looks like is determined by your genes" [p. 299]). Such conflicting messages may be confusing to adolescent readers (Ballentine and Ogle, 2005).

Screen media

In an analysis of popular children's videos and books, Herbozo et al. (2004) reported that body-related messages were conveyed an average of 8.7 times per video and 2.8 times per book. Thinness was a positive female trait in 60 percent of videos, and muscularity a positive male trait in 32 percent of videos. Greenberg et al. (2003) coded the body sizes of 1,018 major child and adult characters in 56 prime-time television programs. Whereas about 5 percent of U.S. women (and 2 percent of men) are underweight, over 30 percent of female characters (12 percent of male characters) were underweight. Not only is underweight on TV over-represented, it is openly praised. Fouts and Burggraf (1999) found that thin female characters in situation comedies were more likely than fat female characters to receive praise, whereas fat characters were more likely to be insulted (if female) or make fun of themselves (if male; Fouts and Burggraf, 2000; Fouts and Vaughan, 2002). Similar gender differences are reflected in global media, with notable differences by country. An analysis of 14,959 human characters in children's television from 24 countries revealed that more females than males were portrayed as very thin, with the greatest percentages in Australia (45 percent of females coded very thin) and the U.K. (37 percent), and the lowest in Hong Kong and Israel (both under 1 percent). In contrast, males were more likely to be portrayed as overweight, especially in Kenya (19 percent coded overweight) and Argentina (17 percent) (Götz and Lemish, 2012).

Internet

Youth engagement with the thin ideal on the internet has been studied most intensively in research on pro-eating-disorder websites. These sites offer resources and opportunities to connect with others who view disordered eating as a lifestyle choice. A content analysis of 12 pro-Ana (anorexia) sites by Norris et al. (2006) revealed themes of control, success, sacrifice, transformation, and coping through religious icons and "thinspirational" photographs of extremely thin bodies. Such sites offer young internet users "trigger pictures" for printing and carrying with them to strengthen their resolve not to eat, thereby extending the web's influence beyond the computer.

Popular theoretical frameworks for explaining effects

Perhaps the most popular framework in work on media and body image is *social comparison theory* (Festinger, 1954), which holds that people are driven to evaluate themselves via comparisons with reasonably similar targets. "Upward" comparisons (in which the target is judged to be superior) can lead to negative self-evaluations and motivate behavioral change. Supporting research reveals that ideal-body media exposure predicts poor body image, disordered eating, and endorsement of the thin ideal most among young audience members who compare their own bodies to those of media personalities (Tiggemann, 2005).

The process of modeling outlined in *social cognitive theory* (Bandura, 2002) has been invoked to explain why young people change their eating and exercise behaviors in response to media messages. If a certain set of ideals is consistently rewarded or unpunished, social cognitive theory predicts that exposure to these ideals will increase motivation to perform the behaviors thought to achieve the depicted ideals and generate the depicted rewards. Because the media thin ideal is associated with positive outcomes (Fouts and Burggraf, 1999), young viewers are given incentives to be thin. Research on children (Dittmar et al., 2006) and adolescents (Harrison, 2001) provides support for the social cognitive theory prediction that exposure is associated with efforts to become thinner.

Eating disorders also have a pronounced emotional component (American Psychiatric Association, 2000) that is often overlooked in rational-choice models of behavior. Over- and undereating help manage unpleasant emotions, which according to *self-discrepancy theory* are experienced when people are reminded of the disconnect between who they are and who they are "supposed" to be (Strauman et al., 1991). Such discrepancies can be activated by media exposure (Harrison, 2001) and are associated with eating pathology. Supporting research by Harrison (2001) showed that self-discrepant adolescents experienced much more negative emotion following exposure to ideal-body television than did non-discrepant adolescents.

Along with these social scientific models are *critical/cultural and feminist views* explaining how media socialize young people, especially girls, to embrace their bodies as loci of control and regulate and discipline their bodies through methods and products promoted in the media (Bordo, 1993). From this perspective, downsizing the body symbolically downsizes the self and constitutes a step toward becoming what Michel Foucault called the "docile body" (Bartky, 1988). Thus while social scientists emphasize thin-ideal media effects on health, critical and feminist theorists emphasize the way media-delivered cultural pressures toward thinness uphold traditional patriarchy.

Research findings

Experiments

A meta-analysis of 25 experiments on girls' and women's body satisfaction by Groesz et al. (2002) revealed moderately decreased body satisfaction among those exposed to thin-ideal media. Television portrayals of the muscular male ideal have also produced increases in depression and muscle dissatisfaction among adolescent boys and men (e.g., Agliata and Tantleff-Dunn, 2004).

Outside the laboratory, Stice et al. (2001) assigned adolescent girls to receive a subscription to *Seventeen* magazine and tracked them for 15 months. Compared to a control group, girls with low levels of social support who received the subscription reported a significant increase in bulimic symptoms.

Surveys

Most cross-sectional surveys of adolescents reveal small-to-moderate positive correlations between exposure to ideal-body television and magazines and variables such as a drive for thinness, body dissatisfaction, and body shame (see Levine and Harrison, 2003). Longitudinal research has shown that thin-ideal internalization is unnecessary for television exposure to predict disordered eating among preadolescent girls and boys (Harrison, 2000a), which suggests that media-body portrayals, or possibly food advertising, may encourage unhealthful dietary control independent of their effect on adoption of the thin ideal.

The few longitudinal studies on media exposure and body image reveal modest but durable long-term correlations. For prepubescent girls, viewing of appearance-focused television programs predicted a decrease in appearance satisfaction one year later (Dohnt and Tiggemann, 2006). Likewise, prepubescent girls' overall television exposure predicted a thinner ideal adult body shape one year later (Harrison and Hefner, 2006). For prepubescent boys, exposure to video gaming magazines predicted an increased drive for muscularity one year later (Harrison and Bond, 2007). Three years after the 1995 introduction of television to the island of Fiji (Becker et al., 2002), disordered eating among adolescent girls was more prevalent than one month after (19 percent versus 8 percent), and vomiting to control weight increased from zero to 7 percent. In qualitative interviews, 77 percent of the girls reported feeling pressured by television to lose weight.

Qualitative methods

Intensive observational or interview methods like those used by Becker et al. (2002) reveal details that purely quantitative studies may miss. Adolescent girls interviewed by Milkie (1999) reported resisting the media-promoted thin ideal but felt pressured to lose weight anyway because they believed their peers embraced this ideal: "They look at her (points to a girl in the magazine) and they think they should look like that because they heard a guy say that she's pretty or whatever." (p. 206). These reports illustrate the complexity of the media-body relationship for adolescents, who may be savvy enough to critique the media-portrayed ideal yet still feel pressured to meet it to gain peer acceptance.

Moderators

Research has revealed five noteworthy moderators that affect young people's vulnerability to ideal-body media: gender, age, race, body image disturbance, and social support. Although research on 6–8-year-olds shows no *gender* difference in the correlation between television viewing and disordered eating (Harrison, 2000b), other studies (e.g., Harrison, 2000a) reveal significant media-disorder relationships for adolescent girls but not boys. This may reflect the fact that the ideal male body is muscular rather than slender, as gaming magazine reading is connected with drive for muscularity among boys (Harrison and Bond, 2007).

Regarding *age*, effects for adolescents are about as large as they are for adults (Grabe et al., 2008; Groesz et al., 2002). Media exposure predicts disordered eating and the idealization of thinness for girls and boys as young as five (Dohnt and Tiggemann, 2006; Harrison, 2000b;

Harrison and Hefner, 2006), but the effect is weaker for younger children than it is for older adolescents and adults.

Research comparing effects by race/ethnicity generally points to stronger relationships for White, Anglo, or European-American youth than those from other ethnic backgrounds. African American girls in Milkie's (1999) investigation reported resisting thin-ideal media pressure. However, in research with African American and Anglo American elementary school girls, Harrison and Hefner (2006) found no race differences. This discrepancy could be due to methodological differences, with the Milkie study using more probing, semi-structured interview techniques to encourage girls to think about how they respond to media. It is also possible that, with depictions of bodies of color becoming increasingly thinner in mainstream magazines (Baker, 2005), the ethnic gap in effects is closing.

Regarding body image disturbance, Groesz et al. (2002) reported much stronger media effects for individuals with pre-existing body issues than for those without. There may be a vicious cycle such that early exposure predicts the development of body image disturbance, which in turn increases vulnerability to thin-ideal media effects. This is especially problematic given that young people with clinically significant eating disorders actively seek out thin-ideal media (Thomsen et al., 2002).

On a more encouraging note, the previously described work of Stice et al. (2001) on *Seventeen* magazine illustrates the protective effect of social support from parents and peers, and underscores the importance of conceptualizing the media as part of a broader environment composed of multiple influences including family, peers, and community.

Ongoing debates in the digital age

After more than 20 years of research including meta-analyses, there is little disagreement that media exposure affects young people's perceptions of their bodies and predicts eating pathology concurrently and over time. Current debates center on whether the effect is strong enough to merit concern given larger effects on obesity. Media-body researchers are often asked if it is not fortuitous that ideal-body media urge young people to lose weight, because then child obesity rates would drop. This question is based on faulty reasoning. Neumark-Sztainer et al. (2007) found that unhealthful weight control tactics like fasting and over-exercising are more, not less, common among overweight children than normal- and underweight children. In desperation, overweight children and teens may use potent weight-loss tactics that are not sustainable over time. Obesity and eating disorders are not opposites; instead they should be viewed as components of a single continuous spectrum of weight-related disorders (Neumark-Sztainer et al., 2007).

A second debate concerns pro-eating-disorder websites as places for youth to provide and receive support (Dolan, 2004). Few people would take issue with online support forums for diabetes or cancer given how isolating these diseases are. Eating disorders are also isolating, yet there are widespread efforts to shut down pro-eating-disorder sites due to fear that they lure youth to a life of disordered eating (Gavin et al., 2008). Adolescent and adult users of a pro-Ana website expressed relief that they could "come out" to their online friends rather than revealing their disorders to offline friends and families (Gavin et al., 2008). The question of whether "coming out" online facilitates healing offline or just prolongs the disorder is a prime topic for future research.

Future directions

Children consume media within home and community contexts, the influence of which has gone underexplored in media-body research. A highly profitable direction for future research would be to attend more to family, peer, and community contexts as moderators and sites for intervention and prevention via media literacy, parental mediation, and fortification against potential effects. The work on social support as a protective factor (Stice et al., 2001) illustrates the power of context. Critics of media-body research have argued that direct effects of media exposure are overestimated (Ferguson et al., 2011; Holmstrom, 2004), and that peer influences and other evolution-driven social dynamics are more powerful predictors of body image and disordered eating (Ferguson et al., 2011). These researchers define "small" effects from a purely psychological (non-clinical) perspective and downplay the profound public-health importance of modest effects (Rutledge and Loh, 2004). They also fail to explain content analyses showing media trends *away* from evolutionarily advantageous body attributes (e.g., the increasingly androgenic body shape of *Playboy* models, Pettijohn and Jungeberg, 2004). Moreover, they fail to acknowledge the role that peers may play in mediating media-generated body ideals, which parallels the role they play in disseminating media-generated fashion trends. Thus, although it may be true that direct media effects are modest, cumulative media effects are larger when the influence of the media as filtered through peers, family, and community agents is added to direct effects. More accurate estimates of total media influence could be provided by research that conceptualizes "media influence" more broadly than direct exposure.

Future research must also attend more to developmental processes so researchers can determine when thin-ideal internalization becomes linked with media exposure and when it becomes a significant mediator between media exposure and eating outcomes (Harrison, 2000b).

In addition, given that research reveals marked differences in media-body ideals from country to country, with the thin ideal receiving the greatest representation in countries that produce and import Westernized media (Götz and Lemish, 2012), more globally-oriented content analyses and effects studies are needed to examine national similarities and differences in the relationship between ideal-body content and body image and eating disturbances worldwide.

Lastly, as work on pro-eating-disorder websites illustrates, young people grappling with body image and disordered eating issues are active seekers of information related to dieting and appearance (Gavin et al., 2008; Thomsen et al., 2002). More work conceptualizing youth *as active agents* in the media-body relationship would help inform intervention and educational efforts designed to harness this activity so children and adolescents can become co-producers of a more healthful relationship with the media.

SEE ALSO in this volume chapter by Bond, Richards, and Calvert.

References

Agliata, D. and Tantleff-Dunn (2004). The impact of media exposure on males' body image. *Journal of Social and Clinical Psychology*, *23*(1), 7–22.

American Psychiatric Association. (2000). *Diagnostic and statistical manual of mental disorders* (4th ed., text revision). Washington, DC: Author.

Baker, C. N. (2005). Images of women's sexuality in advertisements: A content analysis of Black- and White-oriented women's and men's magazines. *Sex Roles*, *52*(1–2), 13–27.

Ballentine, L.W. and Ogle, J.P. (2005). The making and unmaking of body problems in *Seventeen* magazine, 1992–2003. *Family and Consumer Sciences Research Journal*, *33*(4), 281–307.

Bandura, A. (2002). Social cognitive theory of mass communication. In J. Bryant and D. Zillmann (Eds), *Media effects: Advances in theory and research*. Mahwah, NJ: Erlbaum, pp. 121–54.

Bartky, S. L. (1988). *Foucault, femininity, and the modernization of patriarchal power*. In I. Diamond and L. Quimby (Eds), Feminism and Foucault: Reflections on Resistance. Boston, MA: Northeastern University Press, pp. 61–85.

Becker, A. E., Burwell, R. A., Gilman, S. E., Herzog, D. B. and Hamburg, P. (2002). Eating behaviors and attitudes following prolonged exposure to television among ethnic Fijian adolescent girls. *British Journal of Psychiatry*, *180*(6), 509–14.

Bordo, S. (1993). *Unbearable weight: Feminism, Western culture, and the body*. Berkeley, CA: University of California Press.

Centers for Disease Control and Prevention (2007). Childhood obesity. Retrieved August 19, 2007, from http://www.cdc.gov/nccdphp/dnpa/obesity/childhood/

Dittmar, H., Halliwell, E. and Ive, S. (2006). Does Barbie make girls want to be thin? The effect of experimental exposure to images of dolls on the body image of 5–8-year-old girls. *Developmental Psychology, 42*(2), 283–92.

Dohnt, H. and Tiggemann, M. (2006). The contribution of peer and media influences to the development of body satisfaction and self-esteem in young girls: A prospective study. *Developmental Psychology, 42*(5), 929–36.

Dolan, D. (2004, June 24). Learning to love anorexia? "Pro-Ana" web sites flourish. *New York Observer*, Retrieved June 24, 2004, from http://www.observer.com/ pages/story.asp?ID=6913

Ferguson, C. J., Winegard, B. and Winegard, B. M. (2011). Who is the fairest one of all? How evolution guides peer and media influences on female body dissatisfaction. *Review of General Psychology, 15*(1), 11–28.

Festinger, L. (1954). A theory of social comparison processes. *Human Relations, 7*(2), 117–40.

Fouts, G. and Burggraf, K. (1999). Television situation comedies: Female body images and verbal reinforcements. *Sex Roles, 40*(5), 473–81.

——(2000). Television situation comedies: Female weight, male negative comments, and audience reactions. *Sex Roles, 42*(9–10), 925–32.

Fouts, G. and Vaughan, K. (2002). Television situation comedies: Male weight, negative references, and audience reactions. *Sex Roles, 46*(11), 439–42.

Gavin, J., Rodham, K. and Poyer, H. (2008). The presentation of "Pro-Anorexia" in online group interactions. *Qualitative Health Research, 18*(3), 325–33.

Gilbert, K. (1998). The body, young children and popular culture. In N. Yelland (Ed.), *Gender in early childhood*. Florence, KY: Taylor & Francis/Routledge, pp. 55–71.

Götz, M. and Lemish, D. (Eds) (2012). *Sexy girls, heroes and funny losers: Gender representations in children's TV around the world*. Frankfurt, Germany: Peter Lang.

Grabe, S., Ward., L. M. and Hyde, J. S. (2008). The role of the media in body image concerns among women: A meta-analysis of experimental and correlational studies. *Psychological Bulletin, 134*(3), 460–76.

Greenberg, B. S., Eastin, M., Hofschire, L., Lachlan, K. and Brownell, K. D. (2003). Portrayals of overweight and obese individuals on commercial television. *American Journal of Public Health, 93*(8), 1342–48.

Groesz, L. M., Levine, M. P. and Murnen, S. K. (2002). The effect of experimental presentation of thin media images on body satisfaction: A meta-analytic review. *International Journal of Eating Disorders, 31*(1), 1–16.

Harrison, K. (2000a). Television viewing, fat stereotyping, body shape standards, and eating disorder symptomatology in grade school children. *Communication Research, 27*(5), 617–40.

——(2000b). The body electric: Thin-ideal media and eating disorders in adolescents. *Journal of Communication, 50*(3), 119–43.

——(2001). Ourselves, our bodies: Thin-ideal media, self-discrepancies, and eating disorder symptomatology in adolescents. *Journal of Social and Clinical Psychology, 20*(3), 289–323.

Harrison, K. and Hefner, V. (2006). Media exposure, current and future body ideals, and disordered eating among preadolescent girls: A longitudinal panel study. *Journal of Youth and Adolescence, 35*(2), 146–56.

Harrison, K. and Bond, B. J. (2007). Gaming magazines and the drive for muscularity in preadolescent boys: A longitudinal examination. *Body Image: An International Journal of Research, 4*(3), 269–77.

Herbozo, S., Tantleff-Dunn, S., Gokee-Larose, J. and Thompson, J. K. (2004). Beauty and thinness messages in children's media: A content analysis. *Eating Disorders: The Journal of Treatment and Prevention, 12*(1), 21–34.

Holmstrom, A. (2004). The effects of media on body image: A meta-analysis. *Journal of Broadcasting and Electronic Media, 48*(2), 186–217.

Holt, M. K. and Espelage, D. L. (2002). Problem-solving skills and relationship attributes among women with eating disorders. *Journal of Counseling and Development, 80*(3), 346–54.

Hudson, J. I., Hiripi, E., Pope, H. G. and Kessler, R. C. (2007). The prevalence and correlates of eating disorders in the National Comorbidity Survey Replication. *Biological Psychiatry, 61*(3), 348–58.

Johnson, J. G., Cohen, P., Kasen, S. and Brook, J. S. (2002). Eating disorders during adolescence and the risk for physical and mental disorders during early adulthood. *Archives of General Psychiatry, 59*(6), 545–52.

Levine, M. P. and Harrison, K. (2003). Media's role in the perpetuation and prevention of negative body image and disordered eating. In J. K. Thompson (Ed.), *Handbook of eating disorders and obesity*. New York: Wiley, pp. 695–717.

Lewinsohn, P. M. (2001, December). *The role of epidemiology in prevention science*. Paper presented at the annual meeting of the Eating Disorders Research Society, Bernalillo, NM.

Milkie, M. (1999). Social comparisons, reflected appraisals, and mass media: The impact of pervasive beauty images on Black and White girls' self-concepts. *Social Psychology Quarterly*, 62(2), 190–210.

Neumark-Sztainer, D., Wall, M., Guo, J., Story, M., Haines, J. and Eisenberg, M. (2006). Obesity, disordered eating, and eating disorders in a longitudinal study of adolescents: How do dieters fare 5 years later? *Journal of the American Dietetic Association*, 106(4), 568.

Neumark-Sztainer, D., Wall, M., Haines, J. I., Story, M. T., Sherwood, N. E. and van den Berg, P. A. (2007). Shared risk and protective factors for overweight and disordered eating in adolescents. *American Journal of Preventive Medicine*, 33(5), 359–69.

Nicholls, D. (2004). Eating problems in childhood and adolescence. In J. K. Thompson (Ed.), *Handbook of eating disorders and obesity*. Hoboken, NJ: Wiley, pp. 635–55.

Norris, M. L., Boydell, K. M., Pinhas, L. and Katzman, D. K. (2006). Ana and the internet: A review of pro-anorexia websites. *International Journal of Eating Disorders*, 39(6), 443–47.

Pettijohn, T. F. II and Jungeberg, B. (2004). Playboy playmate curves: Changes in facial and body feature preferences across U.S. social and economic conditions. *Personality and Social Psychology Bulletin*, 30(9), 1186–97.

Rutledge, T. and Loh, C. (2004). Effect sizes and statistical testing in the determination of clinical significance in behavioral medicine research. *Annals of Behavioral Medicine*, 27(2), 138–45.

Sands, E. R. and Wardle, J. (2003). Internalization of ideal body shapes in 9–12-year-old girls. *International Journal of Eating Disorders*, 33(2), 193–204.

Stice, E., Agras, W.S. and Hammer, L.D. (1999). Risk factors for the emergence of childhood eating disturbances: A five-year prospective study. *International Journal of Eating Disorders*, 25(4), 375–87.

Stice, E., Spangler, D. and Agras, W. S., (2001). Exposure to media-portrayed thin-ideal images adversely affects vulnerable girls: A longitudinal experiment. *Journal of Social and Clinical Psychology*, 20(3), 270–88.

Strauman, T. J., Vookles, J., Berenstein, V., Chaiken, S. and Higgins, E. T. (1991). Self-discrepancies and vulnerability to body dissatisfaction and disordered eating. *Journal of Personality and Social Psychology*, 61(6), 946–56.

Sypeck, M. F., Gray, J. J., Etu, S. F., Ahrens, A. H., Mosimann, J. E. and Wiseman, C. V. (2006). Cultural representations of thinness in women, redux: Playboy magazine's depiction of beauty from 1979 to 1999. *Body Image*, 3(3), 229–35.

Thomsen, S.R., McCoy, J.K, Gustafson, R.L. and Williams, M. (2002). Motivations for reading beauty and fashion magazines and anorexic risk in college-age women. *Media Psychology*, 4(2), 113–35.

Tiggemann, M. (2005). Television and adolescent body image: The role of program content and viewing motivation. *Journal of Social & Clinical Psychology*, 24(3), 361–81.

Zipfel, S., Lowe, B., Deter, H. C. and Herzog, W. (2000). Long-term prognosis in anorexia nervosa: Lessons from a 21-year follow-up study. *Lancet*, 355(9205), 721–22.

28

MEDIA AND OBESITY

Bradley J. Bond, Melissa N. Richards, and
Sandra L. Calvert

The developed world is experiencing an unprecedented childhood obesity crisis in which nearly 20 percent of children living in both the United States and Europe are obese (World Health Organization, 2012). Serious health problems associated with obesity (e.g., diabetes, heart disease, stroke, and certain cancers) have sparked projections that US children will have shorter life spans than their parents for the first time in modern history (Olshansky et al., 2005). The global prevalence of childhood obesity has largely been attributed to environmental factors, such as media exposure. This chapter examines the relationship between media exposure and childhood obesity, including the mechanisms by which media may contribute to or curtail the obesity epidemic.

The contribution of media to childhood obesity

Longitudinal studies have linked media exposure to childhood adiposity. An analysis of a nationally representative sample of UK children revealed that heavy media exposure during childhood predicted higher body mass indices at the age of 30 (Viner and Cole, 2005). For each additional hour of television consumed on the weekend at age 5, the risk of adult obesity increased by 7 percent. Although the relationship between media exposure and adiposity is complex, scholars have proposed five major mechanisms by which media may contribute to childhood obesity. These are (1) food advertising's influence on increased caloric intake, (2) overeating during exposure, (3) lower metabolic rates during media exposure, (4) increased sedentary behavior during exposure, and (5) media disrupting sleep patterns (American Academy of Pediatrics, 2011).

Food advertising

Among the mechanisms by which media exposure could contribute to childhood obesity, food advertising has received the most attention and empirical support. The US food industry spends approximately $2 billion per year advertising to children (Teinowitz, 2008), nearly triple what the United States Department of Agriculture spends on nutrition education and promotion (Institute of Medicine, 2006).

Content analyses have consistently found that most televised food advertisements targeted to children fall into one of five categories: (1) sugar-coated cereals, (2) candy/sweets, (3) salty snacks, (4) soft drinks, and (5) fast-food restaurants (Institute of Medicine, 2006). One content analysis of over 50,000 food advertisements showed that 98 percent of food advertisements viewed by children were for foods high in fat, sugar, or salt (Powell et al., 2007). Stitt and Kunkel (2008) found that only 3 percent of advertised foods on US television fit the nutritional guidelines from the Department of Health and Human Services for high-nutrient/low caloric foods that should be consumed often. The over-abundance of television advertisements for low-nutrient foods is not unique to the United States; 84 percent of food advertisements targeting New Zealand children promoted low-nutrient foods (Wilson et al., 2006).

The increasing popularity and accessibility of the internet is prompting food marketers to expand to online venues to reach children. Content analyses of online media reveal similar patterns in food marketing to those of television. Seven of the ten most popular children's websites analyzed by Alvy and Calvert (2008) contained food ads, most often for foods high in calories and low in nutritional value. The media advertising landscape, then, is saturated with foods that are low in nutritional value. When a child picks up a remote control or double-clicks a mouse, the child will likely be exposed to foods that are high in fat, sugar, or salt. Children, particularly the youngest ones, may be especially vulnerable when exposed to marketed food products because they do not understand the persuasive intent of commercial content (Calvert, 2008).

Systematic reports by the National Academies (Institute of Medicine, 2006), the UK Food Standards Agency (Hastings et al., 2003), and the European Commission (Matthews et al., 2005) concluded that certain kinds of advertisements directed at children increase the risk for adiposity, that food marketers spend considerable monies distributing these kinds of commercials, and that children before age 8 have considerable difficulty understanding commercial intent. Specific marketing techniques, including branded characters and product placement, are often used to blur the lines between entertainment and advertising to child audiences, thereby increasing product demands and purchases while fostering brand loyalty (Calvert, 2008).

Marketing food to children

Branded characters are media personalities created by a company to promote a specific product (e.g., Tony the Tiger promotes Kellogg's Sugar Frosted Flakes) or already popular licensed characters that are used for marketing (e.g., Shrek promotes McDonald's Happy Meals). Children 2 to 6 years of age recognize branded characters and associate them with products (Calvert, 2008). Associating a branded character with a food product can create positive feelings toward the food, even influencing perceptions of taste. In one experimental study, children who saw popular media characters on a cereal box liked the taste of the breakfast cereal more than children who saw a nearly identical cereal box without those media characters (Lapierre et al., 2011).

Product placement surreptitiously integrates brands into entertainment media content to increase brand awareness. Exposure to product placement can increase a consumer's familiarity with a product, resulting in an affinity for a given brand (Calvert, 2008). One of the most successful food product placements occurred when the film character E.T. ate Reese's Pieces, as national sales of the candy subsequently increased nearly 66 percent (Tylee, 2005). Product placement is increasingly prevalent in today's media landscape. For example, children view about five times as many product placements as they do traditional television advertisements for Coca-Cola products (Speers et al., 2011).

Advergames incorporate branded products into the content of online games to foster favorable attitudes toward products (Calvert, 2008). Advergames generally promote poor-nutrient foods. The manufacturers of Cheetos, for example, allow visitors to their website to choose an allegiance and fight the ultimate battle: crunchy vs. puffy cheese curl snacks. On ClubBK, Burger King's website for children, users create avatars that can be employed each time they play advergames. Purchasing food products at Burger King gives children points they can redeem for virtual accessories for their avatars. These accessories can then improve the child's game performance.

Viral marketing creates a "buzz" about products by encouraging individuals to pass on product information by word-of-mouth in an effort to maximize exposure to a promotional message (Calvert, 2008). Two fast-food chains, Wendy's and Burger King, recently created humorous web-videos with the intent to make them "go viral" and be passed on from person-to-person via the internet, especially among younger audiences (Howard, 2005).

Theoretical explanations for advertising and marketing effects

Several cognitive and behavioral theories are well suited to predict why children may be vulnerable to marketing techniques. Taken together, the cognitive and behavioral theoretical approaches reflect a common theme: young children have difficulty recognizing and understanding that the intent of commercial messages is to sell them products.

Classical conditioning describes the implicit and unconscious relation that develops between a stimulus and a response. In the case of food marketing, the advertisement can create positive emotional experiences that become associated with an actual product or with a branded character that represents that product (Calvert, 2008). For example, the positive associations found by Lapierre et al. (2011) between branded characters and perceptions of better cereal taste could be the result of associating positive feelings with the character.

According to **social cognitive theory**, children can learn behaviors by observing social models (Bandura, 2002). In order for a behavior to be cognitively acquired, a child must observe the behavior of others, learn the consequences of that behavior, and encode that information to determine the appropriateness of imitating the observed behavior in future situations. Behavior that is perceived as leading to reward is more likely to be imitated than behavior that is punished. For example, if children view a television commercial where other children are rewarded for eating a candy bar, the viewers may be more likely to imitate the observed behavior and request or purchase a candy bar for themselves.

The **information processing model** describes how stimuli are received, interpreted, stored, and retrieved (Calvert, 2008). In this model, the child has limited cognitive resources to deploy at any given time. For instance, when children play advergames they must invest cognitive resources to win the game. As such, children may only process the advertising messages implicitly, making it difficult to simultaneously defend themselves against any embedded commercial messages. This distraction may be compounded by the emotional and entertaining experiences of gaming, which may decrease children's ability to build a rational defense against marketed products. Although it could be argued that the advertisement would go unprocessed, research supports that implicit processing through mere exposure can influence familiarity with a product and later preference for that product (Bornstein, 1989).

The **processing of commercialized media content model** proposes that significant pressures weaken individuals' defenses against advertisements throughout childhood and adolescence (Buijzen et al., 2010). Before age 5, children perceive advertisements primarily as entertainment, failing to understand their persuasive intent to sell. Due to limited cognitive ability, automatic responses to bright colors or lively music can create positive attitudes toward the advertised product. By middle childhood (ages 6–9), a child can understand the persuasive intent of an advertised message, though intent is still sometimes difficult to discern. During late childhood (ages 10–12), a child becomes more critical of persuasive messages, yet peer influences can interfere with the ability to defend against an advertisement. During adolescence (ages 13–16), youth gradually achieve the levels of processing needed to be critical of commercial messages, but peer pressure and identity formation can still influence adolescent consumers.

In the **persuasion knowledge model**, consumers use their knowledge of persuasive tactics to interpret, evaluate, and respond to advertisements (Friestad and Wright, 1994). Recognizing the intent of marketers allows consumers to critically analyze, discount, and reject the advertised message. However, if consumers are not consciously aware of the persuasive intent of an advertisement, their cognitive defenses are lowered and they will process the message differently. For example, the stealth marketing techniques used in viral marketing campaigns make consumers more vulnerable to the marketers' messages than a more obvious television commercial or print advertisement (Calvert, 2008).

Overeating during media use

Food marketing may influence the consumption of poor-nutrient foods, but mere exposure may prime an individual to eat simply by stirring up appetite. When people eat on television, those at home may do so too—likely due to priming appetitive thoughts or to imitation of observed on-screen food consumption. Studies in the United States and China support the claim that food advertising may facilitate overeating; specifically, exposing children to *any* food advertising increased consumption of food, including foods that were not even advertised to the children (Harris et al., 2009; Parvanta et al., 2010). More research is needed to empirically support the hypothesis that children overeat during media exposure which depicts food being consumed.

Decreased metabolic rates

Do metabolic rates drop when children view television? One experimental study found that watching television reduced children's resting energy expenditure more than sleeping did, leading the authors to suggest that metabolic rates are lower when watching television than when engaged in other sedentary behaviors (Klesges et al., 1993). However, these results have not been replicated and have generally been considered a weak explanation for any relation between media exposure and childhood obesity.

Media as a sedentary behavior

Time is a zero-sum phenomenon; there are only 24 hours in a day. According to the displacement effect, the amount of time spent with media influences the total time available for other pursuits, including physical activity (Mutz et al., 1993). However, a meta-analysis yielded weak relations between television viewing and both body fat percentage and lower levels of physical activity among children, leading the authors to question a displacement effect (Marshall et al., 2004).

Media, sleep patterns, and obesity

Media exposure could also increase obesity because it disrupts children's sleep. Two relationships— one between shorter sleep duration and obesity (Cappuccio et al., 2008) and another between disrupted sleep patterns and media exposure (Owens et al., 1999)—have been documented. However, the causal patterns between media exposure, sleep patterns, and obesity are not well understood. Time spent with media may displace time needed for sleeping, screens may emit light or noise that disrupts sleeping patterns, media content may over-stimulate children immediately prior to scheduled sleep time, or perhaps children who are heavy media consumers spend less time engaged in physical activity, subsequently leading to both obesity and sleep troubles (Wolfson and Richards, 2011).

Using media to promote health

Exposing children to healthy messages on television could influence their diet and levels of physical activity. Children who viewed public service announcements for healthy foods were more likely to select fruits and juice as snacks than children who did not view the announcements (Gorn and Goldberg, 1982). If marketing devices like product placement and branded characters can increase the desire for low-nutrient foods among youth, the same marketing techniques could potentially increase the desire for high-nutrient foods. For example, children who viewed a Popeye cartoon in the morning were more likely to select spinach for lunch than children who had not viewed the cartoon (Harris and Baudin, 1972), a finding consistent with social cognitive theory.

Product packaging also influences children's desires to consume high-nutrient foods, perhaps through positive associations with branded characters created through classical conditioning. When shown a chocolate bar/broccoli pairing with no branded characters on the packaging, 22 percent of 3- to 5-year-old children preferred the broccoli to the chocolate bar. When images of *Sesame Street*'s Elmo character were on the vegetable's packaging, however, 50 percent of children chose the broccoli (Cole et al., 2010).

Online gaming experiences could modify the dietary habits of children by marketing healthier foods and beverages and by promoting active lifestyles. For example, 9- to 10-year-old children from low-income families were more likely to select healthy snacks after playing a PacMan advergame in which they gained points for consuming bananas and juice and lost points for consuming sodas and chips, when compared to children who played the advergame with the opposite incentives (Pempek and Calvert, 2009). This study suggests that persuasive gaming messages may improve children's health behaviors via classical conditioning.

Exergames are a physically active form of gaming increasingly considered an important venue for stemming the obesity epidemic. In a review of exergame studies involving children and adolescents, Biddiss and Irwin (2010) found that energy expenditure and heart rate during exergame play were on average 222 percent and 64 percent higher than resting rates, respectively. Cooperative exergame play with a peer has also been found to increase weight loss for overweight and obese adolescents (Staiano et al., in press).

Policy options and recommendations

Media literacy

Media literacy refers to the ability of individuals to critically analyze the production techniques and impact of media messages. Improving media literacy is a potential school-based method of reducing the influence of media on children's consumption of poor-nutrient foods and sedentary behaviors (Institute of Medicine, 2006). Although the results of several studies on media literacy interventions are promising (see Dennison et al., 2004), the efficacy of a national school-wide curriculum in the United States remains unknown.

Practitioner training

The doctor's office may be fertile ground for providing parents with the knowledge and resources needed to understand the influence of media on health so that parents can regulate their children's media consumption. The American Academy of Pediatrics (2011) urges pediatricians to counsel parents on monitoring media accessibility (e.g., monitoring length of viewing, monitoring the content of programs viewed, removing televisions from children's bedrooms) because physicians are trusted sources of information who may influence parental behaviors.

Advertising restrictions

Sweden, Norway, and Finland have prohibited commercial sponsorship of children's television programs, Ireland has banned the use of cartoon characters to promote foods, and France has passed legislation requiring healthy messages to accompany advertisements for foods and beverages high in sugar, salt, or artificial color (Institute of Medicine, 2006). The primary argument for a federal ban on advertising poor-nutrient foods in the US lies in the cognitive inability of children to distinguish persuasive messages from entertainment, but advertising restrictions are complicated by the possibility of reduced financial support for children's programming and First Amendment protections for advertisers (Institute of Medicine, 2006).

Financial incentives

Tax revenues on poor-nutrient food ads could be used to fund nutrition education campaigns and programs (Institute of Medicine, 2006). Taxing food advertisements may be difficult, however, given the political unpopularity of taxes and the likely backlash from the food and beverage industry. For example, Coca-Cola spent nearly $10 million to lobby against marketing restrictions and food taxes in 2010 (Center for Responsive Politics, 2011). Alternatively, governments could encourage the marketing of high-nutrient foods through subsidies.

Recommendations for future research

The most common method of quantifying media exposure is participants' self-reports of media use, but the validity of this method is questionable. Developing more valid measures of media exposure will allow researchers to analyze relationships between media exposure, obesity, and interventions more accurately. Vandewater and Lee (2009) note that new technologies, from wearable bands that would detect screen media use to mobile event recorders, may provide researchers with novel, innovative methods of tracking media consumption.

More experimental studies are needed, especially in the area of intervention and the influence of newer media. Studies in these areas could move the needle forward in our understanding of how media exposure contributes to obesity. They could also provide evidence for the establishment of media literacy and intervention programs as a way to stem the childhood obesity epidemic.

Children are living in a world where individuals with genetic dispositions toward obesity are very likely obese, largely because of an obesogenic environment that encourages the expression of genetic obesity (Wadden et al., 2002). As such, assessments of mediators and moderators in the relationship between media exposure and childhood obesity are also needed.

Race is a possible moderating variable that has been understudied. African American children spend more time with media than Caucasian children (Rideout et al., 2010) and have higher rates of obesity than Caucasian children (Anderson and Whitaker, 2009). Studies also demonstrate that television programming popular with African American audiences is more likely to contain low-nutrient food advertisements than television programming popular with general audiences (Tirodkar and Jain, 2003). However, the role of race as a moderator in the relationship between television exposure and adiposity has yet to be strongly supported by empirical evidence.

Conclusions

Obesity rates continue to escalate throughout the developed world. Although eliminating the childhood obesity epidemic is a complex puzzle composed of many critical genetic and environmental influences, the influence of food advertising on children's preferences, requests, and consumption of high fat and low-nutrient foods has received considerable empirical support. The same marketing techniques used to sell unhealthy products, however, can also be used to improve the health of children and adolescents. Concerted long-term research, educational, and policy efforts are needed to transform the media environment from one that may be increasing obesity to one that produces healthy outcomes for the youngest and most vulnerable citizens of our world.

SEE ALSO in this volume chapter by Harrison and chapter by Jordan and Gilmore.

References

Alvy, L. M. and Calvert, S. L. (2008). Food marketing on popular children's web sites: A content analysis. *Journal of the American Dietetic Association, 108*(4), 710–13.

American Academy of Pediatrics (2011). Policy statement—children adolescents, obesity, and the media. *Pediatrics, 128*(1), 201–8.

Anderson, S. and Whitaker, R. (2009). Prevalence of obesity among US preschool children in different racial and ethnic groups. *Archives of Pediatric and Adolescent Medicine, 163*(4), 344–48.

Bandura, A. (2002). Social cognitive theory of mass communication. In J. Bryant and D. Zillmann (Eds), *Media effects: Advances in theory and research.* Hillsdale, NJ: Lawrence Erlbaum, pp. 121–53.

Biddiss, E. and Irwin, J. (2010). Active video games to promote physical activity in children and youth: A systematic review. *Archives of Pediatrics and Adolescent Medicine, 164*(7), 664–72.

Bornstein, R. F. (1989). Exposure and affect: Overview and meta-analysis of research, 1968–1987. *Psychological Bulletin, 106*(2), 265–89.

Buijzen, M., Van Reijmersdal, E. A. and Owen, L. H. (2010). Introducing the PCMC model: An investigative framework for young people's processing of commercialized media content. *Communication Theory, 20*(4), 427–50.

Calvert, S. L. (2008). Children as consumers: Advertising and marketing. *The future of children, 18*(1), 205–25.

Cappuccio, F. P., Taggart, F. M., Kandala, N. B., Currie, A., Peile, E., Stranges, S. and Miller, M. A. (2008). Meta-analysis of short sleep duration and obesity in children and adults. *Sleep, 31*(5), 619–26.

Center for Responsive Politics (2011). Annual Lobbying by Coca-Cola Company. Retrieved from http://www.*opensecrets*.org/lobby/clientsum.php?id=D000000212

Cole, C. F., Kotler, J. and Pai, S. (2010). "Happy healthy Muppets": A look at Sesame Workshop's health initiatives around the world. In P. A. Gaist (Ed.), *Igniting the power of community: The role of CBOs and NGOs in global public health.* New York: Springer, pp. 277–94.

Dennison, B. A., Russo, T. J., Burdick, P. A. and Jenkins, P. L. (2004). An intervention to reduce television viewing by preschool children. *Archives of Pediatrics and Adolescent Medicine, 158*(2), 170–76.

Friestad, M. and Wright, P. (1994). The persuasion knowledge model: How people cope with persuasion attempts. *Journal of Consumer Research, 21*(1), 1–30.

Gorn, G. J. and Goldberg, M. E. (1982). Behavioral evidence for the effects of televised food messages to children. *Journal of Consumer Research, 9*(2), 200–5.

Harris, M. B. and Baudin, H. (1972). Models and vegetable eating: The power of Popeye. *Psychological Reports, 31*(2), 570.

Harris, J. L., Bargh, J. A. and Brownell, K. D. (2009). Priming effects of television food advertising on eating behaviors. *Health Psychology, 28*(4), 404–13.

Hastings, G., Stead, M., McDermot, L., Forsyth, A., MacKintosh, A. M., Rayner, M., Godfrey, C., Caraher, M. and Angus, K. (2003). *Review of research on the effects of food promotion to children.* Glasgow, UK: Centre for Social Marketing.

Howard, T. (2005, May 19). 'Viral' ads are so fun you pass'em along. *USA Today.* Retrieved from http://www.usatoday.com/money/advertising/2005-05-19-viral-usat_x.htm

Institute of Medicine (2006). *Food marketing to children and youth: Threat or opportunity?* Washington, D.C.: The National Academies Press.

Klesges, R. C., Shelton, M. L. and Klesges, L. M. (1993). Effects of television on metabolic rate: Potential implications for childhood obesity. *Pediatrics, 91*(2), 281–86.

Lapierre, M. A., Vaala, S. E. and Linebarger, D. L. (2011). Influence of licensed spokescharacters and health cues on children's ratings of cereal taste. *Archives of Pediatric & Adolescent Medicine, 165*(3), 229–34.

Marshall, S. J., Biddle, S. J. H., Gorley, T., Cameron, N. and Murdey, I. (2004). Relationships between media use, body fatness, and physical activity in children and youth: A meta-analysis. *International Journal of Obesity, 28*(10), 1238–46.

Matthews, A., Cowburn, G., Rayner, M., Longfield, J. and Powell, C. (2005). *The marketing of unhealthy food to children in Europe.* Brussels: European Heart Network.

Mutz, D. C., Roberts, D. F. and van Vuuren, D. P. (1993). Reconsidering the displacement hypothesis: Television's influence on children's time use. *Communication Research, 20*(1), 51–75.

Olshansky, S. J., Passaro, D. J., Hershow, R. C., Layden, J., Carnes, B. A., Brody, J., Hayflick, L., Butler, R. N., Allison, D. B. and Ludwig, D. S. (2005). A potential decline in life expectancy in the United States in the 21st century. *The New England Journal of Medicine, 352*(11), 1138–45.

Owens, J., Maxim, R., McGuinn, M., Nobile, C., Msall, M. and Alario, A. (1999). Television-viewing habits and sleep disturbance in schoolchildren. *Pediatrics, 104*(3), e27.

Parvanta, S. A., Brown, J. D., Du, S., Zimmer, C. R., Zhao, X. and Zhai, F. (2010). Television use and snacking behaviors among children and adolescents in China. *Journal of Adolescent Health, 46*(4), 339–45.

Pempek, T. A. and Calvert, S. L. (2009). Tipping the balance: Use of advergames to promote consumption of nutritious foods and beverages by low-income African American children. *Archives of Pediatrics & Adolescent Medicine, 163*(7), 633–37.

Powell, L. M., Szcypka, G. and Chaloupka, F. J. (2007). Exposure to food advertising on television among US children. *Archives of Pediatric & Adolescent Medicine, 161*(6), 553–60.

Rideout, V., Foehr, U. and Roberts, D. (2010). *Generation M2: Media in the lives of 8–18-year-olds.* Washington DC: The Henry J. Kaiser Family Foundation.

Speers S. E., Harris, J. L. and Schwartz, M. B. (2011). Child and adolescent exposure to food and beverage brand appearances during prime-time television programming. *American Journal of Preventive Medicine, 41*(3), 291–96.

Staiano, A. E., Abraham, A. A. and Calvert, S. L. (in press). Adolescent exergame play for weight loss and psychosocial improvement: A controlled physical activity intervention. *Obesity.*

Stitt, C. and Kunkel, D. (2008). Food advertising during children's television programming on broadcast and cable channels. *Health Communication, 23*(6), 573–84.

Teinowitz, I. (29 July 2008). FTC study: Dollars spent on marketing to kids much lower than thought. *Advertising Age.* Retrieved from http://adage.com/article/news/ftc-studydollars-spent-marketing-kids-lower-thought/129974/

Tirodkar, M. A. and Jain, A. (2003). Food messages on African American television shows. *American Journal of Public Health, 93*(3), 439–41.

Tylee, J. (2005). Is product placement the future? *Campaign,* March 18, 19.

Vandewater, E. A. and Lee, S. (2009). Measuring children's media use in the digital age: Issues and challenges. *American Behavioral Scientist, 52*(8), 1152–76.

Viner, R. M. and Cole, T. J. (2005). Television viewing in early childhood predicts adult body mass index. *The Journal of Pediatrics, 147*(4), 429–35.

Wadden, T. A., Brownell, K. D. and Foster, G. D. (2002). Obesity: Responding to the global epidemic. *Journal of Consulting & Clinical Psychology, 70*(3), 510–15.

Wilson, N., Signal, L., Nicholls, S. and Thomson, G. (2006). Marketing fat and sugar to children on New Zealand television. *Preventative Medicine, 42*(2), 96–101.

Wolfson, A. and Richards, M. (2011). Young adolescents: Struggles with insufficient sleep. In M. El-Sheikh (Ed.), *Sleep and development: Familiar and socio-cultural considerations.* New York: Oxford University Press, pp. 265–99.

World Health Organization (2012). *World health statistics.* Geneva, Switzerland: Author.

29

MEDIA AND SUBSTANCE ABUSE: ALCOHOL, SMOKING, AND DRUGS

Dina L.G. Borzekowski

A considerable number of youth around the globe experiment with and use tobacco, alcohol, and drugs; such use is associated with short- and long-term negative health consequences. After presenting how one may encounter environmental media messages about substances, this chapter discusses how children become familiar with and are influenced by these messages. The chapter concludes with recommendations on how the media environment may be changed to lessen the impact of media messages about tobacco, alcohol, and drugs.

Patterns of tobacco, alcohol, and drug use among youth

Youth experimentation with and use of tobacco, alcohol, and recreational drugs has been and remains commonplace. In many countries, substance use by youth is so widespread and accepted that it is no longer considered a deviant behavior (Erickson and Hathaway, 2010).

Globally, tobacco is used by over a billion men and 250 million women (Shafey et al., 2009). Practically all adult smokers begin smoking during adolescence. For example, many Chinese men begin smoking around age 14 and, of those who will ever smoke, practically all have done so by age 25 (Kenkel et al., 2009). Worldwide, one in five young adolescents (age 13 to 15 years) smokes and between 80,000 to 100,000 youth start smoking every day (Campaign for Tobacco-Free Kids, 2011). But, patterns of use are changing. Smoking is increasing in the developing world but decreasing in developed countries (Shafey et al., 2009; WHO, 2011). Among men, smoking rates are half of what they were four decades ago in the U.S. and Japan (U.S.: 44 percent in 1970 and 23 percent in 2008; Japan 78 percent in 1970 and 40 percent in 2007) (Shafey et al., 2009). In contrast, nearly 60 percent of the male population of China, Yemen, Russia, Indonesia, and Afghanistan are now smokers (Shafey et al., 2009).

Two billion people around the world are regular consumers of alcohol. The highest consumption rates are in Europe, Africa, and the former Soviet States (WHO, 2004). In 2001, the annual alcohol consumption per capita varied from 19.5 liters in Uganda to 16.2 in the Czech Republic, 14.5 in Ireland, 13.9 in the Republic of Moldova, 10.4 in the United Kingdom, and 8.5 in the United States (WHO, 2004). Among youth, alcohol is used more than any other substance (U.S. DHHS, 2007). Although alcohol use among U.S. high school students decreased from 50 percent in 1999 to 42 percent in 2009, one quarter of students still engage in episodic or binge drinking (CDC, 2009). Similar patterns of alcohol consumption are observed in other countries, including the U.K., Denmark, France, and some Mediterranean nations (The Lancet, 2008).

The use of recreational drugs is highest in North America, Western Europe, and Oceania (WHO, 2010). In the U.S., marijuana use among high school students declined from 27 percent in 1999 to 21 percent in 2009 (CDC, 2009). Cocaine use among youth has remained steady (between 2–4 percent) for the last two decades, while current use percentages have been higher for inhalants (12 percent), hallucinogenic drugs (8 percent) and ecstasy (7 percent) (CDC, 2009). Worldwide, recreational drugs are used by a minority of the population, with cannabis the most commonly used drug (between 3–4 percent of adults) (WHO, 2010).

Substantial long- and short-term health consequences are associated with substance use. Most of the leading causes of death (heart disease, cancer, stroke, lung disease) are strongly associated with tobacco use, accounting for 12 percent of male deaths and 6 percent of female deaths world-wide (WHO, 2009). The primary short-term problem with substance use is its association with other risky behaviors. For example, tobacco use is highly associated with future use of alcohol, marijuana, and other recreational drugs – serving as a "gateway drug" (Golub and Johnson, 2001).

Globally, 6.0 percent of male and 1.1 percent of female deaths can be attributed to alcohol consumption (WHO, 2009). Among young people, alcohol significantly contributes to the top three leading causes of death in the United States – accidents, homicide, and suicide. Adolescents who are heavy users start drinking earlier and are more likely to engage in behaviors that pose a risk to themselves or others, including driving under the influence of alcohol, riding with intoxicated drivers, getting injured in fights, having unplanned and unprotected sex, and using tobacco, marijuana, and other recreational drugs (Hingson et al., 2006).

As tobacco and alcohol use are strongly associated with the use of recreational drugs, so is the use of one type of recreational drug with the use of other recreational drugs. Adolescent substance use is linked to immediate dangers (i.e., car accidents, fighting, truancy), as well as long-term developmental disruptions (i.e., risky sexual behavior, dropping out of school) (Weinberg et al., 1998).

Media as one of the determinants of adolescent substance use

There are many determinants associated with adolescents' use of tobacco, alcohol, and other recreational substances (Bronfenbrenner, 1989; Kulig J.W. and the Committee on Substance Abuse, 2005). Among individual, family, peer, school, community, and socio-cultural influences, media use and messages play a significant and important role in predicting substance use.

Media contribute to adolescents' perceptions and behaviors by functioning as a 'super-peer' (Strasburger, 2004). Media are a ubiquitous and pervasive source of health information for youth, and offer both pro- and anti-substance use messages that can influence adolescent behavior. Media may encourage substance use by portraying tobacco, alcohol, and drug use as normative, or promote use with creative advertisements or informative stories about where and how to obtain recreational substances. Like friends, media can dissuade use; comprehensive, theory-based anti-substance use campaigns and programs have been delivered through print, radio, television, and internet sources (Borzekowski and Rickert, 2001; Kurtz et al., 2001).

Media messages about smoking, drinking, and drug use

To understand the impact of messages, it is critical to know the ways that children and youth encounter messages about substance use. Such messages have existed throughout history. Images of smoking can be found on pottery dating back to the eleventh century (Petrone, 1996), references to drinking appear throughout the Old and New Testament (Hanson, 1995), and reports about marijuana use can be found in Chinese writings from c. 2737 BC (Tiersky, 1999).

Today, media messages about tobacco, alcohol, and drugs remain pervasive. Motion picture and television characters smoke, drink or use recreational drugs to convey power, sex appeal, wealth, and rebellion – recall Humphrey Bogart in *Casablanca* (1942), Gloria Swanson in *Sunset Boulevard* (1950), James Dean in *Rebel Without a Cause* (1955), Al Pacino in *Scarface* (1983), or even Blake Lively in *Gossip Girl* (2007). Interestingly, one of the "smokiest" films ever made was *101 Dalmatians* (1961); in fact, the majority of Disney animated feature films from 1937 to 1997 portrayed tobacco (56 percent) and alcohol (50 percent) use (Goldstein et al., 1999).

It is not just Hollywood offering these images. Among the top-grossing films in the U.K. from 1989 to 2008, researchers found that 86 percent had at least one alcohol portrayal and 35 percent featured a recognizable alcohol brand (Lyons et al., 2011). Of the biggest box office Bollywood movies from 2006–8, 60 percent portrayed tobacco use (Arora et al., 2011).

Chinese television showed an average of 8.6 portrayals of smoking per hour between 2001 and 2003 (Li et al., 2006). In a content analysis of popular prime-time television programs broadcast in the U.S. 1998–99 season (Christenson et al., 2000), characters used tobacco in 19 percent and consumed alcohol in 71 percent of the episodes. Only a quarter of the episodes expressed a negative message about either tobacco or alcohol (Christenson et al., 2000).

Among the 200 most popular movies in 1996–97, researchers found that 22 percent of movies rated PG13 showed recreational drug use, often normalizing or even glamorizing it (Roberts et al., 1999). In the leading adolescent- and adult-targeted prime-time programs, 21 percent of the shows included mentions and/or use of recreational drugs (Christenson et al., 2000). In popular music, nearly 90 percent of rap songs have at least one reference to substance use, compared to rock (23 percent) and pop (14 percent). These references were often associated with positive attributes rather than negative consequences (Primack et al., 2008).

Like receptive media, interactive media can be a powerful source for positive and negative information and messages about tobacco, alcohol, and drugs. While tobacco and alcohol company websites require visitors to verify their age before entering, there is concern over how effective these screen pages are from keeping adolescents offline. A nationally representative study of around 800 American 12- to 17-year-olds revealed that almost half admitted to lying about their age at one time or another to access a website or online account (Lenhart et al., 2011). While it is unclear whether tobacco brand websites offer content that appeal to youth, alcohol brand sites tend to feature cartoons, graphics, games, downloadable material, and references to popular cultures (Gordon, 2011). Viral videos containing substance use messages can be shared quickly and widely. This is an emerging area of interest and it will be important to monitor the level of exposure youth have to internet messages about tobacco, alcohol, and drugs.

Awareness of media messages and substance use

Even very young children are aware of environmental messages about tobacco, alcohol, and recreational drugs. In the early 1990s, when the cartoon figure Joe Camel was used to market cigarettes, as many 6-year-olds recognized Joe Camel as recognized Mickey Mouse (Fischer et al., 1991). In 1995, 25 percent of 3-year-olds, 41 percent of 4-year-olds, 63 percent of 5-year-olds, and 72 percent of 6-year-olds could accurately identify Joe Camel (Mizerski, 1995). Children also had strong familiarity with alcohol brands; more kindergarteners could identify the Budweiser logo than the Energizer bunny (Henke, 1995) and preteens were more likely to know the Budweiser frogs than Tony the Tiger, Smokey the Bear, or the Mighty Morphin' Power Rangers (Lieber, 1996).

The effect of exposure to media messages about substance use

Studies show that children's exposure to media messages promoting substance use leads to positive attitudes toward, and use of, tobacco and alcohol (Botvin et al., 1991). A rigorous meta-analysis of 401 studies offers evidence of the relationship between exposure and tobacco use (Wellman et al., 2006). Across time, geography, methodologic designs, and outcome measures, exposure to pro-tobacco messages increases the odds of having positive attitudes about tobacco use and more than doubles the odds of initiating tobacco use. Not surprisingly, positive family and peer attitudes and behaviors contribute to increasing the odds of smoking uptake. While a similar meta-analysis has yet to be published on the impact of alcohol messages, there is a substantial literature indicating that higher exposure to alcohol advertising leads to earlier initiation and greater drinking among youth. In a longitudinal study of German youth, greater exposure to movie depictions of alcohol use, above and beyond baseline covariates, increased the likelihood of initiating use and participating in binge drinking (Hanewinkel and Sargent, 2009). A set of interesting experiments conducted in the Netherlands found that males (but not females) consumed more alcohol if they watched movies containing drinking scenes (Koordeman et al., 2010).

Strategies to alter the impact of media messages promoting substance use

Changing the messages

To alter the impact of media on youth uptake of substances, one strategy is to change the messages conveyed through traditional and interactive media. Messages about the negative effects of smoking, drinking, and illegal drug use could be incorporated into plotlines, as was done with the 'designated driver' campaign, without altering the entertainment value of a program. Public health organizations and coalitions, such as the Hollywood, Health & Society project out of the USC Annenberg Norman Lear Center as well as the Entertainment Industries Council, Inc., continue to help influence scripts by including accurate and realistic messages about the problems involved with substance use.

Counter ads

Another strategy to reduce the influence of pro-substance use messages is to offer counter messages. Following the Master Settlement Agreement (1998) between tobacco companies and 46 U.S. states, great efforts have been made to disseminate creative and hard-hitting anti-smoking messages. Examining the short-term effects of television advertisements from the Florida 'Truth' campaign, youth who had intermediate and high levels of exposure to the campaign were less likely to initiate smoking than those who were not aware of the campaign (Sly et al., 2001). Using a pre/post quasi-experimental design with a national sample, Farrelly et al. (2005) found an inverse dose-response relationship, where youth who had greater exposure to the "Truth" campaign had higher smoking prevalence rates.

Problematically, teenagers are 400 times more likely to see pro-alcohol advertisements than public service announcements discouraging underage drinking (MADD, 2004). Given the high appeal of pro-alcohol media messages, there is a call to create well-produced public service announcements (PSAs) that effectively gain the attention and resonate with adolescent audiences. Perceived realism, desirability, and similarity are constructs that have been suggested for creating higher quality and more effective alcohol PSAs for young people (Andsager et al., 2001).

U.S. efforts to create anti-substance campaigns have focused on illegal substances, rather than on tobacco and alcohol. The National Institute of Drug Abuse (NIDA) has allocated nearly $200 million a year for PSAs targeting illegal drugs and several programs have demonstrated some progress. In Kentucky, for example, a public service campaign resulted in a 27 percent decline in marijuana use among adolescents defined as "sensation seekers," those individuals who are attracted to novel, exciting, and stimulating life experiences (Palmgreen et al., 2001). Although criticized in the public press, the "fried egg" PSA (a message that compared drug use with sizzling your brain like an egg on the stove) aired by the Partnership for a Drug Free America (PDFA) proved effective (Reis et al., 1994). Not only has the PDFA published outcomes data (PDFA, 2003), but independent researchers have confirmed the efficacy of these messages (Strasburger and Wilson, 2002).

Regulations

Regulatory policies have had only minimal influence on changing the pro-smoking messages reaching youth. Comparing cross-sectional data from large youth panels in 2000, 2002, and 2004 (the years following the Masters Settlement), researchers observed declines in youth-reported exposure to pro-tobacco messages in all media channels except the internet (Duke et al., 2009).

It is thought that only complete and international bans will prevent youth exposure to positive messaging around substance use. In response to the globalization of tobacco use, the WHO's Framework Convention on Tobacco Control (FCTC) treaty currently obliges its 168 national parties to prohibit all forms of tobacco advertising and sponsorship (WHO, 2011). If nations invest in and implement the FCTC's recommendations, there is a strong likelihood that children will see fewer messages and be less likely to initiate tobacco use (Wipfli et al., 2004).

In contrast to emerging tobacco controls and regulations, there are many fewer restrictions on alcohol messaging and promotions. To control alcohol messages reaching youth, mainly two approaches are used: 1) the alcohol industry's voluntary codes and 2) the media's general codes on advertising (Babor, 2010). With the industry using a variety of interactive media, point-of-sale marketing, promotions and sponsorships, voluntary codes seem ineffectual and inefficient (Babor, 2010). Studies have shown that the alcohol companies' phrase "drink responsibly," which is rarely dominant in their messaging, is largely ineffective as most youth think that they are already drinking responsibly (Austin and Hurst, 2005). General advertising codes, which cover alcohol as well as other products, have been ineffectual in changing the frequency or general appeal of the pro-drinking messages. In Europe, a few countries officially restrict the amount and content of alcohol messages. Investing the impact of policies, Saffer and Dave (2002) showed that an increase of one type of ban (amount or content) can reduce consumption by 5 to 8 percent. There is optimism that comprehensive bans can greatly alter the initiation and frequency of youth drinking.

References

Arora, M., Mathur, N., Gupta, V. K., Nazar, G. P., Reddy, K. S. and Sargent, J. D. (2011). Tobacco use in Bollywood movies, tobacco promotional activities and their association with tobacco use among Indian adolescents. *Tobacco Control*, doi: 10.1136/tc.2011.043539.

Andsager, J. L., Austin, E. W. and Pinkleton, B. E. (2001). Questioning the value of realism: Young adults' processing of messages in alcohol-related public service announcements and advertising. *Journal of Communication*, 51(1), 121–42.

Austin, E. W. and Hurst, S. J. T. (2005). Targeting adolescents? The content and frequency of alcohol and non alcohol beverage ads on magazine and video formats. November 1999–April 2000. *Journal of Health Communication*, 10, 769–85.

Babor, T. (2010). *Alcohol: No Ordinary Commodity*. New York, NY: Oxford University Press.

Borzekowski, D. L. G. and Rickert, V. I. (2001) Adolescent cybersurfing for health information: A new resource that crosses barriers. *Archives of Pediatrics & Adolescent Medicine*, 155(7), 813–17.

Botvin, E. M., Botvin, G. J., Michela, J. L., Baker, E. and Filazzola, A. D. (1991). Adolescent smoking behavior and the recognition of cigarette advertisements. *Journal of Applied Social Psychology*, 21(11), 919–32.

Bronfenbrenner, U. (1989). Ecological systems theory. In R. Vasta (Ed.), *Six Theories of Child Development*. Greenwich, CT: JAI Press.

Campaign for Tobacco-Free Kids. (2011) Toll of tobacco around the world. Washington, D.C. Available at http://www.tobaccofreekids.org/research/factsheets/pdf/0366.pdf (accessed December 12, 2011).

CDC (Centers for Disease Control and Prevention) (2009). Youth Risk Behavior Survey. Available at: http://www.cdc.gov/yrbs. Accessed on February 14, 2012.

Christenson, P. G., Henriksen, L. and Roberts, D. F. (2000). *Substance Use in Popular Prime-time Television*. Washington, D.C., Office of National Drug Control Policy.

Duke, J. C., Allen, J. A., Pederson, L. L., Mowery, P. D., Xiao, H. and Sargent, J. D. (2009). Reported exposure to pro-tobacco messages in the media: Trends among youth in the United States, 2000–2004. *American Journal of Health Promotion*, 24(3), 195–202.

Erickson, P. G. and Hathaway, A. D. (2010). Normalization and harm reduction: Research avenues and policy agendas. *International Journal of Drug Policy*, 21(2), 137–39.

Farrelly, M. C., Davis, K. C., Haviland, M. L., Messeri, P. and Healton, C. G. (2005). Evidence of a dose-response relationship between "truth" antismoking ads and youth smoking prevalence. *American Journal of Public Health*, 95(3), 425–31.

Fischer, P. M., Schwartz, M. P., Richards, J. W., Goldstein, A. O. and Rojas, T. H. (1991). Brand logo recognition by children aged 3 to 6 years: Mickey Mouse and Old Joe the Camel. *Journal of the American Medical Association*, 266(22), 3145–53.

Goldstein, A. O., Sobel, R. A. and Newman, G. R. (1999). Tobacco and alcohol use in G-rated children's animated films. *Journal of the American Medical Association*, 281(12), 1131–36.

Golub, A. and Johnson, B. D. (2001). Variation in youthful risks of progression from alcohol and tobacco to marijuana and to hard drugs across generations. *American Journal of Public Health*, 91(2), 225–32.

Gordon, R. (2011). An audit of alcohol brand websites. *Drug and Alcohol Review*, 30(6), 638–44.

Hanewinkel, R. and Sargent, J. D. (2009). Longitudinal study of exposure to entertainment media and alcohol use among German adolescents. *Pediatrics*, 123(3), 989–95.

Hanson, D. J. (1995). *Preventing Alcohol Abuse: Alcohol, Culture and Control*. Westport, CT: Praeger.

Henke, L. L. (1995). Young children's perceptions of cigarette brand advertising symbols: Awareness, affect, and target market identification. *Journal of Advertising*, 24(4), 13–28.

Hingson, R. W., Heeren, T. and Winter, M. R. (2006). Age at drinking onset and alcohol dependence: age at onset, duration, and severity. *Archives of Pediatric and Adolescent Medicine*, 160(7), 739–46.

Kenkel, D., Lillard, D. R. and Liu, F. (2009). An analysis of life-course smoking behavior in China. *Health Economics*, 18(S2), S147–S156.

Koordeman, R., Anschutz, D. J., van Baaren, R. B. and Engels, C. M. E. (2010). Effects of alcohol portrayals in movies on actual alcohol consumption: An observational experimental study. *Addiction*, 106(3), 547–54.

Kulig, J. W. and the Committee on Substance Abuse (2005). Tobacco, alcohol, and other drugs: the role of the pediatrician in prevention, identification, and management of substance abuse. *Pediatrics*, 115(3), 816– 21.

Kurtz, M. E., Kurtz, J. C., Johnson, S. M. and Cooper, W. (2001). Sources of information on the health effects of environmental tobacco smoke among African-American children and adolescents. *Journal of Adolescent Health*, 28(6), 458–64.

The Lancet (15 March 2008). Calling time on young people's alcohol consumption. *The Lancet*, 371(9616), 871.

Lenhart, A., Madden, M., Smith, A., Purcell, K., Zickuhr, K. and Rainie, L. (2011). Teens, kindness, and cruelty on social network sites. (November 9, 2011). Available at http://www.pewinternet.org/Reports/2011/ Teens-and-social-media.aspx, accessed on December 7, 2011.

Li, Z., Jiang, Y. and Yang, Y. (2006). The incidence and context of tobacco use in popular movies and teleplays in recent years in China. Poster presentation at the 13th World Conference on Tobacco OR Health. July 12–14, Washington D.C.

Lieber, L. (1996). Commercial and character slogan recall by children aged 9 to 11 years: Budweiser frogs versus Bugs Bunny. Berkeley, CA: Center on Alcohol Advertising.

Lyons, A., McNeill, A., Gilmore, I. and Britton, J. (2011). Alcohol imagery and branding, and age classification of films popular in the UK. *International Journal of Epidemiology, 40*(5), 1411–19.

Mizerski, R. (1995). The relationship between cartoon trade character recognition and attitude toward product category in young children. *Journal of Marketing, 59*(4), 58–70.

MADD (Mothers Against Drunk Driving) (2004, May 26). *Latest CAMY study shows TV alcohol ads outnumber responsibility ads 226 to 1* (press release). Available at http://madd.org/news/0,1056,8239,00.html. Accessed on September 30, 2005.

Palmgreen, P., Donohew, L., Lorch, E. P., Hoyle, R. H. and Stephenson, M. T. (2001). Television campaigns and adolescent marijuana use: tests of sensation seeking targeting. *American Journal of Public Health, 91*(2), 292–96.

PDFA (Partnership for a Drug-Free America) (2003). *Partnership Attitude Tracking Study, Teens 2003.* New York: PDFA.

Petrone, G. S. (1996). *Tobacco Advertising: The Great Seduction with Values.* Atglen, PA: Schiffer.

Primack, B., Dalton, M. A., Carroll, M. V., Argawal, A. A. and Fine, M. J. (2008). Content analysis of tobacco, alcohol, and other drugs in popular music. *Archives of Pediatrics and Adolescent Medicine, 162*(2), 169–75.

Reis, E. C., Duggan, A. K., Adger, H. and DeAngelis, C. (1994). The impact of anti-drug advertising. *Archives of Pediatrics & Adolescent Medicine, 148*(12), 1262–68.

Roberts, D. F., Henriksen, L. and Christenson, P. G. (1999). *Substance Use in Popular Movies and Music.* Washington D.C.: Office of National Drug Control Policy.

Saffer, H., and Dave, D. (2002). Alcohol consumption and alcohol advertising bans. *Applied Economics, 34*(11), 1325–34.

Shafey, O., Eriksen, M., Ross, H. and Mackay, J. (2009). *The Tobacco Atlas, 3rd edition.* Atlanta, GA: The American Cancer Society.

Sly, D. F., Hopkins, R. S., Trapido, E. and Ray, S. (2001). Influence of a counteradvertising media campaign on initiation of smoking: The Florida "truth" campaign. *American Journal of Public Health, 91*(2), 233–38.

Strasburger, V. C. (2004). Children, adolescents, and the media. *Current Problems in Pediatric and Adolescent Health Care, 34*(2), 51–113.

Strasburger, V. C. and Wilson, B. J. (2002). *Children, Adolescents, and the Media.* Thousand Oaks, CA: Sage.

Tiersky, M. (1999). Medical marijuana: Putting the power where it belongs. *Northwestern University Law Review, 93*(2), 547–96.

U.S. DHHS (Department of Health and Human Services). (2007). *The Surgeon General's call to action to prevent and reduce underage drinking.* Washington D.C.: US DHHS.

Weinberg, N. Z., Rahdert, E., Colliver, J. D. and Glantz, M. D. (1998). Adolescent substance abuse: A review of the past 10 years. *Journal of the American Academy of Child and Adolescent Psychiatry, 37*(3), 252–61.

Wellman, R. J., Sugarman, D. B., DiFranza, J. F. and Winickoff, J. P. (2006). The extent to which tobacco marketing and tobacco use in films contribute to children use of tobacco. *Archives of Pediatric and Adolescent Medicine, 160*(12), 1285–96.

WHO (World Health Organization) (2011). WHO report on the global tobacco epidemic. Geneva, Switzerland: WHO.

——(2010). ATLAS on Substance Use (2010). Geneva, Switzerland: WHO.

——(2009). Global health risks: Mortality and burden of disease attributable to selected major risks. Geneva, Switzerland: WHO.

——(2004). Global status report on alcohol 2004. Geneva, Switzerland: WHO.

Wipfli, H., Stillman, F., Tamplin, S., Luiza da Costa e Silva, V., Yach, D. and Samet, J. (2004). Achieving the Framework Convention on Tobacco Control's potential by investing in national capacity. *Tobacco Control, 13*(4), 433–37.

30

MEDIA AND LEARNING
ABOUT THE SOCIAL WORLD

Jeanne Prinsloo

It is surprising that there has been a relative scarcity of research into the relationship between the media and children learning about the social world, given the amount of attention devoted to the potential ill effects of the media and the anxiety this gives rise to in popular debates. This concern is premised on the assumption that children learn from the media and so they impact on their ideas, attitudes, values, sets of behaviours, and even desires. At the heart of this is an anxiety about what precisely children are learning from the media as a consequence of the time and attention they devote to them.

What is striking is that where studies have addressed learning about the social world, they have tended to be confined to issues of gender and, by extension, violence (of boys) and sexualisation (of girls), at times linked to consumer culture. Much less frequently has research addressed the development of perceptions of other kinds of identities in children's social worlds and how they come to develop ideas of the 'Other' along lines of race, ethnicity, class, nationality and age. This chapter presents a brief and consequently partial overview of different ways in which such social learning is studied and the kinds of knowledge that have been produced.

While different research traditions have produced different kinds of knowledge on the topic, they concur that the media play an important role in the way children come to understand the world. However, their understanding of this relationship differs both in relation to how childhood is conceived and in terms of the power attributed to the media. This can be roughly broken down into two research approaches. There is the idea of the vulnerable child who is researched within an effects tradition (primarily in the USA), and the construct of a more competent or active child informed by a cultural tradition. The former tradition tends to adopt a structuralist and the latter a poststructuralist approach that draws on structuralist understandings while allowing for complexity and ambiguities.

Before looking more carefully at these two traditions, the issue of learning itself is introduced. In the studies on the topic the underpinning ideas draw from social psychology and developmental theories, in particular from Piaget's account of incremental learning. Certain aspects of his theory inform many of these studies as they address the process of acquiring ideas or knowledge about the social world, and their incremental development or subsequent rejection (Lemish, 2007).

Piaget's theory of incremental learning

Piaget's theory of equilibration (1954) seeks to explain how people, faced with the plethora of seemingly random events, establish order and predictability by testing out understandings about the world to make sense of them. It is achieved through organising ideas and experiences through cognitive structures referred to as 'schema'. Faced with new ideas or experiences, the child seeks to make sense of them by fitting or assimilating them into an existing schema (e.g., heroes in crime fiction are white). When the schema proves inadequate (e.g., a white villain) the child needs to find a way to deal with the cognitive conflict set up. The schema needs to be adapted or a new more functional one created to resolve the discomfort, a process referred to as accommodation (e.g., villains can be black or white). Learning is understood as being achieved through the development of schema. New experiences are measured against the existing schema and confirm or trouble them, and become more complex.

Piaget's model of such cognitive work is theorised as occurring at the level of the individual, or in other words in isolation, and is critiqued for its omission of a social dimension; the role of others in providing solutions for the disequilibria experienced; its omission of an emotional dimension; and the assumption of a universal child whose intellectual development conforms to the stages he proposed. Mindful of these limitations, a theory of incremental learning is valuable when considering how children develop concepts and so learn about their social world. This understanding informs both research traditions discussed.

The vulnerable child and the effects tradition

The mass media approach is argued to have its roots in social psychology with its focus on the 'crowd'. Underpinned by a concern with the vulnerability and suggestibility of the masses, researchers sought to identify the effects of media on them. This approach subsequently informed research around children, a cohort considered even more vulnerable and suggestible due to their age and relative immaturity. This focus on the media's impact on the vulnerable child has predominated particularly in the USA, and when issues of diversity have been factored in the concerns have been with the 'Other' child, that is, not the white middle class boy child, but the female, working class or black child. The focus on race has generally been framed in terms of black children, termed as 'minority', racial or ethnic children. 'Black' in these circumstances thus signifies 'not white' and therefore is inclusive of various racial and ethnic categorisations. This research generally adopts a socialisation framework to consider how children are socialised to view themselves and others, and how they learn to function as a member of a group and to participate in wider social relationships.

While the effects tradition draws on various theories in investigating the socialising effects of the media, Cultivation Theory and Social Learning Theory most often inform the studies into children learning about the social world. Both are concerned with how children adopt particular attitudes and beliefs based on media prototypes and so acquire scripts for various social situations.

Cultivation theory

Cultivation theory, as the term suggests, proposes that the media cultivate particular perceptions of social realities and the more time a person is exposed to television, for example, the more likely it is that the person's perceptions will match those articulated in the programmes. The 'drip' model refers to the subtle incremental development of ideas and beliefs as a consequence of the repetition of particular repertoires.

In contrast, the 'drench' model proposes that a strong significant character can have an immediate and dramatic impact on viewers under certain conditions, challenging existing schema and leading to changes in attitudes both among the in-group and the out-group. For this reason, an unusual and meaningful portrayal is seen as potentially powerful. The portrayal of African-American Cosby in the 1980s TV series, *The Cosby Show*, as an affluent, successful doctor in contrast to the usual working class, non-authoritative roles scripted for most black actors resulted in positive perceptions among white viewers. This is consistent with the parasocial interaction hypothesis (Mastro and Ortiz, 2008). If positive contact between members of different groups results in positive attitudinal changes, parasocial interaction refers to the positive encounter with a media character which can similarly improve attitudes toward the out-group.

Social learning theory

Social learning theory is based on Bandura's social cognitive approach (2001) which argues that the performance of particular behaviours serves as a model for people to imitate. The media, and TV as the media form most researched, provide symbolic models and the child can acquire a repertoire of behaviours and attitudes through observing these models and recognising that certain behaviours are either validated or exact penalties. These models work as influential schema for processing ideas about social groupings, particularly those they personally seldom encounter (Asamen and Berry, 2012). Viewers are argued to be more likely to model the behaviours of characters they perceive as similar to themselves and consequently for 'racial/ethnic minority children' (Mastro and Ortiz, 2008) racial/ethnic images increase in importance due to their infrequency (compared with white characters), while the predominance of depictions of subordinate or deviant roles provides cause for concern.

Stereotypes and social roles

Both cultivation and modelling theories assume the media have an impact on children through fostering particular social roles and stereotypes. Informed by social psychology, the idea of social roles presumes that an individual will occupy a position in the group which s/he belongs to and which is defined in reference to the roles occupied by others. A social role incorporates a set of stereotypes and thus the expectation that a person will act in a particular way given particular circumstances. Certain groups are consistently portrayed as having negative characteristics and negative stereotyping is framed as misrepresentation. The concern is with the sets of ideas and 'faulty attitudes' (Asamen and Berry, 2012, p. 369) children might acquire as a consequence of their engagement with or 'exposure' to the media. Two implicit assumptions inform this line of argument: first, that it is possible to represent the world accurately or correctly (the media can provide a window on the world); and, second, that this would be necessarily desirable anyway in spite of the extreme social inequalities that prevail globally.

Research findings within the effects tradition

Within the broad effects tradition three kinds of studies have been undertaken and they investigate the amount of time children are 'exposed' to a particular popular media form (frequently television but more recently social media too); the degree of diversity of representations they are exposed to; and preferences in terms of programmes or sets of representations. Many studies begin by establishing the diversity of the United States population statistically along lines of race, ethnicity or other cultural markers which are termed 'minorities' and might make reference to African-American,

Latinos, Asians, and Native Americans (more occasionally) although the terminology to describe different groupings varies considerably. These minority statistics are held against those of a 'majority' that is white but not disaggregated further (e.g., Graves, 1996). The studies implicitly or explicitly advocate multiculturalism or cultural pluralism, are underpinned by a concern for human rights, and employ quantitative methods, frequently Content Analysis.

Investigations into the amount of time that different social groupings are exposed to media might produce slightly different results as a consequence of which children, which media forms and in which year the study was undertaken, but they concur about the broad pattern that Hispanic and black children are heavier television viewers than white children in the USA. Class is occasionally acknowledged as a factor, for example when parents' education levels and occupational status are found to be a reliable predictor of children's viewing patterns. Generally the findings show that black and working class children in the USA watch more TV than white middle class children. The research focus on time spent 'exposed' to a medium derives from the concern that the media cultivate particular attitudes and behaviours as a consequence, and here black and working class children are viewed as more vulnerable, with the media impacting on their suggestible minds. The tendency to focus on race or ethnicity arguably obscures structures of class. Working class children watch more television in part because they do not have access to the alternatives that are available to middle class children, to what Walkerdine refers to as their 'full-diary syndrome' (1999, p. 10), which reduces the amount of time available for media engagement.

The focus on the time spent with media in the context of the present discussion makes sense if what children are exposed to poses reasons for concern. Thus studies have investigated the content, mostly of television, using quantitative methods to establish the extent to which the medium represents diversity, and then they correlate these statistics with the racial or ethnic demographics mentioned above. While the findings vary in relation to the channel, the nature of broadcasting, etc., they identify 'visible racial-ethnic groups' (Graves, 1996) as underrepresented in contrast to an abundance of white representations, and argue that the social world of television in the USA is predominantly white, male and middle class, with African-Americans portrayed in a higher proportion relative to the population than the other minorities, including Asians, Latinos and Native Americans. There is an assumption again that the media should or even could provide an accurate reflection of the social world.

In contrast to the focus on content that children in the USA might be exposed to in general, a study was undertaken to investigate the content of television made specifically for children that was broadcast in twenty-four countries (Götz and Lemish, 2012). While the primary focus was on gender it included 'skin colour' as a variable. The findings attest to the dominance of whiteness in representations made for children, with 72 percent of the human characters white ('Caucasian'), 12 percent Asian, 6 percent black, 3 percent Latina/o and 2 percent South-East Asian. National differences were recorded with the UK having the highest percentage of black characters, Malaysia and Hong Kong having none at all, and in South Africa, a country where 9 percent of the population is white, an overwhelming 90 percent of male characters were white, in contrast to 60 percent of the female characters (pp. 30–31). The hegemony of whiteness that pervades television in the USA inserts itself in the children's domain globally too.

Beyond the quantitative discrepancy in terms of numbers, research has considered role portrayals on television of different groups to establish limited diversity. Studies frequently suggest the media provide powerful schema for understanding of social groups that viewers seldom encounter in an absence of other knowledge. The various studies undertaken over decades attest that in addition to whites being disproportionately represented, they tend to be represented in what are framed as more positive portrayals. Several studies report similar findings: white people tend to be assigned starring roles with positive portrayal. Latinos were less frequently portrayed and more likely to be lawbreakers as were African-Americans. They were also assigned victim status more frequently, for example, to every one hundred powerful Asian portrayals there were four hundred depicted as victims of violence (Graves, 1996).

Occupational variations again find that white people are represented more frequently in middle class jobs, the other groupings are more likely to be blue collar workers, and African-Americans are represented in prime time situation comedies, etc. In addition, there is a degree of ghettoisation as different groups tend to be represented as acting within their own group.

The research studies that consider children's preferences identify the characters they prefer for various reasons. Some research suggests that black American children have a preference for particular white characters, a finding that is scarcely surprising considering that most characters are white. At the same time, studies have found that African-American children and youth are more likely to choose to view programmes featuring African-Americans. The attention to preferences links to the uses and gratifications research approach, which allows that viewers seek out media that provides for the gratification of particular needs. For example, attention has been given to how immigrants use media in the process of acculturating to a new country, and to nurturing social identities (Mastro and Ortiz, 2008).

Cultural approaches

Critiques of the effects tradition of research from within cultural studies propose that it is informed by conservative agendas. The concerns articulated most clearly are that 'minority' children are 'misrepresented' and are exposed to excessive viewing. The implication is that they will assume these lower status roles and regard themselves and other race groups in particular ways. It therefore stands accused of adopting a deficiency model (Lemish, 2007) in relation to working class and black children. Additionally, it fails to trouble the construct of whiteness as 'a speaking position that does not recognise itself as "raced"' (Dyer, 2000, p. 540) and to recognise that racism fundamentally shapes the lives of white people too. In spite of the assumptions of objectivity underpinning such quantitative studies, the identification and selection of positive roles (status, wealth, individualism rather than nurture, service, community) speaks the discourse of and complicity with global capital and its imperialist histories.

If, consistent with the well-known sender-message-receiver model of communication, effects theory research focuses on what mass media do to children, interpretive approaches consider what children do with the media. If the former includes a concern with how working class and black children learn about social roles that impact on identity construction, both of themselves and others, the latter retains the focus on identity and includes two epistemologically different approaches. A humanist approach celebrates the viewer as competent and active, as a rational individual who makes sense of the media. It however pays less attention to power relationships or learning about 'others'. A critical cultural studies approach, also referred to as 'transformative' (Asamen and Berry, 2012), is cognisant of the unequal power relations and historical contexts in which media are both produced and consumed. The audience is understood as one moment in a dynamic circuit of culture which incorporates production, representation and reading/reception processes in relation to the lived world of the viewer (Johnson, 1985). Issues of identity are central in this equation and thus inclusive of class, race, etc.

In contrast to the idea of the stable sociological subject assumed in effects research, the postmodern subject is understood as in process and engaging with both hegemonic and contesting sets of representations. Rather than employing the disease metaphor of 'exposure' to media as in the effects model, interaction is framed as negotiation of meanings. While 'learning' is not explicitly referenced, the principle of organising ideas according to schema retains its purchase as a process of assimilation and accommodation of ideas, emotions and desires, so involving the social, cultural, psychic and cognitive.

The emphasis on meaning as the outcome of socially and historically specific interactions calls for holistic approaches to negotiations of text within specific contexts. Qualitative textual analysis interrogates the ideological or discursive nature of the representations, while audience research seeks to understand the social processes through which children both produce meanings and gain pleasure from these media texts. Consistent with the qualitative and smaller-scale nature of many research projects, the methods include case studies, ethnographic approaches, focus groups and interviews.

Hodge and Tripp's (1986) careful pioneering work into children and television in Australia provides an example of an integrative approach; they incorporated a social semiotic approach to analysing both the children's programmes and their discussions of them. Interestingly, this research direction developed from the recognition that they commenced their Australian study with aboriginal children who had been removed from their families and placed in foster care from a sense of them being deficient. They had made the assumption that they would be more likely to be vulnerable to the ill effects of media representations. They conclude that their expectations were based on ignorance and prejudice and argue that, should many of these children be imprisoned in later life, 'the probable causes will not be the unreality of television, but the harsh realities of their own lives, struggling against the odds in a white world' (1986, p. 142). They recognise that the children make meaning but that this meaning is both formally and ideologically constrained by the texts they encounter and the contexts in which they encounter them. Unlike the humanist tendency, children are recognised as active producers of meaning, but in circumstances not of their own making.

That learning is constrained by the texts they encounter and the contexts in which they encounter them is made explicit in the comparative work undertaken into how children negotiated the meanings about the war on Iraq in 2003 in Germany, Israel and the USA (Lemish and Götz, 2007). The research revealed that the children relied heavily on national news reporting for their knowledge and tended to accept the dominant framing of the events. US children viewed the war as a personal confrontation between the two leaders Saddam Hussein and George Bush, the German children subscribed to the prevailing position articulated in the German media opposing the war, while Israeli children assimilated this war into their understandings of the Israeli/Arab conflict. The socio-cultural and political contexts significantly influenced how they negotiated these events occurring elsewhere particularly as the children had little other knowledge about the events.

Audience studies have developed interesting insights on how young people learn to negotiate the hegemonic discourses they encounter in the media in relation to their lived worlds. Central to this work is the understanding that identity is not merely acquired but performed and these studies draw on a range of theories relating to identity, notably Foucault's conceptualising of the subject. Again it must be noted that there is limited research that addresses issues of social learning outside of gender, particularly within a cultural frame. Consistent with this, Walkerdine (1999) reflects on her own working class childhood and argues that popular culture texts play a central role in constructing desire particularly in relation to working class girls. It is they who tend to engage in talent and beauty contests as moments of fantasy, of escape and of transformation. For working class girls who want more than they have, these media scenarios present alternative fantasies and desires that take a particular social and cultural form. Paradoxically, popular cultural forms thus propose an escape from class constraints, but an escape that enacts a further subjectification, this time as sexualised girls.

How young people mediate ideas and behaviours posed by powerful contesting discourses is described in studies of those located on the margins of late-modernity and global culture as a consequence of their class, cultural, geographical or religious locations. As a result of their liminal location, they recognise culture as a site of contestation and struggle. Such studies frequently draw on postcolonial concepts to address these complex encounters. Examples include Durham's work with South-Asian teen girls who mediate their 'American' (gendered) identity alongside their Indianness. She argues that their 'grappling with these issues of culture and difference vis à vis the media environment demanded the exercise of imaginative agency in carving out a space of gender/sexual agency' (2004, p. 155). Several similar imaginative negotiations are recounted, for example when a South African youth brought up in a conservative rural Xhosa family context negotiates American soap operas to consider more satisfying ways to conduct his personal relationships, and in ways that his traditional and Western values could coexist (Strelitz, 2001). Such accounts speak of young people's complex learning about the worlds they live in with their contesting discourses. They provide localised narratives that make evident the constraints and the structural nature of the power relations they inhabit in a way that effects research cannot as the questions they pose exclude these answers. The little narratives are argued to be valuable in that they propose new ways to consider how children and young people learn from the media. They stand in contrast to broader research projects that interrogate children's use and learning from the media.

This chapter has presented an overview of the research relating to social learning of the other and consequently the self. Common to both the effects and the cultural traditions is a concern with the representations children encounter, but they differ in their assumptions both of childhood as well as how media function in their lives. What becomes very clear is the scarcity of sustained research and knowledge about how children learn about diversity in their worlds and how much there is to be learnt. As most studies have been undertaken in the USA and the negative aspects have been foregrounded, it is reasonable to suggest the need for more intellectual work in this field – for large scale research projects into children's learning as well as and particularly in combination with attention to local situations, contextualised within global and local power relations.

SEE ALSO in this volume chapter by Elias and chapter by Rivera and Valdivia.

References

Asamen, J. K. and Berry, G. L. (2012). Television, children, and multicultural awareness: Comprehending the medium in a complex multimedia society. In D. G. Singer and J. L. Singer (Eds), *Handbook of children and the media*. London: Sage, pp. 363–78.

Bandura, A. (2001). Social cognitive theory of mass communication. *Media psychology*, *3*(3), 265–69.

Durham, M. G. (2004). Constructing the "new ethnicities": Media, sexuality, and diaspora identity in the lives of south Asian immigrant girls. *Critical studies in media communication*, *21*(2), 140–61.

Dyer, R. (2000). The matter of whiteness. In L. Back and J. Solomos (Eds), *Theories of race and racism*. London: Routledge, pp. 539–48.

Götz, M. and Lemish, D. (Eds) (2012). *Sexy girls, heroes and funny losers: Gender representations in children's TV around the world*. Frankfurt, Germany: Peter Lang.

Graves, S. B. (1996). Diversity on television. In T. M. MacBeth (Ed.), *Tuning in to young viewers: Social science perspectives on television*. London: Sage, pp. 61–86.

Hodge, B. and Tripp, D. (1986). *Children and television. A semiotic approach*. Oxford: Polity Press.

Johnson, R. (1985). What is cultural studies anyway? *Social Text*, *16*(1), 38–80.

Lemish, D. (2007). *Children and television. A global perspective*. Oxford: Blackwell.

Lemish, D. and Götz, M. (2007). *Children and media in times of war and conflict*. Cresskill, NJ: Hampton.

Mastro, D. and Ortiz, M. (2008). Media and communication theories. Implications for a multicultural perspective. In J. K. Asamen, M. L. Ellis and G. Berry, L (Eds), *The Sage handbook of child development, multiculturalism and media*. London: Sage, pp. 191–203.

Piaget, J. (1954). *The construction of reality in the child* (trans. Margaret Cook). New York: Basic Books.

Strelitz, L. (2001). Global media, local meanings. *Communication*, 27(2), 49–56.

Walkerdine, V. (1999). Violent boys and precocious girls: Regulating childhood at the end of the millennium. *Contemporary issues in early childhood*, 1(1), 3–23.

31

CHILDREN AND THE NEWS: RETHINKING CITIZENSHIP IN THE TWENTY-FIRST CENTURY

Cynthia Carter

Introduction

It has become something of a truism that children, no matter where they live in the world, regard the news as "boring", refusing to read newspapers, tune into television or radio news, or search out news on the internet.[1] One consequence of this view is that limited research has been undertaken examining children's relationship to the news and its role in facilitating the development of their informed and active citizenship. Clearly, the term "boring" is in urgent need of unpacking as it is ideologically loaded with assumptions about children's civic apathy, which runs the risk of becoming a self-fulfilling prophecy. If adult news is "boring", it is because it represents a world of adults doing largely incomprehensible things, where children's interests and opinions are rarely regarded as noteworthy (unless they are doing something bad) or valuable (extra-ordinarily good) and are thus largely absent. When news is produced with children's civic development in mind, it has the potential to enable them as citizens and empower them to develop an ongoing interest in the world (Carter and Messenger Davies, 2005).

As Lemish (2007a) suggests, if children are citizens ("being") rather than citizens in the making ("becoming") then they "need access to the mediated public domain of television news – both as an audience whose needs and interests are taken into consideration as well as participants whose opinions and concerns are being voiced" (2007a, pp. 136–37). This chapter assesses the contributions of research investigating the role of news, both adults' and children's, in facilitating or hindering children's development and participation as citizens.

Defining childhood and children's citizenship

As already noted, there are those who regard children as "citizens in the making" whilst others see them as already citizens with rights and responsibilities. Each position rests on certain conceptions of the child which establish different stances on children's citizenship and their relationship to the news.

For some, childhood is marked by a series of psychological and physical developments (Piaget, 1969). It is presumed to be a period of innocence and vulnerability gradually leading to adulthood; lack of worldly experience makes children susceptible to corruption (by "bad" adults) so it becomes the responsibility of adults ("good" ones) to protect them. Some take the view, to varying degrees, that children ought to be shielded from the news, particularly violent events, because prolonged exposure may lead to psychological trauma (Cantor and Nathanson, 1996). Children are not generally deemed to be citizens since they have no right to vote or to be held responsible for their actions in the same way as adults.

For others, childhood is regarded as a social construction and therefore an arbitrary and changing category (Ariès, 1962; Jenks, 1992). Studies examining children's civic engagement in demonstrations against the Iraq war, for instance, challenge the view that they are apathetic and unlikely to follow the news (Cushion, 2007). Children are disenfranchised because adults do not know how to speak to them to tap into their willingness to participate as citizens in the public sphere (Bennett, 2008, p. 2).

Bennett (2008) has proposed that there are at least two distinct conceptual approaches shaping scholarly study of children's citizenship and the news. In the first, associated with developmental models described above, it is assumed that children's political awareness and ability to cope with the news builds as they mature. In Bennett's second approach, linked to social construction theories of childhood also outlined above, children are regarded as citizens but are nevertheless disenfranchised by the news, thus undermining their interest in the news and in political participation.

Adult news

Scholars have investigated the role of the news media in children's political socialisation, potential negative effects of news exposure, representation, and the child audience. The studies examined here illuminate how children's citizenship tends to be regarded by adults; as political naives whose news consumption needs encouragement to prepare them for adult life; innocents in need of protection from a violent world; menacing figures; or helpless victims of violence.

News and children's political socialisation

Research on children's political socialisation goes back at least five decades. Early studies presumed that this entailed learning and internalising accepted norms, values, attitudes and behaviours of the prevailing political system. It was a top-down model of communication that assumed "what was thought necessary for citizens to learn was a single set of facts, beliefs and behaviours reflecting a unified political system" (McLeod, 2000, p. 46). Families, schools and news media were to be the "conduits in transmitting to the neophyte citizens what mature citizens knew and practiced" (2000, p. 46). The view of the child is that of a passive recipient of information passed on by authoritative, adult sources.

By the 1970s, researchers examined youth political socialisation in relation to news and interpersonal communication through developmental stages (Conway et al., 1975). Rather than passively absorbing political news content, children ought to be encouraged to express their views as they mature as a way of becoming increasingly political. From the 1990s to the present, concerns over declining civic knowledge, political participation, and news consumption have prompted scholars to re-engage with pertinent issues (McLeod, 2000, p. 57; see also Deth et al., 2011).

Negative effects of news violence

In contrast to those who emphasise the importance of news in children's political socialisation, others warn that care is needed when exposing children to adult news. Violent news stories, in particular, may cause children emotional harm. Certain facts and images are deemed to be inappropriate for specific age groups (van der Molen and Konijn, 2007). Scholars have examined how traumatic news content might lead children to experience negative emotional effects (van der Molen, 2004). Such studies have generated a number of important insights into children's responses to news and raised awareness about the possible short- and long-term emotional harm children may experience after exposure to violence in the news (Cantor and Nathanson, 1996; Hoffner and Haefner, 1993).

Much of this research has emerged from the fields of psychology and medicine. Assumptions are made about the need for adults to protect children from the news and develop coping strategies. Children may internalise frightening stories, leading to fears that bad things will happen to them (Moyer-Gusé and Smith, 2007). A related concern is that without protection, children may perceive the world to be a "confusing, threatening, or unfriendly place" (Gavin, 2011). The recommended therapeutic response is to encourage parents and other adults to talk to children about the news, in age-appropriate ways, to give emotional support and allay fears.

Summers and Winefield's (2009) study of children's anxieties after exposure to terrorism news suggests that mothers who are given "Coping and Media Literacy" training, instructing them how best to discuss such news, are able to reduce their children's fears (2009, p. 575). Adults are directed to give "calm, unequivocal, but limited information" by which Gavin (2011) means "delivering the truth, but only as much truth as a child needs to know". The discourse is primarily one of individual, psychological intervention to ensure that emotional harm is limited. Less emphasis tends to be placed on contributing to children's political knowledge and understanding of events.

Representing children

Children's images are frequently used to symbolise the brutality of war, famine and genocide to arouse adult sympathy and humanise events (Carter and Messenger Davies, 2005, p. 229). For example, a UK *Guardian* newspaper story published in 2003 reported on the 11-year-old Iraqi boy, Ali Ismaeel Abbas's loss of both arms and 14 family members in a bomb attack on Baghdad. As Carter and Messenger Davies suggest,

> Compounding this representation of Ali as a symbol of the suffering child was the absence of his voice telling us what had happened to him. Like the majority of children used to illustrate news stories about war and disaster, Ali was not interviewed or quoted in the article; he was not allowed to tell his own "story".
>
> *(2005, p. 230)*

Aqtashi et al.'s (2004) research on the representation of Palestinian children and the Intifada across six news outlets in the US, UK, Israel and Qatar found that there were very few stories about them. As the researchers suggest, "The issue of deselection is a real one. Palestinian children and their suffering and experiences have a precarious place on the periphery of the dominant news narrative" (2004, p. 404). When they do show up in the news, they tend to be framed within discourses of violence and conflict and thus in discursive terms do not exist outside these frames.

Researchers have also sought children's views on their news representation. Carter et al.'s UK *Newsround* study (2009) found that whilst some express anger over their exclusion from the news, others offer explanations. "I think all children's ideas are important, just as important as adults, they just don't let us say anything because they think that adults' ideas are more sensible than children's" (Nat, Bournemouth, boy aged 9) (2009, p. 26). Cerys (Cardiff, girl aged 15) suggests that the demonisation of some children in the news also plays a role in their exclusion, observing that, "Our views aren't treated as important, and because of YOB culture, and knife crime in the news, we aren't often asked our opinions" (Carter et al., 2009, 26). Children interviewed in Messenger Davies's UK (2004) study of the defunct children's news programme *First Edition* concluded that adults appear to think that children are never central to what is happening in the world.[2] As one boy remarked, "Children basically aren't seen in adult news – they don't care really. But I saw kids carried off in stretchers during the Iraqi war" (2004, p. 65).

News audiences

Lemish's (1998) research with kindergarten-aged children in the US and Israel also challenges the view that children find adult news to be boring. Interest in the news is related to the socio-political context (if it is seen to be important to everyday life) and parental mediation – an inclination towards protectiveness in the US and exposure and family discussion in Israel (1998, p. 502). American children tend to be less interested in news, whilst Israeli children's interest grows with age. A sociocultural understanding of the context of children's news consumption suggests that children in each country are "socialized into very different sets of expectations toward their news media and its role in a democratic society" (1998, p. 501).

In a comparative Israel-US-Germany study of children's responses to the early days of the Iraq war (with Götz, 2007; Seiter, 2007); Lemish (2007b) found that Israeli children closely followed the news. They did not challenge the hegemonic view that the war was necessary and in the political interests of Israel. Götz's (2007) research with German children confirmed their opposition, along with adults, to the war. "Yet", Götz concludes, "the danger of this hegemonic discourse was that it led children to develop a simplistic idea of good and evil that decreed that Saddam Hussein was 100% good and George Bush was 100% bad" (2007, p. 33). In contrast, Seiter's (2007) interviews with American children revealed the extent to which they were protected from the news, which did not make them less fearful, but more, since they felt they were not in possession of the facts. The Bush administration produced a magazine to be used in schools, *Time for Kids*, which personalised the war as a struggle between good and evil, reducing "complex historical events to simple narratives […] responsible for the simplistic view of the war adopted by many students" (2007, p. 49).

A Portuguese study which interviewed 500 children of different ages, classes and social backgrounds concluded that they avidly followed both adult and children's news "not only because it allowed them to be 'updated' but also as a way of occupying their time", much like the adult audience (Ponte, 2008). And yet, this interest often goes unacknowledged.

Children's news

Whilst scholars have investigated children's news production, content and audiences, the corpus of research remains limited. Again, as with adult news, there is a view that most children do not follow children's news and therefore it is not worth investigating. Whether or not children engage with it, in many countries around the world broadcasters have developed children's news programmes and related websites precisely because they believe it to be important to children's social and civic development.

News production

Hirst (2002) maintains that the dearth of children's news programmes in the UK is partly due to their high cost compared to dramas, cartoons or other types of shows which can be sold, resold and endlessly repeated worldwide. Additionally, advertisers appear to prefer promotional slots next to "fun" programmes rather than "serious" ones, thereby providing even less incentive to create factual programmes.

Matthews' (2008) UK study of *Newsround* found that in order to maximise audiences, producers chose to highlight "entertaining" stories over "serious ones", and emotional reactions over reasoned ones (2008, pp. 269–72). Stories are simplified, sometimes resulting in de-contextualising events, making them more "palatable" rather than "intelligible" (2008, p. 274). Positively, highlighting how events might impact on children's lives means that their views are included when they are not in adult news (Matthews 2003, p. 139). Nevertheless, the programme tends to exaggerate children's participation, creating a false impression of their contribution to civic life (Matthews, 2008).

In their comparative study of the coverage of the first days of the Iraq war by the German children's news programme *logo!* and its Dutch counterpart *Jeugdjournaal*, Nikken and van der Molen (2007) found that producers took different presentational approaches. Reporters for *logo!* openly expressed an anti-war sentiment whilst *Jeugdjournaal* reporters did not. Also, *logo!* was more cautious in its reports (using graphics, animations) than *Jeugdjournaal*, which incorporated more distressing material (including real images of American prisoners). Similarly, each used pictures of George Bush and Saddam Hussein to simplify the war. Both countries' producers took their job seriously, spending more time than usual to cover the issues. Children's news has a vital role to play, the authors argue, "in developing the political awareness and empowerment of children", and that broadcasters at all times should budget enough air time for these informational programmes (2007, p. 196).

News content

One of the strengths of children's news is that it often emphasises understanding and context in the stories it reports (Buckingham, 2000, p. 45). However, assumptions are made about children's news interests, knowledge, and cognitive abilities, which are regarded as different and less developed than adults' (Alon-Tirush, 2012). Producers tend to believe that there is a narrow range of topics children find engaging, which some scholars regard as insufficiently challenging (Matthews, 2010). Topics typically covered include schools, the environment, bullying, school dinners, and animals. In Carter et al.'s (2009) UK research, children noted a much wider array of interests including immigration, war, healthy food, fair trade, animal testing, after school care, healthcare, speeding cars, partisan politics, and much more. Thirteen-year-old Samer from Cardiff insisted that "(kids) have things to say about recycling, animals, pollution and everything" (2009, p. 26).

In Israel, children's news has developed because it is believed that children need to follow the news in order to develop as citizens (Alon-Tirush, 2012). Nevertheless, children are also regarded as innocent and vulnerable so content must be "presented in a gentle, balanced manner that will not cause unbearable emotional load. Including soothing, reassuring (at times even optimistic) aspects is viewed as vital" (2012, p. v). Emphasis is therefore placed on constructing "age appropriate" news.

Children are framed as active "consumer citizens" on the US children's news programme *Nick News* (Banet-Weiser, 2007). Because it is a weekly programme, its content tends to be more in depth and challenging than daily news, focusing on issues which producers regard as central to children's developing sense of identity, "issues of race, of fear, of popularity, of discrimination" (2007, p. 14). Nevertheless, content tends to privilege personal (consumer) politics over traditional (party) politics (2007, p. 135).

The child news audience

Nikken and Götz's (2007) comparative research on children's postings about the Iraq war on children's websites in the Netherlands and Germany concludes that they are important avenues through which children are able to participate in deliberative democracy. In both countries most children opposed the war, wanted it stopped, expressed strong emotions, did not appear to be particularly fearful, and showed concern about the impact of war on ordinary people. Children, argue the authors, "should also be given the opportunity to participate in contemporary debates. By writing to a children's channel or program, children can become politically active and very much involved in their own society" (2007, p. 117).

Similarly, Carter (2007) examined children's email and message board postings on the *Newsround* website in the early days of the Iraq war in 2003, as well after the bombings in London in 2005. With regard to Iraq, she found a range of opinions, with some supporting it whilst others challenged its legality and morality. Children were aware of how their anti-war protests were represented in adult news and were upset that adults regarded their views and actions as ill-informed. "Young people repeatedly state", Carter notes, "that they want to be accepted as citizens who possess legitimate points of views and rights" (2007, p. 132). Many children went on to the message boards in July 2005 to discuss the bombings in London, with a number making links between this event and Britain's support for the Iraq war. Such message boards are valuable resources for children's development as citizens "where many must feel they are being listened to and their views are valued" (2007, p. 138).

Online news and children's citizenship

Much is being made of the potential of online environments to draw children to the news (Bakker and de Vreese, 2011). Some argue that unlike old media, they offer welcoming forms of democratic participation for young citizens. Children's growing participation online demonstrates that they are not inevitably apolitical. Instead, many are increasingly choosing to exercise citizenship across a range of platforms and forums where their views are acknowledged and valued: on social media such as Facebook and Twitter, demonstrations, and single issue campaigns (Thorsen et al., 2010).

However, others caution that such claims tend to assume that new technologies offer inherently democratic spaces which encourage and support children's citizenship. Although it may be tempting to think that children who use the internet to keep up to date with the news are actively engaged in civic life, research suggests this is not necessarily true (Messenger Davies et al., 2014). Some argue that children first need improved civic education and media literacy to critically engage with the news (Livingstone et al., 2007). ICTs do not produce citizens. Instead they provide spaces which may be used to develop new citizenship practices bridging the public and private spheres, linking news, entertainment, and political communication in ways that do not simply lead to ever more commercialised and limited forms of citizenship (Hermes, 2006, p. 295).

Conclusions

Issue-oriented campaigns and demonstrations and evolutionary and revolutionary political change have become part of the everyday news landscape. Some children now regularly participate in a wide variety of actions on local, national and global stages. Passive, top-down models of news provision from journalists to audiences are giving way to more interactive and participatory forms of citizen engagement. That said, even in children's news the use of children's voices continues to be "highly circumscribed" (Buckingham, 2000, p. 56; see also Carter et al., 2009).

It is unfair to presume that the mainstream news media should have the sole responsibility to inform children and to motivate them to active citizenship, although they do have an important role to play in supporting deliberative democracy. As the boundaries between news producers and consumers, professional and citizen journalists, adult and child audiences become increasingly blurred, new opportunities arise to democratise politics in terms of gender, class, ethnicity, religion, nationality and generation. Exciting, innovative and interactive news formats, including those produced by children, using old and new media, are challenging adult assumptions about children's political apathy and are offering important opportunities for children's enfranchisement as citizens.

SEE ALSO in this volume chapter by Austin and chapter by Papaioannou.

Notes

1 I use the term "children" to refer to people below the age of 18. The term "young people" is often used to refer to children in their teen years (see Jenks, 1992).
2 Interview material used by Messenger Davies (2004) came from a pilot study conducted with school children in Glasgow 2002–3 with Cynthia Carter, Stuart Allan and Karin Wahl-Jorgensen, funded by the Cardiff School of Journalism, Media and Cultural Studies, Cardiff University, UK.

References

Alon-Tirush, M. (2012). Children's news in Israel: Texts, creators and audiences. Unpublished PhD dissertation, Tel Aviv University.

Aqtashi, N. A., Seif, A. and Seif, A. (2004). Media coverage of Palestinian children and the Intifada. *Gazette: The International Journal for Communication Studies, 65*(5), 383–409.

Ariès, P. (1962). *Centuries of childhood*. New York: Vintage.

Bakker, T. P. and de Vreese, C. H. (2011).Good news for the future? Young people, internet use, and political participation. *Communication Research, 38*(4), 451–70.

Banet-Weiser, S. (2007) *Kids rule! Nickelodeon and consumer citizenship*. Durham: Duke University Press.

Bennett, W. L. (2008). Changing citizenship in the digital age. Civic life online: Learning how digital media can engage youth. In W. L. Bennett (Ed.), *The John D. and Catherine T. MacArthur Foundation series on digital media and learning*. Cambridge, MA: MIT Press, pp. 1–24.

Buckingham, D. (2000).*The making of citizens: Young people, news and politics*. London: Routledge.

Cantor, J. and Nathanson, A. (1996). Children's fright reactions to television news. *Journal of Communication, 46*(4), 139–52.

Carter, C. (2007). Talking about my generation: A critical examination of Children's BBC *Newsround* web site discussions about war, conflict and terrorism. In D. Lemish and M. Götz. (Eds), *Children and media in times of war and conflict*. Creskill: Hampton Press, pp. 121–42.

Carter, C. and Messenger Davies, M. (2005) 'A fresh peach is easier to bruise': Children, young people and the news. In S. Allan (Ed.), *Journalism: Critical issues*. Maidenhead: Open University Press, pp. 224–38.

Carter, C., Messenger Davies, M., Allan, S., Mendes, K., Milani, R. and Wass, L. (2009). *What do children want from the BBC? Children's content and participatory environments in an age of citizen media*. Retrieved from http://www.bbc.co.uk/blogs/knowledgeexchange/cardifftwo.pdf

Conway, M. M., Stevens, A. J. and Smith, R. G. (1975). The relation between children's media use and children's civic awareness. *Journalism Quarterly, 52*(3), 531–38.

Cushion, S. (2007). Protesting their apathy?: An analysis of British press coverage of young anti-Iraq war protestors. *Journal of Youth Studies, 10*(5), 421–34.

Deth, J. W van, Abendschön, S., and Vollmar, M. (2011). Children and politics: An empirical reassessment of early political socialization. *Political Psychology, 32*(1), 147–74.

Gavin, M. L. (2011). How to talk to your child about the news. *KidsHealth*. Retrieved from http://kidshealth.org/parent/positive/talk/news.html#

Götz, M. (2007). "I know that it's Bush's fault:" How children in Germany perceived the war in Iraq. In D. Lemish and M. Götz (Eds), *Children and media in times of war and conflict*. Creskill, NJ: Hampton, pp. 15–36.

Hermes, J. (2006). Citizenship in the age of the internet. *European Journal of Communication, 21*(3), 295–309.

Hirst, C. (2002). Watch out John Craven, here's Jimmy Neutron: Why isn't commercial TV interested in news programmes for children? *The Independent*, 8 February. Retrieved July 1, 2012, from http://www.independent.co.uk/news/media/watch-out-john-craven-heres-jimmy-neutron-641552.html

Hoffner, C. and Haefner, M. (1993). Children's affective responses to news coverage of the war. In B. S. Greenberg and W. Gantz. (Eds) *Desert Storm and the mass media*. Creskill, NJ: Hampton, pp. 364–80.

Jenks, C. (1992). *The sociology of childhood*. Aldershot: Ashgate.

Lemish, D. (1998). What is news?: A cross-cultural examination of kindergartners' understanding of news. *Communication: European Journal of Communication Research, 23*(4), 491–504.

——(2007a). *Children and television: A global perspective*. Oxford: Blackwell.

——(2007b). "This is our war": Israeli children domesticating the war in Iraq. In D. Lemish and M. Götz (Eds), *Children and media in times of war and conflict*. Creskill, NJ: Hampton, pp. 57–74.

Livingstone, S., Couldry, N. and Markham, T. (2007). Youthful steps towards civic participation: Does the internet help? In B. D. Loader (Ed.), *Young citizens in the digital age: Political engagement, young people and new media*. London: Routledge, pp. 21–34.

McLeod, J. M. (2000). Media and civic socialization of youth. *Journal of Adolescent Health, 27*, 45–51.

Matthews, J. (2003). Cultures of production: The making of children's news. In S. Cottle (Ed.), *Media organization and production*. London: Sage, pp. 131–46.

——(2008). A missing link? *Journalism Practice, 2*(2), 264–79.

——(2010). *Producing serious news for citizen children*. Lewiston: Edwin Mellen.

Messenger Davies, M. (2004). Innocent victims, active citizens, *Mediactive, 3*, 55–66.

Messenger Davies, M., Carter, C., Allan, S. and Mendes, K. (2014). News, children and citizenship: User-generated content and the BBC's *Newsround* website. In H. Thornman and S. Popple (Eds), *Content cultures: Transformations of user generated content and public service broadcasting*. London: IBTaurus, pp. 15–36.

Moyer-Gusé, E. and Smith, S. L. (2007). "TV news and coping: Parents' use of strategies for reducing children's news-induced fears. In D. Lemish and M. Götz (Eds), *Children and media in times of war and conflict*. Creskill, NJ: Hampton, pp. 267–86.

Nikken, P. and Götz, M. (2007). Children's writings on the internet about the war in Iraq: A comparison of Dutch and German submissions to guestbooks on children's TV news programs. In D. Lemish and M. Götz (Eds), *Children and media in times of war and conflict*. Creskill, NJ: Hampton, pp. 99–120.

Nikken, P. and van der Molen, J. H. (2007). "Operation Iraqi Freedom" in the children's news: A comparison of consolation strategies used by Dutch and German news producers. In D. Lemish and M. Götz (Eds), *Children and media in times of war and conflict*. Creskill, NJ: Hampton, pp. 177–99.

Piaget, J. (1969). *The origins of intelligence in the child*. New York: International University Press.

Ponte, C. (2008). Children in the news, children and the news – Notes from a Portuguese research project. *News on Children, Youth and Media: International Clearinghouse* (1). Retrieved July 1, 2012, from http://www.nordicom.gu.se/cl/publ/letter.php?id=97#Children%20%3Ci%3Ein%3C/i%3E%20the%20News,%20Children%20%3Ci%3Eand%3C/i%3E%20the%20News%20-%20Notes%20from%20a%20Portuguese%20research%20project

Seiter, E. (2007). U.S. children negotiating the protective silence of parents and teachers on the war in Iraq. In D. Lemish and M. Götz (Eds), *Children and media in times of war and conflict*. Creskill, NJ: Hampton, pp. 37–56.

Summers, J. and Winefield, H. (2009). Anxiety about war and terrorism in Australian high-school children. *Journal of Children and Media, 3*(2), 166–84.

Thorsen, E., Allan, S. and Carter, C. (2010). The first ten years of BBC online. In G. Monaghan and S. Tunney (Eds), *Web journalism: A new form of citizenship?*. Eastbourne: Sussex Academic Press, pp. 116–25.

van der Molen, J. W. (2004). Violence and suffering in television news: Toward a broader conception of harmful television content for children. *Paediatrics, 112*(6), June, 1771–75.

van der Molen, J. H.W. and Konijn, E. A. (2007). Dutch children's emotional reactions to news about war in Iraq: Influence of media exposure, identification, and empathy. In D. Lemish and M. Götz (Eds), *Children and media in times of war and conflict*. Creskill, NJ: Hampton, pp. 75–98.

32
PROCESSES AND IMPACTS OF POLITICAL SOCIALIZATION

Erica Weintraub Austin

Despite alleged apathy and ignorance among young people (e.g., Bennett and Rademacher, 1997), adults 18–29 may hold the keys to victory for many politicians because they currently comprise almost a quarter of eligible voters in the United States and have become a potent force for change internationally, such as in the Arab Spring movement (Social Capital Blog, 2012; Schwartz, 2011). Efforts to stiffen voting eligibility in the U.S. have been criticized as targeting young people and minorities, whose turnout rates have been increasing and associate with early voting and same-day registration (Berry, 2011; Employment and Training Institute, 2011; McDonald, 2011). These trends make political socialization a compelling topic for examination.

The socialization process

Socialization to public affairs is well under way by the third grade (e.g., Niemi and Hepburn, 1995), but children do not simply assimilate into the existing milieu. They seek information and information sources that can promote learning, engage in activities that facilitate the process (such as media use), and continually evaluate their progress toward these goals in a reciprocal process of interaction (O'Keefe and Reid-Nash, 1987). Products of socialization include relevant knowledge, confidence and abilities for action, motivations, behaviors themselves, and self-reflection about one's actions.

The role of personal, environmental and behavioral factors

Consistent with social cognitive theory (Bandura, 2001), current socialization models assume that personal, environmental and behavioral factors interact asymmetrically, at different times, and with unequal strength depending on the content, context and individual factors (Grusec and Davidov, 2010). Meanwhile, competencies and decision-making styles learned in one context may be applied in another. In public affairs socialization processes, parents often exert little direct influence but nevertheless play an important role.

The role of media

Few families discuss politics and public affairs regularly. Young adults in one study reported that only 16 percent of their parents regularly discussed politics (Andolina et al., 2006). This cedes a great deal of civic education to children's rapidly evolving and increasingly independent media environment, in which they consume approximately 11 hours of media per day in the USA (Rideout et al., 2010). For example, 73 percent of teens with access used social networking web sites in 2010 as compared to 55 percent in 2006 and 65 percent in 2008 (Lenhart et al., 2010). The same survey found that most 12–17-year-olds have and multitask with a cell phone and that almost all go online.

The focus of this energy includes public affairs. Only one-third of U.S. 15–25-year-olds surveyed by Andolina et al. (2006) regularly followed traditional news outlets, but 62 percent of 12–17-year-olds sought news and political info online (Lenhart et al., 2010). They also learn from news satire such as late-night talk shows (Hollander, 2005; Meroney, 2000) just as 6–17-year-olds used to rank front-page news second only to comics (Gollin and Anderson, 1980)—showing that youth interest in humor over "real news" is nothing new. Meanwhile, much useful online discussion of politics happens in forums in which political discussion is incidental rather than the primary purpose (Wojcieszak and Mutz, 2009).

Scholars differ about how much viewers learn from such programming, but these differences stem partly from sampling differences that reflect diversity in maturation levels and experience with public affairs content. Television, for example, has been found to level the playing field for political knowledge because of its lower demand on cognitive resources (Eveland and Scheufele, 2000). In addition, some learning from TV news occurs relatively passively (Krugman and Hartley, 1970; Zhao and Chaffee, 1995). Continuing preferences for entertainment, however, can increase knowledge gaps (Prior, 2005). Entertainment programming and television therefore represent useful gateways for public affairs information but have limited value as ongoing primary sources (Bennett, 2004; Burgess et al., 2006).

Making the most of media

The extent to which children and adolescents gain public affairs knowledge, competencies and attitudes from their media use likely depends on their skills for understanding the intent behind, and the form, content and context of, various types of programming, often referred to as *media literacy* (e.g., Aufderheide, 1993; Austin et al., 2006; Kahne et al., 2012; Livingstone, 2003). The fact that late-night comedy assists young adults' recognition of public affairs information more than their free recall while also enhancing recall among the younger adult viewers (Hollander, 2005) suggests that these sources are most useful for those who have the most to learn. Adolescents, with a newly developed ability to understand persuasive intent, implied information and satire (Flavell et al., 2002) may find these sources especially interesting and influential.

Programs such as late-night comedy certainly play an informative role. Exposure to late-night comedy is associated with increased attention to a presidential campaign (Feldman and Young, 2008), including hard news sources. Moreover, the depth of information provided by programs such as *The Daily Show* and broadcast network newscasts including *NPR* can be comparable, and the knowledge base of their users reflects this (Fox et al., 2007a; Kohut, et al., 2007; PublicMind Poll, 2011).

Nevertheless, the most important variable facilitating knowledge gain may be the use of multiple sources—not the use of particular sources. In their analysis, Kohut et al. (2007) found that regular audiences of programs attracting the most knowledgeable viewers tended to use an average of seven sources for their news, compared to an *average* of 4.6 sources for the full sample. Xenos and Becker (2009) also found that young adults who watched *The Daily Show* tended to seek additional information from other news sources. Using multiple sources provides the opportunity to compare and contrast alleged facts but requires an ability to do so, making media literacy a vital skill for political socialization.

Beyond knowledge gain

Knowledge is only one important outcome of information source use. Attitudes and efficacy toward civic participation comprise other important socialization outcomes ultimately predictive of political behavior. High levels of TV exposure may predict lower levels of trust and civic engagement among teens and young adults, but moderate levels seem less problematic (Milner, 2002; Romer et al., 2009). Moderate viewing, after all, still leaves room for outside discussion and activity. In other words, viewing offers benefits but is likely to have downsides in isolation. Young people appear to benefit especially from participatory media and expect to be heard (Bennett, 2004; Burgess et al., 2006; Livingstone et al., 2007; Rheingold, 2007).

More controversy has developed over the alleged effects of late-night satire. Some (e.g., Baumgartner and Morris, 2006), believe *The Daily Show* primarily increases cynicism, characterized by rejection of content and closure to information sources (Cappella and Jamieson, 1997; Pinkleton and Austin, 2004). Critics charge that programs such as *The Daily Show* may increase individuals' belief in their own expertise (internal efficacy) but simultaneously decrease their trust and confidence in the system (cynicism), diminishing their belief that they can and should participate in the public affairs system (external efficacy), regardless of their ability to provide that input. According to this view, satire and entertainment media increase *apathy*—a lack of willingness to exert some degree of effort to participate in even the most basic aspects of the political process (Bennett, 1986; Johnson-Cartee and Copeland, 1991)—even while it increases internal efficacy.

Internal efficacy, however, seems to be a more powerful predictor than cynicism of civic participation and can be improved by use of such programming (Hoffman and Thomson, 2009; Holbert et al., 2007). Similarly, Pinkleton and Austin (2004) found that use of television news among young adults predicted political participation even while satisfaction with it as a source associated with apathy. Overall, nontraditional sources of public affairs information appear to serve an effective educational role, somewhat dependent on use with a skeptical attitude (e.g., Pinkleton and Austin, 2004; Pinkleton et al., 2012) and openness to additional information sources (e.g., Kohut et al., 2007). Indeed, use of this type of programming may help young people develop media literacy and an ability to critically assess civic affairs information, especially when such programs spark discussion and additional learning. Feldman and Young (2008), for example, demonstrated that viewing late-night comedy increased attention to political news and a resilience to the instability of campaign events. Young people actually may learn more from satire than from straight newscasts, because of the complementary roles of negative and positive information on attention and memory. In particular, positive information—cued by humor— enhances memory (Fox et al., 2007; Lang, 2006; Lang et al., 2004) and can compensate for the negativity inherent in so much political coverage. *The Daily Show* has been called "the best critical media literacy program on television" (Trier, 2008, p. 424) and has won awards from organizations such as the National Association for Media Literacy Education (NAMLE, 2005).

The family's role

Seeing substantive discussions taking place in an environment that does not seem stultifying, such as in the media or at school, can motivate adolescents to have discussions that promote their own learning, including within their family. McDevitt (2005), calls this *developmental provocation*.

McDevitt and others (e.g., Chaffee et al., 1970; Chaffee and Yang, 1990; Tolley, 1973) have suggested that news and other media sources spur learning but that conversations motivate active processing and can shape opinions as well as cognitions. Adolescents can gain both information and self-confidence through such conversations, including their attempts to influence their parents.

Thus, despite concerns that parents have either given up or lost their ability to influence their children, research suggests parents still occupy a privileged role (e.g., McLeod and Shah, 2009; McDevitt, 2005). Through parents and other credible individuals, media effects tend to be channeled through interpersonal discussion that assists meaning construction through reflection and contextualization (Kim and Kim, 2008; Southwell and Yzer, 2007). Young people tend to look beyond media to establish and extend the meaning of information they encounter and develop confidence (e.g., Hively and Eveland, 2009).

When children are young, parents play a more obvious role, acting as important role models, providing information about how the world operates and providing reinforcement of appropriate or inappropriate behaviors. As the child's world enlarges to include school, peers and the media, parents increasingly play a more indirect role as counterbalancing and contextualizing influences. Parents especially guide the development of children's communication competence, the ability to use information resources strategically (Burleson et al., 1995; Chaffee et al., 1973).

Family communication norms help explain media-specific discussions and effects. The *Family Communication Patterns* (FCP) Model, developed by Jack McLeod and Steve Chaffee, has been especially important for scholars studying routes to parental influence on media effects. The FCP model proposes that parents teach children how to manage and interpret information in general, which in turn affects the way children approach and internalize any information source.

The FCP model conceptualizes parent–child communication as taking place along two relatively independent dimensions. The first, called *socio orientation*, reflects the parent's desire for harmonious interpersonal relationships through the emphasis of conformity and control. The second dimension, called *concept orientation*, reflects an emphasis on sharing and challenging ideas. Ironically, children in families low on socio orientation and high on concept orientation may model their parents more than those from families emphasizing conformity. Meanwhile, children from families emphasizing both orientations can experience internal conflict because open discussion seems important but so does family harmony and control. Children from concept-oriented families tend to watch more public affairs programming, know more about public affairs, get more involved in civic activities, are more skeptical of advertising, and have parents more likely to discuss media (Chaffee et al., 1973).

Clearly, active parental discussion about media also plays an important role. Parental mediation generally is defined as communication from primary caregivers about the content of media used by children (Austin, 1993; Nathanson, 1999). It has been linked to children's increased understanding of television, including their attention to political affairs news and political involvement (Austin, 1993; Austin and Pinkleton, 2001). Parents and primary caregivers, however, can emphasize different types of active mediation, including *positive active mediation* and *negative active mediation* (Austin et al., 1999). Positive active mediation refers to endorsement and support of content, whereas negative active mediation refers to counter-reinforcing comments. Mediation without any valence can be misinterpreted, while negative mediation helps to teach critical viewing skills and activate skepticism.

The need to take young people seriously

In sum, young people have the potential to become engaged and important forces in civic affairs. Because they also tend to represent a particularly diverse demographic, young people pre- and post voting age can serve as effective messengers in communities that have language and cultural barriers to campaign participation (Kawashima-Ginsberg, 2011; Shea, 2004). Meanwhile, voting turnout among young adults in the U.S.—while lower than among older adults—has risen steadily since 2000 (CIRCLE, 2010; Lopez et al., 2005; Lopez et al., 2007; Trichter and Paige, 2004), and young people tend to get involved in civic affairs in ways that go far beyond electoral politics (Kawashima-Ginsberg, 2011; Schwartz, 2011). Their involvement tends to be predicted by their knowledge of the process, their understanding of how to participate and their belief that their participation matters (Austin et al., 2008; Green, 2004; Livingstone et al., 2007; Young Voter Strategies, 2011). The predictors of their knowledge, attitudes and behaviors relevant to civic affairs therefore represent an important topic for continued attention.

SEE ALSO in this volume chapter by Carter and chapter by Papaioannou.

References

Andolina, M., Keeter, S., Zukin, C. and Jenkins, K. (2006). The civic and political health of the nation: A generational portrait. *CIRCLE Foundation and The Pew Research Center study*. Retrieved from http://www.civicyouth.org.

Aufderheide, P. (1993). National leadership conference on media literacy. Conference report. Washington, D.C.: Aspen Institute.

Austin, E. W. (1993). Exploring the effects of active parental mediation of television content. *Journal of Broadcasting & Electronic Media*, 37(2), 147–58.

Austin, E. and Pinkleton, B. (2001). The role of parental mediation in the political socialization process. *Journal of Broadcasting & Electronic Media*, 45(2), 221–40.

Austin, E. W., Bolls, P., Fujioka, Y. and Engelbertson, J. (1999). How and why parents take on the tube. *Journal of Broadcasting & Electronic Media*, 43(2), 175–92.

Austin, E. W., Chen, Y., Pinkleton, B. E. and Quintero Johnson, J. (2006). The benefits and costs of Channel One in a middle school setting and the role of media literacy training. *Pediatrics*, 117(3), 423–33.

Austin, E. W., Van de Vord, R., Pinkleton, B. E. and Epstein, E. (2008). Celebrity endorsements and their ability to motivate young voters. *Mass Communication and Society*, 11(4), 420–36.

Bandura, A. (2001). Social cognitive theory of mass communication. In J. Bryant and D. Zillmann (Eds), *Media effects: Advances in theory and research*. Mahwah, NJ: Erlbaum, pp. 121–53.

Baumgartner, J. and Morris, J. S. (2006). The *Daily Show* effect: Candidate evaluations, efficacy, and American youth. *American Politics Research*, 34(3), 341–67.

Beck, P. A. (1977) The role of agents in political socialization. In S. A. Renshon (Ed.) *Handbook of Political Socialization*. New York and London: Free Press, pp. 122–27.

Bennett, S. E. (1986). *Apathy in America, 1960–84: Causes and consequences of citizen political indifference*. Dobbs Ferry, NY: Transnational.

Bennett, S. E. and Rademacher, E. W. (1997). The "age of indifference" revisited: Patterns of political interest, media exposure, and knowledge among Generation X. In S. C. Craig and S. E. Bennett (Eds), *After the boom: The politics of Generation X*. Lanham, MD: Rowman and Littlefield, pp. 21–42.

Bennett, W. L. (2004). *Civic Learning in Changing Democracies: Challenges for Citizenship and Civic Education*. Seattle: Center for Communication and Civic Engagement. Retrieved at http://depts.washington.edu/ccce/assets/documents/bennet_civic_learning_in_changing_democracies.pdf

Berry, D. B. (November 25, 2011). Debate heats up on Voter ID laws. *Montgomery Advertiser*. Retrieved at http://www.montgomeryadvertizer.com/article/20111125/NEWS02/111250306/Debate-heats-up-voter-ID-laws

Burgess, J., Foth, M. and Klaebe, H. (2006). Everyday Creativity as Civic Engagement: A Cultural Citizenship View of New Media. In *Proceedings: CommunicationsPolicy & Research Forum*, Sydney, Australia. Retrieved at http://eprints.qut.edu.au/5056/1/5056_1.pdf

Burleson, B. R., Delia, J. G. and Applegate, J. L. (1995). The socialization of person-centered communication: Parents' contributions to their children's social-cognitive and communication skills. In M. A. Fitzpatrick and A. L. Vangelisti (Eds), *Explaining family interactions*. Thousand Oaks, CA: Sage, pp. 34–76.

Cappella, J. N. and Jamieson, K. H. (1997). *Spiral of cynicism: The press and the public good*, New York: Oxford University Press.

Chaffee, S. H. and Yang, S. (1990). Communication and political socialization. In O. Ichilov (Ed.), *Political socialization, citizenship education, and democracy*. New York: Teachers College, Columbia University, pp. 137–57.

Chaffee, S. H., Ward, L. S. and Tipton, L. P. (1970). Mass communication and political socialization. *Journalism Quarterly*, 47(4), 647–59, 666.

Chaffee, S., McLeod, J. and Wackman, D. (1973). Family communication patterns and adolescent political participation. In J. Dennis (Ed.), *Socialization to politics: Selected readings*. New York: Wiley, pp. 349–64.

CIRCLE (Center for Information and Research on Civic Learning and Engagement) (2010). Quick Facts About Youth Voting. Jonathan M. Tisch College of Citizenship and Public Service at Tufts University. Retrieved at http://www.civicyouth.org/quick-facts/youth-voting/

Employment and Training Institute (2011). Research Update: Voter Photo ID Law Court Cases Utilize ETI Research. University of Wisconsin-Milwaukee, 161 W. Wisconsin Avenue, Suite 6000, Milwaukee, WI. Retrieved at http://www4.uwm.edu/eti/2007/VoterID.htm

Eveland, W.P., Jr. and Scheufele, D.A. (2000). Connecting news media use with gaps in knowledge and participation. *Political Communication*, 17(3), 215–37.

Feldman, L. and Young, D. G. (2008). Late-night comedy as a gateway to traditional news: An analysis of time trends in news attention among late-night comedy viewers during the 2004 presidential primaries. *Political Communication*, 25(4), 401–22.

Flavell, J. H., Miller, P. H. and Miller, S. A. (2002). *Cognitive development* (4th Edition). New York: Prentice Hall.

Fox, J. R., Koloen, G. and Sahin, V. (2007a). No joke: A comparison of substance in *The Daily Show with Jon Stewart* and broadcast network television coverage of the 2004 presidential election campaign. *Journal of Broadcasting & Electronic Media*, 51(2), 213–27.

Fox, J. R., Park, B. and Lang, A. (2007b). When available resources become negative resources: The effects of cognitive overload on memory sensitivity and criterion bias. *Communication Research*, 34(3), 277–96.

Gollin, A. and Anderson, T. (1980). *America's children and the mass media*. New York: Newspaper Advertising Bureau.

Green, D. R. (2004). The Effects of an Election Day Voter Mobilization Campaign Targeting Young Voters. CIRCLE Working Paper 21. Jonathan M. Tisch College of Citizenship and Public Service at Tufts University. Retrieved at http://www.civicyouth.org/PopUps/WorkingPapers/WP21Green.pdf

Grusec, J. E. and Davidov, M. (2010). Integrating different perspectives on socialization theory and research: A domain-specific approach. *Child Development*, 81(3), 687–709.

Hively, M. H. and Eveland, W. P. (2009). Contextual antecedents and political consequences of adolescent political discussion, discussion elaboration and network diversity. *Political Communication*, 26(1), 30–47.

Hoffman, L. H. and Thomson, T. L. (2009). The effect of television viewing on adolescents' civic participation: Political efficacy as a mediating mechanism. *Journal of Broadcasting and Electronic Media*, 53(1), 3–21.

Holbert, R. L., Lambe, J., Dudo, A. D. and Carlton, K. A. (2007). Primacy effects of *The Daily Show* and national TV news viewing: Young viewers, political gratifications, and internal political self efficacy. *Journal of Broadcasting & Electronic Media*, 51(1), 20–38.

Hollander, B. (2005). Late-night learning: Do entertainment programs increase political campaign knowledge for young viewers? *Journal of Broadcast & Electronic Media*, 49(4), 402–15.

Johnson-Cartee, K. S. and Copeland, G. A. (1991). *Negative political advertising: Coming of age*. Hillsdale, NJ: Lawrence Erlbaum Associates.

Kahne, J., Lee, N. and Feezell, J. T. (2012). Digital media literacy education and online civic and political participation. *International Journal of Communication*, 6, 1–24.

Kawashima-Ginsberg, K. (2011) Understanding a Diverse Generation: Youth Civic Engagement in the United States. The Center for Information and Research on Civic Learning and Engagement. Jonathan M. Tisch College of Citizenship and Public Service at Tufts University. Retrieved at http://www.civicyouth.org/wp-content/uploads/2011/11/CIRCLE_cluster_report2010.pdf

Kim, J. and Kim, E. J. (2008). Theorizing dialogic deliberation: Everyday political talk as communicative action and dialogue. *Communication Theory*, 18(1), 51–70.

Kohut, A., Morin, R. and Keeter, S. (2007). Public knowledge of current affairs little changed by news and information revolutions: what Americans know: 1989–2007. Washington, D.C.: Pew Research Center for the People and the Press.

Krugman, H. E. and Hartley, E. L. (1970). Passive learning from television. *Public Opinion Quarterly*, *34*(2), 184–90.

Lang, A. (2006). Motivated cognition (LC4MP): The influence of appetitive and aversive activation on the processing of video games. In P. Messaris and L. Humphries (Eds), *Digital Media: Transformation in Human Communication*. New York: Peter Lang, pp. 237–54.

Lang, A., Sparks, J. V., Bradley, S. D., Lee, S. and Wang, Z. (2004). Processing arousing information: Psychophysiological predictors of motivated attention. *Psychophysiology*, *41*(1) (Suppl.), S57–S81.

Lenhart, A., Purcell, K., Smith, A. and Zickuhr, K. (2010). Social media and young adults. Pew Internet and American Life Project. Retrieved at http://www.pewinternet.org/Reports/2010/Social-Media-and-Young-Adults/Summary-of-Findings.aspx

Livingstone, S. (2003). *The changing nature and uses of media literacy*. Media@LSE electronic working papers, 4. London, UK: London School of Economics and Political Science. Retrieved at http://eprints.lse.ac.uk/13476/

Livingstone, S., Couldry, N. and Markham, T. (2007). Youthful steps towards civic participation: does the internet help? In B. Loader (Ed.), *Young citizens in the digital age: Political engagement, young people and new media*. London: Routledge, pp. 21–34.

Lopez, M. H., Kirby, E. and Sagoff, J. (2005). *The Youth Vote 2004*. College Park, MD: Center for Information and Research on Civic Learning and Engagement. Retrieved from http://www.civicyouth.org/PopUps/FactSheets/FS_Youth_Voting_72-04.pdf

Lopez, M., Marcelo, K. and Kirby, E. (2007). Youth voter turnout increases in 2006; Medford, MA: Center for Information & Research on Civic Learning & Engagement. Retrieved July 17, 2007, from http://www.civicyouth.org/PopUps/FactSheets/FS07_2006MidtermCPS.pdf

McDevitt, M. (2005). The partisan child: Developmental provocation as a model of political socialization. *International Journal of Public Opinion Research*, *18*(1), 67–88.

McDonald, Michael P. (2011). *United States Elections Project*. Retrieved at http://elections.gmu.edu/Turn-out_2010G.html.

McLeod, J. M. and Shah, D. V. (2009). Communication and political socialization: Challenges and opportunities for research. *Political Communication*, *26*(1), 1–10.

Meroney, J. (2000). Late-night politics. *The American Enterprise*, *11*, 251.

Milner, H. (2002) *Civic literacy: How informed citizens make democracy work*. Hanover, NH: University Press of New England.

NAMLE (National Association for Media Literacy Education) (2005). Media literate media awards: 2000–2009. Retrieved at http://namle.net/2009/09/23/media-literate-media-awards-2000-2005/

Nathanson, A. I. (1999). Identifying and explaining the relationship between parental mediation and children's aggression. *Communication Research*, *26*(6), 124–43.

Niemi, R. G. and Hepburn, M. A. (1995). The rebirth of political socialization. *Perspectives on Political Science*, *24*(1), 7–16.

O'Keefe, G. J. and Reid-Nash, K. (1987). Socializing functions. In C. R. Berger and S. H. Chaffee (Eds), *Handbook of communication science*. Newbury Park: Sage, pp. 419–45.

Pinkleton, B. E. and Austin, E. W. (2004). Media perceptions and public affairs apathy in the political inexperienced. *Mass Communication and Society*, *7*(3), 319–37.

Pinkleton, B. E., Austin, E. W., Zhou, Y., Willoughby, J. F. and Reiser, M. (2012). Perceptions of news media, external efficacy, and public affairs apathy in political decision making and disaffection. *Journalism & Mass Communication Quarterly*, *89*(1), 23–39.

Prior, M. (2005). News vs. entertainment: How increasing media choice widens gap in political knowledge and turnout. *American Journal of Political Science*, *49*(3), 577–92.

PublicMind Poll (2011, November 21). Some News Leaves People Knowing Less. Fairleigh Dickinson University's PublicMind Poll, Farligh Dickinson University, Madison, New Jersey. Retrieved at http://publicmind.fdu.edu/2011/knowless/

Rheingold, H. (2007). Using Participatory Media and Public Voice to Encourage Civic Engagement. In *Civic Life Online: Learning How Digital Media Can Engage Youth*, (pp. 97–118). Boston, MA: Massachusetts Institute of Technology. Retrieved at http://www.mitpressjournals.org/doi/pdf/10.1162/dmal.978026 2524827.097

Rideout, V. J., Foehr, U. G. and Roberts, D. F. (2010). *Generation M2: Media in the lives of 8-to 18-year-olds*. Kaiser Family Foundation. Retrieved at http://www.kff.org/entmedia/upload/8010.pdf

Romer, D., Jamieson, K. H. and Pasek, J. (2009). Building social capital in young people: The role of mass media and life outlook. *Political Communication*, *26*(1), 65–83.

Schwartz, S. (2011). Youth and the "Arab Spring." Retrieved at http://www.usip.org/publications/youth-and-the-arab-spring

Shea, D. M. (2004). Throwing a Better Party: Local Mobilizing Institutions and the Youth Vote. CIRCLE Working Paper 13. Jonathan M. Tisch College of Citizenship and Public Service at Tufts University. Retrieved at http://www.civicyouth.org/PopUps/WorkingPapers/WP13shea.pdf

Social Capital Blog (2012). Twitter, Facebook and YouTube's role in Arab Spring (Middle East uprisings). Retrieved at http://socialcapital.wordpress.com/2011/01/26/twitter-facebook-and-youtubes-role-in-tunisia-uprising/

Southwell, B. G. and Yzer, M. C. (2007). The roles of interpersonal communication in mass media campaigns. In C. Beck (Ed.), *Communication Yearbook 31*, 420–62.

Tolley, H. (1973). *Children and war: Political socialization to international conflict*. New York: Teacher's College Press, Columbia University.

Trichter, J. and Paige, C. (2004). First-time voter's post-election study: Was it good for them? Retrieved at http://appserv.pace.edu/emplibrary/pace_poll_111804.pdf

Trier, J. (2008). Media literacy: *The Daily Show with Jon Stewart:* Part I. *Journal of Adolescent and Adult Literacy*, *51*(5), 424–27.

Wojcieszak, M. E. and Mutz, D. C. (2009). Online groups and political discourse: Do online discussion spaces facilitate exposure to political disagreement? *Journal of Communication*, *59*(1), 40–56.

Xenos, M. A. and Becker, A. B. (2009). Moments of Zen: Effects of *The Daily Show* on information seeking and political learning. *Political Communication*, *26*(3), 317–32.

Young Voter Strategies (2011). YOUNG VOTER MOBILIZATION TACTICS: A compilation of the most recent research on traditional & innovative voter turnout techniques. Young Voter Strategies.org, The George Washington University, The Graduate School of Political Management, Washington, D.C. Retrieved at http://www.civicyouth.org/PopUps/Young_Voters_Guide.pdf

Zhao, X. and Chaffee, S. H. (1995). Campaign advertisements versus television news as sources of political issue information. *Public Opinion Quarterly*, *59*(1), 41–65.

33

MEDIA, ADVERTISING, AND CONSUMERISM

Children and adolescents in a commercialized media environment

Moniek Buijzen, Esther Rozendaal, and Eva A. van Reijmersdal

In the first decade of the new millennium, children and adolescents' commercial media environment has changed dramatically. Advertisers have rapidly adopted new advertising techniques including branded websites, brand placement in video games, and viral marketing in social media (Buijzen et al., 2010; Calvert, 2008). Those new practices are fundamentally different from traditional advertising. Notably, non-traditional advertising practices typically rely on affect-based mechanisms and are often embedded within program or editorial content (Calvert, 2008; Wright et al., 2005), which may have important consequences for young people's understanding and processing of advertising.

Importantly, the affect-based and integrated commercial media environment poses new challenges for young people's advertising literacy (currently conceptualized as advertising-related knowledge and understanding). For example, when a commercial message is embedded within an "advergame" – an advertiser-sponsored online game – children may be less ready to process the message critically, and to resist its persuasive appeal (Owen et al., 2013). In this chapter, we review the state of the art of the international research literature on young people and persuasion, focusing specifically on today's commercial media environment. We focus on three important themes: (1) persuasion processes, (2) persuasion and resistance, and (3) advertising literacy.

Child and adolescent processing of persuasive messages

Drawing upon the rich theoretical and empirical work on adult persuasion processes, Buijzen et al. (2010) developed a framework for children and adolescents' Processing of Commercial Media Content (PCMC). Similar to dominant adult persuasion models (Eagly and Chaiken 1993; Meyers-Levy and Malaviya, 1999; Petty and Cacioppo 1996), the PCMC framework assumes that persuasion can occur through several processes. Under some conditions, people process a persuasive message systematically and carefully (referred to as the systematic process) and at other times, they rely on simple cues or shortcuts, using low-effort mechanisms to respond to a message (the heuristic process). In addition, a third even less elaborate process was distinguished, the automatic process, which is characterized by a primacy of automatic, affective, and unconscious reactions.

The three persuasion processes are characterized by varying levels of *cognitive elaboration* in response to a message – that is, the recipients' level of processing of the available information in the immediate persuasion context (Petty and Cacioppo 1996). Cognitive elaboration, in turn, relates to the recipients' motivation and ability to process the message effortfully (Eagly and Chaiken 1993). Systematic, heuristic, and automatic persuasion processing may each lead to attitude formation or change, which may in turn affect consumer behavior. However, the specific mediating mechanisms via which attitude change may occur differ in accordance with the processing route taken.

Systematic persuasion processing is based on relatively extensive, deliberate and effortful cognitive elaboration. For systematic processing to occur, people must be highly motivated and able to process all available information. When children and adolescents are concerned, it is relevant to distinguish between two levels of systematic processing. At the most elaborate level, critical systematic processing, an awareness of the persuasive nature of the message is involved, with the recipient actively applying the relevant persuasion knowledge or advertising literacy. Children who do not yet possess the relevant persuasion knowledge and information processing skills are unlikely to reach this level of processing. At a less elaborate level, noncritical systematic processing involves a high awareness of the message or brand, without awareness of its persuasive intent. In the systematic process, persuasion mechanisms leading to attitude change involve active learning mechanisms and formulation of cognitive responses, such as pro- and counter-argumentation to message claims and deliberation over the message source (Petty et al., 2005).

Heuristic persuasion processing is characterized by a moderate level of cognitive elaboration. Compared to the systematic process, the recipient uses merely moderate to low motivation and ability to process the message. Within the heuristic process, the recipient looks for an easy way to form an overall evaluation of the product or brand and relies on relatively simple and low-effort decision strategies. Therefore, advertising defenses are less likely to affect this type of processing, when compared to systematic processing (Livingstone and Helsper, 2006). The mechanisms leading to persuasion involve relatively passive learning and information retrieval mechanisms, such as social learning and consumer cultivation (Shrum et al., 2005). Current marketing practices, particularly those aimed at children, rely heavily on this type of processing, given the increased focus on emotion- and entertainment-based strategies in persuasive messages rather than information and rational argumentation.

Finally, in *automatic persuasion processing*, advertising exposure leads to attitude change without explicit attention to or awareness of the persuasive communication (Meyers-Levy and Malaviya, 1999): Recipient motivation and ability to process are not required. Advertising defenses are unlikely to be activated, because recipients are often unaware that they are being targeted. Highly embedded and stealth forms of marketing rely on this type of processing. Explicit recall of the persuasive message and the advertised product or brand will be low, yet implicit brand memory and attitude changes can be detected, for example through implicit recognition and association tests (Owen et al., 2010; Yang and Roskos-Ewoldsen, 2007).

In the automatic persuasion process, persuasion occurs through implicit and affect-based learning mechanisms, such as evaluative conditioning (i.e., pairing a brand with affectively laden stimuli such as celebrity endorsers or pleasant pictures) and affect transfer (i.e., the positive affect associated with the media experience transfers to the brand). In this process, brand exposure leads to more fluent processing when the brand is encountered again. This facilitated processing fluency leads to a sense of familiarity, which in turn may result in positive affect toward the brand. For example, the positive affect associated with an entertaining advergame (i.e., an online game designed to promote a brand) becomes transferred to the brand (i.e., brand attitude change) outside conscious awareness (Van Reijmersdal et al., 2012).

Persuasion and resistance in the commercialized media environment

The effects of advertising on children and adolescents have often been divided into two general types: intended effects (e.g., children's brand preferences, purchase requests, consumption) and unintended effects (e.g., materialistic orientations, parent–child conflicts, unhealthy eating habits). The most important precursor of both types of effects is advertising-induced change of attitude toward the product or brand. Because each level of processing can lead to attitude change, systematic, heuristic, and automatic processing may each lead to intended and unintended effects.

However, even though the level of processing may not affect the type and strength of the persuasion outcome, it may have consequences for the occurrence of children's *resistance* to persuasion. Resistance, in the child and advertising literature mostly referred to as advertising defenses, dovetails with the concept of advertising literacy (knowledge and understanding of advertising). As indicated above, the retrieval and application of advertising-related knowledge requires the most elaborate level of processing; critical systematic processing. At this level, an awareness of the persuasive nature of the message is involved, with the recipient actively retrieving and applying the relevant advertising knowledge as a defense against persuasion.

In short, for resistance to occur, children should process the message at the most elaborate level (Buijzen et al., 2010; Rozendaal et al., 2011). The likelihood of critical systematic elaboration is determined by the recipient's ability and motivation to process a message, which in turn is predicted by the characteristics of the message, its context, and the recipient (Petty et al., 2005). In the current commercial media environment, several factors may withhold children from processing persuasion at the most elaborate level. Importantly, the nature of contemporary advertising, combined with children's limited consumer experience and cognitive skills, makes it difficult to engage in critical systematic processing.

Elaboration difficulties associated with the commercial media environment

Two characteristics of today's commercial media environment may limit young people's motivation and ability to process a message on the critical systematic level: the affect-based nature and the integration of persuasive messages within the medium context. First, content analyses have revealed that the advertisements young people are most likely to see do not employ classic informational appeals. Rather than presenting arguments or discussing the benefits associated with owning the product, child-directed advertising employs emotional appeals, fast-paced editing techniques, and dynamic formal features (Wicks et al., 2009).

With regard to emotion-based advertising, there are several tactics that marketers frequently rely upon. First, there is the consistent focus on fun and play in advertisements, with scenes filled with happy and excited children. Second, child-directed advertising often employs popular media characters that children feel a great deal of affinity and loyalty towards, including well-known celebrities such as *SpongeBob Squarepants* and *Dora the Explorer*. Third, many nontraditional advertising techniques rely on the mechanism of processing fluency, evaluative conditioning, and affect-transfer, such as advergames that are merely designed to evoke happy and aroused feelings, which are then transferred to the advertised brand.

Such affect- and emotion-based persuasion mechanisms all link to lower-level processing, in particular automatic processing. Thus, the emotional content will distract children from using relevant advertising knowledge as a critical defense. In other words, the affect-based nature of children and adolescents' commercial media environment is likely to limit their motivation and ability to process an advertising message elaborately and, accordingly, to retrieve and apply their conceptual advertising knowledge as a defense.

The same difficulties apply to integrated advertising formats, in which the persuasive message is embedded within the medium context. Buijzen et al. (2010) distinguished between three types of message-context integration. First, format integration refers to the level of integration between the message format and the editorial context. Examples include advertorials in magazines or websites which are designed to resemble editorial articles or website content. Second, thematic integration refers to the conceptual fit or congruence between the persuasive message and its context. This may include, for example, placement of ads around thematically congruent content, such as placement of the *Bridgestone* brand logo in a car racing game, or an advertisement for *Barbie* dolls and toys in the *Barbie* magazine.

Third, narrative integration refers to the semantic or conceptual relevance of the persuasive message within the narrative of the surrounding media context. For example, children's programs based on brands, such as *Bratz* and *Pokémon*, can each be seen as program-length commercials for the corresponding action figures and other brand extensions, including toys, magazines, and music. The level of integration between the persuasive message and its context is likely to have important consequences for the persuasion process. Crucially, integration links to the ability to recognize the message and its persuasive intent (Friestad and Wright, 1994). When the persuasive message is highly integrated with the editorial context, its persuasive nature will be recognized less easily, which in turn is unlikely to lead to critical systematic processing.

In sum, due to their affect-based and integrated nature, nontraditional advertising messages rely heavily on low levels of message elaboration and, therefore, children are unlikely to retrieve and apply their advertising knowledge as a critical defense (Buijzen et al., 2010; Nairn and Fine, 2008; Owen et al., 2013). Indeed, findings of several studies confirm that children's knowledge of nontraditional advertising formats does not influence the actual or intended effects of these formats (Mallinckrodt and Mizerski, 2007; Owen, et al., 2013; Van Reijmersdal et al., 2012).

Elaboration difficulties associated with maturation

In addition to the difficulties that are related to the commercial media environment, young people's motivation and ability to process an advertising message on a critical systematic level will be further limited by their relatively immature advertising and consumer skills (e.g., advertising literacy, marketplace experience, brand memory, and consumption autonomy). For example, children under age 8, who are not yet able to recognize the commercial nature and persuasive intent of an advertising message (Rozendaal et al., 2010), will be less likely to process this message on a critical systematic level. Further, critical systematic processing requires domain-specific knowledge which these children often still lack.

In addition, children's immature cognitive abilities are likely to limit their motivation and ability to process persuasive messages at the critical systematic level. Specifically, to actually enact their advertising knowledge as a defense, children will need to master the "stop and think" response (Lapierre, 2009), which involves the cognitive control to *stop* and recognize the persuasive nature of the message, and to *think* about the persuasive message in some considerable depth to help defend against it. Young people's ability to "stop and think" may depend upon the development of two cognitive abilities: *executive functioning* and *emotion regulation*, which do not fully mature until mid-adolescence. Rozendaal et al. (2011) have argued that without the development of these two abilities children will not be able to exercise adequate control of cognitions (i.e.; the "stop" part of "stop and think"), which would allow for critical evaluation of advertising (i.e.; the "think" part of "stop and think"), and thus engage in critical systematic persuasion processing.

Executive functioning is defined as the "higher order, self-regulatory, cognitive processes that aid in the monitoring and control of thought and action" (Carlson, 2005; p. 595). Executive functioning involves a set of skills that develop throughout childhood. Specifically, three aspects of executive functioning are relevant for critical systematic processing: inhibitory control (the ability to withhold or delay a pre-planned response and to interrupt a process that has already started), attentional flexibility (the ability to fluidly shift attention under cognitively or affectively taxing conditions), and working memory (the part of memory that keeps information immediately accessible for the planning and completion of complex tasks).

When translating these insights to the ability for critical systematic processing, it is plausible that young people with immature executive functioning will have a difficult time using advertising knowledge as a defense while processing advertising. Specifically, because children are less able to control inhibitions, they will be more likely to immediately respond to the perceptually salient and appealing features of the message. Then, because these children have a hard time shifting and controlling their attention, they will be unable to shift their attention away from the affect-based message to focus on their advertising knowledge. Finally, due to their immature working memory abilities, children under the age of 12 will be unable to process the persuasive message and, at the same time, retrieve and apply their advertising knowledge as a critical defense.

Emotion regulation is defined as "the behaviors, skills and strategies, whether conscious or unconscious, automatic or effortful, that serve to modulate, inhibit and enhance emotional experiences and expressions" (Calkins and Hill, 2007, p. 160). This can include subduing or amplifying negatively or positively valenced emotions. With so much of the content in contemporary advertising centered on emotional cues, one would expect that children's ability to process these messages depends on their ability to modulate emotional responses to the message. Children with less of an ability to control affect via emotion regulation are more likely to be overwhelmed by emotional cues, such as happy children or popular media characters. Yet, as children mature and develop the ability to use effective emotion regulation strategies, they become less likely to get caught up in the message's emotional appeal. In the course of adolescence (ages 12–18), they become capable of controlling the emotional impulses that are evoked by the advertisement and become more likely to process the message on the critical systematic level.

Advertising literacy in the commercialized media environment

Current insights in youth's persuasion processing call for a revision of the conceptualization of advertising literacy. In the child and advertising literature advertising literacy is generally defined as knowledge of advertising intent and tactics. Based on various theoretical models (e.g., Wright et al., 2005), seven knowledge components of advertising literacy can be identified:

1 recognition of advertising – differentiating advertising from other media content;
2 recognition of advertising's source – understanding who pays for advertising messages;
3 perception of intended audience – understanding the concept of audience targeting and segmentation;
4 understanding advertising's selling intent – understanding that advertising tries to sell products;
5 understanding advertising's persuasive intent – understanding that advertising attempts to influence consumers' behavior by changing their mental states;
6 understanding advertisers' persuasive tactics – understanding specific persuasion strategies used by advertisers;
7 understanding advertising's bias – being aware of discrepancies between the advertised and the actual product.

However, this focus on conceptual knowledge might be too narrow a conceptualization. In the broader context of media, literacy has been defined as "the ability to access, analyze, evaluate, and create messages across a variety of contexts" (Christ and Potter, 1998, p. 7). In other words, the concept of literacy should not only entail the ability to identify and understand media messages, but also to deal with those messages critically. Drawing on progressing insights into persuasion processing, we have demonstrated in this chapter that conceptual advertising knowledge alone does not automatically result in the ability to critically deal with the current commercial media environment.

There is a need for a reconceptualization of advertising literacy that contends with the changes in the commercialized media environment. Specifically, Rozendaal et al. (2011) proposed to extend the current conceptualization of advertising literacy (i.e., focusing on *conceptual advertising literacy*) with two dimensions. First, *advertising literacy performance* takes into account the actual use of conceptual knowledge of advertising while being exposed to it. The insights presented in this chapter suggest that even if children have the necessary conceptual advertising knowledge in place, it does not necessarily follow that they actually retrieve this knowledge when confronted with advertising and apply it as a critical defense. Therefore, the theoretical distinction between conceptual advertising literacy (i.e., having advertising knowledge) and advertising literacy performance (i.e., retrieving and applying advertising knowledge) should be emphasized more strongly.

Second, *attitudinal advertising literacy* includes low-effort, attitudinal mechanisms that can be effective in reducing children's advertising susceptibility under conditions of low elaboration. Assuming that children primarily process advertising on a less elaborate level, they might need attitudinal rather than cognitive defenses. For example, general critical attitudes toward advertising (e.g., skepticism and disliking of advertising) have been shown to automatically generate negative affect when processing a specific advertisement, which, in turn, is transferred to the advertisement and advertised brand (Zuwerink and Devine, 1996). This suggests that general critical attitudes might be more successful in altering children's responses to advertising messages. For critical attitudes to function as an attitudinal defense, children are less dependent on executive functioning and emotion regulation skills because they operate via a less cognitively demanding mechanism. Thus, attitudinal defenses can be successful in reducing children's advertising susceptibility, even when they are not motivated and able to process an advertising message elaborately (Rozendaal et al., 2012).

Setting the agenda for future research

Based on the extended 3-dimensional definition of advertising literacy (i.e., conceptual advertising literacy, advertising literacy performance, attitudinal advertising literacy), we propose four focal points for the research agenda. First, future research should focus on advertising literacy performance by investigating the conditions under which children retrieve their conceptual advertising literacy and use it as a defense against advertising. Second, future research should further examine if and how children's attitudinal advertising literacy can alter children's responses to persuasive messages. Third, there is a need to understand the specific ways in which literacy affects the persuasion process, for example investigating the assumption that conceptual and attitudinal advertising literacy operate via different mechanisms (i.e., high versus low elaboration).

Finally, future research should reveal if and how interventions aimed to stimulate advertising literacy can change the persuasion process in children. Scholars could draw from the more developed adult persuasion and information processing literatures. Incorporating findings and theories from the adult literature (while also keeping in mind the tremendous developmental differences between children and adults) into the child literature would represent an enormous step forward for the field and would, at the same time, offer compelling tests of how these theories apply to developmental contexts.

SEE ALSO in this volume chapter by Buckingham and chapter by Chan.

References

Buijzen, M., Van Reijmersdal, E. A. and Owen, L. H. (2010). Introducing the PCMC model: An investigative framework for young people's processing of commercial media content. *Communication Theory*, 20(4), 427–50.

Calkins, S. D. and Hill, A. (2007). The emergence of emotion regulation: Biological and behavioral transactions in early development. In J. Gross (Ed.), *Handbook of emotion regulation*. New York: Guilford, pp. 229–48.

Calvert, S. L. (2008). Children as consumers: Advertising and marketing. *The Future of Children*, 18(1), 205–34.

Carlson, S. M. (2005). Developmentally sensitive measures of executive function in preschool children. *Developmental Neuropsychology*, 28(2), 595–616.

Christ, W. G. and Potter, W. J. (1998). Media literacy, media education, and the academy. *Journal of Communication*, 48(1), 5–15.

Eagly, A. H. and Chaiken, S. (1993). *The psychology of attitudes*. Fort Worth, TX: Harcourt Brace Jovanovich College Publishers.

Friestad, M. and Wright, P. (1994). The persuasion knowledge model: How people cope with persuasion attempts. *Journal of Consumer Research*, 21(1), 1–31.

Lapierre, M. A. (2009, November). Intervening against interventions: Children's developing cognition and its impact on the efficacy of advertising interventions. Paper presented at the convention Consumer Culture & the Ethical Treatment of Children: Theory, Research & Fair Practice, East-Lansing, MI.

Livingstone, S. and Helsper, E. J. (2006). Does advertising literacy mediate the effects of advertising on children? A critical examination of two linked research literatures in relation to obesity and food choice. *Journal of Communication*, 56(3), 560–84.

Mallinckrodt, V. and Mizerski, D. (2007). The effects of playing an advergame on young children's perceptions, preferences, and requests. *Journal of Advertising*, 36(2), 87–100.

Meyers-Levy, J. and Malaviya, P. (1999). Consumers' processing of persuasive advertisements: An integrative framework of persuasion theories. *Journal of Marketing*, 63(4), 45–60.

Nairn, A. and Fine, C. (2008) Who's messing with my mind? The implications of dual-process models for ethics of advertising to children. *International Journal of Advertising*, 27(3), 447–70.

Owen, L. H., Lewis, C., Auty, S. and Buijzen, M., (2013). Is children's understanding of non-traditional advertising comparable to their understanding of television advertising? *Journal of Public Policy and Marketing*. Advance online publication, doi: 10.1509/jppm.09.003

——(2010, June). *The role of personal salience in children's implicit processing of brand placements in movies*. Paper presented at the Annual Conference of the International Communication Association, Singapore.

Petty, R. E. and Cacioppo, J. T. (1996). *Attitudes and persuasion: Classic and contemporary approaches* (New ed.). Boulder, CO: Westview Press.

Petty, R. E., Cacioppo, J. T., Strathmann, A. J. and Priester, J. R. (2005). To think or not to think: Exploring two routes to persuasion. In T. C. Brock and M. C. Green (Eds), *Persuasion: Psychological insights and perspectives*. Thousand Oaks, CA: Sage, pp. 81–116.

Rozendaal, E., Buijzen, M. and Valkenburg, P. M. (2010). Comparing children's and adults' cognitive advertising competences in the Netherlands. *Journal of Children and Media*, 4(1), 77–89.

——(2012). Think-aloud process superior to thought-listing in increasing children's critical processing of advertising. *Human Communication Research*, 38(2), 199–221.

Rozendaal, E., Lapierre, M. A., Van Reijmersdal, E. A. and Buijzen, M. (2011). Reconsidering advertising literacy as a defense against advertising effects. *Media Psychology*, 14(4), 333–54.

Shrum, L. J., Burroughs, J. E. and Rindfleisch, A. (2005). Television's cultivation of material values. *Journal of Consumer Research*, 32(3), 473–79.

Van Reijmersdal, E. A., Rozendaal, E. and Buijzen, M. (2012). Effects of prominence, involvement, and persuasion knowledge on children's cognitive and affective responses to advergames. *Journal of Interactive Marketing*, 26(1), 33–42 DOI: 10.1016/j.intmar.2011.04.005

Wicks, J. B., Warren, R., Fosu, I. and Wicks, R. H. (2009). Dual modality disclaimers, emotional appeals and production techniques in food advertising airing in programs rated for children: Is there a good balance? *Journal of Advertising*, *38*(4), 93–105.

Wright, P., Friestad, M. and Boush, D. M. (2005). The development of marketplace persuasion knowledge in children, adolescents, and young adults. *Journal of Public Policy & Marketing*, *24*(2), 222–33.

Yang, M. and Roskos-Ewoldsen, D. R. (2007). The effectiveness of brand placements in the movies: Levels of placements, explicit and implicit memory, and brand choice behavior. *Journal of Communication*, *57*(3), 469–89.

Zuwerink, J. R. and Devine, P. G. (1996). Attitude importance and resistance to persuasion: It's not just the thought that counts. *Journal of Personality and Social Psychology*, *70*(5), 931–44.

34

MEDIA AND GENDER IDENTITIES

Learning and performing femininity and masculinity

Sharon R. Mazzarella

Introduction

One of the first concepts I teach in my classes when I introduce the topic of gender is the difference between biological *sex* and the cultural construct of *gender*. While sex is determined by biology—X and Y chromosomes that make one born a girl or a boy—gender is socially constructed. As Butler (1990; 1993) and other scholars have explained, gender is learned and then performed. The culture in which we are born and grow up teaches us how to perform femininity and masculinity, and while such performativity may be related to one's biological sex, it is not always so. The construction of children's gender identity is a function of a variety of interacting forces including cultural artifacts such as media content. Children and adolescents learn how to enact particular gender roles from models including media characters, and also use media technologies to perform their own gender identity. Reviewing a range of English-language research studies, this chapter addresses both of these topics.

Theoretical grounding

The theories and methodologies employed by scholars studying media and children's gender roles vary based on the questions being asked. For example, most scholars seeking to understand the *effects* of such content employ quantitative methods—content analysis, experiments, and/or surveys. Such studies typically are grounded in Cultivation and/or Social Learning/Social Cognitive Theories. Cultivation Theory (e.g., Gerbner et al., 1980) asserts that media, particularly television, cultivate ideas about reality in the minds of viewers. Heavy viewers, which children in most developed countries are, are more likely to be affected by the reality cultivated by the television world. In fact, cultivation research has consistently documented a relationship between TV viewing and gender-stereotyped views of the world (Signorielli, 1997). Social Learning/ Cognitive Theory (Bandura, 1977, 1994) proposes that children are more likely to attend to and learn from models with whom they can relate, who are similar to them—thus they are more likely to identify with someone of their own sex, especially another child.

While a large body of the research on media and children's gender roles is guided by the above two theories, other scholars approach the topic from a critical/cultural perspective, grounding their scholarship in the theories of Judith Butler and/or other Feminist Theories. For example, Girls' Studies has greatly influenced the way many Media Studies scholars examine the relationship between girls and cultural artifacts including media. Girls' Studies scholars tend to incorporate critical/cultural methods and theories as they seek to understand how girls themselves navigate and incorporate such artifacts into their identity work. These scholars use in-depth interviews, focus groups, observational studies, and so on—methods that enable scholars to understand the relationship between young people and the artifacts rather than the effects of the artifacts on them.

The reader will notice that when I provided an example of more qualitative approaches to the study of media and children's gender roles, I spoke only of Girls' Studies. While Girls' Studies has influenced how scholars study the relationship between girls and media, the establishment of a tradition of Boys' Media Studies has been slow to develop (Wannamaker, 2011). What scholarship exists is found primarily in sociology, education, and English/literacy studies (e.g., Newkirk, 2002; Wannamaker, 2008). Wannamaker's recent anthology (2011) is an anomaly in its attempt to foreground Communication and Media Studies scholarship on the topic. However, while the book was published in a Media Studies book series and appears in the publisher's "communication" list, only a handful of chapter authors are Communication and Media Studies scholars. The majority are from English or other related disciplines.

Gendered messages in media content consumed by young people: youth as media characters

While scholars have studied gendered messages in a range of media content forms targeted to young people (including teen magazines, music lyrics, and music videos), for the sake of space, this section will highlight the most prolific and long-running of such research programs—gender roles in television programs and commercials.

Television programs

Scholarly interest in the gender roles found in children's television goes back to the 1970s. Studies from that era as well as more recent studies (e.g., Aubrey and Harrison, 2004; Götz and Lemish, 2012; Smith and Cook, 2008; Thompson and Zerbinos, 1995), have primarily documented the underrepresentation and stereotyping of female characters. More recent studies have documented *some* positive changes (Baker and Raney, 2007; Lemish, 2010; Smith and Cook, 2008).

For example, in one of the most often cited studies of children's programs in the U.S., Thompson and Zerbinos (1995) found males were likely to be physically and verbally aggressive, more ingenious, and more task-oriented while females were more relationship-oriented, more affectionate and more likely to need and ask for help. In one recent study of gender roles in U.S. children's programs, Aubrey and Harrison (2004) found that male characters in programs watched by young children outnumbered female characters by more than 2:1, a statistic echoed in a more recent study of U.S. children's television (Smith and Cook, 2008), a recent study of U.S. children's superhero cartoons (Baker and Raney, 2007), and in a comparative study of children's television across 24 countries (Götz and Lemish, 2012).

While Aubrey and Harrison (2004) found more gender neutrality than previous studies, male characters were still shown in more active pursuits, while females were more likely than males to be attractive and frail. Continuing this discussion of character physical appearance, Smith and

Cook (2008) found that females in U.S. children's television programs were four times more likely than males to be shown in sexy attire and to have unrealistic body shapes, while Baker and Raney (2007) found that U.S. female superheroes were more attractive and appearance-obsessed.

In an extensive comparative study of children's television programs across 24 different countries, Götz and Lemish (2012) documented the continuation of gender stereotypes in terms of role, age, and body type. Boy characters were more likely to be antagonists; girls were more likely to be members of a group or team; adult characters were more likely to be male; teen characters were more likely to be female; and female characters in general were more likely than male characters to be thin, with blonde or red hair. Based on their analysis, the authors assert that these and other findings support "our argument that gender on children's television around the world is constructed in similar ways, and as such it should be examined, criticized, and reconstructed in ways that are more reflective both of reality, as well as, supportive of the vision of increasing social equity" (p. 44).

As Thompson and Zerbinos (1995) have documented, children's television often presents extremes of gender roles—sometimes stereotypical, sometimes challenging stereotypes. Similarly, Aubrey and Harrison (2004, p. 112) conclude that "On the whole, studies of television's effects on children's gender-role learning have suggested that the medium can contribute to *both* traditional and nontraditional gender-role learning."

While the above studies have addressed children's programs/cartoons, other scholars have looked at television programs popular with or marketed to adolescents. For example, Signorielli (1997, p. 1) examined messages about gender in U.S. media content, including television programs, targeted to teenage girls. The results, she reports, "illustrate the dual role media plays." Echoing Thompson and Zerbinos (1995), she argues that popular teen girl media content" offer[s] girls many positive role models" (p. 30) while simultaneously containing "stereotypical messages about appearance, relationships and careers" (p. 30).

These findings have been confirmed recently in research conducted on two popular U.S. teen programs. Van Damme (2010) found that girls in *Gossip Girl* and *One Tree Hill* were more likely to be portrayed as passive, victims, sexual objects, emotional, looks-obsessed, sneaky, and thin with other characters often remarking on their physical appearance. Boys, on the other hand, were more likely to be portrayed as active, heroes, rational, physically forceful. Interestingly, as did Signorielli, Van Damme found that while there were many "stereotypical gender scripts," "more positive and emancipative discourses regarding female and male characters are also found" (p. 88).

The results of one recent, large-scale project have detailed the role television producers around the world can play in bringing about a more comprehensive and sustained change in television gender portrayals (Lemish, 2010). Based on her interviews with 135 "quality" children's television producers from 65 different countries, Lemish (2010) exposes the struggle (e.g., economic pressure) many such producers encounter when attempting to produce programs that challenge gender stereotypes. Still, based on her interviews, she has reason to be optimistic as she concludes that "television images have the power" to break out of the gender binary, and work "toward advancing gender equality, if we act to do so" (p. 177).

Television commercials

Commercials airing during children's programs have also historically presented a gender-stereotyped world with boy characters portrayed as more active, aggressive and outdoors and girl characters portrayed as more passive and domestic. Taken as a whole, the body of research on this topic has documented some changes in female portrayals over the years (notably a greater presence), yet most stereotypes continue to exist. At one point, studies of U.S. children's television commercials documented a nearly 3:1 overrepresentation of males to females (Larson, 2001). While more recent studies have found a more equitable distribution, single-sex boy ads still predominate (Larson, 2001). A longitudinal analysis conducted by Maher and Childs (2003) documented that while females have attained an increased presence rate in children's television commercials, "males still outnumber females in all major gender measures" of current day children's advertising (p. 79).

Larson (2001) found that girl characters in single-sex U.S. children's commercials were more likely to be portrayed in stereotypical domestic settings while boys were more likely to be shown outside of the home. Girls were more often portrayed in cooperative situations while boys were in more competitive roles. These findings echo those found in numerous other studies of U.S. television commercials (e.g., Davis, 2003; Smith 1994).

Gender-role stereotyping such as the kind mentioned above has been found in international and cross-cultural studies of children's advertising as well. For example, studies of children's commercials in the UK (Furnham et al., 1997; Furnham and Saar, 2005; Lewin-Jones and Mitra, 2009); Poland (Furnham and Saar, 2005); and Australia (Brown, 1998) document the same underrepresentation of females and portrayals of active boys outside of the home and passive, domestic girls.

Variations in young people's preference for media content: youth as media consumers

According to the "Media Practice Model"—the idea that identity formation is a key motivation in the selection of, attention to, and interpretation of media—as adolescents take on the developmental task of creating a sense of self, they may use the media as sources of models (Brown and Pardun, 2004). According to Brown and Pardun (2004), sex is a significant predictor of such choices. For example, Garitaonandia et al. (2001) studied 6–16-year-olds in 12 European countries and found that 9–13-year-old girls were more interested in soap operas with no interest in televised sports. Boys, on the other hand, manifested a strong interest in televised sports. Similarly, in a longitudinal analysis of 9–12 year-olds in Belgium, Roe (1998) also found comparable sex differences with girls choosing music, talk, quiz, children's programs and soap operas while boys preferred science/tech, sports, and movies. In their study of television program watching by young people in the U.S., Brown and Pardun (2004) found that girls and boys watch very different programs. Specifically, they found "girls watch shows featuring teen girls struggling with teen relationships while boys watch boys behaving badly" (p. 276)—a difference the authors attribute to the purposeful search for mediated gender-role models.

Research has also documented differences in girls' and boys' preferences for reading. Scholars studying the relationship between U.S. boys and reading (Newkirk, 2002; Pirie, 2002) agree that the reading habits of boys and girls differ with boys tending to prefer things like science fiction, graphic novels, fantasy, informational books on hobbies, sports and the like. Boys also tend to view reading as a feminine activity, especially because books often focus on emotions (Pirie, 2002). Wannamaker (2008) offers new ways of thinking and talking about books popular with boys, arguing that such texts (including Captain Underpants, the Harry Potter novels, manga, etc.) often rely on depictions of the abject, which "create opportunities to make dominant masculinity visible as a social construct" (back cover).

Another difference related to young people's gendered preferences for media relates to their use of digital technologies. This topic is explored in the next section.

Young people's use of media/technology as related to gender identity negotiation: youth as media producers

Gendering technology: the digital divide?

Kelly et al. (2006) remind us of "the link between technological competence and the construction of gendered identity" (p. 5). In fact, such technological competence has historically been gendered male, and has served as a source of hegemonic masculine power often denied to females. This is particularly relevant when examining the relationship between young people and digital technologies. Most recent studies, in a range of countries, have found little evidence of a gendered digital divide in terms of access, but there do appear to be some differences in how digital technologies are used (Lenhart and Madden, 2005; Livingstone and Helsper, 2007; Mertens and d'Haenens, 2010)—typically some studies show that boys are more likely to use computers for gaming, for example, and girls for blogging and other such creative pursuits.

The internet

While much of the early work examining girls and computer/internet technology focused on content created for girls, more scholars have begun to study content created by girls. Focusing on personal home pages created by girls, Stern's groundbreaking work has shown how girls use these "safe" spaces as forms of "constructed self-presentations" (1999, p. 23), the content of which has proven to be as varied as girls themselves. Including Stern, a range of Girls' Studies scholars have examined the internet as a space fostering girls' self-expression, community building, and identity play. For example, scholars have investigated how the web sites girls create function as forms of identity expression, self-disclosure, communication, and community building (Bortree, 2005; Vickery, 2010). Others have documented how girls use organizational and commercial web sites or social networking sites to explore their identities in general (Weaver, 2005) and their sexual identities in particular (Driver, 2007; Grisso and Weiss, 2005; Stokes, 2010). Still others have highlighted the role of instant messaging in girls' identity development and peer networking (Stern, 2007).

For example, based on their interviews with Canadian teen girls, Kelly et al. (2006) found that various online activities (including chat rooms, IM and role-playing games) allowed girls to "rehearse different ways of being before trying them out offline" (p. 3). Similarly, Bae (2010) looked at how diasporic Korean girls in the U.S. use their personal home pages on the Korean social networking site Cyworld to construct a culturally hybrid form of ethnic feminine identity. Through her survey of teenage girls in New Zealand, Weaver found that nzgirl.co.nz members "identify the site as appealing to a normative feminine subjectivity, but as extending the boundaries of that subjectivity through public informational address" (2005, p. 95).

While much of the research on young people and digital technologies has focused specifically on girls, according to Facer et al. (2001), some boys use their digital knowledge as "the basis for alternative constructions of masculinity, in which expertise in this area compensates for other, more traditionally male qualities such as physical prowess" (p. 210). In an extensive study of computer technologies and gendering, Holloway et al. (2000) found that British students' attitudes toward and use of computers were "negotiated through competing masculinities and femininities in the classroom context" (p. 617). They specifically explain the differences between the "techno boys" versus "the lads" at one school in which the former were highly proficient with computer technology on a range of levels while the latter mostly played games and surfed the web.

Other digital technologies

One of the primary differences in girls' and boys' use of computer technology has generally been considered to be game playing, in part because girls do not see such pursuits as included in a feminine gender identity. As a result, academics, activists, and game designers have begun to focus on girls and computer gaming. For example, Jenson and de Castell (2011) created a school game club for both girls and boys in the Toronto area. Based on their three-year longitudinal study, the authors showed how the gender differences found in earlier studies of young people's gaming practices "were far less evident and some of these were no longer present at all, once the girls had been afforded genuine access, support, a 'girls-gamer' model, and the right to choose what, when and with whom they would play" (p. 175). Similarly, Kim's (2009) study of Japanese "women's games" (games produced and marketed exclusively for girls and women in Japan) found that such games are important in that female players "can experiment with and enact various female identities and female fantasies through the medium of electronic games" (p. 184).

While nearly ubiquitous with young people in the developed world, there has not been much research on gender and mobile phones. In one such study of middle schoolers in the U.S., Cotton et al. (2009, p. 1180) found that "when controlling for affinity and skill, there are no significant gender differences in more traditional communicative uses of the mobile phone" typically thought to be used more by girls than by boys. However, as with the internet, there were differences in how boys and girls used their phones with boys more likely to use their phones for game playing, music listening, video sharing and the like.

Concluding thoughts

The study of media and young people's gender roles has had a prominent place in Media Studies Scholarship for several decades. While the majority of early scholarship focused primarily, but not exclusively, on the content and effects of media targeted to children and adolescents, reception studies have become more prevalent in recent years along with a focus on young people as producers of media content. Similarly, scholars across the globe have made more of an effort to become familiar with and learn from scholarship conducted outside of their home countries, so that we now have a more comparative, though still incomplete, picture of media and gender roles across countries. There is still a need for more cross-cultural analysis, but we are moving in the right direction. Across the globe, aided by the international, interdisciplinary Girls' Studies movement, more research has been focused on content targeted to or produced by girls, but there is a growing need for comparable research on boys. Finally, as digital technologies continue to expand and evolve, scholarship needs to keep pace in order to inform our understanding of how the young use these technologies in their gender identity work.

SEE ALSO in this volume chapter by Lemish.

References

Aubrey, J. S. and Harrison, K. (2004). The gender-role content of children's favorite television programs and its links to their gender-related perceptions. *Media Psychology*, 6(2), 111–46.

Bae, M. S. (2010). Go Cyworld!: Korean diasporic girls producing new Korean femininity. In S. R. Mazzarella (Ed.), *Girl wide web 2.0: Revisiting girls, the Internet, and the Negotiation of Identity*. New York: Peter Lang, pp. 91–113.

Baker, K. and Raney, A. A. (2007). Equally super?: Gender-role stereotyping of superheroes in children's animated programs. *Mass Communication and Society*, 10(1), 25–41.

Bandura, A. (1977). *Social learning theory*. Englewood Cliffs, NJ: Prentice Hall.

——(1994). Social cognitive theory of mass communication. In J. Bryant and D. Zillmann (Eds), *Media effects: Advances in theory and research*. Hillsdale, NJ: Lawrence Erlbaum Associates, pp. 61–90.

Bortree, D. S. (2005). Presentation of self on the Web: An ethnographic study of teenage girls' weblogs. *Education, Communication & Information*, 5(1), 25–39.

Brown, B. A. (1998). Gender stereotypes in advertising on children's television in the 1990s: A cross-national analysis. *Journal of Advertising*, 27(1), 83–96.

Brown, J. D. and Pardun, C. J. (2004). Little in common: Racial and gender differences in adolescents' television diets. *Journal of Broadcasting & Electronic Media*, 48(2), 266–78.

Butler, J. (1990). *Gender trouble: Feminism and the subversion of identity*. New York: Routledge.

——(1993). *Bodies that matter: On the discursive limits of sex*. New York: Routledge.

Cotton, S. R., Anderson, W. A. and Tufekci, Z. (2009). Old wine in a new technology, or a different type of digital divide? *New Media & Society*, 11(7), 1163–86.

Davis, S. N. (2003). Sex stereotypes in commercials targeted toward children: A content analysis. *Sociological Spectrum*, 23(4), 407–24.

Driver, S. (2007). *Queer girls and popular culture: Reading, resisting, and creating media*. New York: Peter Lang.

Facer, K., Sutherland, R., Furlong, R. and Furlong, J. (2001). What's the point of using computers? *New Media & Society*, 3(2), 199–219.

Furnham, A., and Saar, A. (2005). Gender-role stereotyping in adult and children's television advertisements: A two-study comparison between Great Britain and Poland. *Communications*, 30(1), 73–90.

Furnham, A., Abramsky, S. and Gunter, B. (1997). A cross-cultural content analysis of children's television advertisements. *Sex Roles*, 37(1/2), 91–99.

Garitaonandia, C., Juaristi, P. and Oleaga, J. A. (2001). Media genres and content preferences. In S. Livingston and M. Bovill (Eds), *Children and their changing media environment: A European comparative study*. Mahwah, NJ: Lawrence Erlbaum, pp. 141–57.

Gerbner, G., Gross, L., Morgan, M. and Signorielli, N. (1980). The "mainstreaming" of America: Violence profile no. 11. *Journal of Communication*, 30(3), 10–29.

Götz, M. and Lemish, D. (Eds) (2012). *Sexy girls, heroes and funny losers: Gender representations in children's TV around the world*. New York: Peter Lang.

Grisso, A. D. and Weiss, D. (2005). What are gURLS talking about?: Adolescent girls' construction of sexual identity on gURL.com. In S. R. Mazzarella (Ed.), *Girl wide web: Girls, the Internet, and the Negotiation of Identity*. New York: Peter Lang, pp. 31–49.

Holloway, S. L., Valentine, G. and Bingham, N. (2000). Institutionalizing technologies: Masculinities, femininities, and the heterosexual economy of the IT classroom. *Environment and Planning: A.*, 32(4), 617–33.

Jenson, J. and de Castell, S. (2011). Girls @ play: An ethnographic study of gender and digital gameplay. *Feminist Media Studies*, 11(2), 167–79.

Kelly, D. M., Pomerantz, S. and Currie, D. H. (2006). "No boundaries"? Girls' interactive, online learning about femininities. *Youth & Society*, 38(1), 3–28.

Kim, H. (2009). Women's games in Japan: Gendered identity and narrative construction. *Theory, Culture & Society*, 26(2–3), 165–88.

Larson, M. S. (2001). Interactions, activities and gender in children's television commercials: A content analysis. *Journal of Broadcasting and Electronic Media*, 45(1), 41–56.

Lemish, D. (2010). *Screening gender on children's television: The views of producers around the world*. New York: Routledge.

Lenhart, A. and Madden, M. (2005). *Teen content creators and consumers*. Washington, DC: Pew Internet & American Life Project. Retrieved January 23, 2006, from http://www.pewinternet.org/

Lewin-Jones, J. and Mitra, B. (2009). Gender roles in television commercials and primary school children in the UK. *Journal of Children and Media*, 3(1), 35–50.

Livingstone, S. and Helsper, E. (2007). Gradations in digital inclusion: Children, young people and the digital divide. *New Media & Society*, 9(4), 671–96.

Maher, J. K. and Childs, N. M. (2003). A longitudinal content analysis of gender roles in children's television advertisements: A 27 year review. *Journal of Current Issues in Research in Advertising*, 25(1), 71–81.

Mertens, S. and d'Haenens, L. (2010). The digital divide among young people in Brussels: Social and cultural influences on ownership and use of digital technologies. *Communications*, 35(2), 187–207.

Newkirk, T. (2002). *Misreading masculinity: Boys, literacy, and popular culture*. Portsmouth, NH: Heinemann.

Pirie, B. (2002). *Teenage boys and high school English*. Portsmouth, NH: Boynton/Cook.

Roe, K. (1998). "Boys will be boys and girls will be girls": Changes in children's media use. *European Journal of Communication*, 23(1), 5–25.

Signorielli, N. (1997). A content Analysis: Reflections of girls in the media. Menlo Park, CA: Kaiser Family Foundation. Retrieved November 29, 2011 from http://www.kff.org/entmedia/loader.cfm?url=/commonspot/security/getfile.cfmandPageID=14517

Smith, L. J. (1994). A content analysis of gender differences in children's advertising. *Journal of Broadcasting & Electronic Media*, *38*(3), 323–37.

Smith, S. L. and Cook, C. A. (2008). *Gender stereotypes: An analysis of popular films and TV*. Research brief written for the Geena Davis Institute for Gender and Media. Los Angeles, CA.

Stern, S. R. (1999). Adolescent girls' expression on web home pages: Spirited, sombre and self-conscious sites. *Convergence: The Journal of Research into New Media Technologies*, *5*(4), 22–41.

Stern, S. T. (2007). *Instant identity: Adolescent girls and the world of instant messaging*. New York: Peter Lang.

Stokes, C. E. (2010). "Get on my level": How Black American adolescent girls construct identity and negotiate sexuality on the Internet. In S. R. Mazzarella (Ed.), *Girl wide web 2.0: Revisiting girls, the Internet, and the Negotiation of Identity*. New York: Peter Lang, pp. 45–67.

Thompson, T. L. and Zerbinos, E. (1995). Gender roles in animated cartoons: Has the picture changed in 20 years? *Sex Roles*, *32*(9/10), 651–73.

Van Damme, E. (2010). Gender and sexual scripts in popular US teen series: A study on the gendered discourses in *One Tree Hill* and *Gossip Girl*. *Catalan Journal of Communication and Cultural Studies*, *2*(1), 77–92.

Vickery, J. R. (2010). Blogrings as virtual communities for adolescent girls. In S. R. Mazzarella (Ed.), *Girl wide web 2.0: Revisiting girls, the Internet, and the Negotiation of Identity*. New York: Peter Lang, pp. 183–200.

Wannamaker, A. (2008). *Boys in children's literature and popular culture: Masculinity, abjection, and the fictional child*. New York: Routledge.

Wannamaker, A. (Ed.). (2011). *Mediated boyhoods: Boys, teens, and young men in popular media and culture*. New York: Peter Lang.

Weaver, K. (2005). Teenage girls and information communication technologies: A case study of nzgirl.co.nc and its members. *Australian Journal of Communication*, *32*(2), 95–107.

35

INTERNET MEDIA AND PEER SOCIABILITY

Gustavo Mesch

Online communication has become central in the social life of late childhood and adolescence. Such extensive use of online communication elicits mixed reactions among adults. Scholars and practitioners have expressed concern that online communication leads to shallow relationships, and risks of online solicitation and cyber-bullying. In contrast, it has also been argued that online communication provides opportunities for identity exploration, access to social support and information, and the opportunity to develop meaningful relationships. In this chapter, we address these issues, reviewing the central theoretical perspectives and recent research findings on the association between online communication and sociability.

The ability of the internet and cell phones to facilitate constant contact, especially with geographically remote individuals, has caught the popular imagination and the empirical attention of researchers studying the sociability of children and adolescents. Prior to the information age, the social choices of children and adolescents were severely restricted by time and place. Their lack of geographical mobility and their requirement to attend school reduced their social circle to friends they met in the neighborhood, at school and at extracurricular activities. Contact with peers was possible at specific times that usually overlapped school and extracurricular activities. However, new communication technologies support constant contact with peers and the formation of new and geographically dispersed contacts. Thus, the central themes that have dominated the research are the extent of the overlap of online and offline peers, the structure of social networks and the effects of online contacts on social involvement. This chapter will discuss these themes and the existing empirical evidence supporting them.

The overlap of online and offline social ties

Children and teens are frequent users of online communication. A study in the U.S. showed that 79 percent of youth ages 12 to 17 had sent messages to friends in the previous week using a social networking site, 69 percent had sent a text message, 56 percent had sent instant messages (IM) to friends, and 44 percent had sent e-mails (Pew Internet and American Life Project, 2009). In Europe, a study of 29 European countries found that 62 percent of children aged 9 to 16 use instant messaging, 11 percent write or read a weblog and 59 percent have a social networking profile (Livingstone et al., 2011). Online communication has become an integral part of the culture of children and youth. Its widespread diffusion is associated with the network effect, indicating that the extensive use of e-mail, instant messaging and social networking sites by teens is the result of its diffusion through social networks, generally face-to-face ones. There is also evidence that people who interact socially eventually use multiple types of communication channels concurrently. In other words, not only is the adoption of specific applications social in nature, but their use may also depend on the nature of existing social networks.

The extent of overlap of online and offline social ties is a central topic of investigation. Early studies were concerned that online ties did not overlap with offline ties, a fact that can have effects on adolescents' social involvement and security. The displacement-reduction hypothesis assumed that participation in online communication motivates children and adolescents to form superficial online relationships mainly with strangers that are less beneficial than their real world relationships (Valkenburg and Peter, 2009).

As children and adolescents have increasingly adopted online communication as a typical mode of everyday communication with their peers, studies have shown an increasing overlap between online and offline ties. For example, the report of the EU Kids Online study indicates that most children (87 percent) who communicate online are in touch with people they already know in person (Livingstone et al., 2011). In a study of emerging adolescents that compared the networks of "friends" in social networking sites, instant messaging and face-to-face, the results showed that there was a partial but substantial overlap between participants in online and offline networks. Half of the closest instant messaging friends' names were also listed as the closest face-to-face friends. Furthermore, 49 percent of respondents' face-to-face friends were also the top social networking site friends. The findings indicate that the offline and online worlds overlap substantially. At the same time, it is important to acknowledge that connectedness does not imply that online and offline connections are identical. Instead, it appears that when communicating online, adolescents may take advantage of online capabilities to communicate concerns and issues that are different from their face-to-face communication with peers (Subramayan et al., 2008).

Another study of adolescents (ages 16 to 19) used interactions in the public space of a social networking site (the "wall") as the unit of analysis and investigated whether the characteristics of online "friends" are similar to or different from the characteristics of young social networkers. The study found that on average only 54 percent of the interactions were with others who belonged to the same ethnic group, and 42 percent were with others of the same gender. While there is strong public concern that ill-intentioned adults will contact children, the results of this study indicate that most of the wall interactions were between individuals belonging to the same age category (74 percent of the interactions). Indeed, propinquity was high, as 89 percent of the interactions were with people from the same state (Mazur and Kozarian, 2011).

In contrast, a study that investigated the association between the strength of ties and type of communication channel among early adolescents in one school took a different approach. The study conducted in Belgium began with the individual's entire face-to-face network to investigate whether the strength of ties predicts the use of face-to-face and online communication. The study distinguished between three types of ties: "very close friend", "just a friend" and a "person I know". In line with previous studies, all media formats (face-to-face, SMS, phone calls, e-mail, IM) were used to maintain strong ties, making it possible for pupils to stay connected with their friends at times when face-to-face communication was not possible. Focusing on individual technologies, the study found that technologies differed in the functions they fulfilled. Texting was used for maintaining strong ties, and telephone calls were associated with close friendships and were used more within cliques. IM served a dual function as it helped to maintain close ties, but was also often used between less close friends (Van Cleemput, 2012). Thus, close friends are more likely to communicate through a variety of communication channels: face-to-face meetings, phone and cell phone conversations, and online communication (Haythornthwaite, 2002).

Online communication and relational closeness

The association between online communication and relational closeness is particularly interesting. Early studies argued that online communication is of lower quality than face-to-face communication and is not well suited to sustaining intimate relationships and conveying personal messages. A longitudinal American study of adolescents examined to what extent using the internet for different activities (visiting chat rooms, using IM, participating in online games) affected the quality of close adolescent relationships (i.e., best friendships and romantic relationships). The study found that the internet activity choice influenced the quality of the relationship later on. More specifically, using instant messenger was positively associated with most aspects of romantic relationships and relationships between best friends. In contrast, visiting chat rooms was negatively related to the quality of the relationship between best friends. Using the internet to play games and for general entertainment predicted a decline in the quality of the relationship between best friends and between romantic partners (Blais et al., 2008). These findings reflect the important and complex functions of online activity and virtual socialization for the development and maintenance of relationships in adolescence in the information age.

More recent studies have concluded that online communication may facilitate the development of intimacy and closeness. The internet attribute hypothesis suggests that certain characteristics of online communication may be conducive to self-disclosure and intimacy (Valkenburg and Peter, 2007). A study based on a large sample of Dutch adolescents aged 12 to 17 years investigated the extent to which online communication stimulated or reduced closeness to friends, and whether intimate disclosure of personal information online affected their closeness in online relationships. The authors found that adolescents perceived online communication as effective in disclosing personal information. Furthermore, online communication with others who were met online proved to have a negative effect on the perceived closeness to friends (Valkenburg and Peter, 2007). An Israeli study with a large representative sample of adolescents provides one possible explanation for the perception of less relational closeness of online ties – the length of communication. Online friends are acquainted for less time than face-to-face ones, so they are still at the phase of relationship development and are therefore perceived to be of lesser depth and breadth (Mesch and Talmud, 2006). Nevertheless, as time goes by, and as the topics of conversation expand from a small number of shared interests to a wide range of broader areas, the perceived connection is assumed to grow closer. A longitudinal study of Dutch adolescents provides an additional explanation of this phenomenon. Valkenburg and Peter (2009) found that the positive effect of online communication on relational quality could be explained by the tendency to increase intimate disclosures and personal information to close friends through this medium. In other words, the positive effects of online communication on closeness to peers might be associated with perceived attributes of the internet. Adolescents' perceptions about online anonymity and the ability to carefully edit messages encourages a lack of inhibition, which in turn increases their online disclosure of intimate and personal information to their peers. Thus, online disclosure enhanced the perception of high-quality relationships (Schouten et al., 2007; Valkenburg and Peter, 2009).

The content of the communications appears to be very important to perceived closeness to friends. A study on the effect of the use of social networking sites for self-esteem and well-being among adolescents found that the use of the friends' networking sites stimulated the number of relationships formed on the site, the frequency with which adolescents received feedback on their profiles and the tone of the feedback (positive or negative). Positive feedback to profiles was positively associated with well-being and self-esteem, while negative feedback diminished self-esteem and well-being (Valkenburg et al., 2006). Thus, online communication has a real effect on relational closeness, but this effect is dependent on self-disclosure, length of the relationship and the positive content of the communication.

Benefits of online communication

Young people conduct their social life both online and offline, and their overlap leads to perpetual communication with peers. When youngsters come home from school, they keep in touch with their school friends and remote friends through online communication. This continuous contact provides a sense of co-presence, of being together with others in a mediated environment – either remote or virtual. Conversations that started at school continue after school through mediated connections. Online communication is often used as an efficient channel to enable multiple social networks to coordinate face-to-face meetings. Short message service (SMS) is used for "micro-coordination", a concept that refers to the instrumental use of mobile phones and online communication to coordinate a meeting by allowing individuals to adjust and readjust the time and place of meeting in real time (Ling and Yttri, 2002). Thus, the most general benefit of being connected online is belonging to social groups and participating in their activities and exchanges. Therefore, we can conclude that adolescents lacking such access are disadvantaged in their ability to be involved in the social activities of their peer group.

At the same time, given the vast majority of young people who do have such access, the question of who benefits the most seems reasonable. One perspective argues that online communication replicates unequal social skills. The "rich-get-richer" hypothesis proposes that those who already have strong social skills and social networks benefit the most from the internet (Kraut et al., 2002). This approach assumes that existing social connections or competence may be an antecedent of frequency of use of online communication. It is reasonable to assume that teens with strong connections to school-based peers use online communication to seek out additional opportunities to interact with them. It is also reasonable to assume that online communication is more prevalent among peer group networks that are very active socially.

However, the social compensation hypothesis provides a different perspective. According to this view, online communication is more beneficial for socially anxious and isolated youth. Online communication may compensate for a lack of social network ties. In addition, socially anxious adolescents may feel more at an advantage in communicating intimate and personal experiences online (Bargh and McKenna, 2004).

Studies have examined introverts' attitudes to online communication, and the association between self-disclosure and the formation of online relationships. Introverts more strongly agreed that online modes of communication offer greater freedom of expression, and they were more likely than extroverts to choose online communication for their interactions with friends (Blais et al., 2008). Another study based on a large sample of Canadian youngsters who completed a survey in Grade 9 and then in Grade 12 found that socially anxious adolescents are more likely to rely on online communication and to report higher friendship quality (Desjarlais and Willoughby, 2010).

In contrast, the social diversification perspective focuses on ICT as a space of social interaction and its meaning for children and youth. This approach emphasizes the potential of ICT for empowering children and young adults as disadvantaged social groups. Unlike other social groups that are geographically more mobile and exposed to a more diverse focus of activity, adolescents lack geographic mobility and are limited to social relationships that involve individuals similar to them. According to this perspective, the internet might support the expansion of social relationships including access to information, knowledge and skills that are unavailable to teens restricted to certain residential areas (Mesch and Talmud, 2010). The internet is not only about communication with existing ties. Although it is true that many adolescents are using the internet as another channel of communication with existing acquaintances, the innovative aspect of the internet is to provide opportunities for activities that induce social interaction, a space for expansion and the diversification of social relationships (Mesch and Talmud, 2010). As Mazur and Kozarian (2011) found in their study of older adolescents, despite the partial overlap of online and offline ties, online communication tends to diversify the structure of peer networks and expose youngsters to others who share their interests regardless of their age, gender or location.

This approach has proven useful in the understanding of the use of online communication among adolescents belonging to socially disadvantaged groups. For example, a study that compared the use of ICT in Israel among Arabs and Jews found that Jewish adolescents living in a Western type of nuclear family and with an individualistic orientation tended to use communication technologies in a way that did not differ greatly from patterns observed in other Western societies. Their choice of using a cell phone, instant messaging or e-mail was dependent among other things on cost considerations. Network expansion was achieved by meeting new buddies online, but with the goal of moving on as fast as possible to cell phone and face-to-face meetings. By contrast, the Arab adolescents used cell phones to maintain local ties at times or in situations where face-to-face communication was not possible. In addition, their use of online communication reflected their living as a minority group in a traditional enclave surrounded by a Westernized Jewish majority. In such an environment, the adolescents used communication technologies to overcome the limitations of residential segregation, and to create ties that crossed gender lines and were not accepted in their collectivistic and traditional society. From their reports, ties with the opposite sex are apparently common, but are kept secret and tend to remain virtual to avoid breaking the rules of their society (Hijazi-Omari and Ribak, 2008; Mesch and Talmud, 2007).

Diversification is very likely to take place, but not at the expense of existing relationships. The use of technologies that require previous acquaintance, and even membership in the same social circle, can be used to coordinate group activities, continue conversations that started at school, express personal and intimate concerns, and provide social support. In that sense, these technologies can support the development of peer group cohesion and the formation of a sense of solidarity and togetherness. At the same time, online communication is used to reach out to strangers and their unique resources. The extent to which online communication is used to access resources not available in the peer group was at the center of a study of online practices of young adolescents in a large rural area in California. The study identified a group of adolescents that relied on the internet for information diversification. In planning their vocational future, these adolescents engaged in social capital-enhancing activities. Using online communication, they were able to communicate with adult professionals outside their personal and parents' social networks. Thus, the study found that online communication with strangers could be a capital-enhancing activity to access information on vocational and professional programs. This activity was of particular importance for adolescents (Robinson, 2011).

Online communication and cyber-bullying

Concomitant with increased use of the internet has been increased reporting on cyber-harassment, sexual solicitation and cyber-bullying (Patchin and Hinduja, 2006; Tokunaga, 2010). Online bullying is an overt, intentional act of aggression against another person; it is willful and repeated harm-doing, making rude or nasty comments about others online, spreading rumors, and distributing short video clips that are offensive or embarrassing to the victim (Rosen, 2007). The measurement of online harassment is still being developed, and the prevalence that various studies have reported differs according to the measure used. A recent large study of fourth to twelfth grade students in the US found that 15.8 percent had posted something online that was embarrassing or threatening, and 11.8 percent reported they had been bullied on the internet or cell phone. The percentage of victims was lower in elementary grades, but increased through middle school and high school (Children Online, 2011). A meta-analysis of 25 published studies concluded that the average percentage reported of children and youth who were bullied was around 20 percent (Tokunaga, 2010). While the prevalence of cyber-harassment and cyber-bullying is not high, it is nevertheless a type of aggression, and its consequences are amplified by the use of constant online communication.

By utilizing information and communication technologies, bullying enjoys the advantage of several characteristics of the medium that transform the essence of the phenomenon as we know it. First, online communication by its very nature might induce bullying behavior. Communication that lacks non-verbal cues, status symbols and proximity to the victim may lead to lack of inhibition and negative perceptions of others, resulting in an increase in online bullying. Second, offenders exploit the internet's relative anonymity through the use of screens or nicknames to hide their true identity. The perpetrators are often schoolmates, and the victim comes to regard the school as a hostile environment to be avoided by not attending classes. Third, the online environment provides a potentially large audience for the aggressive actions, a potential that might appeal to perpetrators, and provide them with positive feedback on their actions. Fourth, the large audience may amplify the negative effects of online bullying on the victim, as the harassment is being watched by all known acquaintances even beyond the school and neighborhood (Mishna et al., 2010).

For several reasons the effects of cyber-bullying might be more pronounced than those of traditional bullying. In traditional bullying the possibility exists of physical separation between the aggressor and the victim, but in cyber-bullying physical separation does not guarantee a cessation of acts such as sending text messages and e-mails to the victim. In addition, when aggressors engage in bullying using technology, they are not aware of the consequences of the aggression. The screen does not allow a view of the victim's emotional expression. Anonymity and the absence of interaction may make the aggressor still less inhibited and increase the frequency and power of cyber-bullying (Tokunaga, 2010).

Conclusion

Based on the evidence presented in this chapter, it is reasonable to conclude that online communication fosters offline links and provides children and adolescents with opportunities to maintain and expand their social ties to new connections. In line with the social diversification perspective, constraints of locale and age can be overcome through online communication, facilitating connections with ties that provide access to valuable resources of information on hobbies, specific interests and vocational prospects. In contrast to early perspectives such as the displacement-reduction hypothesis, online communication is rarely an escape from offline contexts; rather, durable online and offline ties are mutually embedded and reinforcing. The technological affordance of online relations, as well as the fact that online relational patterns are embedded in the general social structure, allows ICT to promote rather than undermine existing social contacts with friends from school, connecting adolescents into local, rather than global, networks. With the passage of time the online/offline comparison is becoming a faded and even false dichotomy. Many ties operate in both cyberspace and the physical realm. They do not exist only online – instead, adolescents use online contact to fill the spells between face-to-face meetings, and to coordinate joint activities and work. Computer-mediated communication supplements, arranges, and amplifies in-person and telephone communications rather than replaces them. The internet offers ease and flexibility regarding whom one communicates with, what medium to choose, when to communicate, and the communication's duration. In reality, online relationships often fill in empty spots in people's lives, a process deemed important especially where residential dispersal and dual careers reduce the availability of leisure and family time. Certainly these conclusions are temporary as internet research is still young. Given that the technology is constantly evolving, more studies should continue investigating the field.

SEE ALSO in this volume chapter by Ling and Bertel and chapter by Lim.

References

Bargh, J. and McKenna, K. (2004). The internet and social life. *Annual Review of Psychology, 55*(1), 573–90.

Blais, J. J., Craig, W. M., Pepler, D. and Connolly, J. (2008). Adolescents online: The importance of internet activity choices to salient relationships. *Journal of Youth & Adolescence, 37*(5), 522–36.

Children Online. (2011). *Research on the internet and cell phone behavior of students 2010–11.* Retrieved 07.03.12 at http://www.childrenonline.org

Desjarlais, M. and Willoughby, T. (2010). A longitudinal study of the relation between adolescent boys and girls' computer use with friends and friendship quality: Support for the social compensation or the rich-get-richer hypothesis? *Computers in Human Behavior, 26*(5), 896–905.

Haythornthwaite, C. (2002). Strong, weak, and latent ties and the impact of new media. *The Information Society, 18*(5), 385–402.

Hijazi-Omari, H. and Ribak, R. (2008). Playing with fire: On the domestication of the mobile phone among Palestinian teenage girls in Israel. *Information, Communication & Society, 11*(2), 149–66.

Kraut, R., Kiesler, S., Boneva, B., Cummings, J., Helgeson, V. and Crawford, A. (2002). Internet paradox revisited. *Journal of Social Issues, 58*(1), 49–74.

Ling, R. and Yttri, B. (2002). Hyper-coordination via mobile phones in Norway. In J. E. Katz and M. A. Aakhus (Eds), *Perpetual contact: Mobile communication, private talk, public performance.* Cambridge: Cambridge University Press, pp. 139–69.

Livingstone, S., Haddon, L., Görzig, A. and Ólafsson, K. (2011). *Risks and safety on the internet: The perspective of European children: Full findings.* LSE, London: EU Kids Online.

Mazur, E. and Kozarian, L. (2011). Self-presentation and interaction in blogs of adolescents and young emerging adults. *Journal of Adolescent Research, 25*(1), 124–44.

Mesch, G. S. and Talmud, I. (2006). The quality of online and offline relationships: The role of multiplexity and duration. *The Information Society, 22*(3), 137–48.

——(2007). Privacy and networking: Ethnic differences in the use of cell phones and IM in Israel. In James Katz (Ed.). *Mobile communication and social change in a global context,* Boston: MIT Press, pp. 313–35.

Mesch, G. and Talmud, I. (2010). *Wired youth: The social world of adolescence in the information age.* Oxford: Routledge.

Mishna, F., Cook, C., Gadalla, T., Daciuk, J. and Solomon, S. (2010). Cyberbullying behaviors among middle and high school students. *American Journal of Orthopsychiatry, 80*(3), 362–74.

Patchin, J. W. and Hinduja, S. (2006). Bullies move beyond the schoolyard: A preliminary look at cyberbullying. *Youth Violence and Juvenile Justice, 4*(2), 123–47.

Pew Internet and American Life Project (2009). Parent/teen cell phone survey 2009. 1615 L St., NW – Suite 700, Washington, D.C. 20036.

Robinson, L. (2011). Information-channel preferences and information-opportunity structures. *Information, Communication and Society, 14*(4), 472–94.

Rosen, L. D. (2007). *Me, MySpace and I: Parenting the net generation.* New York: Palgrave.

Schouten, A. P., Valkenburg, P. M. and Peter, J. (2007). Precursors and underlying processes of adolescents online self disclosure: Developing and testing an "internet attribute perception" model. *Media Psychology, 10*(2), 292–315.

Subramayan, K., Reich, S., Waechter, N. and Espinoza, G. (2008). Online and offline social networks: use of social networking sites by emerging adults. *Journal of Applied Developmental Psychology*, *29*(6), 420–33.

Tokunaga, R. (2010). Following you home from school: A critical review and synthesis of research on cyberbullying victimization. *Computers in Human Behavior*, *26*(2), 277–87.

Valkenburg, P. M., and Peter, J. (2007). Preadolescents' and adolescents' online communication and their closeness to friends. *Developmental Psychology*, *43*(2), 267–77.

Valkenburg, P. and Peter, J. (2009). Social consequences of the internet for adolescents: A decade of research. *Current Directions in Psychological Science*, *18*(1), 1–5.

Valkenburg, P. M., Peter, J. and Schouten, A. P. (2006). Friend networking sites and their relationship to adolescents' well-being and social self-esteem. *Cyber-Psychology and Behavior*, *9*(5), 584–90.

Van Cleemput, K. (2012). Friendship type, clique formation and the everyday use of communication technologies in a peer group. *Information, Communication and Society*, *15*(8), 1258–77.

PART IV

CONTEXTS AND COMMUNITIES

EDITOR'S INTRODUCTION

Children's media use is embedded in contexts and cannot be fully understood independent of them. Contexts comprise physical spaces, such as bedrooms, and social arrangements, such as families and peer groups. In addition, there are much larger social constructions of communities to be considered; for example, nationality, ethnicity, class, and immigrant status. Authors presented in this part of the handbook explore how various contexts in which children grow up and their media use and meaning are intertwined in complicated ways.

Amy I. Nathanson's chapter opens with a discussion of the most central and common of children's contexts – the family. She discusses trends in caregiver–child co-use patterns, media in family life, the effects of media on family interaction, and parental mediation. Special attention is devoted to the prominence of background television in the household and how it affects family dynamics and children's outcomes. Questions are raised about the possibility for new technologies to alter family hierarchies and a call is issued for continued research in this area.

Rivka Ribak's discussion of media and spaces explores the dynamics of the extended family context, as it reaches outside of the physical home, given that the control of spatiality is implicated in processes of maturation. Young people are defined by the spaces which they are allowed or not allowed to occupy. The media, in general, and mobile telephones, in particular, play a growing role in constructing these spaces. Ribak explores the ways in which mobile phones are used by parents and children to maintain and expand the distance between them, and how mobile phone use is involved in practices of being outside the home, on the city street, or in school. It suggests that studies vary to the extent that they interpret distance as a threat or as a challenge, and construct the mobile phone as a medium for control or sociality.

Siân Lincoln discusses a specific physical space within the family context – the child's bedroom. The concept of a "bedroom culture" first appeared in youth cultural discourses as a way to account for girls' invisibility in street-based youth cultures. Primarily located in the home, specifically in a bedroom, girls engage in bedroom culture through reading magazines and listening to music. This space is easily accessible and relatively unchallenging, so girls could also attend to their household responsibilities. In contemporary contexts of "risk," in which depictions of the dangerous streets prevail alongside the challenges of rapid development and accessibility of media technologies, the bedroom has taken on new significances for young people. Consequently, more recent studies of bedroom culture reveal a dynamic use whereby the media in particular enable young people to explore, display, and represent aspects of their rapidly changing lives in their bedrooms.

As children mature, peer culture gradually gains significant importance. **Sun Sun Lim**'s chapter suggests that when young people interact, they absorb the peer culture that underpins and sustains their relationships with each other. The ways in which young people integrate their media consumption into their peer culture is the focus of this chapter. Specifically, it examines how young people incorporate media content into their peer interactions and appropriate a variety of communication platforms to socialize with their peers, thus generating distinctive traits, norms, practices, codes, and shared identities that make up their unique peer culture(s). Lim covers three salient ways in which young people around the world today interact with one another: face-to-face, via the mobile phone, and over the internet's myriad communication channels. Thus, the chapter provides a closer examination of youth subcultures that are media-based and media-facilitated.

We turn here our attention to two specific groups of children characterized by an additional layer of identity-work. **Michelle M. Rivera** and **Angharad N. Valdivia** examine the role of media in the lives of minority children. Through a transnational lens, they explore the unique ways in which the hybrid identities of minority children complicate more rigid theoretical and conceptual frameworks of existing media research in this area. They pose relevant research questions relating to understudied areas of media and minority children, including the ways in which minority children negotiate media in their daily lives as both active audiences and creators of media. They also consider the complexities of minority identities for children in the current global moment and suggest expanding the minority category beyond a concentrated focus on racial and ethnic identity.

A complementary perspective is offered by **Nelly Elias** in her discussion of media and immigrant children. She describes these children's struggle with integration into a new socio-cultural environment, as well as bonding with their diasporic communities and the conflicting demands entailed by bridging between different cultures. As such, she proposes, media are highly significant in their integration process and their hybrid identity construction, as they enable these youngsters to connect to their original culture and at the same time to learn the norms and values of their host society. Accordingly, this chapter examines media uses of immigrant youth vis-à-vis their parents' attempts to maintain some cultural continuity and family cohesion, and highlights the role of three major media identified in the research literature: television, internet, and books.

The last three chapters in this section focus on the active role children and youth have, or can have, in the media environment. **JoEllen Fisherkeller**'s chapter provides an overview accompanied by case study illustrations of young people creating media on their own while involved in projects in different parts of the world. Young people's media production is dependent on a variety of circumstances and situations, including: motivations and intentions, competencies, available resources, and social support. Because of the diversity of young people in any locale and the diversity of socio-cultural contexts within which they live, there is a tremendous amount of diversity in why, what, and how young people produce media. Likewise, the roles that adults play, directly or indirectly, in young people's productions of media are diverse.

A more specific case of civic engagement by youth via the media is the focus of the chapter by **Tao Papaioannou**. She reviews current research exploring the role of web 2.0 technologies in facilitating civic interests and expression among youth. She too suggests that some research indicates that the characterization of youth as being uninterested in public life may be inaccurate as it does not recognize the ways in which youth incorporate civic interests and media content into their everyday lives. In view of participation opportunities that new media offer and ways in which young people are utilizing online tools, important questions are emerging about whether and how youth use digital technologies to contribute to the public sphere online and strategies that can be developed to promote online participation among youth.

Finally, **Jean Stuart** and **Claudia Mitchell** tackle the topic of media and social change. This chapter considers ways in which children and young people are contributing to official dialogue around issues of concern to their everyday lives. There is growing consensus among those involved in social programming that programs are doomed to failure unless young people are given a more significant voice in participating in policy dialogue about their own well-being. Ways of addressing the critical issue of the participation of children and young people include use of visual and other arts-based methodologies such as photovoice, participatory video, drawing and map making, and digital storytelling, as tools and methods of both research and engagement. They argue that such participatory visual approaches extend beyond simple interventions, in that they yield collections of visual data in the form of photos, videos, and digital stories that can be employed by both youth communities and researchers in documenting and studying their involvement in addressing various social issues.

36

MEDIA AND THE FAMILY CONTEXT

Amy I. Nathanson

The family exerts a tremendous influence on children's media use, shaping their consumption patterns, attitudes toward the media, and vulnerability from exposure. Likewise, the media can shape family life, including the physical location of family members in the household and the quality of exchanges that occur within the family unit (Lee and Chae, 2007; Pasquier, 2001; Pempek et al., 2011; Rideout et al., 2010). The purpose of this essay is to consider the relation between children's media use and the surrounding family context.

Family co-use of media

The ways in which mass media are consumed within the family context have shifted in some ways. Children are using a variety of media more (Rideout et al., 2010), with some youngsters, such as Korean youth, reporting that the internet is more important than television (Lee and Chae, 2007). Rideout et al. (2010) found significant increases between 1999 and 2009 in the percentage of 8–18-year-olds in the U.S. who had televisions, DVD players, computers, and internet access in their bedrooms. Some parents report that a primary reason for installing a television in their young child's bedroom is to allow multiple family members to watch their own shows at the same time (Rideout and Hamel, 2006), suggesting that television use has become more of an individual activity rather than a way of spending time together as a family. The trend toward increasing media use in the bedroom may not hold in all Western countries, however, as Dutch children are significantly less likely than British children to have media devices in their bedrooms (van der Voort et al., 1998). In addition, children and adolescents are increasingly using "personal media" such as cell phones, iPods/MP3 players, and laptop computers (Rideout et al., 2010).

From another perspective, things are still very much the same as they have been. Television remains the dominant medium that children both use (Rideout et al., 2010) and share with family members (Rideout and Hamel, 2006). Although television can be a solitary activity, the majority of U.S. parents report that when children of all ages watch television they do so with someone else (Rideout et al., 2003), including the parent (Gentile and Walsh, 2002). In a cross-cultural survey, Pasquier (2001) also found that the majority of European children report watching television with a family member. In addition, the content that is co-viewed remains a mix of adult-directed (Rideout and Hamel, 2006) and child-directed content (Mendelsohn et al., 2008). Sharing media can be a bonding experience between parents and adolescents (Coyne et al., 2011; Rideout and

Hamel, 2006). As children mature, co-using media tends to decrease in frequency as children gain more independence (Sang et al., 1992).

Research on the effects of co-use on children is sparse and relatively dated. From the work that has been done, we know that the effects of co-use on children are mixed and dependent on the type of material that is shared. In the case of educational television, coviewing has a beneficial effect by increasing children's learning (Reiser et al., 1984; Salomon, 1977). Perhaps the presence of an adult communicates to children that the content is important, thereby resulting in increased levels of attention. This could explain why coviewing of violent material is related to aggression (Nathanson, 1999) and coviewing of general television is related to endorsement of stereotypical sex roles (Rothschild and Morgan, 1987). In addition, coviewing educational material with infants can lead to more and better parent–child interaction (Pempek et al., 2011).

Although there is not much work on sibling coviewing, it appears that it may operate differently. Sibling coviewing does not increase comprehension of the shared material (Haefner and Wartella, 1987), but elevates enjoyment levels and positive feelings (Wilson and Weiss, 1993). It is unclear how this emotional effect might shape children's learning from the coviewed material. More work is needed to understand how the presence of siblings shapes children's co-use of media.

Media in family life

Background television

Scholars in the U.S. have become increasingly interested in the concept of "background television" and its effects on infants and toddlers. The definition of background television is unclear as scholars have yet to define its distinguishing characteristics. It is most often measured by asking parents how often the television is left on regardless of whether anyone is watching it or not. However, background television has also been defined according to the relationship between the content and the viewers available in the household. From this perspective, background television is identified when children are present while adult-directed content is on. "Foreground television," then, is child-directed content that is available when child viewers are present. Future work should consider the conceptual boundaries of the background television concept so that scholars investigating this topic can operate from a common understanding.

Surveys have shown that background television is quite common in the U.S., with sizeable percentages of parents reporting that the television is on for half or most of the day regardless of whether someone is attending to it or not (Masur and Flynn, 2008; Rideout and Hamel, 2006). Television is also regularly left on during family meal times (Gentile and Walsh, 2002; Roberts et al., 1999); however, it is unclear whether this exposure is due to background television or intentional viewing.

The likelihood of living in a household with prevalent background television exposure depends on a number of factors whose influence varies according to the age of the children in the household. According to Rideout and Hamel (2006), young children are more likely to be exposed to background television if their parents believe that educational television is very important. Parents who report relying on television as a babysitter to their infants or preschoolers are also more likely to keep the television on regardless of whether anyone is watching. The sheer availability of televisions in the household, including in the child's bedroom, is also important, especially among preschoolers and early school-age children. Finally, certain demographic factors contribute to households with high background television use, such as being in single-parent-led households, having just one child, and having less income.

Scholars have become increasingly concerned about the effects of the near-constant presence of television on infants and toddlers. Background television may be especially distracting since it contains language and sound effects that may be difficult for young children to ignore (Goodrich et al., 2009).

Mothers report that television is often on while their infants or young children are playing in the room (Masur and Flynn, 2008), leading some scholars to explore the effects of background television on young children's play behavior. Schmidt et al. (2008) examined solitary play among infants and toddlers in the presence of adult-directed television. They found that children played for a shorter amount of time and used a less sophisticated form of play when background television was on compared to when it was off.

Other work has found a relationship between background television and lower reading ability among young children (Vandewater et al., 2005). Vandewater et al. (2005) found that parents in "heavy-television households" in which the television is on always or most of the time read to their children less than parents in other household types, while Rideout et al. (2003) found that children in these households also played outside less than other children. Perhaps the constant presence of television limits opportunities for other types of entertainment and learning.

Background television also alters the quantity and quality of interactions between children and their caregivers (Mendelsohn et al., 2008; Stoneman and Brody, 1983). Kirkorian et al. (2009) observed parents with their infants or toddlers while they interacted either in the presence of adult-directed television or without any television on. They found that when the television was on, parents were less likely to interact with their youngsters. In addition, when parents did interact in the presence of background television, they were passive and relatively inattentive to their children.

Television as a babysitter

Many parents report using child-directed television to occupy or entertain their child so the parents may get a break or accomplish other tasks in the house. Rideout et al. (2003) found that almost half of U.S. parents who participated in a survey based on a nationally representative random sample reported that they are likely to sit their young child in front of the television when they have something important that they need to do.

Research has found that infants and young children who spend more time with television, and especially non-educational television, experience many undesirable outcomes, including lower verbal intelligence (Tomopoulos et al., 2010; Zimmerman and Christakis, 2005) and poor executive function (Barr et al., 2010), although some of these findings are inconsistent. However, content is important, as young children who view educational, age-appropriate television can experience boosts in language development and learning (Linebarger and Vaala, 2010; Linebarger and Walker, 2005; Vandewater, 2011).

Research has not explicitly considered what it means for parents to use television as a babysitter. Perhaps parents who rely on television as a babysitter come to regard television as a superior information and entertainment source for their children. As a result, the question becomes whether using television in a babysitter-like way could alter parents' attitudes toward the medium's value. Parents may inflate their opinions of television in an effort to prevent cognitive dissonance. That is, in order to maintain consistency in their behaviors and attitudes, parents may convince themselves that the television they regularly place their children before provides excellent learning and entertainment opportunities, perhaps even better than other options. We already know that parents with few rules surrounding children's television viewing have positive attitudes toward television (Nathanson, 2001); as a result, the question becomes whether relying on television causes changes in parents' attitudes.

Effects of media on family interaction

Media have the potential to bring families closer together as they provide opportunities for shared experiences and mutually experienced positive affect. Despite this potential, it appears that media mostly diminish family interaction when members are in the same room or instigate family members to separate from each other to enjoy media independently and in isolation (Livingstone, 2007), often as part of a "bedroom culture" (Bovill and Livingstone, 2001).

Several scholars have speculated that educational material may encourage parents to interact with their children and thereby enhance the learning potential of this type of exposure (Kirkorian et al., 2009). The reasoning behind this hypothesis is that parents will respond to educational television by asking their children questions about the material and reinforcing the messages conveyed. In fact, some technologies have been developed, such as the "Mommy bar," to provide explicit prompts for coviewing caregivers to engage their children at critical points in the program (Fisch et al., 2008).

However, there is evidence that even foreground television nearly silences coviewing parents compared with other activities. Nathanson and Rasmussen (2011) observed mothers and their toddlers or preschoolers while they either watched a prosocial, age-appropriate television program, played with toys, or read books together. They found that mothers who viewed television made significantly fewer comments to their children than mothers who either read books (above and beyond the words they read) or played with toys. In addition, television produced the lowest quality of communication between the dyads.

As noted earlier, video games are often cited as a source of positive caregiver–child interaction, especially between fathers and sons (Rideout and Hamel, 2006). Likewise, family-oriented game systems that permit multiple players to participate in fun, non-violent competitions, such as the Wii system, are often purchased for the purpose of providing entertainment for the entire family. Although there has not been much research on the effects of these technologies on family interaction, there is evidence that game systems tend to be used individually or among friends in both the U.S. (Kaiser Family Foundation, 2002) and in Europe (Pasquier, 2001), even though game systems are often placed in public spaces (Aarsand and Aronnson, 2009). Caregiver–child co-playing is a relatively rare phenomenon, despite the reports that parents believe that video games can bring them closer to their children.

One technology that not only has the potential to promote increased caregiver–child interaction but also does appear to facilitate this connection is mobile phones. Both parents and adolescents report that they use cell phones to stay connected to one another (Blair and Fletcher, 2011). This technology also gives both parents and adolescents a sense of control in regulating interactions.

Parental mediation

Thus far, I have described the mostly unintentional consequences of using mass media within a family context. In this final section, I describe "parental mediation," or the more intentional efforts performed by caregivers to mitigate, regulate, or generally shape the way that children use and respond to media.

Active mediation

The most heavily studied dimension of parental mediation is active mediation which refers to parents' communication with children about media. Active mediation has been linked with many positive effects among children and adolescents, including decreased aggression, better school performance, and better critical viewing skills (Nathanson, 2001). In laboratory settings, children who hear adults provide active mediation while they are viewing television learn more from educational television in both the U.S. and the Netherlands (Reiser et al., 1984; Valkenburg et al., 1998), express more acceptance of non-traditional sex roles (Corder-Bolz, 1980; Nathanson et al., 2002), and report less approval of aggressive characters and have fewer aggressive feelings (Corder-Bolz, 1980; Nathanson and Cantor, 2000) than children who view without active mediation.

Developmental differences are important to consider, as younger and older children process and respond to adult mediation in unique ways. Nathanson and Yang (2003) found that asking older elementary-school-aged children questions while viewing an aggressive program was the most effective method for promoting their critical viewing. However, younger elementary-school-aged children benefited more from the straightforward statements compared with the questions.

Newer technologies, because many of them are used in isolation or at least away from the family setting, may be difficult for parents to mediate (Livingstone, 2007; Livingstone and Helsper, 2008). Moreover, the traditional conceptualization of parental mediation may not easily apply to some new technologies, such as the internet (Livingstone and Helsper, 2008). In fact, mediation practices that typically work for television, like active mediation, do not appear to reduce vulnerability to online internet risks among adolescents in the U.K. and the U.S. (Livingstone and Helsper, 2008; Mesch, 2009).

Restrictive mediation

The second dimension of parental mediation is restrictive mediation which refers to the rules parents set and enforce regarding children's media consumption. Parents are more likely to have rules for media use than they are to use active mediation (Nathanson, 2001). This may be because instituting rules can be done relatively quickly and does not require parents to co-use the media or otherwise be knowledgeable about the content that the child is viewing.

The biggest effect of restrictive mediation is reducing children's media exposure (Nathanson, 2001). As a result, any other positive effects that are observed in conjunction with restrictive mediation must be considered in light of the reduced exposure. Research has found that children and adolescents whose parents have media-use rules are less aggressive, endorse fewer sex stereotypes (Rothschild and Morgan, 1987), get better grades in school, and are better able to understand television plots compared with other children (Desmond et al., 1985).

Restrictive mediation may exert an influence in other ways beyond simply reducing media exposure. Nathanson (1999) found that children whose parents restricted their violent television exposure were less likely to believe that such content was important and worthy of their attention. As a result, parents who institute viewing rules may socialize their children into beneficial attitudes toward media that may reduce the children's vulnerability to the material. In addition, the presence of rules may communicate parental interest and involvement. The positive feelings that children have from knowing their parents are involved may also serve as a protective factor during media exposure.

However, rules can backfire, especially as children mature and enter adolescence. There is evidence that adolescents whose parents have strict media-use rules seek out the restricted content more outside of the household (Shin and Hu, 2011) and are more aggressive in general (Nathanson, 2002). These adolescents also report a weaker parent–adolescent bond (Nathanson, 2002). Even younger children may rebel against rules if they are too strict.

Parents' regulation of the internet has become increasingly interesting to scholars. Parents report mixed feelings when it comes to their children's internet use, both noting its educational and social benefits and expressing concern over the content their children may encounter (Livingstone, 2007). Parents may use filters to regulate content, check their children's viewing histories, or place the computer in a common area within the house so that the parent can observe the child's activities (Livingstone, 2007; Mesch, 2009). Pasquier (2001) found that European parents are least likely to restrict computer use, compared with other media.

Conclusion

When we consider the relationship between children and the media, it is important to place this association within the broader family context. Even if children consume media alone, their family continues to shape their interpretation and responses to the content they use. Family dynamics can shape children's vulnerability to the media and, likewise, media use can influence family dynamics. These issues should be explored and, because most of our knowledge is based on American samples, continued work outside of the U.S. would be very beneficial.

As newer technologies continue to become adopted into families, future work should explore whether and how these media shape family dynamics, including the power dynamics between parents and children. Could it be that technology-savvy adolescents attain greater power in media-rich households? Continued research in this area will help us answer these questions.

SEE ALSO in this volume chapter by Ribak, chapter by Lincoln, and chapter by Elias.

References

Aarsand, P. A. and Aronnson, K. (2009). Gaming and territorial negotiations in family life. *Childhood – A Global Journal of Child Research, 16*(4), 497–517.

Barr, R., Lauricella, A., Zack, E. and Calvert, S. L. (2010). Infant and early childhood exposure to adult-direct and child-direct television programming. *Merrill Palmer Quarterly: Journal of Developmental Psychology, 56*(1), 21–48.

Blair, B. L. and Fletcher, A. C. (2011). "The only 13-year-old on planet Earth without a cell phone": Meanings of cell phones in early adolescents' everyday lives. *Journal of Adolescent Research, 26*(2), 155–77.

Bovill, M. and Livingstone, S. (2001). Bedroom culture and the privatization of media use. In S. Livingstone and M. Bovill (Eds), *Children and Their Changing Media Environment*. Mahwah, NJ: Lawrence Erlbaum Associates, pp. 179–200.

Corder-Bolz, C. R. (1980). Mediation: The role of significant others. *Journal of Communication, 30*(3), 106–18.

Coyne, S. M., Padilla-Walker, L. M., Stockdale, L. and Day, R. D. (2011). Game on … girls: Associations between co-playing video games and adolescent behavioral and family outcomes. *Journal of Adolescent Health, 49*(2), 160–65.

Desmond, R. J., Singer, J. L., Singer, D. G., Calam, R. and Colimore, K. (1985). Family mediation patterns and television viewing: Young children's use and grasp of the medium. *Human Communication Research, 11*(4), 461–80.

Fisch, S. M., Ackerman, A., Morgenlander, M., McCann Brown, S. K., Fisch, S. R. D., Schwartz, B. B. et al. (2008). Coviewing preschool television in the US: Eliciting parent-child interaction via onscreen prompts. *Journal of Children and Media, 2*(2), 163–73.

Gentile, D. A. and Walsh, D. A. (2002). A normative study of family media habits. *Applied Developmental Psychology, 23*(2), 157–78.

Goodrich, S. A., Pempek, T. A. and Calvert, S. L. (2009). Formal production features of infant and toddler DVDs. *Archives of Pediatrics and Adolescent Medicine, 163*(12), 1151–56.

Haefner, M. J. and Wartella, E. A. (1987). Effects of sibling coviewing on children's interpretations of television programs. *Journal of Broadcasting & Electronic Media, 31*(2), 153–68.

Kaiser Family Foundation (2002). *Key facts: Children and video games.* Menlo Park, CA: The Henry J. Kaiser Family Foundation.

Kirkorian, H. L., Pempek, T. A., Murphy, L. A., Schmidt, M. E. and Anderson, D. R. (2009). The impact of background television on parent-child interaction. *Child Development, 80*(5), 1350–59.

Lee, S. J. and Chae, Y. G. (2007). Children's Internet use in a family context: Influence on family relationships and parental mediation. *CyberPsychology & Behavior*, *10*(5), 640–44.

Linebarger, D. L. and Walker, D. (2005). Infants' and toddlers' television viewing and language outcomes. *American Behavioral Scientist*, *48*(5), 624–45.

Linebarger, D. L. and Vaala, S. E. (2010). Screen media and language development in infants and toddlers: An ecological perspective. *Developmental Review*, *30*(2), 176–202.

Livingstone, S. (2007). Strategies of parental regulation in the media-rich home. *Computers in Human Behavior*, *23*(2), 920–41.

Livingstone, S. and Helsper, E. J. (2008). Parental mediation of children's internet use. *Journal of Broadcasting & Electronic Media*, *52*(4), 581–99.

Masur, E. F. and Flynn, V. (2008). Infant and mother-infant play and the presence of the television. *Journal of Applied Developmental Psychology*, *29*(1), 76–83.

Mendelsohn, A. L., Berkule, S. B., Tomopoulos, S., Tamis-LeMonda, S., Haberman, H. S., Alvir, J. and Dreyer, B. P. (2008). Infant television and video exposure associated with limited parent–child verbal interactions in low socioeconomic status households. *Archives of Pediatric and Adolescent Medicine*, *162*(5), 411–17.

Mesch, G. S. (2009). Parental mediation, online activities, and cyberbullying. *CyberPsychology and Behavior*, *12*(4), 387–93.

Nathanson, A. I. (1999). Identifying and explaining the relationship between parental mediation and children's aggression. *Communication Research*, *26*(2), 124–43.

——(2001). Mediation of children's television viewing: Working toward conceptual clarity and common understanding. In W. B. Gudykunst (Ed.), *Communication Yearbook 25*. Mahwah, NJ: Lawrence Erlbaum Associates, pp. 115–51.

——(2002). The unintended effects of parental mediation of television on adolescents. *Media Psychology*, *4*(3), 207–30.

Nathanson, A. I. and Cantor, J. (2000). Reducing the aggression-promoting effect of violent cartoons by increasing children's fictional involvement with the victim: A study of active mediation. *Journal of Broadcasting & Electronic Media*, *44*(1), 125–32.

Nathanson, A. I. and Yang, M-S. (2003). The effect of mediation content and form on children's responses to violent television. *Human Communication Research*, *29*(1), 111–34.

Nathanson, A. I. and Rasmussen, E. E. (2011). TV-viewing compared to book-reading and toy-playing reduces responsive maternal communication with toddlers and preschoolers. *Human Communication Research*, *37*(4), 465–87.

Nathanson, A. I., Wilson, B. J., McGee, J. and Sebastian, M. (2002). Counteracting the effects of female stereotypes on television via active mediation. *Journal of Communication*, *52*(4), 922–37.

Pasquier, D. (2001). Media at home: Domestic interactions and regulation. In S. Livingstone and M. Bovill (Eds), *Children and Their Changing Media Environment*. Mahwah, NJ: Lawrence Erlbaum Associates, pp. 161–77.

Pempek, T. A., Demers, L. B., Hanson, K. G., Kirkorian, H. L. and Anderson, D. R. (2011). The impact of infant-directed videos on parent-child interaction. *Journal of Applied Developmental Psychology*, *32*(1), 10–19.

Reiser, R. A., Tessmer, M. A. and Phelps, P. C. (1984). Adult-child interaction in children's learning from *Sesame Street*. *Educational Communication and Technology Journal*, *32*(4), 217–23.

Rideout V. and Hamel, E. (2006). *The media family: Electronic media in the lives of infants, toddlers, preschoolers and their parents*. Menlo Park, CA: Henry J. Kaiser Family Foundation.

Rideout, V. J., Vandewater, E. A. and Wartella, E. A. (2003). *Zero to six: Electronic media in the lives of infants, toddlers, and preschoolers*. Menlo Park, CA: The Henry J. Kaiser Family Foundation.

Rideout, V. J., Foehr, U. G. and Roberts, D. F. (2010). *Generation M2: Media in the lives of 8-to 18-year-olds*. Menlo Park, CA: The Henry J. Kaiser Family Foundation.

Roberts, D. F., Foehr, U. G., Rideout, V. J. and Brodie, M. (1999). *Kids & the media @ the new millennium*. Menlo Park, CA: The Henry J. Kaiser Family Foundation.

Rothschild, N. and Morgan, M. (1987). Cohesion and control: Adolescents' relationships with parents as mediators of television. *Journal of Early Adolescence*, *7*(3), 299–314.

Salomon, G. (1977). Effects of encouraging Israeli mothers to co-observe *Sesame Street* with their five-year-olds. *Child Development*, *48*(3), 1146–51.

Sang, F., Schmitz, B. and Tasche, K. (1992). Individuation and television coviewing in the family: Developmental trends in the viewing behavior of adolescents. *Journal of Broadcasting & Electronic Media*, *36*(4), 427–41.

Schmidt, M. K., Pempek, T. A., Kirkorian, H. L., Lund, A. F. and Anderson, D. R. (2008). The impact of background television on the toy play behavior of very young children. *Child Development*, *79*(4), 1137–51.

Shin, W. and Hu, J. (2011). Parental mediation of teenagers' video game playing: Antecedents and consequents. *New Media & Society*, *13*(6), 945–62.

Stoneman, Z. and Brody, G. H. (1983). Family interactions during three programs: Contextualist observations. *Journal of Family Issues*, *4*(2), 349–65.

Tomopoulos, S., Dreyer, B. P., Berkule, S., Fierman, A. H., Brockmeyer, C. and Mendelsohn, A. L. (2010). Infant media exposure and toddler development. *Archives of Pediatrics & Adolescent Medicine*, *164*(12), 1105–11.

Valkenburg, P. M., Krcmar, M. and de Roos, S. (1998). The impact of a cultural children's program and adult mediation on children's knowledge of and attitudes toward opera. *Journal of Broadcasting & Electronic Media*, *42*(3), 315–26.

van der Voort, T. H. A., Beentjes, J. W. J., Bovill, M., Gaskell, G., Koolstra, G. M., Livingstone, S. and Marseille, N. (1998). Young people's ownership and uses of new and old forms of media in Britain and the Netherlands. *European Journal of Communication*, *13*(4), 457–77.

Vandewater, E. A. (2011). Infant word learning from commercially available video in the US. *Journal of Children and Media*, *5*(3), 248–66.

Vandewater, E. A., Bickham, D. S., Lee, J. H., Cummings, H. M., Wartella, E. A. and Rideout, V. J. (2005). When the television is always on: Heavy television exposure and young children's development. *American Behavioral Scientist*, *48*(5), 562–77.

Wilson, B. J. and Weiss, A. J. (1993). The effects of sibling coviewing on preschoolers' reactions to a suspenseful movie scene. *Communication Research*, *20*(2), 214–48.

Zimmerman, F. J. and Christakis, D. A. (2005). Children's television viewing and cognitive outcomes: A longitudinal analysis of national data. *Archives of Pediatric and Adolescent Medicine*, *159*(7), 619–25.

37

MEDIA AND SPACES

The mobile phone in the geographies of young people

Rivka Ribak

Studies of children and media rarely foreground space (but see Holloway and Valentine, 2000a, 2000b; Ito and Okabe, 2001). Space, however, is where communication takes place, and it is implicated in the process of maturation. To a large extent, young people are defined by the spaces they are allowed or not allowed to occupy, whether because they are constructed as a threat or as threatened by others, or because their movement is restricted as long as they depend on their parents for transportation and economic support (Holloway and Valentine, 2000a, 2000b; James et al., 1998; Livingstone, 2002). Thus issues relating to youths' spatial practices and experiences are inherent in their perception of self and in adults' understanding of their predicament. As Doreen Massey noted, "the control of spatiality is part of the process of defining the social category of 'youth' itself" (1998, p. 127).

The notion of domestication (Silverstone et al., 1992) offers a spatial lens for considering media adoption and use within households. Specifically, it asks how communication technologies are appropriated by family members, how they are placed in domestic spaces and incorporated into members' rhythms, and how use becomes valuable in their social relations; importantly, it also highlights the doubly articulated nature of media, which have both material and symbolic dimensions. Developed in the heyday of television, the notion of domestication invites us, in an age of mobile and ubiquitous media, to complement the study of children's bedroom and living room media use with a study of the *outside* – the street, the school, the shopping mall (see e.g., Thomas, 2005; Wakeford, 2003). This paper, then, adopts the framework of domestication to explore young people's media use outside the home, and reflect upon the ways in which their use of mobile technologies complicates the relationships between intimacy and distance, mobility and maturation, medium and content.

Young people have been early and keen adopters of mobile media (notably the Walkman, see du Gay et al., 1997), receiving or purchasing devices and using them in both conventional and innovative ways. Personal, location-based technologies, in particular, can be seen as metaphors for, and actual tools of maturation, separation and individuation – as well as control and surveillance (Green, 2001; Ribak, 2009). Already in 1998, Gillard et al. (1998) documented the transition to cordless telephones among young Australians. This new device, they noted, enabled teens to evade their parents' eavesdropping by taking the receiver to their bedroom or to the veranda: "I am not allowed ... because they don't want the neighbors hearing what I talk about 'cause apparently it's embarrassing" (p. 142). The quintessential scenario depicted in this account is prescient in that it explores the spatial ramifications of young people's use of what seems today a rather limited form of mobile telephony, and introduces the protagonists of the studies this paper will discuss: (estranged) teens, their (intimate) friends and the (liberating) telephone vis-à-vis (nosy) parents, against the backdrop of the (bourgeois) family home, the corridor with the landline telephone base, and the porch with its outdoor air and its elusive promise of privacy.

This discussion will suggest that space is interpreted in research on young people's media use outside the home in two distinctive yet complementary ways: When the home is a metaphor of safety and connection, the distance from it is a void that needs to be overcome. In this context, the mobile phone may be likened to a bridge over troubled water. Alternatively, when the home is a place of oppression and control, the street becomes a meaningful site of teen creativity, sociality and liberation. Here, the mobile phone is a means for the intense experience of particular places; it allows young people to stay out farther and longer, to express themselves, to locate their friends, to individuate and to grow.

Potential space

Donald Winnicott coined the term "potential space" when referring to the growing ability of children to move away from their mothers. For Winnicott (1965; 1971), this ability originated in "the child's first creation" – the object which the child selected and invested with meaning, which stands for the mother and is transitional in this sense. Gradually children recognize and allow others into this "potential space" – the distance that is tolerated or desired between them and their parents which is, in metaphor and in practice, the meeting place of the social and the individual, a site of cultural production and meaning making (Ribak, 2009; Silverstone, 1993). How do teens and their parents use the mobile phone in the context of such potential spaces?

> I have a 17-year-old, and the worst thing I know is when she goes downtown. I am so afraid, but I have to accept this, you know. But it helps that she has a mobile telephone because she can call if something happens. It is not to control my daughter that she should take her mobile telephone when she goes out, but it is, ahh, [for her safety?] "If something happens, call home and we'll come immediately!" you know. Because she needs to go out and experience Oslo. She has to learn about the world.
>
> *(Ling, 2004, p. 100)*

Teenagers' parents are torn between their responsibility for what they perceive as their children's safety and the cultural requirement that they separate and allow them to become independent individuals. For Rich Ling's (2004) Norwegian interviewees, the mobile phone provides a means for negotiating these seemingly conflicting demands. Like a discrete "umbilical cord," the phone enables parents to let their children go out *and* be safe. And, on a more practical level, it allows for short-term, on-the-move micro-coordination of transportation logistics (Ling and Yttri, 2002). Offering greater availability and flexibility to their children, parents with mobile phone connection can redirect trips that have already started; they can "soften" time by letting their kids know when they will be late or early; they can progressively set the exact meeting place; and, if they miss one another, they can reschedule and relocate their meeting point.

Letting go, however, is not a universal requirement. Thus Margaret Nelson (2010) found that American professional middle class parents effectively and emotionally do not let their kids go, but rather seek intimacy and prolonged connection. The privileged parents she interviewed reject tracking technologies that would allow them to locate their kids, because they *know* where their kids are and they trust them – and if they do not, they read their messages and journals: "Text messaging, I'm definitely reading them. She knows I am" (p. 125). As opposed to middle and working class parents, among privileged parents the notion of safety expands to cover a wide spectrum of situations – such as being "hit on" by a boy at a party – which are thereby defined as emergencies and require immediate responsiveness. Within this parent–child intimacy, the mobile phone is deployed by both parties to negotiate family rules and practices (see also Henderson et al., 2002; Ling and Yttri, 2002):

> I wanted her to go because I wanted her to be exposed, and I wanted her to be comfortable – everyone probably smokes pot and drinks at some point – and not to be freaked out. She was going to go, and then at the last minute – I'm probably a bad mother – I said, "I'm lonely, come home." And she came home. She was ambivalent.
>
> *(Nelson, 2010, p. 124)*

Nelson observes that the child does not know what the final decision will be, but must "remain in constant contact and participate in constant discussion" (2010, p. 169). In her account, the privileged child's world is made up of unexpected and unanticipated shifts, whereas in working and middle class families there is greater clarity about rules and about the ways in which technologies may be used in order to keep them.

Studies that focus on teens rather than their parents offer a mixed picture. Certainly teens feel that the mobile phone allows them to become less dependent on their parents: they are not required to tell them in advance where they plan to go, they can stay out farther and longer, and they may manipulate the conversation so as to calm their parents regardless of their actual whereabouts (Henderson et al., 2002; Ling, 2004). All three practices suggest that the mobile phone is important as an object that provides the potential for conversation, rather than for the actual conversations that are conducted through it (Ribak, 2009). In other words, parents – and teens – can tolerate distance because they know they *can* call, rather than because they *do* call. This may explain, in turn, why violations of this implicit understanding are resisted while compliance is valued and reciprocated. Whereas parents who intrude on their children are filtered, lied to etc. (Campbell, 2006), parents who text are more likely to be texted back (Oksman and Turtiainen, 2004), and parents who avoid calling may actually be rewarded with a call (Ribak, 2009).

But these teen–parent–mobile phone practices imply, too, that teens' sense of greater independence, although pervasive, cannot be taken at face value. While teens indeed do not need to inform their parents that they are going out ahead of time, this license is conditional on teens being constantly available and responsive (Campbell, 2006; Ling and Yttri, 2002; Nelson, 2010). The irony in this dependent independence is made clear in the following reflection, where parent–child distance is contingent on the (mediated) proximity of the parents:

> The mobile phone reinforces the sense of independence because you can allow yourself to be where you want and everything, and you know that if worst comes to worst, you have your mobile with you. So it's independence, like, that you can do anything you want and you are much freer in some sense. The mobile offers some security that you can be free and do what you want, because if anything happens, then you can simply call your parents. It sort of guards you … it's like you're never alone.
>
> *(Girl, aged 17, Ribak, 2009, p. 191)*

In some cases it is the parents who leave. The mobile phone enables what Rakow and Navarro (1993; Ling and Yttri, 2002) termed "remote mothering," referring, in the early days of mobile telephony, to those situations in which North American mothers could be available to their kids while in their car or at work. The "parallel shifts" (Rakow and Navarro, 1993, p. 153) that were thereby created acquire global proportions among transnational families. Madianou and Miller (2011) find that the possession of mobile phones by Filipina migrant worker mothers in the UK helped them to fulfill specific mothering responsibilities, such as checking that children had returned from a night out and that they had done their homework. While some kids resent the technological constraint and others think it is precisely *mediated* distance that allows for the expression of intimacy, it is evident that mobile phones facilitate mother–child communication – "she literally calls every day" (p. 466) – but at the same time justify the prolongation of the mothers' migration. The mothers feel that the technology enables them to stay away, but overcome distance and retain their maternal role.

In Jamaica, transnational family ties are compounded by child shifting, whereby children live with relatives of their biological mother or father. In these circumstances, the mobile phone helps overcome the separation between childcare and biological parentage, allowing mothers to stay in touch with their children, and new connections to be forged between children and their fathers (Horst and Miller, 2006). Divorce or parental separation (Henderson et al., 2002; Ling, 2004; Livingstone, 2002) are additional situations in which the mobile phone helps teens and their parents overcome distance:

> The mobile is really important for me and I take really good care of it. It's like my whole life is in the palm of my hand. I save all the important messages. My dad sent me a text message three minutes into the New Year. I often bomb [call and immediately hang up] my parents and they call me back. I don't see my dad so often, but he sometimes gives me a call just to ask how I'm doing. My big brother sometimes sends me funny messages that we have a good laugh from, especially if I'm with my friends. And I am in contact through the mobile with my half big sister a lot.
>
> *(Girl, aged 16, Oksman and Turtiainen, 2004, p. 332)*

Concern over the distance that separates children from their parents underlies these accounts, which highlight the growing significance of the telephone amongst ever more mobile families. In these studies, it is distance as such, rather than the particular places one travels to, and the connection as such, rather than the actual conversation, which are consequential for both young people and their parents.

Teen's places

How does the mobile phone mediate the experience of teens' outside places (Gagen, 2004; Holloway and Valentine, 2000a, 2000b) – the city and the school (James et al., 1998)?

Studies in the industrialized West have been noting the decline of street culture (Livingstone, 2002): the dearth of public funding for skating rinks, playgrounds and youth clubs; the privatization and corporation of spaces in which young people used to hang out; and the metamorphosis of the street corner into the shopping mall as sites of leisure and sociability (Childress, 2004; Lieberg, 1995; Malone, 2002; Thomas, 2005). These processes underlie both the domestication of teens and media (Haddon, 2004; Hoover et al., 2004; Livingstone, 2002), and the growing importance of mobile phones as safety devices (Clark, 2009; Nelson, 2010; Pain et al., 2005).[1]

A UK study focusing on the urban geographies of young people's safety highlights the importance of the mobile phone in this context. Pain et al. (2005) found that to avoid crime happening to them, 45 percent of the boys they interviewed, and 61 percent of the girls, made sure they had their mobile phone with them. The mobile phone was perceived as a safety device particularly as girls grew older: at 16, 74 percent of the girls, and only 37 percent of the boys, took their mobile phone with them to prevent exposure to crime. This finding suggests that the mobile phone is meaningful to young people as they go out on the street; and that with different street experiences, these meanings differ along age and gender lines. Interestingly, whereas anecdotal evidence suggests that when feeling threatened, women hold the mobile phone as a sign of connection and communication, Cohen et al. (2008) found that the Israeli girls they interviewed used the mobile phone to abate the sense of danger in a very concrete way:

> When I walk at night, sometimes I return from the Girl-Scouts, and I have to walk alone a bit. Many times I call my mom or a friend and talk to her on the mobile … it gives me a sense that I am more protected, that if something would have happened to me, there would be someone who would know.
>
> *(girl aged 15, p. 84)*

Thus the mobile phone helps teens to symbolically confront potential danger; while in fact providing an actual link to teens' parents, who can come to their rescue when needed.

In Japan, teen mobile phone use leads to the disappearance of urban anonymity. Ito and Okabe (2001; Okabe and Ito, 2006) offer a rich account of the ways in which young people use mobile phones in a flow of movement and sociality while shopping, walking, riding the bus and the train, or in some restaurant or karaoke spot. This smooth, arguably ludic and improvisational way of coordinating motion through urban space is echoed in this European description:

> If you have a mobile telephone, you can change plans along the way. You do not need to agree to meet either; you can just call whenever you want actually … you can agree where and when you are going to meet and if there is a change you say you will meet in another place.
>
> *(Boy, aged 17, Ling and Yttri, 2002, p. 158)*

Ito and Okabe, however, call attention to the power geometry (Massey, 1993) expressed in the ways in which different social groups are hierarchically located in relation to flows of media, people, capital and mobility itself. They argue that the fluid freedoms of the street need to be analyzed in conjunction with parental surveillance, adult monitoring and social norms and rules. From this perspective, teens' street mobile phone use is constrained by public transportation regulations that prescribe the use of "manner mode" – silent texting as the preferred mode for personal communication in the public sphere (Ito and Okabe, 2001, p. 15; Baron, 2008).

The tension between conforming and resisting spatial discipline and regimes of control is even more pronounced in the context of schools (James et al., 1998), in which mobile phone use is severely restricted if not altogether banned. Within this highly controlled environment (Holloway and Valentine, 2000a, 2000b), teens use mobile phones in a wide variety of locations, from the classroom itself: "When the teacher is facing the blackboard, I quickly type" (Ito and Okabe, 2001, p. 13); through the school library, back yard, cafeteria and toilets: "If she has an emergency, she can go to the bathroom and call me" (Nelson, 2010, p. 120; see also Horst and Miller, 2006; Green, 2001); to places outside the school grounds, on the way to and from school. The latter play an important role when free movement is otherwise restricted (Hijazi-Omari and Ribak, 2008).

Gagen (2004) calls attention to the distinction between places of childhood – the spaces and institutions through which childhood is negotiated – and children's places, namely the creative ways through which children appropriate and recreate adult spaces. Studies on teen mobile phone use in specific locations explore how places of childhood and children's places co-construct one another.

Spatial constructions

Lamenting the disappearance of the urban child's "first time" navigation of the city streets – that rite of passage that communicated: "You are on your own and responsible. If you are frightened, you have to experience those things" (Turkle, 2008, p. 127), Sherry Turkle argues that contemporary children are "phone-tethered to their parents" such that they are not allowed to experience being alone – and therefore, to cross the threshold of independence. For Israeli Palestinian teenage girls, at the same time, receiving a mobile phone from illicit boyfriends was in itself a rite of passage – one, however, that did not entail additional freedom of movement. Indeed "it was the boyfriends who were mobile and who resided now outside their girlfriends' towns and villages to an extent that challenged traditional marital conventions; whereas the girls remained at home – and used their phones under their pillows" (Hijazi-Omari and Ribak, 2008, p. 159).

What these two accounts suggest is that while mobile phones are profoundly involved in transforming young people's experience of the spaces they are allowed to occupy, the implications of their use are complicated and circumscribed. Thus whereas the contraction of potential space may be seen as a hindrance to the maturation of some, mediated parent–child communication may be the closest (and preferred) approximation of family life for others. By the same token, whereas the outside is a threat to some, it is an adventure for others. This suggests, in turn, that childhood and parenting, communication technologies and the spaces in which they are used, need to be studied with growing sensitivity to the cultural and political–economic dynamics that underlie user practices. What consists of healthy maturation in particular cultural contexts? How do specific spaces and geographies of children interact with the media they use? What applications and devices are available to them in different places, and how are these articulated in the economics of media ownership and consumption?

Interestingly, studies of the commercial representation of young people's media use, such as Campbell's work on teenage girls' interpretations of ads displaying contexts of mobile phone use (Campbell, 2006) and Bain's analysis of the spaces in which white teenage girls are depicted in Hollywood films (Bain, 2003), may be offering insightful starting points.

SEE ALSO in this volume chapter by Drotner, chapter by Ling and Bertel, and chapter by Nathanson.

Note

1 Note that "stranger danger" is less prevalent, and that mobile phones can also be used to "expand the tyrannical spaces in which bullying may take place" (Pain et al., 2005, p. 825).

References

Bain, A. L. (2003). White western teenage girls and urban space: Challenging Hollywood's representations. *Gender, Place and Culture, 10*(3), 197–213.

Baron, N. S. (2008). *Always on: Language in an online and mobile world.* New York: Oxford University Press.

Campbell, R. (2006). Teenage girls and cellular phones: Discourses of independence, safety and 'rebellion'. *Journal of Youth Studies, 9*(2), 195–212.

Childress, H. (2004). Teenagers, territory and the appropriation of space. *Childhood, 11*(2), 195–205.

Clark, L. S. (2009). Digital media and the generation gap. *Information, Communication & Society, 12*(3), 388–407.

Cohen, A. A., Lamish, D. and Schejter, A. (2008). *The wonder phone in the land of miracles: Mobile telephony in Israel.* Cresskill, NJ: Hampton Press.

du Gay, P., Hall, S., Janes, L., Mackay, H. and Negus, K. (1997). *Doing cultural studies: The story of the Sony Walkman.* London: Sage.

Gagen, E. A. (2004). Landscapes of childhood and youth. In J. S. Duncan, N. C. Johnson and R. H. Schein (Eds), *A companion to cultural geography.* Malden, MA: Wiley-Blackwell, pp. 404–19.

Gillard, P., Wale, K. and Bow, A. (1998). The friendly phone. In S. Howard (Ed.), *Wired-up: Young people and the electronic media.* London: UCL Press, pp. 135–51.

Green, N. (2001). Who's watching whom? Monitoring and accountability in mobile relations. In B. Brown, N. Green and R. Harper (Eds), *Wireless world: Social and interactional aspect of the mobile age.* London: Springer, pp. 32–45.

Haddon, L. (2004). *Information and communication technologies in everyday life: A concise introduction and research guide.* Oxford: Berg.

Henderson, S., Taylor, R. and Thomson, R. (2002). In touch: Young people, communication and technologies. *Information, Communication & Society, 5*(4), 494–512.

Hijazi-Omari, H. and Ribak, R. (2008). Playing with fire: On the domestication of the mobile phone among Palestinian teenage girls in Israel. *Information, Communication & Society, 11*(2), 149–66.

Holloway, S. L. and Valentine, G. (2000a). Children's geographies and the new social studies of childhood. In S. L. Holloway and G. Valentine (Eds), *Children's geographies: Playing, living, learning.* London: Routledge, pp. 1–22.

——(2000b). Spatiality and the new social studies of childhood. *Sociology, 34*(4), 763–83.

Hoover, S. M., Clark, L. S. and Alters, D. F. (2004). *Media, home, and family.* New York: Routledge.

Horst, H. A. and Miller, D. (2006). *The cell phone: An anthropology of communication.* Oxford: Berg.

Ito, M. and Okabe, D. (2001). *Mobile phones, Japanese youth, and the re-placement of social contact.* Proceeding of the annual meeting of the Society for Social Studies of Science.

James, A., Jenks, C. and Prout, A. (1998). *Theorizing childhood.* Cambridge: Polity Press.

Lieberg, M. (1995). Teenagers and public space. *Communication Research, 22*(6), 720–44.

Ling, R. (2004). *The mobile connection: The cell phone's impact on society.* Amsterdam: Morgan Kaufmann.

Ling, R. and Yttri, B. (2002). Hyper-coordination via mobile phones in Norway. In J. E. Katz and M. Aakhus (Eds), *Perpetual contact: Mobile communication, private talk, public performance.* Cambridge, UK: Cambridge University Press, pp. 139–69.

Livingstone, S. M. (2002). *Young people and new media: Childhood and the changing media environment.* London: Sage.

Madianou, M. and Miller, D. (2011). Mobile phone parenting: Reconfiguring relationships between Filipina migrant mothers and their left-behind children. *New Media & Society, 13*(3), 457–70.

Malone, K. (2002). Street life: Youth, culture and competing uses of public space. *Environment and Urbanization, 14*(2), 157–68.

Massey, D. (1993) Power-geometry and a progressive sense of place. In J. Bird, B. Curtis, T. Putnam, G. Robertson and L. Tickner (Eds) *Mapping the futures: Local cultures, global change.* London: Routledge, pp. 59–69.

——(1998). The spatial construction of youth cultures. In T. Skelton and G. Valentine (Eds), *Cool places: Geographies of youth cultures.* London: Routledge, pp. 121–29.

Nelson, M. K. (2010). *Parenting out of control: Anxious parents in uncertain times.* New York: New York University Press.

Okabe, D. and Ito, M. (2006). Keitai in public transportation. In M. Ito, D. Okabe and M. Matsuda (Eds), *Personal, portable, pedestrian: Mobile phones in Japanese life.* Cambridge, MA: The MIT Press, pp. 205–18.

Oksman, V., and Turtiainen, J. (2004). Mobile communication as a social stage: Meanings of mobile communication in everyday life among teenagers in Finland. *New Media & Society, 6*(3), 319–39.

Pain, R., Grundy, S. U. E., Gill, S., Towner, E., Sparks, G. and Hughes, K. (2005). 'So long as I take my mobile': Mobile phones, urban life and geographies of young people's safety. *International Journal of Urban and Regional Research, 29*(4), 814–30.

Rakow, L. F. and Navarro, V. (1993). Remote mothering and the parallel shift: Women meet the cellular telephone. *Critical Studies in Mass Communication, 10*(2), 144–57.

Ribak, R. (2009). Remote control, umbilical cord and beyond: The mobile phone as a transitional object. *British Journal of Developmental Psychology*, *27*(1), 183–96.

Silverstone, R. (1993). Television, ontological security and the transitional object. *Media, Culture & Society*, *15*(4), 573–98.

Silverstone, R., Hirsch, E. and Morley, D. (1992). Information and communication technologies and the moral economy of the household. In R. Silverstone and E. Hirsch (Eds), *Consuming technologies: Media and information in domestic spaces*. London: Routledge, pp. 15–31.

Thomas, M. E. (2005). Girls, consumption space and the contradictions of hanging out in the city. *Social & Cultural Geography*, *6*(4), 587–605.

Turkle, S. (2008). Always-on/Always-on-you: The tethered self. In J. E. Katz (Ed.), *Handbook of mobile communication studies*. Cambridge, MA: The MIT Press, pp. 121–38.

Wakeford, N. (2003). The embedding of local culture in global communication: Independent internet cafés in London. *New Media & Society*, *5*(3), 379–99.

Winnicott, D. W. (1965). *The maturational processes and the facilitating environment: Studies in the theory of emotional development*. London: Hogarth Press.

——(1971). *Playing and reality*. London: Tavistock Publications.

38

MEDIA AND BEDROOM CULTURE

Siân Lincoln

The teenage bedroom: a space for girls

The concept of a 'bedroom culture' was first introduced to youth cultural studies in the 1970s by Angela McRobbie and Jenny Garber (1975). They set out to 'add on' the missing dimension of gender to accounts written by the Centre for Contemporary Cultural Studies that primarily documented the subcultural activities of young white males using the concept of social class. In their now canonical paper 'Girls and subcultures', McRobbie and Garber outlined the reasons why teenage girls were absent in these accounts and what they were doing as an alternative. For example, McRobbie and Garber cited methodological issues between male researchers working with female participants, their interactions with whom were recorded as being difficult because the girls were mostly 'giggly' and 'passive' (p. 1). As a consequence girls were frequently considered as 'hangers-on', associated to subcultures only through their boyfriends. However, McRobbie and Garber surmised that teenage girls' invisibility in these accounts did not mean that they were not participating, but rather that their subcultural lives were being lived out in an alternative domain: that of the home.

More specifically, McRobbie and Garber argued that teenage girls were primarily using the home as a site for youth cultural activities because pursuits such as listening to music and reading magazines fitted, necessarily, into their everyday domestic roles and responsibilities. In this respect, girls, McRobbie and Garber argued, did not necessarily have the time and the space of their male counterparts to give the level of commitment required to be a 'member' of a street-based subculture, but instead opted for a culture that could be accommodated easily in their domestic environment and responsibilities, and into their leisure time. 'Bedroom culture' by definition was low maintenance and could easily be dipped in and out of by the teenage girl, requiring little more than a record player and permission to invite friends.

In McRobbie and Garber's account teenage girls could participate in bedroom culture through their engagement in the media and their associated commercial products and goods that were marketed specifically to female teenagers. These included media texts such as teenage girls' magazines and pop music that, McRobbie argues in her later work, cater to a distinct girl culture (1991, p. 11). In her analyses of such texts McRobbie illustrates how teenage girls' magazines, especially *Jackie*, provide 'maps of meaning', through which a particular feminine ideology is presented, one that encourages the romantic encounter with a male counterpart, but within the 'safe' worlds of fantasy and romance, rather than in real life, on the dangerous streets. Through a coding of *Jackie*, McRobbie demonstrated how (heterosexual) 'womanhood' and 'girlhood' (1991, p. 84) was mapped out through popular teen media and mapped on to the lives of their young teen readers. This 'map', according to McRobbie, was one that was essentially 'closed', in the sense that the uses of teenage girls' magazines were predominantly dictated through their pages with little room for interpretation or adaptability by the teenager girl in the 'real world'. In this sense, then, McRobbie identified a set of 'codes' operating in *Jackie* that, she argued, enforced this structured femininity. These codes included: the code of 'romance', the code of fashion and beauty, the code of pop music and the code of personal life.

What McRobbie's codes revealed was that the teenage girl was expected to pursue and aspire to that all important moment of the romantic encounter that would eventually open up the pathway to life as a wife and a mother. In pursuing this, the teenage girl was able to use magazines as a resource, picking up tips on fashion and beauty in her quest to attract a man. Further, such magazines provided a reference point to overcome common issues and problems associated with growing up and becoming independent. To this extent, engaging in bedroom culture was a solitary activity as undertaking various forms of beautification in the quest of finding a man was best done alone, or at least that's what the pages of magazines such as *Jackie* would tell their readers.

What McRobbie's analyses also revealed was the seemingly passive way in which teenage girls engaged with media texts. For example, discussions about pop music in teenage girls' magazines tended to focus on the male pop idol and associated poster-gazing (1991, p. 126), rather than the teenage girl as a gig-goer, a musician or as someone who was genuinely interested in the music itself. Instead, listening to pop music was a useful mechanism through which to create or further enhance the fantasy worlds of love and romance; to fantasise about that romantic clinch with a famous pop star or idol.

McRobbie and Garber's study is now considered to be canonical in the field. It is noted to be particularly ground-breaking because it addressed the position of young women in youth cultures as well as bringing the context of the domestic into the equation: youth cultures and subcultures could exist in the private domain as well as the public. Further, although not explicitly addressed in their study, the media were considered integral to teenage girls' youth cultures in private space, playing a key role in the construction of a bedroom culture and the shaping of teenage girls' leisure time.

Public fears, private youth cultures: media in the home

However, despite the importance of this work and despite some recognition in youth studies in the 1980s that the private domain of the home was an important youth cultural space, studies of youth culture in the domestic sphere, or in bedroom culture specifically, were somewhat elusive until the 1990s when a renewed interest in home-based youth cultures began to re-emerge. There are a number of reasons for this, many of which are related to the media in some way, but I will note three possible reasons here. First, in recent times there has been much debate in the mass media about how public spaces such as the local streets and parks (or other recreational areas) are no longer considered safe spaces of play for young people, but rather are deemed 'risky', dangerous and spaces to be avoided (Valentine and McKendrick, 1997). For example, in their 1999 UK study *Young people, new media* that documented young people's relationships with new media as part of their everyday lives, Livingstone and Bovill (1999) reported that both parents and children expressed fears about using public spaces, fears which, they argued, were contributing to a relocation of leisure time back into the home. Such fears according to Livingstone and Bovill were articulated by parents and children through the discourses of race, ethnicity, social class and gender, but notably fears about public spaces were intensified by the media. For example, they noted that parents felt the news was a source of anxiety, heightening their fears about what goes on in the streets, but also, paradoxically, parents themselves were perpetuating this myth by using the news as a point of reference for their children about 'what might happen' if they strayed too far from home. More recently, James (2007) has noted other global concerns that have also contributed to heightened feelings of risk and danger associated with public spaces:

> In past times, when security issues and terrorist threats were not the dominant issues they are today, children were much freer to 'play outside' and roam the streets or the countryside with relatively little adult interference or supervision. A British study showed 'that the radius within which children roam freely around their homes has shrunk by almost 90% since the 1970s'.
>
> (p. 36 quoted in Abbott-Chapman and Robertson, 2009, p. 421)

Second, this shift of leisure time back into the home has also brought with it a pressure for young people to consume (Rose, 1999) and a pressure on parents to purchase (Lincoln, 2012). The cost of media technologies has fallen dramatically in the UK in recent years, making equipment such as televisions, gaming consoles, personal computers, laptops, mobile phones, and portable listening devices such as the iPod more affordable. This means that parents who are concerned about the safety of their children and who prefer to see them spending their leisure time within the vicinity of the home are able to purchase a range of equipment that provides entertainment. The 'personalised media environment' that this practice creates, Livingstone (2007) argues, is often taken for granted by young people who find themselves using different pieces of technology for different forms of entertainment and communication.

Finally, young people are said to be growing up in a 'risk' society (Beck 1992) whereby it can be argued that the breakdown of traditional institutions such as the nuclear family has meant that young people are 'obliged to become more flexible ... to reflect upon their abilities, inclinations and opportunities, and to plan their own futures' (Roberts, 2009, p. 74). Consequently, youth cultures and spaces of youth cultures have arguably become more fragmented, individualised, ambiguous and blurred. Indeed, the mediated nature of contemporary bedroom culture whereby young people's private spaces are filled with different types of media technologies has led to a blurring of the public and private realm (Reimer, 1995), the interplay of which flows in and out of young people's bedrooms as they interact with different media technologies and forms (Lincoln, 2005).

Teenage bedroom culture: consumption, identity and the media

Room culture scholars (Steele and Brown, 1995; see also, Baker, 2004; James, 2001; Kearney, 2007; Larson, 1995; Lincoln, 2004, 2005, 2012) argue that while dominant public discourses about young people, their bedrooms and media use tend to be framed within the context of the 'lazy couch potato', mindlessly engaging in computer game playing, TV watching etc., young people are in fact using the media in active, original, dynamic and complex ways both inside and outside the home. This argument is a far cry from the rather passive, insular model of bedroom culture reserved only for the teenage girl described in earlier studies.

In their research on adolescent room culture, and using the Adolescent Media Practice Model, Steele and Brown explore how young people use the media as an integral part of their identities and interactions. They argue that young people 'appropriate and transform media messages and images to help them make sense of their lives' (p. 551), with the media providing a key resource through which young people live out their everyday cultural lives. Their research highlighted the many ways in which the media have become embedded into the everyday, ordinary lives of young people, both in public and private realms. Importantly, they conclude that young people's use of the media is never static. As young people encounter different social and cultural experiences, their media practices shift and change accordingly and this is captured in their personal bedroom spaces. Young people's usage of the media, according to Steele and Brown, is typified through 'the moment to moment interface between media and teenagers who come already armed with a sense of how the world is' (p. 567).

While Steele and Brown focus upon the ways in which the media are key resources with which young people mark out their changing identities in their bedrooms, Larson (1995) argues that young people's uses of the media are influenced by the spaces available to them to use the media in. Further, he argues that young people's *experiences* of the media differ greatly depending on those spaces. Ultimately, he argues that 'it is in their solitary bedroom lives where media has some of its most significant functions, where public and private are woven together' (p. 536). Using the specific examples of television and music Larson notes that relatively little attention had been paid to the private contexts of young people's engagement in media such as music. However, Larson argues that in fact young people engage more fully in media practices when they are on their own rather than with friends and that in their bedrooms young people are likely to have more authentic meaningful interactions and experiences with the media. Larson argues that the media are a key resource through which identities are drawn. Music for example, is a key source in the realisation of 'real' identities, while television is used by young people when they wish to 'turn off' from their selves and their lives for a short time (1995, p. 544).

Bedrooms and beyond: contemporary approaches to bedroom culture and the media

While early studies of bedroom culture relied primarily on the structural categories of gender, studies of bedroom culture since the mid 1990s have drawn on a range of conceptual tools such as age, identity and biography (as well as gender and class) (Harris 2001; see also, Henderson et al., 2007) that illustrate more readily the complexities of young people's uses of their bedrooms and the role of the media in it. Such categories are arguably more fluid and able to capture the ever-changing nature of youth culture as well as how youth culture is engaged in both as a collective pursuit and an individual one by young people, male and female. Lincoln (2004, 2005, 2012) uses the concept of 'zoning' as a tool through which to capture the dynamic, evolving and changing nature of contemporary youth culture and how youth cultural activities and practices are articulated in bedroom spaces, for example, through the posters on the wall or through a CD collection. Taking her theoretical cues from McRobbie, Lincoln proposes that young people's bedrooms are key identity spaces that can be understood as a collection of zones. These zones interweave and overlap, flow from one to another, from the public to private, the physical to the virtual reflecting the very nature of contemporary youth culture whereby young people are interacting in both online and offline cultural worlds. According to Lincoln, a 'zone' is:

> A physical and visual arrangement of furniture, technical equipment, beauty products, school books, in fact any item that is 'contained' within bedroom space. It is orientated by the social activities that take place within that space, therefore it may not be fixed in physical or cognitive activities; zones can overlap and integrate. The zone can also become a mediated and fluid construction, enhanced through technologies such as the

TV or the sound system, the mobile phone and the internet; therefore the space of the bedroom is a fluid and dynamic cultural domain ... [a zone] is constructed by teenagers themselves who occupy the space of the bedroom and who select from their 'pick and mix' culture ... and their immense cultural choices.

(2004, p. 97)

Importantly, rather than being constructed by the media, as argued by McRobbie and Garber (1975) and McRobbie (1991), contemporary bedroom culture is derived from them (Lincoln, 2004) and thus a bedroom is a space that is worked upon by young people in order for it to consistently represent a young person's ever-changing cultural interests. For Lincoln, mediated zones created through, for example, music are central to young people's bedroom culture and through different media technologies the experiences of engaging in music in the bedroom are multiple, each technology creating a different listening experience and varying forms of bedroom culture that can depend on a young person's feelings or mood. Using portable listening devices such as iPods allows a young person to experience music in a highly personal and intense fashion, 'zoning' it in such a way that listening to the music is at its most private through those small white headphones (Lincoln, 2012). Additionally, such technologies allow for the creation of individual, personalised play lists that yet again make for an experience of personal space that is unique and can be adapted accordingly to a young person's feelings or mood as well as to whether the space is being used socially with friends or on one's own. Alternatively, young people with televisions in their bedrooms may use them as a form of background noise or 'wallpaper', as part of everyday routines or as a way to create a sense of familiarity and comfort in their space. On the other hand, the bedroom may be used for more deliberate viewing, away from parents and siblings where a television show or movie can be enjoyed in isolation. In each instance, the viewing experience is different and, thus, so is the experience of bedroom culture which can be very personal. The intensity of bedroom cultures is regulated through young people's interactions and their zoning of their personal space.

If a bedroom for a young person is to be understood as a personal and private space, the intensity of which is ultimately controlled by them through the interaction of different 'zones' and in which they can live out their everyday social and cultural lives, it is evident that in a contemporary context such spaces do not merely exist for young people in physical spaces. In recent years new mediated forms of communication such as social networking have emerged and sites such as MySpace, Facebook and Twitter have become almost ubiquitous in the social and cultural worlds of young people growing up in Western societies. Such sites require their users to create online profiles or identities and to 'work on' their spaces to the extent that they become representations of their users. As an integral part of young people's daily interactions and communications, such profiles will be constantly updated and revised to reflect the ever-changing social and cultural worlds of their users who can regulate who 'enters' their spaces, either accepting or rejecting 'friends' (boyd, 2006, 2008). In this respect, scholars such as Brown et al. (1994), boyd (2008), Hodkinson and Lincoln (2008) and Pearson (2009) have suggested that the spatial metaphor of a young person's bedroom provides a useful framework through which to explore social networking media as personal, mediated spaces of youth identities that represent the worked upon, constantly changing nature of contemporary youth cultural identities. Hodkinson and Lincoln (2008) argue, using the example of online journals, that the interactions by young people in such virtual spaces can be understood as a 'virtual bedroom', that is, they are personalised spaces and spaces of ownership and control for a young person (albeit within the parameters set by the sites' owners). In exploring this metaphor further, Lincoln (2012) argues that social networking sites such as MySpace and Facebook may have a basic generic layout, but are personalised by the user through the addition of content. On sites such as MySpace, this personalisation can be achieved through the application of 'wallpaper', music and photographs selected by its young user as well as other forms of decoration such as emoticons used to represent visually the current mood of the user. However, in reflecting upon the extent to which such spaces allow a young person to present an 'authentic' identity, Lincoln (2012) concludes that young people consider the personal space of their bedrooms as a more authentic representation of themselves in comparison to social networking sites; a physical space in their family home that is shut away from the constant gaze of peers and the doors of which can be opened and closed at a young person's discretion. This theme of authenticity in personal and private identity spaces is one that warrants further research in the context of young people, bedroom cultures and the media.

Producing and creating culture? Future explorations in teenage bedroom culture

In the main, studies of bedroom culture and the media to date have focused predominantly around issues of consumption (Kearney, 2007). While indeed as I have demonstrated there has been a theoretical shift from bedroom cultures shaped by the media and passively consumed by the teenage girl to bedroom cultures that are derived from the media and shaped by young people's individual, dynamic interactions, the role of the media is predominantly understood through the discourse of consumption. Kearney critiques recent room culture scholarship on this basis. She argues that given the accessibility of new media technologies to young people in contemporary Western society, greater emphasis should be placed on forms of media *production* within personal spaces such as bedrooms. Indeed, such spaces are often hubs of creative activity as scholars such as Anita Harris (2001) and Sarah Louise Baker (2004) have demonstrated in studies of young people making music in their bedrooms. Bedrooms are spaces in which, for example, aspiring DJs and musicians write, compose and broadcast music, distributing it for free via sites such as YouTube. Further, analyses of media production reveal to an even greater extent the creative, innovative ways in which young people not only use their own personal spaces as sites of identity, but also the ways in which they use the media within them in personalising their experiences of bedroom culture. And while the concept of media production in young people's bedrooms is by no means new (young people have used such spaces for writing music, books, poetry, even teenage diaries for decades), the rapid developments in media technologies and their ubiquity in contemporary youth cultures both inside and outside of the home certainly warrant further academic research, exploration and study.

SEE ALSO in this volume chapter by Mazzarella.

References

Abbott-Chapman, J. and Robertson, M. (2009). Adolescents' favorite places: Redefining the boundaries between public and private space. *Space and Culture*, *12*(4), 419–34.

Baker, S. L. (2004). Pop in(to) the bedroom: Popular music in pre-teen girls' bedroom culture. *European Journal of Cultural Studies*, *7*(1), 75–93.

Beck, U. (1992). *Risk society: Towards a new modernity*. London: Sage.

boyd, d. (2006). Friends, friendsters and top 8: Writing community into being on social network sites. *First Monday*, *11*(12), (accessed 06/11/10).

——(2008). *Taken out of context: American teen sociality in networked publics*. Unpublished doctoral dissertation, University of California, Berkeley.

Brown, J., Dykers, C., Steele, J. and White, A. (1994). Teenage room culture: Where media and identities intersect. *Communications Research, 21*(6), 813–27.

Harris, A. (2001). Revisiting bedroom culture: New spaces for young women's politics. *Hecate, 27*(1), 128–39.

Henderson, S., Holland, J., McGrellis, S., Sharpe, S. and Thomson, R. (2007). *Inventing adulthoods: A biographical approach to youth transitions.* London: Sage.

Hodkinson, P. and Lincoln, S. (2008). Online journals as virtual bedrooms: Young people, identity and personal space. *YOUNG, the Nordic Journal of Youth Research, 16*(1), 27–46.

James, K. A. (2001). "I just gotta have my own space!": The bedroom as a leisure site for adolescent girls. *Journal of Leisure Research, 33*(1), 71–90.

James, V. (2007.) Lost in the concrete jungle. *Geographical, 79,* 34–38.

Kearney, M. C. (2007). Productive spaces girls' bedrooms as sites of cultural production spaces. *Journal of Children and Media, 1*(2), 126–41.

Larson, R. (1995). Secrets in the bedroom: Adolescents' private use of media. *Journal of Youth and Adolescence, 24*(5), 535–50.

Lincoln, S. (2004). Teenage girls' bedroom culture: Codes versus zones. In A. Bennett and K. Kahn-Harris (Eds), *After subculture: Critical studies in contemporary youth culture.* Basingstoke: Palgrave Macmillan, pp. 94–106.

——(2005). Feeling the noise: Teenagers, bedrooms and music. *Leisure Studies, 24*(4), 399–414.

Lincoln, S. (2012). *Youth culture and private space.* Basingstoke: Palgrave Macmillan.

Livingstone, S. (2007). From family television to bedroom culture: Young people's media at home. In E. Devereux (Ed.), *Media studies: Key issues and debates.* London, Sage, pp. 302–21.

Livingstone, S. and Bovill, M. (1999). *Young people, new media: Summary report of the research project 'children, young people and the changing media environment'.* London. United Kingdom: London School of Economics, Media@LSE.

McRobbie, A. (1991). *Feminism and youth culture from Jackie to Just Seventeen.* Basingstoke, Macmillan.

McRobbie, A. and Garber, J. (1975). Girls and subcultures. In A. McRobbie (1991). *Feminism and youth culture from Jackie to Just Seventeen.* London: Macmillan, pp. 1–15.

Pearson, E. (2009). All the world wide web's a stage: The performance of identity in online social networks. *First Monday, 14*(3), p. n/a.

Reimer, B. (1995). The media in public and private spheres. In J. Fornas and G. Bolin (Eds), *Youth culture in late modernity.* London: Sage, pp. 58–71.

Roberts, K. (2009). *Youth in transition: Eastern Europe and the West.* Basingstoke: Palgrave Macmillan.

Rose, N. (1999). *Governing the soul: The shaping of the private self.* London: Free Associations Books.

Steele, J. R. and Brown, J. D. (1995). Adolescent room culture: Studying media in the context of everyday life. *Journal of Youth and Adolescence, 24*(5), 551–76.

Valentine, G. and McKendrick, J. (1997). Children's outdoor play: Exploring parental concerns about children's safety and the changing nature of childhood. *Geoforum, 28*(2), 219–35.

39

MEDIA AND PEER CULTURE

Young people sharing norms and collective identities with and through media

Sun Sun Lim

As children and adolescents develop, they are socialized by their peers as well as by adults. These peer groups play the critical socializing functions which imbue in children a sense of their peers' norms, values and behavioral patterns (Handel et al., 2007). While young people imbibe the adult cultures that surround them, they also absorb the peer culture that underpins and sustains their interactions and relationships with other young people (Brown and Klute, 2003). Peer culture encompasses norms and conventions, shared interests and activities, social and instrumental interaction and the unique modes of communication deployed in all of the aforementioned elements. During the periods of adolescence and early adulthood in particular, peer culture assumes an important role in young people's lives because their emotional center shifts away from the family (Arnett, 2010). Key constituents of young people's peer culture, given the priorities of their life stage, often include shared interests and involvement in leisure pursuits such as play, sports, shopping and media (Larson and Verma, 1999). Print, broadcast and online media constitute an increasingly important part of young people's lives in both industrialized and developing countries and are invariably woven into their peer culture (Arnett, 2010). The ways in which young people integrate their media consumption into their peer culture is the focus of this chapter. Specifically, this chapter will discuss how young people incorporate media content into their peer interactions and appropriate a variety of communication platforms to socialize with their peers, thus generating distinctive traits, norms, practices, codes and shared identities that make up their unique peer culture(s). The chapter is structured according to the three salient ways in which young people around the world today interact with one another: face-to-face, via the mobile phone and over the internet's myriad communication channels. The chapter then provides a closer examination of youth subcultures that are media based and media facilitated. Throughout the chapter, effort has been made to draw examples from as wide a geographical scope as possible.

Media in face-to-face peer culture

Face-to-face interactions with peers are a key facet of youth development as they gradually mature and shift from the social world of their families, towards that of their peer groups. As Pasquier (2008) observes, "[c]ultural preferences and practices are at the very heart of the organization of youth sociability, the base on which one elaborates individual and collective identities"(p. 457). Indeed, extensive research has gone into how media content and devices are appropriated by young people for socialization with peers, as both material for conversation and as a platform for communication.

Prior research has found that as young people interact in school and in leisure settings, media content is often commandeered as a topic of discussion. A qualitative study of young people in Finland, Switzerland and Spain found that media content lubricates conversation and play, with older children chatting about popular television programs and computer games for example, while younger children engage in role-play where they model themselves after characters drawn from popular culture (Suess et al., 1998). Notably, the teens who were studied felt compelled to watch every episode of a popular television program so that they could participate in discussions about the programme that were likely to take place in school the next day. Indeed, alongside parental mediation of young people's media consumption, peer interaction about media content also generates norms about what constitutes acceptable content for the group and determines which media they should consume (Nathanson, 2001). Similarly, Pasquier (2008) observes that the enjoyment of music assumes a crucial role in the lives of young people, and by implication, peer approval of one's musical tastes is key to peer acceptance. For example, she found an active disavowal of classical music which has a dated image amongst young people in France, in favor of trendier genres such as rap and grunge rock. To avert marginalization by their peers therefore, adolescents tend to subscribe to peer-endorsed musical cultures and the accompanying standards and injunctions.

Media content's ability to traverse different social milieu and technological platforms is what makes it an excellent source of connection for young people in their peer interactions. In analyzing the worldwide popularity of Pokémon, Buckingham and Sefton-Green (2003) discovered that children could engage with Pokémon via television cartoons, computer games and trading cards, and translate this knowledge into social interaction, be it of a playful, friendly or competitive nature. This "portability" (Buckingham and Sefton-Green, 2003, p. 388) of children's knowledge about the cartoon thus entrenched Pokémon as a prime ingredient in their peer culture. With growing convergence across media genres and platforms, the portability of media content will become even more palpable, further enlarging the roles that media will assume in young people's peer cultures.

Shared media use is another important way in which media content infuses young people's peer culture. With the rapid diffusion of portable media devices such as mobile phones, MP3 players, laptop computers and hand-held video games, as well as media devices that encourage shared usage such as multi-player video game machines and tablet computers, face-to-face encounters with peers are likely to involve a physical convergence around these devices, and a joint viewing of media content. As observed by Suoninen (2001) of European youth, visiting friends to play electronic games or watch videos is a popular activity, with some teenagers planning special video nights where they watch a series of movies that may not have met with parental approval, thus fostering a thrilling sense of shared deviance. The rising ubiquity of smartphones with location-based services and always-on, always-available internet access in some countries has also introduced a culture of documenting face-to-face peer interactions and sharing amongst the peer group. Singaporean teen girls, for example, take camera phone photographs during outings with friends and share them on-the-spot via Bluetooth or Facebook for their friends to view and access (Lim and Ooi, 2011). Through this instantaneous capture and dissemination of peer encounters, these young people construct shared memories that serve to enhance their sense of group identity.

Mobile phone peer culture

Another dominant mode of peer interaction amongst young people today is mobile phone communication. Conventions and trends in peer-to-peer communication via text, voice or photos constitute the cultural dimensions of young people's mobile phone interactions with their networks of friends. Mobile phone peer culture comprises idiosyncratic communication practices and linguistic codes in the form of truncated, alphanumeric text-ese, which come with their own tacit rules of adoption and standards of social acceptability (Thurlow and Brown, 2003).

On an instrumental level, young people's use of the mobile phone to identify their friends' whereabouts and micro-coordinate serendipitous gatherings has created a peer culture where "mobility and flexible scheduling are central" (Castells et al., 2007). Ling and Yttri (2002) noted from their study of Norwegian teens that this practice of vaguely specifying where to meet before progressively firming up appointments, while not unique to young people, is especially developed amongst teenagers. Such flexibility hinges on always being accessible to others, which in turn creates an always-on intimate community that keeps in perpetual intermittent contact, with its members constantly updating one another on all aspects of their personal life, from the mundane to the weighty (Ito, 2004). This culture of communication also enables young people to engage in a live, stream-of-consciousness narration of daily events that enables them to live out and share in each others' lives, as seen in a Canadian study (Caron and Caronia, 2007). Clearly, these communication processes are of more than instrumental value, and serve to fortify the socio-emotional aspects of relationship-building amongst young people. Indeed, Taylor and Harper (2003) identified the "gifting" function of text messages amongst young people in Britain. While not laden with meaning in and of themselves, text messages are exchanged in a process of performativity where young people display their commitment to friendship, thereby seeking to cement social ties. For instance, the communication culture within a peer group can comprise forwarding text messages from one peer to multiple other members of a peer group network, with an expectation of reciprocity within the network. Such activities help to establish shared conventions and meanings amongst a group of peers, thus forging a sense of collective identity (Green and Haddon, 2009).

Apart from the communicative functions of mobile phone communications, the mobile phone's role as an item of signification is also important amongst young people. With its constant presence, portability and ease-of-adornment, the mobile phone is ideal for this purpose. Young people have been observed to personalize their phones through physical embellishments or the use of accessories, as noted in a US study (Katz and Sugiyama, 2005). Among close-knit peer groups, there is a culture of embellishing phones in a way that marks a shared peer identity as evidenced for example in Japanese street youth practices (Okada, 2006) and amongst young Korean females (Hjorth, 2009).

Online peer culture

Online communication platforms enable young people to extend their peer interaction beyond their face-to-face encounters with one another. This multitude of online platforms, including discussion forums, instant messaging, social networking services such as Facebook and foursquare, and virtual worlds such as Club Penguin and Webkinz, each with its own set of affordances, communication cues, styles and rhythms, offers additional means by which young people can nurture their peer cultures. These platforms are too numerous and varied to systematically review in the present chapter; however, key findings relating to young people's online peer culture will be highlighted.

First, extant research demonstrates that online interactions extend the face-to-face relationships of physically proximate peers and are used to showcase and assert their group identities. Indeed, it is unproductive to regard young people's online interactions as separate and distinct from their offline, face-to-face relationships. As Boudreau (2007) discovered from her study of Girls' Room, a message board created by a group of teen girls in Montreal, the message board rapidly evolved from a site where they chatted about the activities of the day into a virtual community where they discussed issues in a more reflective manner. Through these online interactions, the girls strengthened their sense of belonging to their offline peer group. A similar finding was drawn from research on the media use of juvenile delinquents in Singapore, though with a notable point of divergence. The study found that a group of delinquent teens who used to congregate at a particular apartment building, but who were subsequently incarcerated for criminal activity, would "meet" each other in an online chat group labeled "715" – the apartment building number – thus remotely sustaining their face-to-face peer culture even while physically absent (Lim et al., 2011).

Second, online interactions provide young people with a relatively less risky environment in which to acquaint themselves with the norms and rules of their peer groups. In her study of American teens' use of MySpace, boyd (2008) argues that social network sites allow young people to "work out identity and status, make sense of cultural cues, and negotiate public life" (p. 120). By observing the mutual interactions, validations and admonishments of peers in the socially-networked online setting, young people learn to interpret social situations and manage their public personae both online and offline. On a related note, Clark (2005) found that American teen girls appreciated instant messaging because it offered them opportunities to initiate interaction with peers that they would not have dared attempt in face-to-face settings, and that the asynchronicity of online communication allowed them to plan in advance what they wanted to say and how they wished to present themselves.

Third, although online peer culture is situated within and shaped by offline culture, the dynamics of the online environment can influence the nature of peer interaction and alter the basis of peer culture. Online interaction can occur in text-based chat rooms or graphically-rich virtual worlds such as Massively Multiplayer Online Role-Playing Games and virtual environments in which young people participate via avatars, e.g. Club Penguin, Webkinz and Whyville. The visual anonymity and disembodiment of online text-based interaction relieves young people of the pressures of self-presentation and impression management (Holloway and Valentine, 2003). As the British teens in Holloway and Valentine's (2003) study attest, in text-based chat rooms the peer culture is built more on shared interests than mutual propinquity, and interactions tend to be on substantive topics rather than the mundane details of everyday face-to-face relationships. With regard to interaction in graphically-rich virtual environments, young people can experiment with their identities as they use the virtual tools available to create personalized avatars that can exercise agency and autonomy. Although expressing one's personality through a disembodied, online instantiation of oneself can be rewarding, online peer interaction then hinges on the appearance of one's avatar (Lim and Clark, 2010). As Lu (2010) discovered from her experience of Neopets.com and Burley (2010) from her explorations of Club Penguin, in these highly visual and visible virtual worlds, one risks social embarrassment if one's avatar is not sufficiently adorned with the "right" virtual accoutrements.

Media and youth subcultures

Youth subcultures arise when peer interaction is of such intensity that it develops into an identifiable subculture with distinct beliefs, values and practices. Media can be a component of youth subcultures either as a focal point for the subculture's interest, or as a conduit for a subculture's members to interact and foster their collective identity. I will refer to the former as media-based subcultures and the latter as media-facilitated subcultures. It should be noted that the two are not mutually exclusive since there are media-facilitated subcultures that are not media based, e.g., online pro-anorexia groups, whereas media-based subcultures are almost always media-facilitated, e.g., fan groups. The internet in particular, given its ubiquity and versatility, has become a prime platform for the assertion of youth subcultures.

In media-based youth subcultures, a keenly shared interest, in particular media genres or media personalities, forms the foundation for peer group interaction. Notable youth subcultures have been centered around different types of music, where their members display strong identification with the attitudes and styles of particular musical genres. The straightedge subculture which has a following in Australia, New Zealand, North America and Europe for example, is largely limited to the punk hardcore music scene, and emerged as a form of resistance against the commercialized and self-indulgent mainstream youth culture (Williams, 2003). Members of face-to-face straightedge groups in Australia often use the internet to amass information about straightedge music and raise awareness about cultural events. Similarly, the "rave" subculture which centers around electronic dance music has embraced the internet to share its anarchist philosophy amongst youths in Australia and beyond (Gibson, 1999). Another salient thread in the study of media-based youth subcultures is the analysis of fandom, particularly amongst teen girls. The dynamics within online fan communities is another interesting manifestation of young people's peer cultures. Mazzarella (2005) studied online communities of Chad Michael Murray fans and found tacit codes of conduct amongst the American teen girl fans, including expectations that they use the fan site platform to express their adoration for the celebrity via posts of fan-art, fan-fiction and fan-graphics, and a concerted collective effort to amass and post as much information about the celebrity as possible, no matter how trivial.

As seen above, young people use the media to facilitate their interactions with peers and particular youth subcultures have been especially empowered by the internet and computer-mediated communication (CMC). CMC affords young people a degree of privacy and anonymity that cannot be experienced in face-to-face communication and provides peer cultures that are considered more "deviant" with a safe and non-judgmental sphere for interaction. The proliferation of online pro-anorexic websites is a case in point. Gailey (2009) observes that involvement in these "pro-ana" websites, blogs and social networking sites reflect a conscious attempt to create or seek community. For anorexics, the internet alleviates feelings of alienation and stigma by providing common spaces to "share ideas, feelings, art, poems, support and friendships" (Gailey, 2009, p. 94). Anorexics use blogs and websites to foster and affirm shared ideologies, while dispensing dieting tips and success stories to motivate and stay accountable to one another. Confessions of overeating or the public display of an individual's diet plan for the week are common sightings on such personal or community blogs. Unbounded by geographical and cultural constraints, the internet thus facilitates an engagement in a community of kindred souls (Polak, 2007). Another group of young people that has found solace online is that of homosexual teens. While they may reject the "subculture" label, this is in effect a marginalized group that has yet to receive mainstream acceptance in many societies (Arnett, 2010). In this regard, the internet has been a boon to young people who are unsure of their sexuality, and doubtful about whom they should turn to for advice on coming to terms with their sexual orientation (Silberman, 2001). Whereas homosexual teens were previously reticent about seeking advice, a plethora of online resources has emerged to provide guidance and safe avenues for them to form online communities of support and advocacy. Again, the discreetness of internet mediated communication enables these otherwise ostracized teens to seek acceptance from empathetic individuals, in a manner that is unlikely to be matched in face-to-face interaction.

Conclusion

The media constitute a cornerstone of young people's peer culture that is at once alluring and difficult for them to disengage from. Be they part of mainstream youth or youth subcultures, young people today are avidly appropriating media content and channels to interact with their peers and in the process they foster norms, conventions, shared practices and collective identities within their peer groups. Yet, as the penetration of internet-ready smartphones rises and technological convergence gains pace, so too will the convergence of young people's face-to-face, mobile and online interactions. With the seamless connection of young people's offline and online interactions, there will be greater opportunity for peer cultures to be invigorated, asserted and shared across multiple realms, both mediated and face-to-face. But will such seamlessness intensify "context collapse" (Wesch, 2009) where people from different realms of one's life converge, further challenging young people's ability to negotiate the competing social expectations imposed by different peer groups? Being constantly connected to their peers both online and off, will young people find the pressure of adhering to peer norms overwhelming and deindividuating? Where and how will young people carve out a personal space for themselves if they seek to resist the influences of media-centered and media-facilitated peer culture? Is it even possible for them to do so? It is imperative that future research considers these questions as it tracks the evolving position of media in young people's peer culture.

SEE ALSO in this volume chapter by Ling and Bertel, and chapter by Mesch.

References

Arnett, J. J. (2010). *Adolescence and emerging adulthood: A cultural approach* (4th ed.). Boston, CT: Prentice Hall.

Boudreau, K. (2007). The girls' room: Negotiating schoolyard friendships online. In S. Weber and S. Dixon (Eds) *Growing up online: Young people and digital technologies*. Hampshire: Palgrave Macmillan, pp. 67–79.

boyd, d. (2008). Why youth (heart) social network sites: the role of networked publics in teenage social life. In D. Buckingham (Ed.) *Youth, identity, and digital media*. Cambridge, MA: MIT Press, pp. 119–42.

Brown, B. B. and Klute, C. (2003). Friendships, cliques and crowds. In R. G. Adams and D. M. Berzonsky (Eds), *Blackwell Handbook of Adolescence*. Malden, MA: Blackwell, pp. 330–48.

Buckingham, D. and Sefton-Green, D. (2003). Gotta catch 'em all: Structure, agency and pedagogy in children's media culture. *Media, Culture & Society*, 25(3), 379–99.

Burley, D. (2010). Penguin life: A case study of one tween's experiences inside Club Penguin. *Journal of Virtual Worlds Research*, 3(2), 2–13.

Caron, A. H. and Caronia, L. (2007). *Moving cultures: mobile communication in everyday life*. Canada: McGill-Queen's University Press.

Castells, M., Fernandez-Ardevol, M., Qiu, J. L. and Sey, A. (2007). *Mobile communication and society*. Boston, MA: MIT Press.

Clark, S. L. (2005). The constant contact generation: Exploring teen friendship networks online. In S. R. Mazzarella (Ed.), *Girl wide web: Girls, the internet and the negotiation of identity*. New York: Peter Lang, pp. 203–22.

Gailey, J. A. (2009). "Starving is the most fun a girl can have": The pro-ana subculture as edgework. *Critical Criminology*, 17(2), 93–108.

Gibson, C. (1999). Subversive sites: rave culture, spatial politics and the internet in Sydney, Australia. *Area*, 31(1), 19–33.

Green, N. and Haddon, L. (2009). *Mobile communications*. Oxford: Berg.

Handel, G., Cahill, S. E. and Elkin, F. (2007). *Children and society: The sociology of children and childhood socialisation*. New York, NY: Oxford University Press.

Hjorth, L. (2009). Cybercute@Korea: The role of cute customisation and gender performativity in a case study of South Korean virtual community, Cyworld mini-hompy. In Y. Kim (Ed.), *Media Consumption and Everyday Life in Asia*. London, Routledge, pp. 203–16.

Holloway, S. L. and Valentine, G. (2003). *Cyberkids: Children in the information age*. London: RoutledgeFalmer.

Ito, M. (2004). *Personal, portable, pedestrian: mobile phones in Japanese life*. Los Angeles: Annenberg Centre for Communication.

Katz, J. E. and Sugiyama, S. (2005). Mobile phones as fashion statements: The Co-creation of mobile communication's public meaning. In R. Ling and P. E. Pedersen (Eds), *Mobile communications: Re-negotiation of the social sphere*. London: Springer-Verlag, pp. 63–81.

Larson, R. W. and Verma, S. (1999). How children and adolescents spend time across the world: Work, play, and developmental opportunities. *Psychological Bulletin, 125*(6), 701–36.

Lim, S. S. and Clark, L. S. (2010). Virtual worlds as a site of convergence for children's play. *Journal of Virtual Worlds Research, 3*(2), 2–19.

Lim, S. S. and Ooi, J. (2011). Girls talk tech: Exploring Singaporean girls' perceptions of technology. In M. C. Kearney (Ed.), *Mediated girlhood: New explorations of girls' media culture.* New York: Peter Lang, pp. 243–60.

Lim, S. S., Basnyat, I., Chan, Y. H., Vadrevu, S. and Koh, K. K. (June, 2011). Mobile phones, the Internet and juvenile delinquency – Managing and resisting delinquent peer networks. Unpublished paper presented at the International Communication Association 2011 ICA Mobile pre?conference workshop. "Seamlessly mobile?: Mobile communication @ a crossroads", Boston, MA.

Ling, R. and Yttri, B. (2002). Hyper-coordination via mobile phones in Norway. In J. Katz and R. Aakhus (Eds), *Perpetual contact: Mobile communication, private talk and public performance.* Cambridge: Cambridge University Press, pp. 139–69.

Lu, S. L. (2010). Growing up with Neopets: A personal case-study. *Journal of Virtual Worlds Research, 3*(2), 2–24.

Mazzarella, S. R. (2005). Claiming a space: The cultural economy of teen girl fandom on the Web. In S. R. Mazzarella (Ed.), *Girl wide web: Girls, the internet and the negotiation of identity.* New York: Peter Lang, pp. 141–60.

Nathanson, A. (2001). Parents versus peers: Exploring the significance of peer mediation of antisocial television. *Communication Research, 28*(3), 251–74.

Okada, T. (2006). Youth culture and the shaping of Japanese mobile media: Personalization and keitai internet as multimedia. In M. Ito, M. Matsuda and D. Okabe (Eds), *Personal, portable, pedestrian: mobile phones in Japanese life.* Cambridge, MA: MIT Press, pp. 41–60.

Pasquier, D. (2008). From parental control to peer pressure: Cultural transmission and conformism. In K. Drotner and S. Livingstone (Eds), *The international handbook of children, media and culture.* London: Sage, pp. 448–59.

Polak, M. (2007). "I think we must be normal … there are too many of us for this to be abnormal!!!": Girls creating identity and forming community in pro-ana/mia websites. In S. Weber and S. Dixon (Eds) *Growing up online: Young people and digital technologies.* Hampshire: Palgrave Macmillan, pp. 81–94.

Silberman, S. (2001). We're teens, we're queer, and we've got email. In D. Trend (Ed.), *Reading digital culture.* Malden, MA: Blackwell, pp. 221–25.

Suess, D., Suoninen, A., Garitaonandia, C., Juaristi, P., Koikkalainen, R. and Oleaga, J. A. (1998). Media use and the relationships of children and teenagers with their peer groups. *European Journal of Communication, 13*(4), 521–38.

Suoninen, A. (2001). The role of media in peer group relations. In S. Livingstone and M. Bovill (Eds), *Children and their changing media environment: A European comparative study.* Mahwah, NJ: Lawrence Erlbaum, pp. 201–20.

Taylor, A. and Harper, R. (2003). The gift of the gab?: A design oriented sociology of young people's use of mobiles. *Journal of Computer Supported Cooperative Work, 12*(3), 267–96.

Thurlow, C. and Brown, A. (2003). Generation Txt? The sociolinguistics of young people's text-messaging. *Discourse Analysis Online.* Retrieved from http://extra.shu.ac.uk/daol/articles/v1/n1/a3/thurlow2002003-paper.html

Wesch, M. (2009). YouTube and you: Experiences of self-awareness in the context collapse of the recording webcam. *Explorations in Media Ecology, 8*(2), 19–34.

Williams, J. P. (2003). The straightedge subculture on the Internet: A case study of style-display online. *Media International Australia Incorporating Culture and Policy, 107*(5), 61–74.

40

MEDIA AND MINORITY
CHILDREN

Michelle M. Rivera and Angharad N. Valdivia

Media are of the utmost importance for minority children as they allow them to bridge their experience as members of a minoritized culture and of a mainstream within which they must exist. Both the children and the media function in a transnational world that has implications in terms of belonging, interpretation, and identity. Of importance is the fact that minority child audiences actively interpret and "filter" global media through their local cultural experiences (Buckingham, 2002, p. 7). This chapter begins with an examination of the category "minority" as this varies across national spaces, foregrounding the concept of minoritization as a verb rather than a natural category or the noun "minority." It then proceeds to examine research on representations of minority children. Next the chapter explores research on minority children's use of the media with policy implications. The chapter ends with suggestions for further research.

Categorization

What counts as a minority in one setting can be a majority in another, and the change can be across geography and time—thus the categorization of minority children becomes more complex in relation to global issues. First, "minorities" refers to different groups of children in different times and settings. Second, in many settings the discourse of minoritization does not exist. This does not mean that there are no minorities but rather that because it is not a frame of research, no data is collected on minority children per se. Third, this category has great overlap with that of immigrant children, as the very status of immigration often results in minoritization. Issues of national origin, race and ethnicity, religion, and regionality are all elements that can render a child a "minority." For instance, in the US until the 2000 Census, an overwhelming majority of studies adopted a binary racial model to study minority children who were assumed to be black in relation to normative white children. Following the 2000 acknowledgement of a growing Latina/o population, the landscape of minority children research began to slowly expand to include children of recent or past Latin American origin. Obviously within Latin America, Latina/o is not a useful category but within individual countries there are ways of minoritizing national indigenous populations as well as regional prejudices against neighboring countries. The same applies to all global regions wherein what counts as a minority in one setting changes across time and space. The Europe-wide EU Kids Online LSE project represents some of the challenges to finding data about minority children and media. Lobe et al. (2007) assert that while multinational researchers need to:

> avoid overstating homogeneity within countries [and so downplaying the importance of socio-demographic, regional or cultural divides within a country], they must also avoid overstating heterogeneity across countries [and so reproducing national stereotypes or exaggerating difference].
>
> *(p. 35)*

Yet there is relatively little attention paid to heterogeneity within countries—the level at which minoritization is usually experienced by children. First, the projects are more attentive to gender than to race, ethnicity, or religion (e.g., Garmendia et al., 2011; Staksrud et al., 2009). Second, the category of "risk" potentially includes minority status through "violent or hateful content." For example Hasebrink et al. (2009) single out one of the risks as "racist/hate material/activities" (p. 7) and "biased information, racism, blasphemy, and health advice" at the intersection of content and values/ideology (p. 8). However other EU Kids Online studies discuss "hateful content" in terms of pornography, and not necessarily race or minority status (e.g., de Haan and Livingstone, 2009) or list racism as one of a series of risks that includes "self-harm, suicide, pro-anorexia, drugs, hate/racism, gambling, addiction, illegal downloading, and commercial risks" (Livingstone and Haddon, 2009, p. 3). In all of the above religious minority status is implicitly part of the content and experience of "hate/racism," reminding us that religious discrimination influences media content and consumption among minoritized children. Particular countries' efforts to track, prosecute, and prevent cyberhate, especially in Belgium, do not elucidate how much of this hate is experienced by minoritized children. Thus we can see the difficulty of writing a chapter on minority children and media across the globe when the definition of minority shifts not only in terms of time and space but also within large research projects.

Given that media circulate transnationally, minority children's identification and engagement with particular characters, situations, and particular media is a dynamic area of study that has to be both global and locally contextual. More complex issues of hybrid identities and popular culture further trouble how minority children and the media are studied.

Precisely because the category of "minority" is dynamic and contextual, research about minority children rarely disaggregates them. For instance, Calvert et al. (2003), do not disaggregate racial or ethnic minority status in their study of minority children and computer use. Moreover religious difference influences children's media consumption and requires more attention (Downing, 2003). This chapter explores a context of transnational flows of media consumed by a heterogeneous and globally dynamic population of minority children. It addresses Buckingham's (2008) calls for scholars to engage a more holistic approach to research on children and the media by examining text, production, and audiences together, thus providing a "wider analysis of the ways in which both … are constructed and defined" (p. 227).

Minority children and representation

Research on media representation finds that dominant culture children are over-represented, sometimes to the extent of the exclusion of any minorities. Since the circulation of children's and general media tends to follow transnational patterns of production and reception, the over-representation of white children in US-produced media is circulated globally. Conversely, the near lack of production of any media, including children's media, in Africa results in the severe under-representation of characters and themes from that continent that might appeal and relate to that huge segment of the global population. Regional production nodes in places such as India, Japan, and the UK, as well as a smaller output from other countries in Asia, Europe, and Latin America follow this pattern of over-representation of white children, with notable but not mainstream circulated media being produced in most settings with increasing attention paid to issues of ethnicity and other minoritized children. Numerous studies focus on representations of minority children in media such as cartoons (Harewood and Valdivia, 2005; Merskin, 2008), television (Seiter and Mayer, 2004) and children's literature (Rice, 2005; Roy, 2008). Schlote and Otremba (2010) find that cultural diversity is represented as a problem. In general, studies of minority children suggest that there has been a change from near exclusion, to symbolic anni-hilation, to a multicultural palette foregrounding white children and backgrounding minority children, to some representations of hybrid and ambiguously ethnic children with the potential of addressing and interpellating a wide range of identities (Valdivia 2009; 2011).

Minority children and media use

Minority children's media use varies in relation to their socio-economic class. Thus the finding is one of intersectionality—ethnicity, class, and other vectors of difference such as religion and region, function together. Unsurprisingly, access to "new" media is highly correlated with socio-economic status (SES) in settings such as the US and many countries with wide income gaps and much more widespread in the wealthier countries of Europe, especially those with relatively strong investment in public education and culture. Recent US census data (U.S. Census Bureau, 2010) revealing more ethnically and racially diverse audiences, whose households tend to be younger and often include children, forecasts an increase of ethnic media (Nielsen Company, 2009, pp. 4–7). In the US, ethnic differences in access to cable, video game ownership, internet, HD-ready technologies, and DVR machines at home roughly map out over the SES of ethnic groups and thus predict the level of access and engagement for ethnic children.

Some national studies focus on the role of media in the lives of children. Rideout (2011) found that media use varies much more significantly by race and SES factors than by gender (p. 12). Younger children (0–8 years of age) in higher income households with highly educated parents average less media usage daily than lower-income children. African American children spend more time than white children with media, yet read slightly more (13 minutes) than white children. Children from lower-income households watch more over the air educational television than the recorded material viewed by higher income children. Researchers attribute this to lower access to cable or satellite among lower-income households. Uneven penetration of digital/new media signals a growing "app gap" (p. 21) emerging across households with greater economic disparities. A statistically significant proportion of lower income families exhibit much less use of newer mobile devices in relation to higher income families' use of digital games, videos, and apps on cell phones, iPods, and iPads. Tablet technology and home computers are more prevalent among children in higher income families. Confirming the intersectionality of SES and ethnicity, Pew Research Center data confirms that teen cell phone users from the lowest household incomes are also the most likely to use their portable handsets to go online (Madden, 2010) while 78 percent of white teens, 75 percent of African American teens, and 68 percent of Hispanic teens have cell phones. Among those who own four or more internet-connected devices, minority groups (10 percent African American, 12 percent Hispanic, and 9 percent "other") lag behind the 69 percent of white adopters of multiple internet-enabled devices.

On the other hand, 22 percent of African American children and 21 percent of Hispanic children are described as more likely to engage in "media multitasking" (watching television while completing homework or listening to music devices while playing a video game) than the 11 percent of white children in this same age range (Rideout, 2011, p. 27). "Generation M" (ages 8–18) (Rideout et al., 2005) comprises young people across ethnic groups with expanded access to media inside and outside of the home through the proliferation of mobile devices, while the increased use of new media has not displaced their heavier use of television and music. Multitasking describes media use among youth populations as opposed to reports and studies that focus on "displacement" narratives about old media technologies (Scantlin, 2008, p. 58). The app gap and notable digital divide point to the salience of SES in predicting online access and use, but signal disparities in use and access among ethnic and racial minorities in the US. More studies are needed that examine minority children as interactive subjects online. Lenhart and Madden (2005 cited in Scantlin 2008, p. 56) found that 12 million young people created content online, mostly at home, by 2010. Based on a Kaiser Family Foundation study focusing especially on minority youth, the *New York Times* reported "If your kids are awake, they're probably online" (Lewin, 2010). Furthermore, Rideout et al. (2010) found that race related disparities of access had increased "substantially" (p. 38) over the past five years in terms of minority youth watching more television on new technological platforms.

Worldwide, scholarship considers the complex intersectional engagement with "new" media. For instance, Hijazi-Omari and Rivka Ribak (2008) study mobile phone use among Palestinian teen girls in Israel, exploring their complex and mediated relationships as they face constraints by men, parents, and community. González Hernández (2008) studies youth in Tijuana as an interpretive community negotiating television viewing across the Mexico–US border. Spry (2010) explores mobile media use in the schools and homes of Australian and Japanese youth and argues that within policy and public discourse around mobile media children's voices are ignored (p. 16), with significant implications as rising adoption rates of "new" media technologies provide minority youth with expanded opportunities for the creation and dissemination of media. This sampling of new research reveals the rich possibilities for learning about minority children and media usage.

Minority children and diasporic use of media

Children become minoritized through voluntary and involuntary mobility across the globe. Issues of diaspora and hybridity also need to be considered in relation to children, media, and the globe. Whether discussing ethnicity, religion, nation, or other minority status, much research assumes distinct and mutually exclusive categories. Widespread population mobility means that children are likely to have many national affinities, either through personal experience or through their parents and culture. The production and circulation of media within globalization articulates children to these transnational and diasporic flows and potentially provides them with an outlet for creative engagement across national boundaries. Living within a minority and a potentially dissenting community can enhance the potential for transnational or "diasporic" communication. Location is contingent given that instantaneous digital communication challenges previous categories of community defined by geographical proximity (Buckingham, 2002). In fact studies suggest that children respond to their minoritized status by consuming transnationally available media with their peers and relatives in their locations of origin and by producing media to distribute at least locally to assert their hybrid subjectivity.

For example, a third generation Jewish child in the US might have diasporically migrated from Germany, to Cuba, and then to the US and thus possess a national, linguistic, racial, and religious identity and affiliations that might be quite diverse and internally contradictory. This child's media consumption might range from Hebrew religious material provided by parents or the local synagogue to contemporary mainstream television in English, salsa and Caribbean music in Spanish from Cuban cousins, digital media from China, and anime material from Japan. This hybrid and diasporic media diet and identity "demands delicate negotiations of race/ethnicity, nation, class, language, culture, and history" (Durham, 2004, p. 141). For children whose consumer and heritage culture overlap (Buckingham, 2002), their potential as cultural creators is likely to be dynamic and hybrid.

Worldwide studies such as that of de Block and Buckingham (2007) explore the mediated experience of children as they face migration and therefore minoritization. In fact this diasporic and hybrid situation seems to encourage the jump from media use to media production as contemporary media technologies provide the potential for the production as well as the consumption of media. For children and youth the dividing line is often blurred with the digital technologies. Vargas (2009) documents transnational teens' media usage and production in their efforts to remain connected, especially girls who had no agency in moving and were usually torn from beloved relatives. Elias and Lemish (2009; 2010) similarly find that Soviet teens in Israel use the internet as a resource to stay connected and develop transitioning identities as they seek to create a safe ground to assuage the loneliness of their transnational lives. Similarly Mayer (2003) illustrates the creativity asserted by Mexican American youth through the production of media. Studies that are able to capture these types of micro-level efforts to retain transnational ties rely on small sample family and group methodology (Katz, 2010; Mayer, 2003; Moran, 2011; Vargas, 2009), yet suggest both the painful disruption and the active use of media on the part of teens to regain a sense of belonging and reimagination of their shifting identities.

Conclusions

Minority children are not a new global phenomenon, but research-wise we are just beginning to study them as such and to develop standardized ways of operationalizing the category. As has been the case with communications technologies, each new technology presents children and youth with new opportunities and challenges. Minoritized children experience additional intersectional issues that result in different uses and production of media in relation to normalized representations of whiteness in relation to all other differences. Ongoing research documents a widening gap of media usage—with minority children using more legacy media in new platforms, as well as differentials in terms of access to new technologies, with SES and minority status functioning in tandem. As most nations begin to acknowledge their increasing racial and ethnic diversity, transnational media corporations are ahead of national efforts to track ethnic trends in media consumption to attract minority audiences. Yet minorities are not easily understood. Hybrid racial and ethnic identities of media consumers complicate data in media reports using monolithic categories, disregarding the hybrid racial make-up of Latina/os or Asians in the US, for example. Where does the Afro-Latino or Blasian child fit in the data set? Minority categories must also be expanded across religion and nation, significant vectors of difference that impact the daily lives and media practices of children. Review of the literature reveals a need for further work in this area. Ethnographic approaches have been useful in bringing awareness to activities taking place in the homes of minority children, such as "media brokering." However, US studies provide data on the adoption rates of media and technologies across ethnic and racial groups, but do not address how technologies are integrated into minority children's daily practices. What are these youth filming, uploading, creating, texting, sexting? What are their skill levels? How are their media practices managed, policed, constrained, and/or enabled within their schools, families, religious institutions? How does identity contribute to media usage and production? Minority children represent the inevitable and prevalent movement of populations and media, and as such are a bellwether as to our ability as nations and cultures to include population flows and acknowledge that diasporas and the resulting hybridity are the norm rather than the exception.

SEE ALSO in this volume chapter by Elias.

References

Buckingham, D. (2002). *Children and Media*. London: UNESCO. Retrieved December 3, 2011 from http://www.european-mediaculture.org/Youth-Culture-Media-Culture.518+M5ff6784e153.0.html

——(2008). Children and media: A cultural studies approach. In K. Drotner and S. Livingstone (Eds), *The international handbook of children, media and culture*. Los Angeles, London, New Delhi, Singapore: Sage, pp. 219–36.

Calvert, S. L., Kotler, J. A., Zehnder, S. M. and Shockey, E. M. (2003). Gender stereotyping in children's reports about educational and informational television programs. *Media Psychology*, 5(2), 139–62.

de Block, L. and Buckingham, D. (2007). *Global children, global media: Migration, media and childhood*. Basingstoke: Palgrave Macmillan.

de Haan, J. and Livingstone, S. (2009). *Policy and research recommendations*. EU Kids Online, London: The London School of Economics and Political Science. Retrieved December 3, 2011 from http://eprints. lse.ac.uk/24387/

Downing, J. H. D. (2003). "Where we should go next and why we probably won't": An entirely idio-syncratic, utopian and unashamedly peppery map for the future. In A. N. Valdivia (Ed.), *The Blackwell companion to media studies*. London: Blackwell, pp. 495–512.

Durham, G. (2004). Constructing the "new ethnicities": Media, sexuality, and diaspora identity in the lives of South Asian immigrant girls. *Critical Studies in Media Communication*, 21(2), 140–61.

Elias, N. and Lemish, D. (2009). Spinning the web of identity: The roles of the internet in the lives of immigrant adolescents. *New Media and Society*, 11(4), 533–51.

——(2010). Media, migration experience and adolescence: The role of television and internet for 6- to 18-year-olds of Russian descent in Germany and Israel. *Televizion*, 23/2010/E, 9–13.

Garmendia, M., Garitaonandia, C., Martínez, G. and Casado, M. A. (2011). *Riesgos y seguridad en internet: Los menores españoles en el contexto europeo. [Risk and safety on the internet: Spanish children in the European context]*. Universidad del País Vasco/Euskal Herriko Unibertsitatea, Bilboa: EU Kids Online. Retrieved December 3, 2011 from http://www2.lse.ac.uk/media@lse/research/EUKidsOnline/Participating Countries/spain.aspx

González Hernández, D. (2008). Watching over the border: A case study of the Mexico-U.S. television and youth audience. In A. N. Valdivia (Ed.), *Latina/o communication studies today*. New York: Peter Lang, pp. 219–36.

Harewood, S. and Valdivia, A. N. (2005). Exploring Dora: Re-embodied Latinidad on the web. In S. R. Mazzarella (Ed.), *Girl wide web: Girls, the internet, and the negotiation of identity*. New York: Peter Lang, pp. 85–103.

Hasebrink, U., Livingstone, S., Haddon, L. and Ólafsson, K. (2009). *Comparing children's online opportunities and risks across Europe: Cross-national comparisons for EU Kids Online (2nd edition)*. London: The London School of Economics and Political Science. Retrieved December 3, 2011 from http://eprints.lse.ac.uk/ 24368/

Hijazi-Omari, H. and Ribak, R. (2008). PLAYING WITH FIRE: On the domestication of the mobile phone among Palestinian teenage girls in Israel. *Information, Communication and Society*, 11(2), 149–66.

Katz, V. S. (2010). How children of immigrants use media to connect their families to the community: The case of Latinos in South Los Angeles. *Journal of Children and Media*, 4(3), 298–315.

Lenhart, A. and Madden, M. (2005). *Teen content creators and consumers*. Washington, DC: Pew Internet and American Life Project. Retrieved December 3, 2011, from http://www.pewinternet.org/Reports/ 2005/Teen-Content-Creators-and-Consumers.aspx

Lewin, T. (2010, January 20). If your kids are awake, they're probably online. *New York Times*. Retrieved June 10, 2012, from http://www.nytimes.com/2010/01/20/education/20wired.html

Livingstone, S. and Haddon, L. (2009). *EU kids online: Final report*. EU Kids Online, London: The London School of Economics and Political Science. Retrieved December 3, 2011 from http://eprints.lse.ac.uk/ 24372/

Lobe, B., Livingstone, S. and Haddon, L. with others (2007). *Researching children's experiences online across countries: Issues and problems in methodology*. EU Kids Online, London: The London School of Economics and Political Science. Retrieved December 3, 2011 from http://eprints.lse.ac.uk/2856/

Madden, M. (2010, June 27). *Four or more: The new demographic*. Pew Internet and American Life Project. Presentation at American Library Association – LITA. Retrieved December 3, 2011 from http://pewinternet.org/Presentations/2010/Jun/Four-or-More – The-New-Demographic.aspx

Mayer, V. (2003). *Producing dreams, consuming youth: Mexican Americans and mass media*. New Brunswick: Rutgers University Press.

Merskin, D. L. (2008). Race and gender representations in advertising in cable cartoon programming. *CLCWeb: Comparative Literature and Culture, 10*(2). Retrieved December 3, 2011 from http://docs.lib.purdue.edu/clcweb/vol10/iss2/10

Moran, K. C. (2011). *Listening to Latina/o youth: Television consumption within families*. New York: Peter Lang.

Nielsen Company. (2009, March). *Ethnic trends in media* (pp. 1–12). Retrieved December 3, 2011 from http://blog.nielsen.com/nielsenwire/media_entertainment/looking-towards-2050-ethnic-trends-in-media/

Rice, P. (2005). It "ain't" always so: Sixth graders' interpretations of Hispanic-American stories with universal themes. *Children's Literature in Education, 36*(4), 343–62.

Rideout, V. J. (2011). *Zero to eight: Children's media use in america*. San Francisco, New York, Washington, D.C., Los Angeles: Common Sense Media, pp. 1–44. Retrieved December 3, 2011 from http://vjrconsulting.com/children-media/

Rideout, V. J., Roberts, D. F. and Foehr, U. G. (2005). *Executive summary – Generation M: Media in the lives of 8–18 year-olds*. Washington, D.C.: The Henry J. Kaiser Family Foundation. Retrieved December 3, 2011 from http://www.kff.org/entmedia/entmedia030905pkg.cfm

Rideout, V. J., Foehr, U. G. and Roberts, D. F. (2010). *Generation M2: Media in the lives of 8-10 year olds*. Washington, D.C.: The Henry J. Kaiser Family Foundation. Retrieved December 3, 2011 from http://www.kff.org/entmedia/8010.cfm

Roy, S. (2008). A critical discourse analysis of representation of Asian Indian folk tales in US-American children's literature. *CLCWeb: Comparative Literature and Culture, 10*(2). Retrieved December 3, 2011 from http://docs.lib.purdue.edu/clcweb/vol10/iss2/10

Scantlin, R. (2008). Media use across childhood: Access, time, and content. In S. L. Calvert and B. J. Wilson (Eds), *The handbook of children, media, and development*. Oxford: Blackwell, pp. 51–73.

Schlote, E. and Otremba, K. (2010). Cultural diversity in children's television: Media analyses of programmes and effective strategies. *Televizion*, 23/2010/E, 4–8.

Seiter, E. and Mayer, V. (2004). Diversifying representation in children's tv: Nickelodeon's model. In H. Hendershot (Ed.). *Nickelodeon nation: The history, politics, and economics of America's only TV channel for kids*. New York: NYU Press, pp. 120–33.

Spry, D. (2010). Angels and devils: Youth mobile media politics, fear, hope and policy in Japan and Australia. In S. H. Donald, T. D. Anderson and D. Spry (Eds), *Youth, society and mobile media in Asia*. London: Routledge, pp. 15–30.

Staksrud, E., Livingstone, S., Haddon, L. and Ólafsson, K. (2009). *What do we know about children's use of online technologies? A Report on Data Availability and Research Gaps in Europe* (2nd edition). EU Kids Online, London: The London School of Economics and Political Science. Retrieved December 3, 2011 from http://eprints.lse.ac.uk/24367/

U.S. Census Bureau (2010). *America's Children: Key National Indicators of Well-Being, 2011*. Retrieved December 3, 2011 from http://www.childstats.gov/americaschildren/demo.asp

Valdivia, A. N. (2009). Living in a hybrid material world: Girls, ethnicity and doll products. *Girlhood Studies: An Interdisciplinary Journal, 1*(3), 173–93.

Valdivia, A. N. (2011). This tween bridge over my Latina girl back: The US mainstream negotiates ethnicity. In M. C. Kearney (Ed.), *Mediated girlhoods: New explorations of girls' media culture*. New York: Peter Lang, pp. 93–109.

Vargas, L. (2009). *Latina teens, migration, and popular culture*. New York: Peter Lang.

41

IMMIGRANT CHILDREN AND MEDIA

Nelly Elias

Introduction: media in immigrant children's "inward" and "outward" integration

Immigration and integration into a new society are among the most complex processes in an individual's life, characterized by numerous losses, confusion, and challenges that eventually lead to significant personal changes. While the research literature usually pays more attention to changes characteristic of adult immigrants, the experience may be no less difficult for children and adolescents. Like their parents, immigrant youngsters miss their familiar culture and previous social networks. In parallel, the more rapid adoption of the new language and culture by immigrant youth may widen cultural gaps between them and older family members, thus weakening parental authority and family cohesion.

Accordingly, a distinction should be made between the two adaptation processes that immigrant youth undergo simultaneously: "Outward" integration (acquiring host language skills, adopting local youth culture, and socializing with local peers) and "inward" integration (instilling native linguistic skills, transmitting the cultural heritage, and spending leisure time together) (Elias and Lemish, 2008a). To succeed at these demanding processes, young immigrants have to maximize the use of the resources at their disposal, including media in the host and native languages. This chapter will provide an overview of the principal media use by immigrant children and adolescents seeking to facilitate their incorporation into the new culture – while attempting to preserve their original cultural identity – and to maintain family unity despite growing cultural gaps.

Media use in immigrant families

Despite the centrality of mass media in contemporary families, the roles of media among immigrant families have received very limited research attention. The few studies conducted to date have shown that the roles and effects of media may be situated along two axes: cultural integration versus preservation of the original language and culture, and family integration versus the escalation of parent–child tensions and the widening of intergenerational gaps.

Regarding the first axis, the research literature shows that immigrant parents, who are often concerned about their children's loss of proficiency in their mother tongue and common cultural heritage, perceive homeland media as a means of maintaining their children's language skills and affiliation with their culture of origin. Children, however, usually reject and resent these efforts. Accordingly, Gillespie's (1995) study of Indian immigrants in London found that when parents used ethnic media as tools for cultural didactics, their teenage children reacted with a certain antagonism. Similarly, a study by Elias and Lemish (2008a, 2011) on media use in immigrant families from the Former Soviet Union in Israel and Germany shows that most of the parents employed Russian media for cultural transmission only during their first years in the host country, ceasing to do so subsequently because they despaired of overcoming children's resistance. The few parents who did succeed at this mission were those who chose media content in Russian that appealed to global youth culture, considering it a more enjoyable way to impart a better command of the Russian language to their children.

Nevertheless, immigrant children might be less resistant to their parents' attempts to improve their native language skills when some cultural brokering is practiced. Thus, Katz's (2010) study of Latin American immigrant families in the US revealed that children and parents tended to watch local news in Spanish together and when parents did not understand the significance of media content (even though it was in their mother tongue), children willingly explained it to them, brokering between different sets of cultural knowledge. These brokering activities were not one-way experiences. Rather, parents and children reported cooperatively negotiating the meanings of particular events to reach shared understandings. In this manner, parents facilitated their children's native language facility by introducing them to more sophisticated Spanish vocabulary and necessary contextual information.

Furthermore, a study focusing on the "cultural integration" pole of the first axis examined how Chinese parents in Canada employed the mass media to facilitate their children's English language learning (Guofang, 2007). It was found that parents intentionally encouraged their children's English language acquisition by purchasing a variety of books, magazines, and video cassettes that suited their children's interests and were beneficial in language learning. In addition, these families watched local channels together, including films with English subtitles, so that the children could read the words as they were spoken.

In parallel, immigrant families must cope with another major challenge – weakening internal family ties. Consequently, homeland television broadcasts are used to preserve family unity, as found by Elias and Lemish (2008a, 2011). Although most children in their study were uninterested in specific Russian talk shows or films, they enjoyed viewing them with their parents for the sake of spending leisure time together. Furthermore, among families of old-timers, in which children refused to watch television in Russian, joint television viewing usually involved programs of global reach and appeal, such as international sporting events, reality shows and Hollywood films. This served to circumvent the tension of choosing between two possibilities – assimilation or preservation of the homeland culture – by finding shelter in what both generations perceived to be a "neutral" cultural background.

On the other hand, several studies point to the intergenerational conflicts provoked by television viewing. Thus, Hargreaves and Mahdjoub's (1997) study on Muslim immigrant families in France revealed that installation of a satellite dish led to an escalation in parent–child disputes. Similarly, Ogan's (2001) study of Turkish immigrants in the Netherlands and Siew-Peng's (2001) study of Chinese immigrants in Britain found that children criticized their parents' intensive viewing of homeland channels, as it prevented them from watching the host television programs that were important for socializing with local peers.

While most studies on media use in immigrant families focused primarily on television, Rydin and Sjöberg (2008) investigated internet use by parents and children among refugee families in Sweden. Their findings provide initial insights into the parents' attempts to recruit the internet for the purpose of strengthening their children's attachment to the home country.

By and large, these attempts were found to be ineffective, as children preferred to use the internet to chat with friends in their immediate vicinity. Furthermore, Katz's (2010) study highlighted the internet's role in immigrant families' instrumental adjustment, noting that most immigrant parents were unable to use host language websites because of language constraints and depended on their children's brokering for practical information about the new surroundings.

Finally, an international project on immigrant children's media production and consumption emphasized the importance of parents' ethnic background and their status in the host society (as migrants or refugees) in investigating media roles in immigrant families. The study showed that immigrant parents differed according to their motivation to maintain their children's affiliation with their culture of origin versus their attempts to facilitate their children's incorporation into the receiving culture. Parents thus developed different media strategies aimed at cultural preservation or assimilation: several parents recreated a familiar cultural atmosphere at home by intensive viewing of homeland channels, while others avoided installation of a satellite dish to avoid interrupting their children's host language acquisition (Christopoulou and de Leeuw, 2004; de Block and Buckingham, 2007).

Media roles in young immigrants' social and cultural adaptation

The research literature reveals that the mass media provide young immigrants with various cultural, social, linguistic, informational, and psychological resources needed for their adaptation. To date, three media have gained special research attention – television, internet, and books. The following sections analyze their roles among immigrant children and teens.

Television

The role of television in immigrant children's lives had drawn some research attention already at the end of the 1980s, when Zohoori (1988) compared television use patterns among immigrant and local children aged 6–12 in the US. The findings showed that immigrant children expressed a stronger belief in the reality of people and events and had a more positive attitude towards educational programs than their local counterparts. In addition, immigrant children suffered from a lack of close relationships with local peers. Hence television characters were among the first Americans to whom they were introduced and with whom they could easily "interact." Similarly, a recent study by Gezduci and d'Haenens (2010) of Moroccan, Turkish and Flemish adolescents aged 12–19 in Flanders revealed that host television news played a more prominent role for Moroccan and Turkish youngsters than for the native youth and that it was viewed primarily because of its perceived credibility and its function as a source of social learning.

The research literature also suggests that host language television provides immigrant children with opportunities for second language learning (Elias and Lemish, 2011; Katz, 2011). Acquisition of the new language is essential for immigrant children, whose parents are usually unable to assist them in this process. Host language television thus becomes a major language learning resource that a 12-year-old girl in Elias and Lemish's (2011) study considered as daily "homework" critical to her adjustment to the new country. Similarly, for immigrant children who arrived in a new country at a very young age, native language television broadcasts were found to be effective in improving mother tongue proficiency (Cruickshank, 2010).

No less important is the role of television in shaping immigrant youth's hybrid identities: Local, global, and ethnic. In this regard, Gillespie (1995) found that exposure to Indian films and dramas ensured some degree of preservation of traditional values among immigrant youth, while British and global television broadcasts enabled them to develop a new cultural identity.

Similarly, two recent studies conducted in the US on Indian teenage girls (Durham, 2004) and on their Mexican counterparts (Mayer, 2003) found that American sitcoms and Indian films or Mexican telenovelas, respectively, played an important role in the immigrant girls' construction of ethnic identities and in maintaining their connection to the distant homeland, while also helping them cope with various tensions experienced as young women of color in the US.

Internet

The literature indicates that because of its unique characteristics, such as cultural and linguistic diversity, accessibility, interactivity, and anonymity, the internet provides the young immigrants with the valuable cultural, social, and emotional resources needed for personal growth and empowerment. Overall, the studies identified three principal functions that the internet fulfills for immigrant youth: (1) A source of information about the new society and about the homeland and its culture; (2) a platform for online contacts with co-ethnics and native-born peers; and (3) a tool for preserving one's native language and improving host language skills.

Source of information and cultural knowledge about the host and the home countries

One particularly urgent aspect of immigrant youth's relocation into a new society is the need to adjust to a new lifestyle and cultural demands. The research literature suggests that immigrant adolescents find the internet a very useful tool in their conscious efforts to satisfy this need. Accordingly, a study by Elias and Lemish (2008b) shows that information sought by Russian immigrant adolescents on the internet extended along a continuum from the macro level of news, politics, and the local culture to the micro level of practical information related to everyday life, behavioral patterns, youth fashions and the like. Moreover, the participants had greater trust in Israeli websites and were more willing to adopt the new values and codes of behavior suggested there than those proposed by Israeli peers or teachers.

Besides constituting a major source of information about the host society, the internet also serves as a window to life in a distant homeland. This role is especially important because, in many cases, up to date news from the homeland may be unavailable or distorted by the host media. The research literature thus indicates that immigrant youth search for online news to obtain information about current events in their countries of origin, while using online cultural resources to preserve and strengthen their original ethnic, religious, and cultural identities (d'Haenens, 2003; Elias and Lemish, 2009; Lam and Rosario-Ramos, 2009; Peeters and d'Haenens, 2005).

The studies thus show that these youngsters' digital practices situate them in a transnational circuit of news and ideas, where they are exposed to diverse political narratives, social expectations, cultural values, and societal experiences. These practices appear to foster formation of their hybrid identity and an ability to see things from multiple perspectives originating in the home and host societies.

Interpersonal communication with co-ethnics and native-born peers

The internet has been lauded for its dual capacity as a mass medium and an interpersonal medium and for its ability to transcend temporal and geographical boundaries. Such versatility renders it particularly attractive to immigrants who suffer a sudden decrease in communication resources due to migration. In this regard, the research literature points to a significant increase in immigrant youngsters' use of e-mail and instant messaging software after arrival in their new country to communicate with family and co-ethnic friends residing in their countries of origin. These strengthened relationships with loved ones were found to bring about psychological stability and support (Fogt and Sandvik, 2008; Kim et al., 2009; Yang et al., 2004). Furthermore, the study by Kim et al. (2009) showed that young immigrants also received social support from new relationships with other youngsters of the same nationality. Most such online relationships appeared to be centered on gaining practical information useful in the young immigrants' daily lives.

Several studies revealed that besides constituting a useful platform for bonding with co-ethnics, the internet is also used to build the young immigrant's first meaningful contacts with local peers (Elias and Lemish, 2009; Kim et al., 2009). The purpose of these online relationships varies from contacts of a romantic nature to instrumental functions, such as improving host language skills or obtaining information about life in the host country. Moreover, Elias and Lemish (2009) emphasize that online contacts with local youngsters were described by immigrant youngsters in far more positive terms than was face-to-face communication with Israeli peers whom they met in the neighborhood or in school.

The internet thus plays an important role in maintaining young immigrants' close relationships with people from the same country of origin. This process, called "bonding social capital" by Putnam (2000), is considered significant because it strengthens ties with family and co-ethnic friends who might be in a position to provide emotional support. At the same time, the internet enables these youngsters to make connections with local residents, thus enhancing "bridging social capital" (ibid.) and ultimately serving as the foundation of sociocultural adaptation to the host society.

Improving native and host language skills

Recent studies by Lam and Rosario-Ramos (2009) and Lee (2006) have explored the role of transnational online networks in native language and literacy maintenance among immigrant youth. Lee (2006) found that Korean immigrant youngsters' social networking provided them with a community of Korean speakers (who were minimally present in their local environments) and a source of motivation to use their heritage language. Similarly, Lam and Rosario-Ramos's (2009) research on internet use among immigrant youngsters – from various countries – in the US found that using their native language online helped most of them maintain or even improve their language proficiency – an observation of particular importance because they seldom used their native languages in writing.

Lam and Rosario-Ramos (2009) also point to the immigrant youngsters' search for opportunities to learn and practice their host language online. Besides reading a wide range of English language online material, many of their participants used chats in English to improve their conversational fluency, vocabulary, and writing skills. Similarly, Elias and Lemish (2009) found that Russian-speaking immigrant adolescents in Israel intentionally sought online contacts with native-born peers to improve their Hebrew language skills. Moreover, their participants mentioned that while they often felt embarrassed in face-to-face communication with local peers because of their partial mastery of the host language, they did not experience such feelings in virtual contacts with young Israelis whom they met online, and who were much more tolerant of their language mistakes.

Books

Books represent a "forgotten" medium in the lives of immigrant youth that has attracted only modest research attention to date. The few studies conducted show that books play an influential role in immigrant youth's coping with relocation difficulties. Thus, Champion's (1993) study of the role of school libraries in easing alienation among students of Hispanic origin in the US found that participation in reading groups helped immigrant students understand themselves and others, absorb the new culture, and gain mastery of the subtleties of the English language. Moreover, young participants reported that books helped them understand that people in all cultures overcame numerous obstacles in the course of their personal transformation. Group reading thus served the immigrant adolescents as a pathway to self-understanding and helped them answer critical questions characteristic of displacement and adjustment to their new surroundings.

While Champion's study was limited to guided reading in the host language, a more recent study by Elias and Khvorostianov (2010) on book reading by Russian immigrant adolescents in Israel focused on reading choices made by the interviewees as part of their leisure activities. First, their participants claimed that they read more books in Israel than they did before immigration. Moreover, their reading patterns reflected the immigrant adolescents' need to express, comprehend, and legitimize their feelings of sadness, loneliness, and helplessness caused by immigration. Through reading psychological books and historical novels, they projected their own emotions onto the books' characters and sought solutions to difficulties they were encountering in Israel. The books thus served as an important psychological resource by helping them cope with displacement, cultural shock, and unwelcome reception.

Finally, a study on media use by immigrant youth in the US revealed that immigrant youngsters from different countries differed significantly in the amount of time they dedicated to reading. For example, Chinese immigrant adolescents spent much more time reading books (50 minutes daily) than did their Latin American counterparts (15 minutes daily) (Louie, 2003). Nevertheless, Elias and Khvorostianov (2010) emphasize that it would be wrong to interpret young immigrants' interest in books (or a lack of it) solely according to their original cultural preferences. On the contrary, their findings show that Russian immigrant adolescents' book reading patterns developed as a response to relocation difficulties and may be perceived as part of the immigrants' adaptation strategy.

Conclusions

The research literature underscores the pivotal role played by mass media in the lives of young immigrants, who struggle with integration into a new sociocultural environment, bonding with their diasporic communities, and the conflicting demands entailed in bridging between these different cultures. As such, media are highly significant in their integration process and their hybrid identity construction, as they enable these youngsters to connect to their original culture and at the same time to learn the norms and values of their host society. This said, research on the role of media among immigrant children and adolescents is still in its formative stages, with certain topics requiring particular attention. For example, most studies conducted to date focus on adolescents, whereas little is known about media uses among immigrant children under 12. The media roles in immigrant family interactions are of significance as well, as they shed light on processes of family "inward" integration and intergenerational cultural transmission. Furthermore, media uses in transnational immigrant families deserve special attention, since children in these families are not only separated from their familiar culture but also from that of the parents and sometimes from the siblings who remained in the homeland. More research is required on young immigrants' reading patterns and use of new internet platforms. Finally, the findings presented in this chapter call for more comparative cross-cultural studies, which will contribute to a better understanding of the media-related aspects of the integration process of young immigrants that are unique to a specific immigrant group, differentiating them from those of a more universal nature.

SEE ALSO in this volume chapter by Rivera and Valdivia.

References

Champion, S. (1993). The adolescent quest for meaning through multicultural readings: A case study. *Library Trends, 41*(3), 462–93.

Christopoulou, N. and de Leeuw, S. (2004). *Home is where the heart is: Family relations of migrant children in media clubs in six European countries*. Institute of Education, University of London.

Cruickshank, K. (2010). Literacy in multilingual contexts: Change in teenagers' reading and writing. *Language and Education, 18*(6), 459–73.

de Block, L. and Buckingham, D. (2007). *Global children, global media: Migration, media and childhood*. Basingstoke: Palgrave Macmillan.

d'Haenens, L. (2003). ICT in Multicultural Society. The Netherlands: a context for sound multiform media policy? *Gazette, 65*(4–5), 401–21.

Durham, M. G. (2004). Constructing the "New Ethnicities": Media, sexuality and diaspora identity in the lives of South Asian immigrant girls. *Critical Studies in Media Communication, 21*(2), 140–61.

Elias, N. and Lemish, D. (2008a). Media uses in immigrant families: Torn between "inward" and "outward" paths of integration. *International Communication Gazette, 70*(1), 23–42.

——(2008b). When all else fails: The Internet and adolescent-immigrants. In K. Drotner (Ed.), *Informal learning and digital media*. Cambridge: Cambridge, UP, pp. 139–57.

——(2009). Spinning the web of identity: Internet's roles in immigrant adolescents' search of identity. *New Media & Society, 11*(4), 533–51.

Elias, N. and Khvorostianov, N. (2010). "People of the Book": Book reading by the FSU immigrant adolescents in Israel. *The Journal of Children and Media, 4*(3), 316–30.

Elias, N. and Lemish, D. (2011). Between three cultures: Media in the lives of immigrant families: The case of Russian-speaking immigrants in Israel and Germany. *Journal of Family Issues, 20*(10), 1–29.

Fogt, A. and Sandvik, M. (2008). 'We represent a potential, not a problem': Young people's media use in diaspora. *Nordicom Review, 29*(1), 111–31.

Gezduci, H. and d'Haenens, L. (2010). The quest for credibility and other motives for news consumption among ethnically diverse youths in Flanders. *Journal of Children and Media, 4*(3), 331–49.

Gillespie, M. (1995). *Television, ethnicity and cultural change*. London: Routledge.

Guofang, L. (2007). Home environment and second-language acquisition: The importance of family capital. *British Journal of Sociology of Education, 28*(3), 285–99.

Hargreaves, A. and Mahdjoub, D. (1997). Satellite television viewing among ethnic minorities in France. *European Journal of Communication, 12*(4), 459–77.

Katz, V. S. (2010). How children use media to connect their families to the community: The case of Latinos in Los Angeles. *Journal of Children and Media, 4*(3), 298–315.

——(2011). *Children being seen and heard: How youth contribute to their migrant families' adaptation*. Barcelona: Aresta Publications.

Kim, K-H., Yun, H. and Yoon, Y. (2009). The Internet as a facilitator of cultural hybridization and interpersonal relationship management for Asian international students in South Korea. *Asian Journal of Communication, 19*(2), 152–69.

Lam, W. S. E. and Rosario-Ramos, E. (2009). Multilingual literacies in transnational digitally mediated contexts: An exploratory study of immigrant teens in the United States. *Language and Education, 23*(2), 171–90.

Lee, J. S. (2006). Exploring the relationship between electronic literacy and heritage language maintenance. *Language Learning and Technology, 10*(2), 93–113.

Louie, F. (2003). Media in the lives of immigrant youth. *New Directions for Youth Development, 2003*(100), 111–30.

Mayer, V. (2003). Living telenovelas/telenovelizing life: Mexican American girls' identities and transnational telenovelas. *Journal of Communication, 53*(3), 479–95.

Ogan, C. L. (2001). *Communication and identity in the diaspora: Turkish migrants in Amsterdam and their use of media*. Lexington Books.

Peeters, A. L. and d'Haenens, L. (2005). Bridging or bonding? Relationships between integration and media use among ethnic minorities in the Netherlands. *Communications, 30*, 201–31.

Putnam, R. (2000). *Bowling alone: The collapse and revival of civic America*. New York: Simon & Schuster.

Rydin, I. and Sjöberg, U. (2008). Narratives about the Internet as a communicative space for identity construction among migrant families. In I. Rydin and U. Sjöberg (Eds), *Mediated crossroads: Identity, youth culture and ethnicity*. NORDICOM: Göteborg University, pp. 193–214.

Siew-Peng, L. (2001). Satellite television and Chinese immigrants in Britain. In R. King and N. Wood (Eds), *Media and migration: constructions of mobility and difference*. London: Routledge, pp. 143–57.

Yang, C., Wu, H., Zhu, M. and Southwell, B. G. (2004). Tuning in to fit in? Acculturation and media use among Chinese students in the United States. *Asian Journal of Communication, 14*(1), 81–94.

Zohoori, A. R. (1988). A cross-cultural analysis of children's television use. *Journal of Broadcasting and Electronic Media, 32*(1), 105–13.

42

YOUNG PEOPLE PRODUCING MEDIA

Spontaneous and project-sponsored media creation around the world

JoEllen Fisherkeller

Introduction

For centuries, young people around the world have been producing media, if we include means of communication such as oral storytelling and singing, drawing and painting, writing, and other ways of representing that precede the development of electronic forms. But certainly, since media such as movies, radio, television, video and computer games, and an array of digital technologies and online networks have emerged, young people have been producing these forms as well. Why young people in different locales create, and when possible, distribute various media depends on their situations and circumstances, which are rooted in the histories, economies, politics, and socio–cultures of different places and times. Thus the reasons young people produce media are quite diverse, and relate to issues of intention, resources, competencies, and social support. These issues also have an impact on what kinds of media young people produce, and how they produce various media in different contexts. Of course the why, what, and how of young people producing media are interrelated, but the sections below will discuss them distinctly as much as possible. In each section, I will also address the roles that adults play in young people's media productions.

Why do young people produce?

A broad array of agendas can drive young people to produce media. Education around the world has historically encouraged young people to produce writing, since being literate (which includes being able to read and write) is generally seen as a valuable means of participating in society and culture. This is still true, so many young people produce writing because they are required to by school, and because they have learned to understand and appreciate the value of being literate via their teachers, parents, and other adults in their lives, as well as their peers (Dyson, 1997, 2003).

At the same time, many young people produce writing on their own, for a variety of reasons. Even before computers and online networks, young people were writing to express themselves personally and aesthetically via diaries and journals, to communicate with others in letters and notes, and to reach a wider audience than perhaps their schoolteachers, by creating and distributing their own magazines (Chu, 1997) or home business advertisements (Hull and Schultz, 2002). The distribution of such media was limited since some wanted to keep their writing private, and getting published was out of reach for so many. With the advent of online networks, these kinds of writing can reach a much wider local and even global audience, and youths with access can engage in producing their own writing that might be driven by an interest, whether overt or covert, in crossing the boundaries of the private and public (Ito et al., 2010; Jenkins, 2006).

The advent of online networks, and the emergence of communication technologies such as movies, radio, television, computers, and video games have had an impact as well on why young people produce media that might include writing but also might involve audio/visual and digital features. The emergence of these media has also prompted many adults in a variety of contexts to create opportunities for youth to create and distribute media, for a variety of reasons.

Young people worldwide with access to newer media technologies have pursued creating and distributing their own audio/visual/digital productions for some of the same reasons they might produce writing on their own: personal and aesthetic; communication; reaching a wide audience. In addition, young people with access and motivation can also participate in a variety of online forums that involve sharing multi-modal media that might include original text, audio and visual forms (Ito et al., 2010; Jenkins, 2006). For example, in Lebanon, Palestinian refugees use computer networks in cybercafés to connect with Palestinians in other regions, and also create cyberleaflets using images of injured or killed children to communicate to the world outside of their refugee camps the strife they experience on a daily basis (Khalili, 2005). But most young people around the world have not had and still do not have access to these newer media technologies as producers. While many young people in different locales might readily consume movies, radio, television, and video games, and related media including magazines, comics, recorded music, and advertisements of all kinds, most do not have the tools or the competencies to create newer media due to issues of socio-economics. This situation has prompted many adults in different parts of the world to sponsor and implement opportunities for young people to create and distribute multiple kinds of media, depending on those adults' agendas, backgrounds, and interests, and to some extent, the needs of youth themselves (Fisherkeller, 2011).

Many different kinds of organizations, institutions, and agencies can be involved in both envisioning and supporting youth media production activities: governments, NGOs, corporate foundations, educational institutions and schools, community-based organizations, non-profit agencies, and commercial enterprises (and perhaps some combination of the above). While these different groups might want to give tools and social support to young people who don't have access to media production, their reasons for providing access are diverse and oftentimes interrelated.

The listing below outlines the variety of reasons why adults worldwide contribute to activities that help youth produce their own media.

Social justice: Many projects around the world want to address issues of social justice, because of the inequities of the local and the global that are technological, but also economic, political, and social. These projects often encourage collective action via media production (such as messaging and storytelling) to redress issues of inequity. These projects are not necessarily connected with a specific formal political group.

Political action: Many projects worldwide are interested in formal political action. They want to explicitly promote their agendas to benefit specific groups, especially youth and under-privileged, under-represented communities. This aspect of youth media production can definitely relate to addressing social justice issues, but might also involve promoting formal political interests that are unrelated to social justice per se.

Arts: Many projects around the world support youth participating in the arts. They provide support for individual self-expression, narratives, and non-narrative aesthetics and artistic movements. These expressions may have personal, social, and even political meanings, but the impetus is to express the self in some way. Personal expression is a principle that drives many youth media production projects worldwide, whether that expression is personal, social, and/or political.

Communication: Many projects want to encourage inter-generational and cross-generational communication. Their media production efforts give youth the means to interact with peers and adults. These interactions might be the explicit focus of a media production, such as youth interviewing their grandparents on video. But also, most often the process of media creation and distribution involves young people working with each other and with adult facilitators to accomplish their goals.

Workforce: Many projects are interested in preparing young people for the workforce. Whether explicitly or implicitly, media production can promote youths' economic development and prepare them for work in the media and communication industries.

Academic support: Many projects want to provide academic support for students who might be struggling in school. Such efforts might encourage drop-out prevention and provide motivation for achievement, academic advancement, and college preparation.

Overall development: Many projects are concerned about overall youth development. Media production can provide supports that contribute to young people's health, well-being, and safety. Likewise, some productions might focus specifically on health and safety issues, leading to awareness, prevention, and positive action.

Recreation: Many projects provide recreation. Media production activities can provide enjoyment and entertainment. Even when young people are working hard on their productions, creating media is regarded as a pleasurable activity.

Community development: Many projects want to encourage community development. They provide support, opportunities, and pathways to positive social change for young people who live in communities that might be beleaguered with problems that are social, economic, environmental, and possibly dangerous.

(see also Fisherkeller, 2011)

Projects worldwide that help youth produce media often have multiple aims and objectives, and the adults who work on these kinds of initiatives hail from a variety of disciplines and professions. Youth media projects can involve adults who might be from the worlds of education, media making, youth development, government, policymaking, industry, advocacy, academia, civic activism, and perhaps some combination of these worlds. Understandably, the conceptual frameworks adults in these worlds draw from are quite diverse, and can vary regionally within the same field.

And the listing of aims and objectives above is not exhaustive. For example, Bellotti (2011) discusses how Christian organizations in Brazil have opened up physical spaces for young people to come together and express their similar and divergent beliefs, discussions that continue online on various sites created by the youths. In addition, in the physical spaces some of the young people are creating and performing their own Christian music (rock, rap, heavy metal), and often selling their CDs, T-shirts, and other paraphernalia in gift shops run by the youths themselves. These music performers are also discussed off and online, in terms of their quality but also their messages. By allowing popular music, dancing, and socializing in the youth spaces, as well as discussions of faith and values, Catholic and Protestant organizations in Brazil have been able to attract young people who were not attending traditional services at church, and often had no safe space to socialize. This serves as a transition to what kinds of media young people produce when given the resources and support.

What do young people produce?

The kinds of media that young people create in different parts of the world are as diverse as the reasons why they produce, and as diverse as young people themselves. Given the right tools and social supports, young people can create videos, films, music, photographs, radio programs, video and computer games, and writing using either analog or digital technologies, or both. Within and across these different forms, also, different genres can be created. For example, young people could create a documentary on a topic, and it could appear as a video, a radio program, or an online blog with accompanying photos. Young people might instead take photos of family and friends, or write lyrics for a love song. And given the new digital media, different forms and genres can be blended and transformed in surprising ways, and online networks can provide a means of distribution that allows youths with access to reach a very wide audience with their creations (see Ito et al., 2010)

What gets produced, however, certainly depends a great deal on the socio-economics of individuals and on the different kinds of resources that funded youth media projects might have at their disposal. Understandably, the agendas of youth media projects play a role as well. Several cases serve to illustrate these points.

Weber and Mitchell (2008) illuminate different cases of adolescents creating media to express their personal and social identities in a variety of ways. In a Canadian project, teens created personal websites via a social media network and worked diligently to maintain their profiles as well as their friendships. Many of the teens adjusted or updated their profile information, photos, journal entries, blog postings, and instant messaging activity on a daily basis. They also encouraged visitors to their sites to comment on features and make suggestions as well, including the "look" of the sites with respect to colors, font choices, and clip art as well as original images and designs. In another case, an African refugee living in London participated in a digital storytelling project, where she wrote about and posted images expressing how much she loved her cellphone, even writing a love poem to her phone. According to the authors, this girl's attachment to her cellphone symbolizes the connections she has to others even when she is not using it, and her use of it signals to others that she is the type of person who can use it. A third case analyzes the creations by girls in South Africa who were asked to produce PowerPoint presentations showing images of their bedrooms taken with digital cameras. The objects in and aspects of their bedrooms that were depicted in their photo slide shows were telling about the meaning of girls' personal belongings as representations of their personal and social selves; images of stuffed animals, media they owned, clothing and accessories, and special spaces for storage indicated the "in-between" nature of the teens' identities.

Asthana's (2011) research focuses on three different youth media projects that provide poor and underprivileged Palestinian youths living in Israel with various media production opportunities. All three projects are funded by a wide range of local, national, and international organizations and agencies that generally seek to relieve the plight of Palestinian youths who are either living in refugee camps or are minorities within Israel by giving these youths different ways to express themselves, represent their reality, and build cross-cultural understandings. The media products that these youths produce include magazines, photography, radio, video, television, and new online media. To produce these media, the young people learn how to use the technologies involved, along with design elements such as scriptwriting, graphic design, and lighting. In all of the media they produce, the young people are representing their experience of everyday life and expressing their sense of identity as Palestinians. Asthana claims that these youths are not only illuminating their experiences rationally, but also affectively. That is, not only do their media products represent how they think, but also how they *feel* as Palestinians living in their situations. He suggests that this is an aspect of youths producing media that is sometimes overlooked.

Another project involves young people in different parts of the world using a special social networking site created by researchers to examine how youths communicate with each other via the site. Given funding by a variety of non-profit organizations, Stornaiuolo et al. (2011) established a social networking site that only the participants in the project have access to, in part to protect the participants' privacy (which would not be protected as easily on commercially provided sites). Young people in India, South Africa, Norway, and the United States, working with educators in each location, learn how to navigate the site, and are encouraged to communicate with the participants in the other locations using multiple forms. They design their own multi-modal profiles, where the educators ask them to reflect on how they are representing themselves as individuals, and also their experiences living in their specific situations. They can write to each other privately as well as communally (via messaging, chat, wallspaces, blogs), upload and share images and photographs, and compose digital stories to share using multiple media. Some of the participants in this project have had little to no experience using computers, thus this project affords them opportunities not available to them at home or even school. More importantly, what the researchers found was that because the youths were communicating with people they did not know in distant places, using multiple media, the young participants in this project were finding out both how similar and how different they might be; thus they gained in their appreciation of and interest in these "others." The researchers take care, though, to point out the role that the educators played in the productions of these young people, since the educators knew the overarching goals of the project and were skilled at guiding the youths to be thoughtful about their creations and exchanges. This leads to a discussion of how young people produce in different kinds of contexts.

How do young people produce media?

As these cases illustrate, the practices of creation and distribution can be similar yet also vary across different kinds of contexts. Obviously, young people must learn how to use various kinds of tools to create and distribute and, as research has shown, they can often teach themselves or learn from each other the technical aspects of communication technologies, if they have access (see Ito et al., 2010; Livingstone, 2002). But the young people participating in the cross-cultural social networking project were guided by educators working primarily in school-based contexts, and they had curricular goals, though they were not necessarily part of the schools' formal curricula. These educators' pedagogical frameworks were student-centered and collaborative, and their practices were specifically designed to encourage reflection and thoughtful interaction on the project, whether regarding technical, social, or cultural aspects of interaction.

This kind of approach to working with young people is common to many projects that help youths produce media of all kinds, both in and out of school contexts. Whether they see themselves as educators or not, quite often adults not only want to provide young people with technical skills and knowledge about production, but they also want to encourage them to be critical, creative, thoughtful, and active members of their local and global communities. Adults in many youth media production projects often see themselves as mentors working collaboratively with young people and other concerned adults. For example, a community radio project in South Africa had several projects for young people of different ages, projects that taught them the technical and intellectual skills for writing, editing, and delivering stories that were relevant to diverse groups of young children, teens, and young adults and their local communities (Bosch, 2007). The adults in this community radio context provided training in the use of studio equipment to broadcast the young people's stories and debates. But for the most part the adults let the young people choose topics of interest to themselves, even though they were interested in developing young people's critical consciousness (Freire, 1973) and suggesting alternatives to the mainstream, given the history of the apartheid system and the flow of popular culture from non-African regions, especially the United States.

However, not all projects take this kind of approach. In Singapore, for example, the state has sponsored school-based and public education initiatives that provide young people with the means to learn to use new digital tools, in the hopes that young Singaporeans can compete in the global marketplace of hi-tech and media industries (Lim et al., 2011). These industries have become a growing presence in the region, and are seen by the state to be contributing to economic growth and modernization processes. In schools and public education institutions, students in Singapore are learning to use a wide array of the newer digital media technologies, and are encouraged to contribute to festivals that showcase their creations. Often the theme of the major festivals is to express national pride and enthusiasm, and media products are judged based on these kinds of expressions. The authors note that while young Singaporeans are learning the skills of new digital media and are able to express themselves in these forums, the educational contexts in which they are learning do not encourage a critical, analytic look at both the tools and the products of digital media. The authors suggest that this is due to the teacher-based, transmission-of-knowledge orientation of Singapore's schooling practices. They make policy suggestions that would lead to school and education reforms to address this situation, hoping that teachers could encourage students' critical, analytic thinking about media and technologies.

The institutional constraints of traditional schooling can make it difficult for some youth media projects to practice student-centered, collaborative kinds of learning and production. However, some schools around the world do have media production as part of their regular offerings, providing usually older young people with the tools, skills, and knowledge to create films, videos, games, television, radio, and web-based media. The pedagogies employed by educators working in these situations can vary regionally and even locally. But often youth media projects happen outside of the formal school day because of the need for teachers to attend to crowded mandated curricula that do not include creative media production other than writing. Yet these projects face many challenges, including finding and maintaining funding, employing adults with relevant expertise and interest, and meeting the needs of youth themselves (Goodman, 2003).

Nonetheless, adults in many fields are calling for integrating youth media production across the formal curriculum of schools so that more and more young people can gain in the skills and knowledge of using multiple media forms, given the powerful roles that media and communication technologies play in local and global economies, politics, and everyday life. Likewise, many people call for more research on projects, whether in or out of school, where young people are learning and able to create and distribute media of all kinds, in order to understand the individual, social, cultural, and educational consequences of their media making. Integrating media production into schooling and conducting research on young people who are creating and distributing media in any context calls for collaborations and partnerships among educators, policymakers, funders, researchers, communities, media industries, and of course, young people themselves. These are challenges, but also opportunities to advance our knowledge of young people growing up in media-saturated worlds within which they need and want to participate.

SEE ALSO in this volume chapter by Stuart and Mitchell.

References

Asthana, S. (2011). Youth media imaginaries in the Arab world: A narrative and discourse analysis. In J. Fisherkeller (Ed.), *International perspectives on youth media: Cultures of production and education*. New York: Peter Lang, pp. 50–67.

Bellotti, K. K. (2011). Media and Christian youth groups in Brazil. In J. Fisherkeller (Ed.), *International perspectives on youth media: Cultures of production and education*. New York: Peter Lang, pp. 68–83.

Bosch, T. E. (2007). Children, culture, and identity on South African community radio. *Journal of Children and Media, 1*(3), 277–88.

Chu, J. Y. (1997). Navigating the media environment: How youth claim a place through zines. *Social Justice, 24*(3), 71–85.

Dyson, A. H. (1997). *Writing superheroes: Contemporary childhood, popular culture, and classroom literacy*. NY: Teachers College Press.

——(2003). *The brothers and sisters learn to write: Popular literacies in childhood and school cultures*. New York, NY: Teachers College Press.

Fisherkeller, J. (Ed.) (2011). Introduction. *International perspectives on youth media: Cultures of production and education*. New York: Peter Lang, pp. 1–21.

Freire, P. (1973). *Education for critical consciousness*. New York: Seabury Press.

Goodman, S. (2003). *Teaching youth media: A critical guide to literacy, Video production, and social change*. NY: Teacher's College Press.

Hull, G. and Schultz, K. (2002). *Schools out! Bridging out-of school literacies with classroom practice*. NY: Teachers College Press.

Ito, M., Baumer, S., Bittannti, M., boyd, d., Cody, R., Herr-Stephenson, B., Horst, H., Lange, P. G., Mahendran, D., Martinez, K. Z., Pascoe, C. J., Perkel, D., Robinson, L., Sims, C. and Tripp, L. (2010). *Hanging out, messing around, and geeking out: Kids living and learning with new media*. Cambridge, MA: MIT Press.

Jenkins, H. (2006) *Convergence culture: Where old and new media collide*. NY: New York University Press.

Khalili, L. (2005) Virtual nation: Palestinian cyberculture in Lebanese camps. In R. L. Stein and T. Swedenburg (Eds), *Palestine, Israel, and the politics of popular culture*. Durham, SC: Duke University Press, pp. 126–49.

Lim, S. S., Nekmat, E. and Vadrevu, S. (2011). Singapore's experience in fostering youth media production: The implications of state-led school and public education initiatives. In J. Fisherkeller (Ed.), *International perspectives on youth media: Cultures of production and education*. New York: Peter Lang, pp. 84–102.

Livingstone, S. (2002). *Young people and new media: Childhood and the changing media environment*. London: Sage.

Stornaiuolo, A., Hull, G. A. and Sahni, U. (2011). Cosmopolitan imaginings of self and other: Youth and social networking in a global world. In J. Fisherkeller (Ed.), *International perspectives on youth media: Cultures of production and education*. New York: Peter Lang, pp. 263–80.

Weber, S. and Mitchell, C. (2008). Imaging, keyboarding, and posting identities: Young people and new media technologies. In D. Buckingham (Ed.), *Youth, identity, and digital media*. Cambridge, MA: MIT Press, pp. 25–47.

43

MEDIA AND CIVIC ENGAGEMENT

The role of Web 2.0 technologies in fostering youth participation

Tao Papaioannou

Civic participation among youth has a powerful normative value for democracy. However, until recently, the interest in public life among youth has been steadily declining. Young people are described as politically apathetic as they are uninterested in the news media, unaware of national and international current affairs and indifferent about participating in the political process (Lopez et al., 2005). The advent of Web 2.0 technologies such as social networking media, YouTube, blogs and Wikis provides young people with new opportunities and different modes of processing information, interacting among one another and participating in communities and society. Political and civic groups are increasingly promoting themselves online, hoping to attract the interest and support of young people who are inclined to use these technologies. While the use of social media such as Facebook in articulating citizens' actions and social change has challenged more traditional participation and public debate practices, important questions are emerging about the potential of these technologies to facilitate civic participation and empower youth.

This chapter reviews current research exploring the role of Web 2.0 technologies in fostering civic interests and participation among youth. It specifically focuses on three issues: (1) reconceptualizing the very notion of civic participation so that it reflects the ways in which young people incorporate their civic interests and media content into their everyday lives; (2) examining whether and how children and teenagers make selective use of digital technologies for civic purposes in view of the participation opportunities that new media offer and the ways in which young people utilize online tools available to them; and (3) identifying strategies to further promote online civic participation among youth. This review includes works that aim to provide new insights into advocacy scholarship and practice, and these works are presented as a new starting point for further research, validation and debate.

Reconceptualizing the notion(s) of civic participation

The public image of young people has historically characterized them as uninterested in the news media and apathetic about participating in civic and political activities. This state of disengagement has left some to wonder if we actually face a civic crisis (Putnam, 2000). However, some research has suggested that this characterization is not entirely accurate as it does not recognize the changing nature of youth citizen identity (Bennett, 2008). Without taking into consideration a growing emphasis on self-actualization in young people's political and civic expression, earlier research on civic engagement arguably had adopted a narrow definition of civic participation. Alternatively, recent studies focusing on the role of new media in civic expression, particularly among children, adolescents and young people of up to 18–19 years of age, are beginning to indicate the potential of new media in possibly contributing to new forms of civic involvement and fostering new understandings of what constitutes participation both on and off line.

Bennett (2008) argues that earlier research on civic engagement has had a narrow focus on the dutiful citizen identity, emphasizing participation in state institutions and knowledge about politics and government. Participation behavior has mainly been examined with a focus on young people's poor exposure to the news media and their voting practice. Youth recognize the significance of civic participation but enact it in ways which are the result of shifts in social and political identity processes, rooted in various global socio-cultural changes over the last several decades. Increased social fragmentation and atomization have led to a change from a group-based society to a networked society, recognizing personalized conceptions of membership and identification. Distrustful of media and politicians, particularly in the context of failing institutions and systems in post-industrial democracies, youth do not necessarily follow politics in the news and do not necessarily view voting as the core democratic act. This difference has "excluded young people from the 'adult' realms of socio-political participation and citizenship" (Weller, 2003, p. 154). On the one hand, this exclusion from mainstream forms of political discourse has produced much of the cynicism and withdrawal among youth from public life; on the other hand, it has led to a "worry about this very personalization or privatization of the political sphere and focus on how to promote public actions that link to government as the center of democratic politics, and to other social groups and institutions as the foundations of civic life" (Bennett, 2008, p. 3).

Experiencing growing personal responsibility and choice, youth are increasingly adopting an actualizing citizen identity. They consider self-actualizing politics more relevant to their individual needs than government and organize their citizen identity around their personal lifestyles. Resistant to older expectations about a citizen's duty, they are drawn to alternative political activities. Instead of joining social organizations and parties, they may join informal or online networks for direct social action on consumer and lifestyle issues. Youth do have a sense of community although their definitions of community are not limited to their local communities as many choose to join or create online communities.

Earl and Schussman (2008) argue that "one must ask whether existing notions of what comprises civic engagement tend to ignore, devalue, and otherwise marginalize ways in which younger citizens are connecting with one another to collectively make a difference in their own worlds" (p. 73). This conceptual bias is evident in the debate of the status of children as citizens (Livingstone, 2009). The traditional approach considers children and teenagers as citizens in development until they have attained the legal age to participate in the political process. The focus of their civic participation is very much on providing opportunities to help them develop interests and skills for their future roles as engaged citizens. Civic participation from this perspective is positioned more as civic education as the political efficacy of children and youth is seriously contested. Research following this approach has conventionally focused on participation in the political process among young adults. When children and teenagers are included, the intention is mainly to identify factors of political socialization in their early lives that would prepare them for active citizenship.

However, among others, Levine (2008), Montgomery (2007) and Jenkins et al. (2006) have critically argued for a perspective of citizenship which acknowledges children and adolescents as citizens with present rights and responsibilities and recognizes the ways in which young people incorporate civic activities and media content into their lives. This view has challenged the traditional approach to civic participation to include – beyond direct involvement in government and national issues – volunteer activities, local and online community engagement, youth philanthropy, social activism, political consumerism and lifestyle politics. Striving to bridge or even transcend the conflicting narratives of whether young people are engaged or disengaged, this notion of civic participation seeks to capture creative developments in youth participation which comprise a wide range of practices and civic learning styles, often in forms of shared activity online.

Considerable empirical evidence has supported this broader perspective. For example, young people are reported to display civic skills in new forms of social activism in the restructuring of local spaces (Weller, 2003) and entertainment-related online petitioning (Earl and Schussman, 2008). One study has found increased levels of volunteer work among high school students who participate in interest-driven online communities (Kahne et al., 2011). A large national-scale survey indicates that American youth are interested in civic engagement with "70% believing the importance of helping the community, 68% already doing something to support a cause on a monthly basis" (MTV Networks, 2006). Analysis of 30 years of trends in American adolescents' civic engagement from 1976 to 2005 reveals that in the last 15 years high school students have been less inclined to participate in conventional and alternative political activities, yet increasingly volunteering in their communities (Syvertsen et al., 2011).

Some research has noted, in particular, many online forms of civic expression, ranging from participating in online communities, protesting in gaming and fan sites, blogging about political and social issues to volunteering online. However, before discussing the role of digital technologies in promoting youth civic participation as part of their e-citizenship, it is important to acknowledge that negative results have also been reported, indicating that young people are disengaged from civic/political activities either formal or informal, volunteer or community-based (Andolina et al., 2002). Although young people are highly aware of their power and rights as consumers, when they are involved in boycotting goods and services, their actions are often for personal reasons rather than socially or politically motivated reasons. Participation among youth in cultural production through digital media contributes to the development of their identities, but such effort arguably represents forms of media rather than civic engagement (Buckingham, 2006). These mixed views suggest the need to further examine participation practices in order to uncover an accurate picture of youth civic identity.

The role of digital technologies in youth civic engagement

The mass media have been simultaneously presented as one of the reasons for young people's disconnection to public life, not entirely fairly (Couldry et al., 2010), and one of the means to engage them. Yet youth are found increasingly turning away from traditional mass media in favor of internet-based information sources. This new communication environment may play a crucial role in fostering youth civic participation (Montgomery, 2007). Rather than considered as the object of media effects, youth are actors in their households and community and co-creators of the meanings and practices of their everyday lives. Young people may well be affirming their sense of community and place through new skills and opportunities that new media may open up for them. Researchers are encouraged to look into ways in which young people make selective use of digital technologies for civic purposes.

A great number of youth initiatives have flourished online such as issue-based networks, campaigns and new social movements. These online opportunities address a wide range of issues including voluntarism, youth philanthropy, voting, racism and tolerance, social activism, patriotism, terrorism and military conflict (Montgomery et al., 2004). Many civic and political activities take place on the platform of Causes on Facebook with successful examples of engaging youth as seen in the "Facebook effect" in the election of President Obama of the U.S. Participation in digital media production can develop young people's public voices through ongoing interaction with engaged audiences (Levine, 2008). A transnational analysis of youth media production and distribution projects argues positively that youth media initiatives contribute to advocacy and empower youth to become expressive participants in their local and global multi-mediated realities (Fisherkeller, 2011).

Against enthusiastic claims such as youth are "taking ownership of the new media as tools for the practice of citizenship" (Montgomery, 2007, p. 207), Livingstone (2003) cautions that

> a few studies are charting interesting initiatives using the internet to stimulate young people's participation, holding out the promise of new opportunities through instances of "best practice", although it remains unclear how and by whom these could be evaluated or more widely implemented.
>
> *(p. 151)*

The internet is transforming certain aspects of civic participation as it provides access to far more information, the capability to reach out to others and opportunities for a greater level of direct and personal involvement. The internet offers an increasingly useful and empowering platform for those who are in the position and willing to take advantage of the networked public sphere. However, there is little empirical support for the claim that technology, and particularly the internet, has brought the majority of the young people (or old) into active civic life, so it is important to acknowledge that the civic potentialities of digital technologies still remain a largely unexplored area with no consensus yet. While empirical data is still very much anticipated, limited evidence seems to suggest that digital media can enable a modest degree of civic engagement for youth and adults (Palfrey and Gasser, 2008).

Results of two large panel studies of youth transitioning from adolescence to early adulthood suggest that participation in online communities is associated with increased participation in volunteering, community problem-solving and protest activities (Kahne et al., 2011). A survey (Livingstone, 2007) of UK children 9–19 years old shows that 22 percent of those who go online weekly have voted online and 8 percent have signed a petition online. Further, 54 percent have visited at least one civic website, and 44 percent have discussed online civic or political issues with peers. In seeking predictors of why some teenagers do not visit civic websites, low levels of online participation are attributed to a lack of interest. Youth indeed use digital media to express their civic interests, but it is most likely to be those who are predisposed to be active in civic life. Those who have already developed civic interests are likely to use the internet as a useful resource for pursuing these interests, and their interaction with these online sources increases with age and online expertise. Another survey of public high school students, ages 14–19, reveals a gap between communication and response (Papaioannou, 2011). While many students, 70 percent, read and forward e-mails about the civic groups they are members of, only a minority consistently participate in the activities organized by these groups online and/or offline or actively campaign for these causes. Moreover, online participation does not necessarily lead to further offline participation.

As online communication does not straightforwardly translate into action online or offline, indicating a participation process more complex than from minimal to more ambitious modes, it is then crucial to identify activities and participation methods that youth find appealing and strategies to further mobilize them.

Identifying strategies to foster online civic participation

Digital technology is not the solution to young people's withdrawal from public life, but it is a possible tool to be used in helping them engage. Instead of treating youth as a homogeneous group, it is useful to draw their civic profile in order to appropriately direct online strategies to their varied interests. Also, an appeal to young people's own agendas and expressions may help narrow the gap between opportunities and response. Participatory learning in which students discover and express their political agenda through participation in digital media production may address the challenges of stimulating and sustaining participation. Ultimately, if society wishes to encourage young citizens to participate, the state must provide them with direct feedback and institutional support.

Research on UK children (Livingstone et al., 2005) has revealed three group identities: the civic-minded, the interactors and the disengaged. The civic-minded group tends to be middle class girls with average online skills. They are more likely to pursue their civic interests online, particularly in areas of charity and human rights. Instead of being drawn into new participation opportunities, they have developed civic interests offline and use the internet as an alternative means to express them. The interactors are often middle class boys who have acquired considerable online skills. They use the internet in many ways but do not particularly pay attention to civic activities. However, the range and depth of information and activities this group tends to engage in suggests the possibility that they might respond to an invitation to participate. The disengaged are the least active in online participation, less likely to interact with sites, visit civic sites or make their own sites. Younger than the other groups, they are the less expert group who make average use of the internet and are disengaged in terms of both access and use.

As the online environment can mobilize civic-minded young people in new ways, civic groups need to enhance online activities which target the specific interests of these young people. Recognizing the influence of offline socialization, future research may investigate the possibilities of combining technology with agents of political socialization through providing opportunities in the online environment for the presence and interaction of young people, family, school and peers. Face-to-face interactions may be crucial for sustaining motivation and participation (Dahlgren and Olsson, 2008). Young people may develop both online and offline relationships with civic groups which have both local presence and international appeal. These projects not only offer young people opportunities to engage with their local communities but also to connect with other locally-based projects to create larger national and global networks. The report of the Knight Commission on the Information Needs of Communities in a Democracy (2009) recommends that technologically savvy young people have advanced digital skills but little connection to public life. This uneven distribution creates an opportunity in which young people can volunteer to help connect a physical community to the networked infrastructure. They can facilitate the leverage of networked technology among community leaders in a scenario described as "Geek Corps for Local Democracy." A geek corps would work as the Peace Corps, helping the young understand and participate in local democracy through local and national networks.

Bridging the gap between opportunities and response entails not only willingness to engage but also an appeal to young people's own agendas and expressions. Civic sites sponsored by governments and NGOs are often seen as inauthentic and uncreative, lacking the spontaneous forms of collective expression found on autonomous sites (youth-built and operated) in entertainment media and games (Coleman, 2008). The "who are you?" perspective found in personalized collective actions on social networks (Bennett and Segerberg, 2011) may be extended into this arena. Instead of following the "who are we?" approach in which the civic groups are in the foreground, trying to gain the attention and interest of young people, the organizers may consider adopting the "who are you?" approach so that their online presence is more about creating a platform which provides youth with the tools to determine their own agendas and methods of participation. The organizers do not own the cause; the supporters do. This approach would allow youth to become the center of attention and permit them to express themselves in their own voices and "have their say" by developing or co-developing strategies to present and brand their own actions.

It is also critical to consider the educational needs and opportunities of disengaged youth. These challenges may be addressed through strengthening the opportunity structures of young people's lives and the communities of practices available to them, one of them being developing literacy curricula in which teachers help students discover their political agenda and use digital and virtual technologies for civic expression (Bers, 2010). Participatory education – teaching students how to use participatory media such as blogs, Wiki, music-photo-video sharing or social networking sites to advocate positions and organize actions around issues young people care about – may draw youth into positive early experiences with citizenship (Rheingold, 2008) and increase online political engagement (Kahne et al., 2012).

An issue perhaps more critical than helping young people find their voice is providing them with direct feedback and institutional support (Livingstone, 2009). Interest groups, peer communities, the mass media and particularly political leaders are all part of the opportunity structures that facilitate and shape young people's participation and their potential public influence. Many political groups are enthusiastic in getting youth to participate; however, not as many are directly interacting with young people and supporting them in order to sustain participation. A substantial gap is evident between the participatory experiences young people are looking for and those provided through political websites (Xenos and Foot, 2008). Opportunities to participate are thus reduced, not only for those who are on the wrong side of the digital or participation divide but also for those who are not heard. Fundamentally, if it is the wish of society to have young citizens willing to participate by means of technology, society must provide institutional support as "what matters is not whether new media are capable of capturing, moderating and summarizing the voice of the public, but whether political institutions are able and willing to enter into a dialogical relationship with the public" (Coleman, 2007, p. 375).

Conclusion

This discussion of the changing nature of youth citizen identity and the role of digital technologies in promoting civic engagement, redefining our notion of citizenship and of civic participation and looking to see which young people are involved and how they choose to participate, will enable us to gain a deeper understanding of young people's civic interests and expression. From this perspective, we can explore action patterns in what online activities interest youth and whether they are engaged in different ways via different online mechanisms. We still must investigate strategies that encourage young people to participate in society and possibly transfer interests in civic spheres online to traditional realms of politics such as voting. Future work may focus on developing criteria and methods for evaluating online participation practices and advances provided by the promotion of "participatory culture" and media education relevant to civic literacy. It is perhaps most important to ask what we can learn about civic life online that might help society encourage, enrich and expand the democratic experiences of youth. Discussing these issues directly with young people will help develop further understanding in a way that values and fosters youth participation.

SEE ALSO in this volume chapter by Carter, chapter by Austin, chapter by Fisherkeller, and chapter by Stuart and Mitchell.

References

Andolina, M. W., Jenkins, K., Keeter, S. and Zukin, C. (2002). Searching for the meaning of youth civic engagement: Notes from the field. *Applied Developmental Science*, 6(4), 189–95.

Bennett, W. L. (2008). Changing citizenship in the digital age. In W. L. Bennett (Ed.), *Civic life online: Learning how digital media can engage youth*. Cambridge, Massachusetts: MIT Press, pp. 1–24.

Bennett, W. L. and Segerberg, A. (2011). *The Logic of Connective Action*. Keynote speech at the 2nd Arts and Social Justice Conference, Nicosia, Cyprus.

Bers, M. U. (2010). Beyond computer literacy: Supporting youth's positive development through technology. *New Directions for Youth Development*, 2000(128), 13–23.

Buckingham, D. (2006). MacArthur online discussions on civic engagement. Retrieved from http://spotlight. macfound.org/resources/Civic_EngagementOnline_Discussions'06.pdf

Coleman, S. (2007). E-democracy: The history and future of an idea. In D. Quah, R. Silverstone, R. Mansell and C. Avgerou (Eds), *The Oxford handbook of information and communication technologies*. Oxford: Oxford University Press, pp. 362–82.

Coleman, S. (2008). Doing IT for themselves: Management versus autonomy in youth E-citizenship. In W. L. Bennett (Ed.), *Civic life online: Learning how digital media can engage youth*. Cambridge, Massachusetts: MIT Press, pp. 189–206.

Couldry, N., Livingstone, S. and Markham, T. (2010). *Media consumption and public engagement: Beyond the presumption of attention*. Hampshire, UK: Palgrave Macmillan.

Dahlgren, P. (2009). *Media and political engagement: Citizens, communication, and democracy*. Cambridge: Cambridge University Press.

Dahlgren, P. and Olsson, T. (2008). Facilitating political participation: Youth citizens, internet and civic cultures. In K. Droter and S. Livingstone (Eds), *International handbook of children, media and culture*. London: Sage, pp. 493–507.

Earl, J. and Schussman, A. (2008). Contesting cultural control: Youth culture and online petitioning. In W.L. Bennett (Ed.), *Civic life online: Learning how digital media can engage youth*. Cambridge, Massachusetts: MIT Press, pp. 71–96.

Fisherkeller, J. E. (2011). *International perspectives on youth media: Cultures of production and education*. New York: Peter Lang.

Jenkins, H., Clinton, K., Purushotma, R., Robison, A. J. and Weigel, M. (2006). Confronting the challenges of participatory culture: Media education for the 21st century. Retrieved from http://mitpress.mit.edu/books/chapters/Confronting_the_Challenges.pdf

Kahne, J., Lee, N. J. and Feezell, J. T. (2011). The civic and political significance of online participatory cultures among youth transitioning to adulthood. DML central Working Papers. Retrieved from http://dmlcentral.net/sites/all/files/resource_files/OnlineParticipatoryCultures. WORKINGPAPERS.pdf

Kahne, J., Lee, N. J. and Feezell, J. T. (2012). Digital media literacy education and online civic and political participation. *International Journal of Communication*, 6, 1–24.

Knight Commission on the Information Needs of Communities in a Democracy (2009). *Informing communities: Sustaining democracy in the digital age*. Washington, D.C.: The Aspen Institute.

Levine, P. (2008). A public voice for youth: The audience problem in digital media and civic education. In W. L. Bennett (Ed.), *Civic life online: Learning how digital media can engage youth*. Cambridge, Massachusetts: MIT Press, pp. 119–38.

Livingstone, S. (2003). Children's use of the internet: Reflections on the emerging research agenda. *New Media & Society*, 5(2), 147–66.

Livingstone, S. (2007). Interactivity and participation on the internet: A critical appraisal of the online invitation to young people. In P. Dahlgren (Ed.), *Young citizens and new media: Strategies for learning democratic engagement*. London: Routledge, pp. 103–24.

Livingstone, S. (2009). *Children and the internet*. Cambridge, UK: Polity.

Livingstone, S., Bober, M. and Helsper, E. J. (2005). Active participation or just more information? Young people's take up of opportunities to act and interact on the internet. *Information, Communication and Society*, 8(3), 287–314.

Lopez, M. H., Kirby, E., Sagoff, J. and Herbst, C. (2005). *The youth vote 2004 with a historical look at youth voting patterns, 1972–2004*. CIRCLE Working Paper 35. College Park, MD: Center for Information and Research on Civic Learning and Engagement.

Montgomery, K. (2007). *Generation digital: Politics, commerce, and childhood in the age of the internet*. Cambridge, Massachusetts: MIT Press.

Montgomery, K., Gottlieb-Robles, B. and Larson, G. O. (2004). *Youth as e-citizens: Engaging the digital generation*. Washington, DC: Center for Social Media, School of Communication, American University. Retrieved from http://www.centerforsocialmedia.org/ecitizens/youthreport.pdf

MTV Networks (2006). Just cause: Today's activism. Retrieved from http://www.mtv.com/thinkmtv/research/pdf/Just.Cause.FNL.APX.pdf

Palfrey, J. and Gasser, U. (2008). *Born digital*. New York: Basic Books.

Papaioannou, T. (2011). Assessing digital media literacy among young people through their use of social networking sites. *Journal of Social Informatics*, 8(15), 36–48.

Putnam, R. D. (2000). *Bowling alone: The collapse and revival of American community*. New York: Simon & Schuster.

Rheingold, H. (2008). Using participatory media and the public voice to encourage civic engagement. In W. L. Bennett (Ed.), *Civic life online: Learning how digital media can engage youth*. Cambridge, Massachusetts: The MIT Press, pp. 97–118.

Syvertsen, A. K., Wray-Lake, L., Flanagan, C., Osgood, D. W. and Briddell, L. (2011). Thirty-Year trends in U.S. adolescents' civic engagement: A story of changing participation and educational differences. *Journal of Research on Adolescence*, 21(3), 586–94.

Weller, S. (2003). Teach us something useful: contested spaces of teenagers' citizenship. *Space and Polity*, 7(2), 153–71.

Xenos, M. and Foot, C. (2008). Not your father's internet: The generation gap in online politics. In W. L. Bennett (Ed.), *Civic life online: Learning how digital media can engage youth*. Cambridge, Massachusetts: The MIT Press, pp. 51–70.

44

MEDIA, PARTICIPATION, AND SOCIAL CHANGE: WORKING WITHIN A "YOUTH AS KNOWLEDGE PRODUCERS" FRAMEWORK

Jean Stuart and Claudia Mitchell

What would it really mean to study the world from the standpoint of children [and youth] both as knowers and as actors?

(Oakley, 1994, p. 25)

Introduction

This chapter is located within the growing body of work in child and youth studies which points to the significance of the participation of children and young people, at least in principle, to contributing to the official dialogue around issues of concern to their everyday lives. Indeed, there is a growing consensus amongst those involved in social programming that unless young people are given a more significant voice in participating in policy dialogue about their own well-being, the programs themselves are doomed to failure (Ford et al., 2003). While there are many different approaches to addressing the critical issue of the participation of children and young people, one area that has received considerable attention over the last decade or more is in the area of participatory and community-based research (particularly in the context of development studies), and the use of visual and other arts-based methodologies such as photovoice, partici-patory video, drawing and map-making, and digital storytelling, as tools and methods of both research and engagement (see Clacherty, 2005; Malone, 2008; Moletsane et al., 2008). These participatory visual approaches go beyond simply being interventions, in that they typically yield vast collections of visual data in the form of photos, videos, and digital stories which researchers can use to document and study various social issues, and which communities themselves might use.

A criticism of this work, particularly in relation to children and young people's participation is that too often it is "adult-led, adult-designed and conceived from an adult perspective" (Kellet et al., 2004, p. 329), and that it often misses the mark in relation to what young people are actually doing on their own (as part of a DIY, do-it-yourself culture), or what they *could* be doing in a participatory research context that is more youth-centered and youth-led. Another criticism is that beyond the initial generation of the visual images, young people are often not involved in actually working with the data other than in relation to creating captions, for example, for the images. At the same time, in the extensive body of work on youth and digital media (see for example Bloustien, 2003; Buckingham and Sefton-Green, 1994; Carrington and Robinson, 2009; De Castell and Jenson, 2003; Jenkins, 2006), it is clear that participation itself is a critical feature of what Henry Jenkins terms a "participatory cultures" landscape in referring to DIY media use and other youth-led online practices. In this context young people, as Carrington and Robinson (2009) point out, typically engage in the "remix" and "replay" of visual and other digital artifacts through You Tube and various social net-working sites. We even think of this landscape as a global "social archive." In engaging in these practices young people often engage further in their own cultural productions.

While there is a great deal of convergence between these two broad areas of study, (1) participatory visual studies with youth and (2) youth-focused digital media studies, what is perhaps most "hopeful" is that both have a great deal to contribute to deepening an understanding of the links between digital media and the idea of "youth as knowledge producers," a term first used by Lankshear and Knobel (2003) to refer to the ways in which young people can simultaneously be resources for each other and play a key role as protagonists in the production of knowledge about their everyday lives. The aim of this chapter is to describe some of the ways in which young people are using media within a social change context through the production of media and media messages, and to consider what difference such approaches make. The chapter prioritizes qualitative and interpretivist methods of media usage and discusses media forums/ tools such as photovoice, digital story-telling, participatory video, blogging, and children's radio.

How are young people producing and using media within a social change context?

Much of the work that we describe in this chapter is located within community-based research that addresses the critical issues determined by the youth participants themselves (e.g., poverty, gender based violence, and HIV and AIDS). Most of our own work addresses these issues in a sub-Saharan African context, working through the Centre for Visual Methodologies at the University of KwaZulu-Natal where we have been testing out participatory approaches and media as tools for addressing social change for close to a decade. Added to our review of work in this context will be a review of projects with marginalized youth in other parts of Africa, North America, Australia, and Nepal.

Photovoice

Photovoice (Wang, 1999) involves giving participants cameras to document issues in their everyday lives. Young people can promote change by using their own photographs to frame, select, and share their perspective on issues affecting them. Mitchell et al. (2006) describe a photovoice project with a policy-making component of the *Friday Absenteeism Project*, which took place in a rural KwaZulu-Natal school in South Africa. Although the school principal and teachers understood why so many grade 6 students were consistently missing from school on Fridays as it was market day in the local community, they needed to better understand the underlying causes in order to find appropriate and relevant solutions to keep the students in school. The students documented what it was like to live in an informal settlement. Their photographs highlighted the poverty afflicting their families. Working for extra income at the market on a Friday ensured that they would have food for the weekend. One of the positive outcomes of the project was that stakeholders extended the school feeding scheme to weekends.

A more recent photovoice study, also linked to the Centre for Visual Methodologies for Social Change but taking place in rural Ethiopia was the *Wake up and Smell the Coffee* project (Mitchell, 2012). Children aged 13 and 14 from two schools in and around Jimma town, the birth place of coffee, used photovoice to study the impact of climate change and other environmental issues on coffee growing. For them the critical concern was sustainability and the fact that as young people they needed to be able to take action to address such issues as deforestation. An important component of this project was the process whereby the participants not only took the photos but also did their own analysis in which they categorized their images according to their relevance to addressing environmental issues. They organized and curated a school-based exhibition "Our precious planet" to which their parents and members of the community were invited, and in so doing helped to raise awareness about the issue of deforestation.

Participatory video and digital storytelling

Narrative is one the oldest and most elemental conduits for conveying meaning, and media work offers many opportunities for the energetic and fresh usage of storytelling to explore or reflect on aspects of identity or to envisage routes to social change. In the *Youth as Knowledge Producers* project at the University of KwaZulu-Natal, in which pre-service teachers explore ways in which arts-based approaches can be used to address education in the era of HIV and AIDS, storytelling has involved a variety of media. For example, responses to a scenario of sexual negotiation constructing two characters as trapped by social patterning were initially framed by using a variety of general magazines for collages to suggest how a young couple could respond differently to sexual advances. In later considerations of how to conduct healthy relationships between boys and girls, stories were considered with the help of image and forum theatre where the audience is encouraged to participate and change the actions of characters. Storyboard planning that followed led to the production of short unedited videos either highlighting crisis points and attitudes in relationships or envisaging solutions (Stuart, 2010).

The sometimes shocking power of video production to voice everyday problems and propose solutions to them was tellingly evident in another South African based project where groups of school children between 14 and 18 years of age were engaged in a participatory video activity. They brainstormed issues they wanted to bring forward, planned a narrative through storyboarding to convey the issue and then created an unedited video through the No-Editing Required (NER) approach (See Mitchell, 2011; Mitchell and De Lange, 2011). At the end of that memorable day five out of the six groups created videos on gender violence. Their work called attention to the prevalence and urgency of attending to this disrespect of children's rights, and also to the need to take these films back to the community for discussion on how to address this problem.

Participatory video was also found to be a powerful tool in Nepal in relation to studying the effects of climate change. Framed within the larger project entitled *Children in a Changing Climate*, children used video cameras to document the impact of climate change on their everyday lives. As Gautam and Oswald (2008) describe in "Children of Nepal Speak Out on Climate Change Adaptation," it is critical to get at how young children's health, education, emotional well-being, and access to water is being impacted in relation to floods, droughts, and landslides, all as a result of changing weather patterns. Children were involved in making participatory videos that showed graphically what they were experiencing, and the results were used to formulate policy-oriented actions that were presented to decision-makers in the area.

Another way to unfold narratives for social change is through digital storytelling. Any still images whether drawn or found and any video clips can be combined with a narrative voice or writing and / or music to convey a message. Following planning with a storyboard these elements are brought together through a programme such as Windows Movie Maker. The medium offers scope for much variety and creativity as Gubrium and Difulvio (2011) describe in their work with Latina adolescent girls in the US. The girls who participated in the project created stories in response to the question, "What does it mean to be a girl in the world?" The stories that the girls produced speak to the issue of "fitting in" and to negotiations of self and identity. The authors conclude that "public health research has the potential to be transformative ... Employing emergent methodologies such as digital storytelling can stimulate new forms of engagement" (2011, p. 46).

Digital storytelling has in some cases been conceptualized as participants telling their story through different media forms over time thus providing insight into complex processes not easily presented in a digital story composed in one media form at a specific time. For example, over a seven year period the *Playing for Life* project in Australia, the UK, the US, and Europe aimed to provide understanding of why and how popular music engagement is important to many psychologically or materially marginalized youth and school dropouts and what is needed to ensure their music activities serve as a pathway to broader social inclusion, including perhaps future employment (Bloustien and Peters, 2011). Digital storytelling about the complex processes young people engage with in relation to music-making emerged when, as co-researchers of their own processes, individuals told their story of music engagement over time through their own participatory video making (or auto-video-ethnography) filmed in private and public spaces, through personal uploads and input on the project and on social network websites and through blogging. These young peoples' individual, complex digital stories formed part of the evidence needed to persuade funders and government policy-makers to support engagement with popular music such as hip hop by showing how music is "serious play" which connects children with the community, promotes collaboration, and fosters skills for sharing knowledge and information on social media networking sites.

Blogging and web 2.0

Further emphasis of the value of new media for social change emerged in a project organized around blogging in relation to addressing challenges in the era of HIV and AIDS in South Africa. As described by Mitchell et al. (2010), school children from a rural KwaZulu-Natal school with limited internet access at their school attended weekend workshops at a university where they were able to set up their own blog sites with technical support, and were able to participate in a novel form of photovoice. Each was able to select a photograph from a collection taken on HIV and AIDS issues by peers in an earlier school photovoice session and, in a second layer of making meaning of the pictures, give an individual opinion on how the challenge represented in the photograph could be addressed in the community in the interest of bringing about social change. In follow-up interviews, the participants commented on how the diary blog can provide a space for individuals to frame and voice their ideas without fear of criticism or ridicule and that in dealing with highly stigmatized diseases such as HIV this is very important. While most did not follow up on the blogging after the workshop because of difficulties with gaining access to the internet in their local environment, they remained hopeful though that they would attain such access. One of the boys in the group commented that he saw the blog as providing him with a space to say what he really thought about male/female relationships without obliging him to act tough in front of his peers in order to maintain what he felt was the cultural norm for boys.

The blogging example above highlights the significance of the internet as an emerging feature of work with participatory visual methodologies. While local exhibitions of photographs produced by young people have proven to be very effective in reaching community members, the internet is of course able to reach a more widespread and diverse audience including policy-makers. They can also reach other young people who are also invited to upload their own messages about healthy living or positive change. In 2007, McGill University, the Gendered Adolescence and AIDS Project of Toronto and the Centre for Visual Methodologies UKZN headed up a project in partnership with UNESCO's Culture and HIV division in Paris to develop a webtool on youth, arts, and HIV and AIDS called YAHAnet, www.yahanet.org. This opened up opportunities for youth-based education and advocacy around sexuality, and in relation to HIV and AIDS education, youth groups were able to upload their video, audio, and image projects to a "community forum" and share their creative ideas with like-minded young people and youth leaders. Because the site provides up-to-date information on arts-based methodologies and on HIV research, it also offers a wider scope of possibilities for youth as knowledge producers (Mitchell et al., 2008; MacEntee et al., 2011).

Children's radio

In rural areas of many developing countries gaining access to new media is difficult but even children as young as nine in these areas have demonstrated that, when participating in media production and given the opportunity and space to explore and share their perspectives on the world around them, they can contribute to social change. In a remote, deeply rural under-resourced area of KwaZulu-Natal, South Africa, 9–17-year-old children, as part of the *Abaqophi BakwaZisize Abakhanyayo* project, learn through children's radio production to document their lives, experiences, and interests (Meintjes, 2009). Growing up in a context of extensive poverty in a district at the epicenter of the HIV and AIDS epidemic, children are frequently confronted with death, many are orphaned, and there is high unemployment with attendant problems such as alcoholism in the community. Through participatory processes the children gain skills with resources such as tape recorders to use radio to tell their own stories, ask questions they'd like answered, and share their views and concerns. This enabled the participants to gain confidence, knowledge and skills, including critical thinking, and the opportunity to express their opinions. By facilitating broadcast and other use of the children's programmes, the project is also able to improve public awareness of issues facing South Africa's children growing up in a context of poverty and the AIDS epidemic, and to challenge adults to consider and address children's needs and experiences appropriately.

What difference does this media work make?

As we have highlighted above, this work is clearly part of an emerging body of child-focused research, but it is also an area that various international NGOs such as UNICEF and Save the Children see as critical, and even national governments such as Australia are seeing this as important through its Australian Youth Strategy (Australian Government, 2010). At the same time there are a number of challenges, most notably the one of showing results or providing evidence that this work is not simply tokenistic. How can young people's productions inform policy? As is noted by Gautam and Oswald (2008), Thompson (2009), and Mitchell et al. (2006), exhibitions and other public displays often have the power to engage audiences in ways that other modes do not. A single image of an unsafe toilet, for example, taken by a group of girls in a primary school in Swaziland in response to an open-ended prompt "feeling safe and not so safe" helped to influence a group of policy-makers working in the area of water, sanitation, and child protection at the UN to include categories related to safety and security in their "healthy school" analysis (Mitchell, 2009). Thus the participation of youth first to engage in analysis, and then second to engage in planning and setting up travelling exhibitions linked to policy discussions at community level and beyond can be a key component of testing out the significance of media in relation to social change.

However there are other challenges and concerns in relation to future work. Clearly access is an issue, particularly since so much of this work is located in "digital divide" communities where there may be limited access to different media forms, equipment, and online access. Sustainability is also an issue. In some of the projects in which we have been involved through the Centre for Visual Methodologies, work in a particular community has taken place over six or seven years. In other projects, the activity has been one that is more of a "one-off" intervention. And while the results may have been fascinating, there may be little long term impact. Another key issue relates to outlets and audiences. It is critical that the photos, videos and other productions be viewed by other community members and especially decision-makers. However there may be no obvious outlet for, and very little ownership by, the children and young people themselves. A promising area for further development is in the use of digital archiving, as part of what might be described as a "digital humanities" movement. Increasingly researchers are using digital technology to develop archives for managing large collections of visual data and for using digital archives to study social issues longitudinally (Mitchell, 2011; Park et al., 2007). Typically, however, community members are not involved in either creating/designing these archives or working with the visual data in the archive. This is a key area for future work with children and young people. Indeed, perhaps the greatest challenge is in relation to actually capturing and learning from the knowledge that is being produced through this kind of work. As noted above, this work is frequently framed as "youth as knowledge producers," but what knowledge, whose knowledge and who can use this knowledge?

SEE ALSO in this volume chapter by Fisherkeller and chapter by Kolucki.

References

Australian Government (2010). National Strategy for Young Australians. Retrieved from http://www. deewr.gov.au/Youth/OfficeForYouth/YouthPrograms/Documents/NatStrat.pdf

Bloustien, G. (2003). *Girl-making*. New York, NY: Berghahn.

Bloustien, G. and Peters, M. P. (2011).*Youth, music, and creative cultures: Playing for life*. New York, NY: Palgrave Macmillan.

Buckingham, D. and Sefton-Green, J. (1994). *Cultural studies goes to school*. New York, NY: Routledge.

Carrington, V. and Robinson, M. (2009). *Digital literacies. Social Learning and Classroom Practices*. London, UK: Sage.

Clacherty, G. (2005). Refugee and returnee children in southern Africa: Perceptions and experiences of violence – A qualitative study of refugee and returnee children in UNHCR operations in Angola, South Africa, and Zambia. Pretoria: UNHCR.

De Castell, S. and Jenson, J. (2003). Serious play. *Journal of curriculum studies*, *35*(6), 649–55.

Ford, N., Odallo, D. and Chorlton, R. (2003). Communication from a human rights perspective: Responding to the HIV/AIDS pandemic in eastern and southern Africa. *Journal of Health Communication*, *8*(6), 519–612.

Gautam, D. and Oswald, K. (2008, November). Child voices: Children of Nepal speak out on climate change adaptation. Research Report: London: Children in a Changing Climate. Retrieved from http://preventionweb.net/files/9735_ChildVoicesnp.pdf

Gubrium, A. C. and Difulvio, G. T. (2011). Girl in the world: Digital storytelling as a feminist public health approach, *4*(2), 28–46.

Jenkins, H. (2006). *Convergence culture: Where old and new media collide*. New York, NY: New York University Press.

Kellett, M. Robinson, C. and Burr, R. (2004). Images of childhood. In S. Fraser, V. Lewis, S. Ding, M. Kellett and C. Robinson (Eds). *Doing research with children and young people*. Thousand Oaks, CA: Sage, pp. 27–42.

Lankshear, C. and Knobel, M. (2003). *New literacies*. London, UK: Open University Press.

MacEntee, K., Labacher, L. and Murray, J. (2011). Rights to expression in the age of AIDS: Girls speak out about HIV and sexuality through digital photography. *Girlhood Studies*, 4(1), 156–67.

Malone, K. (2008) Every Experience Matters, An evidence based research report on the role of learning outside the classroom for children's whole development from birth to eighteen years. Commissioned by Farming and Countryside Education for UK Department Children, School and Families, Wollongong, Australia.

Meintjes, H. (2009). *Growing up in a time of AIDS: the Abaqophi BakwaZisize Abakhanyayo children's radio project*. Case Study prepared on behalf of Clacherty and Associates for the Regional Inter Agency Task Team on HIV and AIDS (RIATT), December 2009.

Mitchell, C. (2009) Geographies of danger: School toilets in sub-Saharan Africa. In O. Gershenson and B. Penner (Eds), *Ladies and Gents*. Temple University Press. London, UK: Routledge, pp. 62–74.

——(2011). *Doing visual research*, London, UK: Sage.

——(2012). Putting people in the picture and keeping people in the picture: What's participation got to do with it? In M. Frąckowiak, L. Olszewski and M. Rosińska (Eds), *Collaboratorium. On participatory social change*, Poznań: Fundacja SPOT, pp. 89–98.

Mitchell, C. and De Lange, N. (2011). Community based video and social action in rural South Africa. In L. Pauwels and E. Margolis (Eds), *Handbook on visual methods*. London: Sage, 171–85.

Mitchell, C., Low, B. and Hoechsmann, M. (2008). Social networks for social change:YAHAnet goes live. *South Africa Gender and Media Diversity Journal*, 4, 118–24.

Mitchell, C., Pascarella, J., De Lange, N. and Stuart, J. (2010). "We wanted other people to learn from us": Girls blogging in rural South Africa in the age of AIDS. In S. Mazzarella (Ed.), *Girl wide web 2.0: Revising girls, the internet and the negotiation of identity*. New York, NY: Peter Lang, pp. 161–82.

Mitchell, C., Stuart, J., Moletsane, R. and Nkwanyana, C. B. (2006). 'Why we don't go to school on Fridays' on youth participation through photovoice in rural KwaZulu-Natal. *McGill Journal of Education*, 41(3), 267–82.

Moletsane, R., Mitchell, C., Smith, A. and Chisholm, L. (2008). Methodologies for *Mapping a Southern African girlhood in the age of AIDS*. Rotterdam, the Netherlands: Sense.

Oakley, A. (1994). Women and children first and last: Parallels and differences between children's and women's studies. In B. Mayall (Ed.), *Children's childhoods observed and experienced*. London: Falmer Press, pp. 28–40.

Park, E., Mitchell, C. and De Lange, N. (2007). Working with digital archives: Photovoice and meta-analysis in the context of HIV & AIDS. In N. De Lange, C. Mitchell and J. Stuart (Eds), *Putting people in the picture: Visual methodologies for social change*. Amsterdam, The Netherlands: Sense, pp. 163–72.

Stuart, J. (2010). Youth as knowledge producers: Towards changing gendered patterns in rural schools with participatory arts-based approaches to HIV and AIDS. *Agenda* (Gender and Rurality), 24(84), 53–65.

Thompson, J. (2009). I am a farmer: Young women address conservation using photovoice around Tiwai Island, Sierra Leone. *Agenda*, 23(79), 65–69.

Wang, C. (1999). Photovoice: participatory action research strategy applied to women's health. *Journal of Women's Health*, 8(2), 85–192.

PART V

COLLABORATIONS AND COMPANIONS

EDITOR'S INTRODUCTION

The last section of the handbook focuses on various additional stakeholders who have had an interest in relationships between children and media, and who have intervened in ways they perceive to be beneficial to young people and society at large.

The first four chapters focus on policymaking. The chapter by **Norma Pecora** maps the history and key issues of media policies for children. She argues that the situation in the US has been dominated by the assumption regarding media effects; namely, media contain inappropriate content that is imposed on a vulnerable audience and influences their behavior. She discusses three historical factors that continue, even today, to inform discussions of digital media. First, an early twentieth century social reformist claim that children need protection; second, the First Amendment guarantee of freedom of speech for the press; and third, the fact that US media industries are part of the for-profit commercial system. Studying these forces enables us to understand the tensions between those who see children as needing protection, the demand by industry for profits, and a government regulatory system that works to please both, but never pleases either.

Katalin Lustyik presents an overview of media regulation systems. She argues that the media children consume on a daily basis can have a considerable impact on their cultural, social, and educational development. For example, the domination of "foreign imports," such as US and Japanese cartoons offered on dozens of dedicated children's television channels, can dwarf domestic production and cultural diversity. The chapter includes descriptions of various government initiatives and some of the legally binding international agreements implemented in different parts of the world to promote cultural diversity and to protect domestic and regional program production in the realm of children's television.

Advertising is a particularly contested policymaking area. **Amy Beth Jordan** and **Joelle Sano Gilmore** discuss how the concern over the effects of exposure to advertising on children's well-being and healthy development has led scholars and advocates to call for bans on advertising to children. In doing so, they examine studies related to the amount and effects of exposure to advertisements, highlighting specific concerns over the marketing of products such as tobacco and junk food that are potentially harmful to children. This analysis is followed by a discussion of government policy and regulation of advertising to children in the US, and the role of industry self-regulation. Finally, they consider alternatives to government policies, including the establishment of alternative funding streams for children's media, media literacy education for children and parents, and the production of high quality public service announcements (PSAs) to counter the effects of advertising and marketing on children and adolescents.

A relatively new concern gaining momentum among the public relates to protecting children online. In analyzing internet policies, **Brian O'Neill** argues that governments worldwide are seeking to introduce policies that restrict the circulation of harmful and illegal content, foster greater digital safety, and encourage more responsible practices by industry and by children themselves. The author discusses the difficulties involved when seeking to ensure that protection does not hinder either the inherent freedom of the internet or the capacity of young people to enjoy the opportunities afforded for learning, communication, and entertainment. Reviewing the background of internet regulation related to children, O'Neill presents the main contours of internet policies for children, including forms of content regulation through classification and labeling, the promotion of self-regulation on the part of industry, and education efforts to stimulate greater digital citizenship among young people.

The next five chapters focus on the benefits of educational and quality media content offered to children. **Shalom M. Fisch** reviews the impacts of educational media, television in particular, on learning. Decades of research have demonstrated that sustained viewing of well-designed educational television series can yield significant benefits for children's knowledge, skills, and attitudes in a range of academic subject areas. Effects have been found among both preschool and school-age children, with consistent effects found across countries. When measured long-itudinally, the impact of educational television series has been found to last for years. This chapter reviews key studies on the impact of educational television, theoretical approaches to explain children's comprehension and learning, and added benefits that can arise when children use television in conjunction with other educational media platforms.

Becky Herr Stephenson devotes specific attention to "new" media and learning. She claims that efforts to understand and expand upon the possibilities for learning with new media have emerged over the last decade in both the public and private sectors. Research in new media and learning has drawn upon diverse paradigms including education, learning sciences, developmental psychology, communication and media studies, and neuroscience (among others). Two frameworks for understanding new media and learning include new media literacies and genres of participation, both of which highlight the importance and interdependence of social and technical skills in learning via new media. Of primary importance for future research on new media and learning are issues of equity in participation, including finding ways to ameliorate the participation gap, methods for bridging informal and formal learning spaces, and ways for new media to support the development of ethical and civic participation by youth.

In her chapter on media literacy education, **Renee Hobbs** argues, first, that two overarching themes have long been identified with this initiative: empowerment and protection. While some scholars and practitioners see media literacy education as a means to address the com-plexities and challenges of growing up in a media- and technology-saturated cultural environ-ment, others see media literacy as a tool for personal, social, cultural, and political empowerment. Thus, a second, key framing question must be asked: Is media literacy education a social movement or an academic field? As a social movement, media literacy is aligned with the communication literature on media effects; while as an academic field, it is grounded in the field of education, with a focus on instructional practices of literacy learning with audio–visual and digital "texts." In her conclusion, she suggests that renewed interest in media literacy as a means of civic engagement may reconcile the productive tension between empowerment and protectionist strands within the media literacy education community.

In analyzing how quality media for children has been defined, **Alexis R. Lauricella, Michael B. Robb,** and **Ellen Wartella** argue that this has proven to be a difficult task historically, as well as today, with advances in children's media technologies. Children's media quality has been identified through awards, ratings, and evaluation of educational content. They conclude that despite great technological changes, there has been little change in how quality is assessed. The authors discuss the importance of including examinations of the child, content, and context in evaluating quality children's media, including relevant challenges. The approaches undertaken by Common Sense Media and the Fred Rogers Center are cited as examples of implementing such processes in examining quality children's media today.

The final section of the handbook contains four additional perspectives that are not always or readily visible in this field. **Barbara Kolucki** discusses how UNICEF, a key stakeholder in the discussion over quality media, has worked over the last 25 years to build a model of communication for children in the developing world. In doing so, she demonstrates the creativity and skills of cross-sectorial teams of specialists working with children and media. The goal of training involved in implementing the UNICEF model is to build confidence and competence in producing age-based, culturally appropriate, holistic, and inclusive communication for children. The model has been developed by the author through UNICEF sponsored trainings in numerous countries, with most of the products having been field-tested or evaluated. This "Master Class" process has been effective in producing communication on a range of topics including early child development, gender equity, disability inclusion, HIV/AIDS, and addressing the psycho-social needs of children living in emergencies.

Cecilia von Feilitzen opens her contribution by mapping extensive examples of international media for children initiatives working to advance quality in children's media. The categories she employs enable us to understand the nature of efforts, such as: interventions seeking better representation of children in the media, protection of children from harmful media content, promotion of awareness, media literacy, and children's right to communication through the media.

The need to reframe media as an issue of health and development is presented by **Michael Rich**. Rich claims that pediatricians and the medical community-at-large have expressed concern about the influences of entertainment screen media on the physical, mental, and social health of children and adolescents for more than half a century. Physicians have urged that research be directed to the positive and negative effects of screen media use on health and development, have lobbied for more child-friendly media content, and have developed clinical and parenting policies related to the use of media. While research on media influences on violence, obesity, sex, smoking, alcohol, and other substance use has grown over the last 25 years, public discourse in regard to children and media has been informed more by opinion than evidence, according to Rich.

Finally, **Linda Simensky** argues from the public media industry perspective that there is a need to bridge scholarship and the industry. She claims that, historically, the children's media industry and academic experts have had a relatively ambivalent relationship. One area where experts and producers have worked comfortably together is public broadcasting. While challenges in this relationship remain, particularly in terms of the added cost and the time it takes to produce a series that is reviewed by experts, Simensky argues that public media have found that the benefits outweigh the challenges, as experts can bring to the production of the series a great deal of knowledge and expertise about the series curricula as well as about children and learning. However, she concludes that, overall, the relationship between the industry and experts could benefit from clarifying their shared goals and through better communication.

45

MEDIA POLICIES FOR CHILDREN: ISSUES AND HISTORIES IN THE US

Norma Pecora

In the United States, the discourse on children and media has been grounded in the assumption of inappropriate media content influencing the behavior of a vulnerable audience. It is argued here that this assumption has its roots in the early twentieth century reformist tradition, beginning with the introduction of motion pictures. Over the decades, this discourse has played out in debates on issues such as inappropriate content that gives rise to criminality and violence and advertising and commercialism. Takanishi (1978), speaking of the emergence of "childhood" as a social concern, offers up a number of examples demonstrating that the "past does influence the present" but warns the reader that "teasing out the variables in this relationship is a highly tortuous and complex task" (p. 10). The reader is also forewarned that the story presented here is an unfinished history of the way citizens' groups,[1] media industries, and policy makers have debated the issues on children and their media in the United States.[2]

There are three factors that come together to inform the discourse on children and their media in the United States, which resonate even today in discussions of digital media and the internet. The first is our long history of the perception that children need protection, an idea that was first introduced in the late eighteenth century with the Progressives and the child saving movement. The second is the even longer history of freedom of speech that is fixed in the First Amendment to the Constitution that states: "Congress shall make no law … abridging the freedom of speech or of the press." And the third is the fact that our media industries are based on a for-profit, commercial system. The tensions between social reformists and citizens' groups, media industries, and policy makers and regulators are grounded in these fundamental precepts. By understanding this, we can step back and come to understand the tensions between those who see children as needing protection, a demand by media industries for profitability through audience, and a government regulatory system that works to please both and never pleases either.

This history begins with the first mass medium available to youth that became a part of our culture in the early 1900s. The era of motion pictures is reported to have begun with a showing at the 1893 Columbian Exposition held in Chicago; movie theaters, as we know them, were well-established by 1910.

The era of moving pictures and the progressive reformers

Many changes occurred in the United States during the beginning of the twentieth century including the introduction of a new political and social movement identified as the Progressives. Men and women who had as their agenda

> the amelioration of poverty, and the purification of politics to embrace the transformation of gender relations, the regeneration of the home, the disciplining of leisure and pleasure ... Progressives wanted not only to use the state to regulate the economy; strikingly, they intended nothing less than to transform other Americans, to remake the nation's feuding, polyglot population in their own middle-class image.
>
> *(McGerr, 2003, p. xiv)*

It was, according to McGerr, "rooted in the day-to-day lives of middle-class men and women in the Gilded Age of the late nineteenth century" (2003, p. xiv). This essay begins with the convergence of the women of the child saving and settlement movement in Chicago who were identified with the Progressive movement and their attempts to use the political system to "discipline" the new leisure adopted by youth – motion pictures. Movies were the first mass entertainment form that was available and affordable to all. According to Fisher (1994) the "modernization of leisure" beginning in the late 1890s brought organized pastimes, commercial entertainment, and private diversions all replacing what had been informal, collective leisure.

While this convergence of circumstances was not unique to Chicago, the city offers an interesting starting point. Chicago was one of the largest movie markets at the time and the city had a large Progressive community that was committed to social reform. Among those most active in this community were a new group of women educated as social workers at the University of Chicago and part of the growing philanthropic middle-class described by McGerr (2003). Women like Jane Addams, co-founder of one of the first settlement houses in the United States; Sophonisba Breckinridge and Edith Abbott, who reformed juvenile courts and education; and Louise de Koven Bowen, a philanthropist and a leader in the child saver movement. Each of these women, with others in Chicago, was committed to "the redemptive powers of reform" (Pearson, 2011, p. 4) and the value of state and federal regulatory authority (Sealander and Sorenson, 2008, p. 8).[3] Perhaps the most significant writing on movies of the time came from Jane Addams' *The spirit of youth and the city streets* (Addams, 1909/1972), whose concern was for the working class and immigrant youth. In this book she spoke of the "dream palaces" where she feared that the stories of the movie heroes would "become the model for reality" (p. 80) and the motion pictures would serve as "a place where people [primarily youth] learn how to think, act, and feel" (p. 93). The stories she recounted were tales of violence and escape, brutality and loss of innocence. While she celebrated the "spirit of youth," Addams called for "protective legislation" (p. 149) and a "code of beneficent legislation" (p. 150).

It was this climate of reform and call for protective legislation that was the hallmark of the Progressive movement and it came to define the discourse on children's media as one of protection for a vulnerable audience from inappropriate content. As a consequence of the work of these women, one of the earliest censorship boards was established. This gave police the power to issue permits to movie theaters that did not show movies determined to be "immoral, obscene or indecent" (Grieveson and Kramer, 2004, p. 135); a shift from previous controls based on licensing. Licensing determined who could show movies; permits were an attempt to control content and, consequently, effect (Grieveson and Kramer, 2004). These early reformists left us a legacy of youth as vulnerable and easily converted to a life of crime by the motion pictures, and regulations based on attempts to control content.

The beginnings of policy and regulation

Chicago's censorship regulation put in place in 1907 represents early attempts to set policy for the motion pictures at the local level (Film Censorship, 2005). Later, as a consequence of the Payne Fund[4] Studies published in 1933, the movie industry established the Motion Picture Production Code to regulate the content of motion pictures. This form of self-regulation to avoid government regulation was put in place in response to the findings of the Payne Fund research. While the Code did not specifically address children or youth, the proponents for the code argued that children were a vulnerable audience and therefore more susceptible to the stories of the motion pictures. W.W. Charters, in a popularized version of the findings from the Payne Fund Studies, claimed that "because children were not conscious of the image as representation, they were more likely to accept the scenes presented to them as real" (Jacobs, 1990, p. 33). This clearly echoes Addam's "model of reality."

The era of radio and advocacy

When nationally-distributed commercial radio broadcasting came into the home in the United States during the 1930s, this discourse on protectionism and reform had been well-established. Building on the model established by the motion picture industry the public discourse on children and radio centered on its consequences claiming, among other concerns, that the radio dramas caused nightmares. However, while the early reformists were concerned about the motion pictures' corruption of youth, the concern with radio turned toward younger children. As a home entertainment, radio was far more readily accessible.

By the 1930s the Progressive movement and its social reform agenda was being replaced by advocacy organizations that relied heavily on public pressure to bring about change.[5] In place of the social reformists, represented by Jane Addams, the debate on protectionism fell to groups such as the Women's National Radio Committee, the General Federation of Women's Clubs, The American Legion Auxiliary, and parent/teacher organizations. These women "opposed programs they believed frightened or 'over-stimulated' children" (Butsch, 2000, p. 232; see also Advocacy groups, 2011). In addition while early concerns addressed children of the working class and immigrants, the polyglot population, these middle-class women turned their attention to their own children (Cravens, 1993, p. 5). One particularly vocal, and successful group, was a citizens' group in Scarsdale, New York who, in 1933, rated the violent content of children's radio programs and found almost all were considered as unacceptable (Cooper, 1996, p. 22). Because of radio's reliance on advertising, concern also turned to advertising products directed toward the child audience (Bruce, 2008).

The move to federal regulation

With the technology of radio, came a new mechanism for regulation. The Federal Communication Commission (FCC) determined that a license to use the public air waves was to be granted to those stations that served the "public interest." However challenges to a license could be brought against a station only by those with a financial interest in the industry. This left out those with a social concern and consequently, the only recourse for citizen groups with a grievance was public pressure (New York Times, 1933). And indeed, several national radio networks did respond to public pressure when, in 1935, the networks put in place standards for children's programming. As with the motion picture code, these self-regulatory policies were an attempt to thwart government intervention. In addition to limiting advertisements, the standards prohibited progam content that: demonstrated a disrespect for authority; rewarded cruelty, greed, or selfishness; exploited others; and encouraged dishonesty or deceit (New York Times, 1935a). These restrictions were remarkably similar to guidelines proposed by the Women's National Radio Committee in 1933 (New York Times, 1935b). In 1939, the FCC released a memorandum warning radio stations that they needed to observe their public interest obligations and shortly thereafter the National Association of Broadcasters announced the adoption of a Code, not unlike the Motion Picture Association of America, that offered guidelines on commercial content and program length advertising as well as some program content (New York Times, 1939). As with the MPAA Code, radio regulation was industry-driven.

During the 1940s the FCC, citizens' groups, and the world turned their attention to the war.

The era of television

In the early 1950s, after World War II, television replaced radio in the home and the regulatory climate changed. A court ruling in the 1960s for the United Church of Christ, regarding the renewal of a Mississippi radio license, opened the way for public citizens to petition the FCC (Shapiro, 2006). Advocacy groups could now seek regulatory remedies for children's broadcasting. This is not to say that children had been ignored. Beginning in 1952, Congress held a number of hearings and inquiries on television and violence. These hearings brought together policy makers, citizens' groups, and industry representatives to examine the effect of television programming, its influence on society, and potential recourse – but there would be no regulation.

According to Cooper (1996), Congressional Hearings served a number of functions including acting "as a forum for citizen groups attempting to bring attention to their cause and influence changes in policy, and for industry officials lobbying for or against regulatory change" (p. 11). However, the industry steadily resisted any form of government regulation leaving oversight yet again to citizens' groups and advocacy organizations. In 1969 Action for Children's Television (ACT) was formed as an advocacy organization concerned specifically with the quality of children's television programming. The group quickly gained national attention in 1970, using the new tool that was the result of the United Church of Christ ruling. They submitted a petition to the FCC asking for content regulation in the form of more diverse programming and age-specific programs. From 1970 until the passage of the Children's Television Act of 1990 (CTA), ACT was the leading advocacy organization for children and television. With the passage of CTA, ACT closed and was replaced by other organizations including the Center for Digital Democracy (established 2001), the Parents Television Council (established 1995), and the Campaign for a Commercial Free Childhood (established 2000). The issues addressed by these various groups have included the new digital technology, quality programming, advertising and commercialism, and television violence.

The government intervenes ... at last

The Children's Television Act required the FCC to regulate children's television using criteria similar to those outlined in the 1970 petition from Action for Children's Television. Over the 20 years of FCC hearings on Docket 19142, opened by the initial ACT petition, some regulations had been put in place including no-host selling and advertising time-limits but little other regulation came from the FCC or Congress until the CTA (see Kunkel and Roberts, 1991; Kunkel and Watkins, 1987). With the Act, and its subsequent refinements, a policy on children and media was finally in place. Regulation required that when a station's license was to be renewed the station must demonstrate that it provided a minimum of three hours of educational programming per week, identified with the symbol E/I, and listed in advance. The station must also limit the amount of commercial time and for programming to children of 12 and under commercials were to be separated from the program by non-commercial or program material (bumpers). These regulations spoke to quality programming and advertising limits but did not directly address the inappropriate content of earlier debates.[6] However, with the rewrite of the Telecomunications Act in 1996, the FCC was given oversight to establish a standard for blocking technology. This technology, the V-chip, allowed parents to set controls on their television to limit inappropriate content from coming into the home. The National Association of Broadcasters, the National Cable Television Association, and the Motion Picture Association of America established a voluntary ratings system based on objectionable and inappropriate material, the TV Parental Guidelines, to be used with the V-chip. In 2007, Congress passed the Child Safe Viewing Act that required the FCC to investigate blocking technology that would work on other forms of distribution platforms including wireless and the internet.

To the future

One hundred years after Jane Addams wrote about the dream palaces (1909/1972), the discourse on children and media has changed little. Jane Addams and the women of Chicago who used the regulatory powers of the city begat the Scarsdale women who used public pressure to regulate radio and they begat Action for Children's Television who used the Federal Communications Commission to regulate television. Often these successes have been through public pressure – the Motion Picture Production Code brings about the National Association of Broadcasters Radio Code which brings about the TV Parental Guidelines – illustrating that the past does indeed inform the future. Although government legislation has been slow in responding to the public discourse with regulatory policy, debates were clearly informed by public pressure. The motion picture industry responded to Progressives and the Payne Fund studies; the radio industry set in place guidelines for children's programming based on pressure from citizens groups such as the Parent Teacher Association of Scarsdale New York; and the tenacity of Action for Children's Television finally achieved formal policy with the Children's Television Act.

As we move to a digital environment and multiple platforms, we find much the same patterns. A coalition of professionals and children's advocacy organizations petitioned the FCC to apply the public interest obligations under analog rules to the new digital environment. The Children's Online Protection Act (COPA) was passed by Congress in 1998 seeking to restrict children's access to inappropriate content; it was quickly struck down by the courts as a violation of the First Amendment. In addition to issues of inappropriate content and advertising limits, which take on new dimensions when directed to the internet, there is now the issue of online privacy. The Children's Online Privacy Protection Act (COPPA) was passed in 1998 giving the Federal Trade Commission (FTC) oversight on internet websites and the information sites are allowed to collect. Most recently the Do Not Track Kids Act has been introduced in the House of Representatives to expand COPPA and cover young people up to the age of 18 (Kahn, 2011). However, during a webcast of the Hearings, the discourse differed little from that of the Progressives of the early twentieth century as those in attendance called for the protection of our children and youth when they go online (Markey, 2011).

In many ways we have come a long way, in others … not so far.

SEE ALSO in this volume chapter by Lustyik, chapter by Jordan and Gilmor, and chapter by O'Neill.

Notes

1 My apologies to all the groups who have worked diligently to bring quality to children's programming; this essay focuses on only a very few of the many organizations that have taken part in this debate.

2 The distinction here is between policy and regulation and is based on the work of Brown (2010) – state policies are the goals one hopes to achieve and regulations are the tools used to achieve those goals.

3 This is unfortunately a very simplistic discussion of what was a very complex time that is well-documented in other sources. There was also an element of social class to the debate as the elite and middle class reformers were, some would argue, "trying to exercise social control over the working class" (Pearson, 2011, p. 5; see also McGerr, 2003).

4 The Payne Fund Studies were heavily influenced by the intellectual climate at the University of Chicago. Nine of the thirteen scholars were trained by or on faculty at the University and many were a part of the Chicago Progressive community.

5 The distinction between reform and advocacy is perhaps somewhat subtle but important. The reform movement as discussed here (1900–1920s) tended to be composed of professional women and philanthropists who saw their role as protecting the civil liberties of those less fortunate and maintaining a social order; the advocacy groups (1930s to today) that followed were often citizens' groups with little power but public attention. Unfortunately they are often of short term duration.

6 Peg Charren, long-time director of Action for Children's Television, recognized the problems of debating media content and claimed that it was better to argue for more programming than to impose standards on content. Consequently the organization avoided the "inappropriate content" debate.

References

Addams, J. (1909/1972). *The spirit of youth and the city streets*. Urbana: University of Illinois Press.

Advocacy groups (2011). Retrieved November 15, 2011, from the *Museum of Broadcast Communications*: http://www.museum.tv/eotvsection.php?entrycode=advocacy groups

Brown, D. H. (2010, December). Associate Professor, Ohio University (*personal interview*).

Bruce, A. L. (2008). Creating consumers and protecting children: Radio, early television and the American child: 1930–60. Ph.D. Dissertation. University of New York at Stony Brook.

Butsch, R. (2000). *The making of American audiences: From stage to television, 1750–1990*. New York: Cambridge University Press.

Cooper, C. A. (1996). *Violence on television: Congressional inquiry, public criticism and industry respons, a policy analysis*. Lanham NY: University Press of America.

Cravens, H. (1993). Child saving in modern America 1870s–1990s. In R. Woolons (Ed.), *Children at risk in America: History, concepts, and public policy*. New York: State University of New York Press, pp. 3–31.

Film Censorship. (2005). Retrieved November 15, 2011, from *Encyclopedia of Chicago*: http://encyclopedia.chicagohistory.org/pages/453.html

Fisher, C. (1994). Changes in leisure activity. *Journal of Social History*, 27(3), 453–82.

Grieveson, L. and Kramer, P. (2004). Cinema and reform: Introduction. In L. Grieveson and P. Kramer (Eds), *The silent cinema reader* (reprint 2006 ed.). New York: Routledge, pp. 135–43.

Jacobs, L. (1990, January). Reformers and spectators: The film education movement in the thirties. *Camera Obscura*, 8(22), 28–49.

Kahn, D. (2011, May 23). *Markey and Barton introduce "Do Not Track Kids Act of 2011"*. Retrieved December 10, 2011, from Inside Privacy: http://www.insideprivacy.com/childrens-privacy/markey-and-barton-introduce-do-not-track-kids-act-of-2011/

Kunkel, D. and Watkins, B. (1987). Evolution of children's regulatory policy. *Journal of Broadcasting and Electronic Media*, 34(1), 367–89.

Kunkel, D. and Roberts, D. (1991). Young minds and marketplace values: Issues in children's television advertising. *Journal of Social Issues*, 47(1), 57–72.

McGerr, M. (2003). *A Fierce Discontent*. New York: Oxford University Press.

Markey, E. (2011, October 5). Opening Statement. Hearing on 'Protecting children's privacy in an electronic world'. House of Representatives, Washington, D.C.

New York Times (1933). Mothers protest about 'bogyman' on radio. February 27, p. 1.

New York Times (1935a). Radio ads curbed by Columbia chain. May 14, p. 10.

New York Times (1935b). Women's radio committee discloses its formula for approval of children's programming. December 29, p. 1.

New York Times (1939). The new code for the broadcasting industry. July 12, p. 7.

Pearson, S. J. (2011). *The rights of the defenseless: Protecting animals and children in Gilded Age America.* Chicago: The University of Chicago Press.

Sealander, J. and Sorenson, J. (Eds) (2008). *The Grace Abbott Reader.* Lincoln: University of Nebraska Press.

Shapiro, S. (2006). United Church of Christ v. FCC: Private attorneys general and the rule of law. *Administrative Law Review, 58*(4), 939–60.

Takanishi, R. (1978). Historical roots of advocacy. *Journal of Social Issues, 34*(2), 8–28.

46

MEDIA REGULATION

The protection and promotion of home-grown children's television

Katalin Lustyik

Introduction

Children growing up in the twenty-first century in most parts of the world are targeted by a "steadily swelling flow of material" (Carlsson, 2006, p. 9). The audiovisual content that they are exposed to today comes from all over the world, but predominantly from the United States, Japan and the United Kingdom and a handful of other countries with a strong investment in children's television, while domestically produced children's shows, if they exist at all, are often marginalized. The programs children consume on a daily basis have a considerable impact on their cultural, social and educational development, which might be especially true of domestic programs that specifically aim to relate to their own world, identities, concerns and futures.

In many countries, where resources limit domestic productions, the general concern is that a great deal of imported media contains characters and messages that, at best, are not relevant to local cultures, and at worst, convey violent or sexual images and mass marketed messages. Nyamnjoh (2002) draws attention to the fact that in many parts of the world, including Africa, children mainly watch programming "conceived and produced without their particular interest in mind" that "seldom reflects their immediate cultural contexts" (p. 43). He further argues that these children become "victims of second-hand consumption" who "must attune their palates to the diktats of undomesticated foreign media dishes" (p. 43).

Among the media dishes offered on an increasing variety of platforms in some parts of the world – that can include print media, radio, television and film screens, internet, mobile technologies, and console-based video games – television still remains the most important mass medium for children worldwide. Transnational media companies targeting children race to offer multiplatform services but they still consider television as the driving force behind their key brands. The globally popular *SpongeBob SquarePants,* for instance, started out as a television series on the US-based Nickelodeon children's channel, soon followed by dedicated websites, video games, theatrical films and a plethora of merchandizing (Hendershot, 2004). Additionally, in the realm of media regulation, traditional broadcast content such as television content remains the most heavily regulated form of media in most countries, although new legislative frameworks aim to cover all audiovisual media services regardless of the delivery platform (ACMA, 2011).

When people think of television regulation and children, what immediately comes to mind is media violence, pornography, the television rating systems and a ban on the advertising of cigarettes, alcohol and, more recently in Europe, "junk food," food with high sugar, fat or salt content. While some chapters of this book examine those areas specifically, this chapter focuses on the regulation of domestic or home-grown children's television content in an international context. Such terms as "home-grown," "domestic" or "locally" produced programs are highly ambiguous and the exact definitions vary worldwide, especially given the complexity of the procedure that involves financing, (co)production and post-production, which are often tied to several nations. Generally however, these terms refer to a program produced within a specific nation – or nations in case of coproduction – or a specific region, and perceived as "an invaluable vehicle for conveying societal history, lore and values" that "affirms the right to control over the portrayal of one's own history, cultures and stories" (Kleeman, 2008).

While this chapter aims to describe various types of government initiatives and legally binding international agreements that have been implemented in different parts of the world to promote home-grown children's television content, it does not pretend to draw any general conclusions valid for the world's some 200 countries. The first section of the chapter provides a brief overview of children's television content regulation, and the second section describes key types of government provision for the protection, promotion and distribution of home-grown children's television content. Concrete examples are selected from Australia, Canada, the European Union Member States, China and Qatar. The third section describes some legally binding regional and international efforts that have been implemented to achieve more cultural diversity in the global television program flow.

Regulating children's television content

The regulatory frameworks in which media organizations operate and the types of provisions designed specifically with children in mind, who constitute the most protected audience group, can vary greatly worldwide. With television channels beamed in from all over the world, some governments struggle to adopt frameworks operable in today's dynamically expanding and intertwined global media landscape. The term "media regulation" can narrowly refer to "legally binding government rules by which media organizations must operate" (McKenzie, 2005, p. 2). It can also broadly refer to "any influences over media operations and media content" (McKenzie, 2005, p. 2) as applied in this chapter, which aims to emphasize how television content regulation is a result of an intricate interplay between more and less visible entities or stakeholders that operate within and beyond the borders of nation states.

Stakeholders involved in children's television content regulation can include government-related agencies such as the State Administration of Radio, Film and Television (SARFT) in China; international and regional political institutions such as the United Nations Educational, Scientific and Cultural Organization (UNESCO) or the European Union (EU); professional and industry associations such as the European Broadcasting Union (EBU); civic/non-profit activist groups such as Save Kids' TV in the United Kingdom; religious, medical and educational organizations such as the Qatar Foundation for Education, Science and Community Development (QF); advertisers, parents and, of course, the media organizations themselves that operate on a national, regional or global level.

Media organizations engage in continuous negotiation with other stakeholders in order to avoid extensive government involvement in their operations and services domestically and internationally. As a result of technological changes, the growth of delivery platforms and the rise of powerful transnational media conglomerations, governments have less control over, and in today's political and economic climate often less inclination and support for, the direct regulation of the media available within their jurisdictions, even if they target young citizens. In many countries today, self- and co-regulation is favored, especially in the case of new media but increasingly so in traditionally heavily regulated areas like children's television (Steemers, 2010).

As the number of pay television channels catering specifically for children have skyrocketed during the last twenty years in many parts of the world (e.g. Chalaby, 2006), young viewers in many countries presumably have access to a wider variety of content. In Poland, for example, households with a cable or satellite subscription can access up to 38 children's channels including Carton Network Poland, Disney Channel Polska, Cbeebies Poland, Boomerang, Al Jazeera Children's Channel, Baby TV and others (MAVISE, 2011). In such saturated markets the question "is there still room – is there still need – for content that roots young people in a unique culture or tradition?" (Kleeman, 2008) is raised more frequently. The UK-based Save Kids' TV strongly supports home-grown content production, finding it "alarming" that first-run locally produced programs constitute less than 1 percent of children's television hours in the UK, with the rest filled with repeats and imports (Blumenau, 2011, p. 2).

The most prominent and trend-setting television networks that are also key exporters are US-based Viacom's Nickelodeon, Time Warner's Cartoon Network and Disney, referred to in industry circles as the "masters of the children's television universe" (Westcott 2008). The majority of their heavily rotated content primarily comes from the United States, Japan and the UK (Lustyik, 2010; Pecora and Lustyik, 2011). These globally circulated programs are often described in rather negative terms and in polar opposition to home-grown content, which is perceived as having been developed with the interests and perspectives of local children in mind to provide them a sense of their own place in an increasingly complex world. As D'Arma and Steemers (2011) point out, "there remains one under-researched question about what is especially valuable about indigenous [home-grown] programming and where is the evidence for us thinking that it is actually better than imports" (p. 14). The argument put forward by a former managing director of the Australian Broadcasting Corporation is rather typical: "I'm not suggesting the influence [of imported US shows] being detrimental, but it's not a national Australian influence and it's not conceived or developed with a view to telling our stories" (Shier, 2001, para 3).

Symbolically, the act of protecting and promoting home-grown children's content is about preserving the last remaining unconquered audiovisual territory from "foreign invaders" for future citizens. In economic terms, as children's television has turned into a dynamically growing enterprise, well-integrated into the global entertainment industry, the production of children's programs has become a valuable or even vital part of many major media production industries in several countries besides the US including the UK, Japan, Australia, Canada and China, that needs to be protected and supported.

The protection and promotion of home–grown children's television

Some countries have regulatory frameworks with specific provisions for the transmission of media aimed at children that are either designed *to limit* potentially harmful audiovisual content such as sexually explicit shows, or *to promote* specific types of content such as educational programs. The various mechanisms these nations use to promote the distribution and production of home-grown content range widely. This section highlights four key approaches or mechanisms:

(1) applying programming quotas to curb imports;
(2) supporting home-grown production;
(3) setting up government-funded local or regional children's channels; and
(4) banning imported programs.

In countries that have a programming or transmission quota of nationally or regionally produced content, a number of factors are taken into consideration for determining the actual percentage of quota. Often public service broadcasters with more substantial commitments to serve the public have higher quotas than commercial broadcasters. In Canada, for example, public broadcasters need to air at least 60 percent of Canadian content daily while commercial broadcasters only have to transmit at least 50 percent. Quotas can be also determined by the age of the target audience: Australian broadcasters, for example, can only schedule Australian-produced programs for preschoolers. Many broadcasters try to circumnavigate the transmission quotas by endlessly repeating the same domestic shows, thus in some countries provisions even specify the percentage of first-run local content. In Australia, 25 hours of the annually required 390 hours of children's programs have to be "first-run" Australian productions (Blumenau, 2011).

Besides transmission quotas and the limitation of repeats, regulatory frameworks can also provide broad obligations for broadcasters to invest a certain percentage of their annual profit in the production and acquisition of locally or regionally produced children's content. For instance, Italian broadcasters have to reserve 10 percent of their annual profit for the acquisition of films and TV programs made for children by European producers (Blumenau, 2011).

Incentives can be also created for broadcasters for the prioritization of home-grown children's television programs. Government legislation can stipulate that a certain percentage of government funding for local television and/or film production must be allocated to children's and young people's programs. The Danish Film Institute (DFI), for example, has a dedicated Children & Youth unit that receives 25 percent of the annual government film subsidies to produce stories from Danish children's perspectives that are broadcast on television as well (Danish Film Institute, n.d). Regular funding sources for the production of children's programs can be allocated by government agencies in partnership with cable/satellite distributors or by private media operators alone such as the Shaw Rocket Fund, set up by Canada's largest telecommunications company, which supports the production of high-quality and creative Canadian children's television content (Shaw Rocket Fund, 2011).

In the Middle East, the Qatar Foundation for Education, Science and Community Development (QF), in partnership with the Al Jazeera Network, not only allocates regular funding for the production of local children's programs, but has also launched pan-Arabic children's television channels with the mission of promoting regional content, since the majority of programming offered across the Arab world consists of foreign imports. QF, funded by the ruling royal family, thrives in the nation of Qatar, which boasts the world's highest economic growth rate as well as the highest GDP per capita (CIA, 2010). Launched in 2005, Al Jazeera Children's Channel (JCC), echoing the mission of the Foundation, was created to make a difference in the lives of Arab youth by promoting "self-esteem, understanding and freedom of thought" (Al Jazeera Children's Channel, 2011). Local content reaching 80 percent is perceived to be crucial, with several shows produced in-house. Home-grown production mainly consists of non-fictional programs with a preference for those that incorporate real children in real life situations with regional relevance (JCC, personal communication 2010). Today the non-commercial Al Jazeera Children's Channel and its offspring, Baraem, targeting preschoolers, reach all 22 Arab countries as free satellite channels and are available in many European and Asian countries' cable and satellite subscription packages (Lustyik and Zanker, 2013).

Banning foreign imports is perhaps the most radical regulatory option for the protection of home-grown children's television. In China, since the adaptation of the Open Policy in the early 1980s, which opened up a window for imported programs (up to 30 percent of transmission time), government officials have been concerned about the growing popularity of Japanese, South Korean and US cartoons (Zhuang, 2008). Additionally, with the launch of

China Central TV's Channel 14 (CCTV 14) dedicated to children in late 2003, Disney and Nickelodeon were also able to establish programming blocks that became immediate top-rating performers. In the world's currently biggest media market with more than 1.3 billion people, the government still largely owns and closely monitors the media and might treat foreign media corporations and programming as "corrupting agents of imperialism" (Ma, 2000, p. 22). The Chinese regulatory agency, the State Administration of Radio, Film and Television (SARFT), has employed a "mixture of restrictive measures"(e.g. "legal limitation, policy directives, administrative rules, mini campaigns and normative guidelines") (Chen and Chan, 1998, p. 656) and post-censorship mechanisms to control and "deflect" transnational media flows (Ma, 2000, p. 28). In 2006, to curb the overwhelming appeal of *SpongeBob SquarePants* and other imported popular shows, SARFT imposed a ban on foreign cartoons during prime time television viewing hours (from 5 pm to 9 pm). The main motivation seems economic rather than simply ideological: to support and protect the domestic animation industry rather than to censor foreign media content adored by Chinese children and even young adults (Zhuang, 2008). Officials came to consider the animation industry not only as a significant "growth industry" but also as a "means of extending China's soft power internationally" (Coonan, 2012). But foreign media companies, especially those targeting children, must not only "negotiate every nuance of programming" with the authorities but with Chinese parents as well who can be "even more restrictive than the government, viewing American-style television as too unruly" (Barboza, 2005).

"Enforcing" cultural diversity

While US and Japanese cartoons can be perceived as "unruly" or violent in some parts of the world, a more general concern is their ubiquity. While the abundance of television channels today has the potential to promote cultural diversity and offer "multidimensional flows of media imagery" (Curtin, 2004, p. 272), children's television is particularly standardized with home-grown content "notoriously under-resourced if not marginalized" (D'Arma and Steemers 2008, p. 1). "Any society that regards provision of indigenous [home-grown] programmes as policy goals" argue D'Arma and Steemers

> should acknowledge that the economics of a multichannel television system dominated by commercially oriented US players is hardly conducive to what might be thought of as desirable outcomes such as range and diversity of content that reflects children's own communities and environment.
>
> *(2011, p. 14)*

While in many countries there are no resources, obligations or incentives for broadcasters to produce or schedule home-grown children's content, even in highly regulated regions such as the European Union (EU) the results have been unsatisfactory. The EU's Audiovisual Media Services Directive (earlier known as the Television without Frontiers Directive, TVWF) requires all television channels – irrespective of the type of channel or the type of transmission mode – to devote a majority (at least 50 percent) of transmission time to European works with additional content requirements placed on broadcasters to reflect linguistic or cultural specificities in each Member State. However, even the monitoring of programming offered on thousands of television channels within the 27 Member States has been an enormous bureaucratic task.

According to a recent European Commission report, the majority of thematic children's channels, especially those that belong to non-EU countries (e.g. Disney Channel España, Cartoon Network Germany, Nickelodeon France) did not fulfill their transmission quota obligations and asked for exemption, arguing that when targeting such a niche audience their media libraries consisted of mainly non-European productions (European Commission, 2010). Even Nickelodeon that has embraced "multiculturalism and diversity on an international scale" provides 75 percent of US originating content on its international channels (Sandler, 2004, p. 65). The expectation for Member States, whose role is to enact enforcement measures against non-compliant television channels within their jurisdictions, to put "stricter enforcement" in place "to ensure effective implementation" (European Commission, 2010, Sect. 1.3) has been largely unfulfilled.

On a broader international level, UNESCO's Convention on the Protection and Promotion of the Diversity of Cultural Expressions (UNESCO, 2005) addressed issues that relate to international media flows and the role of nation states. The Convention, which received overwhelming international support, became a legally binding agreement in 2007, reaffirming the sovereign right of nations to adopt policies that protect their cultural industries and promote the diversity of cultural expressions within their jurisdictions. The Convention was described as a "buffer against US cultural domination" (Agence France Press, 2005), and from the US perspective, as a " barrier" aimed to shield healthy "competition from cultural imports" (Will, 2005, p. A17). The US rejection of the Convention was not surprising given the country's position as the largest media content supplier for the rest of the world and its nearly impenetrable domestic media market that is dominated by home-grown content for both children and adult audiences.

Conclusion

While there seems to be international support for creating and sustaining a balance between the protection of local cultural production and the cross-border flow of cultural products, there is little consensus on how it could be achieved and enforced (Magner, 2004). This chapter has described various national initiatives, legislative frameworks and international agreements that have been implemented to support home-grown program production with the focus on children's television content. As discussed earlier, some countries use a combination of protective policies and incentives, and others – with or without restrictive policies in place – have responded by establishing national or regional children's television channels aimed to promote themes and values deemed appropriate for their audience. Many countries do not have any provisions in place.

While nations, depending on their wealth and size, and economic and political clout, still have some control through direct and indirect means to regulate the flow of audiovisual content targeting children living within their jurisdictions, it is an increasingly challenging or seemingly impossible task to do so in the current global media economy. "The rapid expansion of broadband-fuelled entertainment, whether online or across cable TV networks," argued a recent Canadian report pessimistically, "has rendered the regulatory framework established to protect and foster Canadian content obsolete" (Sturgeon, 2010, p. 1). Nations that regard provision of home-grown content for children as a worthy policy goal are certainly in a difficult position, and are forced to vigilantly and continuously compare and revise policies to avoid them becoming obsolete.

SEE ALSO in this volume chapter by Pecora, chapter by Jordan and Gilmore, and chapter by O'Neill.

References

ACMA (Australian Communications and Media Authority) (2011). *International approaches to audiovisual content regulation: A comparative analysis of the regulatory frameworks.* Occasional paper. Australian Communications and Media Authority. Retrieved from http://acma.gov.au

Agence France Press (2005, October 20). US isolated over 'protectionist' UN culture convention. Retrieved from Lexis-Nexis database.

Al Jazeera Children's Channel (2011). Retrieved from http://www.jcctv.net

Barboza, D. (2005, Dec. 29). Nick's cultural revolution. *The New York Times.* Retrieved from http://www.nytimes.com

Blumenau, J. (2011, April). *Children's Media Regulations. A report into state provisions for the protection and promotion of home-grown children's media.* Retrieved from http://www.savekidstv.org.uk/

Carlsson, U. (2006). Foreword. In C. von Feilitzen and U. Carlsson (Eds), *Regulation, Awareness, Empowerment.* Göteborg: The UNICEF International Clearinghouse on Children, Youth and Media, pp. 9–10.

Chalaby, J. K. (2006). American Cultural Primacy in a New Media Order. *The International Communication Gazette, 68*(1), 33–51.

Chen, H. and Chan, J. M. (1998). Bird-caged press freedom in China. In J. Chang (Ed.), *China in the Post-Deng Era.* Hong Kong: The Chinese University Press, pp. 645–68.

CIA (Central Intelligence Agency) (2010). Qatar. *The World Factbook.* Retrieved from https://www.cia.gov/library/publications/the-world-factbook/index.html

Coonan, C. (2012, June 4). China: Gold rush toward more productions. *Variety.* Retrieved at http://www.variety.com/article/VR1118054438?refcatid=1050

Curtin, M. (2004). Media Capitals: Cultural Geographies of Global TV. In. L. Spigel and J. Olson (Eds), *Television After TV.* Chapel Hill, NC: Duke University Press, pp. 270–302.

Danish Film Institute. (n.d). *Children & Youth.* Retrieved from http://dfi.dk

D'Arma, A. and Steemers, J. (2008). Children's television: the soft underbelly of public service broadcasting. Conference paper. RIPE@2008, Germany. Retrieved from http://www.uta.fi/jour/ripe/2008/papers/Steemers_D_Arma.pdf

D'Arma, A. and Steemers, J. (2011). Localisation Strategies of US owned Children's Television Networks in Five European Markets. *Journal of Children and Media, 6*(2), 1–17.

European Commission (2010, Sept. 23). *Ninth Communication on the application of Articles 4 and 5 of Directive 89/552/EEC as amended by Directive 97/36/EC and Directive 2007/65/EC, for the period 2007–2008.* Staff Working Document. Retrieved from http://eur-lex.europa.eu

Hendershot, H. (2004). Nickelodeon's Nautical Nonsense: The Intergenerational Appeal of SpongeBob SquarePants. In H. Hendershot (Ed.), *Nickelodeon Nation: The history, politics and economics of America's only TV channel for kids.* New York: New York University Press, pp. 182–208.

JCC, personal communication (2010). Interviewee did not wish to be identified. Doha, Qatar, April 4, 2010.

Kleeman, D. W. (2008). Local and global: Conflict or complement. Speech given at BakaForum 2008. Retrieved from http://www.centerforchildrenandmedia.org/

Lustyik, K. (2010). Transnational Children's Television: The case of Nickelodeon in the South Pacific. *International Communication Gazette, 72*(2), 171–90.

Lustyik, K. and Zanker, R. (2013). Is there local content on television for children today? In A. N. Valdivia (Gen. Ed.) and S. R. Mazzarella (Ed.), *The international encyclopedia of media studies. Vol. 3: Content and representation.* Oxford, UK: Blackwell, pp. 179–202.

Ma, E. (2000). Rethinking media studies: The case of China. In J. Curran and M. Park (Eds), *De-westernizing media studies.* New York, NY: Routledge, pp. 21–34.

Magner, T. (2004). Transnational Media, International Trade and the Idea of Cultural Diversity. *Continuum: Journal of Media and Cultural Studies, 18*(3), 380–97.

MAVISE (2011). Database of TV companies and TV channels in the EU and candidate countries. Retrieved from http://mavise.obs.coe.int/

McKenzie, R. (2005). Comparing Media regulation between France, the United States, Mexico and Ghana. *Comparative Media Law Journal, 6*, 129–70. Retrieved from http://www.juridicas.unam.mx/publica/rev/indice.htm?r=comlawj&n=5

Nyamnjoh, F. B. (2002). Children, Media and Globalisation: A Research Agenda for Africa. In C. Von Feiltizen and U. Carlsson (Eds), *Children, Young People and Media Globalisation.* Göteborg: The UNICEF International Clearinghouse on Children, Youth and Media, pp. 43–52.

Pecora, N. and Lustyik, K. (2011). Media Regulation and the International Expansion of Nickelodeon. *Journal of Children and Media, 5*(1), 4–19.

Sandler, K. S. (2004). A Kid's Gotta Do What a Kid's Gotta Do: Branding the Nickelodeon Experience. In H. Hendershot (Ed.), *Nickelodeon Nation: The history, politics and economics of America's only TV channel for kids.* New York: New York University Press, pp. 45–68.

Shaw Rocket Fund. (2011). About us. Retrieved from http://www.rocketfund.ca

Shier, J. (2001, Aug. 8). Children's TV At Risk of US Takeover. *The Sydney Morning Herald.* Retrieved from the Lexis-Nexis database.

Steemers, J. (2010). The BBC's role in the changing production ecology of preschool television in Britain. *Television New Media, 11*(1), 37–61.

Sturgeon, J. (2010, Jan 29). CRTC rules become 'ineffective.' *National Post.* Retrieved from http://www.nationalpost.com/story-printer.html?id=2498233

UNESCO (2005). *Convention on the Protection and Promotion of the Diversity of Cultural Expressions.* Retrieved from http://www.unesco.org

Westcott, T. (2008, Jan. 31). Masters of the children's television universe. *Screen Digest.* Special Report.

Will, G. F. (2005, Oct. 12). Dimwitted Nod to 'Diversity.' *The Washington Post,* A17.

Zhuang, P. (2008, Feb. 21). TV blackout on cartoon made abroad extended. *South China Morning Post.* Retrieved from Lexis-Nexis database.

47

CHILDREN AND ADVERTISING POLICIES IN THE US AND BEYOND

Amy Beth Jordan and Joelle Sano Gilmore

Background

The ubiquity of advertisements and children's high exposure rates have led to concern about the effects of advertising on children and have prompted advocates to consider what can be done to reduce exposure or inoculate children to its negative effects (Schor, 2004). In the US, children are exposed to between 24,000 and 30,000 advertisements each year on television alone (Kunkel and Castonguay, 2011). Other industrialized countries report smaller yet impressively high estimates as well (Shah, 2010). In this chapter we provide a brief overview of policy related to advertising to children, including discourse about the fairness of marketing to children, types of advertisements that elicit the most concern, and efforts to mitigate the potential harms of excessive exposure to advertising.

Public discourse about advertising aimed at children is often dominated by opposing views. Advocacy groups and policy makers argue that children are innocent, vulnerable and in need of protection from marketing (Linn and Novosat, 2008; Schor, 2004). Researchers have found that children under 8 years old do not effectively comprehend persuasive marketing messages and that most children under 4 years old do not easily or consistently discriminate between television advertisements and programming (Institute of Medicine, 2006). These findings have been used to justify limits on advertising to younger children in many countries (Caraher et al., 2006). However, Rozendaal et al. (2009) found that Dutch children between the ages of 8 and 12 lack adult levels of advertisement comprehension, and suggest that older children also deserve protection from marketing.

Media and advertising executives argue that children are sophisticated and savvy consumers who deserve the right to engage in the market (Snyder, 2011), and there is some research to support this position (Buckingham, 2009). Furthermore, industry executives argue that restrictions on advertising to children deny companies their right to inform children about their products. In the US (and in many countries) commercial speech is protected speech. (For a review of this argument, see Graff, 2008.) Nonetheless, as illustrated in Table 47.1, countries around the world offer a diversity of advertising policies.

Table 47.1 Advertising policies

Country/Countries	Policy
Brazil	Advertising aimed at children may not be morally offensive, suggest inferiority of a child to other children, or encourage children to "embarrass" parents into buying a product.
Sweden & Norway	No advertising during children's television programming No advertising directed at children under 12
Greece	No toy advertisements between 7 and 10 p.m.
Denmark, Finland, & Austria	No advertising during children's television programming
Belgium (Flemish region)	No advertising in the five minutes preceding and following children's television programming
Nigeria &Thailand	Advertising aimed at children for food products must be approved by national government.
United Kingdom	No advertising for calorie-dense, low nutrient ("junk") foods during children's programming
Israel	Advertising aimed at children may not take advantage of children's innocence, beliefs, imagination, or lack of experience.
Australia	No advertising during television programming aimed at preschoolers
Quebec, Canada	No advertising aimed directly at children during programming where children make up at least 5% of the audience No advertising aimed at children and adults equally during programming where children make up at least 15% of the audience
USA	Advertising during children's programming limited to 10.5 minutes per hour on weekends and 12 minutes per hour on weekdays There must be clear divisions between program content and advertisements (bumpers) No advertisements featuring characters during a program featuring the same characters (host selling)

Sources: Caraher, Landon, and Dalmeny, 2006; Delgado and Foschia, 2003; http://eatbettermovemore.org; www.ofcom.org/uk; Wolberg, 2010

The economic structure of children's media

The production and distribution of children's television shows is expensive – a single episode of a children's television program can cost up to several hundred thousand dollars (Cahn et al., 2008). In many countries, including the US, the production of children's television programming is largely dependent on funding from advertisers (Shah, 2010). Similarly, "advergames" (i.e., advertising messages featuring trade characters and logos in game format) and advertisements on the internet frequently fund the creation and sustainability of children's websites (Kunkel and Castonguay, 2011).

During television's nascent phase in the US, children's media producers struggled to secure funding from advertisers because children were not viewed as valued consumers (Kline, 1993). However, over the decades children have come to be recognized for the influence they have over household purchases and the significant dollars they themselves spend (Henry and Borzekowski, 2011). Researchers estimate that teenagers spend around $160 billion each year, and that children under age 12 spend around $18 billion and influence an additional $200 billion of their parents' purchases including anything from food to automobiles (American Academy of Pediatrics, 2006; Schor, 2004). This purchasing power and influence has led companies to spend over $15 billion on advertising aimed at children each year, most of it airing during children's television programming (Shah, 2010). In addition to providing vehicles for advertisements, many children's media providers derive profits from licensing and merchandising the characters from children's programs (Schor, 2004). As children's media is highly dependent on funding from advertisers who now see children as an important market (Shah, 2010), some worry that the current economic structure of children's media would likely collapse if all advertising to children was banned and if alternative funding structures were not put into place (Shah, 2010; Schor, 2004).

Product concerns

Advocates and researchers have raised specific concerns over advertisements for unhealthy and/or potentially dangerous products that are aimed at children. Numerous studies have suggested that exposure to tobacco and alcohol advertising increases the likelihood that youth will consume these products (e.g., Biener and Siegel, 2000; Mosher, 2012). The associated health risks have led policy makers to ban tobacco and alcohol advertising aimed at children in most countries (World Health Organization, 2003). However, children are still exposed to alcohol and tobacco advertising on billboards and in televised sporting events where children make up a percentage of the audience (Common Sense Media, 2009). In the US, alcohol advertising is also prevalent in public transportation venues that are often used by children and adolescents as a means to get to school (Gentry et al., 2011).

Amid growing concerns about childhood obesity and the associated health risks, several countries are considering or have implemented bans on unhealthy food and beverage advertising targeting children. In countries like the US, researchers have repeatedly found that advertising during children's television programming is dominated by marketing for fast food and sugary cereals (Harrison and Marske, 2005), which is connected to greater consumption of these foods (Hastings et al., 2003). In 2006, the Institute of Medicine concluded that television advertising of foods influences children's food preferences, purchase requests and diets (Institute of Medicine, 2006).

Specific bans on food and beverage advertising aimed at children exist in several countries, including the United Kingdom, which implemented a ban on advertising high fat, salty and sugary products on television programs that have a large youth audience (Dhar and Baylis, 2011). In Quebec, fast food advertising has been banned in all media targeted to children (Quebec Consumer Protection Act, 1980). Combining data from the Canadian food expenditure survey (FoodEx) and the household expenditure survey (FamEx) from 1984 to 1992, Dhar and Baylis compare fast food purchases by households in Ontario. They estimate that the ban has reduced fast food purchases among those affected by the ban by 13 percent per week (Dhar and Baylis, 2011).

Concerns have arisen about children being exposed to age-inappropriate content such as advertisements for violent movies and video games intended for older audiences (American Academy of Pediatrics, 2006) and sexual content (Common Sense Media, 2009). In the US previews for R-rated movies (intended for older audiences) are banned from G-rated movies (general audience, appropriate for children), but children are still exposed to advertising for PG-13 films (intended for those over age 13) and for violent video games (American Academy of Pediatrics, 2006). Critics have also pointed to the overturning of a ban on condom commercials before 9:00 p.m. in the United Kingdom (Laughlin, 2010) and the abundance of advertisements for erectile dysfunction medication in the US as examples of age-inappropriate advertising (Common Sense Media, 2009).

US public policy and advertising to children

In the US, much of the philosophical tension regarding how much say the government should have about media content stems from the constitution's First Amendment protection against government interference in free speech, including commercial speech. Courts have repeatedly had to weigh the rights of commercial entities to say what they please against the need to protect vulnerable citizens, such as children. This balancing act is complicated even further because many government regulations apply only to broadcast television and not to non-broadcast media such as the internet or cable television. The need to protect both the free speech rights of advertisers and special vulnerabilities of children has given rise to a fluid media policy mix of federal mandates and industry self-regulation in many countries. In the section that follows, we examine advertising policy in the US, and the ways in which government regulation and industry self-regulation interact.

Federal Trade Commission

In the US, the Federal Trade Commission is mandated to protect children from unfair and deceptive marketing practices. The Commission's enforcement activities targeting advertising to children have typically focused on *how* products are advertised, rather than *whether* they are advertised. For example, the Commission has brought cases challenging nutritional claims for foods that are likely to be appealing to children. In one case, it challenged a television ad for the Klondike Lite Ice Cream Bar for saying that it was 93 percent fat free (Beales, 2004). The FTC alleged that the claim was false because the entire bar, including the chocolate coating, actually contained 14 percent fat and each bar actually contained 10 grams of fat per serving. They argued that the ad was misleading since a reasonable consumer – especially a child consumer – is not going to eat the bar without its chocolate coating.

The Federal Trade Commission has also been active in ensuring that children do not disclose private information unknowingly. In 1999, pursuant to the Children's Online Privacy Protection Act, the FTC issued its COPPA Rule governing the online collection of personal information from children under the age of 13. The Rule requires commercial web sites and online services to obtain verifiable parental consent before collecting personal information. For this reason, social networking sites such as Facebook do not allow children under 13 to register as users, though as danah boyd et al. (2011) point out, this is easily circumvented. Xanga, a social network site that was judged to "knowingly" collect information from children, was fined $1 million for violating COPPA (Jordan, 2008).

Federal Communications Commission

The Federal Communications Commission also has a role in regulating advertising to children over the broadcast and cable media. The Children's Television Act (CTA) of 1990 limits the amount of advertising during children's programming to 10½ minutes per hour on weekends and 12 minutes on weekdays (Children's Television Act, 1990). In addition, it requires commercial content to be separated from program content through what have come to be known as "bumpers" (in which there is a visual and/or auditory break), although the efficacy of these program separators is in dispute (An and Stern, 2011). The CTA also prohibits stations from including TV advertisements during the program or in spots adjacent to the beginning and end of the program in which the character appears (deemed "host selling").

Recently, the Federal Communications Commission has begun discussing the possibility of regulating embedded advertising in television programs, a practice often referred to as "product placement." Though this advertising strategy is banned in the UK, it is widespread in adult programming in the US (for example, judges during the television program *American Idol* are virtually always seen with Coca-Cola products). However, product placement is typically not used in children's programs due to concern that the shows would be fined for host selling. Cain (2011) argues that one solution to the dilemma is to add a new rating to the current content descriptors that air during programs, which currently include ratings like "S" for sexual content and "FV" for fantasy violence. This descriptor, IPP, would convey to audiences that the show contains "integrated paid promotions."

Industry self-regulation

Self-regulatory practices are common in an industry that is wary of government intervention. Signs of potential governmental regulatory activity often stir the industry to preemptive self-censorship, as has been the case with advertising hard liquor on commercial broadcast stations. If advertisers see new policymaking on the horizon, they will propose new self-regulatory measures. Some scholars call this dynamic "regulation by raised eyebrow" (Kunkel, 1988; Starr, 2004).

The Children's Advertising Review Unit (CARU) of the Council of Better Business Bureaus is the industry's self-monitoring group (Snyder, 2011). It seeks voluntary compliance from marketers by recommending a code of ethical practices to its members. In addition, CARU receives and acts upon complaints of deceptive or misleading advertising on a case-by-case basis. For example, in June 2011 CARU recommended that Reebok discontinue claims made in print advertising that suggested its Zigtech sneakers help children perform better in sports. Reebok responded by saying that it disagreed, but that the company supports "CARU's efforts to promote self regulation" (CARU News, 2011).

Steps toward self-regulation have also been made in food marketing. Alarmed by a sharp rise in childhood obesity, policymakers, the public and health professionals have challenged food industry marketing practices (Sharma et al., 2010). In response, the major food industry players promised to change, and, since 2006, have issued a series of highly publicized pledges through CARU including making significant shifts in what kinds of foods are promoted in children's television programming. At least two systematic content analyses have found that the landscape of food marketing has remained virtually unchanged, however, despite these pledges (Kunkel et al., 2009; Yale Rudd Center, 2011). Other countries, such as Thailand, have developed their own self-regulation initiatives (Thailand Children's Food and Beverage Initiative, 2008), though the impact of these initiatives has not been assessed.

Beyond policy

Advocacy groups, scholars and politicians have spent decades working to decrease children's exposure to advertising, especially for harmful products. As advertising is the main funding source of children's media, it is unlikely to go away anytime soon. Thus, alternative approaches to protecting children from the detrimental effects of advertising may be warranted.

Media literacy

Some have suggested that educating children about advertising's persuasive intent may decrease its deleterious effects (Hobbs, 2011). This argument is manifested in the field of media literacy, defined as "the ability to understand how mass media work, how they produce meanings, how they are organized and how one uses them wisely" (Abdullah, 2000, p. 1). Media literacy can teach youth how to identify advertisers' specific techniques (e.g., appeals to fun) as well as how to identify the target audience of an advertisement (Hobbs, 2011). Hobbs (2011) found that media literacy education significantly impacted adolescents' ability to analyze an advertisement, and An and Stern (2011) concluded that media literacy education was effective in increasing school-aged children's ability to recognize an advergame on the internet as having commercial purposes.

Despite the potential of media literacy to effectively inoculate children, a number of studies suggest that the ability to recognize and understand the persuasive nature of advertisements does not, in and of itself, decrease their effects on children. Livingstone and Helsper (2006) conducted a meta-analysis of studies researching the impact of food and beverage advertisements on children and similarly concluded that older children were often more affected than younger children by the advertisements despite being able to identify them and understand their purpose.

An alternative strategy in media literacy efforts may be to target parents. Horgan (2011) argues that families have unique values, interests and needs and that parents can convey their belief systems through media, including mediated advertisements, in ways that are consistent with the family's priorities. Beyond acting as role models, parents can encourage media education in everyday settings if given the proper knowledge base, motivations and skill set to do so (Horgan, 2011). An interesting example of this has been the EU Project klicksafe.de, which aims to improve safety on the internet by "strengthening media competence." Televised PSAs, such as "Where's Klaus" (http://www.youtube.com/watch?v=RHgXOCDVWOw), encourage parents to become more involved with their children's media use.

Media literacy – whether conveyed by parents or schools – can be an appealing alternative or complement to media policy. It does not offend the free speech sensibilities that many cultures highly value, and it does not hold media makers strictly accountable for the effects of media content on children. At the same time, it is seen as an opportunity to develop critical thinking skills in young people, and empower not only the young audiences but also the teachers and parents who are concerned about their well-being.

Funding for commercial-free programming and PSAs

Establishing alternatives to advertising as a main funding source for children's media can be another avenue by which to address the over-commercialization of childhood. Producers in Canada and France, for example, earn "points" by hiring their own citizens to fill positions related to children's television programming – from actresses and animators to storyboard creators and directors (Cahn et al., 2008). Points that producers gain translate into subsidies from the federal government thereby helping to fund production costs for children's television programming.

Levi (2010) describes another potentially viable answer to the issues of funding children's television in the US. She argues for a "pay or play" alternative to the educational programming requirements of the CTA, which would allow broadcast stations to pay a fee to fund children's educational programming on the Public Broadcasting Service (PBS) in lieu of airing the required "core" programming. Such a model could encourage the production of quality, commercial-free children's educational programming.

Leveraging advertising for good

The same elements that make an ad campaign successful with children can be leveraged to increase attitudes, beliefs and behaviors that improve children's health and well-being. In France, researchers tested a framework for pro-nutrition PSAs aimed at children (Hota et al., 2010). Specifically, they were able to increase the "child-relevance" of a campaign by using popular elements from commercial children's food advertising – bright colors, an appealing child protagonist, and engaging animation and music. Such techniques resulted in higher personal relevance of the advertising message for the child, which, in turn, led to more careful processing of the nutritional message and greater consistency between nutritional attitudes and behaviors. Similarly, Linebarger and Piotrowski (2008) found that children as young as preschool were able to retain pro-health messages in public service announcements, particularly when the themes were reinforced through repetition and paired with programs that featured the same themes as the PSAs.

Conclusion

Advertising remains the main funding source of children's media. Concerns over children's exposure to advertisements for potentially harmful products and the belief that young children are unable to understand advertising's persuasive intent have led advocates and researchers to call for industry restraint and government. Also, activists and scholars have encouraged the development of alternative funding sources for children's media. As government intervention varies by country and industry, media literacy education for children and parents and investment in well-executed PSAs may be viable options for those concerned with advertising's effect on children to consider.

SEE ALSO in this volume chapter by Buckingham, chapter by Chan, and chapter by Bond, Richards, and Calvert.

References

Abdullah, M. H. (2000). Media literacy. *ERIC Digest D152* (rep. no. EDO-CS-00-03; ERIC Document Reproduction Service No. 442 147).

American Academy of Pediatrics. (2006). Children, adolescents, and advertising. *Pediatrics*, *118*(6), 2563–69.

An, S. and Stern, S. (2011). Mitigating the effects of advergames on children. *Journal of Advertising*, *40*(1), 43–56.

Beales, J. H. (2004). Advertising to Kids and the FTC: A regulatory retrospective that advises the present. Remarks before the George Mason Law Review 2004 Symposium on Antitrust and Consumer Protection, Competition, Advertising, and Health Claims: Legal and Practical Limits on Advertising Regulation. Accessed 12/3/2011 via http://www.ftc.gov/speeches/beales/040802adstokids.pdf

Biener, L. and Siegel, M. (2000). Tobacco marketing and adolescent smoking: more support for a causal inference. *American Journal of Public Health*, *90*(3), 407–11.

boyd, d., Hargittai, E., Schultz, J. and Palfrey, J. (2011). Why parents help their children lie to Facebook about age: Unintended consequences of the Children's Online Privacy Protection Act. *First Monday*, *16*(11). Retrieved from http://www.uic.edu/htbin/cgiwrap/bin/ojs/index.php/fm/article/view/3850/3075

Buckingham, D. (2009). Beyond the competent consumer: The role of media literacy in the making of regulatory policy on children and food advertising in the UK. *International Journal of Cultural Policy*, *15*(2), 217.

Cahn, A., Kalgian, T. and Lyon, C. (2008). Business models for children's media. In S. L. Calvert, and B. J. Wilson (Eds), *The handbook of children, media, and development* (1st ed.). Oxford, U.K.: Blackwell, pp. 27–48.

Cain, R. M. (2011). Embedded advertising on television: Disclosure, deception, and free speech rights. *Journal of Public Policy and Marketing*, *2*(226), 238.

Caraher, M., Landon, J. and Dalmeny, K. (2006). Television advertising and children: Lessons from policy development. *Public Health Nutrition*, *9*(5), 596.

CARU News (June 7, 2011). CARU recommends Reebok discontinue certain claims for Zigtech sneakers; company agrees to do so. Retrieved from http://www.caru.org/news/DocView.aspx?DocumentID=8637

Children's Television Act (1990). Pub. L. *No. 101–437, 104 Stat. 996* (codified at 47 U.S.C. 303a-303b (2006)).

Common Sense Media (2009). Study reveals one in six ads during football broadcasts inappropriate for kids. Retrieved 1/5/2012 from http://www.commonsensemedia.org/about-us/news/press-releases/common-sense-media-report-reveals-one-six-ads-during-football-broadcast

Dhar, T. and Baylis, K. (2011). Fast food consumption and the ban on advertising targeting children: The Quebec experience. *Journal of Marketing Research*, *48*(5) (October), 799–813.

Delgado, R. and Foschia, P. (2003). Advertising to children in Brazil. *Advertising and Marketing to Children*, April–June, 1–4.

Gentry, E., Poirier, K., Wilkinson, T., Nhean, S., Nyborn, J. and Siegel, M. (2011). Alcohol advertising at Boston subway stations: An assessment of exposure by race and socioeconomic status. *American Journal of Public Health*, *101*(10), 1936–41.

Graff, S. K. (2008). First Amendment implications of restricting food and beverage marketing in schools. *The Annals of the American Academy of Political and Social Science*, *615*, 158–76.

Harrison, K. and Marske, A. L. (2005). Nutritional content of foods advertised during the television programs children watch most. *American Journal of Public Health*, *95*(9), 1958.

Hastings, G., Stead, M., McDermott, L., Forsyth, A., MacKintosh, A. M., Rayner, M. and Angus, K. (2003). *Review of research on the effects of food promotion to children*. Glasgow: University of Strathclyde.

Henry, H. K. M. and Borzekowski, D. (2011). The nag factor. *Journal of Children and Media*, *5*(3), 298–317.

Hobbs, R. (2011). The state of media literacy: A response to Potter. *Journal of Broadcasting and Electronic Media*, *55* (3), 419–30.

Horgan, M. J. (2011). Parents and other adults: Models and monitors of healthy media habits. In D. Singer and J. Singer (Eds), *Handbook of children and the media*. Thousand Oaks, California: Sage, pp. 661–80.

Hota, M., Chumpitaz Caceres, R. and Cousin, A. (2010). Can public-service advertising change children's nutrition habits? *Journal of Advertising Research*, *50*(4), 460–77.

Institute of Medicine (2006). Food Marketing and the Diet of Children and Youth. Washington DC: National Academies Press.

Jordan, A. (2008). Children's media policy. *The Future of Children*, *18*(1), 235–53.

Kline, S. (1993). *Out of the garden: Toys, TV, and children's culture in the age of Marketing*. London: Verso.

Kunkel, D. (1988). From a raised eyebrow to a turned back: The FCC and children's product-related programming. *Journal of Communication*, *38*(4), 90–108.

Kunkel, D. and Castonguay, J. (2011). Children and advertising: Content, comprehension, and consequences. In D. Singer and J. Singer (Eds), *Handbook of children and the media* (Second ed.). Thousand Oaks, CA: Sage Publications, pp. 36–37.

Kunkel, D., McKinley, C. and Wright, P. (2009). *The impact of industry self-regulation on the nutritional quality of foods advertised on television to children*. A report commissioned by Children Now.

Laughlin, A. (2010, March 16). Tighter rules coming for violent game ads. *Digital Spy*. Retrieved 11/14/2011 from http://www.digitalspy.com/media/news/a208958/tighter-rules-coming-for-violent-game-ads.html

Levi, L. (2010). A "pay or play" experiment to improve children's educational television. *Federal Communications Law Journal*, *62*(2), 1.

Linebarger, D. and Taylor Piotrowski, J. (2008). Evaluating the educational potential of health PSAs with preschoolers. *Health Communication*, *23*(6), 516–25.

Linn, S. and Novosat, C. L. (2008). Calories for sale: Food marketing to children in the twenty-first century. *The Annals of the American Academy of Political and Social Science*, *615*(1), 133.

Livingstone, S. and Helsper, E. J. (2006). Does advertising literacy mediate the effects of advertising on children? A critical examination of two linked research literatures in relation to obesity and food choice. *Journal of Communication*, *56*(3), 560–84.

Mosher, James F. (2012). Joe Camel in a bottle: Diageo, the Smirnoff brand, and the transformation of the youth alcohol market. *American Journal of Public Health*, *102*(1), 56–63.

Quebec Consumer Protection Act (1980). Retrieved 1/3/1980 from http://www2.publicationsduquebec.gouv.qc.ca/dynamicSearch/telecharge.php?type=2&file=/P_40_1/P40_1_A.html

Rozendaal, E., Buijzen, M. and Valkenberg, P. M. (2009). Do children's cognitive advertising defenses reduce their desire for advertised products? *Communications*, *34*(3), 287.

Shah, A. (2010). Children as consumers. *Global Issues*. Retrieved 11/15/2011 from http://www.globalissues.org/article/237/children-as-consumers

Schor, J. (2004). *Born to buy: The commercialized child and the new consumer culture* (1st ed.). New York: Scribner.

Sharma, L. L., Teret, S. P. and Brownell, K. D. (2010). The food industry and self-regulation: standards to promote success and to avoid public health failures. *American Journal of Public Health*, *100*(2), 240–46.

Snyder, W. (2011). Making the case for enhanced advertising ethics: How a new way of thinking about advertising ethnics may build consumer trust. *Journal of Advertising Research*, *51*(3), 477–83.

Starr, P. (2004). *The creation of media: Political origins of modern communications*. New York: Basic Books.

Thailand Children's Food and Beverage Initiative (2008). Retrieved from https://www.ifballiance.org/sites/default/files/Thai%20Pledge%20Fact%20sheet%20Eng%2021-05-08.pdf

Wolberg, D. (2010). Advertising and marketing to children in Israel. *Young Consumers, 11*(1), 90–92.

World Health Organization (2003). Framework Convention on Tobacco Control. May 21.

Yale Rudd Center for Food Policy & Obesity (2011). *Evaluating sugary drink nutrition and marketing to youth.* Retrieved from http://www.yaleruddcenter.org/resources/upload/docs/what/policy/SSBtaxes/SSBStudies_Marketing_to_Youth.pdf

48

INTERNET POLICIES

Online child protection and empowerment in a global context

Brian O'Neill

Introduction

Children's use of the internet has in the first decade of the twenty-first century become a matter of major policy concern. With increasing numbers of young people going online at ever-younger ages and through diverse platforms, governments, NGOs and industry stakeholders have demonstrably increased the attention given to matters of safety and child protection online whilst grappling with rapidly changing trends and technological developments. Policy in this area is most often framed in terms of the need to balance the hugely important opportunities the internet offers children whilst recognising that as minors they require protection. In addition, internet policy for children cannot be separated from international debates on the regulation of the internet, internet freedom and growing trends towards censorship and control of information.

This chapter briefly reviews the principal contours of internet policy for children, charting the growing international consensus on the need to balance digital opportunities for young people with the attendant risks they inevitably encounter. Internet use here refers to all online activities undertaken by children and all the connected devices employed for going online.

Early approaches to online child protection

In what may be called the first phase of internet policy and regulation during the decade of the 1990s, the principal trend pursued was in fact that the internet should not be regulated at all and that, as a nascent medium, technological innovation would be best served by as little interference as possible. In contrast to a medium such as television where its impact on children was always a matter of public concern (Gunter and McAleer, 1997), the main policy priority in the early years of the internet was to promote greater access, harnessing educational opportunities and competitive economic advantage. However, as Lawrence Lessig notes, it did not take long for policymakers to become concerned about the rapid proliferation of pornography and other kinds of unsuitable content universally regarded as harmful for children (Lessig, 2006).

Efforts to introduce internet-specific legislation included the ill-fated Communications Decency Act of 1996 (CDA) in the United States, intended to restrict access by minors to online pornography or other explicit content and to regulate indecency and obscenity on the internet according to 'community standards'. As initially passed by the US Congress in 1996, the CDA imposed criminal sanctions on anyone who:

> knowingly (A) uses an interactive computer service to send to a specific person or persons under 18 years of age, or (B) uses any interactive computer service to display in a manner available to a person under 18 years of age, any comment, request, suggestion, proposal, image, or other communication that, in context, depicts or describes, in terms patently offensive as measured by contemporary community standards, sexual or excretory activities or organs.
>
> *(Telecommunications Act of 1996, Pub. L. No. 104–104, tit. 5, 110 Stat. 56, 133–43, Sec. 502)*

Subsequently, its provisions against indecency were successfully challenged in the US Supreme Court (Reno v. ACLU), and an amended CDA without indecency provisions passed into US law. A further effort to restrict access by minors to pornography or any material that might be harmful to them was proposed in 1998 with the Child Online Protection Act (COPA) though it also was the subject of an injunction and never took effect. The final and ultimately successful measure, the Children's Internet Protection Act (CIPA), was signed into law in 2000 and required US schools and libraries as a condition of federal funding to use internet filters to restrict access by children to harmful online content.

A somewhat different approach emerged in Europe. The *Green Paper On The Protection Of Minors And Human Dignity In Audio-visual And Information Services* (European Commission, 1996a), for instance, was an early attempt to address child protection in the context of a converged media environment. At the same time, the communication on illegal and harmful content on the internet (European Commission, 1996b) laid the ground for a multi-stakeholder approach in tackling the problem of how to regulate content, observing that without effective controls, trust and confidence in the new communications environment would be damaged, constraining the potential benefits of the information society. The introduction of a multiannual Safer Internet Action Plan (European Commission, 1999, 2004) provided a further platform for the development of child protection policies, preferring where possible collaborative arrangements between stakeholders rather than direct legislative intervention. Accordingly, in parallel with the rapid expansion of the internet in the years following 2000, an ambitious series of measures to protect minors evolved through industry self- and co-regulation, filtering and content classification, networks of hotlines and helplines, as well as awareness-raising strategies and education about internet safety. Thus, it was recognised that there was no single solution to the challenges raised by mass use of the internet as well as the fact that, more and more, children and their families would be required to assume greater levels of responsibility for their own safety.

An emerging consensus on matters that affect children may be observed in the first 15 years or so of internet policy and regulation. There is, for instance, a common identification by governments and regulators around the world that children require protection from content that may be harmful to their development and this is the area that has attracted the most attention. In addition, online communication and participation in services originally designed for adults are also agreed to be risky. Similarly, children's own actions where young people themselves may be perpetrators of harmful behaviour are another area of risk. In response, a variety of strategies has emerged to regulate content and behaviour, whilst recognising that multiple actors share the responsibility for providing appropriate protective measures.

Regulating content

Protecting children from unsuitable content that may be harmful for their development is a cornerstone of internet policy for children. Determining which content is unsuitable for children and for which age groups, however, is contested. Illegal content, such as extreme xenophobic material and child sexual abuse imagery, falls into the category of illegal content in almost all jurisdictions. In such instances, what is deemed illegal in the offline world is illegal in the online world also and the only issue is one of ensuring effective compliance and the operation of applicable laws. For other content that may be deemed potentially harmful, but not illegal, provisions for protection vary considerably. Such content risks may include violent or gory online content as well in video games, 'adult' and other pornographic content, racist content or forms of hate speech, and forms of commercial content that may target children in ways for which they are not prepared (Livingstone and Haddon, 2009).

Regulation of content features prominently in the national audio-visual policy schemes of most countries and to some extent in online policy frameworks (OECD, 2011). A general ban on illegal content, offline and online, for instance, is provided for on a near-universal basis. In the United States and Canada, there is a tendency not to have internet-specific legislation governing content while others including Japan, Turkey and Korea have passed dedicated laws governing online content. Between these extremes, most European countries, and Australia and New Zealand, rely to a large extent on the application of existing laws augmented by 'soft' legislation in the form of self- and co-regulatory schemes to enforce age restrictions on content.

Content regulation regimes typically rely on forms of international cooperation between law enforcement, industry and other public–private partnerships in monitoring and suppressing, where applicable, illegal and criminal online content. Mandatory filtering at a national level is applied in only a limited number of countries (Turkey, and proposed in Australia). More frequently, it is applied on a voluntary basis, for instance, as recommended for countries within the European Union under the 2011 Directive on combating the sexual exploitation of children and child pornography (European Union, 2011). Filtering at the level of the internet service provider for content that is not illegal but is recognised as unsuitable for children is always voluntary, even in a country such as Turkey where overall strict censorship applies (OSCE, 2010).

Labelling and classification

An area of specific policy attention since the late 1990s has been the attempt to develop appropriate classification schemes for labelling online content in a way that will better enable parents to make judgements on the suitability of content and to make filtering systems more effective. In the European Union, developing effective and transparent labelling systems has been a feature of safer internet policy since the development of the first Safer Internet Action Plan. Concerns about the effects of violent video game content led to the first voluntary rating system for console games developed by the UK-based Entertainment Leisure Software Publishers Association (ELSPA) in 1994. However with the proliferation of nationally-based classification systems and consequent consumer confusion, the so-called Pan European Game Information system (PEGI) was introduced in 2003. The development of PEGI marks a shift from a legislatively-based classification system based on age-ratings, familiar to the traditional media environment, to one based on labelling, content descriptions and indications of age appropriateness (McLaughlin, 2007). The system is a voluntary one operated by manufacturers and game developers and includes age rating symbols (3+, 7+, 12+, 16+ and 18+) and content descriptors (bad language, discrimination, drugs, fear, gambling, sex and violence). Often seen as a success story for the approach of co-regulation, it has been adopted by most countries in Europe, with strong support from the European

Commission, and reinforces the legislative basis of games classification in countries such as Ireland and the UK.

Less successful have been attempts to extend content classification and labelling systems to the online sphere. PEGI Online, an addition to the PEGI system, was designed specifically for online gaming content using a similar labelling system and supported by an industry code of practice. The system has limited participation however. Other efforts to promote ratings systems for online content have included the Internet Content Rating Association (ICRA), the internationally structured self-regulation initiative (Machill et al., 2002). This content description system was intended to allow web developers to self-label content using categories such as:

- The presence or absence of nudity
- The presence or absence of sexual content
- The depiction of violence
- The language used
- The presence or absence of user-generated content and whether this is moderated
- The depiction of other potentially harmful content such as gambling, drugs and alcohol.

This descriptive classification scheme is operated by the self-completion of a questionnaire (the ICRA Questionnaire) and is intended for use with filtering systems to facilitate and support parental guidance in relation to young people's access to online content. First established in 1994, the system has gained limited industry support and as of 2010 has been absorbed within the Family Online Safety Institute (FOSI) organisation.

Contact risks

Contact risks in which children may be harmed by coming into contact with others via the internet is another area with which internet policy has been particularly concerned. In the main, the contact risks addressed by policymakers have been those in which children have been participants in adult-initiated activity, as an extension of those risks to children from exposure to content that is not age appropriate. 'Stranger-danger' and the risk of abuse of children by adults they may encounter online, while extremely rare, have created significant public anxiety and have subsequently featured in policy debates concerning the protection of children online. Legislative responses have focused on the most extreme forms of risk such as grooming and child sexual abuse facilitated via internet communication. In many countries, new legislative provisions outlawing cybergrooming as a new type of criminal offence have been developed (OECD, 2011, p. 33). The risks of mobile internet use and social networking have also received attention in developing countries where computer and broadband internet use is low but access to mobile phones is high (Beger et al., 2011).

Another dimension of contact risk that has received less attention is that of children's exposure to commercial communication (DCFS/DCMS, 2009). Where in traditional media, restrictions on advertising to children are well established, this is an aspect of the online world that is much less developed. Online gambling, however, in most countries cannot be offered to children. More generally, commercial communication is the subject of self-regulation and only in the Scandinavian countries is advertising to children banned.

Children as actors and perpetrators

The internet is also an interactive environment, especially so for children who are often enthusiastic participants in social media platforms, and the originators of content across the myriad of web 2.0 services available to them. As such, internet policy has had to address questions of conduct initiated by children themselves where youth behaviour has led to new areas of risk and potential harm. Cyber harassment and cyberbullying, arising, more often than not, out of contact between peers, has attracted substantial attention as a persistent and at times intractable aspect of young people's online behaviour (Erdur–Baker, 2010). Cyberbullying – where it does not fall into the category of criminal harassment to which existing laws apply – is primarily addressed through awareness-raising strategies, focusing in particular on the offending and hurtful behaviour of perpetrators, coping strategies for victims and educational policies for target populations (Hinduja and Patchin, 2009; Shariff and Churchill, 2010). Relatedly, the phenomenon of 'sexting' or sending/receiving sexual messages via electronic communication, whether wanted or unwanted, is another area of contact risk that has received research and policy attention (Lenhart, 2009; Ringrose et al., 2012). It has received a more varied response, ranging from criminal prosecutions based on laws pertaining to possession of child pornography (Sacco, 2010) to a policy of 'turning a blind eye' to risky youthful practices.

Potentially harmful user-generated content is a relatively new area of risk where children and young people access or even originate content that includes racist or hate speech, drug-taking and the promotion of anorexia/bulimia, or talk about ways to commit suicide. While such content is subject to the terms of use adopted by the service providers concerned, calls for greater vigilance by hosting companies alongside increasing pressures towards content censorship are evident (Deibert, 2008).

Of course, the one area in which youth conduct has been the subject of most sustained policy action has been in relation to copyright infringement and illegal downloading of copyright content. US Federal Law in the form of the Digital Millennium Copyright Act (1998) exempts internet intermediaries from liability for content carried on their networks. However, increasing pressure from the music industry to tackle apparently widespread copyright infringement through peer-to-peer file sharing has focused efforts on requiring internet service providers (ISPs) to block access to sites facilitating illegal downloading and to cut off access to offending downloaders. This has been fiercely resisted by civil liberties groups opposed to any form of intermediary blocking and efforts to implement the so-called graduated response or 'three strikes policy' in different national jurisdictions, such as France and the United Kingdom, continue to be deeply contested (Ryan, 2010).

Alternative regulatory policy approaches

Legislation-based policy approaches to child protection online provide just one dimension of what is recognised as a complex set of public policy challenges. As such, a host of alternative regulatory instruments and strategies has been developed to address concerns for children's safety (Lievens, 2010). Given the open and dynamic nature of the internet, and the wide cultural variation in moral standards relating to children's exposure to online content, much policy emphasis has been placed on the importance of parents deciding what is best for their children. An early initiative in this regard was the promotion of technical solutions or software-based parental controls to restrict children's web surfing. Despite concerns over their effectiveness as well as their suitability for older children and teenagers, parental controls have been a core feature of internet policy in many countries since the late 1990s and continue to be recommended as an important ingredient in the overall mix of digital safety (Deloitte and European Commission, 2008; Thierer, 2009).

Industry supported self-regulatory agreements have undoubtedly been amongst the most important non-legislative initiatives designed to promote safer internet practice. In the European context, safer use of mobile communications as well as safer social networking have been the two key sectors in which industry providers have, with Commission support, developed a code of practice regarding child safety (European Commission, 2009; GSMA, 2007). Deemed to be the best equipped to respond to rapid changes in technology and the marketplace, industry operators outline their public commitments towards implementation of the agreed code or set of principles, which is then independently evaluated (see Donoso, 2011). Self-regulation, for long a foundation of new media policy, is however coming under increasing scrutiny due to perceived shortcomings in meeting public interest needs as well as difficulties associated with monitoring effectiveness and implementation (Bonnici and De Vey Mestdagh, 2005; Phillips, 2011).

Of most significance in the non-regulatory approach to internet safety has been the emphasis on awareness-raising and education. The education of young internet users is recognised as essential to empowering users and encouraging safer, more responsible online behaviour. Awareness-raising campaigns, with both public and private sector input, have been widely used to draw attention to issues of security and safety, while promoting specific safety messages regarding online use. Educational reinforcement in partnership with national education systems is seen as vital to improving levels of digital literacy and encouraging self-governing behaviour on the part of children and young people (Eurydice, 2009; Safer Internet Programme, 2009). Concepts such as digital citizenship are intended to reflect the importance of the rights and responsibilities of children as social actors in the online world (Mossberger et al., 2008; Passey, 2011) as well as recognising that the best form of protection for young people is self-empowerment (O'Neill and Hagen, 2009).

Conclusion

Despite the evident importance now attached to the agenda of digital safety, and the strong consensus among international agencies both in combating abuses and in promoting online safety (ITU, 2009; UNICEF, 2011), unevenness remains a characteristic of the internet policy landscape with substantial differences at a geo-political level between proponents of an open internet, free of restrictions, whether for neo-liberal economic reasons or based on libertarian principles of free expression, and a more regulated and, in some cases, overtly controlled network. This occurs at a time of rapid internet expansion across the globe and the demonstrable proliferation of new, more accessible means of going online. Children's interests are often located somewhere in the middle of such developments, both as the early adopters and digital explorers of new technologies, and also as the subjects of intense debate on the need for protection, or even as justification for extreme forms of restriction. It is all the more important from a policy perspective, therefore, that children's welfare in the online world be incorporated as part of a wider policy in a converged media environment. This implies that promoting equality of access and participation duly takes into account appropriate levels of protection afforded to all citizens, as well as those representing the best interests of the child, and that standards applying in the media environment as a whole are the outcome of a critical and reflective debate on the values of a responsible and ethical (digital) citizenship.

References

Beger, G., Hoveyda, P. K. and Sinha, A. (2011). From "What's your ASLR?" to "Do you wanna go private?" New York: UNICEF.

Bonnici, J. P. M. and De Vey Mestdagh, C. N. J. (2005). Right vision, wrong expectations: The European Union and self-regulation of harmful internet content. *Information & Communications Technology Law*, 14(2), 133–49.

DCFS/DCMS (2009). *The Impact of the Commercial World on Children's Wellbeing Report of an Independent Assessment*. London: DCFS/DCMS.

Deibert, R. (2008). *Access denied: the practice and policy of global Internet filtering*. Cambridge, MA: MIT.

Deloitte and European Commission (2008). Safer internet: Protecting our children on the net using content filtering and parental control techniques. Luxembourg: European Commission Safer Internet Programme.

Donoso, V. (2011). Assessment of the implementation of the safer social networking principles for the EU on 14 websites: Summary report. Luxembourg: European Commission, Safer Internet Programme.

Erdur-Baker, Ö. (2010). Cyberbullying and its correlation to traditional bullying, gender and frequent and risky usage of internet-mediated communication tools. *New Media & Society*, *12*(1), 109–25.

European Commission (1996a). Green paper on the protection of minors and human dignity in audiovisual and information services. Brussels: European Commission.

——(1996b). Illegal and harmful content on the internet COM(96)487. Brussels-Luxembourg: European Commission.

——(1999). A multiannual community action plan on promoting safer use of the internet by combatting illegal and harmful content on global networks. 4-year work programme 1999–2002. Luxembourg: European Commission Safer Internet Programme.

——(2004). Safer internet action plan. Update of the work programme 2003–4 for the year 2004. Luxembourg: European Commission Safer Internet Programme.

——(2009). Safer social networking principles for the EU. Luxembourg: European Commission Safer Internet Programme.

European Union (2011). Directive 2011/92/EU of the European Parliament and of the Council of 13 December 2011 on combating the sexual abuse and sexual exploitation of children and child pornography, and replacing Council Framework Decision 2004/68/JHA. Retrieved from http://eur-lex.europa.eu/LexUriServ/LexUriServ.do?uri=OJ:L:2012:026:0001:0021:EN:PDF

Eurydice (2009). Education on online safety in schools in Europe. Brussels: Education, Audiovisual and Culture Executive Agency.

GSMA (2007). European framework for safer mobile use by younger teenagers and children. Brussels: GSMA Europe.

Gunter, B. and McAleer, J. (1997). *Children and television, 2nd Edition*. London: Routledge.

Hinduja, S. and Patchin, J. W. (2009). *Bullying beyond the schoolyard: preventing and responding to cyberbullying*. London: Corwin.

ITU (2009). Child online protection. Geneva: International Telecommunication Union.

Lenhart, A. (2009). Teens and sexting: How and why minor teens are sending sexually suggestive nude or nearly nude images via text messaging. Washington, D.C.: Pew Internet & American Life Project.

Lessig, L. (2006). *Code: version 2.0* (2nd ed.). New York: Basic Books.

Lievens, E. (2010). *Protecting children in the digital era: the use of alternative regulatory instruments*. Leiden: Martinus Nijhoff.

Livingstone, S. and Haddon, L. (Eds) (2009). *Kids online: Opportunities and risks for children*. Bristol: Policy Press.

Machill, M., Hart, T. and Kaltenhuser, B. (2002). Structural development of Internet self-regulation: Case study of the Internet Content Rating Association (ICRA). [DOI: 10.1108/14636690210453217]. *Info*, *4*(5), 39–55.

McLaughlin, S. (2007). Violent video games – Can self regulation work? *Communications Law: Journal of Computer Media and Telecommunications Law*, *12*(5), 157–67.

Mossberger, K., Tolbert, C. J. and McNeal, R. S. (2008). *Digital citizenship: the internet, society, and participation*. Boston, MA: MIT Press.

O'Neill, B. and Hagen, I. (2009). Media literacy. In Sonia Livingstone and L. Haddon (Eds), *Kids online: Opportunities and risks for children*. Bristol: Policy Press, pp. 229–39.

OECD (2011). *The protection of children online. Risks faced by children online and policies to protect them*. Paris: OECD Working Party on Information Security and Privacy.

OSCE (2010). Report of the OSCE representative on freedom of the media on Turkey and internet censorship. Vienna: Organization for Security and Co-operation in Europe.

Passey, D. (2011). Internet Safety in the Context of Developing: Aspects of Young People's Digital Citizenship. Lancaster: National Education Network Safeguarding Group.

Phillips, L. (2011, 16 March). EU to force social network sites to enhance privacy. *The Guardian*. Retrieved from http://www.guardian.co.uk/media/2011/mar/16/eu-social-network-sites-privacy

Ringrose, J., Gill, R., Livingstone, S. and Harvey, L. (2012). A qualitative study of children, young people and 'sexting'. London: NSPCC.

Ryan, J. (2010). Internet access controls: Three strikes 'graduated response' initiatives. Dublin: Institute of International and European Affairs.

Sacco, D. T. (2010). Sexting: Youth practices and legal implications. Boston, MA: Berkman Center for Internet and Society.

Safer Internet Programme (2009). *Awareness report on the status of online safety education in schools across Europe*. Luxembourg: European Commision, SIP.

Shariff, S. and Churchill, A. H. (2010). *Truths and myths of cyber-bullying: international perspectives on stakeholder responsibility and children's safety*. New York: Peter Lang.

Thierer, A. (2009). *Parental controls & online child protection: A survey of tools and methods*. Washington, DC: The Progress & Freedom Foundation.

UNICEF (2011). Child safety online – Global challenges and strategies. Florence: UNICEF Innocenti Research Centre.

49

LEARNING FROM EDUCATIONAL TELEVISION

Shalom M. Fisch

Research in numerous countries has shown that children spend tremendous amounts of time using media – often more than in any activity other than sleeping (e.g., Groebel, 1999). Despite the rapidly growing reach of interactive media, survey data from the United States indicate that children continue to use television far more than any other medium (Rideout et al., 2010). From the standpoint of harmful effects of media, such as televised violence, these statistics may appear daunting. However, for educational television, they represent a vast opportunity. Just as violent media content can produce negative effects, educational media content can – and does – produce significant positive effects.

This chapter examines educational television as a tool for informal education (i.e., substantive educational content delivered primarily outside the classroom). It reviews key studies on the impact of such media, theoretical approaches to explain children's comprehension and learning, and the added benefits that can arise from combined use of multiple educational media platforms.

What do children learn from educational television?

Decades of research have demonstrated clearly that both preschool and school-age children learn from well-produced educational television series. A sizable research literature has documented effects on knowledge, skills, and attitudes in various academic subject areas, such as literacy, mathematics, science, social studies, and others (e.g., Fisch, 2004; Kirkorian and Anderson, 2011). Programs designed to contribute to children's socioemotional development also have been found to promote prosocial behavior among young viewers, but that research is beyond the scope of this chapter. (See Mares and Woodard, 2001.)

Perhaps the most prominent – and certainly the most extensively researched – example of an educationally effective television series is *Sesame Street*. The earliest indications of *Sesame Street*'s educative power emerged in a pair of experimental/control, pretest/posttest studies conducted by the Educational Testing Service (ETS) after its first two seasons of production (Ball and Bogatz, 1970; Bogatz and Ball, 1971). Each study found that, among 3- to 5-year-olds, heavier viewers of *Sesame Street* showed significantly greater pretest-posttest gains on an assortment of academic skills related to the alphabet, numbers, body parts, shapes, relational terms, and sorting and classification. The areas that showed the greatest effects were the ones that had been emphasized most in *Sesame Street* (e.g., letters). These effects held across age, sex, geographic location, socioeconomic status (SES) (with low–SES children showing greater gains than middle-SES children), native language (English or Spanish), and whether the children watched at home or in school.

These findings were challenged by critics of *Sesame Street*, most notably by Thomas Cook and his colleagues (1975). They argued that the effects observed in the ETS studies did not merely reflect the effect of watching *Sesame Street*; instead, these researchers felt that the effects reflected a combination of viewing and parents' involvement in the viewing experience. In fact, Cook's point was not without merit, as subsequent research has shown that young children's learning from television can be affected by parental coviewing and commentary (e.g., Reiser et al., 1984). Yet, parental involvement was not solely responsible for the ETS findings. Even when Cook et al. conducted a re-analysis of the ETS data, controlling for other potentially contributing factors such as mothers discussing *Sesame Street* with their child, the ETS effects were reduced but many remained statistically significant. Such effects could not simply be explained through parental involvement; *Sesame Street* itself made a significant contribution.

Sesame Street was found to hold long-term benefits for viewers as well. One component of the Bogatz and Ball (1971) study was a follow-up on a subset of the children who had participated in their earlier study. Teachers rated their students on several dimensions of school readiness (e.g., verbal readiness, quantitative readiness, attitude toward school, relationship with peers) without knowing their prior viewership of *Sesame Street*. Results indicated that those children who had been frequent *Sesame Street* viewers were rated as better prepared for school than their non- or low-viewing classmates.

More than 25 years later, the immediate and long-term effects of *Sesame Street* were confirmed by other data. A three-year longitudinal study of low-SES preschoolers found that after controlling statistically for background variables such as parents' level of education, native language, and preschool attendance, preschool viewing of educational programs – and *Sesame Street* in particular – predicted time spent in reading and educational activities, letter-word knowledge, math skills, vocabulary size, and school readiness on age-appropriate standardized achievement tests. Also, as in the earlier Bogatz and Ball (1971) study, teachers more often rated *Sesame Street* viewers as well-adjusted to school (Wright et al., 2001). A second study was a correlational analysis of data representing approximately 10,000 children from the U.S. Department of Education's National Household Education Survey. Although the data were correlational (and, thus, can suggest but not prove causality), results indicated that preschool *Sesame Street* viewers were more likely to be able to recognize letters of the alphabet and tell connected stories when pretending to read; these effects were strongest among children from low-income families, and held true even after the effects of other contributing factors (e.g., parental reading, preschool attendance, parental education) were removed statistically. In addition, first and second graders who had viewed *Sesame Street* as preschoolers were more likely to be reading storybooks on their own and less likely to require remedial reading instruction (Zill, 2001).

Finally, the longest-term impact of *Sesame Street* was found in a "recontact" study that examined high school students who either had or had not watched educational television as preschoolers; the bulk of this viewing had consisted of *Sesame Street*. Results showed that high school students who had watched more educational television – and *Sesame Street* in particular – as preschoolers had significantly higher grades in English, mathematics, and science. They also used books more often, showed higher academic self-esteem, and placed a higher value on academic performance. These differences held true even after the students' early language skills and family background variables were factored out (Anderson et al., 2001; Huston et al., 2001).

Because few (if any) educational series enjoy the 42-year longevity of *Sesame Street*, other series have not been researched as extensively or over as long a period of time. Nevertheless, numerous studies show that *Sesame Street* is not alone in helping children learn. Research on educational series for both preschool and school-age children has shown that educational television can enhance children's knowledge, skills, and attitudes in a wide variety of subject areas. These include the effects of U.S. series such as *Between the Lions* and *The Electric Company* on children's language and literacy skills; *Square One TV* and *Cyberchase* on children's use of mathematics and problem-solving; *3–2–1 Contact* and *Bill Nye the Science Guy* on the understanding of science and technology; children's news programs on knowledge of current events; and preschool series such as *Blue's Clues* and *Barney & Friends* on more general school readiness (see Fisch, 2004; Kirkorian and Anderson, 2011 for reviews of the literature). Together, this body of research stands as compelling evidence for television's power to educate.

Apart from the sizable literature on learning among preschool and school-age children – and spurred on by both the emergence of "baby videos" such as *Baby Einstein* and the American Academy of Pediatrics' (2001, 2011) calls to discourage any television viewing among children below the age of 2 years – an emerging body of research has begun to evaluate whether children under 2 can learn from television as well. Most experimental studies in this area have assessed learning through one of several methods: imitating behaviors shown on-screen, attempting to find a hidden object in a room after watching someone hide it on-screen, or learning words (spoken words or baby sign language) from a video. Together, these studies show that, not surprisingly, infants and toddlers learn more from live instruction than from a video screen (see Richert et al., 2011). However, some studies have found that young children can imitate simple behaviors or acquire some information from video, although they learn more from either live instruction or coviewing with a parent or other adult who provides live support for the video's lessons (e.g., Dayanim and Namy, 2011; Meltzoff, 1988; Vandewater, 2011). Richert et al. (2011) attribute the advantage of live instruction or coviewing to the idea that young children learn via social interaction and contingent feedback, both of which can be provided by a live partner, but are less likely when viewing a video alone.

How does learning compare across countries and cultures?

Consistent with the data discussed above, research conducted outside the United States has also shown evidence of the impact of educational television. Significant learning from educational television can be seen, for example, in the effects of *Al Manaahil* (Jordan, Morocco, and Tunisia) on children's literacy; *Owl TV* (UK) or *Australia Naturally* (Australia) on knowledge of science; or *Jeugdjournaal* (Netherlands) on knowledge of current events. Many other examples exist as well (see Fisch, 2004; Kirkorian and Anderson, 2011 for reviews of the literature).

The presence of such effects in a variety of countries raises the question of how children's learning from television compares across countries and cultures. A partial answer can be found in research on international co-productions of *Sesame Street*. Under the co-production model, a local production team in a given country collaborates with the staff of Sesame Workshop (producers of the U.S. *Sesame Street*) to craft an educational curriculum that responds to the needs of children in that country, and create a version of *Sesame Street* that is both true to the spirit of *Sesame Street* and culturally appropriate for local audiences. Although each production's curriculum may contain unique topics due to local needs (e.g., aesthetics in China, mutual respect and understanding in a joint Israeli–Palestinian co-production), they also typically share common areas, such as literacy and mathematics. Comparable effects in these areas have been found among viewers of *Sisimpur* in Bangladesh (Lee, 2007), *Susam Sokagi* in Turkey (Sahin, 1990), *Rua Sésamo* in Portugal (Brederode-Santos, 1993), and *Ulitsa Sezam* in Russia (Ulitsa

Sezam Department of Research and Content, 1998), among others. (See Cole et al., 2001 for a review of many of these studies.)

Still, although these studies examined learning in comparable subject areas, they do not provide a direct comparison of learning across countries because different televised segments were shown in each country. A more direct comparison was conducted in a multinational study of children's learning from *Panwapa*, a set of videos, online games, and hands-on activities (translated into several languages) that was designed to introduce 4- to 7-year-old children to aspects of global citizenship. Research assessed learning from *Panwapa* in China, Egypt, Mexico, and the U.S. Comparisons across countries revealed many striking similarities in what children learned from *Panwapa* – and in how they learned, as well. Similar types of comments and behavior were observed among children in different countries as they used *Panwapa* materials, and significant learning was found in all four countries. At the same time, however, culture and prior knowledge also played a role. Children often connected most immediately to material with which they felt a personal connection (e.g., reacting most to on-screen children and places that were familiar in some way). Conversely, learning effects were often stronger in areas in which children had less prior knowledge and, thus, more room to grow. For example, significant effects on understanding of economic disparity appeared in the U.S., perhaps because, on average, the United States has a higher economic standard of living. Yet, effects regarding knowledge about foreign languages were stronger in Egypt, Mexico, and China, perhaps because more of the U.S. children already used foreign languages with their families at home. Finally, because parents and teachers served as gatekeepers for children's experience with *Panwapa*, adult attitudes had the potential either to facilitate *Panwapa*'s effects (e.g., when adults shared the value *Panwapa* placed on diversity) or to mitigate them (e.g., in cultures where technology is not considered an age-appropriate educational tool for preschoolers, or when parental prejudice conflicted with *Panwapa*'s messages about diversity). Thus, it appears that the benefits of educational media can indeed reach across countries and cultures. However, to best understand learning from television, these effects must be considered within the context of all of the other influences present in a child's world (Fisch et al., 2010).

Theoretical approaches

In contrast to the extensive empirical research literature, there have been far fewer attempts to construct theoretical models of the cognitive processing responsible for such effects. Fisch's (2000, 2004) *capacity model* has its roots in information processing theory and cognitive psychology. From this perspective, television programs are seen as complex audiovisual stimuli that require viewers to integrate a range of visual and auditory information in real time as they watch. Educational television programs pose even greater processing demands, because these programs typically present narrative (i.e., story) content and educational content simultaneously, so the two must compete for the limited resources available in working memory. Thus, the model predicts that comprehension of educational content will be stronger, not only when the resource demands for processing the educational content are low, but when the resource demands for processing the narrative content are low as well.

In addition, the model argues that comprehension is affected by *distance*, the degree to which the educational content is tangential to the narrative (in which case the two compete for working memory resources) or integral to it (in which case the two complement each other, so competition is reduced). Thus, comprehension of educational content typically would be stronger when the educational content is integral to the narrative than when it is tangential to it.

Beyond comprehension, the capacity model has also been applied to help explain *transfer of learning* from educational television (i.e. applying concepts or skills learned from a television program to a new problem or situation). Outside the context of television, Bransford et al. (1999) have argued that successful transfer requires several key elements, including a rich understanding of the subject matter that has been presented, a representation of the knowledge that is abstracted beyond its original context, and a match between the representation of the knowledge and the new situation in which it might be applied. Yet, applying these principles to educational television would almost seem to produce a contradiction under the capacity model: According to the capacity model, one of the chief ways to enrich comprehension (as is required for transfer) is to maintain a small distance between narrative and educational content. However, content that is overly tied to a narrative context may not be represented abstractly enough to transfer to new problems in different contexts (e.g., Cognition and Technology Group at Vanderbilt, 1997).

A solution may lie in maintaining a small distance between narrative and educational content, but also presenting the same educational content several times in several different narrative contexts (a principle known as *varied practice* in the education literature; e.g., Gick and Holyoak, 1983). Consider, for example, an episode of *Sesame Street* in which several different segments present the letter *B* in the context of several different words, such as *ball*, *box*, and *boy*. Multiple treatments of the same underlying content can contribute toward a more abstract representation of the concepts involved, and also may encourage a sense of these concepts as applicable in a broader variety of situations, thus encouraging transfer (Fisch, 2004).

The above models shed light on immediate cognitive processing and subsequent educational outcomes. By themselves, however, they are not sufficient to explain longer-term effects, particularly if the eventual outcomes bear little resemblance to the educational content that was presented on television (as in, e.g., effects of preschool viewing of *Sesame Street* on high school performance). Huston et al.'s (2001) *early learning model* explains the long-term effects of educational media, and how such media might interact with all of the other influences in children's lives. Under this model, three facets of early development are proposed as pathways by which long-term effects can result: (a) learning pre-academic skills, particularly those related to language and literacy, (b) developing motivation and interest, and (c) acquiring behavioral patterns of attentiveness, concentration, non-aggressiveness, and absence of restlessness or distractibility. These factors contribute to early success in school, which then plays a significant role in determining children's long-term academic trajectories (e.g., placement in higher ability groups, more attention from teachers, greater motivation to do well). In addition, these early successes may also affect the types of activities in which children choose to engage; for example, good readers may choose to read more on their own. Each of these outcomes can then result in further success over time. In this way, the model posits a cascading effect in which early exposure to educational television leads to early academic success, which in turn contributes to a long-term trajectory of success.

Cross-platform learning

As the above research demonstrates, children learn from educational television (and new media). Today, however, it is increasingly common for projects to span more than one media platform; for example, an educational television series might be accompanied by a related Web site, hands-on outreach materials, or even a museum exhibit or live show. This raises questions as to how learning from combined use of multiple, related media platforms (i.e., cross-platform learning) compares to learning from a single medium.

Recent research, using the school-age mathematics series *Cyberchase*, found that combined use of the *Cyberchase* television series and online games produced more consistent improvement in children's mathematical problem-solving than use of either medium alone. Moreover, the study found that, compared to children who played online *Cyberchase* math games without watching the TV series, children who used multiple media also employed significantly more mathematically sophisticated strategies to play the online games. Thus, the data suggest that the added value of cross-platform learning stems from two factors: (1) Exposing children to similar educational content in multiple contexts not only reinforces learning, but also helps children recognize that the math content can be applied in a wide variety of situations; (2) Children who use multiple media can use transfer of learning to apply the content learned from one medium to help them *while they are in the process of learning from the other* (e.g., applying mathematical content learned from a television series to aid in playing an online mathematical game), resulting in richer, more sophisticated engagement with the latter medium. Indeed, it is quite possible that cross-platform learning may not only permit but facilitate transfer. For example, encountering *Cyberchase* characters in an online game might lead children to think of other times when they saw the same characters (e.g., on television), thus facilitating transfer of learning from one medium to another (Fisch et al., in press).

Conclusion

Despite critics who claim (often without evidence) that television destroys children's attention spans or turns them into "zombie viewers," research has shown that television is neither inherently good nor bad for children. Rather, the effects of a program depend upon numerous factors, not the least of which is its content. As the late researcher John Wright was fond of saying, "Marshall McLuhan appears to have been wrong. The *medium* is not the message. The *message* is the message!" (Anderson et al., 2001, p. 134).

Apart from its value in contributing to researchers' understanding of children's interaction with media, research on the impact of educational media holds practical implications as well. On one level, data on the impact of a particular media product are of great interest to its production team, to gauge the degree to which their efforts have been successful. At the same time, evidence of children's learning from educational media has also been critical for funding agencies interested in accountability and in the evolution of public policy regarding children's media.

Yet, perhaps the most important impact of such research lies in its ability to inform the creation of new programming. By identifying what "works" – approaches and production techniques that contribute to the effectiveness of existing programming – research can help producers incorporate the most effective techniques as they create new material. When used well, research enables material to be tailored directly to the needs, interests, and abilities of its target audience. In this way, research can help ensure that future educational series will be as appealing, age-appropriate, and educationally powerful as possible.

SEE ALSO in this volume chapter by Herr Stephenson and chapter by Peppler.

References

American Academy of Pediatrics (2001). Children, adolescents, and television. *Pediatrics, 107*(2), 423–26.
——(2011). Media use by children younger than 2 years. *Pediatrics, 128*(5), 1040–45.
Anderson, D. R., Huston, A. C., Schmitt, K. L., Linebarger, D. L. and Wright, J. C. (2001). Early childhood television viewing and adolescent behavior. *Monographs of the Society for Research in Child Development, 66*(1), 1–147.
Ball, S. and Bogatz, G. A. (1970). *The first year of Sesame Street: An evaluation.* Princeton, NJ: Educational Testing Service.
Bogatz, G. A. and Ball, S. (1971). *The second year of Sesame Street: A continuing evaluation.* Princeton, NJ: Educational Testing Service.

Bransford, J. D., Brown, A. L. and Cocking, R. R. (Eds) (1999). *How people learn: Brain, mind, experience, and school*. Washington, DC: National Academy Press.

Brederode-Santos, M. E. (1993). *Learning with television: The secret of Rua Sésamo*. [English translation of Portuguese, Brederode-Santos, M. E. (1991). *Com a Televiso o Segredo da Rua Sésamo*. Lison: TV Guia Editora.] Unpublished research report.

Cognition and Technology Group at Vanderbilt (1997). *The Jasper Project: Lessons in curriculum, instruction, assessment, and professional development*. Mahwah, NJ: Lawrence Erlbaum.

Cole, C. F., Richman, B. A. and McCann Brown, S. K. (2001). The world of *Sesame Street* research. In S. M. Fisch. and R. T. Truglio (Eds), *"G" is for "growing": Thirty years of research on children and Sesame Street*. Mahwah, NJ: Lawrence Erlbaum, pp. 147–79.

Cook, T. D., Appleton, H., Conner, R. F., Shaffer, A., Tamkin, G. and Weber, S. (1975). *Sesame Street revisited*. New York: Russell Sage Foundation.

Dayanim, S. and Namy, L. L. (2011, March). Impact of video viewing on infant learning: Using baby signs as an experimental approach. Paper presented at the biennial meeting of the Society for Research in Child Development, Montreal, Canada.

Fisch, S. M. (2000). A capacity model of children's comprehension of educational content on television. *Media Psychology, 2*(1), 63–91.

——(2004). *Children's learning from educational television: Sesame Street and beyond*. Mahwah, NJ: Lawrence Erlbaum.

Fisch, S. M., Lesh, R., Motoki, E., Crespo, S. and Melfi, V. (in press). Cross-platform learning: How do children learn from multiple media? In F. C. Blumberg (Ed.) *Learning by playing: Frontiers of video gaming in education*. New York: Oxford University Press.

Fisch, S. M., Hsueh, Y., Zhou, Z., Xu, C. J., Hamed, M., Khader, Z., Langsten, R., Noriega, G. M., Cespedes, A. H., Druin, A. and Guha, M. L. (2010). Crossing borders: Learning from educational media in four countries. *Televizion, 23*(1), 42–45.

Gick, M. L. and Holyoak, K. J. (1983). Schema induction and analogical transfer. *Cognitive Psychology, 15*(1), 1–38.

Groebel, J. (1999). Media access and media use among 12-year-olds in the world. In C. von Felitzen and U. Carlsson (Eds), *Children and media: Image, education, participation*. Göteborg, Sweden: UNESCO, pp. 61–68.

Huston, A. C., Anderson, D. R., Wright, J. C., Linebarger, D. L. and Schmitt, K. L. (2001). *Sesame Street* viewers as adolescents: The recontact study. In S. M. Fisch and R. T. Truglio (Eds), *"G" is for "growing": Thirty years of research on children and Sesame Street*. Mahwah, NJ: Lawrence Erlbaum, pp. 131–44.

Kirkorian, H. L. and Anderson, D. R. (2011). Learning from educational media. In S. L. Calvert and B. J. Wilson (Eds), *The handbook of children, media, and development*. West Sussex, UK: Wiley-Blackwell, pp. 188–213.

Lee, J. H. (2007). The educational and cultural impact of *Sisimpur*. *Televizion*, 20/2007/E, 51–53.

Mares, M. L. and Woodard, E. H. (2001). Prosocial effects on children's social interactions. In D. G. Singer and J. L. Singer (Eds), *Handbook of children and the media*. Thousand Oaks, CA: Sage, pp. 183–205.

Meltzoff, A. (1988). Imitation of televised models by infants. *Child Development, 59*(5), 1221–29.

Reiser, R. A., Tessmer, M. A. and Phelps, P. C. (1984). Adult-child interaction in children's learning from *Sesame Street*. *Educational Communication and Technology Journal, 32*(4), 217–23.

Richert, R. A., Robb, M. B. and Smith, E. I. (2011). Media as social partners: The social nature of young children's learning from screen media. *Child Development, 82*(1), 82–95.

Rideout, V. J., Foehr, U. G. and Roberts, D. F. (2010). *Generation M²: Media in the lives of 8- to 18-year-olds*. Menlo Park, CA: Kaiser Family Foundation.

Sahin, N. (1990, September). Preliminary report on the summative evaluation of the Turkish co-production of Sesame Street. Paper presented at the International Conference on Adaptations of *Sesame Street*, Amsterdam, The Netherlands.

Ulitsa Sezam Department of Research and Content (1998, November). Preliminary report of summative findings. Report presented to the Children's Television Workshop, New York, NY.

Vandewater, E. A. (2011). Infant word learning from commercially available video in the US. *Journal of Children and Media, 5*, 248–66.

Wright, J. C., Huston, A. C., Scantlin, R. and Kotler, J. (2001). The Early Window project: *Sesame Street* prepares children for school. In S. M. Fisch and R. T. Truglio (Eds), *"G" is for "growing": Thirty years of research on children and Sesame Street*. Mahwah, NJ: Lawrence Erlbaum Associates, pp. 97–114.

Zill, N. (2001). Does *Sesame Street* enhance school readiness?: Evidence from a national survey of children. In S. M. Fisch and R. T. Truglio (Eds), *"G" is for "growing": Thirty years of research on children and Sesame Street*. Mahwah, NJ: Lawrence Erlbaum Associates, pp. 115–30.

50

NEW MEDIA AND LEARNING

Becky Herr Stephenson

New media and learning

"New media" have been defined broadly as information and communication technologies and the practices and contexts associated with their use (Lievrouw and Livingstone, 2006). These new media take diverse forms, for example, images, audio, and video found on the internet, interactive games accessed through mobile devices, or spaces and practices related to sharing one's media creations. In the United States, youth tend to rank among the heaviest users of certain new media. For example, a 2010 survey by the Kaiser Family Foundation found that young people in between the ages of 8 and 18 in the United States spend an average of more than seven hours per day using media (Rideout et al., 2010). While this statistic includes "old media" such as television, the report notes that such media are often accessed through "new" modes such as mobile or online media. Looking specifically at teens aged 12–17 in the US, the Pew Internet & American Life Project reports that 73 percent of online teens in the US use social network sites (Lenhart et al., 2010) and 27 percent record and upload video to the internet (Lenhart, 2012a). Another Pew study on teens, mobile phones, and texting reports that 23 percent of teens aged 12–17 own a smart phone and the average teen sends about 60 text messages per day (Lenhart, 2012b).

Lievrouw and Livingstone, along with many other researchers of new media, note that new media are more than just technologies. They are, as Buckingham (2008) describes, "cultural forms" that "convey images and fantasies, provide opportunities for imaginative self-expression and play, and serve as a medium through which intimate personal relationships are conducted ... " (p. 74). Similarly, researchers from the Digital Youth Project described later in this chapter have identified new media as part of young people's media ecologies, described as the constellation of "everyday [media] practices of youth, existing structural conditions, infrastructures of place, and technologies [that] are all dynamically interrelated ... " (Horst et al., 2009, p. 31). Within such media ecologies, important social interactions, including building and maintaining friendships and aspects of flirting and dating, as well as cultural and civic participation such as media making and discussion/debate, move fluidly between mediated and non-mediated spaces.

Youths' adoption of new media is not limited to teens in the United States. For example, a 2010 survey conducted by Ofcom (Children's Media Literacy in the Nations) reflected high levels of new media ownership and use among families with children aged 5 to 15 throughout the United Kingdom (Ofcom, 2010). In China, the China Internet Network Information Center has estimated that the majority (62 percent) of the country's 384 million internet users were under 30 years of age as of 2010 (Wallis, 2011). Writing about India, Nayar and Bhide (2008) describe the country's rapidly changing media landscapes as being unique in their "youthfulness, both in terms of its [new media's] use and its propellants" (p. 329).

It is within this context, in which new media represent essential tools and practices for youth's participation in social, cultural, and civic life, that efforts over the last decade to understand and expand the possibilities for learning with new media have occurred. Researchers working within diverse paradigms—including education (e.g., Buckingham, 2007; Knobel and Lankshear, 2007; Marsh, 2005; Steinkuehler, 2010), learning sciences (e.g., Barron et al., 2009), developmental psychology (e.g., Staiano et al., 2012), communication and media studies (e.g., Ito et al., 2009; Jenkins et al., 2006; Seiter, 2005), and neuroscience (e.g., Dye and Bavelier, 2010)— have undertaken studies aimed at understanding learning with new media. Organizations in both the public and private sectors have created products designed to leverage characteristics of new media identified as beneficial for learning, for example, motivation and low consequences for failure (Gee, 2003; Hoffman and Nadelson, 2010). As Sonia Livingstone described in her 2011 keynote at the Digital Media and Learning conference, identifying opportunities for learning with new media is a shared interest among multiple sectors, including:

> … educators, political scientists, and civic activists who seek to reinvigorate tired, even failed, institutions of learning and participation with the exciting potential of the digital. Participants also include those keen to ask what children and youth need and deserve, especially now that the digital seems to overturn generational hierarchies and unsettle authoritative adult structures with the exuberance of youthful creativity. … technologists and designers fascinated by what can be made and done and hoping to see new ways of thinking and acting enabled by new means of connecting people and ideas … [and] scholars …
>
> *(Livingstone, 2011, p. 1)*

In the United States in particular, new media have been posited as an important resource in addressing concerns about children's academic achievement and preparation for future work and civic participation (U.S. Department of Education, 2010). Many efforts to use new media for learning have emerged as responses to a perceived "participation gap," a problematic difference in social, cultural, and civic participation between youth with access to new media and those without (Jenkins et al., 2006).

Much of the research, innovation, and intervention in the field of new media and learning has been supported by foundation funding. Particularly influential in this space has been the MacArthur Foundation, which since 2006 has funded approximately $85 million in initiatives related to developing a field of digital media and learning, including funding research (including the projects described later in this chapter), supporting the formation of the Digital Media and Learning (DML) Hub at the University of California, Irvine to coordinate efforts among researchers and other organizations working in the DML space, and supporting professional gatherings such as an annual conference (MacArthur Foundation, 2011).

The next section of this chapter looks at two frameworks for understanding learning with new media: the new media literacies, as described by Project New Media Literacies (NML), and genres of participation, as described by researchers on the Digital Youth Project. Both frameworks combine the language of skills and literacies to identify technical proficiencies *and* social practices conducive to successful learning with and through new media. Further, both frameworks value situated learning, a theory of learning that emphasizes the value of activities that are meaningful and engaging within the learner's specific context and experience, as well as activities that encourage learners to develop expert identities through practice.

Tools for understanding learning in participatory cultures: new media literacies and genres of participation

Both the new media literacies and genres of participation take as a starting point the assumption that young people are living and learning within participatory cultures, defined by Jenkins et al. as:

> ... a culture with relatively low barriers to artistic expression and civic engagement, strong support for creating and sharing creations, and some type of informal mentorship whereby experienced participants pass along knowledge to novices. In a participatory culture, members also believe their contributions matter and feel some degree of social connection with one another (at the least, members care about others' opinions of what they have created).
>
> *(2006, p. xi)*

Participatory cultures take the forms of formal and informal affiliations in online communities, including social network sites and games, as well as spaces for producing and sharing media or information and for receiving mentorship on such production from peers. As Jenkins and colleagues note, opportunities to be a part of participatory cultures are important, forming a kind of "hidden curriculum" (p. xii) that may influence youth's future success in school and adult life.

The social and technical skills necessary for access to participatory cultures have been identified by Project NML researchers as the new media literacies, and include play, performance, simulation, appropriation, multitasking, distributed cognition, collective intelligence, judgment, transmedia navigation, networking, and negotiation. These literacies are broader than just technical skills; all involve social practices and critical approaches to understanding media in addition to technical proficiencies.

Taking a situated learning approach, the learning that takes place with new media in participatory cultures is the participation itself. Children and youth who participate in online spaces such as fan communities or multiplayer online games (MMORPGs) learn things such as how to communicate with others through the specific channels and accepted norms of the community, how to share resources and knowledge using online tools such as Wikis or blogs, and how to create, circulate, and critique media (among numerous other things). These kinds of participation—again, called literacies because of their combination of technical skills and social/cultural competencies—have not always been recognized as valuable within traditional educational institutions; however, organizations and advocates looking ahead to children's future professional and civic participation have eagerly adopted new media literacies, considering them essential to future success.

Building upon the frameworks for participatory cultures and the new media literacies put forth by Project NML, the Digital Youth Project (see Ito et al., 2009), a three-year collaborative ethnographic study carried out by a team of 28 researchers and collaborators, sought to document and categorize young people's uses of new media in order to better understand the informal opportunities for learning presented by different types of new media use. The project produced 23 unique case studies, most of which focused on teenagers (although *youth* was broadly defined to include participants up to the age of 25). Each case study looked at some aspect of how young people used new media in their everyday lives, for example, acquiring and sharing media such as music and movies, using technology for maintaining friendships, flirting, and dating, and technology use within families.

Upon review of the ethnographic data, researchers identified several types of participation that seemed to traverse the diverse sites represented by the case studies. More than just techniques for using new media, the observed types of participation involved different purposes for using new media as well as different modes of engagement and social connection. The term "genres of participation" was chosen to identify these modes of engagement in order to recognize both the individual's role in deciding how to use new media and the influence of social structures on those decisions. Genres of participation emphasize the multiple ways a person may participate in different spaces—or within the same space—as well as the likely possibility that one's participation may change over time. The concept can be understood as a response to both the opportunities and challenges presented by the current technological landscape, as it calls attention to the continuities and slower changes that exist in participation in general, rather than focusing on the use of one particular technology or media format.

A key distinction made by the Digital Youth Project is between genres that are friendship-driven and genres that are interest-driven. Friendship-driven genres of participation tend to center around relationships with friends from school, neighborhood, church, or other activities and institutions. When young people move online to spaces in which they participate in friendship-driven ways, their online activities very closely resemble the activities in which they are involved offline. For example, using instant messaging to continue conversations with friends after school or posting on friends' profiles on social network sites are examples of friendship-driven participation.

In interest-driven participation, existing friendships do not determine participation. Activities that allow young people to practice or demonstrate a particular skill or to dig into a particular interest—belonging to a sports team, theater troupe, band, or choir, among others—are offline examples of interest-driven participation. Online spaces offer countless opportunities for interest-driven participation, including participation in media fandoms, gaming communities, and sites for sharing art, writing, or digital media productions. Young people who engage in interest-driven participation often make friends through these sites, much as members of a community sports team may begin as anonymous neighbors and end as a group of close friends. Interest-driven and friendship-driven genres of participation are dynamic and are not mutually exclusive.

In addition to the main distinctions between interest-driven and friendship-driven participation, researchers identified three sub-genres to further describe ways of approaching media and technology. These three sub-genres, hanging out, messing around, and geeking out, each carry with them characteristics relating to the type and intensity of engagement with media and technology and, in many cases, represent particular types of learning trajectories associated with the development of technological and social skills. For example, hanging out emphasizes social connection among friends; through this genre of participation, learning centers on communication through various (mediated and non-mediated) channels and practices. By hanging out online on social network sites, for example, youth learn—and challenge—norms and expectations around sociability and communication with others. Messing around, a genre identified by researchers when reviewing subjects' responses to questions about how they initially learned a particular technical skill or social practice, represents a mode of participation that privileges investigation and trial-and-error problem solving over communication or social connection. Messing around can be understood as a transitional genre between the primarily social hanging out and the primarily interest-driven geeking out. "Geeking out" is used to describe intensive, focused participation within a particular online community or practice (such as gaming or media production). Like messing around, geeking out involves a level of social connection, often in the form of mentor relationships, but privileges interest-driven participation and learning above social connection.

Keeping in mind the lenses of skills, literacies, and genres of participation the next sections of this chapter briefly examine two areas of primary interest for research and development in new media and learning: gaming and social media.

Games and learning

Games are a frequent entry point to new media for children and youth, as they are often introduced to kids' media ecologies before other new media such as online sites or media production tools (Ito et al., 2009; Salen, 2008). Although strong anti-games discourse exists, related in part to a legacy of psychological effects research in the 1980s and 1990s that was concerned with identifying the negative effects of games and in part to new concerns about game addiction due to the immersive nature of new games (Peppler and Kafai, 2010), enthusiasm for games as tools for learning is high among many educators, researchers, developers, and policymakers.

Video game design that aligns with best learning practices identified by learning scientists, including goal directed behavior, active engagement, decision making, extended commitment, repeated practice, and opportunities to fail and try again, can make video games fertile ground for learning and metacognition. James Paul Gee has hailed video games as new media that "externalize the way in which the human mind works and thinks in a better fashion than any other technology we have" (Gee, 2008, p. 200). Indeed, observing young people play games often yields excellent examples of genres of participation and new media literacies in practice, among them play, performance, and collective intelligence. As Ito and Bittanti (2009) point out, the cultivation of social networks through recreational gaming should be understood as a learning outcome of gaming, just like the development of in-game skills and more general technical expertise.

Shaffer et al. (2005) emphasize video games' potential for supporting play and performance, writing "video games are important because they let people participate in new worlds. They let players think, talk, and act in new ways. Indeed, players come to *inhabit* roles that are otherwise inaccessible to them" (p. 105). Online games offer a valuable context for learning to practice collective intelligence, as players connect with and rely upon others to solve in-game quests and problems. Further, auxiliary materials developed around games (such as Wikis or walk-through videos) represent repositories of collective intelligence, putting the wisdom of the crowd at a player's fingertips.

In an effort to identify areas of growth for learning with and through video games, as well as to consider solutions to long-standing gender disparities in gaming, Peppler and Kafai (2010) have proposed the notion of "gaming fluencies." Gaming fluencies emphasize multiple aspects of gaming—game play, the ability to read games critically, opportunities to participate in social networks around games, and the ability to design/produce games—as the optimal way to approach learning through and about games.

Communicating and connecting through new media: social media and learning

A second area of great interest around new media and learning is the role of social media. Social media comprise a diverse category of new media, ranging from online sites such as Facebook, Bebo or Orkut to mobile technologies and apps that integrate social media into games or everyday tasks like reading online articles. With increasingly ubiquitous internet access in many countries around the world, it is possible for youth to enact large parts of their social lives online, often moving seamlessly between online communication and connection with others in physical spaces.

Social media open up opportunities for connected learning—communication, collaboration, and sharing among learners in different spaces—potentially allowing learning to be recognized anytime and anywhere, rather than being limited to activities that take place in formal educational environments. Both the new media literacies and genres of participation described earlier in this chapter emphasize the value of social networks for learning, not only because they expand the information available to users (collective intelligence), but because they frequently offer authentic opportunities for civic and cultural participation that might not otherwise be open to youth (Ito et al., 2009; Jenkins et al., 2006).

Two primary areas of learning through social media include the development of written literacy (defined broadly to include writing with different types of media) and identity formation/performance. As Jackie Marsh's (2011) study of children's participation in the virtual world Club Penguin indicates, even young children are capable of using multi-modal practices to communicate with friends, including sending "postcards" (private messages) and instant messaging, often blending written text and emoticons to get their messages across. While social media applications tend to vary in the specific communication practices they foster and value, they all offer opportunities to learn to use multimedia for communication.

Much research on social media conducted with teens has focused on the ways in which young people use social network sites to play with and express aspects of their identities. For example, drawing from prior research in interpersonal communication and psychology, danah boyd (2008) describes teens' processes of impression management in online social networks, wherein much of the information conveyed to others in face-to-face communication is not available because cues from one's body are not present. In this context, youth need to learn to present themselves using text, images, sounds, and other media, rather than corporeal symbols and signals.

Conclusion

There is much left to be understood about new media and learning. In addition to considering changes to children's media ecologies as innovative new media enter the marketplace and classroom, a number of pressing issues related to equity and participation with new media exist. Finding ways to address inequalities in access to new media—including approaches to closing the participation gap between young people with robust access to participatory cultures and those without and methods for bridging informal and formal learning spaces—is of prime importance, as is considering ways for new media to support youth's development of ethical and civic participation. In years to come, the shared interest among diverse sectors in understanding these and other issues related to new media and learning will surely be an asset to improving educational outcomes and possibilities.

SEE ALSO in this volume chapter by Livingstone, chapter by Peppler, and chapter by Fisch.

References

Barron, B., Martin, C. K., Takeuchi, L. and Fithian, R. (2009). Parents as learning partners in the development of technological fluency. *International Journal of Learning and Media*, 1(2), 55–77.

boyd, d. (2008). Why youth (heart) social network sites: The role of networked publics in teenage social life. In D. Buckingham (Ed.), *Youth, identity, and digital media*. Cambridge, MA: MIT Press, pp. 119–42.

Buckingham, D. (2007). *Beyond technology: Children's learning in the age of digital culture*. London: Polity Press.

——(2008). Defining digital literacy: What do young people need to know about digital media? In C. Lankshear and M. Knobel (Eds), *Digital literacies: Concepts, policies and practices*. New York: Peter Lang, pp. 73–90.

Dye, M. W. and Bavelier, D. (2010). Differential development of visual attention skills in school-age children. *Vision Research*, 50(4), 452–59.

Gee, J. P. (2003). *What video games have to teach us about learning and literacy*. New York: Palgrave Macmillan.

Gee, J. P. (2008). Learning theory, video games, and popular culture. In K. Drotner and S. Livingstone (Eds), *The international handbook of children, media, and culture*. London: Sage, pp. 196–212.

Hoffman, B. and Nadelson, L. (2010). Motivational engagement and video gaming: a mixed methods study. *Educational Technology Research and Development, 58*(3), 245–70.

Horst, H., Herr Stephenson, B. and Robinson, L. (2009). Media ecologies. In M. lto, S. Baumer, M. Bittani, d. boyd, R. Cody, B. Herr-Stephenson et al. *Hanging out, messing around, and geeking out: Kids living and learning with new media.* Cambridge, MA: MIT Press, pp. 29–78.

Ito, M. and Bittanti, M. (2009). Gaming. In M. Ito, S. Baumer, M. Bittanti, d. boyd, R. Cody, B. Herr-Stephenson et al. *Hanging out, messing around, and geeking out: Kids living and learning with new media.* Cambridge, MA: MIT Press, pp. 195–242.

Ito, M., Baumer, S., Bittanti, M., boyd, d., Cody, R., Herr Stephenson, B. et al. (2009). *Hanging out, messing around, and geeking out: Kids living and learning with new media.* Cambridge, MA: MIT Press.

Jenkins, H., Clinton, K., Purushotma, R., Robinson, A. J. and Weigel, M. (2006). Confronting the challenges of participatory culture: Media education for the 21st century. The John D. and Catherine T. MacArthur Foundation. Retrieved from http://www.digitallearning.macfound.org/.../JENKINS_WHITE_PAPER.PDF

Knobel, M. and Lankshear, C. (2007). *A new literacies sampler.* New York: Peter Lang.

Lenhart, A. (2012a). Teens and online video. Washington, DC: Pew Internet & American Life Project. Retrieved from http://pewinternet.org/Reports/2012/Teens-and-online-video.aspx

Lenhart, A. (2012b). Teens, smartphones & texting. Washington DC: Pew Internet & American Life Project. Retrieved from http://pewinternet.org/Reports/2012/Teens-and-smartphones.aspx

Lenhart, A., Purcell, K., Smith, A. and Zickuhr, K. (2010). Social media & mobile internet use among teens and young adults. Washington, DC: Pew Internet & American Life Projet. Retrieved from http://pewinternet.org/Reports/2010/Social-Media-and-Young-Adults.aspx

Lievrouw, L. A. and Livingstone, S. (2006). Introduction to the first edition (2002) The social shaping and consequences of ICTs. In L. A. Lievrouw and S. Livingstone (Eds), *Handbook of new media: The social shaping and consequences of ICTs.* London: Sage. Retrieved from http://sage-ereference.com/

Livingstone, S. (2011). Digital learning and participation among youth: Critical reflections on future research priorities. *International Journal of Learning and Media, 2*(2–3), 1–13.

MacArthur Foundation (2011). *Exploring digital media and learning.* Chicago: MacArthur Foundation. Retrieved from http://www.macfound.org/media/article_pdfs/DML_BUFF_MARCH_2011.PDF

Marsh, J. (Ed.) (2005). *Popular culture, new media and digital literacy in early childhood.* London: RoutledgeFalmer.

Marsh, J. (2011). Young children's literacy practices in a virtual world: Establishing an online interaction order. *Reading Research Quarterly, 46*(2), 101–19.

Nayar, U. S. and Bhide, A. (2008). Contextualizing media competencies among young people in Indian culture: Interface with globalization. In K. Drotner and S. Livingstone (Eds), *The international handbook of children, media, and culture.* London: Sage, pp. 328–35.

Ofcom (2010) *Children's media literacy in the nations: Summary report.* London: Ofcom. Retrieved from http://stakeholders.ofcom.org.uk/market-data-research/media-literacy/medlitpub/medlitpubrss/childrens medialitsummary/

Peppler, K. A. and Kafai, Y. B. (2010). Gaming fluencies: Pathways into a participatory culture in a community design studio. *International Journal of Learning and Media, 1*(4), 1–14.

Rideout, V., Foehr, U. G. and Roberts, D. F. (2010). Generation M2: Media in the lives of 8- to 18-year olds. Menlo Park: Kaiser Family Foundation. Retrieved from http://www.kff.org/entmedia/upload/8010.pdf

Salen, K. (2008). Gaming literacies: A game design study in action. *Journal of Educational Multimedia and Hypermedia, 16*(3), 301–22.

Seiter, E. (2005). *The Internet playground: children's access, entertainment, and mis-education.* New York: Peter Lang.

Shaffer, D. W., Squire, K. R., Halverson, R. and Gee, J. P. (2005). Video games and the future of learning. *Phi Delta Kappan, 87*(2), 104–11.

Staiano, A., Abraham, A. and Calvert, S. (2012). Competitive versus cooperative exergame play for African American adolescents' executive function skills: Short-term effects in a long-term training intervention. *Developmental Psychology, 48*(2), 337–42.

Steinkuehler, C. (2010). Video games and digital literacies. *Journal of Adolescent & Adult Literacy, 51*(1), 61–63.

U.S. Department of Education (2010). *Transforming American education: Learning powered by technology.* Washington, D.C.: U.S. Department of Education. Retrieved from http://www.ed.gov/sites/default/files/netp2010.pdf

Wallis, C. (2011). New media practices in China: Youth patterns, processes, and politics. *International Journal of Communication, 5*, 406–36.

51

MEDIA LITERACY

Renee Hobbs

A number of competing approaches to media literacy are now in wide circulation in the United States and around the world. Empowerment and protection have long been identified as the two overarching themes in the media literacy education community, reflecting a dynamic and generally productive tension between those who see media literacy education as a means to address the complexities and challenges of growing up in a media- and technology-saturated cultural environment and those who see media literacy as a tool for personal, social, cultural and political empowerment.

Contributing to these distinctive perspectives is the rise of a community of scholars and practitioners who are advancing new knowledge about the nature of the practice of teaching and learning *about* and *with* mass media, popular culture and digital media. As media literacy initiatives are implemented in the family (Mendoza, 2009) as well as in elementary and secondary education and in informal learning spaces, including summer programs, museums, libraries and cultural institutions, a body of research is emerging that offers insight on the consequences and impact of such practices. In a systematic review of over 150 empirical studies in the field, Martens (2010) notes that many communication scholars position media literacy education as a solution to the problem of negative media effects like media violence, gender and racial stereotyping, and bias in the news.

A key framing question must be asked: is media literacy education a social movement or an academic field? *Social movements* arise in response to changing social norms and values (Blumler, 1969) as a form of political participation where people engage in a sustained public effort to make social change, using communicative action to raise awareness, build strategic alliances, and, ultimately, to challenge and reform some aspects of contemporary culture. *Academic fields* generally emerge when those working at the intersections of existing disciplines find the need to reconfigure themselves into a distinct discourse community with shared vision, goals and passion for creating new knowledge (Lauter, 1999). Emergent knowledge communities develop a collective body of foundational knowledge that provides boundaries for a theoretical, methodological and evaluative framework and an infrastructure for dialogue, debate and the dissemination of knowledge (Dirks, 1996).

Although the term "media literacy" has been aligned with both the literature on media effects (e.g., Singer et al., 1980) and the instructional practices of literacy learning (Hobbs, 1998; Lemke, 2006; Postman, 1970) over the past few decades, the inquiry-focused approach to media literacy education, with its critical examination of news, advertising, entertainment, issues of representation, and media ownership, has been challenged by two new approaches. One is focused on digital learning primarily in informal out-of-school or online contexts; another approach positions media literacy as a means to promote increased student motivation and engagement in school through the use of digital technologies or popular culture. The use of mobile media, social media and new technologies for teaching and learning is creating new opportunities for digital and media literacy education in the context of elementary and secondary education, but there are some concerns about what actual learning outcomes actually may result from the use of technology tools for transmission-based (not inquiry-based) learning.

Media literacy as a social movement

In North America and in some European and Asian countries, media literacy advocates are generally aligned with parents, educators, scholars, health professionals and cultural critics who are frustrated by shifting social norms. Issues of concern may include aggression and cyberbullying; gender and racial stereotypes; bias, gossip and sensationalism in the news; pornography, sexting and online sexual behavior; video game and mobile media addiction; materialism and the commercialization of childhood; the rise of celebrity culture; and changing conceptualizations of personal and social identity in relation to the internet and social media (Frau-Meigs and Torrrent, 2009; Gurak, 2001). These issues offer profound challenges to the practice of raising children and educating youth in contemporary society. In particular, media literacy is conceptualized as a means to address the particular challenges associated with growing up in an always-on wireless broadband environment in an era when parental control and government regulation are thought to be of limited value (Livingstone et al., 2011).

As a social movement, media literacy is sometimes conceptualized as a form of protection in response to a "wide range of potentially negative effects on individuals" (Potter, 2010, p. 681). In general, those who see media literacy as a social movement are motivated by a sense that unrestrained capitalism has victimized children and young people, crafting techniques to titillate youth with sex and violence and infiltrating and shaping children's online social and emotional worlds to compel them to spend more and more time online (Bakan, 2011).

While this approach to media literacy has been roundly criticized as a form of moral, cultural or political defensiveness (Buckingham, 2003), it continues to have traction in the United States and some other countries, especially in relation to the ever-changing forms of contemporary digital technology, mass media and popular culture. For example, consider the work of writer, Jennifer Pozner, author of *Reality Bites Back*. When she appeared on the American TV show, *CBS Early Show*, to promote her new book, which looks at the history and popularity of reality TV programs such as *Survivor*, *American Idol* and *Jersey Shore* through a media literacy lens, the program offered the perspectives of Matt Otto, a New York City school principal who has observed his own students frequently re-enacting some of the aggressive and mean-spirited behaviors depicted on some reality shows. He explained that certain behaviors have become more acceptable to students who watch these shows, noting that students may see these aggressive, attention-getting actions as the closest possibility they have to becoming famous. One authentic solution to this problem is to provide opportunities for young people to discuss and analyze problematic media representations with parents, teachers and other caring adults (Pozner, 2011). A number of youth and media advocacy groups are allied with the social movement conceptualization of media literacy. For example, as part of their advocacy efforts for media literacy, Girl Scouts USA conducted survey research with girls ages 11–17, finding that about half of the sample are regular viewers of reality TV shows and that regular viewers accept and expect a higher level of drama, aggression and bullying in their own lives (Girl Scouts USA, 2011).

While youth media practitioners and advocates have been active in conceptualizing media literacy as a form of social activism, scholars working from within the media effects paradigm have also made considerable progress in exploring how media literacy may mitigate the negative impact of media messages on attitudes and behavior. Several studies have examined how media literacy education programs improve health outcomes, by reducing, among others, substance abuse (Austin et al., 2005), smoking (Banerjee and Greene, 2007), and aggressive behavior (Byrne, 2009; Scharrer, 2005; 2006; Webb et al., 2010). Other studies have shown how media literacy education affects adolescents' knowledge and attitudes regarding sexuality (Galician, 2004; Pinkleton et al., 2008), advertising (Livingstone and Helsper, 2006), as well as racial and gender stereotypes (Ramasubramanian, 2007).

Video games and online social media, like traditional mass media and popular culture before it, are being framed in terms of both the *opportunities and risks* they offer to children and young people. In a large multinational study aimed at understanding European children's risky and safer uses of the internet, the EU Kids Online project discovered that, contrary to much of the rhetoric offered by scholars and technology specialists, children and young people with more digital skills have a greater likelihood of exposure to risks, including identity theft, cyberbullying, exposure to hate sites, self-harm sites, sexual images and pornography, violations of privacy, unwanted exposure to advertising, and more (Livingstone et al., 2011). While recognizing the importance of promoting media literacy education in schools, researchers have found that simply teaching digital skills will not necessarily reduce online risk. To address these issues, service learning or community advocacy approaches emphasize the role of discussion, facilitated by young adults who work with younger children to explore mass media and popular culture in ways that activate awareness and support the development of metacognitive and reflective thinking (Cooks and Scharrer, 2007).

Media literacy as an interdisciplinary academic field

Those who see media literacy as an academic field include an international group of scholars with interests in the intersection of media studies, education and human development (Cappello et al., 2011). The essential components of media literacy pedagogy involve the processes of accessing, analyzing, composing, reflecting and taking action in ways that activate creativity, collaboration, critical thinking and communication skills (Barron et al., 2010; Hart and Hicks, 2002; Hobbs, 2006; Lemke, 2006; Rheingold, 2008; Tyner, 2004).

As an academic field, the general emphasis is on the development of interdisciplinary theoretical frameworks and the implementation and evaluation of practical programs that enable children and young people to learn about all forms of mass media, popular culture and digital media as a dimension of an expanded conceptualization of literacy. In both school and non-school settings, practitioners generally implement and develop programs based on their own interests and motivations for media literacy in relationship to the unique needs of their students (Hobbs, 2011a), resulting in highly varied practice that includes the use of digital media, discussions about and exploration of advertising, news, and entertainment media, generally paired with some form of informal or formal media production activities, including video production.

Reflecting a conceptualization of literacy as consisting of both "reading" and "writing," those who see media literacy as an academic field tend to emphasize the instructional or pedagogical values associated with the habits of mind linked to the critical analysis of mass media, digital media and popular culture, especially when combined with media composition activities involving visual, print, sound and digital media tools and technologies (Beach, 2007). Instead of viewing media literacy as a social movement, it is seen here as a distinct set of pedagogical practices (including close analysis of media "texts," cross-media comparison, keeping a media diary and multimedia composition) that help learners build awareness of the constructedness of the media and technology environment, deploy strategies useful in the meaning-making process, understand the economic, political and historical context in which media messages circulate, and appreciate the ways messages influence attitudes and behavior (Wilson et al., 2011).

Theoretically, the academic field approach is aligned with semiotic, critical/cultural, constructivist or empowerment perspectives, which are four theoretical frameworks that reflect a fundamental re-articulation of the "active audience" tradition. Scholars and educators in media literacy generally work at the intersections of existing disciplines, including communication, education, human development, technology studies, sociology, literacy education, art history, technology/information policy, writing and rhetoric, library and information studies, journalism, social work and other fields (Hobbs, 2011b).

At the present time, there are a set of overlapping and distinct discourse communities associated with media literacy, each reflecting the shape of various established disciplinary traditions. *Critical literacy* and *new literacies* scholars may see themselves as distinct in relation to those with interests in *information literacy* or *digital learning*, for example, with each group having a set of core texts that are foundational to their work (Hobbs, 2010; Lemke, 2006; Tyner, 2004).

However, as a result of the rise of interdisciplinary scholarship over the past ten years, more and more scholars in the fields of English education and media studies are reading and building on each other's work (Beach, 2007). In 1996, the National Council of Teachers of English (NCTE) endorsed a resolution that "viewing and visually representing are a part of our growing consciousness of how people gather and share information. ... Teachers should guide students in constructing meaning through creating and viewing nonprint texts." As a result of interdisciplinary mingling, a set of foundational concepts regarding *authors and audiences, messages and meanings and representation and reality* are widely shared (Hobbs, 2006). These concepts support and extend scholarship and provide an infrastructure for dialogue and debate across knowledge communities.

Worldwide momentum for media literacy as a dimension of media policy and as an academic discipline is increasingly evident. Frau-Meigs and Torrent (2009) catalogued the current state of the field in a 2009 book, *Mapping Media Education Policies*, which outlined progress made in countries including Austria, Brazil, Spain, South Korea, Finland, Argentina and Turkey. At the Education, Youth and Culture meeting held in Brussels in 2009, the Council of the European Union formally adopted a policy on a European approach to media literacy in the digital environment, "embedded in a package of measures to ensure an effective European single market for emerging audiovisual media services" (O'Neill, 2010, p. 328). Recognizing the increased competitive environment of the audiovisual sector that results from an inclusive knowledge society, the Council noted that the education system must better support people's ability to access, understand, evaluate, create and communicate media content as part of lifelong learning. They noted

> The responsible and informed use of new technologies and new media requires citizens to be aware of risks and to respect relevant legal provisions, but most literacy policies should address such questions in the context of a generally positive message.
>
> *(Council of Europe, 2007, p. 2)*

The Council recommended the progressive development of criteria to assess the levels of media literacy in member states, beginning in 2011, a task that has been initiated by a number of federal agencies with support from key European scholars. Some scholars question, however, the extent to which European media literacy education will balance the "consumer" orientation (promoting the use of media) with the "citizenship" orientation (empowering critical analysis and active participation), especially given the recalcitrance of the formal education sector in many European nations (O'Neill, 2010).

In the United States, support for digital and media literacy education exists unevenly at the state and local level. Although nearly all states include media literacy learning outcomes in their state education standards, each of the more than 15,000 school districts must decide whether and how media literacy education is implemented. In general, such work happens only as a result of initiatives taken by individual enthusiast teachers or school leaders (Hobbs, 2011a).

However, media policymakers have explicitly addressed the need for media literacy for the wider population, not just children and youth. For example, the FCC's "Future of Media" initiative sought public comment on this question: "What kinds of digital and media literacy programs are appropriate to help people both use new information and communication technologies effectively and to analyze and evaluate the news and information they are receiving?" (Barnett, 2010). The Knight Commission's influential report, "Informing Communities: Sustaining Democracy in a Digital Age" identifies media literacy in relation to enhancing the information capacity of individuals, particularly in relation to citizenship (Knight Commission, 2009). And it's impossible to overstate the influence of the John D. and Catherine T. MacArthur Foundation, which has invested more than $80 million in research on digital media and learning, in supporting a variety of diverse research and practical projects that are transforming the field.

The future of digital and media literacy

When the Educational Testing Service, the company that administers the high-stakes SAT test required for admission to American colleges (Steinberg, 2011) used a question inviting students to critically analyze the genre of reality TV, it asked students to write an essay in response to the prompt:

> Reality television programs, which feature real people engaged in real activities rather than professional actors performing scripted scenes, are increasingly popular. These shows depict ordinary people competing in everything from singing and dancing to losing weight, or just living their everyday lives. Most people believe that the reality these shows portray is authentic, but they are being misled. How authentic can these shows be when producers design challenges for the participants and then editors alter filmed scenes? Do people benefit from forms of entertainment that show so-called reality, or are such forms of entertainment harmful?

While media literacy educators cheered at the news, educators who prioritize the need to transmit core knowledge and emphasize that knowledge is foundational to the development of literacy competencies (Hirsch, 2011) were less than satisfied. Some educational leaders object to digital and media literacy's emphasis on activating and extending students' prior knowledge from their experience with mass media and popular culture. This tension continues to limit the application of digital and media literacy in elementary and secondary educational institutions around the world (Cappello et al., 2011).

However, scholars have begun to develop strategies for evaluating media and technology resources in search of those that "support, conceptualize and extend" student learning without simply adding "glitz and glamor in an electronic learning environment" (Coiro et al., 2006, p. 154). In one project, researchers developed a three-year longitudinal study to examine a learning environment intentionally designed to provide urban youth with tools and learning opportunities that would allow them to create, collaborate and communicate with new media production technologies. The program offered a series of after-school clubs in graphic design, digital broadcasting, movie making, music recording and remixing, and video game development. Results show that, with effective mentoring, students are able to shift their sense of identity to position themselves as authors (Barron et al, 2010). Scholarly inquiry on the practices that contribute to youth empowerment are a vital part of research in digital and media literacy education.

Today, media literacy education has characteristics of both a social movement and a field of inquiry. Even after 20 years of scholarship and practice, problems of definition continue, largely as a result of the dynamic social media landscape which has introduced new competencies, knowledge and skills associated with the rise of the internet, digital technologies and social media. There is also a growing disconnect between practitioners, policymakers and scholars about the conceptualization of "digital literacy" in relation to mass media and (especially) popular culture. While the U.S. federal government defines digital literacy quite narrowly as the technical skills associated with using the internet to search for jobs and access social services (Digital Literacy, 2011), other educators conceptualize digital literacy as the knowledge and skills needed to use social media, including creative and collaborative skills (Jenkins et al., 2007) or the sense of social responsibility associated with responsible online use (Common Sense Media, 2010). Still others frame digital literacy as more closely rooted in the concept of media and information literacy, with emphasis on the skills of using digital tools and technologies to use, access, analyze, evaluate and communicate messages in a wide variety of forms (Hobbs, 2010).

Perhaps the future of digital and media literacy as both a social movement and an academic field can be seen most clearly when it is framed as a citizenship skill. Media literacy is commonly recognized as a tool for strengthening young people's participation in civic and political life (Benkler, 2007; Jenkins et al., 2007; Rheingold, 2008), enabling young people to seek out information on relevant issues, evaluate the quality of the information available, and engage in dialogue with others to form coalitions (Bennett, 2008). One study found that nearly half of high school students from 21 high schools in California had engaged in various classroom activities designed to support media literacy competencies, including critically analyzing the trustworthiness of websites, using the internet to get information about political or social issues, and creating content for the web. These activities are associated with higher rates of online politically driven participation (Kahne et al., 2010). Over the next few years, it will be interesting to see how the productive tension between the protectionist and empowerment strands of the media literacy community evolve and change as a result of research and scholarship, practice in the field, changes in media and technology and philanthropic and cultural funding priorities.

SEE ALSO in this volume chapter by von Feilitzen.

References

Austin, E. W., Pinkleton, B. E., Hust, S. J. T. and Cohen, M. (2005). Evaluation of an American Legacy Foundation/Washington State Department of Health media literacy pilot study. *Health Communication*, 18(1), 75–95.

Bakan, J. (2011). *Childhood under siege*. New York: Simon & Schuster.

Banerjee, S. and Greene, K. (2007). Antismoking initiatives: Effects of analysis versus production media literacy interventions on smoking-related attitude, norm, and behavioral intention. *Health Communication*, 22(1), 37–48.

Barnett, J. (2010). The FCC's Future of Media Project. Nieman Journalism Lab. Retrieved May 6, 2011 from http://www.niemanlab.org/2010/01/the-fccs-future-of-media-project/

Barron, B., Levinson, A., Martin, C., Mertl, V., Stringer, D. and Rogers, M. (2010). Supporting young new media producers across learning spaces: A longitudinal study of the Digital Youth Network. Proceedings of the International Conference of the Learning Sciences, 2, 203–10.

Beach, R. (2007). *Teaching media literacy.* Thousand Oaks: Corwin/Sage.

Benkler, Y. (2007). *The wealth of networks.* New Haven: Yale University Press.

Bennett, W. L. (2008). Civic life online: Learning how digital media can engage youth. John D. and Catherine T. MacArthur Foundation Series on Digital Media and Learning, Cambridge, MA: MIT Press.

Blumler, J. (1969). *Social interactionism: Perspective and method.* Englewood Cliffs, NJ: Prentice-Hall.

Buckingham, D. (2003). *Media education: Literacy, learning and contemporary culture.* Cambridge UK: Polity Press.

Byrne, S. (2009). Media literacy interventions: What makes them boom or boomerang? *Communication Education, 58*(1), 1–14.

Cappello, G., Felini, D. and Hobbs, R. (2011). Reflections on global developments in media literacy education: Bridging theory and practice. *Journal of Media Literacy Education, 3*(2), 66–73.

Coiro, J., Karchmer-Klein, R. A. and Walpole, S. (2006). Critically evaluating educational technologies for literacy learning: Current trends and paradigms. In M. McKenna, D. Reinking, L. D. Labbo and R. D. Kieffer (Eds), *Handbook of Literacy and Technology* (2nd edition). Mahwah, NJ: Lawrence Erlbaum, pp. 145–61.

Cooks, L. and Scharrer, E. (2007). Communicating advocacy: Learning and change in the media literacy and violence prevention project. In L. Frey and K. Carragee (Eds), *Communication activism: Media and performance activism, Vol. 2.* Cresskill, NJ: Hampton Press, pp. 129–54.

Council of Europe (2007). Recommendation CM/REC-2007-11 of the Committee of Ministers to Member States on Promoting Freedom of Expression and Information in the New Information and Communications Environment. Strasbourg: Council of Europe.

Digital Literacy (2011). Digital Literacy. Retrieved December 20, 2011, from http://digitalliteracy.gov

Dirks, Arthur L. (1996). Organization of knowledge: The emergence of academic specialty in America. Retrieved December 2, 2011 from http://webhost.bridgew.edu/adirks/ald/papers/orgknow.htm

Frau-Meigs, D. and Torrent, J. (2009). *Mapping media education policies in the world: Visions, programmes and challenges.* Paris: UNESCO.

Galician, M. (2004). *Sex, love and romance in the mass media: Analysis and criticism of unrealistic portrayals and their influence.* Mahwah, NJ: Lawrence Erlbaum.

Girl Scouts USA (2011). Real to Me: Girls and Reality TV. Retrieved December 1, 2011 from http://www.girlscouts.org/research/publications/girlsandmedia/real_to_me.asp

Gurak, L. (2001). *Cyberliteracy: Navigating the Internet with awareness.* New Haven: Yale University Press.

Hart, A. and Hicks, A. (2002). *Teaching media in the English curriculum.* Stoke-on-Trent, UK: Trentham Books.

Hirsch, E. D. (2011). Beyond comprehension. *American Educator, 34*(4), 30–36.

Hobbs, R. (1998). The seven great debates in the media literacy movement. *Journal of Communication, 48*(1), 16–32.

——(2006). Multiple visions of multimedia literacy: Emerging areas of synthesis. In M. McKenna, L. Labbo, R. Kiefer and D. Reinking (Eds), *International Handbook of Literacy and Technology, Volume II.* Mahwah, NJ: Lawrence Erlbaum, pp. 15–28.

——(2010). *Digital and media literacy: A plan of action.* Washington DC: Aspen Institute.

——(2011a). *Digital and media literacy: Connecting culture to classroom.* Thousand Oaks, CA: Corwin/Sage.

——(2011b). The state of media literacy: A response to Potter. *Journal of Broadcasting and Electronic Media, 55*(3), 419–30.

Jenkins, H., Clinton, K., Purushotma, R., Robison, A. and Weigel, M. (2007). *Confronting the challenges of participatory culture: Media education for the 21st century.* Chicago IL: The John D. and Catherine T. MacArthur Foundation.

Kahne, J., Feezel, J. T. and Lee, N. (2010). Digital Media Literacy Education and Online Civic and Political Participation. DML Central Working Papers. Youth and Participatory Politics. November 8, 2010.

Knight Commission (2009). Informing Communities: Sustaining Democracy in a Digital Age. Aspen Institute, Washington, D.C.

Lauter, P. (1999). Reconfiguring academic disciplines: The emergence of American Studies. *American Studies, 40*(2), 23–28.

Lemke, J. (2006). Toward critical multimedia literacy: technology, research and politics. In M. McKenna, L. Labbo, R. Kiefer and D. Reinking (Eds), *International Handbook of Literacy and Technology, Volume II.* Mahwah, NJ: Lawrence Erlbaum, pp. 3–14.

Livingstone, S. and Helsper, E. (2006). Does advertising literacy mediate the effects of advertising on children? A critical examination of two linked research literatures in relation to obesity and food choice. *Journal of Communication, 56*(3), 560–84.

Livingtone, S., Haddon, L., Gorzig, A. and Olafsson, K. (2011). EU Kids Online: Final Report. Retrieved at http://www2.lse.ac.uk/media@lse/research/EUKidsOnline/EU%20Kids%20III/Reports/D1.5AAnnual Report1,301012public.pdf

Martens, H. (2010). Evaluating media literacy education: Concepts, theories and future directions. *Journal of Media Literacy Education, 2*(1), 1–22.

Mendoza, K. (2009). Surveying parental mediation: Connections, challenges and questions for media literacy. *Journal of Media Literacy Education, 1*(1), 28–41.

O'Neill, B. (2010). Media literacy and communication rights: ethical individualism in the New Media environment. *International Communication Gazette, 72*(4–5), 323–38.

Pinkleton, B. E., Austin, E. W., Cohen, M., Chen, Y. C. and Fitzgerald, E. (2008). Effects of a peer-led media literacy curriculum on adolescents' knowledge and attitudes toward sexual behavior and media portrayals of sex. *Health Communication, 23*(5), 462–72.

Postman, N. (1970). The politics of reading. *Harvard Educational Review, 40*(2), 244–52.

Potter, J. (2010). The state of media literacy. *Journal of Broadcasting & Electronic Media, 54*(4), 675–96.

Pozner, J. (2011). *Reality bites back.* Berkeley, CA: Seal Press.

Ramasubramanian, S. (2007). Media-based strategies to reduce racial stereotypes activated by news stories. *Journalism & Mass Communication Quarterly, 84*(2), 249–64.

Rheingold, H. (2008). Using participatory media and public voice to encourage civic engagement. In W.L. Bennett (Ed.). *Civic life online: Learning how digital media can engage youth.* The John D. and Catherine T. MacArthur Foundation Series on Digital Media and Learning, Cambridge, MA: MIT Press, pp. 97–118.

Scharrer, E. (2005). Sixth graders take on television: Media literacy and critical attitudes about television violence. *Communication Research Reports, 22*(1), 325–33.

——(2006). "I noticed more violence:" The effects of a media literacy program on knowledge and attitudes about media violence. *Journal of Mass Media Ethics, 21*(1), 70–87.

Singer, D. G., Zuckerman, D. M. and Singer, J. L. (1980). Helping elementary school children learn about TV. *Journal of Communication, 30*(3), 84–93.

Steinberg, J. (2011, March 18). Your comments on SAT's reality show moment. The Choice. *New York Times.* Retrieved December 1, 2011 from http://thechoice.blogs.nytimes.com/2011/03/18/reality-sat-comments/

Tyner, K. (2004). Beyond boxes and wires: Literacy in transition. *Television and New Media, 4*(4), 371–88.

Webb, T., Martin, K., Afifi, A. and Kraus, J. (2010). Media literacy as a violence prevention strategy: A pilot evaluation. *Health Promotion Practice, 11*(5), 714–22.

Wilson, C., Grizzle, A., Tuazon, R., Akyempong, K. and Cheung, C. (2011). *Media and information literacy curriculum for educators.* UNESCO: Paris.

52

CHALLENGES AND SUGGESTIONS FOR DETERMINING QUALITY IN CHILDREN'S MEDIA

Alexis R. Lauricella, Michael B. Robb, and Ellen Wartella

Today, children of all ages consume large quantities of media content on a variety of platforms (Common Sense Media, 2011; Rideout et al., 2010). With media technologies ranging from televisions to mobile devices, our ability to determine what is "quality" media for young children has only become more challenging. Given the historical and current interest in evaluating and labeling quality children's media, this chapter seeks to address the positive and negative factors that should be examined and included when trying to understand what is meant by quality children's media.

Awards, ratings, and educational content

Historically, awards have been a popular way of determining quality media for children. Awards for children's media focus on excellence in production, entertainment, and storyline. The Emmys, The George Foster Peabody Awards, and the British Academy of Film and Television Arts Awards have evaluated media for a general audience since the mid 1900s, and include specific awards for quality children's programming. The Prix Jeunesse, Japan Prize, and Parents' Choice Awards focus on evaluating and honoring high quality children's media specifically (Japan Prize, n.d.; Kleeman, 2004; Parents' ChoiceAwards, n.d.; Prix Jeunesse, n.d.). While award programs may serve as a proxy for identifying "quality" media for children, their criteria for selection often vary, making it challenging to compare programs across award types.

An ongoing tension is whether quality is determined by the prevalence of positive content, an absence of negative content, or some combination of both. Many rating systems in the US, like those for movies (MPAA, n.d.), television (FCC, n.d.; 2003), and video games (ESRB, n.d.) work to warn parents about the potential harm in their media choices by indicating age restrictions and content descriptions (Gentile, 2008). A high-quality, educational movie or television program may contain "negative" content such as violence or inappropriate language, but the absence of objectionable content in a piece of media does not necessarily imply quality.

More recently, children's media, especially television programs, have been rated based on their educational content. In the 1990s the United States Congress passed the Children's Television

Act (Children's Television Act, 1990), which required commercial broadcasters to provide programming specifically for children. The goal was that the programming would be high-quality and educational (Glaubke et al., 2008). The FCC (Federal Communications Commission) later required that shows must: "have education as a significant purpose" and "be labeled as 'E/I' to identify the program to the public as educational/informational for children" (Glaubke et al., 2008). The federal regulation that children's programming be "educational" further enhanced the expectation that high-quality programming for children be educational.

Understanding quality television through research

Research studies are another approach to determining quality. In the late 1990s, researchers (Alexander et al., 1998) attempted to define "quality children's television" by examining the characteristics of programs awarded the George Foster Peabody Award. Through an analysis of these programs, the authors determined that most of the award-winning programs were educational (25 percent) or dramatic (28 percent), and very few were animated. They noted that the claims for quality have changed over the last 50 years of awards for children's programming and that industry leaders include production features and even humor in their definitions of quality, whereas the Children's Television Act focuses more on educational value to determine quality.

As part of an evaluation of the state of children's television programming in the United States, Jordan (1996) developed a "quality index," calculated by evaluating ten different program elements that either contribute to, or detract from, the quality of a program. Factors that contribute to quality include: having content that is understandable and appropriate for the target audience, providing an enriching pro-social lesson or theme that is clear and understandable, and making the lesson integral to the story and/or pervasive throughout the program. Factors that detract from quality include: verbal or physical violence, sex or sexual innuendo, gender, ethnic or racial stereotyping, "bad" language, and images of characters engaged in unsafe behaviors that were not contradicted in the narrative. Coders also rated the program as "negative," "neutral," or "positive" based on the level to which they would recommend that a child watch the program. The report indicated that preschool children in the US were well-served with quality media but that programming for 6- to 11-year-olds was of poorer quality overall with little educational value, and tended to be violent, stereotypical, and lacking diversity and production value (Jordan, 1996). A recent study examined the factors that children identify in quality television content (Plenk, 2009). Children identified the following as important factors: subject matter, title, authentic and relatable characters, entertainment value, and production techniques and style.

Determining quality children's media: child, content, context

Defining quality media has never been a simple task (Lemish, 2010; Mikos, 2009) and new media technologies make the task even harder. As shown above, there is not one set definition of quality children's media and no existing formula to determine what could be quality children's media for all age groups and platforms. Rather, it may be more appropriate to examine three separate but related factors that influence the quality of any media experience: the child, the content, and the context (for additional reading on this topic, see Guernsey, 2011).

First, the developmental abilities and age of the child are important for determining the quality of media. We know from television research that programs like *Sesame Street* are educational for preschool-aged children, and viewing is associated with a range of positive academic outcomes (Anderson et al., 2001; Kirkorian and Anderson, 2009); however, because of a range of cognitive limitations, children younger than two may not learn from the same programs in the same way (see Anderson and Pempek, 2005 for review). Depending on the age of the child watching, even well-established educational programs may vary in their educational value and perceived quality.

Beyond cognitive ability, other developmental abilities are crucial for the success of any children's media experience. Children must be able to manipulate and control the media technology in order to use it in a meaningful way. For example, multitouch technology is much easier for young children to control (Buckleitner, 2010) than more traditional computers that rely on a mouse or keyboard. If a toddler does not have the motor control to operate a computer mouse efficiently, it is difficult to make computer content that is of high quality for the child (Lauricella et al., 2009). However, the same content may be considered very high quality for elementary school-aged children who have mastered their mouse control skills (Donker and Reitsma, 2007).

A second major consideration is the content itself. It is well established that viewing violent television content is associated with a range of negative outcomes for children, including increased aggressive behavior, thoughts, and emotions (Anderson et al., 2003). Conversely, watching quality educational television programs with content that is developmentally appropriate has been associated with positive outcomes including better academic achievement (Fisch, 2004a), improved problem solving skills (Kirkorian and Anderson, 2009), and learning of prosocial lessons (Mares et al., 2009). Other features, such as interactivity, can also positively influence the quality of the media experience. Programs like *Dora the Explorer* simulate interaction, encouraging children to respond and directly interact with the television content, improving engagement and learning (Calvert et al., 2007). Newer digital media like computer games, video games, and mobile apps require interaction for the game to proceed, which has been shown to improve content learning (Calvert et al., 2007; Fisch, 2004b; Lauricella et al., 2010).

Third, even with age-appropriate, engaging, and impactful content, it is important to examine the context of media use to fully understand the quality of the experience, including the goals of the parent or user and the social or interactive nature of the engagement. Parents often have a range of goals for their children's media experiences. For example, a parent may want their child to develop literacy skills and might provide the child with a traditional story-book to read. Depending on the reading ability of the child, this parent may opt to jointly read the storybook with their child to enhance the child's learning and the quality of the media interaction. By contrast, if a parent is searching for a tool to keep a child busy while they get something done, a more interactive media experience, like a computer game that requires the child's interaction and response, may provide a higher quality experience since the computer or device can provide basic scaffolding and interaction for the child while the parent is busy.

Joint media engagement has been cited as a desirable quality when using media (Chiong, 2009; Lemish and Rice, 1986; Takeuchi and Stevens, 2011). Interactions between adult caregivers and young children during use of media products can help children process information that they might not otherwise understand. Caregivers may also scaffold children's learning by engaging in language-rich interactions around media experiences, and by extending and elaborating on information embedded in the media. Alternatively, joint play around certain media experiences with siblings or children of similar abilities may provide opportunities for children to practice self-regulation skills like turn-taking, tolerating frustration, impulse inhibiting, etc. (Zap and Code, 2009). Playing video games that do not offer traditional educational content or lessons may help to provide other benefits (Ritterfeld and Weber, 2009) like improved problem solving skills or opportunities to practice and develop social emotional or executive function skills like sharing, empathy, and inhibiting behavior.

Evaluating children's media

Challenges

There are several challenges in determining what is meant by quality in children's media today, rendering a definition of "quality" extremely difficult. First, digital technology use occurs across multiple platforms and is increasingly mobile. A glance at the major media platforms of the last century reveals the tremendous expansion of technology platforms available to consumers (Gutnick et al., 2011). Children are playing with iPads in the car, playing games on a computer at school, and watching DVDs in the backseat of minivans. Beyond the mobility and extension of the actual media technology devices, the contexts in which children are using media are constantly changing and thus influencing the quality of the experience. The quality of a piece of media is fundamentally affected by the environment and interaction occurring around the device. A quality e-book may be enhanced with parent interaction and scaffolding whereas playing a computer game with friends may be more influential for practicing and developing emotion regulation skills like turn-taking.

To complicate matters, the same or similar content is increasingly available across multiple platforms, changing the nature of a child's media experience. More specifically, a single media property can be a transmedia production, crossing multiple platforms and capitalizing on the unique affordances of each platform (Shuler, 2011), making an assessment of quality more challenging. For example, *Sid the Science Kid* is a television property developed to teach science skills to preschool-aged children, but it also encompasses an extensive website with games, videos, and print activities (PBS Kids, n.d.). Also, users can download *Sid the Science Kid* apps for smartphones and tablet computers. The characters and content span multiple platforms but there is variation in the types of engagement and accessibility of the material, making it very hard to universally determine whether *Sid the Science Kid* can be deemed "quality" across all platforms.

One of the most significant challenges in understanding quality media is a lack of scientific research, especially around newer media technologies. A range of platforms, programs, and content bases need to be explored in order to understand if the content presented on a new media platform, like a touchscreen computer, can be understood and manipulated appropriately by children in a way that results in a quality media experience. Identifying commonalities and differences across media may provide some guidance, even in the absence of substantial research (Fisch, 2004b). Extensive research on children's television programming has helped to provide television producers with production techniques and content tips that have been scientifically tested to promote learning and comprehension from television. Specifically, we know that young children struggle to follow basic film editing techniques like cuts, but they can comprehend zooms and pans (Smith et al., 1985). Other components of successful educational television include the importance of repetition (Barr et al., 2007; Crawley et al., 1999), familiarity with characters (Krcmar, 2010; Lauricella et al., 2011), and encouraging interaction between the on-screen character and the child at home, as in *Dora the Explorer* (Calvert et al., 2007). While television research may inform the development of interactive media, the lack of a systematic research base and rapid pace technological innovation makes it difficult to understand what production features will promote engaging and educational experiences for children at different developmental levels.

Approaches

Despite challenges, two formal approaches typify current efforts to understand what is meant by "quality" in children's media. In the United States, Common Sense Media has taken one approach: create a universal rating system for children's media. The goal of Common Sense Media[1] is to rate as many individual pieces of media as possible, based on age appropriateness, and with respect to several content categories (Common Sense Media, n.d.). Reviewers rate movies, games, apps, websites, television shows, books, and music on scales of educational value, ease of use, violence, sex, language, consumerism, drinking, drugs, and smoking, and privacy and safety. Reviewers also provide an overall rating on a five-point scale, and an assessment of whether the reviewers consider a piece of media to be age appropriate. For example, the mobile app *This is My Story (And I'm Sticking To It)* is designated as age appropriate for children as young as four years old, rates as four stars overall, and earns a top five-point score on educational value and ease of use, with a reviewer noting, "kids learn spelling, reading, and sentence structure through filling in the blanks on simple stories with labeled images."

An alternative approach to rating and examining every possible media experience is to establish principles or definitions that help adults better differentiate and choose media based on its quality. Kolucki and Lemish (2011) recently created a "resource pack" for UNICEF with goals of encouraging the production of quality communication with children and inspiring readers to seek out appropriate communication tools and approaches. Kolucki and Lemish (2011) provide four general principles to develop quality communications with children. First, communication must be age-appropriate and child-friendly. Second, communication should address the child holistically, meaning that communication must be balanced and address all of the child's developmental needs. Third, communication should be positive and strengths-based, that is, the communication should focus on the strengths rather than the deficits of each child and it should move them forward and help them experience new things. Finally, communication should address the needs and abilities of all children, even those who are the most disadvantaged. The expectation of this fourth principle is that children should be provided with experiences in which they can see people that are like themselves reflected in a positive light and also they should see positive portrayals of children who are different from them.

Similarly, the Fred Rogers Center[2] is engaged in creating a "Framework for Quality" to define and describe children's media. In 2011, the Fred Rogers Center held two round-tables, bringing together children and media researchers, digital media creators, and early childhood educators to discuss the concept of what is quality in digital media for children today. The goal of these round-tables has been to create a framework to define and describe quality children's media that is applicable to all media. Though currently in development, the Framework starts by considering the nature of children's development, including the interplay of social, emotional, and intellectual development, children's social and cultural contexts, and the importance of human relationships for supporting learning and development. The Framework intends to highlight the affordances of digital media products such as interactivity or depth of engagement that typify a quality product. The goal of the Framework is to provide adults with information that can be applied consistently across media as they select and assess the content and types of media engagement best suited for their children. A second goal is to describe properties that digital media professionals can apply to the design of content regardless of platform, genre, or purpose (Fred Rogers Center for Early Learning and Children's Media, 2011).

Conclusion

Understanding children's quality media is a complex but important task. Ratings, awards, and evaluating educational content can provide parents with resources to help inform their decisions about their children's media content. Examining the intersection between the age-appropriateness of material for the child, characteristics of content, and the social experiences of the context of use is another way in which quality can be examined. Although there is no simple definition for "quality children's media," efforts by groups such as Common Sense Media, UNICEF, and the Fred Rogers Center can inform parents, educators, and media creators about the pieces that are important to completing the quality children's media puzzle.

SEE ALSO in this volume chapter by Kolucki, chapter by Fisch, and chapter by von Feilitzen.

Notes

1 Common Sense Media is an advocacy group in the United States that provides age-based media reviews and information and education with a goal of helping families and educators make informed media choices. For more information, see www.commonsensemedia.org.
2 Established in 2003 under the leadership and guidance of Fred Rogers (of the United States television program, *Mister Rogers' Neighborhood*), the Fred Rogers Center for Early Learning and Children's Media is an international resource for addressing issues affecting young children, birth to age five. The Fred Rogers Center seeks to advance the fields of early learning and children's media by acting as a catalyst for communication, collaboration, and creative change. For more information on the Center, and the Quality Framework Initiative, see www.fredrogerscenter.org.

References

Alexander, A., Hoerrner, K. and Duke, L. (1998). What is quality children's television? *Annals of the American Academy of Political and Social Science*, *557*(1), 70–82.

Anderson, C. A., Berkoqitz, L., Donnerstein, E., Huesmann, R., Johnson, J. D., Linz, D., Malamuth, N. M. and Wartella, E. (2003). The influence of media violence on youth. *American Psychological Society*, *4*(3), 81–110.

Anderson, D. R. and Pempek, T. (2005). TV and very young children. *The American Behavioral Scientist*, *48* (5), 505–22.

Anderson, D. R., Huston, A. C., Schmitt, K. L., Linebarger, D. L. and Wright, J. C. (2001). Early childhood television viewing and adolescent behavior: The recontact study. *Monographs of the Society for Research in Child Development*, *66*(1), p.i–vii+1–154.

Barr, R., Muentener, P., Garcia, A., Fujimoto, M. and Chavez, V. (2007). The effect of repetition on imitation from television during infancy. *Developmental Psychobiology*, *49*(2), 196–207.

Buckleitner, W. (November, 2010). A taxonomy of multi-touch interaction styles, by stage. *Children's Technology Review*, *18*(11), 10–11.

Calvert, S. L., Strong, B. L., Jacobs, E. L. and Conger, E. E. (2007). Interaction and participation for young Hispanic and Caucasian girls' and boys' learning of media content. *Media Psychology*, *9*(2), 431–45.

Children's Television Act (CTA) (1990). Publ. L. No. 101–437, 104 Stat. 996–1000 codified at 47 USC Sections 303a, 303b, 394.

Chiong, C. (2009). *Can Video Games Promote Intergenerational Play & Literacy Learning?* New York, NY: The Joan Ganz Cooney Center at Sesame Workshop.

Common Sense Media (2011). Zero to eight: Children's media use in America. A Common Sense Media Research Study. Available at http://cdn2-www.ec.commonsensemedia.org/sites/default/files/research/zerotoeightfinal2011.pdf

Common Sense Media. (n.d.). Behind the Common Sense Media ratings system. *Common Sense Media*. Retrieved November 15, 2011, from http://www.commonsensemedia.org/about-us/our-mission/about-our-ratings

Crawley, A. M., Anderson, D. R., Wilder, A., Williams, M. and Santomero, A. (1999). Effects of repeated exposures to a single episode of the television program *Blue's Clues* on the viewing behaviors and comprehension of preschool children. *Journal of Educational Psychology*, *91*(4), 630–37.

Donker, A. and Reitsma, P. (2007). Young children's ability to use a computer mouse. *Computers & Education*, *48*(1), 602, 617.

ESRB (Entertainment Software Review Board) (n.d.). Entertainment Software Review Board Game Ratings & Decipher Guide. Retrieved from http://www.esrb.org/ratings/ratings_guide.jsp on November 29, 2011.

FCC (Federal Communications Commission) (2003). In the matter of children's television obligations of digital television broadcasters: Notice of proposed rule making. FCC MM Docket No. 00–167.

FCC (Federal Communications Commission Website) (n.d.). Federal Comunications Commission Guidelines Website. Retrieved from http://transition.fcc.gov/vchip/#guidelines on November 29, 2011.

Fisch, S. M. (2004a). *Children's learning from educational television: Sesame Street and beyond*. Mahwah, NJ: Lawrence Erlbaum.

——(2004b). Characteristics of effective materials for informal education: A cross-media comparison of television, magazines, and interactive media. In M. Rabinowitz, F. C. Blumberg and H. Everson (Eds), *The design of instruction and evaluation: Affordances of using media and technology*. Mahwah, NJ: Lawrence Erlbaum.

Fred Rogers Center for Early Learning and Children's Media (2011). *A Statement on the Development of a Framework for Quality Digital Media for Young Children*. Latrobe, PA: Saint Vincent College.

Gentile, D. A. (2008). The rating systems for media products. In S. L. Calvert and B. J. Wilson (Eds) *Handbook of children, media, and development*. Malden, MA: Blackwell, pp. 527–51.

Glaubke, C. R., Wilson, B. J. and Kunkel, D. (2008). Educationally/Insufficient? An Analysis of the Availability & Educational Quality of Children's E/I Programming. Oakland, CA: ChildrenNow.

Guernsey, L. (2011, October 25). Screen time young kids and literacy: New data begs questions. *Huffington Post*. Retrieved from http://www.huffingtonpost.com/lisa-guernsey/kids-media-consumption_b_1029945.html

Gutnick, A. L., Robb, M., Takeuchi, L. and Kotler, J. (2011). *Always connected: The new digital media habits of young children*. New York, NY: The Joan Ganz Cooney Center at Sesame Workshop.

Japan Prize (n.d.). Japan Prize 2011: International Contest for Educational Media. Retrieved from http://www.nhk.or.jp/jp-prize/english/index.html on November 1, 2011.

Jordan, A. B. (1996). The state of children's television: An examination of quantity, quality, and industry beliefs. *The Annenberg Public Policy Center Report Series*. Philadelphia, PA: University of Pennsylvania.

Kirkorian, H. L. and Anderson, D. R. (2009). In S. L. Calvert and B. J. Wilson (Eds) *Handbook of Children, Media, and Development*. Oxford, UK: Blackwell, pp. 268–89.

Kleeman, D. W. (2004). PRIX JEUNESSE as a force for cultural diversity. In D. G. Singer and J. L. Singer (Eds) *Handbook of children and media*. Thousand Oaks, CA: Sage, pp. 521–31.

Kolucki, B. and Lemish, D. (2011). Communicating with children: Principles and practices to nurture, inspire, excite, educate and heal. Perseus. Retrieved fromhttp://www.unicef.org/cbsc/files/CwC_Web(2).pdf

Krcmar, M. (2010). Can social meaningfulness and repeat exposure help infants and toddlers overcome the video deficit? *Media Psychology*, *13*(1), 31–53.

Lauricella, A. R., Barr, R. F. and Calvert, S. L. (2009). Emerging computer skills: influences of young children's executive functioning abilities and parental scaffolding techniques in the US. *Journal of Children and Media*, *3*(3), 217–33.

Lauricella, A. R., Gola, A. A. H. and Calvert, S. (2011). Toddlers' learning from socially meaningful video characters. *Media Psychology*, *14*(2), 216–32.

Lauricella, A. R., Pempek, T. A., Barr, R. and Calvert, S. L. (2010). Contingent computer interactions for young children's object retrieval success. *Journal of Applied Developmental Psychology*, *31*(5), 362–69.

Lemish, D. (2010). *Screening gender on children's television: The views of producers around the world*. New York and Abingdon: Routledge.

Lemish, D. and Rice, M. (1986). Television as a talking picture book: a prop for language acquisition. *Journal of Child Language*, *13*(2), 251–74.

Mares, M-L., Palmer, E. and Sullivan, T. (2009). In S. L. Calvert and B. J. Wilson (Eds), *Handbook of Children, Media, and Development*. Oxford, UK: Blackwell, pp. 268–89.

Mikos, L. (2009). Quality is a matter of perspective: Thoughts on how to define quality in children's television. *Televizion*, *22/2009/E*, 4–6.

MPAA (Motion Picture Association of America) (n.d.). Motion Picture Association of America: What each rating means webpage. Retrieved from http://www.mpaa.org/ratings/what-each-rating-means

Parents' Choice Awards (n.d.). Parents' Choice Awards Website. Retrieved from http://www.parents-choice.org/aboutawards.cfm on November 30, 2011.

PBS Kids (n.d.). Sid the Science Kid. Retrieved from http://pbskids.org/sid/ on November 1, 2011.

Peabody Awards (n.d.). Peabody Awards Overview & History. Retrieved from http://www.peabody.uga.edu/overview_history/index.php on November 1, 2011.

Plenk, A. (2009). "I think it's very good because ... " Children's perspectives on quality in film and television. *Televizion*, *22/2009/E*, 21–25.

Prix Jeunesse (n.d.). Prix Jeunesse International. Retrieved from http://www.prixjeunesse.de/ on February 13, 2012.

Rideout, V. J., Foehr, U. G. and Roberts, D. F. (2010). Generation M^2: Media in the lives of 8-to 18-year olds. Menlo Park, CA: Henry J. Kaiser Family Foundation.

Ritterfeld, U. and Weber, R. (2009). Video games for entertainment and education. In P. Vorderer and J. Bryant (Eds), *Playing video games: motives, responses, and consequences.* E-library: Taylor & Francis, pp. 471–90.

Shuler, C. (2011, April 27). De-Buzzifying a Buzz Word. *Cooney Center Blog.* Retrieved November 15, 2011, from http://www.joanganzcooneycenter.org/Cooney-Center-Blog-144.html

Smith, R., Anderson, D. R. and Fischer, C. (1985). Young children's comprehension of montage. *Child Development, 56*(4), 962–71.

Takeuchi, L. and Stevens, R. (2011). *The new coviewing: Designing for learning through joint media engagement.* New York, NY: The Joan Ganz Cooney Center at Sesame Workshop.

Zap, N. and Code, J. (2009). Self-regulated learning in video game environment. In R. E. Ferdig (Ed.) *Handbook of research on effective electronic gaming in education.* Hershey, PA: Information Science Reference, pp. 738–57.

53

UNICEF AND COMMUNICATION FOR DEVELOPMENT

An integrated approach to developing capacity to produce communication for and with children

Barbara Kolucki

Introduction to UNICEF

UNICEF is the acronym for the United Nations Children's Fund, established in 1946 to provide food, clothing and health care to children who were facing famine and disease in, primarily, post-World War II Europe.[1] Its mandate was expanded in 1950 to address the needs of children and women in developing countries. It is unique among UN organizations in its partnerships with governments and grassroots organizations, forged to promote, protect and help realize the rights of children worldwide. UNICEF works to uphold the Convention on the Rights of the Child (CRC) as well as other UN Conventions, such as those supporting Women and Persons with Disabilities.[2] The current organizational priorities include: child survival and development; basic education and gender equity; HIV/AIDS and children; child protection; and policy advocacy and partnerships for children.

A brief overview of communication in UNICEF

In the 1950s and 1960s, UNICEF's corporate communication efforts centered on establishing a brand for the organization, which had a dual mission of building infrastructure and reaching mothers and children with supplies. Mass campaigns addressed disease eradication using Information, Education and Communication materials. During the next two decades, under the rubric of the Children Survival and Development Revolution, emphasis shifted to several primary health care measures. Social marketing techniques, which utilize commercial marketing methods to promote social issues, were developed to inform and mobilize communities to take actions that would prevent death, disease and illness among children under 5. In the 1990s, with the signing of the UN Convention on the Rights of the Child and the first World Summit for Children, special advocacy and media projects were developed, and children started being considered among the target audiences of the new communication efforts. Also by that time, communication for development, focused on using communication channels of many types, was being used to encourage participation and support community empowerment with a view to achieving behavior and social change. For example, one landmark project, the *Meena Animation Series*, was launched in South Asia to promote gender equity and child rights for young girls. A similar project for girls aged 13–15 years, the *Sara Communication Initiative*, was launched in Africa.

This era initiated a number of media initiatives aimed at promoting children's rights and, more recently, expanded to include children and youth themselves in the process of media production, including:

- Voices of Youth (VOY) – an online network connecting children from around the globe, informing them about their rights and providing a forum for interaction. Although UNICEF continues to focus on reaching the most marginalized children and youth who oftentimes have little or no access to electronic media, it simultaneously keeps pace with the growing social media trends and utilizes mobile phones, YouTube, Facebook, MySpace, Twitter, Flickr and Scribd.
- Media Activities and Good Ideas by, with and for Children (MAGIC) – an email group for professionals and organizations working in the field of media and children. It is designed to identify resources and good practice as well as providing a searchable online database.
- One Minute Juniors Project – a video initiative where youth from around the world produce a 60 second spot addressing an important personal, national or global issue.

Strategic shifts in communication approaches and processes[3]

From 2000 onwards, communication efforts were revitalized in an effort to change existing attitudes and behaviors with regard to health, nutrition, hygiene, education and protection issues such as child immunization, polio eradication, hand washing, child marriage and many others. The outbreak of the "Avian Flu" pandemic in 2005 provided a global opportunity to expand the focus of communication activities beyond the promotion of positive and measurable behavior change, and explore issues of actively engaging families and communities to drive broader social change. As a result, over the last several years, UNICEF has expanded its earlier communication work under the title "Communication for Development" (C4D) to include initiatives "in which people come together as equals and dialogue – so that all children, families and communities have access to the information, skills, technologies and processes they need to generate solutions; are empowered to make informed choices, reach their full potential; and participate meaningfully in decisions affecting their lives and realize their rights."[4]

The field of C4D encompasses several shifts in approaches to development work (Gill, 2009). Instead of a one-way transmission of messages, it focuses on dialogue and engagement; instead of a beneficiary driven approach, it focuses on a human rights approach. Expert-driven solutions are replaced with community-driven solutions. And rather than communicating solely with adults, it focuses on communication with children and adults as agents of social change.

UNICEF's new and expanded focus on communication for and with children

From the historical summary above, one can see that UNICEF has a great deal of experience in communicating *about* children. Over the years, it also experimented with projects where children were used to pass on a message, using what is called the "Child-to-Child" approach.[5] A key component of the new C4D approach is the recognition that children can be powerful agents of change and transformation, regardless of who they are, where they live or the difficulties they face.

Several articles in the CRC underscore the communication rights of children to be heard, to express themselves and to have communication be accessible and supportive of their cultural context. UNICEF's C4D approach provides a platform for the expression of these rights: children's voices, needs, interests and opinions are valued, nurtured and brought to the fore.

Until recently, the communication priorities of most development agencies have been focused on the survival, health and nutrition needs of children, and to a lesser extent, on promoting basic education and developing school-readiness skills. What has been neglected and only recently expanded is a more holistic approach to child development. Whether living in conditions of material poverty, in conflict or emergency situations, with abuse or trauma, or with gender or disability discrimination, the emotional and spiritual needs of children are increasingly being seen as critical to their survival and optimal development.

Developing communication that gives children more than a "single story"

Nigerian author Chimamanda Adichie talks about the critical importance of having more than a single story of who and what we are or should be.[6] For children in the developing "majority" world, the images and communication they receive can often be divided into two categories. The first is an imported image projecting a view that is primarily white, middle or upper class, and often stereotypical with regard to the presentation of gender, ethnicity and ability. Whether in cartoons, films or books, this imagery is a reflection of children and communities that, for the most part, do not look like or live lives like the majority. The other commonly communicated image is one that seems integral to the development or fund-raising fields: an image of poverty, where the most disadvantaged children are presented as victims in need of help.

If we believe that media reflect who and what are valued in society, what do these images tell children? Some would surely conclude: "*I am not reflected at all.*" Or, "*When I do see myself, I am disempowered, disadvantaged and in need of help.*" These responses suggest isolation, self-doubt, and self-devaluation – polar opposites of the confidence and spirit needed for personal and social empowerment and transformation.

Providing all children developmentally and culturally appropriate communication that is positive and inclusive, changes the "single story" to one that reflects the diversity, potential, and resilience of children and their families around the world. This is the human rights principle that serves as the basis of C4D's focus on communicating for, about and with children.[7]

Building national capacity in communicating with children

Over the last 25 years, a model of communication for children has been built. Since the 1980s, "master classes" have taken place in over 20 countries with the support of the local UNICEF office. These workshops focus on:

- Identifying and nurturing indigenous creative talent to produce communication for and with children. Rather than adapting products or messages from another part of the world, local producers know local context and needs and can truly reflect their culture.
- Bringing participants from all sectors together, often for the first time. Representatives from health, education, child protection and the creative media attest to the value added when this holistic and intersectoral approach is used in production.
- Adding to the global resources and expertise in the field of developing communication for and with children on sensitive topics and including the most marginalized children.

Communication that reaches and empowers children on sensitive topics

What are some of the topics addressed at these workshops? Each country has specific priorities based on local realities. Some countries have children and families living with conflict. Others have experienced natural disasters and emergencies. And all countries need to engage children on topics such as tolerance and conflict resolution; living with or being affected by HIV/AIDS; illness and death; inclusion of children and adults with disability; and dealing with trauma and abuse. In most instances, little if any communication for and with children has been produced on these topics. Of those produced, most materials on these topics reflect adult views of children's needs, or are not appropriate for the youngest children.

The process – as well as outcomes of capacity building

Capacity building in developing communication for and with children includes several components. These often include high level advocacy with Ministers and managers of broadcasting and publishing houses, demonstrating through practice how communicating with children fits into the overarching communication for development needs in a country.

These capacity building workshops are meant to be a model for future communication processes and productions. One priority is that communication should address the critical needs of and involve children and adults who are most vulnerable and marginalized. Many children in the countries where UNICEF works live with hardships difficult for many to imagine. It is critically important that their voices are heard, that their humanity is validated and that their creativity and resilience enrich the workshop process and productions. This means that youth, people with a range of disabilities, those living with HIV/AIDS and from ethnic and other minority groups participate in every aspect of the training.

Participants learn about some of the latest research in the field of child development in general and "sensitive topics" in particular. They learn how to translate this research into simple, practical and creative communication. The developmental stages of different age groups of children are reviewed along with communication implications.

Participants evaluate dozens of communication products on these topics and discuss relevance to the local culture. In a typical week-long workshop, an astounding number of draft productions are on display. They often include several children's books, posters, television live-action spots, short pieces of animation and radio.

Children's participation comes in many forms. Youth are part of the workshop itself. Younger children often contribute ideas for production, along with their voices and non-professional acting talent. After the workshop, pretesting of all prototypes takes place with children.

Specific communication examples from UNICEF country offices

Capacity building workshops have been held in several countries in Asia, Africa, Central and Eastern Europe and the Pacific. What follows is a summary of the uniqueness and outcomes in a few of the countries where UNICEF's expanded approach to developing communication for and with children on a range of sensitive topics has been successful:

Myanmar

Myanmar experienced the Asian tsunami in 2004 and Cyclone Nargis in 2008, both of which were devastating disasters. The first of a series of media production and Training of Trainers (TOT) workshops was held soon after the tsunami. Participants voiced concern about not only the survival but the psycho-social needs of children affected. Many were displaced, had lost family members and, understandably, were afraid of water. The workshop considered how to validate and incorporate children's fears, whether of water, going to the doctor, or new experiences. A range of media was produced, including low-literacy books for infants and preschool children, along with a series of animation spots for young children. The communication was gender-progressive, disability inclusive, and incorporated ethnic and economic diversity. The TOT used and built upon these materials, expanding the holistic early childhood approach throughout the country.

The books were so popular with all age groups that the government ministries, early childhood NGOs and UNICEF produced a "box library" as part of a "Let's Read Initiative." This was sent to pre-schools and primary schools throughout the country as well as to hospitals, orphanages and day-care centers. Over 35,000 classrooms have been reached, impacting an estimated 1,400,000 children, while more than 280,000 children have benefited from NGO distribution of the books in six ethnic languages.[8]

South Africa

Poverty and HIV/AIDS are just two critical issues facing children in South Africa. In 2003, the UNICEF country office requested workshops to address the holistic needs of orphans and vulnerable children, emphasizing the psycho-social needs of children infected and affected by HIV/AIDS.

As in many countries, children in South Africa were exposed to little or no media addressing this sensitive topic. The impact of stress and trauma on young children was often underestimated and issues relating to illness and death were not openly discussed with them. Similarly, communication relating to stigma and discrimination was rare.

The workshops were unique in two ways. Some of the first media for young children addressing loss related to death were developed, requiring a review of what kinds of messages are developmentally appropriate and culturally relevant for very young children. Second, the combined experiences of the disability movement around the world were used as positive examples in the process of developing media that addressed prejudice and inclusion. Examples of communication about and with children and adults with disabilities were shown as role models of innovation, adaptation and resilience. This approach was used as a positive example for communication related to HIV/AIDS.

Kyrgyzstan

In 2005, an animated preschool educational TV series was developed called *The Magic Journey*. The initial overarching goal was to further the developmental needs of young children in the hopes of providing school-preparedness skills. It was based on children's books in the Kyrgyz language featuring a local girl, Akylai, and boy, Aktan, learning through stories, rhymes and play. The series was produced by the Kyrgyz National Broadcasting Company with leadership from the local UNICEF country office and support from the Soros Foundation, the Aga Khan Foundation and the Asian Development Bank. In one short year, the series became the most watched TV program on the local channel.

The UNICEF Representative requested that the series be analyzed in terms of developmental appropriateness and quality. Subsequent workshops recommended the incorporation of:

- more interactivity and entertainment as opposed to didactic presentations;
- using supportive, encouraging adults as opposed to adults who provided lessons and answers to children;
- integration of local children's ideas and live-action spots together with animation;
- explicit and implicit ethnic and disability inclusion compared to very little diversity;

- expanded and gender-progressive roles compared with previous more typical gender portrayals;
- songs and children's voices compared with no songs and primarily adult voice-overs.

An evaluation of the series was conducted by the Centre for Effective Education, Queen's University, Belfast, which included a large scale national survey to elicit interviews indicating qualitative and quantitative responses. The evaluation showed that the series was highly successful in reaching the target audience, with 60 percent of all Kyrgyz children viewing the program daily. Many of the key messages recognized and remembered reflected the educational goals identified by the production team. Children responded very well to the singing and musical segments, and rated the new character using a wheelchair as the third most popular character, after the two main characters, Akylai and Aktan (Eakin and Connolly, 2011).

Fiji/Pacific Islands

This is a multi-country program office, with the most disadvantaged families generally located in remote rural areas and outer islands. High levels of violence and abuse toward children, high transmission rate of the HIV virus, natural disasters and climate change are among critical issues.[9]

The 2010 workshop included representatives from Fiji, Vanuatu, the Solomon Islands and Kiribati. Capacity building focused on HIV/AIDS, sanitation and hygiene and how communication can meets specific needs and be inclusive, gender-progressive.

Several adolescents and adults from the Fiji Association of the Deaf as well as individuals with visual impairment joined others with a common interest in learning how to excel in producing communication for and with children and youth.

The workshop began with some trepidation, as most participants had never met or spoken with so many individuals who have disabilities. When these creative people shared their life stories, taught a bit of sign language and contributed ideas for productions, the results were unique as well as exciting. Books, posters, radio and TV spots on a range of topics were either "signed" or used captioning, and featured deaf and hearing impaired non-actors along with those who were non-disabled.

UNICEF's resource package on communicating with children

UNICEF's Communication for Development (C4D) Unit commissioned a resource package entitled "*Communicating with Children: Principles and Practices to Nurture, Inspire, Excite and Heal*" (Kolucki and Lemish, 2011).The objective was to build upon the pioneering work done around the world, and develop simple, practical guidelines and principles for the production of holistic, inclusive, developmentally and culturally appropriate communication.

The product is a web-based and print resource package with the following components:

- a review of why and how to communicate directly with children in diverse environments with varied degrees of media access;
- an overview of the positive and negative influences of media with emphasis on the positive potential, especially for children in the majority world;
- a mapping of different developmental stages, characteristics and needs of early years, middle years and early adolescent years, with implications for communication for each age group;
- four central principles supported by guidelines for each, which can serve as a "checklist" for producing and evaluating communication for and with children;
- a list of how to avoid common pitfalls in developing communication for children;
- over 70 international examples of positive practice, references and resources that apply the suggested principles and guidelines. These can be summarized in Box 53.1 (see also Lemish and Kolucki, 2013).

Box 53.1 Principles and guidelines of quality communication for children

Principle 1: Communication for children should be age-appropriate and child-friendly

1a   Use child-appropriate language, characters, stories, music and humor
1b   Encourage and model positive interaction and critical thinking
1c   Use special effects judiciously and wisely

Principle 2: Communication for children should address the child holistically

2a   Use an integrated rather than single issue approach to communication
2b   Offer positive models for adults in their relationships with children as full human beings
2c   Create "safe havens"

Principle 3: Communication for children should be positive and strengths-based

3a   Build self-confidence as well as competence
3b   Use positive modeling
3c   Include children as active citizens learning about and modeling social justice and mobilization
3d   Do no harm

Principle 4: Communication for children should address the needs of all, including those who are most disadvantaged

4a   Reflect the dignity of each and every child and adult
4b   Be inclusive: celebrate and value all types of diversity
4c   Ensure communication is free of stereotypes
4d   Reflect and nurture the positive aspects of indigenous cultures and traditions

Some examples of good practice communication

Although several examples from well-known international production houses are included in the Resource Package, the majority are those produced in UNICEF-supported countries. In addition to being locally produced, most are low-budget, address topics specific to the work of UNICEF, with emphasis on meeting the holistic needs of the most marginalized children. Examples that follow the principles and guidelines presented in the Resource Package include:

- *Maldivian Babies:* a children's book featuring a diverse group of children who are healthy, curious, beautiful and confident. In contrast to the more typical examples of such publications, the book includes a premature newborn, various children with disabilities and dark-skinned children, among others
- *Medine:* a book from Turkmenistan about a young girl visiting her grandparents. Together, in a child-appropriate and friendly way, they make their home and surroundings "mosquito and malaria free"

- *Deaf People Can Do Everything but Hear!* TV spots from China portraying children (and adults) who are deaf but who express and have the same desires, dreams and talents as all children
- *One, Two, Three, Four:* an animation spot from Myanmar portraying a nurturing father using daily activities to teach his daughter about nutrition and early learning.

Lessons learned and recommendations for the future

Children are powerful agents of change! They can pass on messages about health but more importantly share their strengths, be models of positive deviance and help touch the hearts and souls of children like themselves.

In order for this to happen, people in every part of the world need to see the value of and learn how to produce communication for and with children that is developmentally and culturally appropriate as well as child-friendly. Even if we are talking about life-threatening or serious issues, it is incumbent upon us to find ways to sensitively develop communication that addresses and responds to these needs. A child living in the most difficult circumstances has the same rights, needs and desires to be entertained, inspired, nurtured and empowered. And every country, regardless of circumstances, has the creative potential to produce exemplary communication that responds to these needs.

What has been done thus far is positive but simply not enough, both in terms of quality and quantity. There are many places on earth where children still have never held a child's book, seen themselves represented positively on television or had an opportunity to express their feelings, opinions and solutions. Yet in reality, many of these individuals, whether disabled, minorities or living in emergencies, have proven to be extremely creative, resilient and competent communicators. It is they who have much to teach us through their participation as active agents of social change.

SEE ALSO in this volume chapter by Lauricella, Robb and Wartella, and chapter by Stuart and Mitchell.

Acknowledgements

The author is particularly grateful to Rina Gill, former Associate Director, Policy and Practice, UNICEF, for sharing perspectives on international development, and for permission to use several of her recent presentations and ideas, especially in sections introducing UNICEF and Communication for Development. Deepest appreciation to Dafna Lemish, co-author of the "Communicating with Children" resource package. Special thanks to Barbara Duncan for her editorial assistance in this project and close collaborative work over three decades. And to UNICEF Staff in New York and around the world – your creativity and wisdom have inspired millions and added tremendous value to my work and life.

Notes

1 See http://www.unicef.org
2 See http://www.un.org/womenwatch/daw/cedaw/, http://www.un.org/disabilities/convention/conventionfull.shtml
3 Personal correspondence and conversations with Ms. Rina Gill, UNICEF, New York, along with review of recent presentations.
4 See http://www.unicef.org/cbsc/index.html
5 See http://www.child-to-child.org/about/approach.html
6 See http://www.ted.com/talks/chimamanda_adichie_the_danger_of_a_single_story.html

7 See also Gill, R. (2011) Keynote presentation, Una Biennial Conference, 12–14 May, Amsterdam. Available at: http://www.unaglobal.org/en/page/about_resources

8 Personal correspondence with Niki Abrishamian and Khin Saw Nyunt of UNICEF-Myanmar

9 See http://www.prixjeunesse.de/themen/newsletter/archive/pdf/2010_2.pdf

References

Eakin, A. and Connolly, P. (2011). *A formative evaluation of the animated children's television series Magic Journey, Kyrgyzstan, Belfast.* Centre for Effective Education, Queen's University, Belfast.

Gill, R (2009). Communication for development: Strategic shifts. Presentation made to the Global C4D Network Meeting, 17–21 May, Cairo, Egypt.

Kolucki, B. and Lemish, D. (2011) *Communicating with children: Principles and practices to nurture, inspire, excite, educate and heal.* NY: Communication for Development Unit, UNICEF. See http://www.unicef.org/cwc

Lemish, D. and Kolucki, B. (2013). Media and early childhood development. In P. Britto, P. Engle, C. Super and N. Ulkuer (Eds), *Early childhood development (ECD) and evidence for policy.* Society for Research in Child Development (SRCD) and UNICEF, pp. 329–47.

54

INTERNATIONAL INITIATIVES CONCERNING CHILDREN AND MEDIA

Networks, associations, organisations, institutions, forums ...

Cecilia von Feilitzen

This chapter gives a few glimpses of existing international and world regional initiatives outside the single media themselves – networks, associations, organisations, institutions, forums, etc. – devoted to children and media. Some initiatives are long-standing. During the past two decades, however, the increasing flow of satellite TV, formatted series, computerised games, the internet, social media, smart phones, new forms of advertising/consumption – and the consecutive awareness of these media's possibilities and risks – has also given rise to more recent initiatives, which in the main aim at defending children's interests that the media often ignore. A vital support for many initiatives is the UN Convention on the Rights of the Child (UN CRC) from 1989, valid for the third of the world's population who are children (under 18 years of age).

The chapter makes no claims to be an exhaustive account. More tips are available at *The International Clearinghouse on Children, Youth and Media*, at Nordicom (2012). It is also important to bear in mind that many more children and media initiatives are of a national/local than international character.

The international initiatives are highly different. For example, are they focusing on "children" and their relations to the media – or on "media" for children? Are they focusing on "children and media" – or is children and media part of a wider engagement, such as children's rights, health issues, communication for social change, or areas relevant to both children and adults? Is the initiative focusing on protection from harmful media content – or rather on supporting children's media literacy? And which is the form of the initiative: an NGO/voluntary/civil/activist one, a public/intergovernmental/UN agency one, a professional media one, a business/private one, a research/information one, or a network of several initiatives?

Promoting quality media for children

Several international initiatives work for quality in children's media: one is the non–profit *International Board on Books for Young People* (IBBY, 2012), founded in 1953. Its mission, manifested through biennial world congresses and other activities, is "to promote international understanding through children's books", "to give children everywhere the opportunity to have access to books with high literary and artistic standards" and "to encourage the publication and distribution of quality children's books, especially in developing countries".

Almost as old as IBBY is the *International Centre of Films for Children and Youth* (Centre international du film pour l'enfance et la jeunesse, CIFEJ, 2012), an independent forum and network founded under the auspices of UNESCO in 1955. Its aim is "to promote excellence in the production of culturally diverse, entertaining, artistic, educational and informative audio-visual media especially designed for children and young people". CIFEJ awards prizes for the best films and supplies information about all world regional and national festivals for children's films. It also administrates the international Kids for Kids Festival, presenting films made by children for children.

Regarding television, the *PRIX JEUNESSE Foundation* (2012) was established in 1964 by the State of Bavaria in Germany, the City of Munich and Bayerischer Rundfunk (Bavarian Broadcasting Corporation).

> The aim of the [...] Foundation is to promote quality in television for the young worldwide. It wants to bring forward television that enables children to see, hear and express themselves and their culture, and that enhances an awareness and appreciation of other cultures.

One main activity of the Foundation is a bi-annual festival, PRIX JEUNESSE International, which awards prizes to the world's best children's and young people's TV programmes. It also has training activities and workshops for producers of child programmes all over the world and facilitates the exchange of children's programmes between countries and channels. The Foundation has partners and projects in all continents, such as *European Broadcasting Union* (EBU), the *Goethe Institute, Deutsche Welle Academy, American Center for Children and Media, Canadian Youth Media Alliance, Midiativa* in Brazil, *Latin American Alliance* (ALA), *Asia-Pacific Broadcasting Union* (ABU), *Asia-Pacific Institute for Broadcasting Development* (AIBD), *Africa Union of Broadcasting* (AUB) Item Exchange, and *Arab States Broadcasting Union* (ASBU). During the 2000s, PRIX JEUNESSE Iberoamericano festivals were initiated in Latin America, inspired by PRIX JEUNESSE International.

Nowadays, most initiatives related to media for children – and children and media – are also online. Apart from the initiatives mentioned in this chapter, there is an abundance of internet initiatives such as websites, communities and social media addressed to children of different ages, which because of linguistic barriers are mostly national ones. Internationally, however, there are (besides Facebook, YouTube, and the like) some school nets, where especially teachers but also pupils may collaborate in projects, visually and at times in a multilingual dialogue (e.g., European Schoolnet, EUN, 2012; GlobalSchoolNet, GSN, 2012).

The rapid development of information and communication technologies (ICTs) is reflected in the independent, not-for-profit initiative *World Summit on Media for Children Foundation* (2012). Its Summits are attended by "key local and global players [... when it comes to] media on all platforms for children and young people. They are also attended by government representatives, NGOs, educators, researchers and business people". The first two World Summits in Melbourne, Australia 1995 and London, UK 1998 were on Television and Children and Television for Children respectively. After the Summits in Thessalonica, Greece 2001, Rio de Janeiro, Brazil 2004, and Johannesburg, South Africa 2007, the latest one in Karlstad, Sweden 2010 was on Media for Children and Youth. Thus, starting from the fact that children's TV programming is threatened in many parts of the world, the 2010 Summit also underlined the importance of high-quality educational digital media for children.

The next World Summit is planned for Kuala Lumpur, Malaysia in 2014. Regional Summits and similar forums have also been arranged in, e.g., Manila, The Philippines 1996, Accra, Ghana 1997, and Toronto, Canada 2000. The African Summits have accentuated the role of radio, which is the dominating medium in large rural areas of the world. Important to mention is that young people, as well, have been invited to the Summits to put forward their own conclusions.

Representing children in the media

Initiatives promoting quality in children's media are, naturally, careful about how children are portrayed in them. But how are children and young people represented in other content? Research shows repeatedly that children are under-represented and stereotyped in such content – and in the news overwhelmingly as victims or perpetrators.

Some initiatives, not having children as their main focus, have commented on this. The *International Federation of Journalists* (IFJ, 2012), aiming to promote "human rights, democracy and pluralism" and defend "press freedom and social justice", has – after several conferences and workshops – adopted IFJ's *Guidelines and Principles for Reporting on Issues Involving Children* at its Annual Congress in Seoul, South Korea, 2001.

Devised for UNICEF (United Nations Children's Fund) by the charity *MediaWise Trust* (2012), the booklet *The Media and Children's Rights: A resource for journalists by journalists* (latest edition 2010) considers "how the UN CRC might impact upon the way children are represented in and by the media".

> [the booklet's] purpose is to generate responsible coverage of children and the impact of adult behaviour and decisions on their lives, as well as to encourage media professionals to consider how best to protect the rights of children and help children to play a role in the mass media.

Also on UNICEF's (2012a, b) website are "Reporting guidelines to protect at-risk children" and *Communicating with Children* from 2011, a resource pack to assist persons communicating with children about their rights and ways to healthy development.

On a world regional level, *Media Monitoring Africa* (2012) launched "Editorial Guidelines and Principles on Reporting on Children in the Media" in 2011. "The guidelines were compiled with the input of children, journalists, editors and various practitioners for African media" and are accompanied by practical tips for media professionals.

It is not possible to summarise the different ethical guidelines here, but examples of such guidelines are: to ensure reporting that is in the best interests of the child; to promote children's rights, including their right of access to media and their right to express their own opinions; to respect children's dignity, privacy and well-being and protect them from harm; and to avoid stereotypes and sensational presentation in material involving children.

Another regional initiative is *Red ANDI* (ANDI Network, 2012), a Latin American network of civil society organisations established in the early 2000s, aiming at "contributing to the journalistic culture and its relationships to entities involved in sustainable development and human/child rights by successively monitoring and analysing the coverage of children's issues, and thereby the country's underlying social problems, primarily in the press". The network sprang out of the 1980s Brazilian not-for-profit independent organisation *ANDI* (Agência de Notícias dos Direitos da Infância, News Agency for Children's Rights, 2012), nowadays having three programmes of media for development: Children and Youth, Inclusion and Development and Communication Policies.

As well as having a long history of using newspapers in the classroom as a teaching tool (Newspaper in Education, NIE), the *World Association of Newspapers and News Publishers* (WAN-IFRA, 2012) also annually awards the World Young Reader Prizes "to innovative newspapers that have devised, in the judges' opinion, the best project or activity in the past 24 months in one or more of the main areas of young reader development". It can be a newspaper content strategy targeting the young, an activity that gives young people the chance to experience professional newspaper journalism, or a public service project in areas such as the environment, literacy, youth civic involvement, etc.

There are a few sources (mostly national research studies) revealing children's own views of the media's images of children. The findings hitherto are similar to reports from youth groups at the World Summits on Media for Children (see above) and conclusions from *Save the Children* (2012), based on talk with children and young people in different continents. Recurrent themes in children's viewpoints are that children want to be taken seriously and to be allowed to speak for themselves.

Regulative media measures

Governmental media regulations and media's self-regulations have mostly been of a national character. But in the increasingly complex, globalised and mediatised world, national media regulations are successively losing their strength and there is a growing trend of guidelines, recommendations, agreements, etc., on a world regional and international level. One aspect in the forefront is children's online safety.

The *Internet Governance Forum* (IGF, 2012) was initiated by the UN Secretary General after the World Summits on the Information Society (WISIS) in 2003 and 2005. The Forum brings together all kinds of stakeholders discussing internet governance. From 2007 onwards, children's online safety has also been on its agenda. Young people are invited to the Forum, as well.

ECPAT International (2012) "is a global network of organisations and individuals working together for the elimination of child prostitution, child pornography and the trafficking of children for sexual purposes" in which context ICTs are well-used platforms. ECPAT cooperates with governments, law enforcement authorities, the technology industry and other NGOs to combat such crimes.

A third example is the non-profit voluntary organisation *Childnet International* (2012), the mission of which "is to work in partnership with others around the world to help make the internet a great and safe place for children".

The activities of the European Commission (EC, 2012 a) can serve as a regional illustration. EC's Safer Internet Programmes 1999–2013 aim to contribute to awareness raising and fighting illegal internet content activities, as well as to cooperation and the exchange of experience and best practices, among other things, through:

- *International Association of Internet Hotlines* (INHOPE, 2012) coordinating a growing network of 41 internet hotlines in 36 countries.
- *Insafe*, a European network of Safer Internet Awareness Centres "promoting safe, responsible use of the internet and mobile devices to young people". *Insafe* also arranges *Safer Internet Day* (2012) which is celebrated in countries outside Europe, as well.
- *European Child Safety Online NGO Network* (eNASCO, 2012) consisting of non-governmental organisations with expertise on child net internet safety.
- *Forum Europe* (2012) bringing together in Child Safety Online Conferences "representatives from all the key stakeholders for a full and frank discussion on existing and future measures undertaken to protect young people online".

- The Communication *Strategy for a Better Internet for Children* (2012) with the purpose of stimulating high-quality online content for children and young people, stepping up awareness
  and empowerment, creating a safe environment for children online, and fighting against
  child sexual abuse and child sexual exploitation.

The *Council of Europe* (COE, 2012) with its 47 member states is another world regional entity
that has produced material and advice on children's internet safety.

Awareness and media literacy

Hand in hand with discussions and regulative measures on online safety goes the manifold of
advice (most often on the national level) seeking to raise awareness of the risks of the internet
among children, parents, schools, child organisations, stakeholders, etc. In parallel, there are
growing demands for media literacy (media education, media literacy education, media and
information literacy, and similar notions). Almost all of the above-mentioned international and
world regional initiatives emphasise the importance of media literacy. One case is the *EU Media
Literacy Expert Group* that has inspired EC (2012b) to define media literacy as "the ability to access
the media, to understand and to critically evaluate different aspects of the media and media
contents, and to create communications in a variety of contexts".

Many other definitions of media literacy exist. There are also kindred concepts, such as
"education for communication" (through the media) and "communication for social change/
development", implying that everyone must learn/be allowed to use the media in order to
participate in the societal process towards increased democracy. That is, communication should
contribute to the empowerment of the audiences and should enable them to participate, from a
bottom-up perspective, in changing their everyday lives and the local community. The latter
concepts are more common in Africa, Asia and Latin America than in richer parts of the world
(where the "independent", "critical" and "media literate" individual often is the model).

Of course, the idea of media literacy is nothing new. Press and film initiatives, for instance, have
tried to promote critical understanding of the media since the middle of the last century. However,
UNESCO (United Nations Educational, Scientific and Cultural Organization) is probably the
organisation that first lifted up media education to the international plane. In 1978, UNESCO
(2012a) published a model for media education based on varying practices in different countries. In
1982, the *Grünwald Declaration on Media Education* was issued at a UNESCO symposium, saying that
"Political and educational systems need to recognise their obligations to promote in their citizens a
critical understanding of the phenomena of communication" (UNESCO, 2012b). After 25 years of
international conferences and declarations, the Grünwald document was reaffirmed in Paris in 2007
by experts, policy-makers, teachers, researchers, NGOs and media professionals from all regions of
the world. It was stated that in spite of the new ICTs, and new research and practices in media
education, media education in most countries had not moved from the phase of experimentation.
The outcome was the UNESCO *Paris Agenda – Twelve Recommendations for Media Education*
(2012c). The recommendations are grouped under four headings dealing with: development of
comprehensive media education programmes at all education levels; teacher training and awareness
raising of the other stakeholders in the social sphere; the important role of research in these contexts;
and the need for stimulating international cooperation and exchange of practices.

After that, "UNESCO has redirected its strategy to treat Media and Information Literacy
(MIL) as a composite concept". The organisation has in 2011 published the *Media and Information
Literacy Curriculum for Teachers* and is developing (2003–12) a set of Information Literacy (IL)
indicators which will allow member states to measure the IL at national and individual levels.

Another UN agency, Alliance of Civilizations (UN AoC, 2012a) has set up a *Media Literacy Education Clearinghouse*, a multilingual database with events, organisations and resources on media literacy education in different countries. This Clearinghouse is also arranging Youth Video Festivals to support 9- to 25-year-olds' own media production.

The UN AoC – with Grupo Comunicar, UNESCO and EC – has also in 2009 published *Mapping Media Education Policies in the World: Visions, Programmes and Challenges*, aiming to provide sources of reference and information on best practices for the implementation of media education (UNESCO, 2012d). Moreover, UNESCO and UN AoC have created a Global Chair on Media and Information Literacy in an international university network (UNITWIN) to enhance media and information literacy and intercultural dialogue (MILID) (UN AoC, 2012b).

Children's media participation

As hinted at, more and more focus in "media literacy" – and its allied concept, "communication for development" – is laid on young people's media participation and personal production. There are a great deal of best practices around the world showing that such participation leads to self-esteem among children, critical understanding and increased media competence, and often knowledge of and interest in the local community. This sometimes also inspires collective action to improve the situation. With that some progress towards civic engagement and increased democracy has been made.

With the internet, many national websites and forums invite children and youths to send in their video productions and the like. But what is there on the international level?

Besides youth forums initiated by the UN agencies mentioned above, UNICEF has offered platforms for children's media participation. In 1995, for example, UNICEF founded *Voices of Youth* (2012) (also on Facebook, Twitter, etc.) as an online place for young people to learn more about development issues (e.g., health, education, human rights) and where they "can share […] thoughts and opinions with thousands of people" representing over 200 countries. Another UNICEF activity was the *International Children's Day of Broadcasting* (2012), which was celebrated for 20 years (ceased after 2011). It began "as a way to get broadcasters to devote airtime to children's issues and has grown over the years to become a celebration of young people's participation in the media". Children over the world have produced radio and television shows broadcast on this day on both private and public, big and small channels.

As regards other kinds of initiatives, the voluntary, non-profitable German-based *Radijojo* (2012) has from 2003 grown to a worldwide multilingual children's radio network and children to children web portal. Children can send in stories, reports, songs and visual material. All themes are welcome: things one likes, things one thinks need to change. Children from over 100 countries have participated.

A world regional initiative is *Young Asian Reporters* (YAR, 2012) established by AMIC (Asian Media Information and Communication Centre) as a follow-up of the second ASEAN Media Forum in 2010. "This network provides a platform for youths to share stories (features/audio/video/photographs) […] and improve their journalistic skills. All stories are given feedback by media experts".

However, due to the exponential rise of the internet, no one has a real overview of how many young people really use it for creating "user-generated" content. According to the survey *EU Kids Online* (2011) such creativity is much less common among European 9- to 16-year-olds with access to the internet than using the internet for school work, playing games, watching video clips, visiting social networks, instant messaging and e-mailing.

Especially, one must bear in mind that only a minority of children, young people and adults in the world use the internet. Even if there are approximately 6 billion mobile-cellular subscriptions in the world, by the end of June 2012 only 34 percent of the world's population was estimated to use the internet. The share of internet users below 25 years of age is hardly bigger. An internet user is here defined as a person who must have 1) access to an internet connection point and 2) the basic knowledge required to use web technology (Internet World Stats, 2012; ITU, 2011). Most children, young people and adults are, thus, still excluded from the web. And of the users, many access the net relatively infrequently due to high costs and lack of infrastructure. These figures are not predicted to rise much in the near future because of difficulties in extending broadband technology.

Consequently, in most corners of the globe traditional media are dominating and much youth media participation occurs via ordinary radio, video, etc. Child participation is one of the key issues of the independent, voluntary organisation *PLAN International* (2012) founded in 1937 and focusing on children's issues. "Plan helps millions of children to learn about their rights and speak out about issues that affect them. Children have the right to take part in decision-making but all too often their involvement is limited or non-existent." As for youth media, PLAN operates almost 60 child media programmes in over 30 countries, especially in Africa, Asia and Latin America. Children produce their own media, such as radio, video and music – and are listened to and seen by real child and adult audiences in their own communities.

Research, knowledge, information

Simultaneously, there are international initiatives concerning children and media focusing on research, knowledge and information. *The International Clearinghouse on Children, Youth and Media* (2012) at Nordicom, University of Gothenburg, provides information about current research and practices in the field through yearbooks, newsletters, reports and a web site. The overall point of departure for the Clearinghouse's efforts is the UN CRC, not least Articles 13 and 17 related to the media. An active global network of researchers, media professionals, politicians, NGOs, media educators, etc., is fundamental to the work. Established in 1997, the Clearinghouse activities are carried out in cooperation with UNESCO by means of a Memorandum of Understanding.

The PRIX JEUNESSE Foundation (mentioned previously) has a sister organisation, *Internationales Zentralinstitut für das Jugend-und Bildungsfernsehen* (The International Central Institute for Youth and Educational Television, IZI, 2012), a department of Bayerischer Rundfunk, Germany. IZI performs often international empirical research on children and television, documents literature on children, youth and educational television, arranges national and international conferences and workshops, and publishes the journal *TelevIZIon*.

The two largest international media researchers' associations give regular attention to children and media: the International Communication Association (ICA, 2012) in its division *Children, Adolescents, and the Media* (CAM), and the International Association for Media and Communication Research (IAMCR, 2012) in its working group *Media Education Research*.

Since 2007, there exists, as well, a scientific peer-reviewed international journal for research on media and young people, *Journal of Children and Media*.

Further initiatives are international databases, for instance, the research *Center on Media and Child Health* (CMCH, 2012) at Boston Children's Hospital and affiliated with the Harvard Medical School and the Harvard School of Public Health, with the vision to "educate and empower both children and those who care for them to create and consume media in ways that optimise children's health and development". A regional example is the non-profit *Advertising Education Forum* (AEF, 2012) focusing on advertising and children.

Two more important international networks will finish these glimpses of international and world regional initiatives concerning children and media. The *Child Rights Information Network*

(CRIN, 2012) is an independent, not-for-profit organisation working for child and human rights. More than 2,100 organisations in 150 countries receive CRIN's newsletters and information. Besides child rights, almost 400 of these organisations are also engaged in children and media.

The Communication Initiative (The CI, 2012) – like many organisations it is also on Facebook and other social media – is a worldwide network focusing on communication and media for social and economic development. "This process is supported by web-based resources of summarised information and several electronic publications, as well as online research, review, and discussion platforms providing insight into communication for development experiences." The CI network process includes *The Communication Initiative: Global* (in English), *La Iniciativa de Comunicación: Latin America* (in Spanish), *Soul Beat Africa* (in English), and several other e-publications. A quick search for children and media on the CI website in May 2012 resulted in several hundreds of items.

Concluding words

The multitude of international initiatives raises, naturally, important questions. Can intergovernmental consensus agreements, networks of child rights organisations, or counter-movements critical of commercial media power ameliorate the prevailing media situation, in which children's rights to communication and participation are too often disregarded and their voices mostly silenced?

Such questions require further analysis. Essential for the analysis are several factors that have not been dealt with in this chapter: How do the international initiatives interplay with national and local ones? How do the initiatives collaborate with the interest groups – children, parents, teachers, voluntary organisations, policy-makers, media professionals, the ICT industry, and researchers? How deeply are the international initiatives rooted in a bottom-up perspective – in children's and other marginalised groups' real needs in their local (social, political, economic, cultural and religious) contexts? How high up on the initiatives' agenda is the fact that many problems with the media in the world are based on inequalities and power relations in the global economy?

References

(All references latest retrieved in May, 2012 (except Internet World Stats retrieved in November, 2012)).

Advertising Education Forum, www.aeforum.org
ANDI, www.andi.org.br
Center on Media and Child Health, www.cmch.tv
Childnet International, www.childnet-int.org
Child Rights Information Network, www.crin.org
The Communication Initiative, www.comminit.com
Council of Europe, www.coe.int/web/coe-portal/what-we-do/media-and-communication/children-and-the-internet
ECPAT International, www.ecpat.net
EU Kids Online, www2.lse.ac.uk/media@lse/research/EUKidsOnline/EU%20Kids%20II%20(2009–11)/EUKidsOnlineIIReports/D4FullFindings.pdf
European Child Safety Online NGO Network, ec.europa.eu/information_society/apps/projects/factsheet/index.cfm?project_ref=SIP-2007-TN-311701
European Commission (a), ec.europa.eu/information_society/activities/sip/policy/intl/index_en.htm
European Commission (b), ec.europa.eu/culture/media/literacy/docs/com/en.pdf
European Schoolnet, www.eun.org
Forum Europe, www.eu-ems.com/summary.asp?event_id=118&page_id=904
GlobalSchoolNet, www.globalschoolnet.org

International Association for Media and Communication Research, iamcr.org

International Association of Internet Hotlines, www.inhope.org

International Board on Books for Young People, www.ibby.org

International Centre of Films for Children and Youth, www.cifej.com/brochure

International Children's Day of Broadcasting, www.unicef.org/videoaudio/video_55906.html

The International Clearinghouse on Children, Youth and Media, Nordicom, www.nordicom.gu.se/clearing house

International Communication Association, www.icahdq.org

International Federation of Journalists, www.ifj.org

International Telecommunication Union, www.itu.int/ITU-D/ict/facts/2011/material/ICTFacts Figures2011.pdf

Internationales Zentralinstitut für das Jugend- und Bildungsfernsehen, www.br-online.de/jugend/ izi/english

Internet Governance Forum, www.intgovforum.org

Internet World Stats, www.internetworldstats.com/stats.htm

Media Monitoring Africa, www.mediamonitoringafrica.org/index.php/programmes/category/children

MediaWise Trust, www.mediawise.org.uk/?page_id=541

PLAN International, plan-international.org/what-we-do/child-participation/child-media

PRIX JEUNESSE Foundation, www.prixjeunesse.de

Radijojo, www.radijojo.de

Red ANDI, www.redandi.org

Safer Internet Day, www.saferinternet.org

Save the Children, www.savethechildren.org.uk/resources/online-library/interviewing-children-guide-journalists-and-others

Strategy for a Better Internet for Children, ec.europa.eu/information_society/activities/sip/policy/index_en.htm

UN Alliance of Civilizations (a), mil.unaoc.org

UN Alliance of Civilizations (b), www.unaoc.org/communities/academia/unesco-unaoc-milid

UNESCO (a), www.unesco.org/ulis/cgibin/ulis.pl?database=&lin=1&futf8=1&ll=1&gp=1&look=default&sc1=1&sc2=1&ref= http://www.unesco.org/ulis/en/advanced_search.html&nl=1&req=2&by=2&au=Minkkinen,%20Sirkka

UNESCO (b), www.unesco.org/education/pdf/MEDIA_E.PDF

UNESCO (c), www.unesco.org/new/en/communication-and-information/media-development/media-literacy

UNESCO (d), unesdoc.unesco.org/images/0018/001819/181917e.pdf

UNICEF (a), www.unicef.org/media/media_tools_guidelines.html

UNICEF (b), www.unicef.org/cwc/index.html

Voices of Youth, www.voicesofyouth.org

World Association of Newspapers and News Publishers, www.wan-ifra.org/articles/2012/05/01/the-world-young-reader-prize-how-to-enter-in-2012

World Summit on Media for Children Foundation, www.wsmcf.com

Young Asian Reporters, www.amic.org.sg/YAR

55

THE MEDICAL COMMUNITY IN THE U.S.: TREATING MEDIA AS AN INFLUENCE ON HEALTH AND DEVELOPMENT

Michael Rich

The medical community has long had a conflicted relationship with media (Rich, 2007). With the rapid proliferation of television and its integration into families' lives during the 1950s, physicians recognized the potential for media to engage, educate, and empower the public to improve their health (American Medical Association, 2000). Yet some in the medical community were wary of the public's enthusiastic embrace of mass entertainment and were concerned that indiscriminate use of media might lead to unhealthy outcomes (Smith, 1952). Each of these reactions arose from—and has been perpetuated to the present by—the medical community's incomplete understanding of how media work, how media affect their users, and how using media in focused, mindful ways could be part of a developmentally optimal, healthy lifestyle.

Since 1947, when the first closed-circuit broadcast of surgery was aired, electronic screen media have been used to educate health professionals. Entertainment television has sporadically attempted to increase health literacy of the general population, whether in the 1946 American Medical Association (AMA)-sponsored "Cavalcade of Medicine" or in today's medical dramas. The challenge is that, in many cases, health education and entertainment fail to marry effectively, with entertainment trumping education. Although there are several notable exceptions—such as the work of Neal Baer, MD, a television writer-producer who trained as a pediatrician and understood how television can effectively inform and empower audiences—popular medical television dramas tend to prioritize narrative over medical accuracy. For example, one study found that such shows rarely portray poorer long-term outcomes of CPR, which could contribute to unrealistically high expectations of resuscitation among viewers (Harris and Willoughby, 2009).

To address this issue and leverage the power of television to promote health literacy, the American Academy of Pediatrics (AAP) founded the Media Resource Team in 1994. This group of Los Angeles-based pediatricians consulted with the television and film industries to serve as a source of accurate medical information to writers and producers, promote positive media messages about children and adolescents, and discourage negative or harmful media content about or aimed at youth. Although they met the leaders of professional guilds and occasionally consulted on the development of programs, their greatest influence was to convince the producers of *America's Funniest Home Videos* not to broadcast clips of children behaving in potentially dangerous ways. Because the costs were not justified by the limited results, the AAP ceased to support the Media Resource Team in the early 2000s.

The danger paradigm

Despite being intrigued by the possibilities that media present for improving health, the medical community has traditionally been most visible and has had the most impact through its concern about media's influences on physical and mental health. Psychologists and educators have voiced such concern since the 1950s. In 1972, the medical community turned its attention to the issue, when the United States Surgeon General published *Television and Social Behavior* (USSG Scientific Advisory Committee on Television and Social Behavior, & National Institute of Mental Health, 1972). This report focused almost exclusively on the effects of exposure to media violence; the consensus statement concluded that some children who viewed violent media were at risk for increases in aggressive behavior. And although many in the research community felt that the summary statements of the Surgeon General's committee of psychologists and television executives fell short of the conclusions warranted by the data, the report awakened the medical community to media as a health concern. In doing so, it laid the foundation for the danger paradigm that persists to the present—a paradigm in which the medical community's job is to prevent potential harmful effects of media use, rather than to evaluate its positive and negative effects and make informed recommendations based on a balanced assessment of the evidence.

This danger paradigm did not originate with the medical community, however. It started decades earlier, when individual academics in the 1930s and 1940s expressed concern about the influences of motion pictures, radio, and comic books on youth. Then, with the rapid penetration of television into homes, the issue came to public attention. U.S. Congressional hearings were convened to determine to what extent radio and TV programs portrayed immorality or glamorized violence and crime (U.S. Congress, 1952). The subcommittee concluded that there was too much violence on television.

Although industry executives insisted that television violence would be limited by the voluntary controls of the new Television Code, a 1954 Gallup Poll indicated that 70 percent of the American public believed television and comic books contributed to adolescent problems (Gallup, 1954). So new hearings were convened by Senator Estes Kefauver, who called upon psychologists, psychiatrists, and public health leaders to testify on whether television viewing contributed to juvenile delinquency. Concerns raised by health experts but supported by scant scientific evidence were countered by network representatives, who argued that any governmental regulation of television content would violate First Amendment rights to free expression. They also reassured the committee that "We are aware of no responsible scientific data or opinion which fixes television as the cause of juvenile delinquency. On the contrary, there is a decided body of opinion that television and films have no causal relationship to juvenile delinquency" (U.S. Congress, 1954, p. 182). They portrayed the widespread concerns as opinion unsupported by data and claimed that the First Amendment-guaranteed right to free expression should be the prevailing value. These arguments polarized the debate and stalemated serious discourse for decades.

Movement begins

Following the 1972 Surgeon General's report, "America's pediatrician" T. Berry Brazelton (1974) observed in an AAP publication that "a child comes away from a television set believing that physical violence is a perfectly acceptable form of self-expression" (p. 10). Maintaining his trademark optimism, however, he suggested that "active participation on the part of the parent, as well as the child, may begin to make television the valuable experience it should be" (Brazelton, 1974, p. 11). The AAP responded to his optimism by developing *A Family Guide to Children's Television*, with Peggy Charren and her advocacy group, Action for Children's Television. It conveyed the new perspective among pediatricians that media use could influence child health and thus should be included in medical histories and addressed in the anticipatory guidance offered in children's annual visits.

Soon after, research on media effects reached the peer-reviewed medical literature when the *Journal of the American Medical Association* published a review of the extant studies on media violence (Rothenberg, 1975). Of 146 peer-reviewed behavioral science papers, which reported findings from 50 studies involving 10,000 children and adolescents, "all showed that violence viewing produces increased aggressive behavior in the young" (Rothenberg, 1975, p. 1043). Specifically, the research demonstrated that children who viewed more media violence showed "decreased emotional sensitivity to media violence" and learned "novel, aggressive behavior sequences" (Rothenberg, 1975, p. 1044). Research did not support Seymour Feshbach's (1961) hypothesis that media violence provided a catharsis and reduced actual violence; several disproved the hypothesis, finding desensitization rather than catharsis. Review of the cumulative findings showed that the risk of subsequent aggression was increased by the level of arousal when viewing media violence and by the similarity of violent scenes to the viewer's actual environments and experiences. Aggressive behavior was found to be inhibited by portrayals of painful and sad outcomes of aggression and by framing violence as morally wrong. Because the findings revealed that children's programs portrayed violence approximately six times as frequently as adult television, and because that violence was often presented as justified or heroic, the author concluded that "immediate remedial action in terms of television programming is warranted" (Rothenberg, 1975, p. 1045).

The American Medical Association (AMA) used these findings to energize the medical community around the issue of television violence. It adopted resolutions stating its concerns, encouraged networks to replace violence with positive programming, and urged the National Institute of Mental Health to fund "objective and applicable measurements of television violence and its effects, and the elucidation of how and to what extent various types and degrees of television violence affect children adversely" (American Medical Association, 1976, p. 80). The following year, the AMA added sexual content to their concerns and authorized nearly a quarter of a million dollars to investigate and determine valid measures of television violence, to monitor television violence and the companies that sponsor it, and to perform content analysis of sex on television (American Medical Association, 1977). Before the House Commerce Subcommittee on Communications, an AMA psychiatrist challenged the television industry to portray healthy, prosocial behaviors, saying

> The television industry cannot have it both ways—claiming that they entertain, facilitate abreaction and release pent-up emotion, yet denying that they shape and influence behavior. Bluntly stated, shaping and influencing behavior that is stimulating the sale of products is precisely one of the major uses of television.
>
> *(American Medical Association, 1977, p. 13)*

After the Surgeon General issued a statement saying that the relationship between televised violence and anti-social behavior was sufficient to warrant immediate response by the medical community (Steinfeld, 1972), the AAP urged pediatricians to "actively oppose television programs emphasizing high degrees of violence and antisocial behavior which detrimentally affect the attitudes and social behavior of children" (American Academy of Pediatrics, 1977, p. 1). Further concluding that advertising to children, who do not yet understand persuasive intent, represented "commercial exploitation of children for profit," the AAP called a "ban on all television advertisements during programs in which a majority of the audience is composed of children under twelve years of age" (American Academy of Pediatrics, 1978, Appendix 9). The AMA consolidated concerns about commercial exploitation and violence a year later, publicly opposing television advertising and programming that exploited children or could negatively affect their health and safety.

Shaping policy

Recognizing the growing need for the medical community to assess and respond to media's influence on children's health and development, the AAP created the Task Force on Children and Television in 1983. It aimed to educate parents about television viewing and its effects on children's knowledge, attitudes, and behavior. Noting concerns about how TV could affect violence, nutrition, school performance, substance use, sexuality, stereotypes, and world-view, the Task Force also focused on media's unrealized potential for beneficial learning. The AAP started to meet regularly with researchers, television executives, and parent groups, establishing a tradition for the medical community of public outreach and advocacy regarding media and child health.

Building on that work and energized by the 1982 National Institute of Mental Health's ten-year follow-up to the Surgeon General's report on television and behavior, which found media violence to be "as strongly correlated with aggressive behavior as any other behavioral variable that has been measured" (National Institute of Mental Health, 1982, p. 6), the AAP began issuing policy statements in the mid-1980s that moved beyond the single issue of media violence and asserted the medical community's responsibility to assess media-related health risks, educate patients, and advocate for health-supportive programming. "Children, Adolescents, and Television" (American Academy of Pediatrics, 1984) was the first of many statements from the AAP and other health professional organizations to focus on media and health outcomes of concern. Acknowledging the dearth of scientific research on media effects, the AAP called on the medical and public health communities to join their academic colleagues in pursuing and publishing scientific inquiry on how media use influences children's physical, mental, and social health.

The research grew significantly in the mid-1980s, when increasing numbers of media effects papers were published in leading health research journals (Rich, 2007). Expanding from no research reports on media during the 1950s and 1960s, and only 12 in the 1970s, there were 34 studies published in 4 out of 6 leading health journals during the second half of the 1980s, 117 in the 1990s, and 450 in the 2000s. This increase motivated parallel increases in public education and policy statements by major health organizations (Schmidt et al., 2008). Due to their focus on children's health and development, pediatricians took the lead, producing 29 original and updated policy statements regarding media effects on health between 1984 and 2011. They addressed clinical concerns from different perspectives, focusing on specific media (television, popular music), health outcomes (violence, substance use, sexual risk behaviors), and developmental issues (attention, imagination, creativity). Other health organizations, from the American Medical Association to the American Academy of Child and Adolescent Psychiatry, followed suit, intermittently issuing policy statements, fact sheets, and strategies for integrating media considerations into clinical practice.

Originally designed as practice recommendations to clinicians, child health policy statements first garnered public attention in 1999, when the AAP recommended discouraging television viewing by children under the age of two. Because the recommendations came from respected child health advocates and contradicted what had become common practice in many U.S. households, the story landed on the front page of *The New York Times*. It ignited a controversy between child advocates and the entertainment industry, which argued that there was little research supporting this recommendation. And parents tended not to follow the recommendations anyway. A national survey in 2003 revealed that only 6 percent of U.S. parents were even aware of AAP recommendations for toddlers' screen time, let alone observing them (Rideout et al., 2003).

What was lost in the debate that erupted was the reality of the pediatrician's role: to provide guidance for children and their parents based on the best available—but not always complete—scientific evidence. That's true whether recommending seatbelt use, treatment for an ear infection, or reduced screen time. Unfortunately, the adversarial nature of the pro-child/pro-media debate forced stakeholders to take sides. When the AAP and other child advocates were again confronted with assertions that media production and consumption are protected by the First Amendment, they fell back into long-established polarized stances that were often informed more by values-based preconceptions than by data.

The need for access to research

The growing wealth of scientific evidence on the positive and negative effects of media on developing minds and bodies barely entered the debate because it was functionally inaccessible to clinicians, parents, teachers, and others who worked with children. Indeed, even a 2000 consensus statement on media violence issued by leading national health organizations at a bipartisan Congressional briefing was able to be dismissed by entertainment industry lobbyists and the general public as unsupported opinion as a result of this missed connection (American Academy of Pediatrics et al., 2000).

The inaccessibility of scientific evidence regarding media effects on health arose from several historical realities. First, media effects research has been conducted across at least 13 disciplines: anthropology, business, communication, criminal justice, critical studies, economics, education, gender studies, medicine, psychology, public health, social work, and sociology. Because media are integrated into so many aspects of contemporary human existence, any discipline that studies humans and their behaviors offers a perspective on how we create and consume media. This diversity of perspectives presents a challenge to establishing a comprehensive evidence base. Because few academics are able to stay current with the scholarship even within their own field, each body of research remains largely within the confines of its discipline. Differences in language and methodology and a competitive academic culture discourage effective interaction, communication, and collaboration.

As a result, research has been pursued in parallel, with similar and even duplicative studies conducted in isolation. And while there is value in reproducing key findings, doing so with an awareness of similar studies in other fields would greatly increase that value—as it did in the *Journal of Children and Media*, an interdisciplinary journal that devoted its February 2012 special issue to the topic of media and child health. A lack of interdisciplinary communication, in contrast, abnegates the opportunity for enriching a study with the complementary perspectives and the reinforcing rigor of other disciplines. In order to raise scholarship to the next level, all extant research must be accessible to all investigators, and consensus must be achieved on what we know and what we need to discover. The resulting possibilities for collaboration would enrich and extend the literature and deepen our respective understandings of how media affect children's health.

Reframing media as a public health issue

In 2002, the Center on Media and Child Health (CMCH) at Boston Children's Hospital (BCH) was established to address that need. Conceived as a resource to all stakeholders seeking to understand and respond to the positive and negative effects of media on children's health, CMCH aimed to abandon the advocacy-driven "us and them" stances that typically characterize the issue.

First, it recognized that media are here to stay, will not be controlled by legislation, and are unlikely to change dramatically in response to the concerns of special interest groups. And media are indeed becoming increasingly ubiquitous and ingrained in society. In the first decade of the twenty-first century, U.S. children's media use exploded, with 2010 data indicating more than 7½ hours of active media use and, with multitasking, 10¾ hours of media exposure each day (Kaiser Family Foundation, 2010). Given children's ever-growing engagement with and immersion in media, CMCH worked to reframe media as an environmental health issue, integrated into so many aspects of children's lives that it influences them as profoundly as the air they breathe and the water they drink. This framework suggests that the key is to improve the media environment in which children develop—and that such work would require all stakeholders, including those who create and distribute the media, to make production and consumption decisions based on scientific evidence about how media affect children's health.

To support all stakeholders in doing this work, CMCH aims to provide the most up-to-date scientific understanding of how media affect their users and to provide evidence-based expertise to all efforts that address children's involvement with media. With this information, responsible producers can create successful media that do no harm and may improve their users. Parents, teachers, and pediatricians can use reliable, valid information to assess the media's effects on children, hold producers accountable for "product safety," and direct children toward health-supporting media. Just as science has guided parenting decisions about good nutrition and car seats, science can guide the production and consumption of media.

To build common ground for the study of media and child health, CMCH has created a comprehensive, up-to-date library of the "state of the knowledge" on these issues. This internationally accessible Database of Research (DoR) is available at www.cmch.tv, for use by researchers, clinicians, educators, parents, policymakers, and anyone interested in media and children's health (Rich and King, 2008). Because these resources are accessible worldwide, they offer a unique entry point for users who otherwise have varying degrees of access to such information. With a uniform nomenclature and format developed by CMCH librarians, the DoR standardizes citations from more than a dozen disciplines to facilitate comparison. In addition, the age group of the subject population, research design, and standardized keywords facilitate categorization by key parameters and accurate subject searching (King et al., 2005). Each citation also includes both a structured abstract for researchers and a synopsis written for the general public. As of 2012, this resource brought together more than 3,800 citations from disparate sources and aims to remain current by adding 25–30 new papers weekly.

CMCH also disseminates up-to-the-minute research findings and news through a blog for researchers (www.cmch.typepad.com/cmch) and translates science into research-based, balanced, practical advice for caregivers through *Ask the Mediatrician* (www.askthemediatrician. org), an interactive question and answer blog for raising healthy children in the Digital Age.

With these and other initiatives, CMCH aims to provide a comprehensive evidence base and effective strategies to all who need them. Its three-pronged approach to supporting the medical community in establishing recommendations for healthy media use includes *investigating* what remains unknown about media influences on child health, *translating* what is known into effective clinical, educational, and parenting strategies, and *innovating* applications for media that support and enhance children's physical, mental, and social health.

The future of media and child health

Media are completely integrated into our environments and our lives. They have a powerful and nearly constant influence on children's health and development. The goal, within both the medical community and the larger network of dedicated researchers, must be to take advantage of the increased scope and rigor of true interdisciplinarity to elevate the consistency and rigor of media effects research. Unbiased evidence can be made relevant to the clinicians, teachers, parents, and media producers who are the agents of change. As with nutrition or sports, media represent both opportunity and risk for children's health and development. If the medical community, and society at large, can move beyond the danger paradigm and make informed choices based on evidence, we can move forward to live, parent, and use media in ways that promote the health, education, and safety of our children.

SEE ALSO in this volume chapter by Scharrer, chapter by Peter, chapter by Harrison, chapter by Bond, Richards and Calvert, and chapter by Borzekowski.

References

American Academy of Pediatrics (1977). *AAP Resolution Concerning the Effects of Television Violence on Children*. Elk Grove Village, IL: American Academy of Pediatrics.

——(1978). *Task Force on Television and Advertising – Action Memorandum*. Elk Grove Village, IL: American Academy of Pediatrics.

——(1984). Children, adolescents, and television. *News and Comment, 35*(12), 8.

American Academy of Pediatrics, American Academy of Child & Adolescent Psychiatry, American Psychological Association, American Medical Association, American Academy of Family Physicians, & American Psychiatric Association (2000). *Joint statement on the impact of entertainment violence on children*. Congressional Public Health Summit.

American Medical Association (1976). Proceedings from *House of Delegates*. Dallas, TX.: American Medical Association

——(1977). Objection to Sex on TV. H-485.999.

——(2000). *E-Health Timeline*. Chicago, IL.: American Medical Association.

Braun, T. and Schubert, A. (2003). A quantitative view on the coming of age of interdisciplinarity in the sciences 1980–99. *Scientometrics, 58*(1), 183–89.

Brazelton, T. B. (1974). TV and children: A pediatrician's advice. *News and Comment, 25*(9), 10–11.

Feshbach, S. (1961). The stimulating effects of a vicarious aggressive activity. *The Journal of Abnormal and Social Psychology, 63*(2), 381–85.

Gallup, G. (1954, November 21). The Gallup Poll: Air Waves Share Blame. *Washington Post and Times Herald*, 1A.

Harris, D. and Willoughby, H. (2009). Resuscitation on television: realistic or ridiculous? A quantitative observational analysis of the portrayal of cardiopulmonary resuscitation in television medical drama. *Resuscitation, 80*(11), 1275–79.

Kaiser Family Foundation (2010). Generation M2: Media in the lives of 8- to 18-year-olds. Menlo Park, CA.: Kaiser Family Foundation.

King, B. E., Gray, S. and Rich, M. (2005, June). NWL – Center on Media and Child Health: Building an e-resource for researchers and the public. Paper presented at the Special Libraries Association, Toronto, Ontario.

National Institute of Mental Health (1982). *Television and behavior: Ten years of scientific progress and implications for the Eighties*. Washington, D.C.: U.S. Government Printing Office.

Rich, M. (2007). Is television healthy? The medical perspective. In N. Pecora, J. P. Murray and E. A. Wartella (Eds), *Children and television: 50 years of research*. Mahwah, NJ: Lawrence Erlbaum, pp. 109–48.

Rich, M. and King, B. E. (2008). Center on Media and Child Health: Scientific evolution responding to technological revolution. *Journal of Children and Media, 2*(2), 183–88.

Rideout, V. J., Vandewater, E. A. and Wartella, E. A.(2003). *Zero to six: Electronic media in the lives of infants, toddlers, preschoolers, and their parents.* Menlo Park, CA: Kaiser Family Foundation.

Rothenberg, M. B. (1975). Effects of television violence on children and youth. *Journal of the American Medical Association, 234*(10), 1043–46.

Schmidt, M., Bickham, D. S., Branner, A. and Rich, M. (2008). Media-related policies of professional health organizations. In S. L. Calvert and B. J. Wilson (Eds). *Blackwell handbook of child development and the media.* Oxford, UK: Blackwell, pp. 503–26.

Smith, A. (1952). Influence of TV crime programs on children's health [comment]. *Journal of the American Medical Association, 150*(1), 37.

Steinfeld, J. (1972). Statement in hearings before Subcommittee on Communications of Committee on Commerce (United States Senate, Serial #92–52, pp. 25–27). Washington, DC: U.S. Government Printing Office.

U.S. Congress (1952). *Investigation of radio and television programs, 1.* Washington, D.C.

——(1954). *Juvenile delinquency (television programs).* Washington, D.C.

USSG Scientific Advisory Committee on Television and Social Behavior, & National Institute of Mental Health (1972). *Television and social behavior: Reports and papers.* Rockville, MD: National Institute of Mental Health.

56

BRIDGING SCHOLARSHIP AND THE MEDIA INDUSTRY

How public broadcasting works with academia

Linda Simensky

Personal introduction

I work on the industry side of children's media, and currently oversee children's programming for PBS, working out of the PBS headquarters in Arlington, Virginia. In the course of my career, I have been in charge of development, mostly of animated series, at both Nickelodeon at the start of Nicktoons and Cartoon Network in its early days. I have been known to dabble in academia, having written chapters for five academic books in addition to having taught and lectured at colleges in the course of my career. I have had a unique vantage point for watching the relationship (and often the non-relationship) between the kids' media industry and the research community over the years.

Although I worked with researchers at both Nickelodeon and Cartoon Network and oversaw more than a hundred focus groups, I had not worked closely with what we think of as "experts," people with advanced degrees either working at research companies or in academia who are knowledgeable on topics ranging from child development to how children learn particular topics. While at Nickelodeon, we invited a few advisors to weigh in on what a child might get out of watching some of our shows. At Cartoon Network, as the channel was considering making preschool shows, we asked an educational expert from a research company about what challenges we could expect to encounter and what kids could gain from watching a cartoon. The information we received in both cases was considered incidental to our decision-making. Rather than thinking much about child development, we mostly focused on funnier jokes, the acquisition of a larger audience, and higher ratings as we produced our series.

The role of academia in commercial versus public broadcasting

In 2003, I moved from commercial media over to public broadcasting to head up the department at PBS that oversees the development and production of the television series for children aged two to eight (see Simensky, 2007). PBS worked closely with advisors of all sorts, particularly on children's programming. Since all children's programming on PBS is educational, advisors developed and reviewed curricula, gave feedback on pitches and series and worked on both the formative and summative research for series. PBS executives and producers are accountable to the American public and understand that it is imperative to get the curriculum right. In my new position, I found myself collaborating with university professors, curriculum writers, child development experts, and researchers who were adept at working with television and web producers to maximize the amount that a viewer could learn from a series or a web site.

I realized that where we ignored these advisors in commercial media, they were providing crucial information to the producers of educational media. By reviewing the educational approach to a particular subject and assessing it for age appropriateness, educational advisors could improve the efficacy of educational media, particularly preschool programming, without detracting from the entertainment value of the episode. This collaboration is necessary when you consider that these forms of educational media could have significant impact on viewers' lives if done correctly. If one of the goals of educational media is to educate its viewers, then parents and teachers are counting on the producers to do the research to confirm that the series are using effective teaching techniques as well as accurate and age-appropriate information. Producers in turn depend on the advisors for feedback and testing to make sure their series are effective.

In an article in the *Journal of Children and Media* (Simensky, 2008), I had the chance to look at the relationship between academia and the industry, particularly with regards to research being done independently. In this piece, I considered if academia was answering the questions that the industry needed answered, or if it was simply going after hot button topics that could get news coverage. I also wondered if it was possible for an independent research study to have results that would be useful to the industry, as opposed to results that would be ignored or denied. I noted that, in my opinion, academia could be judgmental and critical when it should be analytical and focused. I also felt the industry could in turn be dismissive and defensive. Ultimately, I concluded that working together could be accomplished through researching topics of mutual interest and presenting results in language the industry could easily understand.

While the educational side of children's media instinctively understands the importance of sharing information and creating a dialogue, this relationship is rare in commercial media beyond preschool programming, particularly where there exists a more adversarial relationship between academia and the media. Nevertheless, there are areas where advisors can contribute to the understanding of kids and media across the entire industry, particularly with regards to what is age appropriate or even what is funny. And yet there is limited collaboration of this sort beyond educational media, public broadcasting, and preschool programming.

As noted earlier, commercial non-educational series produced for viewers aged 6–11 or 9–14 rarely work with child development experts or curriculum advisors at any point during the development or production process. It is hard in some cases to see what advisors would bring to the process of commercial production. The added time needed for experts to weigh in or make adjustments and the extra expenses are seen as obstructions to making the series in a timely manner. The end result is that it takes less time to produce a non-educational series, although the animation process is still extremely time-consuming regardless of the content.

In addition, many commercial television producers feel that advisors are not successful at collaboration – that advisors tend to be literal and usually don't bring much insight to a humorous cartoon or an action series. Their feedback is not always easily understandable by non-academicians. The two groups don't always share the same goals.

While it's not crucial for commercial producers to work with experts, there certainly are times when everyone involved would benefit from a better understanding of age appropriateness or what a viewer might get out of watching a show. Even the opportunity to read relevant studies would be beneficial for the industry.

Obstacles to collaborations

There are certainly logical reasons why advisors are not involved with certain types of programming. While they have a very specific role to play with educational programming, particularly preschool programming, it is not clear to everyone in the media industry what these advisors can bring to other types of series.

It is important to consider that the inclusion of advisors adds to the cost of the series and the length of time it takes to produce the material. Working with advisors can add up to two years to the development process as well as extra time to the production process. While every television series is different and requires a unique set up, production on a series, particularly an animated series, takes a significant amount of time. Animation, regardless of whether it's 2D or 3D, whether it is done by hand or using a computer program, requires painstaking frame-by-frame work that cannot be done any more quickly than studios currently do it. In addition, when producing an educational series, the research and testing that go into the formative period of an educational production add at least a year or more to the process. For an educational preschool or early elementary school-age children's series, if everything moves as quickly as possible, it takes approximately two and a half to three years from the generation of a series idea to the point where a series is ready to premiere. For a commercial, non-educational children's series, if everything moves as quickly as possible, it takes approximately two years from the generation of a series idea to the point where a series is ready to premiere. A commercial series can take a full year less than an educational series to produce.

The curriculum specialists and advisors for a series usually include experts on all facets of the particular topic for the series (i.e., areas of science, math or reading.) While still in the formative stages of development, producers try to have a variety of advisors with different areas of expertise on a particular topic work on their show. Generally, these teams of advisors also include at least one child development expert, one school or preschool teacher who teaches the series curriculum to children in the target age, and one or two college professors who are experts on the topic. At times, finding the right experts for a project can take up to two months. Sometimes an advisory board is assembled; this can involve additional experts. In the formative stages of some shows, as many as 10 to 15 advisors may weigh in with feedback.

Finding the right advisors can be a complicated process. According to producer Carol Greenwald (who produces the series *Arthur, Curious George* and *Martha Speaks* for PBS) of WGBH, the PBS station in Boston, it is important to find the advisors who have the best feel for the material and have a range of experience. Most importantly, she notes that advisors must also like the show idea and believe that children can be taught through media (Greenwald, 2012).

The contributions of advisors

The advisors weigh in at various points in the production process, starting at the very beginning, since the idea of the series and the curriculum need to be integrated early on. The advisors review the curriculum, which is written by a curriculum writer, and then review the series proposal, the document that explains the basic idea for a series. This document features an overall explanation of what the series is about, character descriptions and designs, background and setting designs, story ideas, an example of a script, the curriculum document, and an explanation of the interactive plan for the series (including a digital plan that includes a web site and games, as well as ideas for apps and other extensions of the series.) At this point, the many advisors on the team sometimes need to resolve their own differences of opinion. Greenwald noted that when the series *Martha Speaks* was being developed, one advisor, a noted vocabulary expert, felt that the series curriculum needed to feature as many vocabulary words as possible in each episode. Conversely, another advisor on the team believed the series needed to focus on a limited number of words used repeatedly throughout the story. The producers had to make an executive decision based on what they felt the stories could best accommodate (Greenwald, 2012).

The advisors also make sure the educational age skew of the curriculum used in the overall idea and in the story ideas matches the age skew of the intended viewers. Many educational series will do the formative testing at this phase and then make adjustments as needed. Following this, frequently, the network commissions an 11-minute or 22-minute pilot. The pilot is then tested in focus groups or through other market research techniques for appeal and efficacy of the teaching of the subject matter. If the pilots test well and the network is generally happy with the overall direction and test results, these pilots then have the possibility to move forward into series, with or without adjustments. When a production is at the piloting stage, the advisors remain involved and continue to give feedback.

Depending on the project, sometimes during the formative testing period, the advisors and producers also will need to consider the socioeconomic status of potential viewers and may need to analyze the difference between middle class viewers and low income viewers in terms of their ability to understand or absorb the curriculum of a series.

Advisors continue to weigh in once a series is in production. For certain kinds of curriculum-based series such as science-based series, a curriculum specialist and/or expert will be assigned a list of topics and will research the topics and the age-appropriate curriculum for each topic. This process takes anywhere from three weeks to three months, is incorporated into the writing schedule, and must be done for each episode. An example of the three-month research process would be the PBS series *Dinosaur Train*. Episodes frequently involve the introduction of a new dinosaur species to viewers; two experts who work on the series generate a new curriculum document for each episode.

At times, producers of a series will need to assess the effectiveness of their series in teaching its curriculum. At that point, the producers will commission summative research to determine how effective a series is. As a note of interest, in addition to adding time to the production process, adding research and/or the curriculum review of scripts adds $5,000 to $10,000 per episode.

The case of PBS

Besides the advisors who work on specific educational series, PBS uses a variety of experts and advisors both on series and as general advisors. The children's programming department includes a Director of Content and Curriculum for the Ready To Learn grant who is in charge of overseeing content development and curriculum integration across multiple media platforms. There is also a PBS Kids Next Generation Media Advisory Board that provides PBS Kids management with strategic counsel regarding research, content and distribution, business development, and educational and community impact for children's media. These board members work with PBS Kids to examine how rapidly evolving technology changes the media and educational landscape and considers the implications for PBS Kids viewers. These advisors meet with the PBS Kids staff annually for a two-day conference at PBS headquarters. In addition, PBS calls on individual board members as needed throughout the year to provide project-based advice relevant to their unique area of expertise.

Every children's series on PBS also creates and maintains a series web site on pbskids.org as well as additional digital experiences such as e-books and apps for such devices as mobile phones and tablets. These sites and apps are considered an integral part of the series experience for viewers and require attention from advisors as well. Advisors also weigh in on outreach materials to assess that the materials are enhancing the learning from the series and digital applications.

Unlike commercial media, PBS also receives a number of grants from government agencies such as the United States Department of Education and the National Science Foundation. These grants frequently require the participation of additional educational experts from academia who have experience and advanced knowledge germane to the subject matter of a particular grant. The people who receive these grants are accountable and must prove that they move the needle, their work is impactful and they are worthy of receiving the funds. The shows, web sites, and apps they work on must be testable, and must show that they can positively impact the viewers who watch or use them.

In addition to the advisors who work on the content side of the grants, the government agencies also use advisors and experts to help choose the projects to receive funding. These government agencies also use independent experts to assess the efficacy of the media or the overall success of the grant. For example, Brian Lekander, the U.S. Department of Education's Program Manager of the Ready To Learn Television grant, is tasked with finding these advisors and experts for both grant application panel reviews as well as quality reviews such as the Government Performance Results Act (GPRA) accountability review and various research reviews. To find qualified experts who have significant practical experience or research backgrounds, the Department of Education has open calls that are widely distributed to the public through Federal Register notices. They also bring in successful reviewers from similar or relevant programs, get recommendations from grantees or via professional networks, and are implementing a new centralized reviewer database, which houses a pool of individuals any program can rely upon. These advisors participate through leadership events such as conferences and symposia, and occasionally in publications (Lekander, 2012).

Lekander noted two major challenges in finding the right advisors. It is critical to find advisors in the community who do not have a conflict of interest or could stand to benefit if a particular production entity is chosen. He has also found that it can be difficult to find advisors who have the right backgrounds and knowledge to review specific topics. For example, he completed a search for reviewers to look at a variety of educational media. In a search for advisors with expertise in early learning and mathematics, he found that the media people did not know math, the math people did not know media, and the technology specialists were not up to speed on either math or media. Most of the early education mathematics experts referred were already connected to one of the grantees being evaluated, leading to conflict of interest concerns. His compromise was to use combinations of people for this particular review. He found ultimately that educators were the most successful reviewers since they were the best at gauging efficacy (Lekander, 2012).

Necessary improvements

Overall, the process of bridging scholarship with the media industry could benefit from a few improvements that could make the experience better and easier for both sides. First, it is crucial for both sides to speak the same language. Frequently, academic material is viewed as impenetrable by the rest of the media industry. It is important to write clearly and directly with the idea in mind that if readers can follow the material, they will be more likely to implement the recommendations.

Also, it is important for both sides to have knowledge about the other's work. The academic experts need to make an effort to understand the production process, for example, or the importance of ratings to the network and why the show must work creatively and aesthetically. Some advisors have expressed that writers are not able to put enough academic content in their stories and then the advisors want to write the stories themselves without understanding what makes a story work creatively.

It helps when both sides understand the goals of the project and can work together. Advisors should feel that the production and creative teams understand them and can implement their suggestions. The members of the creative team in turn need to feel that they are getting helpful and useful advice from the advisors, as opposed to direction they disagree with and negative feedback. And it is important for advisors to have an appreciation of television, web sites and apps, and the belief that these platforms can be used to effectively impart knowledge.

Finally, it is necessary for academic experts to have a forum to share their findings with the industry and to have opportunities to hear from experts through conferences, dialogues in forums, and even conversations in casual settings.

SEE ALSO in this volume chapter by Fisch.

References

Greenwald, C. (29 May, 2012). Telephone interview with author.

Lekander, B. (8 June, 2012). Telephone interview with author.

Simensky, L. (2007). Programming children's television: The PBS model. In J. A. Bryant (Ed.), *The children's television community*. NJ: Lawrence Erlbaum, pp. 131–46.

——(2008). Peering out from the trenches: Reflections on the industry–academic relationship. *Journal of Children and Media, 2*(2), 180–83.

SUBJECT INDEX

NAME INDEX

C

Go, J. 153
Godfrey, C. 239
Gokee-Larose, J. 230
Gola, A. H. 45, 174, 177, 207, 431
Goldberg, M. E. 99, 101, 236, 238
Goldenberg, E. 177
Golding, P. 142, 146
Goldstein, A. O. 242, 245
Gollin, A. 264, 268
Golub, A. 241, 245
Goncalo, J. 198
Gonzales, H. 39, 45
González Hernández, D. 332, 334
Goodman, S. 349, 350
Goodrich, S. A. 174, 175, 177, 301, 304
Goonasekera, A. 209, 215
Gootman, J. 147
Gordon, R. 242, 245
Gorley, T. 239
Gorn, G. J. 236, 238
Gorzig, A. 37, 110, 118, 119, 133, 215, 293, 424
Gottlieb-Robles, B. 358
Gotz, M. 27, 29, 62, 67, 167, 186, 188–91, 225, 229, 230, 250, 252–54, 258, 260–62, 280, 281, 285
Grabe, S. 224, 227, 230
Graff, S. K. 386, 393
Gram, M. 142, 143, 146
Grant, J. 105, 106, 110
Graves, S. B. 250, 251, 254
Gray, J. J. 231
Gray, M. L. 150, 153
Gray, S. 176, 457
Green, C. L. 138
Green, D. R. 267, 268
Green, E. 157, 161
Green, J. 92, 154
Green, N. 127, 128, 132, 307, 311, 313, 324, 327
Greenberg, B. S. 225, 230
Greene, K. 419, 423
Greenfield, P. 187, 191
Greenhow. C. 194, 199
Greenwald, C. 461, 462, 464
Greenwood, C. 178
Greer, C. 26, 29
Grela, B. 45, 177
Gresle-Favier, C. 158, 162
Grewal, I. 76, 80
Grieveson, L. 372, 376
Griffin, C. 60
Grimes, S. M. 114, 118
Grimm, L. 156, 162
Grinter, R. 128, 132
Grisso, A. D. 283, 285
Grixti, J. 76, 79, 80
Grizzle, A. 424
Groebel, J. 209, 215, 403, 409

Groesz, L. M. 226–28, 230
Gross, L. 212, 215, 285
Grugeon, E. 137, 139
Grundy, S. U. E. 313
Grusec, J. E. 263, 268
Gubrium, A. C. 362, 364
Guernsey, L. 426, 431
Guha, M. L. 152, 154, 409
Guilford, J. P. 194, 199
Gunter, B. 57, 60, 209, 215, 285, 395, 401
Guo, G. 222
Guo, J. 231
Guofang, L. 337, 342
Gupta, V. K. 244
Gurak, L. 418, 423
Gustafson, R.L. 231
Gutnick, A. L. 428, 431

H

Haberman, H. S. 305
Haddon, L. 37, 110, 118, 119, 127–30, 132, 133, 215, 293, 310, 313, 324, 327, 330, 334, 335, 397, 401, 424
Haefner, M. 257, 261, 300, 305
Hagen, I. 400, 401
Hahlweg, K. 185
Haines, J. 231
Hainey, T. 125
Hakansson, P. A. 192
Hall, S. 63, 67, 313
Halliwell, E. 230
Halperin, J. M. 185
Halverson, R. 416
Hamagami, F. 53
Hamburg, P. 229
Hamburger, M. 223
Hamby, R. H. 184
Hamed, M. 409
Hamel, E. 171, 177, 299, 300, 305
Hamelink, C. J. 77, 80
Hammer, L.D. 231
Handel, G. 322, 327
Hanewinkel, R. 243, 245
Haninger, K. 209, 215, 216
Hansen, C. H. 218, 222
Hansen, M. 156, 162
Hansen, R. D. 218, 222
Hanson, D. J. 242, 245
Hanson, K. G. 305
Harewood, S. 331, 334
Hargittai, E. 113, 118, 149, 154, 392
Hargreaves, A. 337, 342
Harper, R. 324, 328
Harrington, K. 223

U

V

W